Keystones of Entrepreneurship Knowledge

Published on the Occasion of the
50th Anniversary of the
International Council for Small Business
ICSB

Blackwell
Publishing

Keystones of Entrepreneurship Knowledge

Edited by
Rob van der Horst
Sandra King-Kauanui
Susan Duffy

Blackwell
Publishing

© 2005 International Council for Small Business

Blackwell Publishing, Inc.
350 Main Street
Malden, MA 02148
USA

Blackwell Publishing, Ltd.
9600 Garsington Road
Oxford OX4 2DQ
United Kingdom

First published 2005 by Blackwell Publishing Ltd.

Library of Congress Cataloging-in-Publication Data is located at the Library of Congress.
Includes bibliographical references.

ISBN-10: 1-4051-3921-8 (alk.paper)
ISBN-13: 978-1-4051-3921-2

Keystones of Entrepreneurship Knowledge

Preface

Some might say that everything has already been written about entrepreneurship and small business. The amount of books, articles, and brochures published over the last decade is really very impressive. One can read about young entrepreneurs, female entrepreneurship, high-tech starters, succession in family businesses, ethnic entrepreneurship and many other subjects in numerous languages. Does the world really need another book?

We think it does, because this is a very special book. It does not bring you new ideas that may be outdated in a few years from now. It brings you what we believe to be the 20 best articles ever published about entrepreneurship and small business. They have borne the test of time, and are still relevant and valuable. They really are the Keystones of Entrepreneurship Knowledge.

With this book the International Council for Small Business (ICSB) celebrates its 50th anniversary. ICSB is the major worldwide organisation bringing together people and organisations that are committed to the advancement of entrepreneurship and small business. Our membership is made up of researchers, policymakers, educators and service providers. Apart from their common interest and knowledge in entrepreneurship, ICSB members have a strong desire to share their knowledge with others. This book is an example of the type of products and services we strive to produce. It provides us an opportunity to achieve the ICSB mission: to share global knowledge with our growing global network.

What will you find in this book? It starts with an article by the President of ICSB, Dr. Sandra King-Kauanui. She gives her reflections on ICSB as an organisation and on its major objective: adding value to its members. Following her article, there is a list of the current ICSB Board of Directors.

The eleven affiliates of ICSB are briefly presented in the next chapter. In almost every part of the world we have an active ICSB affiliate. When members join an affiliate, they also become a member of the ICSB. If you are interested in becoming a member, there is contact information provided for each affiliate. For those living outside of affiliated regions of the world, we invite you to join ICSB through the International Office.

The next four chapters make up the core of the book. They contain the 20 'best' articles on entrepreneurship and small business ever published in a scientific journal or book since ICSB was founded. These articles have been selected by two eminent scientists and educators for each of the four fields that form the pillars of ICSB: research, public policy, education and service provision. Our associate editors consider these papers to be the best articles of the last 50 years. The eight associate editors are:

Research
Roy Thurik: Erasmus University Rotterdam, The Netherlands; Free University Amsterdam, The Netherlands; EIM Business & Policy Research, Zoetermeer, The Netherlands; Max Planck Institute for Research into Economic Systems, Jena, Germany.
J. Hanns Pichler: Vienna University of Economics and Business Administration, Austria.

Public Policy
Lois Stevenson: Industry Canada; University of Ottawa, Canada.
David Storey: Warwick Business School, United Kingdom.

Education
George Solomon: George Washington University, USA.
Kevin Hindle: Australian Graduate School of Entrepreneurship, Swinburne University of Technology, Melbourne, Australia.

Service Provision
Colin Dunn: RMIT University, Melbourne, Australia.
Michael Schaper: The inaugural Small Business Commissioner of the Australian Capital Territory, Canberra, Australia.

At the beginning of each of these four chapters, the associate editors provide an introduction, including the rationale for article selection and an explanation of why the articles are still relevant for the present generation of researchers, policy-makers, educators and service providers.

In the next chapter the International Office of ICSB is presented. On a day-to-day basis, the International Office plays a central role in the organisation. In the article the role and staff of the International Office are highlighted.

The last chapter is an overview of the history of ICSB. Bob Brockhaus, a past ICSB president and, for many years, the Executive Director of the ICSB, leads us through 50 years of ICSB's past to the present.

The editors are grateful to the people and organisations that have made this book possible: the authors of the original published works, the associate editors, the publishers and the organisations that gave permission to re-publish the articles and chapters, the authors of additional chapters, and the staff of our publisher, Blackwell Publishing.

Writing, reading and talking about entrepreneurship and small business is never boring. It is about people: people who take the initiative to start a business, to launch a new product, to grow. Sometimes they fail, often they succeed. Entrepreneurship has become an extremely important issue around the globe. In many emerging economies, such as former Central and Eastern European States, Africa, Latin America and Asia, entrepreneurship has become one of the most important ways to secure income for large groups of people: For 50 years ICSB has been the prime organisation advancing entrepreneurship worldwide. We are ready to continue that role into the future as we create global knowledge through global networks. We hope you enjoy the book.

Rob van der Horst, Senior Vice-President Research and Publications
Sandra King-Kauanui, President
Susan Duffy, Executive Director

ICSB: Creating Global Knowledge through Global Networks

by Sandra King-Kauanui, ICSB President

I am both honored and enthused to be the president of the International Council for Small Business (ICSB) as we come to our 50th anniversary. This is an exciting time for ICSB. It is a time to reflect on the past, assess the present, and envision the future. With the dedication of many individuals over the last five decades, ICSB has grown and prospered around the world. Today, we have 11 affiliates from around the globe and more than 2,300 members. Our conferences have continued to grow larger and more globally oriented. ICSB's research publication, the *Journal of Small Business Management* (*JSBM*), is well respected in the field.

As I reflect on where we are today, it is clear to me that ICSB has grown well beyond an organization that merely provides a conference once a year. We have become an organization that can provide unique resources to support all of our members as they work to advance entre-preneurship worldwide. Our goal is to continue to build ICSB through connection with, and support for, the four pillars of our membership: researchers, policymakers, educators, and service providers. As I envision the future, our challenge must be to continue to create an environment rich in the resources that our members need to continue their work in advancing small business and entrepreneurship around the globe.

To meet our objective of adding value to our members, I have spent some time reflecting on the structure of ICSB. I see ICSB as a system made up of three inter-dependent and fluid parts.

As illustrated in the diagram, it is through the creation and dissemination of global knowledge and the building of strategic networks that our members are able to further the advancement of entrepreneurship worldwide. Because of ICSB's unique composition, we have not only survived but have also grown over

the last 50 years. Today, our challenge is to decide how we will continue to move ICSB forward for the next five decades. I believe the answer lies in finding new ways of *adding value* to the system. To do this effectively, we must identify specific leverage points that will provide us with the greatest impact to our global system. To gain a better understanding of how we plan to proceed into the future, we can look at each part of the system separately.

The first part of the system is our *members*. Without our members, the system (ICSB) does not exist. It is extremely important that ICSB uses its relationship with our affiliates, their members, and our nonaffiliated members to provide the resources required. Because we know that our affiliate members are researchers, policymakers, service providers, and educators, we must commit to support all four constituent groups. Therefore, all of our new initiatives will be considered in light of *all* of our varied members' needs. In supporting all of our members and their needs, we believe it will help our affiliates increase their membership. In addition, we are supporting affiliates' growth through the addition of new chapters. These new chapters will not only increase the affiliates' membership, but they will also provide new networks and additional resources for all of our members. In the future, some of these chapters will eventually grow into affiliates.

The second part of the system is the *creation of global knowledge*. To assure that we are providing support for *all* of our members and supporting our goal of creating global knowledge, we are in the process of reviewing and, in some cases, redesigning our existing publications. We are also working on new publications to incorporate research and application in practice, policy, and education. In addition, the board has approved funds for a new website that will provide member-only access to valuable resources. The website will provide a place for our members to share knowledge, create relationships, and build best practices.

The third link to our system is the *strategic networks* that ICSB has built and continues to build with other organizations. We are again trying to keep all four constituents in mind as we build strategic alliances with other organizations. These alliances will provide our members with valuable resources for their work. To date, we have created alliances with Quantum Leaps Inc., the International Small Business Congress, the World Association for Small and Medium Enterprises, the Organization for Economic Co-operation and Development, and the Direct Selling Education Foundation. With our new website, we hope to provide our members with more information on how they can utilize these alliances.

All of these initiatives, building a diverse membership, generating knowledge in multiple areas of SME development, and building strategic networks, will meet our objective of "*adding value to our members.*"

On a personal note, I will end with saying how excited I am to be part of this organization. Like others before me who have served this great organization, I have created many lifetime friendships as a result of my involvement with ICSB. Although we are certainly more than an association with a conference, I have found that attending the ICSB World Conference is an excellent way to become more involved with the organization. It has also provided me with rich resources that I have used in my own work in advancing entrepreneurship.

The 2005 World Conference is extremely special as we are celebrating our 50th anniversary in Washington, D.C. We are not only celebrating our past, but we are also introducing many new things that our executive team has been working on to move our organization forward. Following is the Board of Directors for ICSB for 2004–2005. It is because of their support this book became a reality.

ICSB Board of Directors 2004–2005

ICSB Affiliates

The International Council for Small Business (ICSB) has the following 11 affiliates across the globe:

ICSB–Brazil
Brazilian affiliate of ICSB

CCSBE
Canadian Council for Small Business and Entrepreneurship

ECSB
European Council for Small Business and Entrepreneurship

ICSB–Japan
Japanese affiliate of ICSB

ICSB–Korea
Korean affiliate of ICSB

ICSB–Puerto Rico and the Caribbean
Puerto Rico and the Caribbean affiliate of ICSB

ICSB–ROC
Republic of China affiliate of ICSB

SAESBA
Southern African Entrepreneurship and Small Business Association

SEAANZ
Small Enterprise Association of Australia and New Zealand

The Entrepreneurship Forum
Singapore affiliate of ICSB

USASBE
United States Association for Small Business and Entrepreneurship

Each affiliate covers a specific geographical area. Members residing in an area not covered by any of the affiliates belong to ICSB International. ICSB has 2,400 members, of which 2,350 are members of an affiliate.

New members join ICSB through their local geographic affiliate. On the following pages all affiliates are briefly presented. You will find the name of the affiliate president (as of July 1, 2005), contact details, and some characteristics of the affiliates. You may contact the appropriate affiliate for any questions you may have.

BRAZIL

Name of the affiliate
ICSB–Brazil
Geographical coverage
Brazil
Year of establishment
1999
President
Sylvio G. Rosa Jr.
Secretariat
Zilah Borelli Rosa ParqTec Alfredo Lopes Street, 1717 13560-460 Sao Carlos Sao Paulo Brazil
Telephone
+55 16 3362 6262
Fax
+55 16 3362 6261

Website
www.icsb-brasil.org.br

Secretariat's email
zilah@parqtec.com.br

Total number of members
35

Characteristics of members
35 percent researchers 45 percent educators 10 percent policymakers 10 percent practitioners, advisors

Strategic alliances
Sebraetec, a technology consultancy service that aims to solve everyday problems of small enterprises. The project has been active for the past five years, involving universities, research institutes, and ICSB/ParqTec. CME—The Business Modernization Center. This is the result of a partnership with Brazilian Small Business Administration (Sebrae). It offers laboratorial infrastructure to help companies develop new products and processes. Genetec. This is a partnership involving ICSB/ParqTec, Brazilian Research Council (CNPq), Softex 2000, University of Sao Paulo, Federal University of Sao Carlos, and Sebrae to promote the creation of new information-technology ventures.

Main activities
Educational programs, including: The MEGA ENTREPRENEURSHIP/MEGA INCUBATION, which is an initiative of ICSB/ParqTec with CNPq. It aims in 2005 to prepare 40 young entrepreneurs to start new high-tech ventures. The project offers training courses to undergraduate and graduated students, faculty members, and researchers.  *www.parqtec.com.br/mega.php*

Canadian Council for Small Business and Entrepreneurship

Conseil canadien de la PME et de l'entrepreneuriat

CANADA

Name of the affiliate
Canadian Council for Small Business & Entrepreneurship/Conseil Canadien de la PME et de l'entrepreneuriat (CCSBE/CCPME)
Geographical coverage
Canada
Year of establishment
1979
President
Annette St-Onge
Secretariat
Acadia Centre for Small Business & Entrepreneurship c/o Ann McGrath Acadia University Wolfville, Nova Scotia Canada B4P 2R6
Telephone
+1 902 585 1776
Fax
+1 902 585 1057
Website
www.ccsbe.org
Secretariat's email
ccsbe.secretariat@acadiau.ca

Total number of members
135

Characteristics of members

40 percent researchers
7 percent educators
14 percent policymakers
39 percent practitioners, advisors
The percentage of educators versus researchers is misleading. The 40 percent of researchers represent the members who are academics and teach in a university setting. Many of these individuals consider themselves educators. The 7 percent of educators represent members who are private trainers or teach in a community college setting.

Strategic alliances

CCSBE/CCPME has a strategic alliance with the APEC IBIZ Small Business Counsellor Certification Program, which represents 43 APEC Certified Business Counselors (CBCs) in Canada; 200 enrolled in the Canadian program and more than 100 worldwide. Many of these CBCs are members or potential members of CCSBE/CCPME.

Main activities

— Annual bilingual (English/French) conference.
— CCSBE/CCPME publishes an academic journal, the *Journal for Small Business & Entrepreneurship*, four times a year and an e-newsletter four times a year.
— Quarterly newsletter: Keeping members informed on events, news, and ICSB-related matters.
— Regional activities: Events designed to bring members together at the provincial level to share their knowledge on regional issues.
— Women in Business Committee: A committee working to support the research and developmental needs of Canadian women entrepreneurs.
— CCSBE/CCPME will be hosting the ICSB Conference in Halifax in 2008.
— Other services to members: CSBE/CCPME offers services to members in Canada's two official languages, French and English.

EUROPE

Name of the affiliate
European Council for Small Business and Entrepreneurship (ECSB)
Geographical coverage
Europe (more than 30 countries)
Year of establishment
1988
President
David Smallbone
Secretariat
European Council for Small Business and Entrepreneurship, Secretariat Small Business Institute, Turku School of Economics and Business Administration Rehtorinpellonkatu 3 20500 Turku Finland
Telephone
+358 2 4814 545
Fax
+358 2 4814 393
Website
http://www.ecsb.org
Secretariat's email
info@ecsb.org
Total number of members
550, including 42 members from Eastern Europe

Characteristics of members

80 percent researchers
40 percent educators
5 percent policymakers
10 percent practitioners, advisors

Strategic alliances

ECSB organizes the RENT Research in Entrepreneurship Conference every year in cooperation with the European Institute of Advanced Studies in Management (EIASM).
ECSB supports the European Doctoral Programme in Entrepreneurship and Small Business Management.

Main activities

— ECSB's main objective is to advance the understanding of entrepreneurship and to improve the competitiveness of small and medium-sized enterprises (SMEs) in Europe. ECSB facilitates the creation and distribution of new knowledge through research, education, and the open exchange of ideas among professions and across national and cultural borders.
— In order to facilitate and enhance the exchange of knowledge within the ECSB membership, ECSB organizes for its members high-quality conferences, such as the RENT Research in Entrepreneurship Conference every year in cooperation with EIASM. In addition, the ECSB supports the organization of special one-day workshops that deal with matters concerning SME and entrepreneurship policy. In 2007, ECSB will also organize the ICSB World Conference (www.icsb2007.org) in cooperation with the Small Business Institute at the Turku School of Economics and Business Administration in Finland.
— ECSB also aims to support the training of new researchers in the field by organizing a doctoral seminar in connection with the RENT conference and by cooperating with the European Doctoral Programme in Entrepreneurship and Small Business Management initiated by ECSB (http://selene.uab.es/edp/).
— The exchange and creation of knowledge among members is also possible at the Internet platform (www.ecsb.org). The Members Area at www.ecsb.org offers members access to information of other members and their expertise. The Internet platform also enables the development of joint projects within the membership. Every year a special virtual workshop, Inter-RENT, is organized at the members forum. The idea of the workshop is to deepen a selected theme from the previous RENT conference. The chair of the workshop selects suitable papers to be developed, improving the possibilities of publication of high-quality articles. The best papers are published in an online Inter-RENT publication.
— Another important field of activity of ECSB is cooperation with various governmental institutions interested in improving the understanding and development of small businesses and entrepreneurship in general.

JAPAN

Name of the affiliate	
ICSB–Japan	
Geographical coverage	
Japan	
Year of establishment	
1999	
President	
Eiichi Erich Kasahara	
Secretariat	
Strategy and Marketing Department Mizuho Information & Research Institute, Inc. Takabashi Square 2-3 Kanda-Nishikicho, Chiyoda-ku Tokyo 101-8443 Japan	
Telephone	
+81 3 5281 5431	
Secretariat's email	
ErichAPRIM@aol.com	
Total number of members	
25	
Characteristics of members	
30 percent researchers 30 percent educators 0 policymakers 40 percent practitioners, advisors	
Main activities	
In 2000, Masayoshi Fukuda, Eiichi Erich Kasahara, and Masahide Teraishi, members of ICSB–Japan, wrote an academic book, published by Bunshindo, one of the major academic publishers in Japan. In 2001, a special prize, the Prize for Promoting Study on SME Management, was given to these three people.	

KOREA

Name of the affiliate	
ICSB–Korea	
Geographical coverage	
South Korea	
Year of establishment	
1987	
President	
In-Ho Kim	
Secretariat	
Joonho Lee, Secretariat Officer Sunyoon Kwon, Assistant Administrator Korea Small Business Institute 16-2, Yoidodong, Yeongdeungpoku Seoul, Korea, 150-740	
Telephone	
Joonho Lee: +82 2 707 9828; Sunyoon Kwon: +82 2 707 9852	
Fax	
Joonho Lee: +82 2 707 9892; Sunyoon Kwon: +82 2 707 9892	
Secretariat's email	
Joonho Lee: johlee@kosbi.re.kr Sunyoon Kwon: sykwon@kosbi.re.kr	
Total number of members	
59	
Characteristics of members	
12 percent researchers 20 percent educators 0 policymakers 68 percent practitioners, advisors	

Main activities
— Every year, regular and irregular meetings are held to discuss the direction of management and improvement in ICSB–KOREA. In addition, the best prize-awarded papers of the ICSB conferences are translated and distributed to the members. — In the near future, several forums will be held to discuss the development of small and medium-sized enterprises. Participants will mainly be ICSB members.

PUERTO RICO AND THE CARIBBEAN

Name of the affiliate	
ICSB–Puerto Rico and the Caribbean	
Geographical coverage	
All of the Caribbean region (all islands in the Caribbean and Central America)	
Year of establishment	
1996–1997	
President	
Nelson J. Perea	
Secretariat	
José M. Romaguera International Entrepreneurship Institute P.O. Box 4545 Mayaguez, Puerto Rico 00681-4545 U.S.A.	
Telephone	
+1 787 265 3802	
Fax	
+1 787 832 5320	
Website	
www.icsbcaribbean.com	
Secretariat's email	
emprende@coqui.net	
Total number of members	
85	

Characteristics of members
10 percent researchers
65 percent educators
8 percent policymakers
17 percent practitioners, advisors

Strategic alliances
Alliance with CEO–Puerto Rico to foster entrepreneurship development among students at the universities. The affiliate maintains other strategic alliances with various trade groups in the Caribbean region that foster entrepreneurship and attend to issues particular to small and medium-sized businesses.

Main activities
— The main activity of the affiliate has been an annual event held to highlight the role of small and medium-sized enterprises (SMEs) in the economy and to foster entrepreneurship. The first such event, held in March 1997 with Dr. David Birch as keynote speaker, was the first official activity of the then-new affiliate. The Annual Entrepreneurship Summit is usually held in March–May.
— As part of the development strategy of the affiliate, various chapters have been established. These chapters have their own leadership that works in coordination with the affiliate to foster entrepreneurship and develop an effective network where researchers, practitioners, policymakers, and educators can come together to discuss, develop, and implement plans for advancing SMEs in their respective regions. Current chapters of the ICSB–Puerto Rico and the Caribbean affiliate are Barbados, Dominican Republic, and Puerto Rico.
— The affiliate has contributed significantly to ICSB on the international level in a variety of ways. These include hosting the ICSB 2002 World Conference held in San Juan, Puerto Rico, and having its members participate very actively in the Board of Directors of ICSB in leadership roles such as president, president-elect, and various senior vice president positions.

REPUBLIC OF CHINA

Name of the affiliate	
ICSB–ROC	
Geographical coverage	
Republic of China	
Year of establishment	
1991	
Acting President	
Kai Yang	
Secretariat	
Yvonne Yu 5th Floor, 6 Roosevelt Rd., Sec. 1 Taipei, Taiwan 100 Republic of China	
Telephone	
+886 2 2321 4261	
Fax	
+886 2 2394 73171	
Secretariat's email	
yvonne-564@yahoo.com.tw	
Total number of members	
56	

SOUTHERN AFRICA

Name of the affiliate
Southern African Entrepreneurship and Small Business Association (SAESBA)
Geographical coverage
Southern Africa–South Africa
Year of establishment
ICSB–SA: 1987; name change to SAESBA: 1999
President
David Moshapalo
Secretariat
Helen Maroleni SENSAS Communications P.O. Box 1507 Gallor Manor 2052 Johannesburg South Africa
Telephone
+27 11 728 0431
+27 11 728 4399
Website
www.saesba.co.za
Secretariat's email
debaloyi@mweb.co.za

Total number of members
94

Strategic alliances

- Business Unity South Africa (BUSA). Interaction with BUSA aims to structure a united business front within South Africa, in general among small businesses.
- Department of Trade & Industry (DTI). The DTI's small, micro, and medium-size enterprise (SMME) program, championed by the Deputy Minister of Trade and Industry, Lindiwe Hendricks, aims to ensure that all sector development policies incorporate the goals of maximizing the contribution of small business to the economy.
- Small Enterprise Development Agency (SEDA). SEDA was launched directly after the 49th ICSB World Conference. It aims to oversee and fulfill small-business development, opportunity, and needs.
- Banks
- Universities and colleges. The University of Pretoria, University of South Africa, University of Kwa-Zulu, Natal, as well the University of Potchefstroom house a vast database of researchers in the SMME field as well as acclaimed academics who contribute intellectually, as well as practically, to South Africa's economy as some of them are solid and successful businesspeople.

Main activities

- Conferences
- Workshops
- Educational programs
- Journal
- Books
- Research
- Newsletter
- Databases
- Other services to members
- As a result of the 49th ICSB World Conference, which was successfully organized, hosted, and run by SAESBA, the minister of economic affairs, Paul Mashtile, mandated three of the board members, namely, David Moshapalo, Danisa Baloyi, and Gerrit Cloete, to investigate and commission an agency that would represent SMMEs. As a result of their research and recommendations, the Gauteng SMME Agency was born. Danisa Baloyi is the chairperson, and David Moshapalo is a director.
- In his State of the Nation address on February 11, 2005, President Thabo Mbeki of South Africa issued a policy statement that emphasis would be placed on the development of SMMEs in South Africa. As a result, in his budget speech on February 23, 2005, the minister of finance, Trevor Manuel, allocated over R1 billion to the development of SMMEs in South Africa.

AUSTRALIA AND NEW ZEALAND

Name of the affiliate
Small Enterprise Association of Australia and New Zealand (SEAANZ)
Geographical coverage
Australia and New Zealand
Year of establishment
1987
President
Michael Schaper
Secretariat
Kathy Griffiths RMIT University Level 16 239 Bourke Street 3000 Melbourne Victoria Australia
Telephone
+61 3 992 55940
Fax
+61 3 992 55599

Website
www.seaanz.asn.au

Secretariat's email
Kathryn.griffiths@rmit.edu.au

Total number of members
338

Characteristics of members
50 percent researchers 20 percent educators 15 percent policymakers 15 percent practitioners, advisors

Strategic alliances
The Australasian Institute of Enterprise Facilitators

Main activities
SEAANZ is an incorporated not-for-profit association that has the objective to advance the development and understanding of small enterprise by: — furthering the development of scholarship, education, and research in small enterprise and enterprise management, including encouraging the application of research findings; — identifying and developing proposals for programs to meet small-enterprise needs; — communicating and disseminating ideas and information on small enterprise and promoting their discussion by the holding of conferences, publishing materials, and other appropriate means; — liaising, including affiliating, with other associations or bodies with similar objectives; — making representations and/or providing commentaries to government or to other bodies on any matter relevant to the association; and — doing all such other things as are conducive or incidental to the attainment of any of the above objectives. SEAANZ endeavors to achieve these objectives through the following mechanisms: conferences, workshops, educational programs, journals, books, research, newsletter, databases, other services to members as and when required.

SINGAPORE

Name of the affiliate	
The Entrepreneurship Forum, ICSB–Singapore	
Geographical coverage	
Singapore	
Year of establishment	
1994	
President	
Wee-Liang Tan	
Secretariat	
Singapore Management University Tanglin P.O. Box 257 Singapore 912409 Singapore	
Telephone	
+65 822 0157	
Fax	
+65 822 0101	
Secretariat's email	
wltan@smu.edu.sg	
Total number of members	
16	
Strategic alliances	
Centre for Corporate Management Development, Singapore	
Main activities	
43rd ICSB Conference Seminars and workshops	

United States Association for Small Business and Entrepreneurship
U.S. Affiliate of the International Council for Small Business

UNITED STATES OF AMERICA

Name of the affiliate
U.S. Association for Small Business and Entrepreneurship (USASBE)
Geographical coverage
All 50 states
Year of establishment
1981
President
Dianne H. B. Welsh dhbwelsh@tampabay.rr.com
Secretariat
Joan Gillman U.S. Association for Small Business and Entrepreneurship Hosting organization: University of Wisconsin 975 University Ave. Suite 3260 53706 Place Madison, Wisconsin U.S.A.
Telephone
+11 608 262 9982
Fax
+11 608 263 0818
Website
www.usasbe.org

Secretariat's email
jgillman@wisc.edu
Total number of members
949
Characteristics of members
75 percent researchers 80 percent educators 10 percent policymakers 20 percent practitioners, advisors
Strategic alliances
— The Coleman Foundation — The John E. Hughes and Jeanne T. Foundation — The Ewing Marion Kauffman Foundation — The Edward Lowe Foundation — Direct Selling Educational Foundation — Acton Institute — International Franchise Educational Foundation — Small Business Institute — NCIIA — CEO — SIFE — DECA — SCORE — National Federation of Independent Business Foundation — Small Business Administration—SBA Office of Advocacy — Entrepreneur Media, Inc. — Southwestern-Thompson Publishing Co.
Main activities
— USASBE's mission is to advance knowledge and foster business development through entrepreneurship education and research. USASBE is interdisciplinary, cross-functional, and globally connected (as an affiliate of the ICSB). USASBE is the premier network for entrepreneurship educators at all student levels, for professional practitioners, for entrepreneurship researchers, and for government policymakers. USASBE offers cutting-edge programs for entrepreneurship education and encourages research that has practical application. — USASBE offers an annual conference in January, papers and workshops, and cutting-edge keynotes as well as educational programs. It offers numerous research awards at the conference, and members receive *Liaison Newsletter* (electronic, quarterly).

— *Entrepreneurship Theory & Practice, Journal of Small Business Management,* and *Entrepreneur* magazine. Members have access to an extensive website that contains current-member contact information, curriculum, syllabi and teaching tools, a large bibliography, and more. The website links to ICSB and its affiliates. In addition, *Journal of International Entrepreneurship* text will be available in August 2005.

Introduction to the Paper Selection

The next four chapters contain twenty seminal articles on entrepreneurship and small business. Each was originally published in a scientific journal or book. These articles have been selected by two associate editors for each of the four fields that form the pillars of ICSB: research, public policy, education and service provision.

Our associate editors consider these papers to be the best articles of the last 50 years. At the beginning of each of these four chapters, the associate editors provide an introduction, including the rationale for article selection and an explanation of why the articles are still relevant for the present generation of researchers, policymakers, educators and service providers.

The twenty articles form a collection of outstanding contributions to our knowledge of SMEs and entrepreneurship. Reading the articles gives you a good impression of how this knowledge has evolved over time. At the same time they create inspiration for further research in the fascinating world of entrepreneurship and small business.

Short Curricula Vitae of the associate editors are presented in Appendix B.

Best Papers in the Field of Research

Introduction
by J. Hanns Pichler and Roy Thurik

Entrepreneurship and small business are related concepts, but they are not synonymous. Entrepreneurship is a type of behavior dealing with opportunities rather than resources that is displayed in businesses large and small and also elsewhere. Small businesses, on the other hand, can be a vehicle for both Schumpeterian entrepreneurs introducing new products and processes that change an industry and for people who run and own a business to provide a living for themselves.

Entrepreneurship and small businesses are important where they overlap, notably in the area of new small and often fast-growing businesses. However, the way in which they matter has evolved over time. During the first decades of the last century, small businesses were both a vehicle for entrepreneurship and a source of employment as well as income. This is the era in which Schumpeter conceived his *Theory of Economic Development* (1912), emphasizing the role of the entrepreneur as the very cause for the dynamics of economic development, in describing how the innovating entrepreneur challenges incumbent firms by introducing new inventions that make existing technologies and products obsolete. This process of creative destruction essentially characterizes what has been called the *entrepreneurial economy*.

During the years after World War II, small business continued to matter, although less on the grounds of economic efficiency than for social and political purposes. At a time when large firms had yet to establish their position they enjoyed in the 1960s and 1970s, small businesses were the main source of employment and hence contributed to social and political stability. However, scholars, economists, intellectuals, and policymakers at the time were convinced that the future lay rather in the hands of large corporations and that small businesses would tend to fade away because of their own inefficiencies. Such view was inspired by Schumpeter's *Capitalism, Socialism and Democracy* (1942), with its specific emphasis on the innovative activities of large and established firms in describing how they outperform their smaller counterparts through a strong positive feedback loop, from innovation to increased research and development (R&D). This process of creative accumulation characterizes what has been called the *managed economy*.

There is ample evidence that economic dynamics gradually shifted from large firms to small firms in the 1970s and 1980s and that entrepreneurial activity provided the key to economic growth and productivity improvements. This return to the *entrepreneurial economy*[1]

---

[1]See Audretsch, D. B., and A. R. Thurik (2001). "What Is New about the New Economy: Sources of Growth in the Managed and Entrepreneurial Economies," *Industrial and Corporate Change* 10(1), 267–315.

was accompanied by a remarkable growth of publications in the fields of entrepreneurship and small-business research being eclectic by nature. The broad range of contributions makes it impossible to cover all aspects within given limits of this chapter on research.

Because entrepreneurship is all about uncertainty and risk, we chose an article in the Knightian tradition. In Kihlstrom and Laffont (1979) the degree of risk aversion and differentiation of risk between being an entrepreneur and a wage earner take on a central role in determining what alternative is being chosen, thus providing the basis for a subsequent influential body of literature about the determinants of entrepreneurship.

In an entirely different tradition, Gartner (1985) stresses that differences among entrepreneurs and their ventures are huge, despite focusing on differences between entrepreneurs and nonentrepreneurs and equally between entrepreneurial and nonentrepreneurial firms. A framework of heterogeneity is provided where occupational choice considers only two alternatives and where heterogeneity constitutes the essence of entrepreneurial activity.

Lumpkin and Dess (1996) return to the firm as unit of observation and introduce the concept of *entrepreneurial orientation*. Because business activity cannot survive without performance, they propose a framework linking entrepreneurial orientation to performance and complementing this also with environmental and organizational factors. This eclectic framework, including a variety of alternatives, is fundamental for

many analyses trying to explain performance differences between entrepreneurial ventures.

Entrepreneurial performance and activities at the macro level of economies are only loosely connected to that at the level of individual endeavor. Baumol (1990) shows that it is the allocation of entrepreneurial activities that determines their effect on the economy. By referring to Schumpeter's views in his *Theory of Economic Development* and also to evidence from historical examples, he shows that existing laws and legal procedures of an economy specify relative payoffs of various entrepreneurial activities, their allocation among competing uses, ranging from productive to even destructive ones, and hence their contribution to productivity growth. Baumol's views are indispensable when trying to link entrepreneurial activity to macroeconomic development and performance.

Lastly, the seminal article of Brock and Evans (1989) is to be mentioned in the given context. Reemphasizing the *entrepreneurial economy* went together with a growing interest in small and young businesses, leading to a new field within economics. The authors were the first to give an idea of what this new field of *small-business economics* might look like by raising the question about the role of small business in modern economies, which still ranks high on the research agenda when investigating firm size and age-related issues. Particularly, the six reasons why the small-business part of the economy gained importance have proven very influential.

Small Business Economics*
by William A. Brock and David S. Evans

The paper presents an overview of small-business economics. Small businesses are shown to comprise a substantial and expanding segment of the U.S. economy. The role of small businesses in the economy is considered from the standpoint of various economic theories of the size distribution of firms. Firm-size related empirical regularities are reviewed and their implications for economic theory is discussed. Several small-business policy issues are discussed, including the role of small businesses in labor, macroeconomic, and regulatory policies, along with a review of research on small-business economics that might help guide these policies.

I. Introduction

Most firms are small compared with the companies that economists usually study. About 13 million of the 17 million corporations, partnerships, and sole proprietorships that filed federal tax returns in 1986 had no employees other than their owner. All but approximately 10 000 of the 4 million businesses with employees had fewer than 500 employees.[1] Businesses that were not among the 10 000 largest businesses employ about half the workforce and produced about a third of the Gross National Product in 1978.[2] A great deal of economic activity therefore takes place among firms about which economists know remarkably little.

These small firms are playing an increasingly important role in the economy. In the United States, the number of new business incorporations increased by 87 percent from 376 thousand in 1976 to 703 thousand in 1986 while real Gross National Product increased by only 39 percent.[3] Between 1975 and 1985 the percent of full-time nonagricultural workers who were self-employed increased from 10.7 percent to 12.0 percent for men and from 3.2 percent to 4.7 percent for women.[4] The share of employment in firms with fewer than 500 employees increased from 51.0 percent in 1976 to 52.9 percent in 1984.[5] The growth of the small-business sector has profound implications for macro-

Originally appeared in *Small Business Economics*, 1989, Volume 1, Number 1.
*We wish to thank Zoltan J. Acs and an anonymous reviewer for helpful comments.
[1]Based on data reported in the U.S. Small Business Administration (1988), pp. 20–21.
[2]Brock and Evans (1986).
[3]*Statistical Abstracts* (1987), p. 357, Table B—95.
[4]Evans and Leighton (1987).
[5]U.S. Small Business Administration (1986).

economic and employment policies. Yet the causes of the surge in small businesses and the effect of this surge on the economy are not well understood.

Small-business economics seeks to better understand why firms come in different sizes, how and why firm behavior varies with size, what determines the formation, growth, and dissolution of small firms, the role of small firms in the introduction of new products and the evolution of industries, and the dynamic relationships among small firms and macroeconomic variables such as output and employment.

None of these questions is new. Many of these questions have been at least touched upon by previous economic studies. Alfred Marshall's (1890) analysis of the advantages and disadvantages of small businesses, Frank Knight's (1921) discussion of the characteristics of the entrepreneur, and Joseph Schumpeter's (1934) examination of the role of the entrepreneur in economic change are classics, while important theoretical contributions have been made in the last decade by Robert Lucas (1978). Richard Kihlstrom and Jean-Jacques Laffont (1979), and Boyan Jovanovic (1982). There are scores of empirical examinations of differential relationships across firm sizes for wages, growth, profitability, and stock-market returns. It is therefore legitimate to ask why a new specialty is required to treat these sorts of questions.

Small-business economics is needed for at least two reasons. Economists have concentrated over-whelmingly on large businesses. The leading textbooks in economics have little or no discussion of small businesses or entrepreneurs. Most empirical research on firms examines large publicly traded companies usually in the manufacturing sector. Although small-business questions could be treated within the confines of existing areas, they have not been nor are they likely to be. Existing work on small businesses is scattered and unfocused. The first *raison d'être* for small-business economics is that there is an unfilled niche for studies of this sector of our economy.

Small firms have special characteristics that are relevant to many important economic questions. Each economic field tends to be aware only of those characteristics that concern its parochial interests. Financial economists know that the efficient markets model breaks down for small firms, labor economists know that smaller firms pay lower wages for apparently comparable workers, and industrial organization economists know that small firms are more likely to fail and have faster and more variable growth than large firms. But there has been little recognition that these regularities may be connected. The second *raison d'être* for small-business economics is that this speciality can help collect, synthesize, and explore these size-related regularities.

We provide an overview of small-business economics in this paper. We present a statistical portrait of small businesses in the United States in the next section. We concentrate on the U.S. because we are most familiar with our own country and data are more readily available on small businesses in the U.S. An important area of future research is to compare and contrast the small-business sectors in industrialized, lesser-developed, and socialistic countries. In the third section we review various economic theories that help explain the static and dynamic role of small businesses in the economy. These theories will provide a useful starting point for small-business studies. The fourth section reviews some of the key empirical characteristics of small firms and discusses their implications for economic theory. We highlight several policy issues raised by recent work on small-business economics in the fifth section. Brief conclusions are presented in the last section.

II. Small Business in America

Supreme Court Justice Stewart could have been talking about small businesses instead of pornography when he said, "I [can't] define [it]. But I know it when I see it." For most questions we shall want to address there is no need to adopt any particular definition of small businesses. Mainly we shall be concerned with how certain economic phenomena vary with firm size or with other factors that are associated with firm size. We shall often find ourselves talking about smaller versus larger businesses. The question we are examining will determine whether the universe for this comparison is an industry, the economy, or some other grouping. If, for example, we are examining market structure, the relevant comparison is probably between smaller and larger firms in the same industry or market. If, to take another example, we are examining wage structures and if these structures are determined by organizational technologies that are more or less the same for all industries, the relevant comparison would probably be between smaller and larger businesses in the economy.

A Snapshot of the Small-Business Sector

That said, it is useful to adopt some purely arbitrary breakdowns for assessing the importance of smaller firms in the economy. In 1983, 89 percent of the 10.7 million sole proprietorships, 74 percent of the 1.5 million partnerships, and 39 percent of the 3.0 million corporations had receipts of less than $100 000.[6] But together these small firms accounted for less than 3 percent of all business receipts reported to the Internal Revenue Service. Thus, while these "microenterprises" are numerous they account for a small fraction of business sales. Even the 99.7 percent of businesses with sales of under $1 million accounted for only 13.8 percent of business sales.

Other definitions of small businesses reveal a more prominent role in aggregate economic activity. In 1977 firms with fewer than 500 employees produced 46.5 percent of business output and firms with fewer than 100 employees produced 34.1 percent of business output.[7] In 1984 firms with fewer than 500 employees accounted for 52.9 percent of all jobs and firms with fewer than 100 employees accounted for 38.9 percent of all jobs.[8] Self-employed workers, who operate most of what would be considered microenterprises, account for a substantial fraction of employment although they account for a miniscule portion of business sales. Haber et al., for example, estimate that 26.4 percent of the nonagricultural workers were employed by firms operated by self-employed individuals. This figure includes the owner, unpaid family workers, and paid workers.[9]

---

[6]Statistical Abstracts of the United States (1987).

[7]Based on a study by Joel Popkin and Associates reported in Brock and Evans (1986). Business output is measured by "gross product originating" which is almost the same as value added. Gross product originating includes employee compensation, net interest, indirect business taxes, and capital consumption allowances. It does not include rents paid to others which are usually included in value added.

[8]See U.S. Small Business Administration (1987), Table A1.25. These figures as based on the Small Business Data Base which is not as comprehensive as Census data. The *1982 Enterprise Statistics* shows that 55.8 percent of employment is in firms with fewer than 500 employees.

[9]Haber et al. report this number as a lower estimate of the fraction of workers employed by private businesses. Note, however, that their calculations do not reflect hours of work. Many of the owners and workers in their calculations work only part time and may have multiple jobs.

These employment figures overstate the importance of small firms for several reasons. First, small firms employ more part-time workers than large firms so that the share of total hours for small firms is probably less than the share of total jobs. Second, small firms pay lower wages than large firms. In 1984 establishments with less than 100 employees accounted for 56 percent of all employment but only 49 percent of all wages.[10] The disparity is probably even greater than these figures suggest since smaller firms typically provide lower fringe benefits than larger firms.[11] Third, smaller firms are more labor-intensive than larger firms and therefore control a smaller share of capital than of employment.[12]

Nevertheless, small firms clearly do play a substantial role in the economy. Running a small business is a major occupation to which labor economists have paid little attention. They employ a sizeable fraction of the labor force if we take small firms to be those with fewer than 500 employees. A randomly selected worker is just as likely to be employed by a small firm (fewer than 500 employees) as a big firm (500 or more employees). Finally, almost half of

business output, as measured by Gross Product Originating, is produced by firms with fewer than 500 employees.[13]

Changes in the Small-Business Sector over Time

Until the last decade the relative importance of small businesses in the economy was on a long secular decline that dates back to the onset of the industrial revolution. Average firm size, as measured by real gross national product per firm, increased from $150 000 in 1947 to $245 000 in 1980.[14] The fraction of the nonagricultural labor force that is self-employed decreased from at least the late 19th century to the early 1970s.[15] The fraction of the nonagricultural workforce that is self-employed decreased from about a fifth of the workforce at the end of World War II to only 6.9 percent in 1970.[16] Between 1958 and 1977 the small-business share of value added declined by 4 percent and the small-business share of employment declined by 6 percent.[17]

This downward trend was reversed according to several measures by the late 1970s. Average Gross National Product per firm decreased from $245 000 in 1980

---

[10]*Statistical Abstracts* (1987), Table 858. Note these figures are for establishments. Some small establishments are operated by large firms.

[11]See Brown and Medoff (1985).

[12]According to IRS data reported in the U.S. Small Business Administration (1987), p. 82 firms with 250 or more employees had $217 thousand of assets per employee and firms with 10–24 employees had $83 thousand of assets per employee.

[13]Based upon 1980 figures reported in Brock and Evans (1986).

[14]Based on GNP data and from the *Economic Report of the President* for 1988 and the number of businesses filing tax returns from the *Statistical Abstracts of the United States for 1988*. GNP figures are in 1982 dollars.

[15]See Blau (1987) and the references cited therein. *Historical Statistics of the United States from Colonial Times to 1970* show that the fraction of the civilian labor force that is self-employed decreased from 19 percent in 1949 to 8.9 percent in 1970. These figures are based on workers under government social insurance programs. The 6.9 percent figures is based on Census information which includes all nonagricultural workers.

[16]Based on data reported in the *Historical Statistics of the United States from Colonial Times to 1970* and *Statistical Abstracts of the United States*.

[17]See Brock and Evans (1986), p. 21. Small firms are defined as those with fewer than 500 employees.

to $210 000 in 1987.[18] The percent of the full-time labor force that is self-employed increased from 6.9 percent in 1975 to 7.4 percent in 1986.[19] The share of employment in small firms has risen from 51.0 percent in 1976 to 52.9 percent in 1984.[20]

The causes of this upswing are an active area of research in small-business economics. Several possibilities are under investigation. First, we appear to be in the midst of a period of "creative destruction", Schumpeter's (1950) description of the process by which entrepreneurs develop new products and processes that displace the traditions of the past. Infant industries are often dominated by smaller firms. Second, recent technological changes, such as those that have decreased computer costs, may have reduced optimal firm size and the minimum scale of entry. Third, the increasing integration of the world economy and the emergence of strong manufacturing sectors in many previously lesser developed countries has increased competitive risks for U.S. manufacturers. Greater variability of sales due to foreign competition and unstable exchange rates may have increased the returns to "flexibility", a key advantage of smaller firms according to a number of authors.[21] Fourth, increased labor-force participation of women and the entry of baby-boomers into the labor market may have increased the supply of exactly those kinds of workers small businesses use most inten-

sively. This increase in supply, together with falling real wage rates during the 1970s and early 1980s, may have given labor-intensive smaller businesses a competitive edge over capital-intensive larger businesses. Fifth, changes in consumer tastes (possibly due to the indulged baby-boomers) may have increased the demand for specialty products at the expense of the mass-produced merchandise made by larger firms. While boutiques are clearly important in retail trade, they may be an increasingly important factor in manufacturing. The growth of specialty kitchen companies like Sub-Zero and Gaggenau is one of many possible examples of such manufacturer boutiques. Sixth, the relaxation of entry regulations in some industries, such as telephone manufacturing, has increased the opportunities for small businesses.[22]

The relative importance of these (and perhaps other) factors is essential for understanding the future role of small businesses in the economy. If the formation and growth of small businesses is due to the development of new products or technologies, then history teaches us that, over time, only a handful of the firms in these new industries will survive.[23] Small businesses are merely transitory and will largely disappear in the long run. There used to be hundreds of small steel, automobile, chemical, and telephone companies when those technologies and products were still young. To the extent that the growth of small businesses is due to a permanent shift in

---

[18] In 1982 dollars.

[19] See Evans and Leighton (1987).

[20] See U.S. Small Business Administration (1987), Table A1.25, which is based on the Small Business Data Base. Figures from the Census Bureau's *Enterprise Statistics* indicate that the share of employment in firms with fewer than 500 employees decreased from 55.1 percent in 1958 to 52.5 percent in 1977 and then increased to 54.1 percent in 1982.

[21] See Mills (1984) and Acs, Audretsch, and Carlsson (1988).

[22] See Shephard (1982) who shows that concentration has decreased in the economy partly because of deregulation.

[23] See Klepper and Graddy (1985).

tastes towards specialty items, small businesses will be more durable. If the formation of small businesses has been due to decreases in wage rates, the aging of the baby-boom generation and decreases in fertility may raise wages and decrease the competitive advantage of small firms. Already, tight labor markets for young workers in many areas are forcing small-business closures and reducing opportunities for growth. Finally, if technological change has reduced optimal firm size, small businesses may be here to stay.[24] Obviously, government policies towards small businesses depend intimately on which of these stories applies to particular industries.

III. The Role of Small Businesses in Market Economies

If an unlimited number of firms had access to the same technology for producing a good and if this technology exhibited decreasing returns to scale beyond some point, it is well known that all firms would be the same size, the universal firm size would be determined by the minimum point on the long-run average cost schedule, the number of firms would be determined by the number required to equate industry supply and demand, and changes in demand or factor prices will lead to entry (e.g. demand increases or factor prices decreases) or exit (e.g. demand decreases or factor prices increase) but never both. This textbook model of industry is at odds with the facts for most industries. Firms come in many different sizes. Many firms earn more than a competitive rate of return so that average cost is not at a minimum. At any point in time some firms are entering while others are exiting. A great deal of effort has gone into trying to reconcile the neo-classical theory of the firm with these realities.

Economists have told several stories about why small businesses coexist with large ones. The first story is that firms have differing access to some scarce factor of production. This factor could be entrepreneurial ability (e.g. Henry Ford), know-how (e.g. methods for producing corn flakes), or a physical resource (e.g. mineral water). Firms with bigger endowments of this scarce factor can produce any given level of output at a lower cost. But, because it is not possible to increase these endowments, diminishing returns eventually set in for all firms. Assuming even the best-endowed firm is small relative to the market, the industry will be competitive and there will be a size distribution of firms that corresponds to the distribution of the scarce resource.

The most sophisticated version of this story, which dates back at least to Jacob Viner (1932), is that presented by Lucas' (1978) important piece on the size-distribution of firms. There is a distribution of managerial ability θ in the population of potential workers and managers. Firm costs are given by $c(q)/\theta$ where $c(q)$ exhibits decreasing returns to scale. Better managers (higher θ's) have lower costs and produce more output in equilibrium. Small businesses coexist with large businesses in this model because at the margin small and large firms are equally efficient even though a large firm can produce any given level of output more efficiently than a small firm can.

The second story is that there is a technological tradeoff between efficiency—the costs of producing a given level of output—and flexibility—the costs of adjusting output—that gives rise to a size distribution of firms. Larger capital-intensive firms can produce a given level

---

[24]See Blau (1987) and Acs *et al.* (1988).

of output at a lower marginal cost than smaller labor-intensive firms can. But smaller labor-intensive firms can adjust their current level of output more easily than larger capital-intensive firms. If demand fluctuates over time there is a tradeoff between efficiency and flexibility. Smaller firms incur higher marginal production costs at a point in time than larger firms but incur lower marginal adjustment costs over time as demand fluctuates. These arguments are due to David Mills (1984) and are elaborated upon in several papers which provide some empirical support for the theory.[25]

The third story is that the size distribution of firms at a point in time is determined primarily by how lucky firms have been over time. Due largely to Herbert Simon, this story rests on the following assumptions. Once firms have reached some technologically determined minimum efficient firm size they have constant returns to scale. All firms that are larger than the minimum efficient size are therefore equally efficient. Firm sales at a point in time are proportionate to past sales plus a multiplicative random disturbance. Over time firms that have received a lot of lucky draws get big and the size distribution of firms becomes skewed with many small firms getting a small portion of sales and a few large firms getting a large portion of sales. It is difficult to displace firms which have built up a big lead over their competitors. For example, in simulations of this sort of model Scherer (1980) found the four-firm concentration ratio increased from an average of 8 percent at the start of an industry to almost 60 percent in what could be considered the long run.

The fourth story is based on Lucas' (1967) seminal analysis of capital-adjustment. He attempted to reconcile several empirical findings. The first was that many real-world production functions seemed to exhibit constant returns to scale. The second was firms even in the same industry come in many different sizes. The third was that firm growth is roughly independent of firm size. He showed that if it is costly to adjust firm size (i.e. if there are capital-adjustment costs) firms will stagger their expansion over time. Larger firms, in effect, have had more time to adjust themselves to previous expansions in demand or reductions in cost. Except for these differences in adjustment, smaller and larger firms are the same.

Several authors have examined the implication of selection—e.g. survival of the fittest—and learning—e.g. entrepreneurs can learn how good from their profit history—on the dynamics of firm growth and industry evolution.[26] The models developed by these authors are especially useful for understanding firm dynamics in new industries.

Jovanovic (1982) assumes that individuals are unsure about their abilities to manage a business but that they can learn about their abilities by observing how well they perform in the rough and tumble of the business world. But, because production is inherently risky it takes time to disentangle one's true ability from chance upswings or downswings in one's business. Individuals alter their behavior over time as they become better informed about their true abilities. People who find out they are better than they initially thought expand while those who find out they are poorer than they initially thought contract and possibly return to an alternative occupation. In this model small businesses coexist with big businesses for two reasons. First, better managers can run

---

[25]See Acs, Audretsch, and Carlsson and the references cited therein.
[26]See Nelson and Winter (1982) who have made a number of seminal contributions to this area over the years.

larger firms more efficiently than poorer managers. Poorer managers specialize in smaller firms and better managers specialize in larger firms. Second, firms start out small but grow over time as their owners learn whether they are good businessmen. Younger firms will tend to be smaller firms.[27]

Ericson and Pakes (1988) call Jovanovic's model the passive learning model because managers do nothing to learn but observe their profits. They develop an alternative model (the active learning model) in which firms can invest in research with risky outcomes. Firms which are successful at this discovery process grow. Small firms have just started this discovery process or have not been very successful at it.[28]

There is certainly an element of truth to each of these stories. Our task for the future is to develop richer theories which can distinguish empirically between the relative importance of these stories in explaining the static and dynamic roles of small businesses in the economy. Consider, for example, the flexibility, capital-adjustment, and learning models. At a point in time small firms might have adopted more flexible— i.e. less capital-intensive—technologies either because they have had less time to adjust their capital stock to demand shifts or because they are less sure of their abilities and therefore incur fewer sunk capital costs to minimize their risk or because fluctuations in demand over time make flexibility desirable. Determining the extent to which firm heterogeneity at a point in time is due to each of these alternative sources will be a challenging task.

IV. Small-Business Regularities and Their Implications for Economic Theory

One of the ways that economic science, like all sciences, progresses is by developing theories that can explain the various empirical regularities we see around us. Our understanding of the world progresses by extending or modifying our theories in response to anomalies, that is to those empirical regularities that do not seem to be consistent with our existing theories, and to regularities that are neither consistent nor inconsistent with our theories. Business size is important to economists in good measure because of the many size-related regularities, often anomalous, that have been uncovered. This section reviews these regularities and discusses some of their implications for economic theory.

Firm Growth and Failure

Recent work by Evans (1987a, 1987b) and Dunne, Roberts, and Samuelson (1987) using large samples of manufacturing firms have found the following relationships between firm growth, firm size, and firm age.[29] (1) Firm growth decreases with firm size for firms of the same age and decreases with firm age for firms of the same size. (2) The variability of firm growth decreases with firm age for firms of the same size and, to a weaker extent, with firm size for firms of the same age. (3) The probability that a firm will fail over a given period of time decreases with firm size for firms of the same age and decreases with firm age for

---

[27]Some of these results are based on fairly special assumptions and might not generalize to richer models.

[28]Also see Nelson and Winter (1982) for models which are similar in spirit.

[29]Many previous studies have documented some aspects of these regularities using smaller samples and without distinguishing separately between size and age effects. For an excellent recent study of firm growth and size see Hall (1987).

firms of the same size. The theory that comes closest to capturing these regularities is due to Jovanovic. Under the particular parametric cases he considers for the technology and the learning process, his theory is consistent with firm growth decreasing with firm age, with the variability of firm growth decreasing with age, and with the probability of firm failure decreasing with size.

Pakes and Ericson (1988) argue, however, that these implications are not robust to more general specifications of the technology and the learning process. Under fairly general assumptions, they show that Jovanovic's model (which they term the passive learning model) implies that (a) the size distribution of firms is stochastically increasing over time (i.e. roughly speaking the average size of survivors increases over time) and (b) past values of firm size have a longlasting effect on future firm size (i.e. there is a high degree of autocorrelation between current and lagged values of firm size). They find that (a) holds for both manufacturing and retail trade but that (b) holds for retail trade but not for manufacturing. They go on to show that their own model (which they term the active learning model) implies (a) and (c) past values of firm size have no longlasting effect on future firm size. Their model is consistent with manufacturing but not retail trade.

Future work in this area will be needed to develop theories that can explain the age-size-growth regularities discussed above and the resulting evolution of the size distribution of firms. The results discussed above suggest that learning considerations will prove important. Individuals must learn about their general abilities as entrepreneurs, learn how to operate particular technologies, learn about location or other aspects of market demand, and learn about new technologies or ways of doing things. Our guess is that the relative importance of these various kinds of learning will vary over the lifecycle of the firm and across different industries. Integrating these kinds of learning considerations with capital adjustment considerations will prove valuable.

Wages and Job Stability

The second set of regularities concern wages, turnover, and other job characteristics across firm size. (1) Smaller firms and establishments pay less than larger firms and establishments even after controlling for observable worker-characteristics such as education and experience and whether the firm or establishment is unionized and the industry in which the individual works.[30] There is mixed evidence on whether the pay differences are due to unobservable worker characteristics. Using a fixed-effects estimator that ostensibly controls for unobservable worker characteristics. Brown and Medoff (1985) find that most of the differential remains while Evans and Leighton (1988) find that virtually all of the differential disappears for firms with more than 25 employees. (2) Small-firm jobs are less stable. Workers in these jobs have shorter tenures, are more likely to quit or to be fired, and are more likely to experience a future spell of unemployment.[31] (3) Small-firm jobs are more likely to be part time and small firms employ a disproportionate number of women, blacks, and teenagers.

The wage-size relationship is especially important because it is inconsistent with the theory of compensating differ-

---

[30]See Brown and Medoff (1985) and Evans and Leighton (1988) for an analysis of a number of datasets.

[31]See Brown and Medoff (1985) and Evans and Leighton (1988) for an analysis of several datasets.

entials which has been center-piece of labor economists since Adam Smith. Brown and Medoff (1985) argue that larger firms and establishments do not appear to get better workers than smaller firms and establishments. Workers at larger firms and establishments appear to get rents (even without the benefit of a union) which are difficult to reconcile with competitive theory.

The finding that wages are apparently not being set equal to marginal value products is broadly consistent with efficiency-wage theory which is the leading alternative to the competitive-wage theory.[32] Efficiency wage theory argues that firms choose the wage to minimize the per-unit cost of labor. Firms may find it profitable to pay supracompetitive wages if, faced with imperfect information about worker quality, higher wages lead to higher quality *on average*. For example, suppose that larger firms have more trouble monitoring workers than do smaller firms. By paying workers more than their reservation wage large firms reduce shirking in the face of imperfect monitoring.[33]

As Brown and Medoff (1985) point out, however, none of the existing theories of labor-market behavior is entirely consistent with the known regularities. For example, it is unclear why larger firms would use supracompetitive wages to deter shirking rather than steep wage-tenure profiles, stock options, or bonuses. Moreover, the efficiency-wage theories do not have very sharp predictions about the precise structure of the wage-size relationship other than that there might be one. Evans and Leighton (1988) have found that the cross-sectional wage-size relationship is due to very small firms (fewer than 25 employ-

ees) paying low wages and very large firms (1000 or more employees) paying high wages. Wages are independent of firm and plant size for firms with 25–999 employees. This sort of finding places important restrictions on the effect of size on personnel technologies for hiring and monitoring workers. Further work is also needed to determine the importance of unobserved worker quality. The findings of Evans and Leighton (1988) suggest that compensating differentials for unobserved worker quality might be almost the whole explanation for the regularities cited above.

Innovation

Schumpeter's conjecture that larger firms are more innovative than smaller firms has stimulated many empirical studies of the relationship between firm size and innovation.[34] While these studies face enormous measurement problems because of the difficulty of quantifying innovation, they tend to show that smaller firms are at least as innovative as larger firms. Scherer (1982) concludes from a review of the qualitative and quantitative evidence that

> A little bit of bigness—up to sales levels of $250 to $400 million at 1978 price levels—is good for invention and innovation. But beyond the threshold further bigness adds little or nothing, and it carries the danger of diminishing the effectiveness of inventive and innovative performance.

Data collected by the U.S. Small Business Administration suggests an even stronger connection between innovation and firm size. The SBA identified innova-

---

[32]See Krueger and Summers (1988) for a recent analysis.
[33]See Bulow and Summers (1984) for a model along these lines.
[34]See Kamien and Schwartz (1975) and F. M. Scherer (1982) for a critical review of the theoretical and empirical literature.

tions from a variety of publications for 1982.[35] They found that firms with fewer than 500 employees generated 36.2 innovations per million employees while firms with 500 or more employees generated 31.0 innovations per million employees. The difference is particularly striking for manufacturing in which firms with fewer than 500 employees generated 32.2 innovations per million employees while firms with 500 or more employees generated 25.5 innovations per employee. A recent analysis of the manufacturing data by Acs and Audretsch (1987) found that the difference between the small-firm and large-firm innovation rates systematically differs across industries. The small-firm innovation rate is relatively higher in industries which have a high proportion of skilled labor, high proportion of large firms, high overall innovation rates, low capital intensity, low concentration, low unionization rates, and more standardized products.

Financial Characteristics

Our final set of regularities concern evidence, on the one hand, that smaller firms have more difficulty obtaining capital and evidence, on the other hand, that smaller firms have abnormally high stock market returns. Several recent papers have found that liquidity constraints bear more heavily on smaller firms, that is smaller firms are more likely to be unable to obtain capital at market interest rates and therefore to be subject to credit rationing. Evans and Jovanovic (1988) find that most individuals who switch from wage work to self-employment face binding liquidity constraints that forces them to use an inefficiently small amount of capital and some individuals are deterred altogether from starting businesses because of binding liquidity constraints. Fazzari,

Hubbard, and Petersen (1987) find that the smaller publicly traded firms face liquidity constraints and that smaller firms have more difficulty obtaining capital during downturns. According to Fazzari *et al.*, smaller firms are more dependent on internal finance or bank loans than are larger firms. The largest firms account for 74 percent of total manufacturing assets over the period of their study but issued 99 percent of all new shares and 92 percent of all new corporate bonds. Changes in liquidity supply therefore bear more heavily on smaller firms who rely more heavily on bank loans. Fazzari *et al.* document that the credit sources for smaller firms dry up more rapidly during downturns than the credit sources for larger firms.

Recent research in finance has tried to explain several anomalies that are directly or indirectly associated with small firms.[36] First, there are deterministic seasonalities in stock market returns. The most famous of these is the January effect. Small firms display excess returns in January. Second, stock returns are negatively correlated at a frequency of 3–5 years. This effect, known as mean reversion, is strongest for small firms and coincides roughly with the business cycle. Third, the random-walk model of efficient securities markets is rejected most strongly for small firms using a variety of tests.

We conjecture that the anomalies found in the finance literature can be explained in good part by the fact that liquidity constraints bear more heavily on smaller firms together with the fact that the availability of liquidity to firms varies seasonally and over the business cycle. The January effect can be explained by the fact that smaller firms have especially high liquidity in January after the Christmas sales season. Mean

---

[35]See U.S. Small Business Administration (1985).
[36]For a review of these see Thaler (1987a, 1987b).

reversion can be explained by the fact that liquidity dries up faster for smaller than for larger firms when the economy goes into a recession. Notably, the 3–5 year frequency of recessions corresponds roughly to the autocorrelation pattern found in the mean-reversion literature. See Brock (1988) for further details.

Explaining the small-firm effects we have examined in this section will help economists not only better understand the role of small businesses in the economy, but also obtain a richer understanding of the operation of markets. These empirical aspects of small firms also have interesting implications for government policies towards small business, a topic to which we now turn.

V. Policy Applications of Small-Business Economics

The expanding role of small businesses in the economy has confronted policy makers with a number of important issues and economists with a plethora of fascinating research questions. We highlight some of the key policy questions that are or should be under investigation by economists. We begin by discussing the role of small firms in the labor market. David Birch's pioneering work on this topic, of course, stimulated much of the early work on small-business economics. We then turn to the relationships among small firms and macroeconomic policies. We conclude by reviewing some of our own research on the differential effect of government policies on small firms.

Small Firms and the Job Market

Birch's (1979) claim that small businesses create a disproportionate share of new jobs piqued the interest of policymakers who, in the high unemployment days of the early 1980s, were interested in new methods for reducing unemployment. While we have not conducted a systematic survey, our casual impression from newspaper accounts in the last decade is that a number of states have adopted programs for small business–loan funds, technology parks, incubator programs, and tax-incentives—at least in part because of their belief that small-business formation would promote jobs and economic prosperity. Policymakers have also expressed interest in programs that stimulate small-business formation by unemployed or otherwise disadvantaged workers. Several Western European countries have adopted programs to stimulate small-firm formation by unemployed workers.[37] These programs, which provide financial and other assistance to unemployed workers who start firms, were a response to chronically high rates of unemployment on the one hand and low rates of business formation on the other hand compared with the United States. In this country several experimental programs have tried to encourage business formation by disadvantaged workers—e.g. low-income, unskilled workers, many of them on welfare.[38] The U.S. Department of Labor is implementing experimental programs in several states to provide financial and managerial assistance to unemployed workers who start small firms.[39]

It is perhaps a good measure of the need for a new specialty in small-business economics that the development and implementation of small-business policies has quickly outpaced economic research that might help guide these policies. To illustrate this point it is helpful to consider some of the unre-

---

[37]See Bendick and Egan (1987) for a summary and critique.
[38]See Balkin (1988).
[39]See U.S. Department of Labor (1987) for a description of the proposed project.

solved issues raised by the job generation literature. The finding that small businesses create a disproportionate share of new jobs, while interesting, begs a number of questions which need to be addressed before we can understand the precise importance of small firms in the labor market. We review some of the research on these questions below.

There are important differences in job characteristics across firm sizes as we have already seen. Smaller-firm jobs pay lower wages, offer fewer job benefits, and are more likely to be temporary or part time. Therefore smaller firms may not have generated a disproportionately large share of new hours worked or new compensation (wages plus fringe benefits) even if they have generated a disproportionately large share of jobs. Unfortunately, this question is not easy to address because the datasets—e.g. Dun and Bradstreet—used to estimate job creation have little or no data on hours of work or compensation.[40]

Job stability also differs across firm sizes. Because small firms are more likely to fail and have more variable growth than large firms, the jobs created by small firms are more likely to disappear than the jobs created by large firms. Dunne, Roberts, and Samuelson (1987) have shown that, when the higher failure rate of small firms is taken into consideration, the expected number of jobs created by small businesses is not disproportionately greater than the expected number of jobs created by large businesses. Their analysis, however, ignores the fact that high small-business exit rates are often accompanied by high small-business formation rates. Thus the jobs lost by failing small businesses may be quickly replaced by jobs created by new small businesses. For example, Massachusetts has had a low unemployment rate in recent years despite the high failure rate of technology-based businesses around Boston. Many of these companies quickly fail. But the workers dismissed from them quickly find jobs with newly formed high technology companies.

Jonathan Leonard (1986) argues that Birch's finding may be a statistical artifact resulting from the expansion of businesses who for whatever reason are less than their optimal sizes and the contraction of businesses who for whatever reason are larger than their optimal sizes. At a point in time small businesses will have a disproportionate number of businesses that are less than their equilibrium size and large businesses will have a disproportionate number of businesses that are greater than their optimal size. Businesses that are too small expand over time and businesses that are too large contract over time giving the appearance that small firms are generating a disproportionate share of new jobs. Many of these new jobs are, in effect, being created by large firms that are temporarily small. Leonard presents data from Equal Employment Opportunity Commission files that suggest that at least part of Birch's finding is a statistical illusion.[41,42]

---

[40]It is not impossible however. The May 1979, 1983, and 1987 Current Population Surveys have information on the size of the firm in which respondents work. It would be possible to use this information to calculate changes in the distribution of working hours and wages across firm sizes between these years.

[41]His results are not sufficiently refined for us to determine how much is an illusion and how much is real.

[42]An important point to keep in mind about Dunne, Roberts, and Samuelson's finding and Leonard's finding, however, is that their datasets do not cover most of the 1980s, a period which has had unusually rapid small business growth.

Lost amidst the controversy over whether small firms create a disproportionate share of new jobs and whether those jobs are worthwhile jobs, is the significance of small-business job creation for government policies. In and of itself the fact that small firms create a disproportionately large share of new jobs does not provide an efficiency justification for government assistance programs to stimulate small-firm formations. For example, government assistance might stimulate the formation of businesses by entrepreneurs who were not sufficiently efficient to make a go of it on their own. The firms started by such entrepreneurs might be less likely to grow and more likely to fail than firms started by entrepreneurs without government assistance.[43] Bendick and Egan (1987) find evidence of just such an effect for the British and French start-up assistance programs for unemployed workers and question whether such programs are a cost-effective means of creating new jobs.

To justify small-business assistance programs on efficiency grounds it is necessary to identify market breakdowns that lead to too few small firms or too few small-firm jobs. A traditional rationale for small-business loan subsidies is that capital-market imperfections lead to small firms getting too small a supply of capital. Until recently, most of the evidence of such imperfections was anecdotal. But, as mentioned earlier, work by Evans and Jovanovic and Fazzari, Hubbard, and Petersen finds that smaller firms are more likely to face liquidity constraints. Depending upon the precise reason for these liquidity constraints—an important topic for further research—government assistance programs to small firms might increase economic efficiency.

Another possible justification for small-firm assistance programs is that other government programs may reduce the number of small firms below the efficient level by imposing fixed costs that bear more heavily on smaller firms. We explore this issue in more detail below when we discuss the optimal design of regulatory programs towards small firms. But it is useful to point out the implication of this problem for the jobs question. Suppose that large firms find it efficient not to hire low-skilled workers.[44] These workers would be unemployed unless they can be absorbed by small firms. But the imposition of fixed costs by various government programs reduces the number of small firms below the efficient level. For example, FICA taxes probably bear more heavily on smaller firms because of the administrative costs in meeting the FICA requirements and because of the increased capital requirements they place on liquidity-constrained small firms. Consequently, an insufficient number of small firms are formed and therefore too few of the unemployed workers are absorbed into small firms. It is *conceivable* that a second-best policy in these circumstances would involve subsidizing the creation of small firms.[45] Much additional work will be necessary before economists will be able to determine whether small-business assistance programs are efficient.

---

[43]Such would be the case in the Lucas and Jovanovic models of small businesses discussed earlier.

[44]This would be possible under some of the efficiency-wage theories.

[45]It is important to note that if there are binding liquidity constraints, subsidized loans may attract "good" entrepreneurs who would have entered but for the constraints. See Evans and Jovanovic for details.

Small Firms and Macroeconomic Policy

The expansion of the small-business sector has potentially important macroeconomic implications. The increase in the fraction of workers employed by small firms which are less able to weather economic downturns suggests that unemployment will increase more rapidly in future recessions. More jobs are likely to be lost because of firm closures and because of layoffs compared with previous recessions.[46] Of course, the flip side of this problem is that unemployment might decrease more rapidly in future upturns to the extent that smaller firms expand more rapidly than larger firms.[47] To help government policymakers address these concerns, more research is needed on the unemployment experience of small versus large firm workers—Do workers at smaller firms experience longer unemployment durations than otherwise comparable workers at larger firms?—and on the historical experience of job loss across firm sizes—Is our conjecture correct that small firm jobs are more fragile during downturns?

The possibility of a high run up in unemployment as a result of recession-induced small business failures and contractions suggests that policymakers might want to exercise more caution in implementing macroeconomic policies that have especially adverse effects on small firms. Evidence that smaller firms are more likely to face liquidity constraints, for example, suggests that policies which increase capital rationing by financial institutions or decrease the amount of self-financing available to firms will have a larger effect on smaller firms. Fazzari, Hubbard, and Petersen argue that the Tax Reform Act of 1986 may have had a more positive effect on investment than is widely believed. Although this Act may have increased the marginal cost of capital it also decreased the tax rate of inframarginal as well as marginal corporate profit. By increasing cash flow the Act may have stimulated investment by liquidity-constrained firms. Changes in the supply of high-powered money in the economy may also have a differential effect on small firms. If there is credit rationing, reductions in the quantity of high-powered money may have a greater effect on the quantity of credit supplied (and thus on the fraction of firms that are liquidity constrained) than on real interest rates.[48] Efforts to reduce inflationary pressures by reducing the money supply may have especially high costs for small firms and their employees. The effect of credit rationing on small firms over the business cycle is an especially interesting area of research.

Small Firms and Regulatory Policy

Many government rules and regulations impose easier requirements on smaller firms or exempt smaller firms from the requirements altogether. The "Mrs. Murphy" exemption to the Civil Rights Act of 1968 is the classic example. Owner-occupied apartment buildings

---

[46]The greater potential instability of jobs is not just a small-business phenomenon. Larger businesses are making greater use of part-time or part-year workers, temporary workers provided by personnel supply services, full-time workers who receive fewer pension and health benefits than regulator employees, and self-employed individuals who work as outside contractors for other businesses. Based on U.S. Labor Department figures reported by Louis Uchitelle (1988).

[47]And, to continue the previous footnote, to the extent that larger firms are more willing to hire temporary workers than permanent workers.

[48]For a discussion see Stiglitz (1987) and the references cited therein.

with four or fewer units—such as the rooming house owned by Mrs. Murphy, an imaginary constituent—are exempt from the nondiscrimination provisions of this act.[49] We have shown (Brock and Evans (1985) and Brock and Evans (1986)) that these measures, rather than being populist attempts to help small businessmen, may be sensible attempts to minimize the social cost of implementing government rules and regulations. The argument is worth going through because it illustrates how the application of a simple model of small businesses (based on Lucas (1978)) can help guide government policies.

Suppose that the cost function for an industry is $c(q, \theta) - c(q)/\theta$ where θ is an index of managerial ability, q is output, and $c(q)$ exhibits decreasing returns to scale.[50] Higher θ's correspond to better managers. At any given price better managers produce more output than poorer managers. The competitive equilibrium (which will exist under certain additional assumptions) for this industry is described by an equilibrium price p' and a marginal manager θ' who breaks even. Individuals with $\theta > \theta'$ operate firms. Those with $\theta < \theta'$ choose their next best opportunity (e.g. wage work). Individuals with higher θ's produce more output and have higher profits. Smaller firms are as efficient at the margin as larger firms in this model and the resulting size distribution of firms maximizes social surplus assuming there are no externalities.

This model can be used to analyze the effect of government regulations on the size distribution of businesses. Without any special treatment for small firms regulations will tend to impose higher costs per unit of output on smaller firms. These regulation-induced scale economies will tend to force smaller firms to close down in equilibrium. Under certain circumstances, the closure of small firms may decrease economic efficiency (as measured by social surplus) even after taking into account the costs of the activity (e.g. pollution) that the regulation was supposed to curtail. Exempting small firms from the regulation or imposing lighter requirements on them might be one way to avoid this welfare loss. Brock and Evans (1985, 1986) discuss several qualifications to this finding and suggestions for designing regulations that take the differential effects of regulation across firm size into account.

VI. Summary

We have tried in this paper to summarize some of what is known and much of what is not known about small businesses. The small-business sector—which a cynic might define as those businesses that economists hardly ever study—is a sizeable and growing part of the U.S. economy. The precise role of small businesses in the economy and the causes of the recent reversal in the secular decline of small businesses is a fertile area of research. Small businesses present a number of conundrums for economists. We have uncovered many facts about smaller businesses which are inconsistent with our theories. Workers at smaller firms getting paid less or smaller listed firms having excess stock market returns in January are two examples. Like most anomalies in science, these facts will help stimulate the development of more refined theories which will have implications well beyond small-business economics. Recent evidence on patterns of growth and failure across different sizes and ages of firms is stimulating the development of richer theories of firm dynamics. Evidence on pay dif-

---

[49]For other examples see Brock and Evans (1986), Chapter 4 and the references cited therein.
[50]For details see Brock and Evans (1986).

ferentials across firm sizes have motivated several theories of firm hiring and monitoring practices.

The paucity of research on small businesses together with the rising importance of small businesses in the economy has created a significant gap between what policymakers would like to know and what economists can say with some confidence. Research on the role of small businesses in the labor market, the relationship between the business cycle and small business formation, dissolution, and growth, and the effects of macroeconomic policies on small businesses will prove especially critical for the sensible formulation of government policies.

References

Acs, Z., Audretsch, D., and Carlsson, B., 1988, "Flexible Technology and Firm Size", RPIE Working Paper, 1988. Case Western Reserve University.

Balkin, S., in press, *Self-Employment for Low Income People*, New York: Praeger Press.

Bendick, M. and Egan, M., 1987, "Transfer Payment Diversion for Small Business Development: British and French Experience", *Industrial and Labor Relations Review* (July), 528–542.

Birch, D., 1979, *The Job Generation Process,* Cambridge, MA.: Center for the Study of Neighborhood and Regional Change, Massachusetts Institute of Technology.

Blau, D., 1987, "A Time Series Analysis of Self-Employment", *Journal of Political Economy* **95** (June), 445–467.

Brock, W., 1988, "The Role of Small Business in Macroeconomics and Finance", unpublished. Department of Economics, University of Wisconsin.

Brock, W. and Evans, D., 1986, *The Economics of Small Businesses: Their Role and Regulation in the U.S. Economy*, New York: Holmes and Meier.

Brock, W. and Evans, D., 1985, "The Economics of Regulatory Tiering", *Rand Journal of Economics* **16** (Autumn). 398–409.

Bulow, J. and Summers, L., 1986, "A Theory of Dual Labor Markets with Application to Industrial Policy. Discrimination, and Keynesian Unemployment", *Journal of Labor Economics* **4** (April), 376–414.

Brown, C. and Medoff, J., 1985, "The Employer Size Wage Effect", unpublished paper.

Dunne, T., Roberts, M., and Samuelson, L., 1987, "The Impact of Plant Failure on Employment Growth in the U.S. Manufacturing Sector", unpublished paper, Pennsylvania State University.

Evans, D., 1986, "The Differential Effect of Regulations across Plant and Firm Sizes", *Journal of Law and Economics* (April).

Evans, D., 1987, "Firm Growth, Size, and Age: Estimates for 100 Manufacturing Industries", *Journal of Industrial Economics* (June).

Evans, D., 1987, "Tests of Alternative Theories of Firm Growth", *Journal of Political Economy* (August).

Evans, D. and Leighton, L., 1987, *Self-Employment Selection and Earnings over the Lifecycle*. Washington, D.C.: U.S. Small Business Administration.

Evans, D. and Leighton, L., 1988, "Why Do Smaller Firms Pay Less", Department of Economies, Fordham University.

Evans, D. and Leighton, L., 1988, "Some Empirical Aspects of Entrepreneurship", Department of Economics, Fordham University.

Evans, D. and Jovanovic, B., in press, "Estimates of a Model of Entrepreneurial Choice under Liquidity Constraints", *Journal of Political Economy.*

Fazzari, S., Hubbard, R., and Peterson, B., 1987, "Financing Constraints and Corporate Investment", NBER Working Paper No. 2387, Cambridge, MA.: National Bureau of Economic Research.

Hall, B., 1987, "The Relationship between Firm Size and Firm Growth in the U.S. Manufacturing Sector", *Journal of Industrial Economics* **35** (June), 567–581.

Jovanovic, B., 1982, "Selection and Evolution of Industry", *Econometrica* **50**(3), 649–670.

Kihlstrom, R. and Laffont, J., 1979, "A General Equilibrium Entrepreneurial Theory of Firm Formation Based on Risk Aversion", *Journal of Political Economy* **59**, 719–48.

Klepper, S. and Graddy, E., 1985, "Industry Evolution and the Determinants of Market Structure", unpubl. paper, Carnegie Mellon University.

Knight, F., 1921, *Risk, Uncertainty, and Profit*, New York: Houghton Mifflin.

Krueger, A. and Summers, L., 1988, "Efficiency Wages and the Inter-Industry Wage Structure", *Econometrica* **56**, 259–294.

Leonard, J., 1986, "On the Size Distribution of Employment and Establishments", NBER Working Paper No. 1951, Cambridge: National Bureau of Economic Research.

Lucas, R., 1967, "Adjustment Costs and the Theory of Supply", *Journal of Political Economy* (August), 321–34.

Lucas, R., 1978, "On the Size Distribution of Business Firms", *Bell Journal of Economics* **9**, 508–23.

Marshall, A., 1961, *Principles of Economics,* London: Macmillan and Company.

Mills, D., 1984, "Demand Fluctuations and Endogenous Firm Flexibility", *Journal of Industrial Economies* (September), 55–71.

Pakes, A. and Ericson, R., 1987, "Empirical Implications of Alternative Models of Firm Dynamics", unpublished paper, Department of Economics. University of Wisconsin.

Scherer, F., 1980, *Industrial Marker Structure and Economic Performance* (2d ed.), Boston: Houghton Mifflin.

Schumpeter, J., 1961, *The Theory of Economic Development*, New York: Oxford University Press (reprint of 1934 edition).

Schumpeter, J., 1950, *Capitalism, Socialism, and Democracy* (3d. ed.), New York: Harper and Row.

Shephard, W., 1982, "Causes of Increased Competition in the Economy. 1939–1980", *Review of Economics and Statistics* (November), 613–626.

Simon, H. and Bonini, C., 1958, "The Size Distribution of Business Firms", *American Economic Review* **48**, 607–17.

Stiglitz, J., 1987, "The Causes and Consequences of the Dependence of Quality on Price", *Journal of Economic Literature* **25** (March), 1–48.

Thaler, R., 1987, "The January Effect", *Journal of Economics Perspectives* **1** (Summer), 197–201.

Thaler, R., 1987, "Seasonal Movements in Security Prices II: Weekend, Holiday, Turn of the Month, and Intraday Effects", *Journal of Economics Perspectives* **1** (Fall), 169–177.

Uchitelle, L., 1988, "Reliance on Temporary Jobs Hints at Economic Fragility", *New York Times*, March 16, 1988, p. 1.

U.S. Department of Commerce, various years, *Statistical Abstracts*, Washington, D.C.: Government Printing Office.

U.S. Department of Commerce, 1972, *Historical Statistics of the United States from Colonial Times to 1970,* Washington, D.C.: Government Printing Office.

U.S. Small Business Administration, various years, *The State of Small Business*, Washington, D.C.: Government Printing Office.

A General Equilibrium Entrepreneurial Theory of Firm Formation Based on Risk Aversion*
by Richard E. Kihlstrom and Jean-Jacques Laffont

We construct a theory of competitive equilibrium under uncertainty using an entrepreneurial model with historical roots in the work of Knight in the 1920s. Individuals possess labor which they can supply as workers to a competitive labor market or use as entrepreneurs in running a firm. All entrepreneurs have access to the same risky technology and receive all profits from their firms. In the equilibrium, more risk averse individuals become workers while the less risk averse become entrepreneurs. Less risk averse entrepreneurs run larger firms and economy-wide increases in risk aversion reduce the equilibrium wage. A dynamic process of firm entry and exit is stable. The equilibrium is efficient only if all entrepreneurs are risk neutral. Inefficiencies in the number of firms and in the allocation of labor to firms are traced to inefficiencies in the risk allocation caused by institutional constraints on risk trading. In a second best sense which accounts for these constraints, the equilibrium is efficient.

I. Introduction

The recent work on the economics of uncertainty has failed to achieve general agreement as to the goals which motivate firm behavior under uncertainty. The criteria guiding firm decision making which have been proposed and studied in the existing literature include expected profit maximization and expected utility of profit maximization as well as maximization of the firm's stock market value. Difficulties with each of these criteria have led to a discussion ("Symposium on the Optimality of Competitive Capital Markets" [1974]) of the conditions under which there exists a criteria for firm decision making which achieves unanimous approval of stockholders. They have also led to the study of other more sophisticated criteria for firm decision making. The paper of Drèze (1974) is one in which this latter approach is taken. Each of these subse-

Originally appeared in *Journal of Political Economy*, 1979, Volume 87, Number 4.

*Research support from the National Science Foundation under grant SOC-76-11583 is gratefully acknowledged. Much of this work was completed while Kihlstrom was a visitor at the Laboratoire d'Econometrie, L'Ecole Polytechnique. Their support for that visit is greatly appreciated. Finally, we also would like to thank Jean Michel Grandmont, Sergiu Hart, Glenn Loury, Robert Lucas, Ed Prescott, Sherwin Rosen, and Hugo Sonnenschein for helpful comments.

quent approaches has achieved only limited success. For example, unanimity can be achieved only in limited technological circumstances. Similarly, the equilibria of Drèze are not always efficient in the "second best" sense of Diamond (1967).

In this paper we construct a competitive general equilibrium theory of the firm under uncertainty which is based on an entrepreneurial model having its historical roots in the work of Knight (1921). The entrepreneurial model permits us simultaneously to use the expected utility maximization criterion and to provide a justification for its use. This is accomplished by assuming that for each firm there is an expected utility maximizing entrepreneur who makes decisions for the firm. Furthermore, the model uses a free-entry assumption to endogenously determine the number of firms and the identity of the entrepreneurs who run them. It also permits us to identify the individual characteristics of individuals who choose to become entrepreneurs.

In the model, individuals are assumed to have a choice between operating a risky firm or working for a riskless wage. There are, of course, many factors which should influence this choice. The most important ones would include entrepreneurial ability, labor skills, attitudes toward risk, and initial access to the capital required to create a firm. The present paper focuses on risk aversion as the determinant which explains who becomes an entrepreneur and who works as a laborer. The equilibrium which is shown to exist has the property that less risk averse individuals become entrepreneurs, while the more risk averse work as laborers.

In addition to providing an explanation for the identity of entrepreneurs, the entrepreneurial model can also be used to study several issues of traditional interest to economists. One of these is the process of firm entry and exit.

Specifically, using the model described below, it is possible to analyze the dynamics of firm entry and exit in a general equilibrium context. This can be done using a formalization of a tâtonnement process which is analogous to that commonly used to study the stability of competitive equilibrium. While our stability analysis is less complete and more special than the analysis in the stability literature for competitive equilibrium, it nevertheless introduces an element, specifically firm entry and exit, which this literature was unable to incorporate. Furthermore, this element is introduced while retaining the general equilibrium framework and the basic price-adjustment process. In our general equilibrium process, as in the tâtonnement process used in the competitive equilibrium literature, prices (in our case, wages) adjust to (labor) market disequilibrium by rising when there is excess supply. Earlier formalizations of the entry-exit process, specifically, those in Quandt and Howrey (1968) and Brock (1972), were partial equilibrium models. They were also based on formalizations of the adjustment process which, while similar in spirit, differed in detail from the tâtonnement price-adjustment process used in the competitive equilibrium framework. For example, in the papers by Quandt and Howrey and by Brock, the dynamic variable is the number of firms in an industry. The industry grows when profits (or excess profits) are positive; it contracts when profits are negative.

Another traditional question which can be investigated using the entrepreneurial model concerns the determinants of the distribution of firm size. Specifically, an entrepreneur's attitude toward risk can be related to the size of the firm which he operates. While it might be conjectured that more risk averse entrepreneurs run smaller firms, this is not always true. However, it does follow when the production function satisfies certain conditions which are spelled out in theorem 3 below.

It is also possible to use this model to study one determinant of the distribution of income between workers and entrepreneurs. Specifically, it can be shown that, under certain conditions, the equilibrium wage level would be depressed if the economy's population became more risk averse.

Finally, it is possible to investigate the efficiency of the equilibrium of the entrepreneurial model. In general the equilibrium is inefficient and the inefficiency takes three forms: risks are maldistributed, firms are operated at the wrong levels, and there is an inappropriate number of firms. It is shown, however, that all of these forms of inefficiency occur because there are institutional constraints embodied in the model which prohibit an efficient allocation of risks when entrepreneurs are risk averse. This is seen in two ways. First, the equilibrium is efficient if, in equilibrium, all entrepreneurs are risk neutral. Second, we follow Diamond (1967) and Radner (1968) and investigate the efficiency of equilibrium in a second best or "limited" sense which permits a less than completely efficient allocation of risks. Although the "limited efficiency" approach taken in this paper is in the same spirit as those adopted by Diamond and by Radner, it employs a different concept of limited efficiency than the ones they employed. Thus we accept the specific institutional constraints imposed by our equilibrium model on the distribution of risk and ask only that, given these constraints, all other decisions be made efficiently (Pareto optimally). The constraints on risk trading imposed in taking this approach are, in fact, stronger than those introduced by Diamond and by Radner. It is possible, however, to show that if, in defining limited efficiency, these constraints are imposed, then the equilibrium is efficient in the limited sense.

Because all of the inefficiencies which may arise in an equilibrium can be traced to the institutional constraints on risk trading, it is reasonable to conjecture that the efficiency properties of the equilibrium will be substantially improved by the introduction of at least some market opportunities for risk sharing among entrepreneurs and between entrepreneurs and workers. The introduction of a stock market in which the entrepreneur can raise capital for the purpose of financing his input purchases would be one way of providing additional opportunities for risk sharing. Sharecropping arrangements provide another device by which risks are, in fact, often shared. This is especially true in agricultural economies. The present paper does not investigate the issues which arise when either of these risk sharing possibilities becomes available. In a subsequent paper (Kihlstrom and Laffont 1978), we have, however, succeeded in studying these extensions of the entrepreneurial model discussed here. The emphasis there is on the stock market as a device for risk sharing. It is specifically shown that the introduction of a stock market does, indeed, result in equilibrium allocations which are efficient in a stronger sense than that considered here. Specifically they are efficient in the sense of Diamond.

This paper concludes with a brief summary of our results and a discussion of their relationship to Knight's above-mentioned entrepreneurial theory.

II. The Model

The set of agents is identified with the interval $[0, 1]$. If $\alpha \in [0, 1]$, individual α has the von Neumann Morgenstern utility function $u(I, \alpha)$ where I represents income, and $I \in [0, \infty]$. For all $I \geq 0$, the first and second derivatives u_I and u_{II} exist and are continuous. The marginal utility u_I is positive and nonincreasing, that is, $u_{II} \leq 0$. Thus all agents are risk averse or indifferent to risk.

We also assume that the Arrow (1971)-Pratt (1964) absolute risk aversion measure is nondecreasing in α. More precisely, if α exceeds β, then agent α is at least as risk averse as agent β in the sense that

$$r(I, \alpha) = -\frac{u_{II}(I, \alpha)}{u_I(I, \alpha)} \geqq -\frac{u_{II}(I, \beta)}{u_I(I, \beta)}$$

$$= r(I, \beta) \qquad (1)$$

for all $I \in (0, \infty)$.

Each agent can become an entrepreneur and use without cost a technology defined by a continuous production function $y = g(L, x)$ where $y \geqq 0$ is output, $L \geqq 0$ is the labor input, and x is the value taken by a nondegenerate random parameter $\bar{x}$ with support $[0, \bar{x}]$, $0 < \bar{x} < +\infty$.

The marginal product g_L is assumed to be continuous and positive on $[0, +\infty) \times (0, \bar{x}]$. The second derivative is continuous and nonpositive on $[0, +\infty) \times [0, \bar{x}]$. Thus g exhibits nonincreasing returns to scale for each x. In addition, $g(0, x) = g(L, 0) = 0$ for all $x \in [0, \bar{x}]$ and $L \in [0, +\infty)$, while $g(L, x) > 0$ on $(0, +\infty) \times (0, \bar{x}]$.

A variety of interpretations of the random variables $\tilde{x}$ is possible. In all of these interpretations, the stochastic distribution of $\tilde{x}$ is assumed to be the same for all firms. On the one extreme we can assume that the random variables which determine the output of each firm are stochastically independent. At the other extreme they can be perfectly correlated. In this case, not only is the distribution of $\tilde{x}$ the same for all firms, but the same random variable $\tilde{x}$ influences the output of all firms. Intermediate cases occur when the $\tilde{x}$s are correlated but not perfectly correlated. In each of these alternative interpretations, all individuals are assumed to have the same beliefs about the distribution of $\tilde{x}$, that is, the distribution of $\tilde{x}$ is objective.

The price of output is 1 and labor is hired at a competitive wage w. It is assumed that the demands of entrepreneurship preclude additional work by agents who choose to operate a firm. Thus agents have a choice. They can become entrepreneurs and receive an uncertain income or they can work and receive the market wage w. If an individual becomes an entrepreneur and employs L workers he will receive profits equal to

$$g(L, \tilde{x}) - wL. \qquad (2)$$

To avoid the difficulties associated with the problem of bankruptcy we assume that all individuals begin with A units of income and that they are unable to hire workers who cannot be paid if $\tilde{x} = 0$. Thus L must be less than or equal to A/w.

An individual who becomes an entrepreneur will choose to employ $L(w, \alpha)$ workers where $L(w, \alpha)$ is the L value in $[0, A/w]$ which maximizes

$$Eu(A + g(L, \tilde{x}) - wL, \alpha). \qquad (3)$$

Our assumptions on u and g guarantee that $L(w, \alpha)$ exists. If either $u_{II} < 0$ or $g_{LL} < 0$, then $L(w, \alpha)$ will be unique. When entrepreneur α faces the wage w and employs $L(w, \alpha)$ workers, his profits are random and equal to

$$\tilde{\pi}(w, \alpha) = g(L(w, \alpha), \tilde{x}) - wL(w, \alpha). \qquad (4)$$

If the wage is w, agent α will choose to be an entrepreneur when

$$Eu(A + \tilde{\pi}(w, \alpha), \alpha) \geqq u(A + w, \alpha). \qquad (5)$$

He will be a worker at wage w if

$$Eu(A + \tilde{\pi}(w, \alpha), \alpha) \leqq u(A + w, \alpha), \qquad (6)$$

and he will be indifferent if the equality holds in (5) and (6).

Equilibrium is reached when the labor market clears. At the equilibrium wage, the labor demanded by all agents who choose to become entrepreneurs equals that supplied by agents who choose to enter the labor market.

Formally, an equilibrium is a partition $\{\Delta, \Gamma\}$ of $[0, 1]$ and a wage w, that is, a pair $(\{\Delta, \Gamma\}, w)$; for which

(E.1) labor supply equals labor demand in the sense that

$$\int_\Delta L(w, \alpha)\mu(d\alpha) = \mu(\Gamma)$$

where μ is Lebesgue measure and

(E.2) for all $\alpha \in \Delta$ (5) holds and for all $\alpha \in \Gamma$ (6) holds.

III. The Existence and Uniqueness of Equilibrium

We can now prove that an equilibrium exists. The first step is to define $w(\alpha)$, the certainty equivalent wage which makes agent α indifferent between the two activities—work and entrepreneurship. Formally, $w(\alpha)$ is defined by

$$Eu(A + \tilde{\pi}(w(\alpha), \alpha), \alpha)$$
$$= u(A + w(\alpha), \alpha). \qquad (7)$$

The properties of $w(\alpha)$ are established in the lemma which follows. These properties will permit us to describe the structure of the equilibrium in a way which simplifies the existence proof. Further interpretive remarks follow the formal statement of the lemma.

Lemma

Assume that for each I, $r(I, \alpha)$ is an increasing function of α.[1] Also assume that either $g_{LL} < 0$ or $u_{II} < 0$. Then:

i) For each $\alpha \in [0, 1]$, $Eu(A + \tilde{\pi}(w, \alpha), \alpha) - u(A + w, \alpha)$ is a continuous monotonically decreasing function of w.

ii) $w(\alpha)$ is a well-defined function of α, that is, for each $\alpha \in [0, 1]$, $w(\alpha)$ exists and is unique. In addition $w(\alpha) > 0$.

iii) If $w > (<) w(\alpha)$, then $Eu(A + \tilde{\pi}(w, \alpha), \alpha) < (>) \mu(A + w, \alpha)$.

iv) If $\alpha > \beta$, then $w(\alpha) < w(\beta)$.

v) If $\beta > (<) \alpha$, then $Eu(A + \tilde{\pi}(w(\alpha), \beta), \beta) < (>) u(A + w(\alpha), \beta)$.

vi) If $0 < w < w(\beta)$, then $L(w, \beta) > 0$.

This is true, in particular, if $w = w(\alpha)$ where $\alpha > \beta$.

Remark 1. Result iv asserts that more risk averse individuals are induced to become workers at lower wages than less risk averse agents. In order to interpret result v, note that agent α will be the marginal entrepreneur if the equilibrium wage is $w(\alpha)$. Result v asserts that all individuals who are more (less) risk averse than the marginal entrepreneur will be workers (entrepreneurs). This result implies that in any equilibrium, there will be a marginal entrepreneur $\hat{\alpha}$ for whom $w(\hat{\alpha})$ is the equilibrium wage. The set of entrepreneurs Δ will be the interval $[0, \hat{\alpha}]$ and the set of workers Γ will be $(\hat{\alpha}, 1]$. The problem of finding an equilibrium then reduces to the problem of finding a marginal entrepreneur $\hat{\alpha}$ for whom E.1 holds when $w = w(\hat{\alpha})$, $\Delta = (0, \hat{\alpha}]$, and $\Gamma = (\hat{\alpha}, 1]$, that is, for whom $\int_0^{\hat{\alpha}} L(w(\hat{\alpha}), \alpha)\mu(d\alpha) = 1 - \hat{\alpha}$.

Proof. (i) The assumptions made about u and g guarantee that $Eu(A + g(L, \tilde{x}) - wL, \alpha)$ is a strictly concave continuous function of L and a continuous function of w.

To prove monotonicity, note first that for each nonnegative L, the monotonicity of u implies that

$$Eu(A + g(L, \tilde{x}) - wL, \alpha)$$
$$< Eu(A + g(L, \tilde{x}) - w'L, \alpha) \qquad (8)$$

---

[1]If $r(I, \alpha)$ is nondecreasing but not strictly increasing the strict inequalities in iii, iv, and v are replaced by weak inequalities.

when $w > w'$. Maximizing over L on each side of inequality (8) implies the inequality

$$Eu(A + \tilde{\pi}(w, \alpha), \alpha)$$
$$= \max_{\frac{A}{w} \geq L \geq 0} Eu(A + g(L, \tilde{x}) - wL, \alpha)$$
$$\leq \max_{\frac{A}{w'} \geq L \geq 0} Eu(A + g(L, \tilde{x}) - w'L, \alpha)$$
$$= Eu(A + \tilde{\pi}(w', \alpha), \alpha) \qquad (9)$$

when $w > w'$. Thus $Eu(A + \tilde{\pi}(w, \alpha), \alpha)$ is nonincreasing and $Eu(A + \tilde{\pi}(w, \alpha), \alpha) - u(A + w, \alpha)$ is monotonically decreasing.

ii) It is easily seen that $Eu(A + \tilde{\pi}(w, \alpha), \alpha) - u(A + w, \alpha) > 0$ when $w \approx 0$. If, on the other hand, w is large, then

$$g(L, x) - wL \leq \max g(L, x) \approx 0$$
$$0 \leq L \leq \frac{A}{w}$$
$$0 \leq x \leq \bar{x} \qquad (10)$$

and equation (6) will hold. Because of the continuity established in i, the intermediate value theorem implies the existence of a positive wage $w(\alpha)$ which satisfies (7). The monotonicity established in i implies the uniqueness of $w(\alpha)$. Monotonicity also implies inequality iii. Figure 1 illustrates the situation.

iv) We use the fact that $w(\alpha)$ is the certainty equivalent of $\tilde{\pi}(w(\alpha), \alpha)$. We also define $w(\alpha, \beta)$ to be the certainty equivalent of $\tilde{\pi}(w(\alpha), \alpha)$ for agent β. Pratt's (1964) theorem 1 is now applied to prove that $\beta > (<) \alpha$ implies $w(\alpha, \beta) < (>) w(\alpha)$. The monotonicity of $u(w, \beta)$ in w then guarantees that

$$Eu(A + \tilde{\pi}(w(\alpha), \alpha), \beta)$$
$$= u(A + w(\alpha, \beta), \beta)$$
$$< (>)u(A + w(\alpha), \beta) \qquad (11)$$

when $\beta > (<) \alpha$.

Figure 1

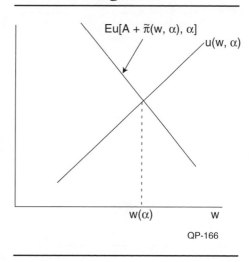

QP-166

Now note that, by definition of $\tilde{\pi}(w, \beta)$,

$$Eu(A + \tilde{\pi}(w(\alpha), \beta), \beta)$$
$$\geq Eu(A + \tilde{\pi}(w(\alpha), \alpha), \beta). \qquad (12)$$

When $\beta < \alpha$ inequalities (11) and (12) combine to yield

$$Eu(A + \tilde{\pi}(w(\alpha), \beta), \beta)$$
$$> u(A + w(\alpha), \beta). \qquad (13)$$

Figure 2 illustrates what is easily proven; that inequality iv is a consequence of inequality (13), the equality defining $w(\beta)$, and the fact that $Eu(\tilde{\pi}(w, \beta), \beta) - u(w, \beta)$ decreases monotonically in w.

v) Inequality v follows immediately from iii and iv.

vi) Since iii implies that $Eu(A + \tilde{\pi}(w, \beta) \beta) > u(A + w, \beta)$, if $w(\beta) > w$, $\tilde{\pi}(w, \beta) = g(L(w, \beta), \bar{x}) - wL(w, \beta)$ must exceed $w > 0$ with positive probability. This is impossible if $L(w, \beta) = 0$. ||

Figure 2

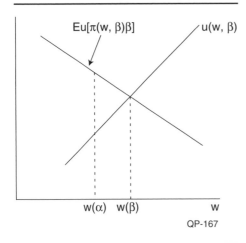

$Eu[\pi(w, \beta)\beta]$

$u(w, \beta)$

$w(\alpha)$ $w(\beta)$ w

QP-167

In the discussion of existence, the analysis is restricted to cases which satisfy assumption A: $u(I, \alpha)$ is everywhere a continuous function of α.

Theorem 1.[2] Assume that for each I, $r(I, \alpha)$ is a nondecreasing function of α. Also assume that either $g_{LL} < 0$ or $u_{II} < 0$. Under assumption A an equilibrium exists.

Proof. Under assumption A it can be shown that our assumptions guarantee that $L(w, \alpha)$ and $w(\alpha)$ are continuous functions of α on $[0, 1]$. Thus for each $w \in [w(0), w(1)]$ and $\hat{\alpha} \in [0, 1]$, $\int_0^{\hat{\alpha}} L(w, \alpha)d\alpha$ exists.

We can now find an $\hat{\alpha}^*$ such that

$$\int_0^{\hat{\alpha}^*} L(w(\hat{\alpha}^*), \alpha)d\alpha = 1 - \hat{\alpha}^*. \quad (14)$$

Note that $\int_0^{\hat{\alpha}} L(w(\hat{\alpha}), \alpha)d\alpha - (1 - \hat{\alpha})$ is a continuous function of $\hat{\alpha}$ which is negative when $\hat{\alpha} = 0$ and positive (by vi of the

lemma) when $\hat{\alpha} = 1$. The intermediate value theorem implies the existence of an $\hat{\alpha}^*$ satisfying 14.

Now we can define

$$(\{\Delta, \Gamma\}, w) = (\{[0, \hat{\alpha}^*], (\hat{\alpha}^*, 1], w(\hat{\alpha}^*)) \quad (15)$$

or

$$(\{\Delta, \Gamma\}, w) = (\{[0, \hat{\alpha}^*), [\hat{\alpha}^*, 1], w(\hat{\alpha}^*)).$$

For these entrepreneur, worker, wage combinations v of the lemma implies that condition E.2 holds while E.1 reduces to (14). ||

The next theorem gives conditions under which the equilibrium is unique.

Theorem 2. Assume that for each I, $r(I, \alpha)$ is a nondecreasing function of α. Also assume that either $g_{LL} < 0$ or $u_{II} < 0$. If, in addition, $L(w, \alpha)$ is a decreasing function of w, then the equilibrium is unique.

Proof. Because of the lemma, and for reasons discussed in remark 1, the equilibrium occurs at an $\hat{\alpha}$ for which (14) holds. In addition, the lemma implies that $L(w, \alpha) > 0$ for all α and all $w \le w(\alpha)$, and that $w(\hat{\alpha}) \ge w(\hat{\alpha}')$ if $\hat{\alpha} < \hat{\alpha}'$. Then since $L(w, \alpha)$ is a decreasing function of w, $\hat{\alpha} < \hat{\alpha}'$ implies

$$\int_0^{\hat{\alpha}'} L(w(\hat{\alpha}'), \alpha)d\alpha = \int_0^{\hat{\alpha}} L(w(\hat{\alpha}'), \alpha)d\alpha$$
$$+ \int_0^{\hat{\alpha}'} L(w(\hat{\alpha}'), \alpha)d\alpha > \int_0^{\hat{\alpha}} L(w(\hat{\alpha}'), \alpha)d\alpha.$$

Thus labor demand at $w(\hat{\alpha})$, $\int_0^{\hat{\alpha}} L(w(\hat{\alpha}), \alpha)d\alpha$, is a strictly increasing function of $\hat{\alpha}$. Furthermore, labor supply at $w(\hat{\alpha})$, $(1 - \hat{\alpha})$, is a strictly decreasing function of $\hat{\alpha}$. Therefore excess demand at $w(\hat{\alpha})$, $\int_0^{\hat{\alpha}} L(w(\hat{\alpha}), \alpha)d\alpha, - (1 - \hat{\alpha})$, is a strictly increasing function of $\hat{\alpha}$ and there can be only one $\hat{\alpha}$ at which excess demand can

---

[2]This theorem can be proved without assumption A. The assumption is made solely to permit a simple existence proof.

equal zero, that is, at which (14) can hold. ||

Conditions under which $L(w, \alpha)$ is a decreasing function of the wage w are discussed in remark 4 at the end of the following section on comparative statics.

IV. Comparative Statics

Having established the existence of an equilibrium, it is now possible to study its properties. Specifically, we can first ask how a firm's size, as measured by its labor demand, is related to the risk averseness of the entrepreneur running the firm. It might be expected that more risk averse entrepreneurs operate smaller firms, that is, use less labor than less risk averse entrepreneurs. Theorem 3 gives conditions under which this expected result obtains. The conditions require that a change in x must affect output and the marginal product of labor in the same way; if an increase in x raises output it must also raise the marginal product of labor. One important special case in which this condition holds occurs when the uncertainty enters multiplicatively

$$g(L, x) = xh(L).^3 \qquad (16)$$

Theorem 3. Assume that $L(w, \alpha) < A/w$. If $g(L, x)$ and $g_L(L, x)$ are both monotonically increasing or both monotonically decreasing functions of x, the $L(w, \alpha)$ is a monotonically decreasing function of α.

The proof is essentially the same as that given in Baron (1970) and is not reproduced.

We can now ask to what extent it is possible to describe the influence of individual attitudes toward risk and of technological parameters on the equilibrium.

In general, not much can be said about the effect of these parameters on the number of firms, a variable of particular interest. But for the purpose of studying the distribution of wealth between workers and entrepreneurs it is important to know how these parameters influence the wage. What can be shown is that, under certain reasonable conditions, an increase in individual risk aversion reduces the wage.

Theorem 4. If (i) in equilibrium, all entrepreneurs are identical, (ii) either $g_{LL} < 0$ or $u_{II} < 0$, (iii) $g(L, x)$ and $g_L(L, x)$ are both monotonically increasing (or decreasing) functions of x, and (iv) $L(w, \hat{\alpha})$ is an interior solution and a decreasing function of w, then an increase in the Arrow-Pratt absolute risk aversion measure $r(I, \hat{\alpha})$ for all I, lowers the equilibrium wage.

Remark 2. The intuitive basis for this result is as follows. Since, in equilibrium, workers are the most risk averse individuals, an economy-wide increase in risk aversion increases the supply of workers and this tends to lower the wage. This tendency is reinforced by demand changes implied by theorem 3 which applies because of assumption iii. Specifically, theorem 3 implies that an increase in the entrepreneurs' aversion to risk reduces the demand for labor.

PROOF.—If, in equilibrium, $L(w, \hat{\alpha})$ is an interior solution, the first-order maximization condition for the marginal entrepreneur is

$$Eu_I(A + g(L, \tilde{x}) - wL, \hat{\alpha})g_L(L, \tilde{x})$$
$$= Eu_I(A + g(L, \tilde{x}) - wL, \hat{\alpha})w \qquad (17)$$

where $L = L(w, \hat{\alpha})$

We also have

---

[3]This is the case considered by Baron (1970). In Baron's paper, x is interpreted as price. Equation (16) is also included in the class of cases studied by Diamond. In Diamond's terminology, (16) represents a case of stochastic constant returns to scale.

$$u(A + w, \hat{\alpha})$$
$$= Eu(A + g(L, \tilde{x}) - wL, \hat{\alpha}) \quad (18)$$

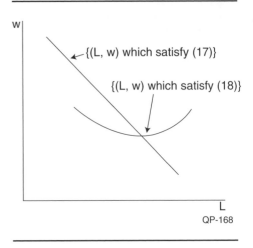

at $L = L(w, \hat{\alpha})$.

The equilibrium conditions (17) and (18) imply relationships between L and w which are described in figure 3. The relationship implied by (17) is downward sloping because of assumption iii. As indicated, (18) implies that w is a function of L which reaches its minimum when it intersects the line defined by (17). This is proved by differentiating (18) implicitly to obtain

$$\frac{dw}{dL} = -\frac{Eu_I(A + g(L, \tilde{x}) - wL, \hat{\alpha}) \times [g_L(L, \tilde{x}) - w]}{u_I(A + w, \hat{\alpha}) + Eu_I(A + g(L, \tilde{x}) - wL, \hat{\alpha})L} \quad (19)$$

The differentiation is justified by the implicit function theorem because the denominator in (19) is positive. The numerator is zero when (17) holds. The second order sufficient condition for the entrepreneurial maximization problem is satisfied because of condition ii. Thus, as reflected in figure 3, the numerator in (19) is positive (negative) and dw/dL is negative (positive) when $L < (>)$ $L(w, \hat{\alpha})$.

Now suppose that $r(I, \hat{\alpha})$ increases for every I, then theorem 3 above guarantees that $L(w, \hat{\alpha})$ is lower for each w. Also, reasoning similar to that employed in the proof of the lemma guarantees that for each L, the wage level w at which (18) holds is also reduced. Thus the r increase affects the relationships between L and w implied by (17) and (18) as shown in figure 4. As a result the equilibrium wage must decline. ||

We can now make several observations which we formalize as remarks.

Remark 3. A similar proof applies if $L(w, \hat{\alpha})$ is always an increasing function of w.

Figure 3

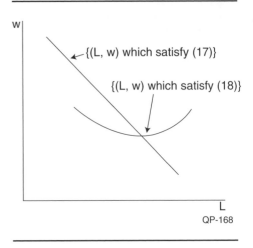

{(L, w) which satisfy (17)}

{(L, w) which satisfy (18)}

QP-168

Figure 4

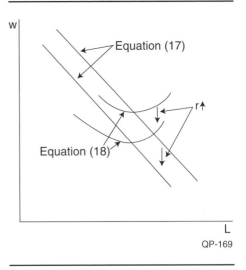

Equation (17)

Equation (18)

QP-169

Remark 4. There are several important cases in which $L(w, \hat{\alpha})$ is indeed a decreasing function of w. These occur when either (*a*) $r(I, \hat{\alpha})$ is a constant function of I, (*b*) $g(L, x)$ and $g_L(L, x)$ are both increasing (or both decreasing) functions of x and $r(I, \hat{\alpha})$ is a nonincreasing function of I, or (c) $g(L,x)$ satisfies (16) and

$$-\frac{Iu_{II}(A + I, \hat{\alpha})}{u_I(A + I, \hat{\alpha})} \leqq 1$$

for all I. The condition imposed on $u(\cdot, \hat{\alpha})$ in c asserts that when $u(A + I, \hat{\alpha})$ is considered as a function of I it has Arrow-Pratt relative risk aversion less than or equal to one.

Proof of remark 4. Implicitly differentiating (17) we obtain

$$\frac{dL}{dw} = -\frac{\begin{array}{c}-LEu_{II}(A + g(L, \tilde{x}) - wL, \hat{\alpha}) \\ \times [g_L(L, \tilde{x}) - w]\end{array}}{D}$$
$$-\frac{-Eu_I(A + g(L, \tilde{x}) - wL, \hat{\alpha})}{D} \quad (20)$$

where $D = Eu_{II}(A + g(L, \tilde{x}) - wL, \hat{\alpha})[g_L(L, \tilde{x}) - w]^2 + Eu_I(A + g(L, \tilde{x}) - wL, \hat{\alpha})g_{LL}(L, \tilde{x})$. The second-order condition for the entrepreneur's maximization problem (which is implied by condition ii of theorem 4) guarantees that the implicit function theorem applies to justify the implicit differentiation. This condition also asserts that the denominator in (20) is negative. In general, the sign of the numerator in (20) is ambiguous since the first term is ambiguous. (The second term is negative.) In case a, however, the first term is

$$LEu_{II}(A + g(L, \tilde{x})$$
$$- wL, \hat{\alpha})[g_L(L, \tilde{x}) - w]$$
$$= - rLEu_I(A + g(L, \tilde{x})$$
$$- wL, \hat{\alpha})[g_L(L, \tilde{x}) - w] \quad (21)$$

which equals zero because of the first-order condition (17). Thus in case a, the numerator is negative as is dL/dw.

In case b, the first term can be shown to be nonpositive by an argument similar to that used by Baron (1970).

In case c, the fact that $h''9(L) \leqq 0$ can be used to obtain

$$[h'(L)L\tilde{x} - wL] \leqq h(L)\tilde{x} - wL \quad (22)$$

and

$$-u_{II}(A + h(L)\tilde{x} \\ - wL, \hat{\alpha})[h'(L)L\tilde{x} - wL] \\ \leqq -u_{II}(A + h(L)\tilde{x} \\ - wL, \hat{\alpha})[h(L)\tilde{x} - wL]. \quad (23)$$

When this inequality is combined with c, the numerator in (20) is negative. ||

V. Dynamics

In this brief section, we consider the stability of a tâtonnement adjustment process similar to that used in studying the stability of competitive equilibrium. In this process, the wage is assumed to adjust to labor market disequilibrium by rising when there is excess demand and falling when there is excess supply. Specifically,

$$\frac{dw}{dt} = \phi\Big[\int_0^{\hat{\alpha}(w(t))} L(w(t), \alpha)d\alpha \\ - (1 - \alpha(w(t)))\Big] \quad (24)$$

where ϕ is a differentiable increasing function such that $\phi(0) = 0$ and where $\hat{\alpha}(w)$ satisfies the equation

$$Eu(\tilde{\pi}(w, \hat{\alpha}(w)), \hat{\alpha}(w)) = u(w, \hat{\alpha}(w)). \quad (25)$$

We define

$$V(w) = \Big(\phi\Big\{\int_0^{\hat{\alpha}(w)} L(w, \alpha)d\alpha \\ - [1 - \hat{\alpha}(w)]\Big\}\Big)^2 \quad (26)$$

to be the Lyapunov function. Then[4]

---

[4]If we assume that u_α and $u_{I\alpha}$ exist and are continuous, repeated application of the implicit function theorem implies that $\hat{\alpha}(w)$ is a differentiable function of w.

$$\frac{d}{dt}V(w(t)) = 2\phi' \left[\int_0^{\hat{\alpha}(w)} L(w, \alpha)d\alpha \right.$$

$$- (1 - \hat{\alpha}(w)) \Big]$$

$$\times \Big\{ [L(w(t), \hat{\alpha}(w(t))) + 1]$$

$$\times \hat{\alpha}'(w(t))$$

$$\left. + \int_0^{\hat{\alpha}(w(t))} \frac{\partial L}{\partial w}(w(t), \alpha)d\alpha \right\}$$

$$\times \left(\frac{dw}{dt} \right)^2. \tag{27}$$

Now $\phi' > 0$ by assumption, and $\alpha'(w(t))$ is negative because of the lemma. Thus if $\partial L/\partial w < 0$, d/dt $V(w(t))$ is negative and $w(t)$ converges to the equilibrium wage.

These results are summarized in the following theorem.

Theorem 5. Assume that for each I, $r(I, \alpha)$ is a decreasing function of α and that either $g_{LL} < 0$ or $u_{LL} < 0$. Also assume that u_α and $u_{I\alpha}$ exist and are continuous. If $L_u(w, \alpha)$ exists and is negative, then $w(t)$ converges to the unique equilibrium wage.

Remark 5. In the standard explanation for firm entry and exit, which does not admit the possibility of uncertain profits, reductions (increases) in profits caused by falling (rising) demand or increases (decreases) in cost result in exit (entry). In our entrepreneurial model demand changes are not explicitly considered and cost changes are introduced by wage changes. In addition, changes in the return to nonentrepreneurial activities, specifically labor, also cause entry or exit. Again these changes are embodied in wage changes.

The fact that returns to nonentrepreneurial activities influence firm entry and exit is a reflection of the general equilibrium nature of our formalization. In this framework, an individual's decision to enter as an entrepreneur or exit to become a worker is made after the expected utility of the random profits available to entrepreneurs has been compared to the utility of the nonrisky wages earned by workers. In the formalizations of Quandt and Howrey (1968) and of Brock (1972), firms decide to enter if (excess) profits can be made. This is appropriate when there is no uncertainty and no opportunity cost to entry other than capital costs. In our model both of these complications are present. Profits are random and the opportunity cost of becoming an entrepreneur is lost wages.

Remark 6. Since the model of the adjustment process studied here is analogous to that employed in the literature on competitive equilibrium, it is subject to the same criticisms. Specifically, the dynamic wage change equations are not explained by an underlying model of maximizing behavior. In the paper by Smith (1974), the dynamic equations which describe the process of firm entry and exit are explicitly obtained from a maximization model.

VI. Efficiency of Equilibrium

In this section, two concepts of efficiency are studied. The first is unconstrained Pareto optimality in the sense of Arrow (1964) and Debreu (1959). The second is a constrained version of Pareto optimality in which the institutional constraints on risk trading implicit in our concept of equilibrium are imposed on all allocations. The reasons for studying constrained optima will be suggested by the analysis of unconstrained optima. We will show that because of the institutional restrictions embodied in our equilibrium concept, asking for unconstrained optimality is, in general, clearly asking for too much. There are, nevertheless, interesting cases in which an equilibrium is efficient in an unconstrained sense. In addition, it is possible to specify the nature of the unconstrained inefficiencies.

Before proceeding to the formal discussion it is convenient to introduce special assumptions which are employed to simplify the analysis of unconstrained efficiency. Specifically, we now assume that $\bar{x}$ is the same random variable for all firms, that is, that the random variations in the firms' outputs are perfectly correlated. This assumption will be sufficient to permit an intuitive explanation of the inefficiencies occurring in our model. Furthermore, a general treatment would take us beyond the scope of the paper. The reader should note however that this assumption is used only in the discussion of unrestricted efficiency. In the subsequent discussion of restricted efficiency, no assumptions are made about the dependence or independence of the returns to different firms.

As a preliminary to the formal discussion, we define an unrestricted feasible allocation as a specification of Γ and Δ and of functions $v : \Delta \to [0, \infty)$ and $y(\cdot, x) : [0, 1] \to [0, \infty)$, for each x, which satisfy the conditions

$$\int_\Delta v(\alpha)\mu(d\alpha) = \mu(\Gamma) \qquad (28)$$

and

$$\int_0^1 y(\alpha, x)\mu(d\alpha)$$
$$= \int_\Delta g(v(\alpha), x)\mu(d\alpha) + A \qquad (29)$$

for each x.

The v specifies the allocation of labor to firms. Equation (28) asserts that labor supply equals demand. The function $y(\cdot, x)$ describes the allocation of income to individuals in each state. The constraints (29) require that, in each state

x, the supply of the commodity equals demand.[5]

The Pareto-optimal allocations can be studied by introducing arbitrary linear social welfare functions. Specifically, let λ be an arbitrary Lebesgue measurable function $\lambda : [0, 1] \to [0, 1]$. The corresponding social welfare function is

$$\int_0^1 \lambda(\alpha)Eu(y(\alpha, \tilde{x}), \alpha)\mu(d\alpha). \qquad (30)$$

If Γ, Δ, v, and $y(\cdot, \cdot)$ are chosen to maximize (30) subject to the constraints (28) and (29), the result is a Pareto-optimal allocation. In order to describe the Pareto optimal allocations, we study the solutions to these maximization problems for arbitrary λ functions.

First notice that it is possible for a planner who wishes to maximize (30) subject to the constraints (28) and (29) to ignore the identity of individuals who become workers and entrepreneurs and concern himself only with the number of entrepreneurs, that is, the number of firms. A similar simplification is possible in choosing v; only the distribution of labor to firms matters; it is unimportant which entrepreneur runs which firm. This makes it possible to establish a convention that facilitates the comparison of efficient allocations with equilibrium allocations. Specifically, we can assume that in making his choice of Γ and Δ, the planner simply chooses an individual $\hat{\alpha}$ ($\hat{\alpha}$ can also be interpreted as the number of firms) and then assigns $\Delta = [0, \hat{\alpha}]$ and $\Gamma = (\hat{\alpha}, 1]$.

The second simplification which is possible in the discussion of unconstrained optimality is introduced because g exhibits decreasing returns to scale. Under this assumption, efficiency

---

[5]Notice that the notation embodies the assumption that the output of all firms is affected by the same random variable $\tilde{x}$. Specifically, a "state of nature" is completely defined by x, the value taken by $\tilde{x}$. If different firms were affected by different random variables, the description of a "state" would have to specify the value taken by each of these variables.

requires that every firm produce the same amount. If this were not true, output in each state x could be increased if labor were transferred from a high output firm to a low output firm. This transfer would increase output because of the differences in labor's marginal productivity (in every state x) which would result from the initial inequality of the outputs of the two firms considered.[6]

Sicne $\gamma(\alpha)$ must be the same for all entrepreneurs (28) reduces to

$$v(\alpha) = \frac{1 - \hat{\alpha}}{\hat{\alpha}} \qquad (31)$$

for all $\alpha \in [0, \hat{\alpha}]$. Using this result, (29) becomes

$$\int_0^1 y(\alpha, x)\mu(d\alpha) = \hat{\alpha} g\left(\frac{1 - \hat{\alpha}}{\hat{\alpha}}, x\right) + A. \qquad (32)$$

The program for obtaining Pareto-optimal allocations reduces to

$$\max_{(\hat{\alpha}, y(\cdot, \cdot))} \int_0^1 \lambda(\alpha) Eu(y(\alpha, \tilde{x}), \alpha)\mu(d\alpha)$$

subject to (32) for all x. The first-order conditions are

$$\lambda(\alpha)\pi(x)u_I(y(\alpha, x), \alpha) = \delta(x),$$
$$\text{for all } \alpha \text{ and all } x \qquad (33)$$

and

$$\int_0^{\tilde{x}} \delta(x)g\left(\frac{1 - \hat{\alpha}}{\hat{\alpha}}, x\right)dx$$
$$= \int_0^{\tilde{x}} \frac{\delta(x)}{\hat{\alpha}} g_L\left(\frac{1 - \hat{\alpha}}{\hat{\alpha}}, x\right)dx \qquad (34)$$

where $\delta(x)$ is the multiplier associated with the resource constraint in state x, and $\pi(x)$ is the value of the objective probability density function at x.

Using the value of $\delta(x)$ defined by (33) and inserting in (34) we obtain, after taking the expectation over x,

$$\frac{1}{\hat{\alpha}} Eu_I(y(\alpha, \tilde{x}), \alpha)g_L\left(\frac{1 - \hat{\alpha}}{\hat{\alpha}}, \tilde{x}\right)$$
$$= Eu_I(y(\alpha, \tilde{x}), \alpha)g\left(\frac{1 - \hat{\alpha}}{\hat{\alpha}}, x\right) \qquad (35)$$

for every α.

Using (33) for two different x values, say x_1 and x_s, and for two different α values, say α and β, we also obtain

$$\frac{u_I(y(\alpha, x_s), \alpha)}{u_I(y(\alpha, x_1), \alpha)} = \frac{u_I(y(\beta, x_s), \beta)}{u_I(y(\beta, x_1), \beta)} \qquad (36)$$

for all s and all α, β.

Condition (35) can be viewed as that which determines the efficient $\hat{\alpha}$, that is, the optimal division of individuals between workers and entrepreneurs. In the special case where (16) holds, that is, when there are stochastic constant returns to scale, (35) reduces to

$$\hat{\alpha} = \left[b'\left(\frac{1 - \hat{\alpha}}{\hat{\alpha}}\right)\right] \bigg/ \left[b\left(\frac{1 - \hat{\alpha}}{\hat{\alpha}}\right)\right] \qquad (37)$$

which is the $\hat{\alpha}$ level which maximizes the output $\hat{\alpha}b$ $((1 - \hat{\alpha})/\hat{\alpha})x$ for every x. The input level $1 - \hat{\alpha}/\hat{\alpha}$ is also the one which would be chosen in an allocation which is efficient in Diamond's second-best sense.

The conditions (36) are those which characterize efficient allocations of contingent claims to the output produced.

---

[6]This result can be derived immediately by writing the Euler equation corresponding to the maximization with respect to $v(\cdot)$. We get $E\delta(\tilde{x})g_L(v(\alpha), \tilde{x}) = \delta_0$ where δ_0 is the multiplier associated with (28) and $\delta(x)$ are the multipliers associated with (29). Thus $E\delta(\tilde{x})g_L(v(\alpha), \tilde{x}) = E\delta(\tilde{x})g_L(v(\alpha'), \tilde{x})$ for all $\alpha \leq \hat{\alpha}$ and $\alpha' \leq \hat{\alpha}$. Since g_L is a decreasing function of L for each x, $v(\alpha') \neq v(\alpha)$ would make this equality impossible.

It is clear from the preceding discussion and from the conditions (35) and (36) that there will be several sources of inefficiency in an equilibrium of the type defined above. The most obvious relates to the point made earlier that in an efficient allocation all firms should be producing equal amounts if returns to scale are diminishing for each x. In general, the equilibrium will be characterized by entrepreneurs who have varying attitudes toward risk. For that reason different entrepreneurs will produce different outputs. This is one source of inefficiency. Note, however, that it will fail to arise if all entrepreneurs have the same utility function and therefore the same attitude toward risk.

A second type of inefficiency arises because of the fact that only entrepreneurs bear risks in equilibrium. This is the institutional constraint on the allocation of risk bearing of which we spoke earlier. Thus, in general, the conditions (36) cannot be satisfied if there are risk averse entrepreneurs. A special case in which this problem does not arise occurs when all entrepreneurs are indifferent to risk. In that case condition (36) holds in equilibrium because of the linearity of entrepreneurs' utility functions and the fact that workers bear no risk. We will return to discuss this case more completely later.

The third source of inefficiency which requires more discussion is the optimal choice of $\hat{\alpha}$. To discuss this problem in an appropriate setting it seems necessary to consider an equilibrium in which all entrepreneurs are the same and produce the same output. This eliminates inefficiencies of the first type mentioned and makes it possible to ask if (35) might be satisfied.

To study this question, recall that (17) is the necessary condition for entrepreneurial expected utility maximization. In general, (17) differs from (35) because, as we shall see below,

$$
\hat{\alpha} E u_I \left(A + g\left(\frac{1-\hat{\alpha}}{\hat{\alpha}}, \tilde{x} \right) \right.
$$
$$
\left. - w\left(\frac{1-\hat{\alpha}}{\hat{\alpha}} \right), \hat{\alpha} \right) g_L\left(\frac{1-\hat{\alpha}}{\hat{\alpha}}, \tilde{x} \right)
$$
$$
\neq w E u_I \left(A + g\left(\frac{1-\hat{\alpha}}{\hat{\alpha}}, \tilde{x} \right) \right.
$$
$$
\left. - w\left(\frac{1-\hat{\alpha}}{\hat{\alpha}} \right), \alpha \right). \qquad (38)
$$

(In an equilibrium in which all entrepreneurs have the same utility function, $L(w(\hat{\alpha}), \tilde{x}) = \dfrac{1-\hat{\alpha}}{\hat{\alpha}}$ since supply equals demand.)

Also recall that, in equilibrium, w satisfies (18) where $L = \dfrac{1-\hat{\alpha}}{\hat{\alpha}}$. Thus w is the certainty equivalent of the random variable $g\left(\dfrac{1-\hat{\alpha}}{\hat{\alpha}}, \tilde{x} \right) - w\left(\dfrac{1-\hat{\alpha}}{\hat{\alpha}} \right)$. When entrepreneurs are risk averse, condition (18) implies that

$$
w = E g\left(\frac{1-\hat{\alpha}}{\hat{\alpha}}, \tilde{x} \right) - w\left(\frac{1-\hat{\alpha}}{\hat{\alpha}} \right) - \rho \quad (39)
$$

where ρ is a positive risk premium. Rearranging, we obtain that

$$
\frac{1}{\hat{\alpha}} w = E g\left(\frac{1-\hat{\alpha}}{\hat{\alpha}}, \tilde{x} \right) - \rho. \qquad (40)
$$

Substituting (40) in (17) yields

$$
\frac{1}{\hat{\alpha}} E u_I (A + g(L, \tilde{x}) - wL, \hat{\alpha}) g_L(L, \tilde{x})
$$
$$
= \frac{1}{\hat{\alpha}} w E u_I (A + g(L, \tilde{x}) - wL, \hat{\alpha})
$$
$$
= [E g(L, \tilde{x})][E u_I (A + g(L, \tilde{x}) - wL, \hat{\alpha})]
$$
$$
- \rho E u_I (A + g(L, \tilde{x}) - wL, \hat{\alpha}) \qquad (41)
$$

where $L = \dfrac{1-\hat{\alpha}}{\hat{\alpha}}$. Risk aversion ($u_{II} < 0$) also implies that

$0 > c = \text{cov}(g(L, \tilde{x}),$
$$u_I(A + g(L, \tilde{x}) - wL, \hat{\alpha}))$$
$$= Eg(L, \tilde{x})u_I(A + g(L, \tilde{x})$$
$$- wL, \hat{\alpha}) - [Eg(L, \tilde{x})]$$
$$\times [Eu_I(A + g(L, \tilde{x}) - wL, \hat{\alpha})] \quad (42)$$

where, again $L = (1 - \hat{\alpha})/\hat{\alpha}$. Combining (41) and (42) we obtain

$$\frac{1}{\hat{\alpha}} Eu_I(A + g(L, \tilde{x}) - wL, \hat{\alpha})g_L(L, \tilde{x})$$

$$= Eg(L, \tilde{x})u_I(A + g(L, \tilde{x}) - wL, \hat{\alpha})$$

$$- c - pEu_I(A + g(L, \tilde{x}) - wL, \hat{\alpha}) \quad (43)$$

with $L = (1 - \hat{\alpha})/\hat{\alpha}$. Note that (43) and (35) are the same if the covariance c equals the negative of $pu_I\left(A + g\left(\frac{1 - \hat{\alpha}}{\hat{\alpha}},\right.\right.$

$\left.\left.\tilde{x}\right) - w\left(\frac{1 - \hat{\alpha}}{\hat{\alpha}}\right), \hat{\alpha}\right)$. In this case the equilibrium is efficient. Otherwise, risk aversion causes two types of errors. One of these, measured by the term

$-pu_I\left(A + g\left(\frac{1 - \hat{\alpha}}{\hat{\alpha}}, \tilde{x}\right) - w\left(\frac{1 - \hat{\alpha}}{\hat{\alpha}}\right), \hat{\alpha}\right),$ is introduced by the "entry condition" (18) and tends to cause the right-hand side (RHS) of (35) to exceed the left-hand side (LHS). The other type of error is measured by c. It enters through the entrepreneurial maximization condition (17) and it tends to make the RHS of (35) smaller than the LHS in equilibrium. To identify the direction of the effect which each of these errors has on the choice of $\hat{\alpha}$ consider the case in which (16) holds so that the optimal choice of $\hat{\alpha}$ is independent of the preferences and the income distribution. Recall that in this case $\hat{\alpha}$ should be chosen to maximize output in each state and that (35) reduces to the first-order condition for this output maximization problem. It is also easy to verify that when the LHS of (35) exceeds the RHS in equilibrium, then the derivative,

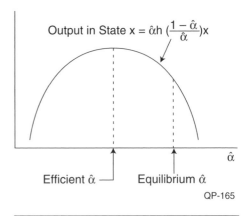

Figure 5

Output in State x = $\hat{\alpha}h \left(\frac{1 - \hat{\alpha}}{\hat{\alpha}}\right)x$

$\hat{\alpha}$

Efficient $\hat{\alpha}$ —⌐   Equilibrium $\hat{\alpha}$

QP-165

$h\left(\frac{1}{\hat{\alpha}} - 1\right)x - \frac{1}{\hat{\alpha}}h'\left(\frac{1}{\alpha} - 1\right)x$, of output with respect to $\hat{\alpha}$ is negative at the equilibrium. It is then clear from figure 5 that in this case the equilibrium $\hat{\alpha}$ is too large to be efficient. Thus there are too many firms in equilibrium when the error, $-c$, introduced by the entrepreneur's equilibrium condition, outweighs

$-pEu_I\left(A + g\left(\frac{1 - \hat{\alpha}}{\hat{\alpha}}, \tilde{x}\right) - w\left(\frac{1 - \hat{\alpha}}{\hat{\alpha}}\right), \hat{\alpha}\right),$

the error introduced by the entry condition. Similar reasoning leads us to conclude that there are too few entrepreneurs when the error introduced by the entry condition outweighs the error introduced by the entrepreneurial first-older condition. These conclusions coincide with intuition. On the one hand risk aversion should cause too few individuals to become entrepreneurs and this should operate through the entry condition. On the other hand risk aversion on the part of those who become entrepreneurs reduces labor demand when (16) holds (recall theorem 3). The error caused by entrepreneurial risk aversion should reduce the equilibrium labor demand and the equilibrium wage. The low wage creates an incentive for too many individuals to become entrepreneurs.

We can now consider several important special cases. The first such case is that in which all entrepreneurs have constant absolute risk aversion in the sense of Arrow-Pratt, that is, $u(I, \alpha_1) = -e^{-rI}$, for some $r > 0$; and the production function is

$$g(L, x) = L^{\gamma}x \qquad (44)$$

where $\gamma \in (0, 1)$. In this case, (35) reduces to

$$\hat{\alpha} = 1 - \gamma, \qquad (45)$$

and the efficient labor input per firm is

$$\frac{1 - \hat{\alpha}}{\hat{\alpha}} = \frac{\gamma}{1 - \gamma}. \qquad (46)$$

The equilibrium conditions (17) and (18) combine to yield

$$0 = \frac{E\tilde{x}e^{-rL\gamma, \tilde{r}}}{Ee^{-rL\gamma, \tilde{r}}} + \frac{1}{r\gamma L^{\gamma-1}(1+L)} \log(Ee^{-r, \tilde{r}L\gamma}) \qquad (47)$$

where $L = (1 - \hat{\alpha})/\hat{\alpha}$.

It can be shown that the RHS of (47) is a decreasing function of L and that it is negative if $\gamma/(1 - \gamma)$ is substituted for L. Thus the efficient L level exceeds the equilibrium level. As a result there are too many firms in equilibrium.

Note that in this class of examples the efficient number of firms approaches zero if γ approaches one, that is, if returns to scale become constant. The limiting case in which returns to scale are indeed constant is one in which, in general, there are too many entrepreneurs. The efficiency analysis just carried out does not apply to this case because it assumes that $g_{LL} < 0$ for all L. (The existence of equilibrium proof does apply if $u_{II} < 0$.) It is possible to analyze this case directly however by substituting

$$g(L, x) = h(L)x = kLx \qquad (48)$$

in (34). The output in state x then becomes $k(1 - \hat{\alpha})x$ which is clearly maximized for each x when $\hat{\alpha} = 1$. Thus the measure of the optimal set of entrepreneurs is zero and almost all individuals should work. This result occurs because the technology set of the economy is the same if there is either one entrepreneur, some larger entrepreneur set of measure zero, or a set of positive measure.

There is one important case in which the equilibrium is efficient. That is the case already mentioned in which all entrepreneurs are indifferent to risk. Since the preceding discussion makes it clear that entrepreneurial risk aversion causes the errors which result in a nonoptimal equilibrium level for $\hat{\alpha}$, it should not now be surprising that the equilibrium is efficient when entrepreneurs are not risk averse. For that case, we have already noted that the distribution of risk is efficient, that is, condition (36) is satisfied. The linearity of the utility function implies then that $u_I(\cdot, \alpha)$ is independent of $y(\alpha, x)$, so that (35) reduce to

$$\hat{\alpha}Eg\left(\frac{1 - \hat{\alpha}}{\hat{\alpha}}, \tilde{x}\right) = Eg_L\left(\frac{1 - \hat{\alpha}}{\hat{\alpha}}, \tilde{x}\right). \qquad (49)$$

For the same reason (17) reduces to

$$Eg_L\left(\frac{1 - \hat{\alpha}}{\hat{\alpha}}, \tilde{x}\right) = w. \qquad (50)$$

In addition, risk indifference implies that $\rho = 0$ so that (40) becomes

$$w = \hat{\alpha} E g\left(\frac{1-\hat{\alpha}}{\hat{\alpha}}, \tilde{x}\right). \qquad (51)$$

Taken together the equilibrium equations (50) and (51) imply (49) and the equilibrium therefore satisfies all of the conditions for efficiency.

The preceding discussion of efficiency suggests that entrepreneurial risk aversion is the source of all of the observed inefficiencies. When entrepreneurs are risk averse the equilibrium is not only characterized by an inefficient distribution of risk; there will, in general, also be too many or too few firms and they will not employ the correct number of workers. In fact, it is well known that an inefficient distribution of risk is inevitable with any equilibrium in which some subgroup of risk averse individuals (in this case, the entrepreneurs) bear all of the risks. Suppose, however, that we concede the inevitability of a maldistribution of risks and ask if, given this kind of inefficiency, the other aspects of the equilibrium might be efficient. Specifically, let us accept the fact that entrepreneurial risks cannot be shared and require only an optimal division of individuals between entrepreneurial activities and labor and of labor between firms. Is it then possible that in this restricted sense the equilibrium is efficient?

In order to pose this question formally we define a restricted feasible allocation to be a specification of Γ, Δ together with two functions $v : \Delta \to [0, \infty)$ and $\xi : [0, 1] \to [-A, \infty)$ which satisfy the equations (28),

$$\int_0^1 \xi(\alpha) d\alpha = 0, \qquad (52)$$

and $A + g(v(\alpha), x) + \xi(\alpha) \geq 0$ for all x and $\alpha \in \Delta$.

The function $v(\alpha)$ specifies the labor to be employed by entrepreneur α, that is, for each $\alpha \in \Delta$, $v(\alpha)$ is α's labor demand. Equation (28) expresses the equality of labor supply and demand. The function ξ specifies the amount of a certain payment made to each α. Equation (52) is a supply-demand equality for these payments. It guarantees that the resources exist to make all payments. The final condition rules out bankruptcy.

The difference between this concept of restricted feasibility and the notion of unrestricted feasibility should be noted. In the definition of unrestricted feasibility, the payments made to individuals are contingent on the state of nature x. As in an Arrow-Debreu economy, the only constraint on the allocation of contingent claims is that supply must equal demand in each state. As a result, risks can be completely reallocated. In contrast, a restricted feasible allocation specifies, for each α, a payment $\xi(\alpha)$ which is not state contingent; it does not permit a reallocation of risks. As a result, the distribution of risks implied by a restricted feasible allocation has two important features. First, as in equilibrium, workers bear no risks; entrepreneurs bear all risks. In addition, the distribution of risk among entrepreneurs is determined by the distribution of labor since, for entrepreneurs, $y(\alpha, x)$ is restricted to equal $A + g(v(\alpha), x) + \xi(\alpha)$. This feature is also shared with equilibrium allocations of risk since, in equilibrium, $y(\alpha, x) = g(L(w, \alpha), x) - wL(w, \alpha) + A$ if α is an entrepreneur. These considerations permit us to observe that the conditions defining restricted feasibility do indeed embody the institutional constraints on risk trading implicit in our equilibrium concept.

It should also be noted that this definition of restricted feasible allocations does not employ any explicit or implicit assumptions about the independence or dependence of the $\tilde{x}$'s which enter the production functions of different firms.

An allocation Λ which is restricted feasible is said to be restricted efficient if there is no other restricted feasible allocation Λ^* which Pareto dominates Λ.

We can now prove that an equilibrium is efficient in the restricted sense just defined. It should first be emphasized again that for this theorem we can and will drop the assumption that the $\tilde{x}$ is the same for all firms. In fact, it is not necessary for the theorem to make any assumptions about the dependence or independence of the random variables which enter different firm's production functions.[7]

Theorem 6. An equilibrium is restricted efficient.

Proof. In an equilibrium allocation

$$
\begin{aligned}
&\Delta = [0, \hat{\alpha}) \\
&\Gamma = [\hat{\alpha}, 1] \\
&v(\alpha) = L(w(\hat{\alpha}), \alpha) \text{ and} \\
&\xi(\alpha) = \begin{cases} -wL(w(\hat{\alpha}), \alpha) & \text{if } \alpha \in \Gamma \\ w & \text{if } \alpha \in \Delta. \end{cases}
\end{aligned} \quad (53)
$$

Now consider some other allocation $\Lambda^* = (\Gamma^*, \Delta^*, v^*, \xi^*)$ which Pareto dominates the equilibrium. To express this domination formally it is necessary to first partition the set of individuals into four sets:

    i) those in $\Delta^* \cap \Delta$,
    i) those in $\Delta^* \cap \Gamma$,
    iii) those in $\Gamma^* \cap \Gamma$, and
    iv) those in $\Gamma^* \cap \Delta$.

If α is in $\Delta^* \cap \Delta$, then Pareto dominance of Λ^* implies that

$$
\begin{aligned}
&Eu(A + g(L(w(\hat{\alpha}), \alpha), \tilde{x}) \\
&\quad - w(\hat{\alpha})L(w(\hat{\alpha}), \alpha), \alpha) \\
&\leq Eu(A + g(v^*(\alpha), \tilde{x}) + \xi^*(\alpha), \alpha). \quad (54)
\end{aligned}
$$

By definition of $L(w(\hat{\alpha}), \alpha)$ then

$$
\xi^*(\alpha) \geq -w(\hat{\alpha})v^*(\alpha). \quad (55)
$$

If α is in $\Delta^* \cap \Gamma$, then again Pareto dominance of Λ^* implies

$$
\begin{aligned}
&Eu(A + g(L(w(\hat{\alpha}), \alpha), \tilde{x}) \\
&\quad - wL(w(\hat{\alpha}), \alpha), \alpha) \\
&\leq u(A + w(\hat{\alpha}), \alpha) \\
&\leq Eu(A + g(v^*(\alpha), \tilde{x}) + \xi^*(\alpha), \alpha) \quad (56)
\end{aligned}
$$

and again (55) holds.

If α is in $\Gamma^* \cap \Gamma$, then

$$
u(A + w(\hat{\alpha}), \alpha) \leq u(A + \xi^*(\alpha), \alpha) \quad (57)
$$

and

$$
w(\hat{\alpha}) \leq \xi^*(\alpha). \quad (58)
$$

Finally, if α is in $\Gamma^* \cap \Delta$, then

$$
\begin{aligned}
u(A + w(\hat{\alpha}), \alpha) &\leq Eu(A + g(L(w(\hat{\alpha}), \alpha), \tilde{x}) \\
&\quad - w(\alpha)L(w(\hat{\alpha}), \alpha), \alpha) \\
&\leq u(\xi^*(\alpha), \alpha) \quad (59)
\end{aligned}
$$

so that (58) holds in this case also.

We have established that for all $\alpha \in \Delta^*$, (55) holds while for all $\alpha \in \Gamma^*$, (58) holds. In fact, a similar argument guarantees that since Λ^* Pareto dominates the equilibrium, there must either be a Δ^* subset of positive measure on which (55) holds with a strict inequality or a Γ^* subset of positive measure on which (58) holds with a strict inequality. Thus

$$
\begin{aligned}
&\int_0^1 \xi^*(\alpha)d\alpha \\
&\quad > [-\int_{\Delta^*} v^*(\alpha)d\alpha + \mu(\Gamma^*)]w(\hat{\alpha}). \quad (60)
\end{aligned}
$$

Inequality (60) implies that Λ^* cannot be restricted feasible. Specifically, because of (60), equations (28) and (52) cannot hold simultaneously. We have therefore shown that the equilibrium is

---

[7]Note that unlike the definition of unrestricted feasibility, the definition of restricted feasibility embodies no implicit assumption about the dependence of the $\tilde{x}$'s faced by different firms.

restricted efficient because it cannot be Pareto dominated by a restricted feasible allocation. ||

Restricted efficiency is similar in spirit to Diamond's (1967) constrained efficiency, that is, efficiency under the given constraints on the risk allocation. Here we have imposed more constraints than in Diamond's model of the stock market since, in our approach, entrepreneurs are not allowed to share any risk with workers or other entrepreneurs. However, we get restricted efficiency without any technological assumption such as those imposed by Diamond's assumption of stochastic constant returns to scale. A similar result is obtained in Kihlstrom and Laffont (1978), where risk sharing is introduced by the existence of markets for shares to firms. The resulting equilibrium is shown to be efficient in the sense of Diamond. The efficiency theorem involves no restrictive assumptions about technology. Specifically, it does not require stochastic constant returns to scale.

VII. Summary

In this paper we have introduced a simple general equilibrium model of firm formation in which production requires entrepreneurial as well as normal labor inputs. Workers receive fixed wages while entrepreneurs receive risky profits. Individuals decide whether to become entrepreneurs or workers by comparing the risky returns of entrepreneurship with the nonrisky wage determined in the competitive labor market. The wage adjusts to the point where the supply of workers is equal to the entrepreneurial demand for labor.

Although we have not discussed the interpretation of the entrepreneurs' contribution to the productive process we have implicitly or explicitly made assumptions about the nature of this contribution. The primary assumption is that the relationship between output and the entrepreneurial labor input is characterized by an indivisibility. Specifically, each firm requires a unit of entrepreneurial labor regardless of how much normal labor it employs and how much it produces. In this sense, the expenditure of entrepreneurial labor can be viewed as a set-up cost. Normally, the nonconvexities introduced by indivisibilities in general and set-up costs in particular cause problems when the existence of equilibrium is studied. In our model, this problem is avoided, as it can be in general (see, e.g., Aumann 1966), by assuming that the set of individuals is a continuum.

One possible interpretation of our model is that the entrepreneur contributes managerial and organizational skills. In Knight's words he performs the "function of exercising responsible control."[8] In fact, our entire model can be viewed as a formalization, for a special case, of Knight's discussion of the entrepreneur.[9] In our model, an entrepreneur is characterized by two activities. He supplies entrepreneurial inputs and bears the risks associated

[8]Knight (1921), p. 278.
[9]Knight's view of the entrepreneur as well as the view formalized here are rather different from that set forth by Schumpeter (1934, 1939). Schumpeter viewed the entrepreneur as an innovator. (See, e.g., the discussion on pp. 132–36 of Schumpeter [1934].) His view of the entrepreneur's contribution and of his compensation is in essence dynamic. He also specifically asserts on p. 137 of Schumpeter (1934) that "the entrepreneur is never a risk bearer." For a more modern discussion of the entrepreneur and his role (or lack of one) in economic theory, see Baumol (1968).

with production. In Knight's treatment the entrepreneur makes the same contributions "with the performance of his peculiar twofold function of (*a*) exercising responsible control and (*b*) securing the owners of productive services against uncertainty and fluctuation in their incomes."[10] Knight's view of the labor market and of an individual's decision to become a worker or an entrepreneur also appears to be similar to that formalized here. This is illustrated by the discussion on pages 273–74 of Knight (1921). Specifically, he asserts that, "the laborer asks what he thinks the entrepreneur will be able to pay, and in any case will not accept less than he can get from some other entrepreneur, or *by turning entrepreneur himself*. In the same way the entrepreneur offers to any laborer what he thinks he must in order to secure his services, and in any case not more than he thinks the laborer will be worth to him, *keeping in mind what he can get by turning laborer himself*."[11] He continues: "Since in a free market there can be but one price on any commodity, a general wage rate must result from this competitive bidding."[12]

Our model represents only a special case of Knight's view because we assume that all individuals are equal in their ability to perform entrepreneurial as well as normal labor functions. They differ only in their willingness to bear risks. Knight emphasizes ability as well as "willingness [and] power to give satisfactory guarantees"[13] as factors determining the supply of entrepreneurs. In our model, the size of the initial income A can be interpreted as a measure of an individual's power to guarantee wages by bearing risk. We have assumed here that all individuals are alike in their possession of this "power." An interesting alternative interpretation can be made by explaining the differences in risk aversion as arising from differences in wealth. Suppose, for example, that all entrepreneurs have the same utility function which is decreasingly risk averse (in the absolute sense of Arrow-Pratt). Then the differences in the willingness to bear risk—that is, to "give satisfactory guarantees" in Knight's words—will be determined by initial wealth. Thus if A varies across individuals, the more risk averse individuals will also be those who initially are the poorest. Assuming that the constraints $L \leq A/w$ are never binding in equilibrium our model can then be reinterpreted as predicting that entrepreneurs are those who are initially wealthy. (Of course the opposite prediction can be obtained by making the less generally accepted assumption that the common utility function is increasingly risk averse.) With this interpretation, the possession of wealth which provides additional power to give satisfactory guarantees also makes an individual more willing to bear risk.

To complete the analogy between our results and Knight's discussion note that our theorem 4, which relates the equilibrium wage to the level of entrepreneurial risk aversion, was in a sense anticipated by the discussion of Knight (1921, p. 283) which concludes that "entrepreneur income, being residual, is determined by the demand for these other [productive] services, which demand is a matter of self-confidence of entrepreneurs as a class. . . ."[14]

---

[10]Knight (1921, p. 278).
[11]Ibid., pp. 273–74 (emphasis added).
[12]Ibid., p. 274.
[13]Ibid., p. 283.
[14]Ibid.

This paper has extended the classical results concerning the existence and stability of equilibrium to the entrepreneurial model. We have also described the nature of the equilibrium's inefficiencies and identified the institutional constraints on risk trading as the source of these inefficiencies. These results establish that it is possible to construct an internally consistent general equilibrium model of entrepreneurially operated firms. In fact, this analysis should only be viewed as a first step in the construction of a general equilibrium entrepreneurial theory of the firm under uncertainty. As presented here it is perhaps best viewed as a description of equilibrium in a world of small businesses or farms.

The next step is to incorporate a stock market into our analysis. Once a stock market is embedded in the model, we can use it to ask interesting questions about the interaction between a modern firm's financial and productive decisions. Furthermore, the introduction of a stock market represents an institutional change that facilitates risk trading and thereby eliminates some of the inefficiencies that occur at an equilibrium. The extension of the model in this direction has been studied in a subsequent paper (Kihlstrom and Laffont 1978).

References

Arrow, Kenneth J. "The Role of Securities in the Optimal Allocation of Risk-Bearing."*Rev. Econ. Studies* 31 (April 1964): 91–96.

———. *Essays in the Theory of Risk Bearing*. Chicago: Markham, 1971.

Aumann, Robert J. "Existence of Competitive Equilibria in Markets with a Continuum of Traders." *Econometrica* 34 (January 1966): 1–17.

Baron, David P. "Price Uncertainty, Utility and Industry Equilibrium in Pure Competition." *Internal. Econ. Rev.* 11 (October 1970): 463–80.

Baumol, William J. "Entrepreneurship in Economic Theory." *A.E.R. Papers and Proc.* 63 (May 1968): 64–71.

Brock, William A. "On Models of Expectations That Arise from Maximizing Behavior of Economic Agents over Time." *J. Econ. Theory* 5 (December 1972): 348–76.

Debreu, Gerard. *Theory of Value.* New York: Wiley, 1959.

Diamond, Peter A. "The Role of a Stock Market in a General Equilibrium Model with Technological Uncertainty." *A.E.R.* 57 (September 1967): 759–76.

Drèze, Jacques. "Investment under Private Ownership: Optimality, Equilibrium Stability." In *Allocation under Uncertainty: Equilibrium and Optimality.* London: Macmillan, 1974.

Kihlstrom, Richard E., and Laffont, Jean-Jacques. "A Competitive Entrepreneurial Model of the Stock Market." Mimeographed. Urbana, Ill.: Univ. Illinois, 1978.

Knight, Frank H. *Risk, Uncertainty and Profit.* New York: Harper & Row, 1965.

Pratt, John W. "Risk Aversion in the Small and in the Large." *Econometrica* 32 (January–April 1964): 122–36.

Quandt, Richard, and Howrey, E. Phillip. "The Dynamics of the Number of Firms in an Industry." *Rev. Econ. Studies* 35 (July 1968): 349–53.

Radner, Roy. "Competitive Equilibrium under Uncertainty." *Econometrica* 36 (January 1968): 31–58.

Schumpeter, Joseph A. *The Theory of Economic Development; An Inquiry into Profits, Capital, Credit, Interest, and the Business Cycle.* Cambridge, Mass.: Harvard Univ. Press, 1934.

———. *Business Cycles; A Theoretical, Historical, and Statistical Analysis of the Capitalist Process.*

Abridged ed. New York: McGraw Hill, 1939.

Smith, Vernon. "Optimal Costly Firm Entry in General Equilibrium." *J. Econ. Theory* 9 (1974): 397–417.

"Symposium on the Optimality of Competitive Capital Markets." *Bell J. Econ. Management Sci.* 5 (Spring 1974): 125–86.

A Conceptual Framework for Describing the Phenomenon of New Venture Creation
by William B. Gartner

A review of the entrepreneurship literature suggests that differences among entrepreneurs and among their ventures are as great as the variation between entrepreneurs and nonentrepreneurs and between new firms and established firms. A framework for describing new venture creation integrates four major perspectives in entrepreneurship: characteristics of the individual(s) who start the venture, the organization which they create, the environment surrounding the new venture, and the process by which the new venture is started.

The major thrust of most entrepreneurship research has been to prove that entrepreneurs are different from nonentrepreneurs (Brockhaus, 1980a, 1980b; Carland, Hoy, Boulton, & Carland, 1984; Collins & Moore, 1964; DeCarlo & Lyons, 1979; Hornaday & Aboud, 1971; Howell, 1972; Komives, 1972; Litzinger, 1965; McClelland, 1961; McClelland & Winter, 1969; Palmer, 1971; Schrier, 1975; Shapero, 1975) and that entrepreneurial firms are different from nonentrepreneurial firms (Collins & Moore, 1970; Cooper, 1979; Smith, 1967; Thorne & Ball, 1981). The basic assumption underlying this research is that all entrepreneurs and their new ventures are much the same. The present paper suggests that the differences among entrepreneurs and among their ventures are much greater than one might expect; in fact, the diversity may be larger than the differences between entrepreneurs and nonentrepreneurs and between entrepreneurial firms and nonentrepreneurial firms. Once the diversity among entrepreneurs and their ventures is recognized, the necessity for finding a way to classify them becomes apparent. Groups sharing similar characteristics must exist within the universe of entrepreneurs and their ventures. How are these groups revealed? Many different characteristics have been employed in past research to describe entrepreneurs and their ventures. Do the characteristics themselves fall into groups? In other words, does one subset of characteristics describe a single aspect of new venture creation, such as the environment surrounding the

Originally appeared in *Academy of Management Review*, 1985, Volume 10, Number 4.

The research leading to this paper was supported in part by a grant from the National Science Foundation and is based on the author's doctoral dissertation. Additional support was provided by the Center for Entrepreneurial Studies, University of Virginia.

new venture, or the features of the organization that results?

This paper attempts to organize the many variables that have been used in past research to describe entrepreneurs and their ventures into a comprehensive framework. Far from being reductive, this new view of the entrepreneurship literature should provide valuable insights into the process of new venture creation by showing it to be a complex and multidimensional phenomenon. Once a clear retrospective analysis of the literature is provided, future research can proceed on more solid footing. Instead of many different researchers palpating different parts of the elephant and reaching reductive conclusions, at least all will know the name, if not the nature, of the beast with which they are dealing.

Much past research has been unidimensional, focusing on a single aspect of new venture creation, and its main purpose has been to show how entrepreneurs or their firms differ from nonentrepreneurs or nonentrepreneurial firms. (In fact, it might be said that unidimensional research goes hand in hand with the attitude that all entrepreneurs and their firms are alike, the task of the unidimensional research being to prove how all things entrepreneurial differ from all things nonentrepreneurial.) It has been consistently pointed out, however, in reviews of literature on entrepreneurs, for example, (Brockhaus, 1982; Glueck & Mescon, 1980; McCain & Smith, 1981) that variables that are assumed to differentiate entrepreneurs from nonentrepreneurs (managers, for instance) frequently do not bear up under close scrutiny. Yet the search for these elusive variables continues, and entrepreneurs and prospective entrepreneurs are subjected to batteries of psychological tests in attempts to isolate the single spring that makes them tick differently from others. As with other aspects of new venture creation, attempts are made to isolate key variables that separate entrepreneurial situations from nonentrepreneurial ones. Pennings (1980, 1982a, 1982b) has explored environments that support new venture creation; Van de Ven (1980) and Kimberly (1979) have focused on the process of venture creation.

This search for key variables is a motivation for research only if the task of entrepreneurial research is taken to be the distinction of entrepreneurs and things entrepreneurial from nonentrepreneurs and nonentrepreneurial situations. If a much different perspective is taken, the perspective that there are many different kinds of entrepreneur and many ways to be one and that the firms they create vary enormously as do the environments they create them in, then the burden shifts. How is each new venture creation different from another? Researchers need to think in terms of a combination of variables that make up each new venture creation (Van de Ven, Hudson, & Schroeder, 1984). The creation of a new venture is a multidimensional phenomenon; each variable describes only a single dimension of the phenomenon and cannot be taken alone. There is a growing awareness that the process of starting a business is not a single well-worn route marched along again and again by identical entrepreneurs (Hartman, 1983). New venture creation is a complex phenomenon: entrepreneurs and their firms vary widely; the actions they take or do not take and the environments they operate in and respond to are equally diverse—and all these elements form complex and unique combinations in the creation of each new venture. It is not enough for researchers to seek out and focus on some concept of the "average" entrepreneur and the "typical" venture creation. New organizational forms evolve through variation, and this variation in new venture creation needs to be studied

(Aldrich, 1979; Hannan & Freeman, 1977; Pfeffer & Salancik, 1978; Weick, 1979). This insistence on variation can be seen, for example, in Vesper (1979), who posits 11 different kinds of entrepreneur, and in a recent study by Cooper and Dunkelberg (1981), which reveals that entrepreneurs in certain industries can be very different from those in other industries.

Once the variation and complexity in new venture creation is recognized, it then is necessary to find a framework for systematically discovering and evaluating the similarities and differences among new ventures (McKelvey, 1982). Once it is no longer assumed that all entrepreneurs and their ventures present a homogeneous population, then other homogeneous subsets within the entrepreneurial universe must be sought out in order that entrepreneurial research can produce meaningful results. A primary value of the framework for describing new venture creation presented here is that it provides a systematic means of comparing and contrasting complex ventures; it provides a way to conceptualize variation and complexity.

A Framework for Describing New Venture Creation

Definitions of key words such as entrepreneur are often various and always a problem in the study of entrepreneurship (Brockhaus, 1980b; Komives, 1969; Long, 1983). Because the entrepreneur is only one dimension of this framework, it seems more important in this paper to define the term "new venture creation." Such a definition can be outlined here with less trepidation, if only because there is less precedent.

New venture creation is the organizing (in the Weickian sense) of new organizations. "To organize is to assemble ongoing interdependent actions into sensible sequences that generate sensible outcomes" (Weick, 1979, p. 3). The definition of new venture creation is synonymous with the definition of the new organization developed by the Strategic Planning Institute (1978; p. 1–2):

a new business venture launched as one of the following:
1. an independent entity
2. a new profit center within a company which has other established businesses, or
3. a joint venture which satisfies the following criteria:
   1. Its founders must acquire expertise in products, process, market and/or technology.
   2. Results are expected beyond the year in which the investment is made.
   3. It is considered a new market entrant by its competitors.
   4. It is regarded as a new source of supply by its potential customers.

The importance of this definition should not be overlooked, because it recognizes the multidimensional aspects of new venture creation. First, it emphasizes that individuals with expertise are a key element of the new venture. At the same time that it recognizes the new venture as an organizational entity, it stresses that the new venture is not instantaneously produced, but evolves over time (beyond a year). The new venture is seen further within the context of its environment: it is forced to seek out resources, and it competes in the market place. All these aspects of the new venture must be kept in mind if it is to be adequately described and classified.

Figure 1 presents a framework for describing the creation of a new venture across four dimensions: (a) individual(s)—the person(s) involved in

Figure 1
A Framework for Describing New Venture Creation

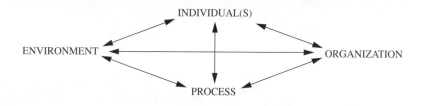

starting a new organization; (b) organization—the kind of firm that is started; (c) environment—the situation surrounding and influencing the new organization; and (d) new venture process—the actions undertaken by the individual(s) to start the venture.

Any new venture is a gestalt (Miller, 1981) of variables from the four dimensions. No new venture creation can be comprehensively described, nor can its complexity be adequately accounted for, unless all of its four dimensions are investigated and an attempt is made to discover how variables from each dimension interact with variables from other dimensions.

This framework is the first to combine the four dimensions of venture creation, though other researchers have sought to combine two or more of the dimensions. This "thinking across dimensions" is especially apparent in the work of those theorists and researchers who have developed entrepreneurial classification schemes. Classifications of entrepreneurs themselves are often based on two dimensions: individual characteristics plus new venture process considerations—the word often used is "style." Danhoff (1949) based his scheme on the entrepreneur's openness to innovation; Cole (1959) on the sophistication of the entrepreneur's decision making tools; and Dailey (1971) according to bureaucratic or entrepreneurial style.

Smith (1967) divided entrepreneurs by a stylistic orientation—craftsman or opportunistic. Filley and Aldag (1980) used management orientation. Vesper (1979, 1980) in two similar classifications differentiated among entrepreneurs by the activities involved in business formation and operation, and in another scheme (1980) by competitive strategy. In Cooper (1979) entrepreneurs are linked to particular environments, and, as cited previously, Cooper and Dunkelberg's (1981) study matches different entrepreneurs and their characteristics to the types of firms they are likely to start. In Vesper's (1979) classification the entrepreneur's type of firm is also a factor, as it is in several other classification studies (Braden, 1977; Filley & Aldag, 1980; Smith, 1967). Recently, Van de Ven et al.'s (1984) empirical study examined educational software firms on the basis of three dimensions: entrepreneurial—background characteristics and psychological attributes of the founding entrepreneurs; organizational—planning and organizational activities undertaken before and after company startup; and ecological—support and resources made available to influence the development of the industry. These classification schemes and frameworks are ways of stepping back to get an overall picture, a process like model-building, which involves integration and synthesis.

Individual(s)

Whether an entrepreneur is viewed as a "captain of industry," a hard-headed risk bearer (Mill, 1848), risk taker (Palmer, 1971) or a "rapacious risk avoider" (Webster, 1976); whether he merely metamorphoses into an entrepreneur at certain moments and is something else the rest of the time (Danhoff, 1949), or whether his need for achievement (McClelland, 1961) and capacity for innovation (Schumpeter, 1934) are always ticking away; whether he is a "displaced person" (Shapero, 1975), something close to a juvenile delinquent (Gould, 1969), or a "man apart" (Liles, 1974) with an absolutely clear-headed (veridical) perception of reality (Schrage, 1965), an aberrant "artist" with an "innate sense of impending change" (Hill, 1982); or whether he is, indeed, that completely political animal, a community builder (Schell & Davig, 1981), the entrepreneur is overwhelmingly perceived to be different in important ways from the nonentrepreneur, and many researchers have believed these differences to lie in the background and personality of the entrepreneur.

One often pursued avenue has been the attempt to develop a psychological profile of the entrepreneur and to measure such psychological characteristics as need for achievement (DeCarlo & Lyons, 1979; Hornaday & Aboud, 1971; McClelland, 1961; McClelland & Winter, 1969; Schwartz, 1976). However, other researchers have not found need for achievement useful in describing entrepreneurs (Brockhaus, 1980b; Litzinger, 1965; Schrage, 1965); still others have questioned the value and validity of using psychological characteristics of any kind to describe entrepreneurs (Brockhaus, 1982; Glueck & Mescon, 1980; Jenks, 1965; Kilby, 1971; McCain & Smith, 1981; Van de Ven, 1980). However, the following psychological characteristics have been used in many studies and may have some validity in differentiating

among types of entrepreneurs (Brockhaus, 1982):

1. Need for achievement
2. Locus of control
3. Risk taking propensity

Some researchers have found it fruitful to look at the entrepreneur's background, experience, and attitudes. Some individual characteristics that may be of value in describing entrepreneurs are:

1. Job satisfaction (Collins & Moore, 1970; Komives, 1972)
2. Previous work experience (Cooper, 1970; Lamont, 1972; Susbauer, 1972)
3. Entrepreneurial parents (Collins & Moore, 1970; Robert & Wainer, 1968; Schrier, 1975; Secrest, 1975; Shapero, 1972; Susbauer, 1972)
4. Age (Komives, 1972; Liles, 1974; Roberts & Wainer, 1968; Secrest, 1975; Thorne & Ball, 1981)
5. Education (Brockhaus & Nord, 1979; Collins & Moore, 1964; Howell, 1972; Roberts, 1969; Susbauer, 1972)

Process

In 1949 Danhoff wrote, "Entrepreneurship is an activity or function and not a specific individual or occupation . . . the specific personal entrepreneur is an unrealistic abstraction" (p. 21). Other theorists have pursued this idea of function and have tried to differentiate the entrepreneurial function from other more routine functions such as the managerial function (Baumol, 1968; Cole, 1965; Hartmann, 1959; Leibenstein, 1968; Schumpeter, 1934). This "dynamic" aspect of the entrepreneur has been acknowledged in the work of eight researchers who have enumerated certain actions that an entrepreneur performs in order to create a new venture. Except for Peterson and Berger (1971), who described the entrepreneurial activities of record producers, these studies were theoretical, that is, based on general observation rather than systematic research. The similarities in their views are summarized here; six common behaviors are listed (the order does not imply a sequence of actions):

1. The entrepreneur locates a business opportunity (Cole, 1965; Kilby, 1971; Maidique, 1980; Schumpeter, 1934; Vesper, 1980).
2. The entrepreneur accumulates resources (Cole, 1965; Kilby, 1971; Leibenstein, 1968; Peterson & Berger, 1971; Schumpeter, 1934; Vesper, 1980).
3. The entrepreneur markets products and services (Cole, 1965; Kilby, 1971; Leibenstein, 1968; Maidique, 1980; Peterson & Berger, 1971; Schumpeter, 1934; Vesper, 1980).
4. The entrepreneur produces the product (Kilby, 1971; Maidique, 1980; Peterson & Berger, 1971; Schumpeter, 1934; Vesper, 1980).
5. The entrepreneur builds an organization (Cole, 1965; Kilby, 1971; Leibenstein, 1968; Schumpeter, 1934).
6. The entrepreneur responds to government and society (Cole, 1965; Kilby, 1971).

Environment

Much of the current concern (Peters & Waterman, 1982) over how to design organizations that keep and encourage innovative individuals is an indirect acknowledgment that entrepreneurs do not operate in vacuums—they respond to their environments. The existence of highly supportive regional entrepreneurial environments (Cooper, 1970; Draheim, 1972; Pennings, 1982b; Susbauer, 1972)—including "incubator organizations"—can, from one perspective, be said actually to create entrepreneurs. The idea of "pushes" and "pulls" from the environment has found its way into many studies of entrepreneurship (Shapero & Sokol, 1982).

In organization theory literature, two different views of the environment have been developed. One perspective, environmental determinism, sees the environment as an outside set of conditions to which the organization must adapt (Aldrich, 1979; Aldrich & Pfeffer, 1976; Hannan & Freeman, 1977). The other perspective, strategic choice, sees the environment as a "reality" that organizations create via the selectivity of their own perceptions (Child, 1972; Starbuck, 1976; Weick, 1979). In the entrepreneurship literature, both perspectives on the environment have been taken. In the present paper those characteristics that are viewed as relatively fixed conditions imposed on the new venture from without are called environmental variables. Variables over which the organization has more control (strategic choice variables) are more readily viewed as characteristics of the organization itself and are treated as such.

In an overview of 17 research papers on environmental variables that influenced new venture creation, Bruno and Tyebjee (1982) found 12 factors that they judged stimulated entrepreneurship:

1. Venture capital availability
2. Presence of experienced entrepreneurs
3. Technically skilled labor force
4. Accessibility of suppliers
5. Accessibility of customers or new markets
6. Governmental influences
7. Proximity of universities
8. Availability of land or facilities
9. Accessibility of transportation
10. Attitude of the area population
11. Availability of supporting services
12. Living conditions

Another study of environmental influences on new venture creation was Pennings' studies of organization birth frequencies (1980, 1982a, 1982b). Pennings found that organization birth rates were high in areas with: high occupational and industrial differentiation; high percentages of recent immigrants in the population; a large industrial base; larger size urban areas; and availability of financial resources.

Another field of research has taken the deterministic perspective regarding the environment and new ventures: industrial economics. Oliver Williamson (1975) explored the process by which the failure of markets to coordinate efficiently the production and distribution of goods and services often resulted in the start-up of organizations to coordinate the production function through administration. Porter (1980) focused on the competitive environment that confronts firms in a particular industry. Porter's work provides five environmental influences on organizations: barriers to entry, rivalry among existing competitors, pressure from substitute products, bargaining power of buyers, and bargaining power of suppliers.

Organization

Despite a bold early attempt by Stauss (1944) to direct the focus away from the entrepreneur and toward his created organization (by claiming, somewhat tortuously, that the firm is the entrepreneur), most subsequent studies of new venture creation have neglected to comment on or even communicate certain characteristics of the organizations on which they focused. The assumption behind this seems to derive from two other assumptions: (a) if all entrepreneurs are virtually alike and (b) they all go through the same process to create their ventures, then (c) the organizations they create must, like widgets, not be of any interest in themselves.

Many research samples in entrepreneurship studies are selected, for example, without regard to type of firm (i.e., manufacturing, service, retail, wholesale). Of the studies that have indicated the type of firm, Smith (1967), Cooper (1970), Collins and Moore (1970), Susbauer (1972), and Braden (1977) studied manufacturing firms, and most focused on high technology manufacturing firms. Litzinger (1965) studied motel firms, and Mescon and Montanari (1981) studied real estate firms. However, researchers in these studies made no attempts to compare the type of firm studied to other types of firm to determine what difference type of firm might make in the process of new venture creation. Cooper and Dunkelberg (1981), Gartner (1982), and Van de Ven et al. (1984) have begun to link type of firm across other dimensions, such as entrepreneurial background and response to environment.

The presence of partners is another firm characteristic suggested by Timmons, Smollen, and Dingee (1977) as a vital factor in starting certain types of firm, and some research has mentioned partners as a characteristic of the firms studied (Cooper, 1970; DeCarlo & Lyons, 1979).

Strategic choice variables are treated here as characteristics of the organization. Porter (1980) identified three generic competitive strategies that firms may "choose": (a) overall cost leadership, (b) differentiation, and (c) focus. Vesper (1980) identified 14 competitive entry wedges: the new product or service, parallel competition, franchise entry, geographical transfer, supply shortage, tapping unutilized resources, customer contract, becoming a second source, joint ventures, licensing, market relinquishment, sell off of division, favored purchasing by government, and governmental rule changes.

Conclusion

Listing each variable of new venture creation under the appropriate dimension of the framework illustrates the potential for a high degree of complexity in the interaction of these variables within the multidimensional phenomenon of venture creation (Figure 2).

The four dimensional conceptual framework can be seen as a kaleidoscope, as an instrument through which to view the enormously varying patterns of new venture creation. Past attempts to differentiate the typical entrepreneur and his/her typical creation from all nonentrepreneurs and all nonnew ventures have, whether intentionally or not, advanced the notion that all entrepreneurs are alike and all new venture creation is the same. However, there clearly is a wide variation in the kinds of new ventures that are started. For example, are there similarities between the creation of a waterbed store by a 20-year old college student and the creation of a personal computer company by three engineers? Are the differences between them more important than the similarities? What is the value of comparing the creation of a pet store by two unemployed physical therapists to the creation of a 5,000-acre business park by four real estate developers? The goal is not to smooth over any differences that might exist among these new ventures or to throw these very different individuals into the same pot in order to extract the typical qualities of the typical entrepreneur. The goal is to identify the specific variables that describe how each new venture was created, in order that meaningful contrasts and comparisons among new ventures can be made.

First must come careful description with an eye to variation. The search for key variables, for general principles, for universally applicable laws of entrepreneurship that has characterized much of the entrepreneurship literature betrays an impatience with the slow methodical process of description. Attention to careful observation and description is the basis of good scientific research (McKelvey, 1982). In what does all this careful description of new ventures result? A collection of uniquely described ventures, each different from all the others? Once good description is achieved, then good comparisons and contrasts can be made, and subsets of similar ventures can be established. These homogeneous populations are needed before any general rules or theories of new venture creation can be postulated. The lack of such homogeneous samples in the past has led to conflicts in the results of research studies.

The conceptual framework presented here provides a way of analyzing past research studies. Each study can be broken down into the types of individuals, organizations, environments, and processes that were investigated. One way in which the framework can be useful is in identifying those aspects of new venture creation neglected by a particular study. New research may then be designed to account for these lacunae. For example, Brockhaus defines his sample of entrepreneurs as:

> Individuals who within three months prior to the study had ceased working for their employers and at the time of the study owned as well as managed business ventures. . . . The businesses whose owners served as participants were selected from the listing of businesses licensed by St. Louis County, Missouri during the months of August and September, 1975 (1980a, p. 39).

Although Brockhaus, unlike other researchers, attempts to close in on the actual entrepreneurial function by interviewing his entrepreneurs within a few months of the creation of their ventures, useful and necessary distinctions among the individuals and their new ventures are not made. One is not sure what types of firms were studied (retail, service, manufacturing, etc.) or whether the St. Louis environment was likely to influence certain types of individuals to

Figure 2
Variables in New Venture Creation

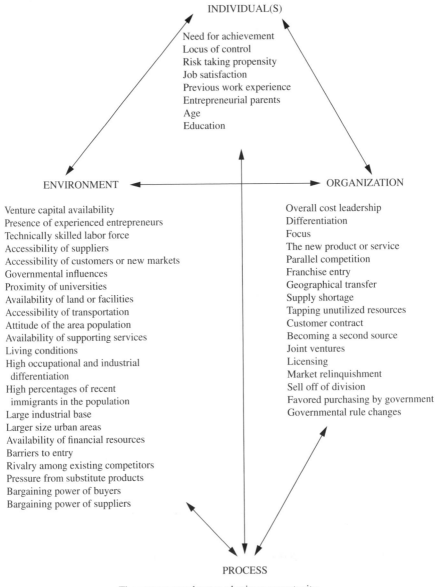

INDIVIDUAL(S)

Need for achievement
Locus of control
Risk taking propensity
Job satisfaction
Previous work experience
Entrepreneurial parents
Age
Education

ENVIRONMENT

Venture capital availability
Presence of experienced entrepreneurs
Technically skilled labor force
Accessibility of suppliers
Accessibility of customers or new markets
Governmental influences
Proximity of universities
Availability of land or facilities
Accessibility of transportation
Attitude of the area population
Availability of supporting services
Living conditions
High occupational and industrial
  differentiation
High percentages of recent
  immigrants in the population
Large industrial base
Larger size urban areas
Availability of financial resources
Barriers to entry
Rivalry among existing competitors
Pressure from substitute products
Bargaining power of buyers
Bargaining power of suppliers

ORGANIZATION

Overall cost leadership
Differentiation
Focus
The new product or service
Parallel competition
Franchise entry
Geographical transfer
Supply shortage
Tapping unutilized resources
Customer contract
Becoming a second source
Joint ventures
Licensing
Market relinquishment
Sell off of division
Favored purchasing by government
Governmental rule changes

PROCESS

The entrepreneur locates a business opportunity
The entrepreneur accumulates resources
The entrepreneur markets products and services
The entrepreneur produces the product
The entrepreneur builds an organization
The entrepreneur responds to government and society

create certain types of firms. Is the process of starting a venture in St. Louis different, or is the process different for certain types of businesses or certain kinds of individuals? Accounting for type of firm, environment, and process in this study would enhance comparison among the individuals in the study and individuals in other studies.

In analyzing results of research studies, a focus on differences in one of the four dimensions might explain conflicting results. For example, studies such as Collins and Moore (1970) suggest that individuals who start firms are social misfits who do not fit into most organizations. Yet other studies such as Cooper (1970) suggest that individuals who start successful firms are good team players. On closer examination it is seen that Collins and Moore studied manufacturing firms that were more like job shops in the 1950s, and Cooper studied high technology firms in the 1960s. High technology industries might require more skills than one individual would be likely to have, necessitating that individuals combine their abilities in teams in order to start an organization successfully.

In addition to providing a means by which past research can be analyzed, the framework outlines a format for future research methodologies and for reporting such research. More careful attention must be paid to the research sample. For example, women entrepreneurs are a popular research topic. If similarities are discovered among women who start firms, are these similarities a result of similar environments? Can differences be attributed solely to psychological or background characteristics? What is the value of research results that are based on such unexamined and possibly heterogeneous sample populations?

Even in a narrowly selected research sample, the framework might be useful in drawing the researcher's attention to considerations inherent in each of the four dimensions, in order that conclusions regarding the virtual sameness of all the members of the sample may not be made too hastily. For example, in a sample of new organizations in the micro-computer industry, a number of considerations might be made. What is the variation among the entrepreneurs in their work backgrounds, education, age? How do competitive strategies used by these new organizations vary? Are there regional or other subenvironments in the industry that cause variations in firms and strategies? What is the variation in the venture creation process: do all individuals devote equal time to financing the organization, hiring personnel, marketing? What differences exist between "new" and "old" firms in this industry?

The brief review of the literature provided earlier is only a running start at a comprehensive analysis and evaluation of the entrepreneurship literature. For example, in a study of individuals who start firms, who are the individuals? Are the individuals in McClelland's samples (McCelland, 1961; McCelland & Winter, 1969) similar to those in Brockhaus (1980a) or Schrage (1965)? More about the similarities and differences within and among past research samples needs to be known. There are many dimensions and variables across which these samples may be compared.

The framework also points up the importance of interactions of variables among dimensions in understanding new venture creation. How does an individual's background influence the type of activities undertaken to start an organization? Does the marketing individual devote his time to marketing instead of manufacturing, and are there some environments or firms that require more marketing? Is the process of starting a retail store similar to that of starting a steel mill? Are entry strategies used by new organizations in the robotics industry similar to those used in the brewery industry?

The framework for describing new venture creation provides the possibility of describing subsets within the unwieldy set of all entrepreneurs and all new ventures. Newly created ventures that display meaningful similarities across the four dimensions could be described and classified together (Gartner, 1982). Significant generalizations regarding some or all new venture creations might emerge, generalizations that do not, however, attempt to mask the variation in new venture creation.

This paper does not purport to answer specific questions about how new ventures are started or provide specific developmental models for new venture creation. No claim is made that the framework or the list of variables is comprehensive; the claim is only that the description of new ventures needs to be more comprehensive that it is at present. A great many more questions are asked here than are answered. However, the paper provides a means of making a fundamental shift in the perspective on entrepreneurship: away from viewing entrepreneurs and their ventures as an unvarying, homogeneous population, and towards a recognition and appreciation of the complexity and variation that abounds in the phenomenon of new venture creation.

References

Aldrich, H. E. (1979) *Organizations and environments*. Englewood Cliffs, NJ: Prentice-Hall.

Aldrich, H. E., & Pfeffer, J. (1976) Environments of organizations. *Annual Review of Sociology*, 76–105.

Baumol, W. J. (1968) Entrepreneurship in economic theory. *American Economic Review*, 58(2), 64–71.

Braden, P. (1977) *Technological entrepreneurship* (Michigan Business Reports, No. 62). Ann Arbor: University of Michigan.

Brockhaus, R. H. (1980a) The effect of job dissatisfaction on the decision to start a business. *Journal of Small Business Management*, 18(1), 37–43.

Brockhaus, R. H. (1980b) Risk taking propensity of entrepreneurs. *Academy of Management Journal*, 23, 509–520.

Brockhaus, R. H. (1982) The psychology of the entrepreneur. In C. A. Kent, D. L. Sexton, & K. H. Vesper (Eds.), *Encyclopedia of entrepreneurship* (pp. 39–59). Englewood Cliffs NJ: Prentice-Hall.

Brockhaus, R. H., & Nord, W. R. (1979) An exploration of factors affecting the entrepreneurial decision: Personal characteristics vs. environmental conditions. *Proceedings of the National Academy of Management*, 364–368.

Bruno, A. V., & Tyebjee, T. T. (1982) The environment for entrepreneurship. In C. A. Kent, D. L. Sexton, & K. H. Vesper (Eds.), *Encylopedia of entrepreneurship* (pp. 288–307). Englewood Cliffs, NJ: Prentice-Hall.

Carland, J. W., Hoy, F., Boulton, W. R., & Carland, J. A. C. (1984) Differentiating entrepreneurs from small business owners: A conceptualization. *Academy of Management Review*, 9, 354–359.

Child, J. (1972) Organizational structure, environment and performance: The role of strategic choice. *Sociology*, 6, 1–22.

Cole, A. H. (1959) *Business enterprise in its social setting*. Cambridge, MA: Harvard University Press.

Cole, A. H. (1965) An approach to the study of entrepreneurship: A tribute to Edwin F. Gay. In H. G. J. Aitken (Ed.), *Explorations in enterprise* (pp. 30–44). Cambridge, MA: Harvard University Press.

Collins, O. F., & Moore, D. G. (1964) *The enterprising man*. East Lansing: Michigan State University.

Collins, O. F., & Moore, D. G. (1970) *The organization makers*. New York: Appleton-Century-Crofts.

Cooper, A. C. (1970) The Palo Alto experience. *Industrial Research*, 12(5), 58–61.

Cooper, A. C. (1979) Strategic management: New ventures and small business. In D. E. Schendel & C. W. Hofer (Eds.), *Strategic management* (pp. 316–327). Boston: Little, Brown.

Cooper, A. C., & Dunkelberg, W. C. (1981) A new look at business entry: Experiences of 1,805 entrepreneurs. In K. H. Vesper (Ed.), *Frontiers of entrepreneurship research* (pp. 1–20). Wellesley, MA: Babson College.

Daily, C. A. (1971) *Entrepreneurial management: Going all out for results.* New York: McGraw-Hill.

Danhoff, C. H. (1949) Observations on entrepreneurship in agriculture. In A. H. Cole (Ed.), *Change and the entrepreneur* (pp. 20–24). Cambridge, MA: Harvard University Press.

DeCarlo, J. F., & Lyons, P. R. (1979) A comparison of selected personal characteristics of minority and non-minority female entrepreneurs. *Journal of Small Business Management*, 17(4), 22–29.

Draheim, K. P. (1972) Factors influencing the rate of formation of technical companies. In A. C. Cooper & J. L. Komives (Eds.), *Technical entrepreneurship: A symposium* (pp. 3–27). Milwaukee, WI: Center for Venture Management.

Filley, A. C., & Aldag, R. J. (1980) Organizational growth and types: Lessons from small institutions. In B. Staw & L. Cummings (Eds.), *Research in organizational behavior* (Vol. 2, pp. 279–320). Greenwich, CT: JAI Press.

Gartner, W. B. (1982) *An empirical model of the business startup, and eight entrepreneurial archetypes.* Unpublished doctoral dissertation. University of Washington, Seattle.

Glueck, W., & Mescon, T. (1980) *Entrepreneurship: A literature analysis of concepts.* Paper presented at the annual meeting of the Academy of Management, Detroit, MI.

Gould, L. C. (1969) Juvenile entrepreneurs. *American Journal of Sociology*, 74, 710–719.

Hannan, M. T., & Freeman, J. (1977) The population ecology model of organizations. *American Journal of Sociology*, 82, 929–964.

Hartman, C. (1983) Who's running America's fastest growing companies? Inc., 5(8), 41–47.

Hartmann, H. (1959) Managers and entrepreneurs: A useful distinction? *Administrative Science Quarterly*, 3, 429–457.

Hill, R. (1982) The entrepreneur: An artist masquerading as a businessman? *International Management*, 37(2), 21–22, 26.

Hornaday, J., & Aboud, J. (1971) Characteristics of successful entrepreneurs. *Personnel Psychology*, 24(2), 141–153.

Howell, R. P. (1972) Comparative profiles—Entrepreneurs versus the hired executive: San Francisco Peninsula semiconductor industry. In A. C. Cooper & J. L. Komives (Eds.) *Technical entrepreneurship: A symposium* (pp. 47–62). Milwaukee, WI: Center for Venture Management.

Jenks, L. (1965) Approaches to entrepreneurial personality. In H. G. J. Aitken (Ed.), *Explorations in enterprise* (pp. 80–92). Cambridge, MA: Harvard University Press.

Kilby, P. (1971) Hunting the heffalump. In P. Kilby (Ed.), *Entrepreneurship and economic development* (pp. 1–40). New York: Free Press.

Kimberly, J. R. (1979) Issues in the creation of organizations: Initiation, innovation, and institutionalization. *Academy of Management Journal*, 22, 437–457.

Komives, J. L. (Ed.). (1969) *Karl A. Bostrum seminar in the study of enterprise.* Milwaukee, WI: Center for Venture Management.

Komives, J. L. (1972) A preliminary study of the personal values of high of high technology entrepreneurs. In A. C. Cooper & J. L. Komives (Eds.). *Technical entrepreneurship: A symposium* (pp. 231–242). Milwaukee, WI: Center for Venture Management.

Lamont L. M. (1972) The role of marketing in technical entrepreneurship. In A. C. Cooper & J. L. Komives (Eds.), *Technical entrepreneurship: A symposium* (pp. 150–164). Milwaukee, WI: Center for Venture Management.

Leibenstein, H. (1968) Entrepreneurship and development. *American Economic Review*, 58(2), 72–83.

Liles, P. R. (1974) *New business ventures and the entrepreneur*. Homewood, IL: Irwin.

Litzinger, W. D. (1965) The motel entrepreneur and the motel manager. *Academy of Management Journal*, 8, 268–281.

Long, W. (1983) The meaning of entrepreneurship. *American Journal of Small Business*, 8(2), 47–59.

Maidique, M. A. (1980) Entrepreneurs, champions and technological innovation. *Sloan Management Review*, 21(2), 59–76.

McCain G., & Smith, N. (1981, Summer) A contemporary model of entrepreneurial style, *Small Business Institute Review*, 40–45.

McClelland, D. (1961) *The achieving society*. Princeton, NJ: Van Nostrand.

McClelland, D., & Winter, D. G. (1969) *Motivating economic achievement*. New York: Free Press.

McKelvey, B. (1982) *Organizational systematics—Taxonomy, evolution, classification*. Berkeley: University of California Press.

Mescon, T., & Montanari, J. (1981) The personalities of independent and franchise entrepreneurs: An empirical analysis of concepts. *Journal of Enterprise Management*, 3(2), 149–159.

Mill, J. S. (1848) *Principles of political economy with some of their applications to social philosophy*. London: J. W. Parker.

Miller, D. (1981) Toward a new contingency approach: The search for organ-

ization gestalts. *Journal of Management Studies*, 18, 1–26.

Palmer, M. (1971) The application of psychological testing to entrepreneurial potential. *California Management Review*, 13(3), 32–39.

Pennings, J. M. (1980) Environmental influences on the creation process. In J. R. Kimberly & R. Miles (Eds.). *The organization life cycle* (pp. 135–160). San Francisco: Jossey Bass.

Pennings, J. M. (1982a) Organizational birth frequencies. *Administrative Science Quarterly*, 27, 120–144.

Pennings, J. M. (1982b) the urban quality of life and entrepreneurship. *Academy of Management Journal*, 25, 63–79.

Peters T. J., & Waterman, R. H. (1982) *In search of excellence*. New York: Harper & Row.

Peterson, R. A., & Berger, D. G. (1971) Entrepreneurship in organizations: Evidence from the popular music industry. *Administrative Science Quarterly*, 16, 97–107.

Pfeffer, J., & Salancik, G. R. (1978) *The external control of organizations*. New York: Harper & Row.

Porter, M. E. (1980) *Competitive strategy: Techniques for analyzing industries and competitors*. New York: Fress Press.

Roberts, E. B. (1969) Entrepreneurship and technology. In W. Gruber & D. Marquis (Eds.). *Factors in the transfer of technology* (pp. 219–237). Cambridge. MA: M.I.T. Press.

Roberts, E. B., & Wainer, H. A. (1968) New enterprise on Rte. 128. *Science Journal*, 4(12), 78–83.

Schell, D. W., & Davig. W. (1981) The community infrastructure of entrepreneurship. In K. H. Vesper (Ed.), *Frontiers of entrepreneurship research* (pp. 563–590). Wellesley, MA: Babson College.

Schrage, H. (1965) The R & D entrepreneur: Profile of success. *Harvard Business Review*, 43(6), 56–69.

Schrier, J. W. (1975) Entrepreneurial characteristics of women. In J. W. Schrier & J. Susbauer (Eds.), *Entrepreneurship and enterprise development: A worldwide perspective* (pp. 66–70). Milwaukee, WI: Center for Venture Management.

Schumpeter, J. A. (1934) *The theory of economic development* (R. Opie, Trans.). Cambridge, MA: Harvard University Press.

Schwartz, E. B. (1976) Entrepreneurship: A new female frontier. *Journal of Contemporary Business.* 5, 47–76.

Secrest, L. (1975) Texas entrepreneurship. In J. W. Schrier & J. Susbauer (Eds.), *Entrepreneurship and enterprise development: A worldwide perspective* (pp. 51–65). Milwaukee, WI: Center for Venture Management.

Shapero, A. (1972) The process of technical company formation in a local area. In A. C. Cooper & J. L. Komives (Eds.), *Technical entrepreneurship: A symposium* (pp. 63–95). Milwaukee, WI: Center for Venture Management.

Shapero, A. (1975) The displaced, uncomfortable entrepreneur. *Psychology Today*, 9(6), 83–88.

Shapero, A., & Sokol, L. (1982) The social dimensions of entrepreneurship. In C. A. Kent, D. L. Sexton, & K. H. Vesper (Eds.), *Encylclopedia of entrepreneurship* (pp. 72–90). Englewood Cliffs, NJ: Prentice-Hall.

Smith, N. (1967) *The entrepreneur and his firm: The relationship between type of man and type of company.* East Lansing: Michigan State University.

Starbuck, W. H. (1976) Organizations and their environments. In M. Dunnette (Ed.), *Handbook of industrial and organizational psychology* (pp. 1069–1123). Chicago: Rand McNally.

Stauss, J. H. (1944) The entrepreneur: The firm. *Journal of Political Economy*, 52(2), 112–127.

Strategic Planning Institute. (1978) *The startup data manual.* Unpublished manuscript. Cambridge, MA: Strategic Planning Institute.

Susbauer, J. C. (1969) *The technical company formation process: A particular aspect of entrepreneurship.* Unpublished doctoral dissertation, University of Texas, Austin.

Susbauer, J. C. (1972) The technical entrepreneurship process in Austin, Texas. In A. C. Cooper & J. L. Komives (Eds.), *Technical entrepreneurship: A symposium* (pp. 28–46). Milwaukee, WI: Center for Venture Management.

Thorne, J. R., & Ball, J. G. (1981) Entrepreneurs and their companies: Smaller industrial firms. In K. H. Vesper (Ed.), *Frontiers of entrepreneurship research* (pp. 65–83). Wellesley, MA: Babson College.

Timmons, J. A., Smollen, E., & Dingee, A. L. M. (1977) *New venture creation.* Homewood, IL: Irwin.

Van de Ven, A. H. (1980) Early planning, implementation and performance of new organizations. In J. R. Kimberly & R. Miles (Eds.), *The organization life cycle* (pp. 83–134). San Francisco: Jossey Bass.

Van de Ven, A. H., Hudson, R., & Schroeder, D. M. (1984) Designing new business startups: Entrepreneurial, organizational, and ecological considerations. *Journal of Management*, 10(1), 87–107.

Vesper, K. H. (1979) Commentary. In D. E. Schendel & C. W. Hofer (Eds.), *Strategic management* (pp. 332–338). Boston: Little, Brown.

Vesper, K. H. (1980) *New venture strategies.* Englewood Cliffs, NJ: Prentice-Hall.

Vesper, K. H. (1981) Scanning the frontier of entrepreneurship research. In K. H. Vesper (Ed.), *Frontiers of entrepreneurship research* (pp. vii–xiv). Wellesley, MA: Babson College.

Vesper, K. H. (1982a) Expanding entrepreneurship research. In K. H. Vesper (Ed.), *Frontiers of entrepreneurship research* (pp. vii–xx). Wellesley, MA: Babson College.

Vesper, K. H. (1982b) Introduction and summary of entrepreneurship research. In C. A. Kent, D. L. Sexton, & K. H. Vesper (Eds.), *Encyclopedia of entrepreneurship* (pp. xxxi–xxxviii).

Webster, F. A. (1976) A model for new venture initiation: A disclosure on rapacity and the independent entrepreneur. *Academy of Management Review*, 1(1), 26–37.

Weick, K. E. (1979) *The social psychology of organizing* (2nd ed.). Reading, MA: Addison-Wesley.

Williamson, O. E. (1975) *Markets and hierarchies, analysis and antitrust implications*. New York: Free Press.

Clarifying the Entrepreneurial Orientation Construct and Linking It to Performance

by G. T. Lumpkin and Gregory G. Dess

The primary purpose of this article is to clarify the nature of the entrepreneurial orientation (EO) construct and to propose a contingency framework for investigating the relationship between EO and firm performance. We first explore and refine the dimensions of EO and discuss the usefulness of viewing a firm's EO as a multidimensional construct. Then, drawing on examples from the EO-related contingencies literature, we suggest alternative models (moderating effects, mediating effects, independent effects, interaction effects) for testing the EO-performance relationship.

For both start-up ventures and existing firms, entrepreneurship carried on in the pursuit of business opportunities spurs business expansion, technological progress, and wealth creation. Entrepreneurial activity represents one of the major engines of economic growth and today accounts for the majority of new business development and job creation in the United States (*Business Week*, 1993). As such, writers in both the scholarly literature (e.g., Covin & Slevin, 1991) and popular press (e.g., Peters & Waterman, 1982) have argued that entrepreneurship is an essential feature of high-performing firms.

Entrepreneurship scholars have developed numerous typologies to describe alternate perspectives of entrepreneurship (e.g., Cooper & Dunkelberg, 1986; Schollhammer, 1982; Webster, 1977). These classification systems typically depict differences in entrepreneurship as the result of various combinations of individual, organizational, or environmental factors that influence how and why entrepreneurship occurs as it does. Although these efforts have served to point out the various dimensions of the entrepreneurial process, they have not led to any widely held consensus regarding how to characterize entrepreneurship. This lack of consensus has impeded progress for researchers toward building and testing a broader theory of entrepreneurship, and has made it especially difficult for them to investigate the relationship of entrepreneurship to performance.

To address this problem, this article draws on prior theory and research to make a distinction between the concepts of entrepreneurship and "entrepreneurial orientation." The distinction is compara-

---

Originally appeared in *Academy of Management Review*, 1996, Volume 21, Number 1.

ble to the one made in the strategic management literature between content and process (Bourgeois, 1980). The early strategy literature equated entrepreneurship with going into business, and the basic "entrepreneurial problem" (Miles & Snow, 1978) was to address the principal question of strategy *content*, that is, "What business shall we enter?" The answer to this question determined a firm's domain and guided its product-market relationships and resource deployments. As the field of strategic management developed, however, the emphasis shifted to entrepreneurial *processes*, that is, the methods, practices, and decision-making styles managers use to act entrepreneurially. These include such processes as experimenting with promising new technologies, being willing to seize new product-market opportunities, and having a predisposition to undertake risky ventures. The trend has been to use concepts from the strategy-making process literature to model firm-level entrepreneurship (Covin & Slevin, 1989, 1991; Miller, 1983). Five dimensions—autonomy, innovativeness, risk taking, proactiveness, and competitive aggressiveness— have been useful for characterizing and distinguishing key entrepreneurial processes, that is, a firm's *entrepreneurial orientation* (*EO*). They do not, however, represent entrepreneurship, which is defined here as *new entry*. That is, new entry explains *what* entrepreneurship consists of, and entrepreneurial orientation describes *how* new entry is undertaken.

The essential act of entrepreneurship is *new entry*. New entry can be accomplished by entering new or established markets with new or existing goods or services. New entry is the act of launching a new venture, either by a start-up firm, through an existing firm, or via "internal corporate venturing" (Burgelman, 1983). New entry is thus the central idea underlying the concept of entrepre-

neurship. Evidence of this is suggested by the large portion of research on entrepreneurship that is devoted to explaining the corollaries and consequences of new venture activity (e.g., Hisrich & Peters, 1989; MacMillan & Day, 1987; Sandberg & Hofer, 1987; Stuart & Abetti, 1987; Vesper, 1980, 1988; Webster, 1977). Although the concept of entrepreneurship as new entry is itself a topic brimming with issues and research questions, in this article we are chiefly concerned with EO, a corollary concept that emerged primarily from the strategic management literature.

An EO refers to the processes, practices, and decision-making activities that lead to new entry. It emerges from a strategic-choice perspective (Child, 1972), which asserts that new-entry opportunities can be successfully undertaken by "purposeful enactment" (Van de Ven & Poole, 1995). Thus, it involves the intentions and actions of key players functioning in a dynamic generative process aimed at new-venture creation. The key dimensions that characterize an EO include a propensity to act autonomously, a willingness to innovate and take risks, and a tendency to be aggressive toward competitors and proactive relative to marketplace opportunities.

All of these factors—autonomy, innovativeness, risk taking, proactiveness, and competitive aggressiveness—may be present when a firm engages in new entry. In contrast, successful new entry also may be achieved when only some of these factors are operating. That is, the extent to which each of these dimensions is useful for predicting the nature and success of a new undertaking may be contingent on external factors, such as the industry or business environment, or internal factors, such as the organization structure (in the case of an existing firm) or the characteristics of founders or top managers. Thus, although some prior research suggests that the dimensions of an EO covary (e.g., Covin & Slevin,

1989), we suggest that autonomy, innovativeness, risk taking, proactiveness, and competitive aggressiveness may vary independently, depending on the environmental and organizational context. This is consistent with Gartner's (1985: 697) perspective regarding new venture formation:

> The creation of a new venture is a multidimensional phenomenon; each variable describes only a single dimension of the phenomenon and cannot be taken alone ... entrepreneurs and their firms vary widely; the actions they take or do not take and the environments they operate in and respond to are equally diverse—and all these elements form complex and unique combinations in the creation of each new venture.

In this article, therefore, we argue that (a) the relationship between EO and performance is context specific and (b) the dimensions of EO may vary independently of each other in a given context.

The purpose of this article is to provide an integrative framework for exploring the relationship between EO and performance by integrating prior theory and empirical findings into a researchable whole. To this end, we first endeavor to delineate and refine the dimensions of EO. Then, consistent with Stinchcombe's (1965) caveat regarding the importance of organizational and environmental factors to the success of new entrants, we propose a contingency framework. Accordingly, the two interrelated objectives of this article are (a) to clarify the nature of the entrepreneurial orientation construct and (b) to suggest a contingency approach to frame research questions and further researchers' understanding of EO-performance relationships.

Before moving on, we briefly address level-of-analysis considerations. The concept of *entrepreneurship* has been applied to many different levels, for example, individuals, groups, and "whole organizations." One of the reasons there has been little agreement on the nature of entrepreneurship and how it contributes to performance is because the term is used in the context of various levels of analysis. Entrepreneurship often is thought to be within the purview of individuals only, because it is frequently associated with the introduction of a revolutionary invention (Kilby, 1971). It is also considered by some theorists to apply primarily to the domain of small businesses because they are responsible for the majority of economic growth and new-job creation via entry into untapped markets (Birch, 1979). Recently, there has also been an emphasis on corporate entrepreneurship as a means of growth and strategic renewal for existing larger firms (Guth & Ginsberg, 1990). Thus, it is important to consider the level of analysis that is used in discussing the EO construct.

New entry as the essential act of entrepreneurship is primarily a firm-level phenomenon. It is analogous to a business-level strategy undertaken by a nondiversified economic unit. Thus, *new entry* refers to actions that may be initiated by an individual, a small firm, or the strategic business unit of a large corporation. As such, this discussion of entrepreneurial orientation will focus at the firm/business-unit level. This firm-level approach is consistent with classical economics in which the individual entrepreneur is regarded as a firm. The small business firm is simply an extension of the individual who is in charge. Applying EO to the nondiversified business unit is also consistent with Schumpeter (1942), who shifted attention away from the individual entrepreneur by arguing that entrepreneurship eventually would be dominated by firms that were capable of devoting more resources to innovation. Addressing EO at the firm level corresponds to the model used in recent work by Covin and Slevin (1991), who emphasized the role of entrepreneurship as firm behavior. In the examples that follow, we have used both small corporations and strategic business units (SBUs) to illustrate EO concepts.

The remainder of this article is divided into four sections. First, we explore the relevant theoretical and empirical literature that relates to the dimensions of an entrepreneurial orientation. Second, we discuss key contingencies that often are associated with the EO-performance relationship. Third, alternate contingency models will be suggested for investigating the performance implications of EO relationships. For illustrative purposes, several examples of contingent relationships suggested by the literature are proposed in this section. In the final section, we suggest avenues for further theory development and empirical research, and we discuss how our proposed framework may be useful in explaining differences in entrepreneurial behavior and performance across firms.

Dimensions of an Entrepreneurial Orientation

Prior researchers have suggested that there is a set of organizational processes from which strategic decisions evolve (Hart, 1992; Rajagopalan, Rasheed, & Datta, 1993). These take the form of patterns or modes that can be characterized and identified across organizations (Hart, 1992). The dimensions of a firm's strategy-making processes may be viewed as encompassing the entire range of organizational activities that involve planning, decision making, and strategic management. Such processes also encompass many aspects of the organization's culture, shared value system, and corporate vision (Hart, 1992; Pascale, 1985). In attempting to identify the vari-

ables that are relevant to organizational modes and models of strategic decision processes, many researchers have focused on delineating the dimensions of strategy making. For example, Miller and Friesen (1978) identified 11 strategy-making process dimensions, including adaptiveness, analysis, integration, risk taking, and product-market innovation. In his study of structural influences on decision-making processes, Fredrickson (1986) proposed dimensions such as proactiveness, rationality, comprehensiveness, risk taking, and assertiveness. Hart's (1992) integrative framework for strategy-making processes combined various dimensions into five "distinctive modes of strategy making": command, symbolic, rational, transactive, and generative. Miles and Snow (1978) considered multidimensional aspects of organizational processes to formulate a typology that includes prospectors, defenders, analyzers, and reactors.

In a similar vein, we believe there is a fundamental set of strategy-making process (SMP) dimensions that underlies nearly all entrepreneurial processes. The study of a firm's entrepreneurial orientation is analogous to Stevenson and Jarillo's (1990) concept of *entrepreneurial management*, in that it reflects the organizational processes, methods, and styles that firms use to act entrepreneurially. With regard to the specific dimensions of EO, Miller (1983) has provided a useful starting point. He suggested that an entrepreneurial firm is one that "engages in product market innovation, undertakes somewhat risky ventures, and is *first* to come up with 'proactive' innovations, beating competitors to the punch" (1983: 771). Accordingly, he used the dimensions of "innovativeness," "risk taking," and "proactiveness" to characterize and test entrepreneurship. Numerous researchers have adopted an approach based on Miller's (1983) original conceptualization (e.g., Covin & Slevin, 1989; Ginsberg,

1985; Morris & Paul, 1987; Naman & Slevin, 1993; Schafer, 1990). For example, Covin and Slevin (1989) investigated the performance of entrepreneurial firms in hostile and benign environments. In their study of 161 small manufacturers, "entrepreneurial strategic posture" was measured using a scale that ranked firms as entrepreneurial if they were innovative, risk taking, and proactive.

Two other dimensions are important aspects of an entrepreneurial orientation. The first is competitive aggressiveness, which captures the distinct idea of "beating competitors to the punch," suggested by Miller's (1983) definition of an entrepreneurial firm. It refers to the type of intensity and head-to-head posturing that new entrants often need to compete with existing rivals. Competitive aggressiveness was highly correlated with entrepreneurship across all levels of risk in a study that used published risk rankings to compare firms in low- and high-risk environments in Eastern Europe, the Commonwealth of Independent States, and the United States (Dean, Thibodeaux, Beyerlein, Ebrahimi, & Molina, 1993).

Another key component of an EO is a tendency toward independent and autonomous action. Start-up firms must exercise intentionality to carry forward the specific actions required to launch new ventures (Bird, 1988; Katz & Gartner, 1988). Layers of bureaucracy and organizational tradition rarely contribute to new-entry activities in existing firms (Kanter, 1983). Instead, it requires the exercise of autonomy by strong leaders, unfettered teams or creative individuals who are disengaged from organizational constraints to lead to new entry. This was the conclusion of Burgelman (1983: 241), who found that, in the case of internal corporate venturing, "the motor of corporate entrepreneurship resides in the autonomous strategic initiative of individuals at the operational levels in the organization."

The next five subsections clarify the dimensions of autonomy, innovativeness, risk taking, proactiveness, and competitive aggressiveness and offer suggestions for how these dimensions might be studied further. Although we view each of these dimensions as salient to an EO, our discussion also reflects the argument that they may vary independently in a given context.

Autonomy

The history of entrepreneurship is filled with stories of self-determined pioneers who had a unique, new idea—a better idea—and made a business out of it. Entrepreneurship has flourished because independently minded people elected to leave secure positions in order to promote novel ideas or venture into new markets, rather than allow organizational superiors and processes to inhibit them. Within organizations as well, it is the freedom granted to individuals and teams who can exercise their creativity and champion promising ideas that is needed for entrepreneurship to occur. Thus, an important impetus for new-entry activity is the independent spirit necessary to further new ventures. As such, the concept of *autonomy* is a key dimension of an entrepreneurial orientation.

Autonomy refers to the independent action of an individual or a team in bringing forth an idea or a vision and carrying it through to completion. In general, it means the ability and will to be self-directed in the pursuit of opportunities. In an organizational context, it refers to action taken free of stifling organizational constraints. Thus, even though factors such as resource availability, actions by competitive rivals, or internal organizational considerations may change the course of new-venture initiatives, these are not sufficient to extinguish the autonomous entrepreneurial processes that lead to new entry: Throughout the process, the organizational player remains free to act independently, to make key decisions, and to proceed.

Discussions of entrepreneurial activity in the strategy-making process literature often emphasize the role of autonomous behavior, but in two distinct contexts. Mintzberg (1973) and Mintzberg and Waters (1985) described an entrepreneurial strategy-making mode, in which decisive and risky actions are taken by a strong leader. This is similar to Hart's (1992) command mode and Bourgeois and Brodwin's (1984) commander model, both of which suggest entrepreneurial behavior that is characterized by centralized vision and strong leadership. This type of autonomy, which may be regarded as auto*cratic* (Shrivastava & Grant, 1985), is common in smaller, owner/manager firms where "the force for pattern or consistency in action is individual vision, the central actor's concept of his or her organization's place in its world. This is coupled with *an ability to impose that vision on the organization through his or her personal control of its actions* (Mintzberg & Waters, 1985: 260, emphasis added).

In contrast, Hart's (1992) integrative framework included a generative mode, wherein strategy making occurs from the entrepreneurial activities of organizational members' generating ideas that are passed on to higher levels of management. Similarly, Bourgeois and Brodwin (1984) described a Crescive model, wherein strategy is initiated within the organization via individual entrepreneurship. These models suggest that the impetus for new ventures often occurs at lower levels in an organization (Bower, 1970) and reflect the importance of autonomy to organization members who might be found in an internal corporate venture setting. In both cases, the freedom to act independently is a crucial dimension of EO.

As the previous discussion suggests, evidence of autonomy in firms may vary as a function of size, management style,

or ownership. For example, in a firm in which the primary decision maker is the owner/manager, autonomy is implied by the rights of ownership. However, the extent to which autonomy is exercised in this case may depend on the level of centralization or the extent of delegation, and this may be related to organizational size. In studies of small firms, researchers have examined the nature and extent of autonomous behavior by investigating how centralized the leadership is and how often managers delegate authority and rely on technical expertise. Miller (1983) found that the most entrepreneurial firms had the most autonomous leaders. That is, in small simple firms, high levels of entrepreneurial activity were associated with chief executives who maintained strong central authority and also acted as the firm's knowledge leader by being aware of emerging technologies and markets. In a study of decision making by 32 Indian firms, Shrivastava and Grant (1985) found a similar strong reliance on *managerial autocracy* among 10 of the firms in which a single key manager was the primary decision making agent. Of these 10 firms, 8 were classified as "entrepreneurial."

To promote *intrapreneurship* (Pinchot, 1985), many large firms have engaged in changes in organizational structure such as flattening hierarchies and delegating authority to operating units. These moves are intended to foster autonomy, but the *process* of organizational autonomy requires more than a design change. Firms must actually grant autonomy and encourage organizational players to exercise it (Quinn, 1979). In some firms, the process involves champions who promote entrepreneurial activity by shielding the new venture innovators from organizational norms or resource constraints that might cause the new enterprise to be rejected. Thus, the exercise of organizational autonomy is often characterized by a two-stage process involving a project *definition* that is carried out by autonomous organizational members and a project *impetus* that is carried out by champions who sustain the autonomous efforts (Bower, 1970). Burgelman (1983) found, for example, that initial internal corporate-venturing efforts were conducted by corporate R&D departments operating outside the confines of the current corporate strategy. Hart (1991) studied the autonomous processes of organizational actors by asking managers the extent to which entrepreneurial efforts based on employee initiative emerges upward from lower levels to help shape the firm's strategic direction.

Burgelman (1983) also found that product champions formed the critical link between project definition and impetus processes. Their role consisted of procuring resources and creating market interest in the new project. Thus, in an organizational setting, it is often the champions that play the most entrepreneurial roles by scavenging for resources, going outside the usual lines of authority, and promoting risk taking on behalf of new ideas and promising breakthroughs (Kanter, 1983; Peters & Waterman, 1982). Shane (1994a) found that experienced organizational champions favored efforts to create autonomy via actions such as bending the rules and bypassing procedures and budgets. These examples may provide useful clues for operationalizing autonomy in future studies.

Innovativeness

Schumpeter (1934, 1942) was among the first to emphasize the role of innovation in the entrepreneurial process. Schumpeter (1942) outlined an economic process of "creative destruction," by which wealth was created when existing market structures were disrupted by the introduction of new goods or services that shifted resources away from existing firms and caused new firms to grow.

The key to this cycle of activity was entrepreneurship: the competitive entry of innovative "new combinations" that propelled the dynamic evolution of the economy (Schumpeter, 1934). Thus "innovativeness" became an important factor used to characterize entrepreneurship.

Innovativeness reflects a firm's tendency to engage in and support new ideas, novelty, experimentation, and creative processes that may result in new products, services, or technological processes. Although innovations can vary in their degree of "radicalness" (Hage, 1980), innovativeness represents a basic willingness to depart from existing technologies or practices and venture beyond the current state of the art (Kimberly, 1981). There are numerous methods by which to classify innovations (see Downs & Mohr, 1976), but perhaps the most useful distinction is between product-market innovation and technological innovation. Until recently, most research has focused on technological innovativeness, which consists primarily of product and process development, engineering, research, and an emphasis on technical expertise and industry knowledge (Cooper, 1971; Maidique & Patch, 1982). Product-market innovativeness suggests an emphasis on product design, market research, and advertising and promotion (Miller & Friesen, 1978; Scherer, 1980). Even this broad categorization may be hard to distinguish; however, because innovativeness frequently represents considerable overlap and blending of product-market and technological innovation, as in the case of technologically sophisticated new products designed to meet specific market demand. In either case, innovativeness is an important component of an EO, because it reflects an important means by which firms pursue new opportunities.

Evidence of firm innovativeness may take several forms. In the broadest sense, innovativeness may occur along a continuum from a simple willingness to either try a new product line or experiment with a new advertising venue, to a passionate commitment to master the latest in new products or technological advances. To capture this range of activity, numerous methods have been employed to measure innovativeness.

For example, in a study of innovative responses to changes in the environment, Karagozoglu and Brown (1988) asked managers from 56 firms about their willingness to discard old beliefs and explore new alternatives and the way in which they valued and rewarded experimentation. The level of expenditures and number of resources dedicated to research and development also represent a firm's involvement in innovation activities. In terms of human resources, Hage (1980) argued that the more professionals and specialists in a firm, such as engineers and scientists, the higher the level of innovation. Miller and Friesen (1982) examined the "technocratization" of firms and found that higher levels of innovativeness were associated with greater reliance on technically trained specialists. Miller (1987, 1988) used R&D costs as a percentage of sales to measure financial resources devoted to innovation. Thus, even though these factors may vary by industry, a simple count of financial or human resources committed to innovation activities may be useful for operationalizing innovativeness. For product-market innovativeness, Miller (1987, 1988) asked members of firms to indicate the percentage of total sales spent specifically on the costs of initiating and implementing product-market innovations. Another frequently used marketing-related method for assessing innovation is to investigate the number of new product or service introductions and the frequency of changes in services or product lines (Covin & Slevin, 1989; Miller & Friesen, 1982).

Regarding technological innovativeness, the emphasis shifts to achieving competencies in the latest technologies and production methods and the development of advanced manufacturing processes. This important aspect of innovativeness is lacking in most of the studies based on Miller's (1983) concept of innovativeness, which focused exclusively on the product-market aspect of innovation activities. Subsequent researchers have endeavored to capture this additional aspect of innovativeness, for example, Zahra and Covin (1993: 452), who focused on "technology policy," that is, the firm's commitment to "acquiring, developing, and deploying technology." In this context, firms were asked to rate the extent to which they emphasize technological development and seek to build a reputation for trying new methods and technologies. Another approach that extended efforts to measure innovativeness was used by Saleh and Wang (1993), who, in a study that compared highly innovative firms to low innovators, supplemented the Miller-based approach with questions about efforts to synthesize disparate efforts across functional lines and flexibility in adapting new processes.

Risk Taking

The early entrepreneurship literature equated the idea of entrepreneurship with working for oneself (i.e., seeking self-employment rather than working for someone else for wages) (Cantillon, 1734; Shane, 1994b). Along with this type of work came the idea of assuming personal risk. Cantillon (1734), who was the first to formally use the term *entrepreneurship*, argued that the principal factor that separated entrepreneurs from hired employees was the uncertainty and riskiness of self-employment. Thus, the concept of *risk taking* is a quality that is frequently used to describe entrepreneurship.

Risk has various meanings, depending on the context in which it is applied. In the context of strategy, Baird and

Thomas identified three types of strategic risk: (a) "venturing into the unknown," (b) "committing a relatively large portion of assets," and (c) "borrowing heavily" (1985: 231–232). The first of these definitions conveys a sense of uncertainty and may apply generally to some types of risk often discussed in the entrepreneurship literature, such as personal risk, social risk, or psychological risk (Gasse, 1982). As a term in financial analysis, *risk* is used in the context of the familiar risk-return trade-off, where it refers specifically to the probability of a loss or negative outcome. This is essentially the definition that Miller and Friesen adopted when they defined *risk taking* as "the degree to which managers are willing to make large and risky resource commitments—i.e., those which have a reasonable chance of costly failures" (1978: 923). Both the notion of high leverage from borrowing and heavy commitment of resources is consonant with this definition of risk taking. Thus, firms with an entrepreneurial orientation are often typified by risk-taking behavior, such as incurring heavy debt or making large resource commitments, in the interest of obtaining high returns by seizing opportunities in the marketplace.

It can be argued that all business endeavors involve some degree of risk, such that it is not meaningful to think in terms of "absolutely no risk." Thus, the range of risk-taking behavior extends from some nominal level—"safe" risks, such as depositing money in a bank, investing in T-Bills, or restocking the shelves—to highly risky actions, such as borrowing heavily, investing in unexplored technologies, or bringing new products into new markets. Beyond this general point of agreement, however, methods of accounting for and measuring risk vary widely. Brockhaus, for example, focused on *risk propensity*, which he defined as "perceived probability of receiving the rewards" associated with the successful outcome of a risky situation (1980: 513). He used an early version of Kogan and Wallach's (1964) choice dilemmas questionnaire that assessed risk preferences by presenting respondents with 12 hypothetical situations and asking them to "choose between a safe alternative and a more attractive but risky one" (Brockhaus, 1980: 514). Sitkin and Pablo (1992), however, in their model of risk behavior, distinguished between risk perceptions, risk preferences, and risk propensity. Their use of the term *risk propensity* "is consistent with Brockhaus's (1980) conceptualization of the term, but it does not conform either to his formal definition (which includes preferences) or to his empirical operationalization (which measures perceptions, rather than propensities or preferences)" (Sitkin & Pablo, 1992: 12–13). Instead, they regard risk propensity as a mediator between risk preferences and risk behavior, arguing that "the *general desire* to avoid or pursue risks (i.e., risk preferences) does not determine *specific risk behaviors*, but rather it affects the *general likelihood* of a person's behaving in more or less risky ways (i.e., risk propensity)" (1992: 15). Other factors also may be important to predicting risk taking, such as how the risk problem is framed (Kahneman & Tversky, 1979), results of past risk taking (Thaler & Johnson, 1990), and the ability to perform under risky conditions (Slovic, Fischhoff, & Lichtenstein, 1980).

These attempts to more clearly understand risk taking stem, in part, from researchers not being able to find consistent patterns when investigating risk taking associated with entrepreneurship. Numerous investigators have reported inconsistencies in the risk-taking propensity of individuals who engage in new entry (e.g., Brockhaus, 1982) and equivocal relationships between risk taking and performance (e.g., Begley & Boyd, 1987). Particularly salient to this study is that most studies of entrepreneurially related risk taking investigate individuals rather than firms. This brings up another type of problem with measuring risk, namely that a risk-averse individual, or one who prefers to study an opportunity thoroughly before embarking on it, may not advocate risk avoidance by the whole firm. That is, an individual aversion to a specific new-venture opportunity may be overcome by either careful study and investigation or confidence in a good idea. The result may be that, at the level of the firm, risks are taken that would not be taken by a firm member.

Effectively operationalizing firm-level risk taking, therefore, remains an area for future development. Presently, however, there is a well accepted and widely used scale based on Miller's (1983) approach to EO, which measures risk taking at the firm level by asking managers about the firm's proclivity to engage in risky projects and managers' preferences for bold versus cautious acts to achieve firm objectives. Venkatraman (1989a) used a similar approach, asking managers the extent to which they followed tried-and-true paths or tended to support only projects in which the expected returns were certain.

Proactiveness

Economics scholars since Schumpeter have emphasized the importance of initiative in the entrepreneurial process. Penrose (1959) argued that entrepreneurial managers are important to the growth of firms because they provide the vision and imagination necessary to engage in opportunistic expansion. Lieberman and Montgomery (1988) emphasized the importance of first-mover advantage as the best strategy for capitalizing on a market opportunity. By exploiting asymmetries in the marketplace, the first mover can capture unusually high profits and get a head start on establishing brand recognition. Thus, taking initiative by anticipating and pur-

suing new opportunities and by participating in emerging markets also has become associated with entrepreneurship. This fourth characteristic of entrepreneurship is often referred to as *proactiveness.*

The term *proactiveness* is defined in *Webster's Ninth New Collegiate Dictionary* (1991: 937) as "acting in anticipation of future problems, needs, or changes." As such, proactiveness may be crucial to an entrepreneurial orientation because it suggests a forward-looking perspective that is accompanied by innovative or new-venturing activity. In an early formulation, Miller and Friesen argued that the proactiveness of a firm's decisions is determined by answering the question, "Does it *shape* the environment (high score) by introducing new products, technologies, administrative techniques, or does it merely react?" (1978: 923). Later, proactiveness was used to depict a firm that was the quickest to innovate and first to introduce new products or services. This is suggested by Miller's description of an entrepreneurial firm as one that is "*first* to come up with 'proactive' innovations" (1983: 771). Although the idea of acting in anticipation of future demand is an important component of entrepreneurship, the idea of being first to market is somewhat narrowly construed. A firm can be novel, forward thinking, and fast without always being first. Miller and Camp (1985), for example, in their study of 84 SBUs, found that the second firm to enter a new market was as pioneering as the first entrant and just as likely to achieve success via proactiveness. Therefore, consistent with Miller and Friesen's (1978) earlier definition, we agree with Venkatraman, who suggested that proactiveness refers to processes aimed at anticipating and acting on future needs by "seeking new opportunities which may or may not be related to the present line of operations, introduction of new products and brands ahead of competition, strategically eliminating operations which are in the mature or declining stages of life cycle" (1989a: 949). Thus, a proactive firm is a leader rather than a follower, because it has the will and foresight to seize new opportunities, even if it is not always the first to do so.

In addition to the previous definition of proactiveness, there also has been a tendency in the entrepreneurship literature to equate *proactiveness* with *competitive aggressiveness*. The terms are often used interchangeably, for example, in the case in which Covin and Slevin (1989) explained that their model of entrepreneurial strategic posture consists of innovativeness, proactiveness, and risk taking which they defined as "characterized by frequent and extensive technological and product innovation, *an aggressive competitive orientation*, and a strong risk-taking propensity by top management" (1989: 79, emphasis added).

Although closely related to competitive aggressiveness, we feel there is an important distinction between it and proactiveness that needs to be clarified. Proactiveness refers to how a firm relates to *market opportunities* in the process of new entry. It does so by seizing initiative and acting opportunistically in order to "shape the environment," that is, to influence trends and, perhaps, even create demand. Competitive aggressiveness, in contrast, refers to how firms relate to *competitors*, that is, how firms *respond* to trends and demand that already exist in the marketplace. The two ideas are similar, because, as Porter (1985) suggested, the market is the playing field for competitors. But proactiveness has more to do with *meeting* demand, whereas competitive aggressiveness is about *competing* for demand. Combining these distinct concepts inappropriately may explain why Stuart and Abetti (1987) found that a variable labeled "strategic aggressiveness," in which they joined the notions of "first-to-market" with a "highly offensive" posture, was not useful as a predictor of new-entrant success.

To further clarify these concepts, it may be useful to consider the proactiveness continuum. We suggest that the conceptual opposite of proactiveness is *passiveness* (rather than *reactiveness*), that is, indifference or an inability to seize opportunities or lead in the marketplace. Reactiveness, in contrast, suggests a response to competitors. This approach is consistent with Chen and Hambrick, who stated that "a firm should be both proactive and responsive in its environment in terms of technology and innovation, competition, customers, and so forth. Proactiveness involves taking the initiative in an effort to shape the environment to one's own advantage; responsiveness involves being adaptive to competitors' challenges" (1995: 457). An EO, therefore, involves both proactiveness in pursuing opportunities and the will to respond aggressively to competitors. Thus Amdahl, when it learned that IBM had introduced a new product just as they were about to proactively enter the large CPU market with a lighter, faster machine, responded by returning to investors to secure an additional $16 million to further upgrade their product line prior to entry (Cooper, Willard, & Woo, 1986).

Previous researchers have operationalized firm-level proactiveness by asking managers about the firm's tendency to lead rather than follow in the development of new procedures and technologies and the introduction of new products or services (e.g., Covin & Slevin, 1989; Miller, 1983). In Venkatraman's STROBE formulation (1989a), he emphasized the scanning aspect of proactiveness as it relates to opportunity seeking and specifically queried managers if they had "strategically eliminated" operations in later stages of their firm-life cycles.

Because proactiveness suggests an emphasis on initiating activities, it is closely related to innovativeness and is likely to covary with it, as in the case of new-product introductions. Morris and Paul (1987), when they conducted a factor analysis on a 12-item innovativeness, risk-taking, proactiveness scale, on the one hand found two main factors, one that captured both innovativeness and proactiveness and another representing risk taking. On the other hand, the products and services that firms proactively bring to the market also may be imitative or reflect low innovativeness. This may be the case, for example, when a firm enters a foreign market with products that are tried-and-true in domestic markets, but uniquely meet unfilled demand in an untapped market.

The proactiveness dimension of EO most closely resembles the ideas suggested by Miles and Snow's (1978) prospector type, about which they stated,

> the Prospector's prime capability is that of finding and exploiting new products and market opportunities. . . . Prospectors are frequently the creators of change in their respective industries. Change is one of the major tools used by the Prospector to gain an edge over competitors. (1978: 551–553)

Summaries of studies that report on efforts to measure the Miles and Snow typology (e.g., Zahra & Pearce, 1990) and recent efforts by scholars to improve prospector measurement techniques (e.g., Conant, Mokwa, & Varadarajan, 1990) also may provide useful clues for measuring proactiveness.

Competitive Aggressiveness

Stinchcombe (1965) suggested that young firms are particularly susceptible to the "liability of newness" and, therefore, must take steps to establish legitimacy and power relative to suppliers, customers, and other competitors. Because new ventures are much more likely to fail than established businesses, many scholars have argued that an aggressive stance and intense competition are critical to the survival and success of new entrants (e.g., MacMillan, 1982; Porter, 1985). Thus, competitive aggressiveness is a fifth dimension of entrepreneurship that is frequently mentioned in the literature.

Competitive aggressiveness refers to a firm's propensity to directly and intensely challenge its competitors to achieve entry or improve position, that is, to outperform industry rivals in the marketplace. As suggested previously, competitive aggressiveness is characterized by responsiveness, which may take the form of head-to-head confrontation, for example, when a firm enters a market that another competitor has identified, or reactive, for example, when a firm lowers prices in response to a competitive challenge. Competitive aggressiveness also reflects a willingness to be unconventional rather than rely on traditional methods of competing. Examples of this and other forms of competitive aggressiveness available to new entrants include adopting unconventional tactics to challenge industry leaders (Cooper et al., 1986), analyzing and targeting a competitor's weaknesses (Macmillan & Jones, 1984) and focusing on high value-added products while carefully monitoring discretionary expenses (Woo & Cooper, 1981). Similarly, Porter (1985) recommended three approaches for aggressively pursuing existing firms: "doing things differently," that is, reconfiguration; changing the context, that is, redefining the product or service and its market channels or scope; and outspending the industry leader. Thus, competitive aggressiveness, which refers to firm responsiveness directed toward achieving competitive advantage, is an important component of an EO. The importance of this variable as a dimension of EO was highlighted in a study of the entrepreneurial processes of U.S. firms in global markets, in which Dean (1993) found that competitive aggressiveness explained considerably more variance (37%) in corporate entrepreneurship than did any other strategy or structural variable analyzed. Evidence of competitive aggressiveness may take several forms. Covin and Covin (1990: 48), for example, asked managers if they adopted a "very competitive 'undo-the-competitors' posture" or preferred to "live-and-let-live." Activities aimed at overcoming rivals may include, for example, setting ambitious market-share goals and taking bold steps to achieve them, such as cutting prices and sacrificing profits (Venkatraman, 1989a) or spending aggressively compared to competitors on marketing, product service and quality, or manufacturing capacity (MacMillan & Day, 1987). The breadth and speed of new entry also may indicate an aggressive posture. A "fast-followers" approach often is used by firms to aggressively bring new products to market. This approach is accomplished by speeding up the product-development cycle time. Miller and Camp found that the most successful aggressive firms were those that did not shy away from broadly defined markets "in terms of the number, sizes, and types of their customers, as well as the breadth of their product line" (1985: 99). Scales developed by Ginsberg (1985) and Khandwalla (1977) also were used to focus on the aggressiveness of competitive processes used by managers to pursue rivals. Based on a review of the literature and our analysis of an entrepreneurial orientation, we suggest

Proposition 1: Autonomy, innovativeness, risk taking, proactiveness, and competitive aggressiveness are salient dimensions of an entrepreneurial orientation.

Independence of the Five Dimensions

Although innovativeness, risk taking, and proactiveness are important dimensions that entrepreneurial firms may exhibit, Miller's (1983) original conceptualization using these three dimensions—which Covin and Slevin (1989) have labeled "a basic, unidimensional strategic orientation" (1989: 79)—implies that only firms that exhibit high levels of all three dimensions should be regarded as entrepreneurial. This approach may be too narrowly construed for explaining some types of entrepreneurial behavior. Research (e.g., Brockhaus, 1980) suggests that entrepreneurs may be very cautious and risk averse under certain conditions. Other research suggests that entrepreneurial firms may benefit more from imitation than from high levels of innovativeness (Nelson & Winter, 1982). In addition, the development of numerous typologies of entrepreneurial behavior suggests that an EO can be best characterized by several dimensions in various combinations. For example, Schollhammer (1982) described five different types of entrepreneurship: acquisitive, administrative, opportunistic, incubative, and imitative. Firms employing the acquisitive type of entrepreneurship achieve new entry into markets by purchasing existing firms. This approach requires little or no innovativeness and, if the acquired firm is an established business, may involve relatively low risk. Cooper and Dunkelberg (1986) suggested that various paths to business ownership constitute different degrees of entrepreneurship. They agreed that starting a business requires initiative, creativity, and personal risk taking, but entrepreneurial owners who obtain their position by promotion or inheritance generally are not required to be innovative or to assume a substantial degree of personal risk. Webster (1977) used a mathematical calculation of the perceived payoff per principal, that is, the expected financial return to new venture participants, for classifying different types of entrepreneurial ventures. This approach makes little reference to the creativity or proactiveness that may be required by entrepreneurial firms and instead focuses primarily on risk.

The previous examples suggest that an attempt to limit entrepreneurial behavior to only those cases in which high levels of all EO dimensions are evident falls short of explaining many types of entrepreneurship. Although we argue here that all five dimensions are central to understanding the entrepreneurial process, they may occur in different combinations, depending on the type of entrepreneurial opportunity a firm pursues. Sony and Matsushita provide an example of how two competitors can differ along dimensions of entrepreneurial orientation. On the one hand, Sony, well known for its entrepreneurial spirit and R&D skills, aggressively pursues first-mover advantages from new-product innovation. Matsushita, on the other hand, takes a very different competitive posture. Its nickname in Japanese is "Maneshita denki," which roughly translates to "electronics that have been copied." Matsushita typically lets Sony and others innovate, but then takes a leadership position based on its skills in manufacturing and marketing (Lieberman & Montgomery, 1988). Thus, Matsushita draws on the innovativeness of others to position itself to be ready to enter a market once rapid growth begins. Although few observers would argue that Sony has a strong EO, we suggest that Matsushita also has a strong EO. That is, it incurs risks through capital investment in plant and equipment, is proactive by entering markets early in the product life cycle, and displays intense competitive aggressiveness through its strategies that are intended to build strong market share. Therefore,

Proposition 2: The salient dimensions of an entrepreneurial orientation—autonomy, innovativeness, risk taking, proactiveness and competitive aggressiveness—may vary independently of each other in a given context.

The Entrepreneurial Orientation-Performance Relationship: Exploring Key Contingencies and Alternate Models

The importance of entrepreneurship to the strategic management of firms has been widely acknowledged in the strategy literature (e.g., Andrews, 1971; Chandler, 1962; Schendel & Hofer, 1979). Miles and Snow (1978) regarded the entrepreneurial problem as a fundamental issue faced by all firms, the solution to which defines an organization's domain, its product-market relationships, and its resource commitments. Those in strategic management are concerned with the performance implications of management processes, decisions, and actions at the level of the firm. Prior theory and research have suggested that an EO is a key ingredient for organizational success. There often appears to be a normative bias, however, toward the inherent value in entrepreneurship and an assumption that for new entry to result in high performance, firms must have a strong entrepreneurial orientation (Collins & Moore, 1970; Covin & Slevin, 1991; Peters & Waterman, 1982; Schollhammer, 1982; Zahra, 1993). This assumption remains largely untested, as suggested by Zahra, who found that there is "a paucity of empirical documentation of the effect of entrepreneurship on company financial performance" (1993: 11). To address this question, we provide Figure 1, an integrative framework for exploring the relationship between entrepreneurial orientation and performance.

Strategic management scholars are concerned with the relationship between key variables—(organizational structures and processes and characteristics of the business environment) and performance. In order to effectively model the EO-performance relationship, the role of contingent variables will be considered. Contingency theory suggests that congruence or fit among key variables, such as environment, structure, and strategy, is critical for obtaining optimal performance (Miller, 1988). Factors such as industry and environmental variables, or the structural and managerial characteristics of an existing firm, influence how an entrepreneurial orientation will be configured to achieve high performance. The contingency relationships that we propose also provide a context for addressing the extent to which dimensions of EO may, under certain conditions, vary independently rather than covary. Thus, the framework suggested by Figure 1 presents factors that may affect the relationship between an EO and performance.

To address these issues, we review EO-related contingencies that have been suggested in the literature. Then, we present alternative models to demonstrate how the role of contingency variables on the EO-performance relationship can be investigated.

Identifying Key Contingencies

The entrepreneurship literature, in referring to the causes of entrepreneurship, often mentions factors such as managerial style, need for achievement, and other social or motivational factors. These may be important corollaries to an entrepreneurial orientation that help explain a firm's performance. Similarly, environmental factors, such as dynamism and munificence, or structural factors, such as the decentralization of decision making, may influence the performance of firms with an entrepreneurial orienta-

Figure 1
Conceptual Framework of Entrepreneurial Orientation

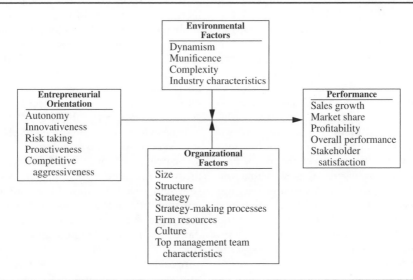

tion. In their model of entrepreneurship as firm behavior, Covin and Slevin (1991) discussed the relationship of strategy, structure, and environment to the EO dimensions of innovativeness, risk taking, and proactiveness. Using these three dimensions, several researchers have verified the importance of viewing the EO-performance relationship in a contingency framework (e.g., Covin & Slevin, 1989; Karagozoglu & Brown, 1988; Zahra & Covin, 1995). In one of the few studies to test a three-way model of environment, structure and EO, Naman and Slevin (1993) found support for a positive relationship between fit and performance for organic firms in a turbulent environment whose style was highly innovative, risk taking, and proactive. In other studies that tested the relationship between contingency variables and individual dimensions of EO, there was also a significant association with performance (e.g., Covin & Covin, 1990; Miller, 1983, 1988).

Contingency theories have been fundamental to furthering the development of the organizational sciences by recognizing the importance of the alignment or fit among key constructs of interest (Burns & Stalker, 1961; Lawrence & Lorsch, 1967; Schoonhoven, 1981; Venkatraman, 1989b). Given the centrality of the EO construct, we consider it necessary to investigate the role of environmental and organizational variables to further our understanding of how EO contributes to performance outcomes. Through such a perspective, we recognize the need to go beyond the investigation of bivariate correlations and examine congtingency relationships. Furthermore, Rosenberg suggested that the introduction of a third variable into the analysis of a two-variable relationship (e.g., EO-performance) helps reduce the potential for misleading inferences and permits a "more *precise* and *specific* understanding" (1968: 100) of the original two-variable relationship.

Table 1 summarizes key contingencies that have been identified in prior research and that are associated with the EO-performance relationship.

Measuring Firm Performance

In investigating the EO-performance relationship, it is essential to recognize the multidimensional nature of the performance construct (Cameron, 1978; Chakravarthy, 1986). That is, entrepreneurial activity or processes may, at times, lead to favorable outcomes on one performance dimension and unfavorable outcomes on a different performance dimension. For example, heavy investment in R&D and product innovation may enable a firm to successfully enter new product-market domains and consequently enhance sales growth in the long run. However, the requisite resource commitment may detract from short-run profitability. Thus, research that only considers a single dimension or a narrow range of the performance construct (e.g., multiple indicators of profitability) may result in misleading descriptive and normative theory building.

Research testing the propositions such as those suggested in this article should include multiple performance measures. Such measures could include traditional accounting measures such as sales growth, market share, and profitability. In addition, indicators of "overall performance" would be useful in incorporating the firm's goals, objectives, and aspiration levels (Kirchhoff, 1978) as well as other elements of broader stakeholder satisfaction. Alternative measures of performance may compete, depending on the size and type of firm and its ownership. For example, new firms often are initiated because key players prefer to work for themselves rather than take direction from an organizational superior. This is consistent with a lifestyle approach (Birley, 1987), whereby effectiveness may be judged by the most basic

Table 1
Contingency Variables Related to the Entrepreneurial Orientation-Performance Relationship

Organizational Factors	Environmental Factors
Structure	Environment
Bahrami & Evans, 1987	Covin & Slevin, 1989
Covin & Slevin, 1988	Karagozoglu & Brown, 1988
Jennings & Lumpkin, 1989	Khandwalla, 1987
Miller, 1983, 1987	Miller, 1983
Naman & Slevin, 1993	Miller & Friesen, 1978
Sandberg & Hofer, 1987	Miller & Friesen, 1983
Slevin & Covin, 1990	Zahra, 1993
Strategy	Zahra & Covin, 1995
Gupta & Govindarajan, 1984	Industry Characteristics
Miller, 1988	Cooper, 1979
Naman & Slevin, 1993	Eisenhardt & Schoonhoven, 1990
Sandberg & Hofer, 1987	MacMillan & Day, 1987
Venkatraman, 1989a	Miller & Camp, 1985
Woo & Cooper, 1981	Porter, 1980
Strategy-Making Processes	Sandberg & Hofer, 1987
Burgelman, 1983	Stuart & Abetti, 1987
Jennings & Lumpkin, 1989	Tushman & Anderson, 1986
Miller & Friesen, 1982	
Schafer, 1990	
Firm Resources	
Birley, 1985	
Ostgaard & Birley, 1994	
Ramachandran & Ramnarayan, 1993	
Romanelli, 1987	
Stevenson & Gumpert, 1985	
Culture	
Burgelman, 1984	
Burgelman & Sayles, 1986	
Kanter, 1982, 1983	
Stevenson & Gumpert, 1985	
Stuart & Abetti, 1987	
Top Management Team Charcteristics	
Begley & Boyd, 1987	
Cooper & Dunkelberg, 1986	
Eisenhardt & Schoonhoven, 1990	
MacMillan, Zemann, & Subbanarasimha, 1987	

type of financial criteria, such as monthly cash flow or mere survival. Thus, a small, privately owned firm may regard its continued existence as a satisfactory indicator of high performance, even though it cannot claim to have a strong return on assets or growth in market share. It also may make a conscious decision not to grow beyond a certain size, in order to maintain control of the business. Thus, factors such as overall satisfaction and nonfinancial goals of the owners may need to be weighted more heavily in evaluating performance, especially among privately held firms.

Other nonfinancial considerations may be important. Factors such as reputation, public image and goodwill, and the commitment and satisfaction of employees may be important to new entrants. Similarly, Zahra (1993) has suggested that the importance of alternate financial and nonfinancial performance measures change at different points in the life of an organization or new venture. This last point is consistent with Quinn and Cameron's (1978) finding that the criteria of effectiveness shift as an organization evolves. Thus, those who investigate the effectiveness and efficiency of an entrepreneurial orientation need to be sensitive to these performance criteria.

Alternate Models Using Dimensions of an Entrepreneurial Orientation

Venkatraman (1989b) and Boal and Bryson (1987) have proposed alternative models for investigating the impact of third variables as a means of exploring contingency relationships. We believe that the models in Figure 2—moderating effects, mediating effects, independent effects, and interaction effects—provide a useful framework for gaining additional insight into the EO-performance relationship. We first concentrate on examples of various "third variables" to illustrate how they might affect the EO-performance relationship. Next, we

provide examples of contingent relationships that incorporate the multidimensional nature of the EO construct.

These four models have been used previously to provide theoretical insight into the planning-performance (Boal & Bryson, 1987), generic strategies-performance (Dess & Rasheed, 1992), and consensus-performance (Dess & Priem, 1995) relationships. We contend, therefore, that our understanding of the EO-performance link can be further enriched by testing alternate contingency models based on prior theory and research and the frameworks suggested by Venkatraman (1989b) and Boal and Bryson (1987). The alternative models presented here serve as examples of possible relationships and provide a framework for introducing propositions that we acknowledge are tentative. We have proposed models that illustrate frequently mentioned relationships in the literature. They are for illustrative purposes and provide a context in which to draw on real-world examples.

The moderating-effects model is shown in Figure 2a. In this model, the form or strength of the EO-performance relationship varies as a function of organizational structure. Burns and Stalker (1961) introduced the idea of organic versus mechanistic organizational structures. From their investigation of 20 Scottish and British industrial firms, they concluded that organizations are arrayed along a mechanistic-organic continuum, which, they argued, constituted "two formally contrasted forms of management system" (Burns & Stalker, 1961; 119). Organic organizations typically are decentralized and informal and have an emphasis on lateral interaction and an equal distribution of knowledge throughout the organizational network. Mechanistic organizations, in contrast, tend to be highly centralized and formal, and they are characterized by a high degree of vertical interaction and specialized differentiation between functions. Khand-

Figure 2
Alternate Contingency Models of the Entrepreneurial Orientation-Performance Relationship

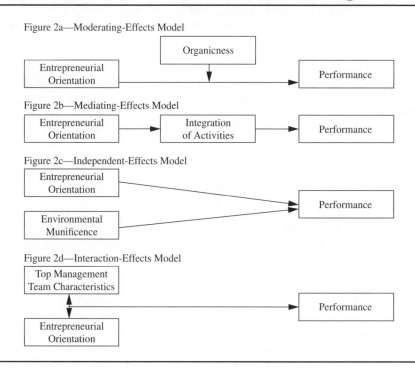

Figure 2a—Moderating-Effects Model

Figure 2b—Mediating-Effects Model

Figure 2c—Independent-Effects Model

Figure 2d—Interaction-Effects Model

walla (1977) argued that an EO needs to be associated with the flexibility inherent in organic organization structures. Similarly, Covin and Slevin (1991) suggested that an EO should be associated with low structural formalization, decentralization, and low complexity. Miller and Friesen (1982) compared the structural attributes of entrepreneurial versus conservative firms. In Covin and Slevin's (1988) analysis of 80 businesses, the "organicness" of the firms' structure was found to moderate the relationship between an entrepreneurial decision-making style and performance. The form of the moderating-effects model suggests that organization structure must be included in order to correctly specify the EO-performance relationship. Therefore,

Proposition 3: The relationship between EO and firm performance will be moderated by the use of an organic structure. Firms with an entrepreneurial orientation that use an organic structure will have higher performance relative to those that do not use an organic structure.

The mediating-effects model is illustrated in Figure 2b. In it, EO is considered an antecedent variable, firm performance is the outcome variable, and the integration of organizational activities is the mediating variable. In this example, we suggest that effective integrating activities and processes intervene in the relationship between EO and performance. Firms with a strong EO will aggressively enter new-product markets and incur greater risks. Such competitive moves will result in their having to cope with more complex and rapidly changing environments. To deal with such environmental demands, Lawrence and Lorsch (1967), Galbraith (1973), and others have argued that such resulting differentiation requires a greater use of integrating structure in order to attain superior performance. This is consistent with Ashby's (1956) law of requisite variety, wherein external complexity should be matched with a corresponding level of complexity in internal processes. Similarly, Kanter (1983) suggested that integrative thinking is vital when creating the type of team environment wherein innovative activities are encouraged and enriched. She argues that

> such organizations reduce rancorous conflict and isolation between organizational units; create mechanisms for exchange of information and new ideas across organizational boundaries; ensure multiple perspectives are taken into account in decisions, and provide coherence and direction to the whole organization. (Kanter, 1983: 28)

In addition, Miller suggested that such activities would include the "extensive use of structural integration devices such as committees and task forces" (1983: 773) and the effective use of rules, planning, and budgeting as well as integrating roles for project activity across functions (Galbraith & Kazanjian, 1986). Also, to integrate activities across business units within a corporation, Porter (1985) suggested the term *horizontal organization*, which consists of horizontal structures, horizontal systems, and horizontal human resource practices. DuPont's nonwovens unit provides an example of a "horizontal organization's"

importance in spurring entrepreneurial activity (*DuPont Annual Report,* 1993). Members of this unit work in networks and teams to gain insights into potential products, and they get together with customers or partners to quickly develop them. Such flexibility enables the nonwovens unit to seek opportunities in a variety of products and markets. For examples, this unit worked with DuPont's automotive unit to evaluate a Tyvek® car cover that was recently introduced in retail markets. The two units continue to work together to design an improved product as well as a cover for new cars en route to dealers. Thus,

Proposition 4: The relationship between EO and firm performance will be mediated by the use of integrating activities. Firms with an entrepreneurial orientation that use integrating activities will have higher performance compared to those that do not use integrating activities.

An independent-effects model is illustrated in figure 2c. In it, EO and environmental munificence are depicted as having independent effects on the dependent variable, firm performance. Environmental munificence may be defined as the profitability or growth rates of the industry in which a firm competes. This relationship is consistent with the traditional industrial organization paradigm (Porter, 1981), which posits that the industry within which a firm competes has a critical impact on its performance. Beard and Dess (1981), Rumelt (1982), and Lieberson and O'Connor (1972) found that a firm's industry context was a significant predictor of performance. We also argue that although EO may have an independent effect on performance, an EO will not interact with the environmental munificence-performance relationship. One may argue that firms or SBUs competing in munificent environments typically will generate additional slack because of relatively higher levels of profits. Such slack resources can be used to facilitate experimentation with new strategies and practices (Bourgeois, 1981), thus enhancing a firm's overall EO. However, we believe that such processes will *not* occur unless the firm has effective integrating mechanisms (Proposition 3) and/or an organic structure (Proposition 4) to facilitate such behavior. In other words, resources, in and of themselves, will not enhance a firm's EO. Therefore,

Propostion 5: Both environmental munificence and EO will have an independent effect on organizational performance.

An interaction-effects model is shown in Figure 2d. In it, characteristics of the top management team (TMT), such as tolerance for ambiguity or need for achievement, are believed to interact to influence firm performance. The interaction model is unique because there is no implication of a main effect on EO (as there is with the moderating-effects model discussed previously). In this case, only an interaction effect is proposed. Tolerance for ambiguity has been defined as "the tendency to perceive ambiguous situations as desirable" (Budner, 1962: 29). Favoring ambiguity such as this is likely to be congruent with the type of innovative, risk-taking behavior suggested by the EO construct. Need for achievement is a person's drive to accomplish difficult tasks and be successful (McClelland, 1961). This type of drive is consistent with the proactiveness and risk-taking characteristic of entrepreneurship. Prior studies by Miller and Droge (1986) and Miller and Toulouse (1986) found that need for achievement interacted with strategy making and organizational structure. It is important to point out that personality factors (such as tolerance for ambiguity and need for achievement) tend to be consistent over

rather long periods of time (Conley, 1984). Behaviors may be reactive to or vary with EO, but personality will be less likely to exhibit such relationships. We believe this distinction raises an interesting empirical question: To what extent would a "strong" EO affect various personality traits of incumbent managers?

Proposition 6: Tolerance for ambiguity and EO will influence organizational performance through their interaction effect. Firms with an EO, in which managers have high tolerance for ambiguity, will have higher performance compared to firms with managers who have low tolerance for ambiguity.

Proposition 7: Need for achievement and EO will influence organizational performance through their interaction effect. Firms with an EO, in which managers have a high need for achievement, will have higher performance compared to firms in which managers have a low need for achievement.

These four models should provide additional insight into the EO-performance relationship. The models also provide an overall framework for the testing of competing theories. For example, we have proposed that in Figure 2c, environmental munificence would have an independent effect on performance. However, Covin and Slevin (1989) suggested and found statistically significant empirical results for the role of environmental hostility, a similar concept, as a moderator in the EO-performance relationship. They defined hostile environments as "characterized by precarious industry settings, intense competition, harsh, overwhelming business climates, and the relative lack of exploitable opportunities" (1989: 75). One could argue that, in hostile environments, resources would be more constrained and would, in turn, lead to greater control, coordination, and interlocking of organizational behavior (Pfeffer & Leblebici, 1973). A smaller resource base also would impede experimentation with new strategies (Bourgeois, 1981) and direct efforts toward conserving limited resources (Chakravarthy, 1982; Richards, 1979). Under such conditions, entrepreneurial behavior would be stifled and, even if viable strategic alternatives were proposed, the allocation of sufficient resources to ensure their proper implementation would become problematic. Thus, the scarcity of resources would adversely affect the relationship between a firm's EO and performance. This example illustrates the need to test alternate models of the role of third variables.

Entrepreneurial Orientation as Multidimensional: How Relationships May Differ

We have focused on alternate models for investigating the EO construct and its relationship to performance. However, consistent with Proposition 2, dimensions of EO may, in fact, vary independently. Accordingly, we provide two examples using Figure 2a to illustrate how relationships may differ when the multidimensional nature of EO is explicitly recognized.

Example 1. As was noted, theory and research suggest that an organic structure provides a desirable structural context for *innovativeness* (Covin & Slevin, 1991; Miller & Friesen, 1982). Thus, the innovativeness dimension of an EO is likely to be positively related to performance when the setting is organic. However, because structural "organicness" suggests decentralization and low formalization, traditional methods of organizational control are relaxed. Such an organizational environment may promote the autonomy and creativity required for innovative behavior. However, an organic structure may

negatively moderate the *competitive aggressiveness*-performance relationship. That is, although an organic structure may contribute to an atmosphere of creativity, it also may detract from a firm's ability to focus intensely enough to effectively compete with industry rivals. With such a structure, it may be more difficult to coordinate and integrate primary and support activities in a firm's value chain (Porter, 1985). The resulting loose coupling (Weick, 1976), implicit in an organic structure, may be detrimental to expanding a firm's product-market domain. Such is the case with Dell Computer Company of Austin, Texas—a firm with 1994 sales of approximately $3 billion. "Until very recently, Dell was a big and growing company with a corner grocery store style of management" (Mack, 1994: 46) without the structuring of activities required for a company that had grown so rapidly. Dell was unable to coordinate its design, manufacturing, sales, and procurement functions. Not surprisingly, Dell had problems controlling costs, a major shortcoming for a firm competing aggressively for market share in what has largely become a commodity business. To turn things around, Dell has hired several experienced managers to rationalize all aspects of its operations, including supplier reductions and improved inventory control. There has been one indication of Dell's successful turnaround: By January 30, 1994, Dell was enjoying a 43% jump in sales with a corresponding 27% drop in inventory compared to the previous year. Thus, to compete aggressively, Dell had to depart from its organic "grocery store" approach. Therefore,

Proposition 8: "Organicness" will moderate the relationship between innovativeness and performance: Among firms with high innovativeness, greater "organicness" will be associated with higher performance.

Proposition 9: "Organicness" will moderate the relationship between competitive aggressiveness and performance: Among firms with strong competitive aggressiveness, greater "organicness" will be associated with lower performance.

Example 2. Quick response has been increasingly recognized as an important form of competitive advantage (Bower & Hout, 1988; Stalk, 1988; Thomas, 1991). A firm following a strategy of quick response may outperform rivals through a variety of competitive means, such as quickly adjusting to market conditions or fast delivery of products and services. The relationship between *proactiveness* and firm performance may be enhanced if a quick-response strategy enables the firm to successfully introduce new products or services. This strategy may help a firm become a first mover (Lieberman & Montgomery, 1988) and provide a source of sustainable competitive advantage (Barney, 1992) if imitation and substitution are difficult for competitors. On the one hand, the competitive advantage of late entrants may be compromised through the diffusion of new technologies throughout the industry. On the other hand, a quick-response strategy may negatively moderate the relationship between *innovativeness* and firm performance. That is, a strategy that emphasizes speed of response without giving attention to the developmental activities and cross-functional coordination (Devanna & Tichy, 1990) needed to effectively develop an innovative new product or service may cause performance to suffer. Further, a firm that responds too quickly to a new innovation may fail to integrate important feedback from the marketplace that would perhaps have helped it to respond with more effective innovative activities. Apple's Newton personal digital assistant (PDA) illustrates the "downside" of com-

bining quick response and innovation (Robello, 1994). Apple's plan was to quickly ensnare market share by building customers' expectations as high as possible, thereby increasing customers' switching costs. However, the product that ex-CEO Sculley had hoped would correct a 1993 third-quarter loss of $188 million did not deliver. Sales were only 1% of Apple's revenues, versus the hoped-for 25%. What went wrong? Most of the model's glitches were related to its lack of promised ability to decipher handwriting. Clearly, Apple could have benefited by closer coordination among its marketing, R&D, production, and engineering professionals. Therefore,

Proposition 10: A quick-response strategy will moderate the relationship between proactiveness and performance: Among firms that are highly proactive, a quick-response strategy will be associated with higher performance.

Proposition 11: A quick-response strategy will moderate the relationship between innovativeness and performance: Among firms that are highly innovative, a quick-response strategy will be associated with lower performance.

Implications for Research and Practice

The term *entrepreneurship* is used broadly and applied in many contexts. Researchers investigating entrepreneurship are still struggling, however, with issues such as "What makes a firm entrepreneurial?" "Can any firm be entrepreneurial?" "What's the difference between entrepreneurship and effective strategic management?" and "When does a firm cease to be entrepreneurial?" Underlying these issues is the basic question, "What is entrepreneurship?" In the interest of addressing this question, our goal has been to illuminate one aspect of this broadly used term—the entrepreneurial orientation construct. By clarifying this concept, distinguishing it from the new entry aspects of entrepreneurship, and using a contingency framework to relate it to performance, we have endeavored to help guide further theory building in this important area. As such, we can begin to address other questions related to the nature of entrepreneurship.

For example, to the question, "What makes a firm entrepreneurial?" we would argue that any firm that engages in an effective combination of autonomy, innovativeness, risk taking, proactiveness, and competitive aggressiveness is entrepreneurial. Thus, an entrepreneurial orientation, as reflected in the organizational processes and decision-making style of a firm, can be a source of competitive advantage or strategic renewal, even for firms that are not involved in launching new ventures. In this respect, an effective EO may be an example of good strategic management. This difference, in fact, further highlights the importance of distinguishing between the EO aspect of entrepreneurship and new entry. New entry is the action that distinguishes entrepreneurial behavior from other types of business activity that might be undertaken to capitalize on an opportunity. For example, it might be good business to purchase a large supply of raw materials that suddenly becomes available at a deeply discounted price, or it may increase efficiency to reorganize a production capability by outsourcing key components of the process. These actions reflect insightful decision making and good management practices rather than entrepreneurship. Defining entrepreneurship as new entry, therefore, represents a somewhat narrower approach to conceptualizing the construct than suggested by Stevenson and Jarillo (1990), who defined it rather broadly as "the process of . . . pursuing opportunities" (1990: 23). In contrast, the idea of entrepreneurship as new entry is more encompassing than the approach taken by Gartner (1988: 26), who argued that "entrepreneurship is the creation of new organizations." We suggest that new entry may occur across a range of firms, from individuals to existing organizations, without necessarily creating a new organization.

The entrepreneurial orientation construct, we believe, represents the *process* aspect of entrepreneurship. Future researchers should consider the extent to which such entrepreneurial processes may predict the nature and success of pursuing opportunities via new entry. Additionally, the relationship of EO to other key predictor variables such as strategies and tactics, industry life cycle, and size are fertile areas for future research. An entrepreneurial orientation may be especially important for small new entrants that are struggling to develop a management team, to organize resources efficiently, and to develop a strategy. During start-up, an EO may be the only thing a young firm has going for it until issues of survival can be satisfied.

Regarding the question, "When does a firm cease to be entrepreneurial?" we would argue again that a firm can choose to maintain an entrepreneurial orientation throughout its life. We also suggest, however, that when members of a firm become overly passive or decline to take risks or exercise creativity in order to capitalize on a market opportunity, they run the risk of losing the entrepreneurial edge. In contrast, the extent to which an EO will be effective in a given context may vary. Both Slevin and Covin (1990) and Miller (1983, 1988) suggested that firms can be too entrepreneurial; that is, they may take risks or incur R&D expenses that are not in accord with the market environment or circumstances in which they are competing. Thus, it is important to employ a contingency framework to evaluate what factors may influence the relationship of an EO to performance.

The idea that the dimensions of EO may vary independently is consistent with the work of prior entrepreneurship scholars, who have proposed different typologies to characterize entrepreneurship. Schollhammer (1982), for example, posited five different types of entrepreneurship: acquisitive, administrative, opportunistic, incubative, and imitative. Within each of these categories, the extent to which autonomy, innovativeness, risk taking, proactiveness, and competitive aggressiveness can contribute positively to performance may vary. In the future, researchers should investigate how entrepreneurial processes influence performance in the different settings, such as those that Schollhammer suggest. Empirical research may reveal unique configurations of the dimensions of EO. For example, Baumol (1986) suggested that entrepreneurial activities fall into two primary categories: *initiating* and *imitative*. Future research may support the idea that the dimensions of EO fall into two broad categories that correspond to Baumol's two types where initiating entrepreneurship proceeds from high levels of innovativeness and proactiveness, whereas imitative new entry is successful because of an emphasis on competitive aggressiveness. Researchers should also investigate whether some dimensions of EO are always present, whereas others vary depending on the context. Future investigators may find, for example, that risk taking and autonomy are needed for all types of new entry, but that innovativeness, proactiveness, and competitive aggressiveness are present only under certain conditions. Additionally, these dimensions may combine to form unique entrepreneurial types. Zahra and Covin (1993), for example, used the concept of an aggressive technological posture, which combines notions of innovativeness and competitive aggressiveness.

Although we have argued in this article for the viability of investigating contingency relationships, we also believe that additional insights can be gained by exploring configurations among an EO and other key constructs. That is, an EO may be more strongly associated with performance when it is combined with *both* the appropriate strategy and the proper environmental conditions. Such an assertion is consistent with Miller's (1988) and others' ideas that a configurational framework has promise for further developing normative and descriptive theory. Additionally, Lenz, in a study of savings and loan associations, concluded that "neither environment, strategy nor organizational structure is sufficient to explain differences in performance . . . organizational performance is determined, in part, by the particular coalignment administrators are able to achieve" (1980: 220–221). Previous research by the authors found that entrepreneurial strategy making, when matched with high environmental uncertainty and a low-cost strategy, was associated with high performance. This was contrary to our hypothesis (Dess, Lumpkin, & Covin, 1995). One might interpret such a finding as suggesting that even when competing on the basis of cost, it may be advisable to proactively scan the environment, take some risks, and innovate. Alternatively, perhaps entrepreneurial orientations are not necessarily inconsistent with overall cost-leadership strategies, unless each is pursued at the extreme. In retrospect, had we viewed the EO as multidimensional, the results and our interpretations may have provided additional insights. That is, risk taking and proactiveness may have been consistent with this configuration but not innovativeness (or other dimensions of EO).

In addition to exploring relationships among EO, strategy, environment, and organizational performance, researchers should investigate the processes through which entrepreneurial behavior enhances a firm's competitive position and performance. Such research should entail fine-grained (Harrigan, 1983) methodologies such as intensive field research and case studies. For example, Burgelman (1983) explored the implications of induced and autonomous entrepreneurial activities among six internal corporate-venturing projects and found that autonomous strategic activities often are initiated by individuals at the operational levels in the organization. Fine-grained methodologies also could provide insight into the role of culture and, in the context of the resource-based model of the firm, complex social processes (e.g., Barney, 1992) associated with the dimensions of an entrepreneurial orientation. Finally, such methodologies also could help to address a more basic question, that is, how to operationalize the various constructs suggested in this article. For example, there are numerous methods employed for measuring the construct "risk taking" (Baird & Thomas, 1985). What is the best method in the context of EO? Prior research suggests that entrepreneurs simply don't "see" the risks that others see, or, alternatively, they see nonentrepreneurial behavior as far more risky. In the future, researchers should help to empirically capture such a construct. The same issue is relevant for all the EO constructs addressed in this article.

Conclusion

Exploring relationships between entrepreneurial behavior and performance is very timely, given the competitive conditions faced by firms of all sizes in today's economy. Our goal has been to build on prior theory and research in order to (a) clarify the multidimensional nature of the EO construct and (b) suggest alternative contingency models that we believe will provide additional insight into the EO-performance relationship. We encourage research efforts

directed at understanding the dimensionality of the EO construct and the role of contingency and configurational approaches in explaining its relationship to performance. Such efforts will contribute to further theoretical development in the field of entrepreneurship. Research to refine measures, explore the underlying processes associated with entrepreneurial activity, and recognize the multidimensional nature of entrepreneurial behavior also will enhance our understanding of EO and its relationship to organizational performance.

References

Andrews, K. R. 1971. *The concept of corporate strategy.* Homewood. IL: Irwin.

Ashby, W. R. 1956. *An introduction to cybernetics.* Englewood Cliffs, NJ: Prentice Hall.

Bahrami, H., & Evans, S. 1987. Stratocracy in high-technology firms. *California Management Review,* 30(1): 51–66.

Baird, I. S., & Thomas, H. 1985. Toward a contingency model of strategic risk taking. *Academy of Management Review,* 10: 230–243.

Barney, J. 1992. Integrating organizational behavior and strategy formulation research: A resource-based analysis. In P. Shrivastava, A. Huff, & J. Dutton (Eds.), *Advances in strategic management:* 39–62. Greenwich, CT: JAI Press.

Baumol, W. J. 1986. Entrepreneurship and a century of growth. *Journal of Business Venturing,* 1: 141–145.

Beard, D., & Dess, G. G. 1981. Corporate-level strategy, business-level strategy, and firm performance. *Academy of Management Journal,* 24: 663–688.

Begley, T. M., & Boyd, D. P. 1987. Psychological characteristics associated with performance in entrepreneurial firms and smaller businesses. *Journal of Business Venturing,* 2: 79–93.

Birch, D. 1979. The job generation process. *MIT program on neighborhood and regional change.* Cambridge, MA: MIT Press.

Bird, B. 1988. Implementing entrepreneurial ideas: The case for intention. *Academy of Management Review*, 13: 442–453.

Birley, S. 1985. The role of networks in the entrepreneurial process. *Journal of Business Venturing*, 1: 107–117.

Birley, S. 1987. New ventures and employment growth. *Journal of Business Venturing*, 2: 155–165.

Boal, K., & Bryson, J. 1987. Representation, testing and policy implications of planning processes. *Strategic Management Journal*, 8: 211–231.

Bourgeois, L. J. 1980. Strategy and environment: A conceptual integration. *Academy of Management Review*, 5: 25–39.

Bourgeois, L. J. 1981. On the measurement of organizational slack. *Academy of Management Review*, 6: 29–39.

Bourgeois, L., & Brodwin, D. 1984. Strategic implementation: Five approaches to an elusive phenomenon. *Strategic Management Journal*, 5: 241–264.

Bower, J. L. 1970. *Managing the resource allocation process.* Boston: Harvard University Press.

Bower, J. L., & Hout, T. M. 1988. Fast cycle capability for competitive power. *Harvard Business Review*, 88(6): 110–118.

Brockhaus, R. H. 1980. Risk taking propensity of entrepreneurs. *Academy of Management Journal*, 23: 509–520.

Brockhaus, R. H. 1982. The psychology of the entrepreneur. In C. A. Kent, D. L. Sexton, & K. H. Vesper (Eds.), *Encyclopedia of entrepreneurship*: 39–71. Englewood Cliffs, NJ: Prentice Hall.

Budner S. 1962. Intolerance of ambiguity as a personality variable. *Journal of Personality*, 30: 29–50.

Burgelman, R. A. 1983. A process model of internal corporate venturing in the diversified major firm. *Administrative Science Quarterly*, 28: 223–244.

Burgelman, R. A. 1984. Designs for corporate entrepreneurship. *California Management Review*, 26(2): 154–166.

Burgelman, R. A., & Sayles, L. R. 1986. *Inside corporate innovation: Strategy, structure and managerial skills.* New York: Free Press.

Burns, T., & Stalker, G. 1961. *The management of innovation.* London: Tavistock.

Business Week. 1993. *Enterprise.* [Special issue].

Cameron, K. 1978. Measuring organizational effectiveness in institutions of higher education. *Administrative Science Quarterly*, 23: 604–632.

Cantillon, R. 1734. *Essai sur la nature du commerce en general* [Essay on the nature of general commerce]. (Henry Higgs, Trans.). London: Macmillan.

Chakravarthy, B. 1982. Adaptation: A promising metaphor for strategic management. *Academy of Management Review*, 7: 35–44.

Chakravarthy, B. 1986. Measuring strategic performance. *Strategic Management Journal*, 6: 437–458.

Chandler, A. D. 1962. *Strategy and structure: Chapters in the history of American industrial enterprise.* Cambridge, MA: MIT Press.

Chen, M. J., & Hambrick, D. C. 1995. Speed, stealth, and selective attack: How small firms differ from large firms in competitive behavior. *Academy of Management Journal*, 38: 453–482.

Child, J. 1972. Organization structure, environment, and performance: The role of strategic choice. *Sociology*, 6: 1–22.

Collins, O., & Moore, D. 1970. *The organization makers.* New York: Appleton-Century-Crofts.

Conant, J. S., Mokwa, M. P., & Varadarajan, P. R. 1990. Strategic types, distinctive marketing competencies, and organizational performance: A multiple measures-based study. *Strategic Management Journal*, 11: 365–383.

Conley, J. J. 1984. Longitudinal consistency of adult personality: Self-reported psychological characteristics across 45 years. *Journal of Personality and Social Psychology*, 47: 1325–1333.

Cooper, A. C. 1971. *The founding of technologically-based firms.* Milwaukee, WI: The Center for Venture Management.

Cooper, A. C., & Dunkelberg, W. C. 1986. Entrepreneurship and paths to business ownership. *Strategic Management Journal*, 7: 53–68.

Cooper, A. C., Willard, G. E., & Woo, C. W. 1986. Strategies of high-performing new and small firms: A reexamination of the niche concept. *Journal of Business Venturing*, 1: 247–260.

Cooper, R. G. 1979. The dimensions of industrial new product success and failure. *Journal of Marketing*, 43: 93–103.

Covin, J. G., & Covin, T. 1990. Competitive aggressiveness, environmental context, and small firm performance. *Entrepreneurship: Theory and Practice*, 14(4): 35–50.

Covin, J. G., & Slevin, D. P. 1988. The influence of organization structure on the utility of an entrepreneurial top management style. *Journal of Management Studies*, 25: 217–234.

Covin, J. G., & Slevin, D. P. 1989. Strategic management of small firms in hostile and benign environments. *Strategic Management Journal*, 10: 75–87.

Covin, J. G., & Slevin, D. P. 1991. A conceptual model of entrepreneurship as firm behavior. *Entrepreneurship: Theory and Practice*, 16(1): 7–24.

Dean, C. C. 1993. *Corporate entrepreneurship: Strategic and structural correlates and impact on the global presence of United States firms.* Unpublished doctoral dissertation, University of North Texas, Denton, TX.

Dean, C. C., Thibodeaux, M. S., Beyerlein, M., Ebrahimi, B., & Molina, D. 1993. Corporate entrepreneurship and competitive aggressiveness: A comparison of U.S. firms operating in Eastern Europe or the Commonwealth of Independent States with U.S. firms in other high-risk environments. In S. B. Prasad (Ed.), *Advances in international and comparative management*: 31–54. Greenwich, CT: JAI Press.

Dess, G. G., Lumpkin, G. T., & Covin, J. G. 1995. *Contingency versus configurational tests of the entrepreneurial orientation construct.* Unpublished manuscript.

Dess, G. G., & Priem, R. L. 1995. Consensus-performance research: Theoretical and empirical extensions. *Journal of Management Studies*, 32: 401–417.

Dess, G. G., & Rasheed, A. 1992. Commentary: Generic strategies. In P. Shrivastava, A. Huff, & J. Dutton (Eds.), *Advances in strategic management*: 409–416. Greenwich, CT: JAI Press.

Devanna, M. A., & Tichy, N. 1990. Creating the competitive organization of the 21st century: The boundaryless corporation. *Human Resource Management*, 28: 455–471.

Downs, G. W., & Mohr, L. B. 1976. Conceptual issues in the study of innovation. *Administrative Science Quarterly*, 21: 700–714.

DuPont Corporation. 1993. *Annual report.* Wilmington, DE: Author.

Eisenhardt, K. M., & Schoonhoven, C. B. 1990. Organizational growth: Linking founding team, strategy, environment, and growth among U.S. semiconductor ventures, 1978–1988. *Administrative Science Quarterly*, 35: 504–529.

Fredrickson, J. 1986. The strategic decision making process and organizational structure. *Academy of Management Review*, 11: 280–297.

Galbraith, J. 1973. *Designing complex organizations*. Reading, MA: Addison-Wesley.

Galbraith, J., & Kazanjian, R. 1986. *Strategy implementation: Structure, systems, and process* (2nd ed.). St. Paul, MN: West.

Gartner, W. B. 1985. A conceptual framework for describing the phenomenon of new venture creation. *Academy of Management Review*, 10: 696–706.

Gartner, W. B. 1988. "Who is an entrepreneur?" is the wrong question. *American Journal of Small Business*, 12(4): 11–32.

Gasse, Y. 1982. Elaborations on the psychology of the entrepreneur. In C. A. Kent, D. L. Sexton, & K. H. Vesper (Eds.), *Encyclopedia of entrepreneurship*: 209–223. Englewood Cliffs, NJ: Prentice Hall.

Ginsberg, A. 1985. Measuring changes in entrepreneurial orientation following industry deregulation: The development of a diagnostic instrument. *Proceedings of the International Council of Small Business*: 50–57.

Gupta, A. K., & Govindarajan, V. 1984. Business unit strategy, managerial characteristics, and business unit effectiveness at strategy implementation. *Academy of Management Journal*, 27: 25–41.

Guth, W. D., & Ginsberg, A. 1990. Guest editor's introduction: Corporate entrepreneurship. *Strategic Management Journal* [Special issue], 11: 5–15.

Hage, J. 1980. *Theories of organizations*. New York: Wiley.

Harrigan, K. R. 1983. Research methodologies for contingency approaches to strategy. *Academy of Management Review*, 8: 398–405.

Hart, S. L. 1991. Intentionality and autonomy in strategy-making process: Modes, archetypes, and firm performance. In P. Shrivastava, A. Huff, & J.

Dutton (Eds.), *Advances in strategic management*, vol. 7: 97–127. Greenwich, CT: JAI Press.

Hart, S. L. 1992. An integrative framework for strategy-making processes. *Academy of Management Review*, 17: 327–351.

Hisrich, R. D., & Peters, M. P. 1989. *Entrepreneurship: Starting, developing, and managing a new enterprise*. Homewood, IL: Irwin.

Jennings, D. F., & Lumpkin, J. R. 1989. Functioning modeling corporate entrepreneurship: An empirical integrative analysis. *Journal of Management*, 15: 485–502.

Kahneman, D., & Tversky, A. 1979. Prospect theory: An analysis of decision under risk. *Econometrica*, 47: 263–291.

Kanter, R. M. 1982. The middle manager as innovator. *Harvard Business Review*, 60(4): 95–106.

Kanter, R. M. 1983. *The change masters: Innovation and entrepreneurship in the American corporation*. New York: Simon & Schuster.

Karagozoglu, N., & Brown, W. B. 1988. Adaptive responses by conservative and entrepreneurial firms. *Journal of Product Innovation Management*, 5: 269–281.

Katz, J., & Gartner, W. B. 1988. Properties of emerging organizations. *Academy of Management Review*, 13: 429–441.

Khandwalla, P. 1977. *The design of organizations*. New York: Harcourt Brace Jovanovich.

Khandwalla, P. 1987. Generators of pioneering innovative management: Some Indian evidence. *Organization Studies*, 8(1): 39–59.

Kilby, P. 1971. Hunting the heffalump. In P. Kilby (Ed.), *Entrepreneurship and economic development*: 1–40. New York: Free Press.

Kimberly, J. R. 1981. Managerial innovation. In P. C. Nystrom & W. H. Starbuck (Eds.), *Handbook of organizational design*, vol. 1: 84–104. New York: Oxford University Press.

Kirchhoff, B. A. 1977. Organization effectiveness measurement and policy research. *Academy of Management Review*, 2: 347–355.

Kogan, N., & Wallach, M. A. 1964. *Risk taking: A study in cognition and personality.* New York: Holt, Rinehart & Winston.

Lawrence, P., & Lorsch, J. 1967. *Organization and environment.* Cambridge, MA: Harvard University Press.

Lenz, R. T. 1980. Environment, strategy, organizational structure, and performance: Patterns in one industry. *Strategic Management Journal*, 1: 209–226.

Lieberman, M., & Montgomery, D. 1988. First-mover advantages. *Strategic Management Journal* [Special Issue], 9: 41–58.

Lieberson, S., & O'Connor, J. 1972. Leadership and organizational performance: A study of large organizations. *American Sociological Review*, 37: 117–130.

Mack, T. 1994. Michael Dell's new religion. *Forbes*, June 6: 45–46.

MacMillan, I. C. 1982. Seizing competitive initiative. *Journal of Business Strategy*, 2: 43–57.

MacMillan, I. C. & Day, D. L. 1987. Corporate ventures into industrial markets: Dynamics of aggressive entry. *Journal of Business Venturing*, 2(1): 29–39.

MacMillan, I. C., & Jones, P. E. 1984. Designing organizations to compete. *Journal of Business Strategy*, 4: 11–26.

MacMillan, I. C., Zemann, L., & Subbanarasimha, P. N. 1987. Criteria distinguishing successful from unsuccessful ventures in the venture screening process. *Journal of Business Venturing*, 2(2): 123–137.

Maidique, M. A., & Patch, P. 1982. Corporate strategy and technological policy. In M. L. Tushman & W. L. Moore (Eds.), *Readings in the management of innovation*: 273–285. Marshfield, MA: Pitman.

McClelland, D. C. 1961. *The achieving society.* Princeton, NJ: Van Nostrand.

Miles, R., & Snow, C. 1978. *Organizational strategy, structure, and process.* New York: McGraw-Hill.

Miller, A., & Camp, B. 1985. Exploring determinants of success in corporate ventures. *Journal of Business Venturing*, 1(2): 87–105.

Miller, D. 1983. The correlates of entrepreneurship in three types of firms. *Management Science*, 29: 770–791.

Miller, D. 1987. Strategy making and structure: Analysis and implications for performance. *Academy of Management Journal*, 30: 7–32.

Miller, D. 1988. Relating Porter's business strategies to environment and structure: Analysis and performance implications. *Academy of Management Journal*, 31: 280–308.

Miller, D., & Droge, C. 1986. Psychological and traditional determinants of structure. *Administrative Science Quarterly*, 31: 539–560.

Miller, D., & Friesen, P. 1978. Archetypes of strategy formulation. *Management Science*, 24: 921–933.

Miller, D., & Friesen, P. 1982. Innovation in conservative and entrepreneurial firms: Two models of strategic momentum. *Strategic Management Journal*, 3: 1–25.

Miller, D., & Friesen, P. 1983. Strategy-making and environment: The third link. *Strategic Management Journal*, 4: 221–235.

Miller, D., & Toulouse, J. 1986. Chief executive personality and corporate strategy and structure in small firms. *Management Science*, 32: 1389–1409.

Mintzberg, H. 1973. Strategy making in three modes. *California Management Review*, 16(2): 44–53.

Mintzberg, H., & Waters, J. A. 1985. Of strategies, deliberate and emergent. *Strategic Management Journal*, 6: 257–272.

Morris, M. H., & Paul, G. W. 1987. The relationship between entrepreneurship and marketing in established firms. *Journal of Business Venturing*, 2(3): 247–259.

Naman, J. L., & Slevin, D. P. 1993. Entrepreneurship and the concept of fit: A model and empirical tests. *Strategic Management Journal*, 14: 137–153.

Nelson, R., & Winter, S. 1982. *An evolutionary theory of economic theory and capabilities.* Cambridge, MA: Harvard University Press.

Ostgaard, T. A., & Birley, S. 1994. Personal networks and firm competitive strategy: A strategic or coincidental match? *Journal of Business Venturing*, 9(4): 281–305.

Pascale, R. 1985. The paradox of "corporate culture": Reconciling ourselves to socialization. *California Management Review*, 27(2): 26–41.

Pfeffer, J., & Leblebici, H. 1973. The effect of competition on some dimensions of organization structure. *Social Forces*, 52: 268–279.

Penrose, E. T. 1959. *The theory of the growth of the firm.* Oxford, England: Oxford University Press.

Peters, T., & Waterman, R. 1982. *In search of excellence.* New York: Harper & Row.

Pinchot, G. 1985. *Intrapreneuring: Why you don't have to leave the corporation to become an entrepreneur.* New York: Harper & Row.

Porter, M. 1980. *Competitive strategy.* New York: Free Press.

Porter, M. 1981. The contributions of industrial organization to strategic management. *Academy of Management Review*, 6: 609–620.

Porter, M. 1985. *Competitive advantage.* New York: Free Press.

Quinn, J. B. 1979. Technological innovation, entrepreneurship, and strategy. *Sloan Management Review*, 20(3): 15–26.

Quinn, R., & Cameron, K. 1983. Organizational life cycles and shifting criteria of effectiveness: Some preliminary evidence. *Management Science*, 29: 33–51.

Rajagopalan, N., Rasheed, A., & Datta, D. 1993. Strategic decision processes: Critical review and future directions. *Journal of Management*, 19: 349–384.

Ramachandran, K., & Ramnarayan, S. 1993. Entrepreneurial orientation and networking: Some Indian evidence. *Journal of Business Venturing*, 8(6): 513–524.

Richards, M. 1979. Commentary. In D. Schendel & C. Hofer (Eds.), *Strategic management*: 80–84. Boston, MA: Little, Brown.

Robello, K. 1994. Newton: Will what fell down go up? *Business Week*, July 11: 41.

Romanelli, E. 1987. New venture strategies in the microcomputer industry. *California Management Review*, 30: 160–175.

Rosenberg, M. 1968. *The logic of survey analysis.* New York: Basic Books.

Rumelt, R. 1982. Diversification strategy and profitability. *Strategic Management Journal*, 3: 359–369.

Saleh, S. D., & Wang, C. K. 1993. The management of innovation: Strategy, structure, and organizational climate. *IEEE Transactions on Engineering Management*, 40(1): 14–21.

Sandberg, W. R., & Hofer, C. W. 1987. Improving new venture performance: The role of strategy, industry structure, and the entrepreneur. *Journal of Business Venturing*, 2: 5–28.

Schafer, D. S. 1990. Level of entrepreneurship and scanning source usage in very small businesses. *Entrepreneurship Theory & Practice*, 5(2): 19–31.

Schendel, D., & Hofer, C. W. 1979. *Strategic management.* Boston: Little, Brown.

Scherer, F. M. 1980. *Industrial market structure and economic perfor-*

mance (2nd ed.). Boston: Houghton-Mifflin.

Schollhammer, H. 1982. Internal corporate entrepreneurship. In C. A. Kent, D. L. Sexton, & K. H. Vesper (Eds.), *Encyclopedia of entrepreneurship*: 209–223. Englewood Cliffs, NJ: Prentice Hall.

Schoonhoven, C. B. 1981. Problems with contingency theory: Testing assumptions hidden within the language of contingency "theory." *Administrative Science Quarterly*, 26: 349–377.

Schumpeter, J. A. 1934. *The theory of economic development.* Cambridge, MA: Harvard University Press.

Schumpeter, J. A. 1942. *Capitalism, socialism, and democracy.* New York: Harper & Brothers.

Shane, S. A. 1994a. Are champions different from non-champions? *Journal of Business Venturing*, 9: 397–421.

Shane, S. A. 1994b. Why do rates of entrepreneurship vary over time? *Academy of Management Best Paper Proceedings*: 90–94.

Shrivastava, P., & Grant, J. H. 1985. Empirically derived models of strategic decision-making processes. *Strategic Management Journal*, 6: 97–113.

Sitkin, S. B., & Pablo, A. L. 1992. Reconceptualizing the determinants of risk behavior. *Academy of Management Review*, 17(1): 9–38.

Slevin, D. P., & Covin, J. G. 1990. Juggling entrepreneurial style and organizational structure—How to get your act together. *Sloan Management Review*, Winter: 43–53.

Slovic, P., Fischhoff, B., & Lichtenstein, S. 1980. Facts versus fears: Understanding perceived risk. In D. Kahneman, P. Slovic, & A. Tversky (Eds.), *Judgment under uncertainty: Heuristics and biases*: 463–489. Cambridge, England: Cambridge University Press.

Stalk, G. 1988. Time-the next source of competitive advantage. *Harvard Business Review*, 66: 41–51.

Stevenson, H. H., & Gumpert, D. E. 1985. The heart of entrepreneurship. *Harvard Business Review*, 85(2): 85–94.

Stevenson, H. H., & Jarillo, J. C. 1990. A paradigm of entrepreneurship: Entrepreneurial management. *Strategic Management Journal* [Special issue], 11: 17–27.

Stinchcombe, A. L. 1965. Social structure and organizations. In James G. March (Ed.), *Handbook of organizations*: 142–193. Chicago: Rand McNally.

Stuart, R., & Abetti, P. A. 1987. Start-up ventures: Towards the prediction of initial success. *Journal of Business Venturing*, 2: 215–230.

Thaler, R. H., & Johnson, E. J. 1990. Gambling with the house money and trying to break even: The effects of prior outcomes on risky choices. *Management Science*, 36: 643–660.

Thomas, P. R. 1991. *Getting competitive: Middle managers and the cycle time ethic.* New York: McGraw-Hill.

Tushman, M. L., & Anderson, P. 1986. Technological discontinuities and organizational environments. *Administrative Science Quarterly*, 31: 439–465.

Van de Ven, A., & Poole, M. S. 1995. Explaining development and change in organizations. *Academy of Management Review*, 20: 510–540.

Venkatraman, N. 1989a. Strategic orientation of business enterprises: The construct, dimensionality, and measurement. *Management Science*, 35: 942–962.

Venkatraman, N. 1989b. The concept of fit in strategy research: Toward verbal and statistical correspondence. *Academy of Management Review*, 14: 423–444.

Vesper, K. H. 1980. *New venture strategies.* Englewood Cliffs, NJ: Prentice Hall.

Vesper, K. H. 1988. Entrepreneurial academics—How can we tell when the field is getting somewhere? *Journal of Business Venturing*, 3: 1–10.

Webster, F. A. 1977. Entrepreneurs and ventures: An attempt at classification and clarification. *Academy of Management Review*, 2: 54–61.

Webster's ninth new collegiate dictionary. 1991. Springfield, MA: Merriam Webster.

Weick, K. E. 1976. Educational organizations as loosely coupled systems. *Administrative Science Quarterly*, 21: 1–19.

Woo, C. Y., & Cooper, A. C. 1981. Strategies of effective low share business. *Strategic Management Journal*, 2: 301–318.

Zahra, S. 1993. A conceptual model of entrepreneurship as firm behavior:

A critique and extension. *Entrepreneurship: Theory ad Practice*, 17(4): 5–21.

Zahra, S, A., & Covin, J. G. 1995. Contextual influences on the corporate entrepreneurship-performance relationship: A longitudinal analysis. *Journal of Business Venturing*, 10: 43–58.

Zahra, S, A., & Covin, J. G. 1993. Business strategy, technology policy and firm performance. *Strategic Management Journal*, 14: 451–478.

Zahra, S. A., & Pearce, J. A. 1990. Research evidence on the Miles-Snow typology. *Journal of Management*, 16: 751–768.

Entrepreneurship: Productive, Unproductive, and Destructive*

by William J. Baumol

The basic hypothesis is that, while the total supply of entrepreneurs varies among societies, the productive contribution of the society's entrepreneurial activities varies much more because of their allocation between productive activities such as innovation and largely unproductive activities such as rent seeking or organized crime. This allocation is heavily influenced by the relative payoffs society offers to such activities. This implies that policy can influence the allocation of entrepreneurship more effectively than it can influence its supply. Historical evidence from ancient Rome, early China, and the Middle Ages and Renaissance in Europe is used to investigate the hypotheses.

It is often assumed that an economy of private enterprise has an automatic bias towards innovation, but this is not so. It has a bias only towards profit. [HOBSBAWM 1969, p. 40]

When conjectures are offered to explain historic slowdowns or great leaps in economic growth, there is the group of usual suspects that is regularly rounded up—prominent among them, the entrepreneur. Where growth has slowed, it is implied that a decline in entrepreneurship was partly to blame (perhaps because the culture's "need for achievement" has atrophied). At another time and place, it is said, the flowering of entrepreneurship accounts for unprecedented expansion.

This paper proposes a rather different set of hypotheses, holding that entrepreneurs are always with us and always play *some* substantial role. But there are a variety of roles among which the entrepreneur's efforts can be reallocated, and some of those roles do not follow the constructive and innovative script that is

Originally appeared in *Journal of Political Economy*, 1990, Volume 98, Number 5.
*I am very grateful for the generous support of the research underlying this paper from the Division of Information Science and Technology of the National Science Foundation, the Price Institute for Entrepreneurial Studies, the Center for Entrepreneurial Studies of the Graduate School of Business Administration, New York University, and the C. V. Starr Center for Applied Economics. I am also very much indebted to Vacharee Devakula for her assistance in the research. I owe much to Joel Mokyr, Stefano Fenoaltea, Lawrence Stone, Constance Berman, and Claudia Goldin for help with the substance of the paper and to William Jordan and Theodore Rabb for guidance on references.

conventionally attributed to that person. Indeed, at times the entrepreneur may even lead a parasitical existence that is actually damaging to the economy. How the entrepreneur acts at a given time and place depends heavily on the rules of the game—the reward structure in the economy—that happen to prevail. Thus the central hypothesis here is that it is the set of rules and not the supply of entrepreneurs *or the nature of their objectives* that undergoes significant changes from one period to another and helps to dictate the ultimate effect on the economy via the *allocation* of entrepreneurial resources. Changes in the rules and other attendant circumstances can, of course, modify the composition of the class of entrepreneurs and can also alter its size. Without denying this or claiming that it has no significance, in this paper I shall seek to focus attention on the allocation of the changing class of entrepreneurs rather than its magnitude and makeup. (For an excellent analysis of the basic hypothesis, independently derived, see Murphy, Shleifer, and Vishny [1990].)

The basic proposition, if sustained by the evidence, has an important implication for growth policy. The notion that our productivity problems reside in "the spirit of entrepreneurship" that waxes and wanes for unexplained reasons is a counsel of despair, for it gives no guidance on how to reawaken that spirit once it has lagged. If that is the task assigned to policymakers, they are destitute: they have no means of knowing how to carry it out. But if what is required is the adjustment of rules of the game to induce a more felicitous allocation of entrepreneurial resources, then the policymaker's task is less formidable, and it is certainly not hopeless. The prevailing rules that affect the allocation of entrepreneurial activity can be observed, described, and, with luck, modified and improved, as will be illustrated here.

Here, extensive historical illustrations will be cited to impart plausibility to the contentions that have just been described. Then a short discussion of some current issues involving the allocation of entrepreneurship between productive and unproductive activities will be offered. Finally, I shall consider very briefly the means that can be used to change the rules of the game, and to do so in a manner that stimulates the productive contribution of the entrepreneur.

I. On the Historical Character of the Evidence

Given the inescapable problems for empirical as well as theoretical study of entrepreneurship, what sort of evidence can one hope to provide? Since the rules of the game usually change very slowly, a case study approach to investigation of my hypotheses drives me unavoidably to examples spanning considerable periods of history and encompassing widely different cultures and geographic locations. Here I shall proceed on the basis of historical illustrations encompassing all the main economic periods and places (ancient Rome, medieval China, Dark Age Europe, the Later Middle Ages, etc.) that the economic historians almost universally single out for the light they shed on the process of innovation and its diffusion. These will be used to show that the relative rewards to different types of entrepreneurial activity have in fact varied dramatically from one time and place to another and that this seems to have had profound effects on patterns of entrepreneurial behavior. Finally, evidence will be offered *suggesting* that such reallocations can have a considerable influence on the prosperity and growth of an economy, though other variables undoubtedly also play substantial roles.

None of this can, of course, be considered conclusive. Yet, it is surely a standard tenet of scientific method that tentative confirmation of a hypothesis is provided by observation of phenomena that the hypothesis helps to explain and that could not easily be accounted for if that hypothesis were invalid. It is on this sort of reasoning that I hope to rest my case. Historians have long been puzzled, for example, by the failure of the society of ancient Rome to disseminate and put into widespread practical use some of the sophisticated technological developments that we know to have been in its possession, while in the "High Middle Ages," a period in which progress and change were hardly popular notions, inventions that languished in Rome seem to have spread like wildfire. It will be argued that the hypothesis about the allocability of entrepreneurial effort between productive and unproductive activity helps considerably to account for this phenomenon, though it certainly will *not* be claimed that this is all there was to the matter.

Before I get to the substance of the discussion, it is important to emphasize that nothing that follows in this article makes any pretense of constituting a contribution to economic history. Certainly it is not intended here to try to explain any particular historical event. Moreover, the analysis relies entirely on secondary sources, and all the historical developments described are well known to historians, as the citations will indicate. Whatever the contribution that may be offered by the following pages, then, it is confined to enhanced understanding and extension of the (nonmathematical) theory of entrepreneurship in general, and not to an improved analysis of the historical events that are cited.

II. The Schumpeterian Model Extended: Allocation of Entrepreneurship

The analysis of this paper rests on what seems to be the one theoretical model that effectively encompasses the role of the entrepreneur and that really "works," in the sense that it constitutes the basis for a number of substantive inferences.[1] This is, of course, the well-known Schumpeterian analysis, whose main shortcoming, for our purposes, is the paucity of insights on policy that emerge from it. It will be suggested here that only a minor extension of that model to encompass the *allocation* of entrepreneurship is required to enhance its power substantially in this direction.

Schumpeter tells us that innovations (he calls them "the carrying out of new combinations") take various forms besides mere improvements in technology:

> This concept covers the following five cases: (1) the introduction of a new good—that is one with which consumers are not yet familiar—or of a new quality of a good. (2) The introduction of a new method of production, that is one not yet tested by experience in the branch of manufacture concerned, which need by no means be founded upon a discovery scientifically new, and can also exist in a new way of handling a commodity commercially. (3) The opening of a new market, that is a market into which the particular

---

[1]There has, however, recently been an outburst of illuminating writings on the theory of the innovation process, analyzing it in such terms as *races* for patents in which the winner takes everything, with no consolation prize for a close second, or treating the process, alternatively, as a "waiting game," in which the patient second entrant may outperform and even survive the first one in the innovative arena, who incurs the bulk of the risk. For an overview of these discussions as well as some substantial added insights, see Dasgupta (1988).

branch of manufacture of the country in question has not previously entered, whether or not this market has existed before. (4) The conquest of a new source of supply of raw materials or half-manufactured goods, again irrespective of whether this source already exists or whether it has first to be created. (5) The carrying out of the new organization of any industry, like the creation of a monopoly position (for example through trustification) or the breaking up of a monopoly position. [(1912) 1934, p. 66]

The obvious fact that entrepreneurs undertake such a variety of tasks all at once suggests that theory can usefully undertake to consider what determines the *allocation* of entrepreneurial inputs among those tasks. Just as the literature traditionally studies the allocation of other inputs, for example, capital resources, among the various industries that compete for them, it seems natural to ask what influences the flow of entrepreneurial talent among the various activities in Schumpeter's list.

Presumably the reason no such line of inquiry was pursued by Schumpeter or his successors is that any analysis of the allocation of entrepreneurial resources among the five items in the preceding list (with the exception of the last—the creation or destruction of a monopoly) does not promise to yield any profound conclusions. There is no obvious reason to make much of a shift of entrepreneurial activity away from, say, improvement in the production process and toward the introduction of new products. The general implications, if any, for the public welfare, for productivity growth, and for other related matters are hardly obvious.

To derive more substantive results from an analysis of the allocation of entrepreneurial resources, it is necessary to expand Schumpeter's list, whose main deficiency seems to be that it does not go far enough. For example, it does not explicitly encompass innovative acts of technology transfer that take advantage of opportunities to introduce already-available technology (usually with some modification to adapt it to local conditions) to geographic locales whose suitability for the purpose had previously gone unrecognized or at least unused.

Most important for the discussion here, Schumpeter's list of entrepreneurial activities can usefully be expanded to include such items as innovations in rent-seeking procedures, for example, discovery of a previously unused legal gambit that is effective in diverting rents to those who are first in exploiting it. It may seem strange at first blush to propose inclusion of activities of such questionable value to society (I shall call them acts of "unproductive entrepreneurship") in the list of Schumpeterian innovations (though the creation of a monopoly, which Schumpeter does include as an innovation, is surely as questionable), but, as will soon be seen, this is a crucial step for the analysis that follows. If entrepreneurs are defined, simply, to be persons who are ingenious and creative in finding ways that add to their own wealth, power, and prestige, then it is to be expected that not all of them will be overly concerned with whether an activity that achieves these goals adds much or little to the social product or, for that matter, even whether it is an actual impediment to production (this notion goes back, at least, to Veblen [1904]). Suppose that it turns out, in addition, that at any time and place the magnitude of the benefit the economy derives from its entrepreneurial talents depends *substantially*, among other variables, on the allocation of this resource between productive and unproductive entrepreneurial activities of the sorts just described. Then the reasons for including acts of the latter type in the list of entrepreneurial activities become clear.

Here no exhaustive analysis of the process of allocation of entrepreneurial activity among the set of available options will be attempted. Rather, it will be argued only that at least *one* of the prime determinants of entrepreneurial behavior at any particular time and place is the prevailing rules of the game that govern the payoff of one entrepreneurial activity relative to another. If the rules are such as to impede the earning of much wealth via activity A, or are such as to impose social disgrace on those who engage in it, then, other things being equal, entrepreneurs' efforts will tend to be channeled to other activities, call them B. But if B contributes less to production or welfare than A, the consequences for society may be considerable.[2]

As a last preliminary note, it should be emphasized that the set of active entrepreneurs may be subject to change. Thus if the rules of the game begin to favor B over A, it may not be just the same individuals who switch their activities from entrepreneurship of type A to that of type B. Rather, some persons with talents suited for A may simply drop out of the picture, and individuals with abilities adapted to B may for the first time become entrepreneurs. Thus the allocation of entrepreneurs among activities is perhaps best described in the way Joan Robinson (following Shove's suggestion) analyzed the allocation of heterogeneous land resources (1933, chap. 8): as the solution of a jigsaw puzzle in which the pieces are each fitted into the places

selected for them by the concatenation of pertinent circumstances.

III. Entrepreneurship, Productive and Unproductive: The Rules Do Change

Let us now turn to the central hypothesis of this paper: that the exercise of entrepreneurship can sometimes be unproductive or even destructive, and that whether it takes one of these directions or one that is more benign depends heavily on the structure of payoffs in the economy—the rules of the game. The rather dramatic illustrations provided by world history seem to confirm quite emphatically the following proposition.

PROPOSITION 1. The rules of the game that determine the relative payoffs to different entrepreneurial activities *do* change dramatically from one time and place to another.

These examples also suggest strongly (but hardly "prove") the following proposition.

PROPOSITION 2. Entrepreneurial behavior changes direction from one economy to another in a manner that corresponds to the variations in the rules of the game.

A. Ancient Rome

The avenues open to those Romans who sought power, prestige, and wealth are instructive. First, it may be noted that they had no reservations about the desirability of wealth or about its pursuit (e.g., Finley 1985, pp. 53–57). *As long as it did not involve participation in*

---

[2]There is a substantial literature, following the work of Jacob Schmookler, providing strong empirical evidence for the proposition that even the allocation of inventive effort, i.e., the directions pursued by inventive activities, is itself heavily influenced by relative payoff prospects. However, it is now agreed that some of these authors go too far when they appear to imply that almost nothing but the demand for the product of invention influences to any great extent which inventions will occur. For a good summary and references, see Abramovitz (1989, p. 33).

industry or commerce, there was nothing degrading about the wealth acquisition process. Persons of honorable status had three primary and acceptable sources of income: landholding (not infrequently as absentee landlords), "usury," and what may be described as "political payments":

> The opportunity for "political moneymaking" can hardly be overestimated. Money poured in from booty, indemnities, provincial taxes, loans and miscellaneous extractions in quantities without precedent in Graeco-Roman history, and at an accelerating rate. The public treasury benefited, but probably more remained in private hands, among the nobles in the first instance; then, in appropriately decreasing proportions, among the *equites*, the soldiers and even the plebs of the city of Rome. . . . Nevertheless, the whole phenomenon is misunderstood when it is classified under the headings of "corruption" and "malpractice", as historians still persist in doing. Cicero was an honest governor of Cilicia in 51 and 50 B.C., so that at the end of his term he had earned only the legitimate profits of office. They amounted to 2,200,000 sesterces, more than treble the figure of 600,000 he himself once mentioned (*Stoic Paradoxes* 49) to illustrate an annual income that could permit a life of luxury. We are faced with something structural in the society. [Finley 1985, p. 55]

Who, then, operated commerce and industry? According to Veyne (1961), it was an occupation heavily undertaken by freedmen—former slaves who, incidentally, bore a social stigma for life. Indeed, according to this writer, slavery may have represented the one avenue for advancement for someone from the lower classes. A clever (and handsome) member of the lower orders might deliberately arrange to be sold into slavery to a wealthy and powerful master.[3] Then, with luck, skill, and drive, he would grow close to his owner, perhaps managing his financial affairs (and sometimes engaging in some homosexual activity with him). The master then gained cachet, after a suitable period, by granting freedom to the slave, setting him up with a fortune of his own. The freedmen, apparently not atypically, invested their financial stakes in commerce, hoping to multiply them sufficiently to enable them to retire in style to the countryside, thereafter investing primarily in land and loans in imitation of the upper classes.

Finally, regarding the Romans' attitude to the promotion of technology and productivity, Finley makes much of the "clear, almost total, divorce between science and practice" (1965, p. 32). He goes on to cite Vitruvius's monumental work on architecture and technology, in whose 10 books he finds only a single and trivial reference to means of saving effort and increasing productivity. Finley then reports the following story:

> There is a story, repeated by a number of Roman writers, that a man—characteristically unnamed—invented unbreakable glass and demonstrated it to Tiberius in anticipation of a great reward. The emperor asked the inventor whether anyone shared his secret and was assured that

---

[3]Stefano Fenoaltea comments that he knows no documented cases in which this occurred and that it was undoubtedly more common to seek advancement through adoption into an upper-class family.

there was no one else; whereupon his head was promptly removed, lest, said Tiberius, gold be reduced to the value of mud. I have no opinion about the truth of this story, and it is only a story. But is it not interesting that neither the elder Pliny nor Petronius nor the historian Dio Cassius was troubled by the point that the inventor turned to the emperor for a reward, instead of turning to an investor for capital with which to put his invention into production?[4] ... We must remind ourselves time and again that the European experience since the late Middle Ages in technology, in the economy, and in the value systems that accompanied them, was unique in human history until the recent export trend commenced. Technical progress, economic growth, productivity, even efficiency have not been significant goals since the beginning of time. So long as an acceptable life-style could be maintained, however that was defined, other values held the stage. [1985, p. 147]

The bottom line, for our purposes, is that the Roman reward system, although it offered wealth to those who engaged in commerce and industry, offset this gain through the attendant loss in prestige. Economic effort "was neither the way to wealth nor its purpose. Cato's gods showed him a number of ways to get more; but they were all political and parasitical, the ways to conquest and booty and usury; labour was not one of them, not even the labour of the entrepreneur" (Finley 1965, p. 39).

B. Medieval China

In China, as in many kingdoms of Europe before the guarantees of the Magna Carta and the revival of towns and their acquisition of privileges, the monarch commonly claimed possession of all property in his territories. As a result, particularly in China, when the sovereign was in financial straits, confiscation of the property of wealthy subjects was entirely in order. It has been claimed that this led those who had resources to avoid investing them in any sort of visible capital stocks, and that this, in turn, was a substantial impediment to economic expansion (see Balazs 1964, p. 53; Landes 1969, pp. 46–47; Rosenberg and Birdzell 1986, pp. 119–20; Jones 1987, chap. 5).

In addition, imperial China reserved its most substantial rewards in wealth and prestige for those who climbed the ladder of imperial examinations, which were heavily devoted to subjects such as Confucian philosophy and calligraphy. Successful candidates were often awarded high rank in the bureaucracy, high social standing denied to anyone engaged in commerce or industry, even to those who gained great wealth in the process (and who often used their resources to prepare their descendants to contend via the examinations for a position in the scholar bureaucracy). In other words, the rules of the game seem to have been heavily biased against the acquisition of wealth *and position* through Schumpeterian behavior. The avenue to success lay elsewhere.

---

[4]To be fair to Finley, note that he concludes that it is *not* really interesting. North and Thomas (1973, p. 3) make a similar point about Harrison's invention of the ship's chronometer in the eighteenth century (as an instrument indispensable for the determination of longitude). They point out that the incentive for this invention was a large governmental prize rather than the prospect of commercial profit, presumably because of the absence of effective patent protection.

Because of the difficulty of the examinations, the mandarins (scholar-officials) rarely succeeded in keeping such positions in their own families for more than two or three generations (see Marsh 1961, p. 159; Ho 1962, chap. 4 and appendix). The scholar families devoted enormous effort and considerable resources to preparing their children through years of laborious study for the imperial examinations, which, during the Sung dynasty, were held every 3 years, and only several hundred persons in all of China succeeded in passing them each time (E. A. Kracke, Jr. in Liu and Golas [1969, p. 14]). Yet, regularly, some persons not from mandarin families also attained success through this avenue (see, e.g., Marsh [1961] and Ho [1962] for evidence on social mobility in imperial China).

Wealth was in prospect for those who passed the examination and who were subsequently appointed to government positions. But the sources of their earnings had something in common with those of the Romans:

> Corruption, which is widespread in all impoverished and backward countries (or, more exactly, throughout the pre-industrial world), was endemic in a country where the servants of the state often had nothing to live on but their very meager salaries. The required attitude of obedience to superiors made it impossible for officials to demand higher salaries, and in the absence of any control over their activities from below it was inevitable that they should purloin from society what the state failed to provide. According to the usual pattern, a Chinese official entered upon his duties only after spending long years in study and passing many examinations; he then established relations with protectors, incurred debts to get himself appointed, and then proceeded to extract the amount he had spent on preparing himself for his career from the people he administered—and extracted both principal and interest. The degree of his rapacity would be dictated not only by the length of time he had had to wait for his appointment and the number of relations he had to support and of kin to satisfy or repay, but also by the precariousness of his position. [Balazs 1964, p. 10]

Enterprise, on the other hand, was not only frowned on, but may have been subjected to impediments deliberately imposed by the officials, at least after the fourteenth century A.D.; and some historians claim that it was true much earlier. Balazs tells us of

> the state's tendency to clamp down immediately on any form of private enterprise (and this in the long run kills not only initiative but even the slightest attempts at innovation), or, if it did not succeed in putting a stop to it in time, to take over and nationalize it. Did it not frequently happen during the course of Chinese history that the scholar-officials, although hostile to all inventions, nevertheless gathered in the fruits of other people's ingenuity? I need mention only three examples of inventions that met this fate: paper, invented by a eunuch; printing, used by the Buddhists as a medium for religious propaganda; and the bill of exchange, an expedient of private businessmen. [P. 18]

As a result of recurrent intervention by the state to curtail the liberty and take over any accumulated advantages the merchant class had managed to gain for itself, "the merchant's ambition turned to becoming a scholar-official and investing his profits in land" (p. 32).

C. The Earlier Middle Ages

Before the rise of the cities and before monarchs were able to subdue the bellicose activities of the nobility, wealth and power were pursued primarily through military activity. Since land and castles were the medieval forms of wealth most highly valued and most avidly sought after, it seems reasonable to interpret the warring of the barons in good part as the pursuit of an economic objective. For example, during the reign of William the Conqueror (see, e.g., Douglas 1964), there were frequent attempts by the barons in Normandy and neighboring portions of France to take over each other's lands and castles. A prime incentive for William's supporters in his conquest of England was their obvious aspiration for lands.[5] More than that, violent means also served to provide more liquid forms of income (captured treasure), which the nobility used to support both private consumption and investment in military plant and equipment, where such items could not easily be produced on their own lands and therefore had to be purchased from others. In England, with its institution of primogeniture (the exclusive right of the eldest son to inherit his father's estate), younger sons who chose not to enter the clergy often had no socially acceptable choice other than warfare as a means to make their fortunes, and in some cases they succeeded spectacularly. Thus note the case of William Marshal, fourth son of a minor noble, who rose through his military accomplishments to be one of the most powerful and trusted officials under Henry II and Richard I, and became one of the wealthiest men in England (see Painter 1933).

Of course, the medieval nobles were not purely economic men. Many of the turbulent barons undoubtedly enjoyed fighting for its own sake, and success in combat was an important avenue to prestige in their society. But no modern capitalist is a purely economic man either. What I am saying here is that warfare, which was of course pursued for a variety of reasons, was *also* undertaken as a primary source of economic gain. This is clearly all the more true of the mercenary armies that were the scourge of fourteenth-century France and Italy.

Such violent economic activity, moreover, inspired frequent and profound innovation. The introduction of the stirrup was a requisite for effective cavalry tactics. Castle building evolved from wooden to stone structures and from rectangular to round towers (which could not be made to collapse by undermining their corners). Armor and weaponry became much more sophisticated with the introduction of the crossbow, the longbow, and, ultimately, artillery based on gunpowder. Military tactics and strategy also grew in sophistication. These innovations can be interpreted as contributions of military entrepreneurs undertaken at least partly in pursuit of private economic gains.

This type of entrepreneurial undertaking obviously differs vastly from the introduction of a cost-saving industrial process or a valuable new consumer product. An individual who pursues wealth through the forcible appropriation of the possessions of others surely

---

[5] The conquest has at least two noteworthy entrepreneurial sides. First, it involved an innovation, the use of the stirrup by the Normans at Hastings that enabled William's warriors to use the same spear to impale a series of victims with the force of the horse's charge, rather than just tossing the spear at the enemy, much as an infantryman could. Second, the invasion was an impressive act of organization, with William having to convince his untrustworthy allies that they had more to gain by joining him in England than by staying behind to profit from his absence by trying to grab away his lands as they had tried to do many times before.

does not add to the national product. Its net effect may be not merely a transfer but a net reduction in social income and wealth.[6]

D. The Later Middle Ages

By the end of the eleventh century the rules of the game had changed from those of the Dark Ages. The revival of the towns was well under way. They had acquired a number of privileges, among them protection from arbitrary taxation and confiscation and the creation of a labor force by granting freedom to runaway serfs after a relatively brief residence (a year and a day) in the towns. The free-enterprise turbulence of the barons had at least been impeded by the church's pacification efforts: the peace and the (later) truce of God in France, Spain, and elsewhere; similar changes were taking place in England (see, e.g., Cowdrey [1970]; but Jones [1987, p. 94] suggests that some free-enterprise military activity by the barons continued in England through the reigns of the earlier Tudors in the sixteenth century). All this subsequently "gave way to more developed efforts to enforce peace by the more organized governments of the twelfth century" (Brooke 1964, p. 350; also p. 127). A number of activities that were neither agricultural nor military began to yield handsome returns. For example, the small group of architect-engineers who were in charge of the building of cathedrals, palaces, bridges, and fortresses could live in great luxury in the service of their kings.

But, apparently, a far more common source of earnings was the water-driven mills that were strikingly common in France and southern England by the eleventh century, a technological innovation about which more will be said presently. An incentive for such technical advances may have been the monopoly they conferred on their owners rather than any resulting improvement in efficiency. Such monopoly rights were alike sought and enforced by private parties (Bloch 1935, pp. 554–57; Brooke 1964, p. 84) and by religious organizations (see below).

The economic role of the monks in this is somewhat puzzling—the least clear-cut part of our story.[7] The Cistercian abbeys are generally assigned a crit-

---

[6]In saying all this, I must not be interpreted as taking the conventional view that warfare is an unmitigated source of impoverishment of any economy that unquestionably never contributes to its prosperity. Careful recent studies have indicated that matters are more complicated (see, e.g., Milward 1970; Olson 1982). Certainly the unprecedented prosperity enjoyed afterward by the countries on the losing side of the Second World War suggests that warfare need not always preclude economic expansion, and it is easy to provide earlier examples. The three great economic leaders of the Western world preceding the United States—Italy in the thirteenth–sixteenth centuries, the Dutch Republic in the seventeenth and eighteenth, and Great Britain in the eighteenth and nineteenth—each attained the height of their prosperity after periods of enormously costly and sometimes destructive warfare. Nevertheless, the wealth gained by a medieval baron from the adoption of a novel bellicose technique can hardly have contributed to economic growth in the way that resulted from adoption of a new steelmaking process in the nineteenth century or the introduction of a product such as the motor vehicle in the twentieth.

[7]Bloch (1935) notes that the monasteries had both the capital and the large number of consumers of flour necessary to make the mills profitable. In addition, they were less likely than lay communities to undergo military siege, which, Bloch notes, was (besides drought and freezing of the waterways) one of the main impediments to adoption of the water mill, since blocking of the waterway that drove the mill could threaten the besieged population with starvation (pp. 550–53).

ical role in the promotion of such technological advances. In some cases they simply took over mills that had been constructed by others (Berman 1986, p. 89). But the Cistercians improved them, built many others, and vastly expanded their use; at least some writers (e.g., Gimpel 1976, pp. 3–6) seem to suggest that the Cistercians were the spearhead of technological advance.

Historians tell us that they have no ready explanation for the entrepreneurial propensities of this monastic order. (See, e.g., Brooke [1964, p. 69] and also a personal communication to me from Constance Berman. Ovitt [1987, esp. pp. 142–47] suggests that this may all have been part of the twelfth-century monastic drive to reduce or eliminate manual labor in order to maximize the time available for the less onerous religious labors—a conclusion with which Bloch [1935, p. 553] concurs.) But the evidence suggests strongly that avid entrepreneurs they were. They accumulated vast tracts of land; the sizes of their domesticated animal flocks were enormous by the standards of the time; their investment rates were remarkable; they sought to exercise monopoly power, being known, after the erection of a water mill, to seek legal intervention to prevent nearby residents from continuing to use their animal-powered facilities (Gimpel 1976, pp. 15–16); they were fierce in their rivalrous behavior and drive for expansion, in the process not sparing other religious bodies—not even other Cistercian houses. There is a "record of pastoral expansionism and monopolies over access established by the wealthiest Cistercian houses . . . at the expense of smaller abbeys and convents . . . effectively pushing out all other religious houses as competitors" (Berman 1986, p. 112).

As with early capitalists, the asceticism of the monks, by keeping down the proportion of the monastery's output that was consumed, helped to provide the resources for levels of investment extraordinary for the period (pp. 40, 83). The rules of the game appear to have offered substantial economic rewards to exercise of Cistercian entrepreneurship. The order obtained relatively few large gifts, but instead frequently received support from the laity and from the church establishment in the form of exemptions from road and river tolls and from payment of the tithe. This obviously increased the *marginal* yield of investment, innovation, and expenditure of effort, and the evidence suggests the diligence of the order in pursuing the resulting opportunities. Their mills, their extensive lands, and their large flocks are reported to have brought scale economies and extraordinary financial returns (chap. 4). Puritanical, at least in earlier years, in their self-proclaimed adherence to simplicity in personal lifestyle while engaged in dedicated pursuit of wealth, they may perhaps represent an early manifestation of elements of "the Protestant ethic." But whatever their motive, the reported Cistercian record of promotion of technological progress is in diametric contrast to that of the Roman empire.

E. Fourteenth Century

The fourteenth century brought with it a considerable increase in military activity, notably the Hundred Years' War between France and England. Payoffs, surely, must have tilted to favor more than before inventions designed for military purposes. Cannons appeared as siege devices and armor was made heavier. More imaginative war devices were proposed: a windmill-propelled war wagon, a multibarreled machine gun, and a diving suit to permit underwater attacks on ships. A pervasive business enterprise of this unhappy century of war was the company of mercenary troops—the *condottiere*—who roamed Europe, supported the side that could offer the most attractive terms, and in lulls between fighting, when unemployment threatened, wandered about thinking up military enterprises of their own, at the expense of the general public (Gimpel 1976, chap. 9; see also McNeill 1969, pp. 33–39). Clearly, the rules of the game—the system of entrepreneurial rewards—had changed, to the disadvantage of productive entrepreneurship.

F. Early Rent Seeking

Unproductive entrepreneurship can also take less violent forms, usually involving various types of rent seeking, the type of (possibly) unproductive entrepreneurship that seems most relevant today. Enterprising use of the legal system for rent-seeking purposes has a long history. There are, for example, records of the use of litigation in the twelfth century in which the proprietor of a water-driven mill sought and won a prohibition of use in the vicinity of mills driven by animal or human power (Gimpel 1976, pp. 25–26). In another case, the operators of two dams, one upstream of the other, sued one another repeatedly at least from the second half of the thirteenth century until the beginning of the fifteenth, when the downstream dam finally succeeded in driving the other out of business as the latter ran out of money to pay the court fees (pp. 17–20).

In the upper strata of society, rent seeking also gradually replaced military activity as a prime source of wealth and power. This transition can perhaps be ascribed to the triumph of the monarchies and the consequent imposition of law and order. Rent-seeking entrepreneurship then took a variety of forms, notably the quest for grants of land and patents of monopoly from the monarch.

Such activities can, of course, sometimes prove to contribute to production, as when the recipient of land given by the monarch uses it more efficiently than the previous owner did. But there seems to have been nothing in the structure of the land-granting process that ensured even a tendency toward transfer to more productive proprietors, nor was the individual who sought such grants likely to use as an argument in favor of his suit the claim that he was likely to be the more productive user (in terms of, say, the expected net value of its agricultural output).

Military forms of entrepreneurship may have experienced a renaissance in England in the seventeenth century with the revolt against Charles I. How that may have changed the structure of rewards to entrepreneurial activity is suggested by Hobsbawm (1969), who claims that at the end of the seventeenth century the most affluent merchants earned perhaps three times as much as the richest "master manufacturers."[8] But, he reports, the wealthiest noble families probably had incomes more than 10 times as large as those of the rich merchants. The point in this is that those noble families, according to Hobsbawm, were no holdovers from an ancient feudal aristocracy; they were, rather, the heirs of the Roundheads (the supporters of the parliamentary, or puritan, party) in the then-recent Civil War (pp. 30–32). On this view, once again, military activity would seem to have become the entrepreneur's most promising recourse.

But other historians take a rather different view of the matter. Studies reported in Thirsk (1954) indicate that ultimately there was little redistribution of property as the result of the

---

[8]The evidence indicates that the wealth of affluent families in Great Britain continues to be derived preponderantly from commerce rather than from industry. This contrasts with the record for the United States, where the reverse appears to be true (see Rubinstein 1980, pp. 22–23, 59–60).

Civil War and the restoration. Rather it is noted that in this period the "patrician élites depended for their political power and economic prosperity on royal charters and monopolies rather than on talent and entrepreneurial initiative" (Stone 1985, p. 45). In this interpretation of the matter, it was rent seeking, not military activity, that remained the prime source of wealth under the restoration.

By the time the eighteenth-century industrial revolution ("the" industrial revolution) arrived, matters had changed once again. According to Ashton (1948, pp. 9–10), grants of monopoly were in good part "swept away" by the Monopolies Act of 1624, and, we are told by Adam Smith (1776), by the end of the eighteenth century they were rarer in England than in any other country. Though industrial activity continued to be considered somewhat degrading in places in which industry flourished, notably in England during the industrial revolution there was probably a difference in degree. Thus Lefebvre (1947, p. 14) reports that "at its upper level the [French] nobility . . . were envious of the English lords who enriched themselves in bourgeois ways," while in France "the noble 'derogated' or fell into the common mass if [like Mirabeau] he followed a business or profession" (p. 11). (See, however, Schama [1989], who tells us that "even a cursory examination of the eighteenth-century French economy . . . reveals the nobility deeply involved in finance, business and industry—certainly as much as their British counterparts. . . . In 1765 a royal edict officially removed the last formal obstacles to their participation in trade and industry" [p. 118].) In England, primogeniture, by forcing younger sons of noble families to resort to commerce and industry, apparently was imparting respectability to these activities to a degree that, while rather limited, may have rarely been paralleled before.

The central point of all the preceding discussion seems clear—perhaps, in retrospect, self-evident. If entrepreneurship is the imaginative pursuit of position, with limited concern about the means used to achieve the purpose, then we can expect changes in the structure of rewards to modify the nature of the entrepreneur's activities, sometimes drastically. The rules of the game can then be a critical influence helping to determine whether entrepreneurship will be allocated predominantly to activities that are productive or unproductive and even destructive.

IV. Does the Allocation between Productive and Unproductive Entrepreneurship Matter Much?

We come now to the third proposition of this article.

PROPOSITION 3. The allocation of entrepreneurship between productive and unproductive activities, though by no means the only pertinent influence, can have a profound effect on the innovativeness of the economy and the degree of dissemination of its technological discoveries.

It is hard to believe that a system of payoffs that moves entrepreneurship in unproductive directions is not a substantial impediment to industrial innovation and growth in productivity. Still, history permits no test of this proposition through a set of anything resembling controlled experiments, since other influences *did*, undoubtedly, also play important roles, as the proposition recognizes. One can only note what appears to be a remarkable correlation between the degree to which an economy rewarded productive entrepreneurship and the vigor shown in that economy's innovation record.

Historians tell us of several industrial "near revolutions" that occurred before *the* industrial revolution of the eighteenth century that are highly suggestive for our purposes (Braudel [1986, 3:542–56]; for a more skeptical view, see Coleman [1956]). We are told that two of the incipient revolutions never went anywhere, while two of them were rather successful in their fashion. I shall report conclusions of some leading historians on these episodes, but it should be recognized by the reader that many of the views summarized here have been disputed in the historical literature, at least to some degree.

A. Rome and Hellenistic Egypt

My earlier discussion cited ancient Rome and its empire as a case in which the rules did not favor productive entrepreneurship. Let us compare this with the evidence on the vigor of innovative activity in that society. The museum at Alexandria was the center of technological innovation in the Roman empire. By the first century B.C., that city knew of virtually every form of machine gearing that is used today, including a working steam engine. But these seem to have been used only to make what amounted to elaborate toys. The steam engine was used only to open and close the doors of a temple.

The Romans also had the water mill, this may well have been the most critical pre-eighteenth-century industrial invention because (outside the use of sails in transportation by water) it provided the first significant source of power other than human and animal labor: "it was able to produce an amount of concentrated energy beyond any other resource of antiquity" (Forbes 1955, 2:90). As steam did in more recent centuries, it offered the prospect of providing the basis for a leap in productivity in the Roman economy, as apparently it actually did during the eleventh, twelfth, and thirteenth centuries in Europe. Yet Finley (1965, pp. 35–36), citing White (1962), reports that "though it was invented in the first century B.C., is was not until the third century A.D. that we find evidence of much use, and not until the fifth and sixth of general use. It is also a fact that we have no evidence at all of its application to other industries [i.e., other than grinding of grain] until the very end of the fourth century, and then no more than one solitary and possibly suspect reference . . . to a marble-slicing machine near Trier."

Unfortunately, evidence of Roman technical stagnation is only spotty, and, further, some historians suggest that the historical reports give inadequate weight to the Roman preoccupation with agricultural improvement relative to improvement in commerce or manufacture. Still, the following quotation seems to summarize the weight of opinion: "Historians have long been puzzled as to why the landlords of the Middle Ages proved so much more enterprising than the landlords of the Roman Empire, although the latter, by and large, were much better educated, had much better opportunities for making technical and scientific discoveries if they had wished to do so" (Brooke 1964, p. 88). It seems at least plausible that some part of the explanation is to be found in the ancient world's rules of the game, which encouraged the pursuit of wealth but severely discouraged its pursuit through the exercise of productive entrepreneurship.[9]

---

[9] It has been suggested by historians (see, e.g., Bloch 1935, p. 547) that an abundance of slaves played a key role in Roman failure to use the water mill widely. However, this must imply that the Romans were not efficient wealth seekers. As the cliometric literature has made clear, the cost of maintaining a slave is not low and certainly is not zero, and slaves are apt not to be efficient and dedicated workers. Thus if it had been efficient to replace human or animal

B. Medieval China

The spate of inventions that occurred in ancient China (before it was conquered by the barbarian Yuan dynasty in 1280) constituted one of the earliest potential revolutions in industry. Among the many Chinese technological contributions, one can list paper, (perhaps) the compass, waterwheels, sophisticated water clocks, and, of course, gunpowder. Yet despite the apparent prosperity of the Sung period (960–1270) (see, e.g., Liu and Golas 1969), at least some historians suggest that none of this spate of inventions led to a flowering of *industry*[10] as distinguished from commerce and some degree of general prosperity. And in China too, as we have seen, the rules did not favor productive entrepreneurship. Balazs (1964, p. 53) concludes that

> what was chiefly lacking in China for the further development of capitalism was not mechanical skill or scientific aptitude, nor a sufficient accumulation of wealth, but scope for individual enterprise. There was no individual freedom and no security for private enterprise, no legal foundation for rights other than those of the state, no alternative investment other than landed property, no guarantee against being penalized by arbitrary exactions from

officials or against intervention by the state. But perhaps the supreme inhibiting factor was the overwhelming prestige of the state bureaucracy, which maimed from the start any attempt of the bourgeoisie to be different, to become aware of themselves as a class and fight for an autonomous position in society. Free enterprise, ready and proud to take risks, is therefore quite exceptional and abnormal in Chinese economic history.

C. Slow Growth in the "Dark Ages"

An era noted for its slow growth occurred between the death of Charlemagne (814) and the end of the tenth century. Even this period was not without its economic advances, which developed slowly, including the beginnings of the agricultural improvements that attended the introduction of the horseshoe, harness, and stirrup, the heavy plow, and the substitution of horsepower for oxen, which may have played a role in enabling peasants to move to more populous villages further from their fields (see White 1962, p. 39 ff.). But, still, it was probably a period of significantly slower growth than the industrial revolution of the eleventh–thirteenth centuries (Gimpel 1976), about which more will be said presently. We have already seen that this was a

---

power by the inanimate power of the waterways, failure to do so would have cut into the wealth of the slaveholder, in effect saddling him with the feeding of unproductive persons or keeping the slaves who turned the mills from other, more lucrative, occupations. Perhaps Roman landowners *were* fairly unsophisticated in the management of their estates, as Finley (1985, pp. 108–16) suggests, and, if so, there may be some substance to the hypothesis that slavery goes far to account for the failure of water mills to spread in the Roman economy.

[10]Also, as in Rome, none of this was associated with the emergence of a systematic body of science involving coherent theoretical structure and the systematic testing of hypotheses on the basis of experiment or empirical observation. Here, too, the thirteenth-century work of Bishop Grosseteste, William of Henley, and Roger Bacon was an early step toward that unique historical phenomenon—the emergence of a systematic body of science in the West in, say, the sixteenth century (see Needham 1956).

period in which military violence was a prime outlet for entrepreneurial activity. While this can hardly pretend to be *the* explanation of the relative stagnation of the era, it is hard to believe that it was totally unimportant.

D. The "High Middle Ages"

A good deal has already been said about the successful industrial revolution (and the accompanying commercial revolution sparked by inventions such as double-entry bookkeeping and bills of exchange [de Roover 1953]) of the late Middle Ages, whose two-century duration makes it as long-lived as our own (see Carus-Wilson 1941; White 1962; Gimpel 1976).

Perhaps the hallmark of this industrial revolution was that remarkable source of productive power, the water mills, that covered the countryside in the south of England and crowded the banks of the Seine in Paris (see, e.g., Gimpel 1976, pp. 3–6; Berman 1986, pp. 81–89). The mills were not only simply grain-grinding devices but accomplished an astonishing variety of tasks and involved an impressive variety of mechanical devices and sophisticated gear arrangements. They crushed olives, ground mash for beer production, crushed cloth for papermaking, sawed lumber, hammered metal and woolens (as part of the "fulling" process—the cleansing, scouring, and pressing of woven woolen goods to make them stronger and to bring the

threads closer together), milled coins, polished armor, and operated the bellows of blast furnaces. Their mechanisms entailed many forms of ingenuity. Gears were used to translate the vertical circular motion of the efficient form of the waterwheel into the horizontal circular motion of the millstone. The cam (a piece attached, say, to the axle of the waterwheel, protruding from the axle at right angles to its axis of rotation) served to lift a hammer and to drop it repeatedly and automatically (it was apparently known in antiquity, but may not have been used with waterwheels). A crank handle extending from the end of the axle transformed the circular motion of the wheel into the back and forth (reciprocating) motion required for sawing or the operation of bellows. The most sophisticated product of all this mechanical skill and knowledge was the mechanical clock, which appeared toward the end of the thirteenth century. As White (1962, p. 129) sums up the matter, "the four centuries following Leonardo, that is, until electrical energy demanded a supplementary set of devices, were less technologically engaged in discovering basic principles than in elaborating and refining those established during the four centuries before Leonardo."[11]

In a period in which agriculture probably occupied some 90 percent of the population, the expansion of industry in the twelfth and thirteenth centuries

---

[11]As was already noted, science and scientific method also began to make an appearance with contributions such as those of Bishop Grosseteste and Roger Bacon. Walter of Henley championed controlled experiments and observation over recourse to the opinions of ancient authorities and made a clear distinction between economic and engineering efficiency in discussing the advisability of substituting horses for oxen. Bacon displayed remarkable foresight when he wrote, circa 1260, that "machines may be made by which the largest ships, with only one man steering them, will be moved faster than if they were filled with rowers; wagons may be built which will move with incredible speed and without the aid of beasts; flying machines can be constructed in which a man . . . may beat the air with wings like a bird . . . machines will make it possible to go to the bottom of seas and rivers" (as quoted in White [1962, p. 134]).

could not by itself have created a major upheaval in living standards.[12] Moreover, it has been deduced from what little we know of European gross domestic product per capita at the beginning of the eighteenth century that its average growth in the preceding six or seven centuries must have been very modest, since if the poverty of that later time had represented substantial growth from eleventh-century living standards, much of the earlier population would surely have been condemned to starvation.

Still, the industrial activity of the twelfth and thirteenth centuries was very substantial. By the beginning of the fourteenth century, according to Gimpel (1976), 68 mills were in operation on less than one mile of the banks of the Seine in Paris, and these were supplemented by floating mills anchored to the Grand Pont. The activity in metallurgy was also considerable—sufficient to denude much of Europe of its forests and to produce a rise in the price of wood that forced recourse to coal (Nef [1934]; other historians assert that this did not occur to any substantial degree until the fifteenth or sixteenth century, with some question even about those dates; see, e.g., Coleman [1975, pp. 42–43]). In sum, the industrial revolution of the twelfth and thirteenth centuries was a surprisingly robust affair, and it is surely plausible that improved rewards to industrial activity had something to do with its vigor.

E. The Fourteenth-Century Retreat

The end of all this period of buoyant activity in the fourteenth century (see the classic revisionist piece by Lopez [1969] as well as Gimpel [1976, chap. 9]) has a variety of explanations, many of them having no connection with entrepreneurship. For one thing, it has been deduced by study of the glaciers that average temperatures dropped, possibly reducing the yield of crops (though recent studies indicate that the historical relation between climatic changes and crop yields is at best ambiguous) and creating other hardships. The plague returned and decimated much of the population. In addition to these disasters of nature, there were at least two pertinent developments of human origin. First, the church clamped down on new ideas and other manifestations of freedom. Roger Bacon himself was put under constraint.[13] The period during which new ways of thinking brought rewards and status was apparently ended. Second, the fourteenth century included the first half of the devastating Hundred Years' War. It is implausible that the associated renewal of rewards to military enterprise played no part in the economic slowdown.

F. Remark on "Our" Industrial Revolution

It need hardly be added, in conclusion, that *the* industrial revolution that began in the eighteenth century and con-

---

[12]But then, much the same was true of the first half century of "our" industrial revolution, which, until the coming of the railways, was centered on the production of cotton that perhaps constituted only some 7–8 percent of national output (Hobsbawm 1969, p. 68). Initially, the eighteenth-century industrial revolution was a very minor affair, at least in terms of investment levels and contributions to output and to growth in productivity (perhaps 0.3 percent per year) (see Landes 1969, pp. 64–65; Feinstein 1978, pp. 40–41; Williamson 1984).

[13]The restraints imposed by the church had another curious effect: they apparently made bathing unfashionable for centuries. Before then, bathhouses had been popular as centers for social and, perhaps, sexual activity; but by requiring separation of the sexes and otherwise limiting the pleasures of cleanliness, the church undermined the inducements for such sanitary activities (see Gimpel 1976, pp. 87–92).

tinues today has brought to the industrialist and the businessperson generally a degree of wealth and a respect probably unprecedented in human history. The fact that this period yielded an explosion of output at least equally unprecedented is undoubtedly attributable to a myriad of causes that can probably never be discovered fully and whose roles can never be disentangled. Yet the continued association of output growth with high financial and respectability rewards to productive entrepreneurship is surely suggestive, even if it can hardly be taken to be conclusive evidence for proposition 3, which asserts that the allocation of entrepreneurship *does* really matter for the vigor and innovativeness of an economy.

V. On Unproductive Avenues for Today's Entrepreneur: A Delicate Balance

Today, unproductive entrepreneurship takes many forms. Rent seeking, often via activities such as litigation and takeovers, and tax evasion and avoidance efforts seem now to constitute the prime threat to productive entrepreneurship. The spectacular fortunes amassed by the "arbitrageurs" revealed by the scandals of the mid-1980s were *sometimes*, surely, the reward of unproductive, occasionally illegal but entrepreneurial acts. Corporate executives devote much of their time and energy to legal suit and countersuit, and litigation is used to blunt or prevent excessive vigor in competition by rivals. Huge awards by the courts, sometimes amounting to billions of dollars, can bring prosperity to the victor and threaten the loser with insolvency. When this happens, it must become tempting for the entrepreneur to select his closest advisers from the lawyers rather than the engineers. It induces the entrepreneur to spend literally hundreds of millions of dollars for a single legal

battle. It tempts that entrepreneur to be the first to sue others before those others can sue him. (For an illuminating quantification of some of the social costs of one widely publicized legal battle between two firms, see Summers and Cutler [1988].)

Similarly, taxes can serve to redirect entrepreneurial effort. As Lindbeck (1987, p. 15) has observed, "the problem with high-tax societies is not that it is impossible to become rich there, but that it is difficult to do so by way of productive effort in the ordinary production system." He cites as examples of the resulting reallocation of entrepreneurship " 'smart' speculative financial transactions without much (if any) contribution to the productive capacity of the economy" (p. 15) as well as "illegal 'business areas' such as drug dealing" (p. 25).

In citing such activities, I do not mean to imply either that rent-seeking activity has been expanding in recent decades or that takeover bids or private antitrust suits are always or even preponderantly unproductive. Rather, I am only suggesting where current rent-seeking activities are likely to be found, that is, where policy designers should look if they intend to divert entrepreneurial talents into more productive channels.

The main point here is to note that threats of takeovers are sometimes used as a means to extract "greenmail" and that recourse to the courts as a means to seek to preserve rents through legally imposed impediments to competition does indeed occur, and to suggest that it is no rare phenomenon. This does, then, become an attraction for entrepreneurial talent whose efforts are thereby channeled into unproductive directions. Yet, to the extent that takeovers discipline inefficient managements and that antitrust intervention sometimes is legitimate and sometimes contributes to productivity, it would seem that it will not be easy to change the rules in a way that discourages allocation of entrepreneurial effort into such activities, without at the same time undermining the legitimate role of these institutions. Some promising proposals have been offered, but this is not a suitable place for their systematic examination. However, a few examples will be reported in the following section.

VI. Changes in the Rules and Changes in Entrepreneurial Goals

A central point in this discussion is the contention that if reallocation of entrepreneurial effort is adopted as an objective of society, it is far more easily achieved through changes in the rules that determine relative rewards than via modification of the goals of the entrepreneurs and prospective entrepreneurs themselves. I have even gone so far as to use the same terms to characterize those goals in the very different eras and cultures referred to in the discussion. But it would be ridiculous to imply that the attitudes of a wealth-seeking senator in Rome, a Sung dynasty mandarin, and an American industrialist of the late nineteenth century were all virtually identical. Still, the evidence suggests that they had more in common than might have been expected by the causal observer. However, even if it were to transpire that they really diverged very substantially, that would be of little use to the designer of policy who does not have centuries at his or her disposal and

who is notoriously ineffective in engendering profound changes in cultural influences or in the structure of preferences. It is for this reason that I have chosen to take entrepreneurial goals as given and to emphasize modification in the structure of the rewards to different activities as the more promising line of investigation.

This suggests that it is necessary to consider the process by which those rules are modified in practice, but I believe that answers to even this more restricted question are largely beyond the powers of the historians, the sociologists, and the anthropologists into whose domains it falls. One need only review the disputatious literature on the influences that led to the revival of trade toward the end of the early Middle Ages to see how far we still are from anything resembling firm answers. Exogenous influences such as foreign invasions or unexpected climatic changes can clearly play a part, as can developments within the economy. But the more interesting observation for our purposes is the fact that it is easy to think of measures that *can* change these rules quickly and profoundly.[14]

For example, the restrictions on royal grants of monopolies imposed by Parliament in the Statute of Monopolies are said to have reduced substantially the opportunities for rent seeking in seventeenth- and eighteenth-century England and may have moved reluctant entrepreneurs to redirect their efforts toward agricultural improvement and industry. Even if it did not succeed to any substantial extent in reallocation of the efforts of an unchanged body of

---

[14]Of course, that still leaves open the critical metaquestion, How does one go about changing the society's value system so that it will *want* to change the rules? But that is not the issue with which I am grappling here, since I see no basis on which the economist can argue that society *ought* to change its values. Rather, I am positing a society whose values lead it to favor productivity growth and am examining which instruments promise to be most effective in helping it to pursue this goal.

entrepreneurs from one of those types of activity to the other, if it increased failure rates among the rent seekers while not impeding others who happened to prefer productive pursuits, the result might have been the same. Similarly, tax rules can be used to rechannel entrepreneurial effort. It has, for instance, been proposed that takeover activity would be reoriented substantially in directions that contribute to productivity rather than impeding it by a "revenue-neutral" modification in capital gains taxes that increases rates sharply on assets held for short periods and decreases them considerably for assets held, say, for 2 years or more. A change in the rules that requires a plaintiff firm in a private antitrust suit to bear both parties' legal costs if the defendants are found not to be guilty (as is done in other countries) promises to reduce the frequency with which such lawsuits are used in an attempt to hamper effective competition.

As has already been said, this is hardly the place for an extensive discussion of the design of rational policy in the arena under consideration. The objective of the preceding brief discussion, rather, has been to suggest that there are identifiable means by which the rules of the game can be changed effectively and to illustrate these means concretely, though hardly attempting to offer any generalizations about their character. Certainly, the few illustrations that have just been offered should serve to confirm that there exist (in principle) testable means that promise to induce entrepreneurs to shift their attentions in productive directions, *without any major change in their ultimate goals*. The testability of such hypotheses indicates that the discussion is no tissue of tautologies, and the absence of references to the allocability of entrepreneurship turned up in extensive search of the literature on the entrepreneur suggests that it was not entirely self-evident.

VII. Concluding Comment

There is obviously a good deal more to be said about the subject; however, enough material has been presented to indicate that a minor expansion of Schumpeter's theoretical model to encompass the determinants of the *allocation* of entrepreneurship among its competing uses can enrich the model considerably and that the hypotheses that have been associated with the model's extension here are not without substance, even if none of the material approaches anything that constitutes a formal test of a hypothesis, much less a rigorous "proof." It is also easy to confirm that each of the hypotheses that have been discussed clearly yields some policy implications.

Thus clear guidance for policy is provided by the main hypothesis (propositions 1–3) that the rules of the game that specify the relative payoffs to different entrepreneurial activities play a key role in determining whether entrepreneurship will be allocated in productive or unproductive directions and that this can significantly affect the vigor of the economy's productivity growth. After all, the prevailing laws and legal procedures of an economy are prime determinants of the profitability of activities such as rent seeking via the litigative process. Steps such as deregulation of the airlines or more rational antitrust rules can do a good deal here.

A last example can, perhaps, nail down the point. The fact that Japan has far fewer lawyers relative to population and far fewer lawsuits on economic issues is often cited as a distinct advantage to the Japanese economy, since it reduces at least in part the quantity of resources devoted to rent seeking. The difference is often ascribed to national character that is said to have a cultural aversion to litigiousness. This may all be very true. But closer inspection reveals that there are also other influences. While in the United States legal institutions such as trebled damages provide a rich incentive for one firm to sue another on the claim that the latter violated the antitrust laws, in Japan the arrangements are very different. In that country any firm undertaking to sue another on antitrust grounds must first apply for permission from the Japan Fair Trade Commission. But such permission is rarely given, and, once denied, there is no legal avenue for appeal.

The overall moral, then, is that we do not have to wait patiently for slow cultural change in order to find measures to redirect the flow of entrepreneurial activity toward more productive goals. As in the illustration of the Japanese just cited, it may be possible to change the rules in ways that help to offset undesired institutional influences or that supplement other influences that are taken to work in beneficial directions.

References

Abramovitz, Moses. *Thinking about Growth, and Other Essays of Economic Growth and Welfare.* New York: Cambridge Univ. Press, 1989.

Ashton, Thomas S. *The Industrial Revolution, 1760–1830.* London: Oxford Univ. Press, 1948.

Balazs, Etienne. *Chinese Civilization and Bureaucracy: Variations on a Theme.* New Haven, Conn.: Yale Univ. Press, 1964.

Berman, Constance H. "Medieval Agriculture, the Southern French Countryside, and the Early Cistercians: A Study of Forty-three Monasteries." *Trans. American Philosophical Soc.* 76, pt. 5 (1986).

Bloch, Marc. "Avènement et conquêtes du moulin a eau." *Annales d'Histoire Économique et Sociale* 7 (November 1935): 538–63.

Braudel, Fernand. *Civilization and Capitalism, 15th–18th Century.* Vols. 2, 3. New York: Harper and Row, 1986.

Brooke, Christopher N. L. *Europe in the Central Middle Ages, 962–1154.* London: Longman, 1964.

Carus-Wilson, Eleanora M. "An Industrial Revolution of the Thirteenth Century." *Econ. Hist. Rev.* 11, no. 1 (1941): 39–60.

Coleman, Donald C. "Industrial Growth and Industrial Revolutions." *Economica* 23 (February 1956): 1–22.

———. *Industry in Tudor and Stuart England.* London: Macmillan (for Econ. Hist. Soc.), 1975.

Cowdrey, H. E. J. "The Peace and the Truce of God in the Eleventh Century." *Past and Present*, no. 46 (February 1970), pp. 42–67.

Dasgupta, Partha. "Patents, Priority and Imitation or, the Economics of Races and Waiting Games." *Econ. J.* 98 (March 1988): 66–80.

de Roover, Raymond. "The Commercial Revolution of the 13th Century." In *Enterprise and Secular Change: Readings in Economic History*, edited by Frederic C. Lane and Jelle C. Riemersma. London: Allen and Unwin, 1953.

Douglas, David C. *William the Conqueror: The Norman Impact upon England.* Berkeley: Univ. California Press, 1964.

Feinstein. C. H. "Capital Formation in Great Britain." In *The Cambridge Economic History of Europe*, vol. 8, pt. 1, edited by Peter Mathias and M. M. Postan. Cambridge: Cambridge Univ. Press, 1978.

Finley, Moses I. "Technical Innovation and Economic Progress in the Ancient World." *Econ. Hist. Rev.* 18 (August 1965): 29–45.

———. *The Ancient Economy.* 2d ed. London: Hogarth, 1985.

Forbes, Robert J. *Studies in Ancient Technology.* Leiden: Brill, 1955.

Gimpel, Jean. *The Medieval Machine: The Industrial Revolution of the Middle Ages.* New York: Holt, Reinhart and Winston, 1976.

Ho, Ping-Ti. *The Ladder of Success in Imperial China, 1368–1911*. New York: Columbia Univ. Press, 1962.

Hobsbawm, Eric J. *Industry and Empire from 1750 to the Present Day*. Harmondsworth: Penguin, 1969.

Jones, Eric L. *The European Miracle: Environments, Economies, and Geopolitics in the History of Europe and Asia*. Cambridge: Cambridge Univ. Press, 1987.

Landes, David S. *The Unbound Prometheus: Technological Change and Industrial Development in Western Europe from 1750 to the Present*. New York: Cambridge Univ. Press, 1969.

Lefebvre, Georges. *The Coming of the French Revolution, 1789*. Princeton, N.J.: Princeton Univ. Press, 1947.

Lindbeck, Assar. "The Advanced Welfare State." Manuscript. Stockholm: Univ. Stockholm, 1987.

Liu, James T. C., and Golas, Peter J., eds. *Change in Sung China: Innovation or Renovation?* Lexington, Mass.: Heath, 1969.

Lopez, Robert S. "Hard Times and Investment in Culture." In *The Renaissance: A Symposium*. New York: Oxford Univ. Press (for Metropolitan Museum of Art), 1969.

McNeill, William H. *History of Western Civilization*. Rev. ed. Chicago: Univ. Chicago Press, 1969.

Marsh, Robert M. *The Mandarins: The Circulation of Elites in China, 1600–1900*. Glencoe, Ill.: Free Press, 1961.

Milward, Alan S. *The Economic Effects of the Two World Wars on Britain*. London: Macmillan (for Econ. Hist. Soc.), 1970.

Murphy, Kevin M.; Shleifer, Andrei; and Vishny, Robert. "The Allocation of Talent: Implications for Growth." Manuscript. Chicago: Univ. Chicago, 1990.

Needham, Joseph. "Mathematics and Science in China and the West." *Science and Society* 20 (Fall 1956): 320–43.

Nef, John U. "The Progress of Technology and the Growth of Large-Scale Industry in Great Britain, 1540–1640." *Econ. Hist. Rev.* 5 (October 1934): 3–24.

North, Douglass C., and Thomas, Robert Paul. *The Rise of the Western World: A New Economic History*. Cambridge: Cambridge Univ. Press, 1973.

Olson, Mancur. *The Rise and Decline of Nations: Economic Growth, Stagflation, and Social Rigidities*. New Haven, Conn.: Yale Univ. Press, 1982.

Ovitt, George, Jr. *The Restoration of Perfection: Labor and Technology in Medieval Culture*. New Brunswick, N.J.: Rutgers Univ. Press, 1987.

Painter, Sidney. *William Marshal: Knight-Errant, Baron, and Regent of England*. Baltimore: Johns Hopkins Press, 1933.

Robinson, Joan. *The Economics of Imperfect Competition*. London: Macmillan, 1933.

Rosenberg, Nathan, and Birdzell, L. E., Jr. *How the West Grew Rich: The Economic Transformation of the Industrial World*. New York: Basic Books, 1986.

Rubinstein, W. D., ed. *Wealth and the Wealthy in the Modern World*. London: Croom Helm, 1980.

Schama, Simon. *Citizens: A Chronicle of the French Revolution*. New York: Knopf, 1989.

Schumpeter, Joseph A. *The Theory of Economic Development*. Leipzig: Duncker and Humblot, 1912. English ed. Cambridge, Mass.: Harvard Univ. Press, 1934.

Smith, Adam. *An Inquiry into the Nature and Causes of the Wealth of Nations*. 1776. Reprint. New York: Random House (Modern Library), 1937.

Stone, Lawrence. "The Bourgeois Revolution of Seventeenth-Century England Revisited." *Past and Present*, no. 109 (November 1985), pp. 44–54.

Summers, Lawrence, and Cutler, David. "Texaco and Pennzoil Both Lost Big." *New York Times* (February 14, 1988).

Thirsk, Joan. "The Restoration Land Settlement." *J. Modern Hist.* 26 (December 1954): 315–28.

Veblen, Thorstein. *The Theory of Business Enterprise.* New York: Scribner, 1904.

Veyne, Paul. "Vie de trimalcion." *Annales: Économies, Societés, Civilisations* 16 (March/April 1961): 213–47.

White, Lynn T., Jr. *Medieval Technology and Social Change.* Oxford: Clarendon, 1962.

Williamson, Jeffrey G. "Why Was British Growth So Slow during the Industrial Revolution?" *J. Econ. Hist.* 44 (September 1984): 687–712.

Best Papers in the Field of Public Policy

Introduction

by David Storey and Lois Stevenson

Policy-oriented research in the entrepreneurship/small-business area has a relatively short history. Small business emerged as a specific public-policy interest in the 1970s and 1980s with the realization that small firms not only enhance competition but also uniquely contribute to the employment and local economic development process. This offered intellectual justification for exploring a wider range of policy impacts on small firms and a rationale for policymakers to intervene in their support. Entrepreneurship as a specific public-policy interest emerged even more recently, since the late 1990s, with increasing knowledge about the importance of new firms to productivity, innovation, and economic growth. This created a void for understanding of the dimensions of entrepreneurship policy as a policy domain and justifications for government actions to stimulate the supply and quality of entrepreneurs and new firms. The five articles in this section, selected for the insights they impart, examine different facets of the role that public policy has played and should potentially play.

In "Entrepreneurship, Small and Medium Sized Enterprises and Public Policies," Storey reviews the contribution of public policies toward small and medium-sized enterprises (SMEs), making the case that public policy can influence SME development, both positively and negatively. The explicit focus of his discussion is on SME rather than entrepreneurship policies. He reviews the rationale for public policy in support

of SMEs (that is, why should governments intervene, how it intervenes, and how effective interventions are assessed), arguing that because of the absence of clear objectives and targets at the beginning of the policy formulation process, the conduct of policy evaluation is difficult. He outlines six progressively sophisticated steps to effective policy/program evaluation that will lead to more systematic approaches to measuring the effects of these policies, providing bureaucrats are more willing to subject their programs to careful scrutiny.

The article by Alistair Nolan of the Organisation for Economic Co-operation and Development (OECD), "Rationales for Public Policy," examines the economic bases and rationale for public policies that aim to encourage self-employment and entrepreneurship and the grounds for designing, implementing, or targeting entrepreneurship policies at the local level. The explicit focus of this review is on entrepreneurship policies. It (1) discusses market failure in connection with the supply of new and small firms, such as financial, business-advisory services; availability of workspaces and business development; and training services; (2) presents a detailed review of empirical and theoretical studies of purported market failures that support entrepreneurship policy measures; and (3) examines other arguments for supporting entrepreneurship (for example, social cost of unemployment). It states that interventions such as supplying information and advice to starters, encouraging awareness of entrepreneurship, and promoting collaborative behavior among firms are unlikely to produce policy failures. It concludes that although several arguments underlie policy rationale, policy effects based on these suffer from a lack of empirical studies of enterprise demographics and local economic development based on the positive externalities of entrepreneurship.

Stevenson and Lundström in "Entrepreneurship Policy for the Future: Best Practice Components" present the early findings from a more extensive, ongoing body of work to discover the dimensions of entrepreneurship policy. This 2001 article was the first to clarify the properties of entrepreneurship policy, the distinctions between small-business policy and entrepreneurship policy, the key components of a framework for entrepreneurship policy measures, and a typology of entrepreneurship policy approaches. It sets out the parameters for a clearer vision of entrepreneurship as a policy domain, where the policy objective is to motivate and stimulate the supply of entrepreneurs through an integrated, comprehensive set of enabling policies that address the awareness, education, skills, start-up assistance, and ease-of-business-entry needs of new entrepreneurs, including provision for tailored approaches to increase entrepreneurship among targeted groups of the population. The impact of this article has been to shed light on the emergence of entrepreneurship policy as an evolution of traditional small-business policy and to lead to an accelerated adoption of entrepreneurship policy frameworks by governments and more attention from the research community.

In "Research Mimicking Policy: Entrepreneurship/Small Business Policy Research in the United States," Dennis provides an excellent overview of entrepreneurship/small-business policy in the United States and its association with policy research and offers observations to enhance our understanding of the direction entrepreneurship/small-business policy research needs to take in the future. He concludes that (1) there is an inadequate body of entrepreneurship/small-business policy research to address most basic policy questions, insufficient funding for this policy research, and a lack of policy-oriented research data; (2) there are gaps in entrepreneurship/small-business research addressing all phases of the policy cycle, particularly at the initial stages; and (3) there is a lack of relevance of most academic research to actual policy issues, notably that produced in business schools. Most of this research reacts to existing policy, is not produced in a timely way to inform or influence policy-thinking on the impacts of a variety of issues on small business (for example, health care or minimum wage), and contributes little to an understanding of the externalities associated with entrepreneurship/small business, leaving policymakers to make decisions affecting small business without appropriate frames of reference. Dennis asserts that more research is required to establish the impacts of alternative policy models, including the development of more rigorous mathematical models to quantify and appraise the impact of small-business support programs. The impact of this article has been to call attention to the ongoing need to bridge the gap between academic research and policy development in the field.

Wren and Storey in "Evaluating the Effect of Soft Business Support upon Small Business Performance" elaborate on the "remarkably undeveloped" nature of the evaluation of small-firm policies and describe a sophisticated case study of how to systematically apply econometric models and robust techniques to the evaluation of "soft" versus "hard" public-policy measures (for example, advisory assistance and gateway services versus subsidized small-business loans and capital grants). The techniques they describe allow the quantification of the effects of a "soft" support measure. They identify issues that need to be considered in such evaluations and how these can be addressed by applying econometric techniques and taking explicit account of selection bias. Because of the greater difficulty in attributing changes in small-business performance to "soft" measures of policy intervention, this area of evaluation is often ignored by governments, even though substantial amounts of public investment are often involved in providing these services. This article contributes substantially to our knowledge base in the area of small-business program evaluation by sharing a methodology for evaluating the effects of initiatives to address market failures based on asymmetric information rather than lack of cash.

In conclusion, whereas Storey focuses on public-policy rationale for supporting SMEs, the OECD article focuses on public-policy rationale for encouraging entrepreneurship. Stevenson and Lundström examine what entrepreneurship policy is, its policy framework, and the types of policies comprising an entrepreneurship policy approach. Dennis points to the lack of policy-oriented entrepreneurship/small-business research being produced by academics, particularly in business schools, and the need to bridge the gap between the research community and the policymaking community to effect more informed policy at the beginning of the policy development cycle. All five articles reference the need for more consideration of the measured impacts of policies and policy measures on the performance of the SME sector and/or the emergence of entrepreneurs and new firms and the ultimate relationship to improvements in economic performance. Wren and Storey, specifically, provide an elaborate case study of how the application of rigorous econometric techniques can produce a quantifiable measure of the effects of "soft" policy measures on the incremental performance of small firms.

Entrepreneurship, Small and Medium Sized Enterprises and Public Policies*

by David J. Storey

Introduction

Governments throughout the world now recognise the important role in economic and social welfare played by smaller enterprises. In countries such as the United States and the United Kingdom there has been a striking change over the past forty years: In the 1960s small scale enterprise was equated with technological backwardness, managerial conservatism and modest economic contributions. This contrasts with the current view that, whilst many small firms do fit the 1960s stereotype, the sector also contains dynamic and innovative enterprises that collectively make a considerable contribution to economic well being (Acs, Carlsson and Karlsson, 1999). The magnitude and nature of this contribution continues to be a subject of discussion amongst scholars (Storey, 1994), but governmental awareness of the role of small enterprises has risen sharply.[1]

Governments can facilitate or impede this contribution and this paper reviews public policies towards SMEs in developed—OECD—countries. It seeks to review the contribution that such policies and programmes have made in those countries. A key focus is on methodologies for assessing the impact of policies.

Section 2 discusses the rationale for the existence of such policies. Section 3 then provides examples of a wide range of such policies. Here a distinction is made between policies that address directly the problems identified by small businesses themselves, and policies that are more closely aligned to the concerns of the public policy makers themselves. Section 4 provides a context for reaching a judgment on the effectiveness of the policies by addressing the issue of policy

Originally appeared in *Handbook of Entrepreneurship Research*, edited by Z.J. Acs and D.B. Audretsch, published by Kluwer Academic Publishers, 2003.

*This paper has benefited from comments received from many individuals. Fundes/IADB financed a version of this paper. Albert Berry, Emilio Zavalos and Maria Vega provided important insights. Presentations were also made to Rotterdam School of Management in the Netherlands, Department of Economics, University of Cork, Ireland. NUTEK in Stockholm and HM Treasury in London. I also valued the comments from Andrew Burke, Denny Dennis and Anders Lundstrom who read and commented upon the paper. However, my initial debt is to the OECD SME Best Practice Working Party and its secretary Marie-Florence Estimé. In my role as Expert to that Committee, I was confronted with these issues on many occasions and the paper clearly stems from that experience.

[1]For example European governments such as Sweden and the Netherlands have produced policy documents on this subject for the first time. Ministry of Economic Affairs (2000). Another illustration, this time from the US, is Audretsch's (2002) observation that policy to promote SMEs became politically bi-partisan in recognising that small businesses were the major source of new job creation in that country.

evaluation. Section 5 reaches some general conclusions on policy effectiveness in the developed economies. Section 6 then widens that discussion to cover not only the technicalities of the evaluation, but also the wider political and economic framework in which it takes place. Section 7 provides an overall conclusion.

However, before beginning any discussion of the rationale for SME policies it is necessary to clarify the definition of SME policies that will be used. Our focus is on public policies; by this we mean those which use taxpayers' funds to directly or indirectly target primarily or exclusively SMEs. Using this definition excludes the wide range of assistance services provided for SMEs by the private sector. Specifically we exclude services to SMEs provided by banks, accountants, lawyers and private sector consultants. The definition also excludes public policies that, although they strongly influence SMEs, do not have such firms as their prime focus. Examples of such policies are macroeconomic policies designed to achieve a benign trading environment of stable growth with low inflation. These are excluded from consideration on the grounds that such a framework seeks to benefit all sizes of firms and not primarily or exclusively SMEs. Other similar examples of excluded policies include banking regulatory policy, except where the specific focus is SMEs.

It is also necessary to emphasise that the prime focus of the review is on SME policies, rather than entrepreneurship policies. Lundstrom and Stevenson (2001) make this distinction. They view SME policies as focused upon existing enterprises, whereas entrepreneurship policies are directed towards individuals. These individuals are considering, are about to, or have recently started a new business. But, since they currently play only a modest role in the policy armoury of developed economies, it is SME policies that will receive the bulk of the coverage in this chapter.

Finally, it has to be emphasised that the review uses the term SME. The term itself is not common parlance in all countries. Most notably the United States continues to use the phrase "small business" rather than SME. Furthermore the precise definition of an SME small business also varies between countries. Until fairly recently the EU definition of an SME corresponded to the US definition of a small business—as one having less than 500 employees. However, in 1996 the EU changed its SME definition so that today an SME is (broadly) defined as having less than 250 workers. Within the SME category the EU also specifically defines Medium sized firms as having 50–249 employees, small firms as having 10–49 employees and Micro-firms as having less than 10 workers. The fact that a small firm in the EU is defined as having a maximum of 49 workers, whereas a small business in the United States has less than 500 employees clearly provides the basis for confusion and difficulties of cross country comparison. These problems are accentuated when further definitional differences from countries such as Japan and Australia are included.[2]

Table 1 makes the important contextual point that, even using identical definitions, the economic contribution of small firms varies widely across OECD countries. Using employment as the measure, it is clear that large firms are considerably more important in the North American countries of Canada and the US, than in the European countries of France and Sweden. This is by no means simply explained by differences in

---

[2]In Australia a small business in manufacturing is defined as having less than 100 employees, whereas in services the upper limit is 20 employees. In Japan an upper limit of 250 employees is used.

Table 1
Percentage Shares of Employees by Size of Enterprise: Whole Economy

	0–19	20–49	50–99	100–499	500+
Canada	20	10	8	16	45
France	31	13	——25——		30
Sweden	31	11	——25——		33
Switzerland	39	12	——25——		24
USA	20	——18——		15	48

Note: Canada data are 1–19 employees, i.e. do not include self-employed without employees.
Source: OECD (2000): table A2, p. 211.

income per head since rich Switzerland has the lowest proportion of employment in large firms. In short, developed economies are not characterised by uniformity in the size distribution of enterprises, but North America has a higher proportion of its employment in large firms than Europe.

Despite the differences in definition of SMEs, and their different economic contribution within the OECD countries, such enterprises exhibit some common characteristics:

- They are generally owned and managed by the same individual or group of individuals.
- They lack market power, having only a small share of markets—or more unusually a bigger share of a tiny or localised market.
- They are legally independent in the sense of not being owned by a larger group of firms.

In some respects such firms may be considered to be at a disadvantage, compared with large firms and it is the efforts by public policy to offset this "disadvantage" which is at the heart of SME policy in developed economies. It is to this issue that we now turn.

"Government intervention is justified only where the private and social costs and benefits (of new firm formation) diverge, or where the existing distribution of income significantly distorts the extent to which willingness to pay reflects an individual or groups demand for a good or service" (Storey, 1982, p. 205).

It is well established that, subject to certain key assumptions, goods and services are allocated efficiently through the price mechanism (Rowley and Peacock, 1974). The key assumptions are competition in the goods market, informed consumers, an absence of externalities and willingness to pay reflecting demand.

In the context of small firm public policy intervention the key assumptions most likely to be contravened are those of perfect information and the absence of externalities.

Three types of information imperfection can occur.

(a) Individuals do not realise (are ignorant of) the private benefits of starting a business.
(b) Small business owners do not realise the private benefits of obtaining

expert advice from "outside" specialists.

(c) Financial institutions are unable to assess accurately the viability of small firms and (on balance) overestimate the risks of lending to this group. Lack of access to finance, in comparison with larger firms, makes it difficult for small (new) firms to develop/start.

In addition, policy intervention can be justified where there is a divergence between private and social returns. Where social returns exceed private returns, positive externalities or spillovers exist. Here firms may not undertake projects which, whilst in the interests of society as a whole, yield the firm insufficient returns. The role of a public subsidy is to make it privately worthwhile for the firm to undertake the project, enabling society as a whole to benefit. In practice, as will be shown, it is difficult to ensure that public programmes succeed in ensuring that *only* those projects with positive externalities are implemented, and that public funds are not used to subsidies projects that would have been undertaken without the subsidy (Lerner, 1999; Wallsten, 2000).

So how does government respond to these information imperfections? This section discusses responses to each of the three information imperfections, and to the presence of externalities, in turn.

(a) Raising the Awareness of Individuals to the Private Benefits of Starting a Business

Governments, in many countries, have sought to raise the awareness of individuals—or groups of individuals—to the private benefits of starting a business. In some instances the focus has been on raising the overall rate of new business formation in an economy.

A prime example of this was the efforts of the Thatcher government which came to power in the UK in 1979 with a clear objective to create an "Enterprise Culture" (Burrows, 1991). The clear message of this administration was to seek to change social attitudes of the UK population. The objective was to shift the UK away from what it perceived to be a "dependency culture"—in which workers relied on large organisations and the state to provide them with employment. Instead the UK was to become a country in which people went out and created their own jobs by starting their own businesses. The dependency culture would be transformed into an "enterprise culture".

Whilst the Thatcher "enterprise culture" was aimed at almost all individuals in the UK, this is the exception rather than the rule. Instead, government initiatives seeking to make certain individuals or groups more enterprising/entrepreneurial are more typical. In Europe much of the focus has been on young people—the young unemployed in Southern Italy (Law 44), young graduates and young people more generally in the UK (STEP, PYBT and LIVEWIRE).[3] In the US, on the other hand, enterprise policy is currently focused upon minorities and females. Implicitly this assumes either the spirit of enterprise is insufficiently endemic within some US citizens and needs encouragement, or it assumes the presence of prejudice/discrimination against such groups.

---

[3]STEP is the Shell Technology Enterprise Programme. This is a work experience programme in a small firm undertaken by undergraduate students. PYBT is the Prince's Youth Business Trust (now Prince's Trust): it provides finance and advice to young people seeking to establish/develop small enterprises. LIVEWIRE is a signposting and advisory service for young entrepreneurs.

Countries with governments seeking to encourage "enterprise", whether in the population as a whole or amongst specific groups, assume there are barriers to the transition of some groups into self-employment/business ownership. One important barrier is lack of awareness. For example, young people may not even consider small business/self-employment as a source of employment for themselves. This is particularly true in "transition" economies, but may also be the case in countries where entrepreneurs have comparatively low social esteem—such as Sweden (Boter et al., 1999). Even in moderately entrepreneurial economies such as the UK, some groups—such as graduates—have traditionally viewed self-employment as inappropriate or insufficiently prestigious (well paid).[4]

One example of a UK-based programme designed to influence the attitudes of young people to self-employment and small business is the Shell Technology Enterprise Programme [STEP]. This seeks to enhance the awareness of college students of the benefits of working in a small business through short-term placements during their summer vacation. A second example of enterprise support to young people is Law 44 which provides a wide range of financial and advisory support to individuals aged 18 to 30 wishing to establish a new business in Southern Italy.

Policies to raise awareness constitute the response of government to what is perceived to be a market failure caused by information imperfections. The more tricky question is whether, from an ethical point of view, this differs from "brain washing/social engineering", since it is a deliberate and conscious act by the State to change the attitudes and aspirations of its people. It is surprising that this question seems to have received little consideration amongst those proposing such policies.

(b) Raising the Awareness of Small Business Owners to the Private Benefits of Obtaining Information from Outside Sources

In almost all developed economies the state provides some forms of subsidised information and advice for smaller businesses. For example, Personal Business Advisors in the UK, the ALMI services in Sweden or SCORE in the United States are all, to different degrees, part-funded by the taxpayer in order to provide advisory services to small firms at below market rates.

The prime market failure being rectified by these subsidised small firm advisory services is imperfect information. The subsidy implies small firm owners are unaware of the private benefits such advice can provide. They therefore tend to purchase a socially sub-optimal quantity of advice, meaning their business is either more likely to fail, or to perform less well than it would do if the subsidised advice were unavailable.

As an illustration, successive UK governments for thirty years[5] have been prepared to subsidise small firms "tasting" of

---

[4]Belfield (1999) finds undergraduate students are keenly aware that small firms pay less well than large and are less likely to provide training opportunities. Westhead (1997) in a survey of UK undergraduates, finds 90 percent view employment in a multinational as highly prestigious, whereas only 20% view self-employment employment in a small firm as prestigious.
[5]Following the recommendations of the Bolton Committee (1971), the UK government established the Small Firms Information Centres. It said, "We should like to see the signposting and information function vested in a single, easily identifiable organisation with a network of local offices in all the most important centres of industry and commerce". In making this recommendation the Committee clearly had in mind an important distinction. This is between

the benefits from advice provided by "external" advisors. This is because it is assumed that, once the firm has obtained the advice, the private benefits to the firm can be more accurately assessed. Given this more informed position, it is assumed that those businesses expecting to gain will be prepared to purchase, without the need for the subsidy.

The second market failure-based justification for subsidising small business advisory services is that the enhanced performance of such businesses yields social benefits (positive externalities). These are discussed in more detail in section (d), below, but, in the current context, externalities occur in the following way. Small businesses which use the advice may be less likely to fail, and/or likely to grow more rapidly. This yields social as well as private benefits—most notably those of additional job creation and the enhancement of the long-term competitiveness of the economy as a whole (Birch, 1979; Department of Trade and Industry, 1998).

In practice, it is often unclear whether it is the "information-imperfections" or the "externality" arguments that underlie the provision of publicly subsidised advice for small firms. It is however important to be clear on the rationale for policy since the two justifications have very different policy implications. Where the case is made for the long-term divergence between social and private benefits there is, in principle, a case for a continuing public subsidy and low charges to be paid by the small firm. But,

where the case is based on the assumption of ignorance of the small firm owner of the private benefits of external advice, the case can only be made for a once-off "taster" subsidy.[6]

It is frequently observed that small firm owners are notoriously reluctant to pay for advice from outsiders. Curran, Berney and Kuusisto (1999), in their discussion of the ability of the UK's Personal Business Advisors to charge fees for their advice, say:

"It is unlikely that substantial additional resources will come from fees since resistance amongst SME owners to paying fees is well-entrenched".

As illustrations of these theoretical issues, two very different approaches to the provision of publicly subsidised information and advice for small firms are now reviewed. The first, defined as the ALMI model, is predicated on the notion that there are positive externalities associated with subsidising small firms to acquire external advice. The second is the Enterprise Initiative (EI) model, which assumes market failure as one where small firms under-estimate the private benefits of external advice.

In presenting these models we reiterate that the different diagnoses of market failure lead to very different "solutions". However, we also show that these attempts to rectify market failure present politicians with important decisions on pricing and the introduction of an appropriate regulatory framework.

subsidising/enhancing the awareness of the availability of advice—which they viewed as acceptable—and subsidising the direct provision of the advice—which they did not. As they say, "Businessmen must be left to accept for good or ill, the consequences of their own judgement". p. 138.

[6]Bolton (1971) was very clear in this matter. It viewed government expenditure to overcome lack of awareness as acceptable. It did not accept the case for subsiding "missionary services designed to overcome prejudice or to persuade businessmen of the value of advisory services against their better judgement".

(i) The ALMI Model. Under the ALMI model, in Sweden, business advice is provided directly to small firms by a public sector organisation, with the cost being covered wholly or primarily by the taxpayer. Hence it implicitly assumes that there are social benefits to the economy as a whole, as well as private benefits to the small enterprise, from the provision of subsidised advisory services. To obtain these social benefits requires a continuing subsidy: otherwise small firms will purchase less information than is socially optimal.

Whilst conceptually simple, the ALMI approach makes it very difficult to assess the "free" market demand for small firm advisory services for the following reasons. First, because provision by a public organisation can lead to "crowding out" of private consultants by the public suppliers who are "cheaper" because they have the benefit of the subsidy. Second, because the public provider has, effectively a monopoly position, suppliers have a reduced incentive to generate satisfied clients in order either to stay in business or to develop their own consultancy business. In short, the public sector is less incentivised. Thirdly, the small business sector may be unwilling to buy services, designed to help them run their own businesses better, from public servants—after all, what do they know about running a business? Whilst this may be a rational or an irrational act, it causes the demand for small firms advisory services to be lower—in an ALMI model—than under full information.

(ii) The Enterprise Initiative (EI) Model. An alternative approach is not to have the advisory services delivered by a public organisation such as ALMI, but rather to subsidise the use of private sector advisors/consultants. The classic example was the UK Enterprise Initiative (EI) which operated between 1988 and 1994. Here the use of approved private sector consultants by small firms to provide information was subsidised from public funds. A maximum of 15 days' use of consultants was permitted per firm. It is therefore an example of a "taster" initiative, based on the view that small firms without the subsidy will purchase a privately sub-optimal quantity of external advice. In EI there is no case for a continuing subsidy—as with ALMI—since the only purpose is a once-off demonstration to the individual small firm of the private benefits of the external advice.

Some of the problems with the ALMI approach are overcome in the EI model because the advisory services are provided by private firms which compete with one another, and which, if they under-perform, will fail. Hence the small firm customer is likely to obtain a better service under EI than ALMI because, in the former case, the advisors/consultants are incentivised.

The EI model, however, also has its problems. First, there needs to be some additional state regulations to ensure that the advisors/consultants who undertake the work for small firms are both suitable and bona fide. Without such regulation of the external consultants, there is limited value in the Initiative since small firms would be purchasing advisory services with the same level of ignorance as in the "free" market. Hence the state checks the bona fides of the consultant, and may also operate a "matching" or "introduction/brokering" service to combine small firms with appropriate consultants/advisors. The problem is that this service is trying to second guess the marketplace and, when matters go wrong—as they inevitably do—the EI is held responsible. This requirement to second guess the marketplace stems from a recognition that markets are at their most effective when the consumer is experienced through repeat purchasing, and least effective when the consumer is purchasing for the first time. As the latter is the case here, the consumer is assumed to benefit from the guidance provided by regulating the consultants.

A second regulatory problem is that of setting the appropriate charging allocation policy, and here it is vital to be clear on objectives. Is the objective to ensure that the maximum possible numbers of firms obtain a "taste" of the benefits of utilising the services of a consultant? Is the object to ensure that those firms that participate in the Initiative demonstrate enhanced performance? Is the object to ensure that, once the subsidy is removed, that small firms are significantly more likely to use an external consultant than prior to participation in the Initiative?

A variety of charging/allocation options are available. The first is that no charge is made to the small firm for the use of the advisor/consultant. This, however, risks the Initiative having a politically unacceptably high budget; more likely is that resources are allocated on an arbitrary basis such as "first come, first served", or providing only a very limited amount of time per firm, neither of which are guaranteed to maximise welfare. Allocating on a "first come, first served" basis, for example, means that take-up will be more heavily concentrated amongst those firms that are most aware or well networked, yet these may not be those most likely to benefit from the provision of information. Indeed, sine they are, by definition, currently comparatively well informed, they may be deemed less likely to benefit than those who are currently poorly informed.

Allocating advisory services in very small quantities may ultimately be self-defeating. This is because the firms know they will not obtain enough advice either to make it worthwhile them applying, or for them to reach an informed judgement about whether the advice was of value. It also makes it difficult for the state to be able to judge whether the provision of the advice has influenced the performance of the firm.

An alternative approach is to restrict use of the Initiative to certain types of firms. These restrictions might eliminate firms in certain sectors, certain regions, or those beyond a specified size or age. Multiple or sequential use of the Initiative might also be prohibited. However, this type of non-price rationing risks being arbitrary and bureaucratic. For example, two firms which are identical in almost all respects may find one excluded from access to advisory services if it has slightly more employees than the other, or is located outside the location boundary or has a slightly different industrial classification. These factors are not necessarily good indicators of whether the firms (or the economy more widely) would benefit from the information services.

In principle, it is desirable for those using information/advice services to pay a charge since this, in part, avoids the problem of non-price rationing discussed above. The EI approach was to require some of the cost of the advisor/consultant to be paid for by the small firm with the remainder being covered by the state. The effective state subsidy rate may be varied so that certain types of small firms, which are thought likely to benefit most from use of the advice, would be more heavily subsidised. The advantage of a charging scheme is that it lowers the cost to the state of the Initiative, but it also "simulates" the market for small firm advisory services. By varying the subsidy the state can make some estimate of the demand for advice. The key disadvantage of charging for such services is that the firms which may benefit from them most may be the least able to pay—because of their precarious financial position.

Relating this then to the objectives of the Initiative, if the objective is to maximise the number of small firms that obtain a "taste" of the benefits of having an advisor/consultant, then it is not appropriate to change. To ensure the budget for the Initiative is politically acceptable a tight restriction would be placed on the amount of time the advisor/consultant provided. In this case, the "jam" would be spread very thinly across many firms. It is not to be expected that there would be any resulting observable change in their performance because the amount of "jam" received by an individual firm is so modest. The use of charges is therefore not compatible with this objective.

However, as noted earlier, a key objective could be to ensure the Initiative leads to an enhanced performance on the part of assisted firms. In this case, it may be appropriate to charge on the grounds that only those firms who themselves believe they will benefit from the Initiative will pay the charge, and that the firm's own judgement is the best indicator of potential benefit. The use of a charge means access to the Initiative is restricted, so that more "jam" is allocated per small firm. For this reason, it is more likely that an observable impact upon firm performance could both be present and be identified by the firm. Charging is therefore compatible with achieving this objective.

A third objective may be to ensure more extensive use of advisors/consultants once the subsidy is removed. Again, the use of charging is compatible with this objective on the grounds that those firms most likely to subsequently use the advisor/consultant will be those perceiving themselves as having benefited from the advice received. This, as argued above, is compatible with a charging strategy.

In summary, the market failure-based rationale for EI is that small firms underestimate the private benefits of obtaining external advice/consultancy. The role of EI was to provide a "once-off" public subsidy to enable the small firm to "taste" the benefits of external advice. Having tasted, the firm would then be an informed consumer, hence overcoming the market failure.

(c) Financial Institutions Are Unable to Assess Accurately the Viability of Small Firms

In a fully informed, efficient capital market, good projects are funded and bad projects are not, irrespective of the resources of the borrower.

What then happens where the financial institution knows some borrowers are more risky than are others, but has imperfect and asymmetric information? This realistically describes three key characteristics of the market for small firm loans. First, financial institutions know that, as a group, small firms are more risky than large. Second, the information available to financial institutions about small firms is less than that available about large firms. Third, the borrower is better informed about the risk of the project than the lender.[7]

If finance markets behaved in a manner similar to conventional markets, then high-risk borrowers would be prepared to pay a price premium over low-risk borrowers to obtain access to funds. For its part, financial institutions would be prepared to lend at this higher, market-clearing, rate.

Yet markets supplying finance to small firms do not behave in this manner. Allocation of funds does not take place through the price mechanism, but instead through rationing (Stiglitz and Weiss, 1981). Thus the high-risk project/

---

[7]In practice, particularly for start-up businesses, this assumption is not necessarily valid. It seems more plausible to argue that the bank, with many years of codified experience in lending (or not lending) to new firms is a better judge of the risk of a new venture than a prospective borrower with no prior business experience. Nevertheless, even in this case, information is asymmetric.

business is not able to obtain funds by offering to pay the price premium; instead the financial institution is more likely to be influenced by the borrower's access to collateral. Hence there may be good projects/businesses, which are prepared to pay a risk premium market rate, but which are denied access to funds because of their own lack of access to collateral. This is referred to as a "funding gap".

The practical significance of the "funding gap" is that if viable (small) businesses are unable to obtain access to funds, because of imperfect information, this leads to welfare losses to society. It therefore provides an, in principle, justification for government intervention.

There are, however, two reasons why evidence of the presence of collateral-based lending to small firms, of itself, may not justify state intervention. The first is that, as Bester (1985) argues, the pledging of collateral can be interpreted as signalling the viability of the project. Thus the low expected return project will have low pledged collateral, and so collateral is viewed as a satisfactory device for signalling the expected value of the project. The problem here is that collateral signals access to wealth, as well as project valuation. Collateral-based lending risks discriminating in favour of the rich and against the poor in a manner unrelated to project valuation. It therefore strengthens rather than reduces the case for intervention.

A second reason why a "gap" does not necessarily justify government intervention is that the inability to borrow from financial institutions may merely reflect a difference between the objective risk assessment of the bank and the consistently (over-) optimistic views of entrepreneurs. De Meza (2002) develops this reasoning in several papers (De Meza and Webb, 1987; De Meza and Southey, 1996). He argues that asymmetric information results in too many low-quality projects being funded. Social welfare would therefore be more enhanced by discouraging entry into entrepreneurship than by government intervention to eliminate "funding gaps".

Nevertheless, the presence of identified funding gaps has been used to justify government intervention in the provision of loans for small businesses. As will be shown later, a frequent form of that intervention is a Loan Guarantee Scheme, examples of which are found in France, Canada, USA, UK. Netherlands, as well as many less developed economies (Llisteri, 1997; Riding and Haines, 1999).

Loan Guarantee Schemes seek to overcome market imperfections in the provision of debt finance for small firms. They focus on ensuring that good projects are not precluded from access to finance through lack of access to collateral. Whilst the details of such schemes vary between countries, the basic principle is that if private banks judge a project to be viable, but only when collateralised, a loan may be made on the LGS. Interest on this loan will be charged at a premium rate but, in the event of default, government generally covers somewhere between 70% and 85% of the loss (KPMG, 1999).

The perception that information imperfections/asymmetry generates "funding gaps" is, of course, not restricted to loan capital. Similar issues apply in the market for private equity. Here the high fixed costs of due diligence can mean that modest sums of seed capital are not provided by financial institutions, or are provided on a socially sub-optimal scale. Public programmes to address these "gaps" exist in a number of countries. Mason and Harrison (2000) review these programmes and make important distinctions between different types of programme. The first is where public money is supplied to formal venture capital funds to encourage them to make investments that would not normally have been made on strict commercial criteria. The second is the provision of tax incentives to wealthy individuals to encourage them to become business angels. A third type of programme uses public money to subsidise the greater awareness of angels and businesses of one another.

(d) Un-Priced External Benefits May Be Present

Many governments have programmes to provide public subsidies to new and small firms in the science and technology sectors. Such programmes are justified on two grounds: The first is that financial institutions, because of information imperfections, are particularly poor at assessing risk in technology-based ventures.

The second ground is that of the presence of spillovers generated by new technology-based firms. The arguments are closely linked to the case for subsidies for Research and Development (Klette et al., 2000). It is that innovating firms, because they cannot fully exclude other firms from modifying or copying their innovation, will be less likely to innovate than is socially optimal. Society is therefore denied the benefits of this innovation, which could be considerable for firms developing new products or services. The role of the public subsidy is therefore to make the innovation more privately worthwhile for the firm, encouraging its introduction, and so enhancing welfare.

The best-known example of such a programme is the Small Business Innovation Research (SBIR) Program (Lerner, 1999; Wallsten, 2000). It began in 1982 and, by 1997, its annual budget exceeded $1 billion. Monies are allocated on the basis of open competition in two phases. In Phase I funds of up to $100,000 can be allocated to the successful firm to "determine the scientific and technical merit of an idea". Up to $750,000 is available to successful firms in Phase II to "develop the idea".[8]

How Does Government Intervene?

Section 2 discussed the rationale for government intervention in support of small and medium-sized enterprises. In order to anchor that rationale in reality, examples of interventions have been presented where appropriate. That approach, however, fails to provide a "big picture" of the considerable variety of approaches and specific initiatives implemented in developed countries. It also ignored the reality that government intervention on behalf of SMEs frequently has a powerful political momentum. This section aims to provide a "big picture" of the nature of intervention. The political discussion is covered in section 4.

A key theme of section 2 was the stark differences in the attitudes of governments in developed countries to the question of public intervention in support of small firms. At one extreme, and clearly different from virtually all other countries in the world,[9] is the United States, where Dennis (1999) can say: "*the United States has no small business or entrepreneurship policy.*"

According to Dennis, the United States, has a competition policy in which Entrepreneurship and small business play a key role, with government acting to ensure neutrality amongst competitors, irrespective of size. He points to the

---

[8]A similar programme operates in the UK. SMART Awards are made to firms undertaking development projects in innovative technologies. In exceptional cases, the amount awarded to a firm could be up to £450,000.

[9]Switzerland is probably the only country, to this author's knowledge, which comes close to the United States in this regard.

opening sentences of the Small Business Act 1953 and comments

> "Small business is not mentioned in its own policy outline until the eightieth word. Three references to competition precede it. Even security is a forerunner. Competition, and implicitly the consumer, is the overriding concern of the law, not entrepreneurial or small business per se."

Yet, even the admits that, whilst the concept is clear, in practice these economic principles become entwined with social objectives. It is also the case that the US has specific SME policies—such as SBDCs and SBIR. Nevertheless, the key philosophical standpoint of the United States is that the role of government is to hold, rather that enter, the ring.

Country members of the European Union, however, broadly take a different view.[10] Here both national governments, and the European Union itself, view small firms as key sources of job creation and competitiveness. They also view themselves as playing a role in promoting economic development by having specific policies to support small firms. They therefore, implicitly or explicitly, view the positive externalities associated with support for SMEs—most notably job creation—as their justification for intervention.

EU countries have therefore introduced an almost bewildering range of policies to assist smaller enterprises. It is certainly not appropriate here to seek to itemise these policy interventions. For this, the interested reader should consult ENSR (1997) for a review of EU policies or OECD (1996, 1997, 1998) for countries outside the EU.

Table 2 provides a structure for examining such interventions without assuming, of course, that they necessarily constitute "best practice". The Table distinguishes between those interventions that respond to the problems articulated by small firms, and the interventions that reflect more closely the agenda of government. The former is shown in the top half of the table and the latter in the lower half. A distinction is also made between generic problems identified on the left-hand side and specific policy interventions on the right.

Table 3 develops this by taking the main areas in table 2 and identifying specific programmes that seek to overcome the problems identified. Table 3 seeks to be illustrative rather than comprehensive, so only some of the topics identified in Table 2 are covered in Table 3. Table 3 is structured similarly to Table 2, with policies relating to the SME Agenda in the top half of the table and those more closely linked to the agenda of government in the lower half of the table.

In selecting the items for inclusion in Table 3 efforts have been made to provide a wide geographical coverage of countries of different sizes and economic philosophies. Even so, there is better coverage of policies in English-speaking countries simply because this material was more accessible to this author.

Despite these biases the table provides a description of programmes that seek to address items of concern to SMEs and to government. It also reaches a broad judgement of the extent to which the programme has been successful, where this judgement about based on factors such as whether, following an

---

[10]Within the EU there is a wide spectrum of opinion with the US position being, on balance, comparatively favoured by the UK and least favoured by France and the Scandinavian countries. Canada may also be taken as an example of a country with some interventionist policies to support SMEs.

Table 2
Policy Areas and Illustrations

SME's agenda	Policies
1. Finance	Loan Guarantee Schemes (USA, Canada & UK)
	Sabatani Act (Italy)
2. Markets/Demand	Europartinairt (EU)
	Trade Fairs (Greece)
	Public Procurement (USA)
3. Admin Burdens	Enterprise & De-Regulation Unit (UK)
	Business Entry Point (Australia)
	Business Administration Courses (Portugal)
4. Premises	Science Parks (Italy, Germany)
	Managed Work Space
	Incubators (Finland)
5. New Tech	Business Innovation Centres (EU)
	SBIR (USA)
6. Skilled Labour	Small Firms Training Loan (UK)
Government's agenda	
1. Entrepreneurial Skills	Advice (ALML Sweden)
	SBDCs (USA)
	Training (Japan)
2. Entrepreneurial Awareness	LiveWIRE (UK)
	Atlantic Canada (Canada)
3. Competitiveness	SBIR (USA)
4. Special Groups	Young People (Law 44—Italy)
	Micro loans to Women (Sweden)
	American Indians (USA)
5. Regional Spatial Issues	Business Birth Rate (Scotland)

evaluation, the programmes life/scale was extended. However, as will be shown in sections 4 and 5 of this chapter, some evaluations are more rigorous than are others. For this reason, judgements on programme success are not based on a set of consistent criteria or appraisal methods.

The budgets of these programmes are often considerable. Despite its protestations, the US government expenditure on small firm programmes is, in absolute terms massive, with the SBIR programme alone having an annual budget of more than 1 billion US$. Details of such budgets are provided later in section 5.

Assessing the Effectiveness of Intervention: Clarification of Objectives

The above section demonstrated that governments intervene in a wide variety of ways in order to assist SMEs. The

Table 3

Illustrations of Public Programmes to Assist SMEs and Enhance Entrepreneurship

Problem	Programme	Description	Country	Evaluation	Success
SME's AGENDA					
1. Access to Loan Finance	Loan Guarantee Scheme	SMEs without access to own collateral obtain access to bank loans by state acting as guarantor	UK, USA, Canada, France, Netherlands	OECD (1997) KPMG (1999) Riding and Haines (2001)	Yes, generally viewed as helpful, but small scale impact on the overall financing of SMEs in most countries
2. Access to Equity Capital	Enterprise Investment Scheme	Tax breaks for wealthy individuals to become business angels	UK	Not of current scheme	Unknown
3. Access to Markets	Europartenariat	Organisation of Trade Fairs to encourage cross-border trade between SMEs	EU	The Sweden Europartenariat was assessed by NUTEK (1998)	General satisfaction amongst firms that participated
4. Administrative Burdens	Units established within government to seek to minimise administrative burdens on smaller firms	Sunsetting Legislation, Deregulation Units	Netherlands, Portugal, UK	No formal evaluations	The view of small firms themselves is that bureaucratic burdens have increased markedly in recent years
5. Science Parks	Property based developments adjacent to universities	Seek to promote clusters of new technology based firms	UK, France, Italy and Sweden	DTI (1994)	Conflicting findings on impact of SPs on performance of firms
6. Managed Workspace	Property provision to assist new and very small firms	Often called business incubators, these provide premises for new and small firms on "easy-terms"	World-wide	United Nations (2000)	General recognition that such initiatives are of value

Table 3
Continued

Problem	Programme	Description	Country	Evaluation	Success
7. Stimulating Innovation and R&D in small firms	Small Business Innovation Research Program	$1 billion per year is allocated via a competition to small firms to stimulate additional R&D activity	USA	Lerner (1999) Wallsten (2000)	Lerner implies SBIR enhances small firm performance, but Wallsten is unable to show it leads to additional R&D
8. Stimulating Training in small firms	Japan Small Business Corporation (JSBC)	JSBC and local governments provide training for owners and managers of small firms. The training programme began in 1963	Japan	None	Unknown
GOVERNMENT'S AGENDA					
1. Entrepreneurial Skills	Small Business Development Corporations (SBDCs)	Counselling is provided by SBDC mentors to small business clients who may be starting a business or be already trading	USA	Chrisman and McMullan (1996)	This study finds SBDC clients have higher rates of survival and growth than might be expected. Reservations over these findings are found in this text
2. Entrepreneurial Awareness	Entrepreneurship Education	To develop an awareness of enterprise and/or an entrepreneurial spirit in society by incorporating enterprise into the school and college curriculum	Australia, Netherlands, but leading area was Atlantic Canada	Lundstrom and Stevenson (2001)	Conventional assessments are particularly difficult here because of the long "lead times"
3. Special Groups	Law 44	Provides finance and mentoring advice to young people in Southern Italy, where enterprise creation rates were very low	Southern Italy	Del Monte and Scalera (2001) OECD (1997) Maggioni et al. (1999)	This is an expensive programme, but most studies show the survival rates of assisted firms to be well above those of "spontaneous" firms

central question of interest to taxpayers and policy-makers is whether such intervention is effective.

It is not possible to even begin to make such an assessment unless the objectives of the policy are clearly specified. This means they have to be formulated in a manner that is, in principle, capable of measurement. Unfortunately, this is rarely the case.

Instead, objectives are specified in very general terms, such as "creating a more enterprising society", or "making this country the most enterprise-friendly country in the world in which to do business". Only if there were tangible measure that underpin these objectives—such as international league tables providing an agreed set of criteria to measure the "enterprise-friendly" nature of a country—would such objectives be "clearly specified". To our knowledge, no such league tables exist.

A second problem is that, even where SME policies are clearly specified, they frequently have multiple objectives, some of which may even compete with one another. Finally, in many cases, the objectives have to be inferred from politicians' statements, rather than being specified in official documents.

Table 4 illustrates some of the above issues. It shows SME policies may have several, and possible conflicting, objectives.

The table makes an important distinction between "intermediate" and "final" objectives. The purpose of the distinction is that policy-makers frequently infer the two are identical, whereas in practice they differ sharply. Row 1 of Table 4 illustrates the point. SME policy in developed economies is normally emphasised most strongly during periods of recession and high unemployment, because small firms are believed to be important sources of

Table 4
Objectives of Small Firm Policy

Intermediate	Final
1. Increase employment	Increase employment Reduce unemployment
2. Increase number of start-ups	Increase number of start-ups Increased stock of firms
3. Promote use of consultants	Promote use of consultants Faster growth of firms
4. Increase competition	Increase competition Increase wealth
5. Promote "efficient" markets	Promote "efficient" markets Increase wealth
6. Promote technology diffusion	Promote technology diffusion Increase wealth
7. Increase wealth	Votes

Source: Storey (1994).

job creation. Clearly, in times of high unemployment, job creation is more highly valued by politicians than in conditions of full employment. In this sense, the link is made that if smaller enterprises generate jobs this will lead to the desirable "final" objective of reducing unemployment.

In practice, this link between job creation and unemployment is, in fact, quite complex. For example, even if small enterprises do generate additional jobs, these are more likely to be low paid, and part-time than such jobs created by larger firms. Small firm owners may also seek different types of workers in terms of skills and motivation from larger firms (Cowling and Storey, 1998). For all these reasons, individuals who are unemployed may not fill the jobs generated by small firms. Instead, small employers may favour individuals from outside the labour force, but who only work part-time. They may also favour individuals who travel into the area/country from outside. So, if for example, the "final" objective of policy is to lower unemployment for young males, then this may not be best achieved by stimulating small enterprises which may employ females or formerly retired workers. It is therefore critical that evaluators are clear whether it is the "intermediate" or the "final" objective that is the ultimate aim of policy.

The remainder of Table 4 provides other examples of possible confusion between "intermediate" and "final" objectives of enterprise policy. Row 2 illustrates that there can be a lack of clarity about whether the objective is to increase the number of start ups or whether it is to increase the total number of firms in the economy. If it is the latter, this, in principle, could be achieved by seeking to lower the death rate of firms. However, the policies to achieve this would be radically different from those designed to raise the birth rate of firms. Similar levels of confusion are apparent from the other "intermediate" and "final" objectives. The interested reader can review these at length in Storey (1994).

The final row of the table emphasises that public policies towards small enterprises have a clear political dimension. They are formulated by politicians who need to take account, not only of the interests of small enterprise owners and their workers but also the wider political agenda, in their efforts to become elected and re-elected. It is therefore naïve to believe that politicians will voluntarily favour the specification of a single target upon which they will be judged, even if that single target could be agreed.

So what may reasonably be expected? The first reasonable expectation is that a broad framework for SME policy could be specified, reflecting political priorities. Such a framework could include commitments to facilitating the access to resources of those wishing to start businesses; to minimising the disadvantages of small scale in dealing with government; to eliminating evidence of discrimination against groups in society, etc.

Within this broad context it is then appropriate to introduce legislation which reflects these broad principles. The critical issue is that the legislation has to have clearly specified objectives or targets which are capable of measurement. It should not be the task of the evaluators to have to infer the objectives of the legislation. That is the responsibility of the legislators.

It is also necessary to set aside funds to enable an assessment of the impact of the legislation to be conducted. Where, for example, substantial public funds are committed there should be a budget of perhaps 0.5% set-aside for evaluation. The legislation should also specify the methodology for the conduct of the assessment. We return to these issues at the end of the following section.

Assessing the Effectiveness of Intervention: The Six Steps

This section will identify, as examples, several major policy interventions, in a number of different countries, which have been the subject of recent scrutiny by academic researches. Many have already been described in section 2 when the rationale for intervention was outlined.

These examples are intended to reflect a diversity of philosophies and approaches to small firm support. Hence they are drawn from the United States, Canada and from the European Union. The interventions seek to address market failures in policy areas such as "start-ups", "finance", "information" and in "research and development".

Our use only of those evaluations conducted by academics is for two reasons; firstly, as Curran et al. (1999) note, these tend to be more critical than those undertaken either by the sponsoring organisation itself or by private sector consultants.[11] The second reason is that, because of the refereeing process, the academic research is expected to ensure all relevant information is in the public domain.

The choice of these programmes is determined exclusively by the availability of academic evaluations, conducted very recently, and which are published in reputable academic journals. As we note in the next section, we cannot necessarily assume that the impact of these programmes is necessarily typical of the small business support programmes either in these countries or elsewhere. Indeed we make a case that,

if anything, these are likely to be amongst the more effective programmes on the grounds that the bureaucrats have allowed (external) evaluations to take place and for the findings to enter the public domain.

Table 5 identifies the programmes, the evaluations of which will be reviewed. It shows that, as well as covering several countries, they are directed towards very different sub-sets of the population of SMEs. For example, as noted in section 3, the SBIR programme is concerned with high-tech small firms, whereas Law 44 is concerned with encouraging the start up of new firms by young people. Some programmes, such as SBLA or SBIR provide finance only, whereas GI and Law 44 provide finance and advice. In contrast, SBDC and EI only subsidise access to expert advice. Taken as a group, however, the evaluations cover many of the generic forms of small business support provided by governments as shown in Tables 2 and 3.

Table 5 also shows that expenditure on such programmes can be substantial. Clearly it is difficult to compare, for example, small firm programme expenditures in a small country such as Ireland with those in the vastly larger United States. Nevertheless, the expenditure on a programme such as SBIR is clearly substantial in absolute terms. It was noted earlier that Wallsten (2000) reports the SBIR total budget in 1998 exceeded 1 billion USDs. The budget is also substantial on a per-enterprise basis, with awards of up to 100,000 USD for Phase I winners and up to 750,000 USD for Phase II winners under the SBIR programme.

SME Enterprise support programmes are also substantial in other countries. For example, Wren and Storey (2002)

---

[11]Curran et al. say, in their review of research on UK Business Links (BLs), "As in evaluations of other SME policies, independent evaluations of BLs by academic researchers have been less favourable than those sponsored by central government or BLs themselves", p. 65.

Table 5
Six Examples of Programme Evaluation

Country	Programme	Functions of Programme	Approximate Annual Expenditure	Currently Operating?	Source of Evaluation
1. United States	Small Business Innovation Research (SBIR)	Grants to High Technology businesses for Research and Development	1.1 billion $US in 1997	YES	Lerner (1999) Wallsten (2000)
2. United States	Small Business Development Centres (SBDCs)	Training and Counselling services	1.39 million $US	YES	Chrisman and McMullan (1996)
3. United Kingdom	Enterprise Initiative Marketing (EI)	Subsidised use of External Marketing Consultants	45 million GBP per annum	NO: ended in 1994	Wren and Storey (2002)
4. Northern Ireland Republic of Ireland	Grant Assistance in Ireland (GI)	Marketing, Training and Investment Grants	20 million GBP in NI approx. similar in Republic	YES	Roper and Hewitt-Dundas (2001)
5. Canada	Small Business Loan Act (SBLA)	Guaranteeing Loans to Small Business	42.5 million SC	YES	Riding et al. (1999)
6. Italy	Law 44	Subsidising new businesses established by young people in S. Italy	Not known	YES	Maggioni et al. (1999) Del Monte and Scalera (2001)

report the scale of budgets associated with several of the programmes in Table 5. For example, the ALMI service in Sweden absorbed 7–8% of that country's net industrial costs: the Law 44 programme in Italy has cost in excess of 300 million ECUs. Finally, the latest estimate of "soft" support to SMEs from the UK government is 650 million GBPs.

Given the substantial sums of public money devoted to SMEs it is surprising that Lerner (1999) can say, with some justification:

> "Despite economists' interest in interactions between governments and firms, the public subsidisation of small firms has attracted virtually no scrutiny."

To review evaluations of these programmes, which clearly exhibit considerable diversity, requires some common framework. This is provided in the current author's earlier work on this topic (Storey, 1999). That paper identified six generic types of evaluation of small business policies in developed countries, shown as Table 6.

The generic types of evaluation are referred to as "Steps" with the least sophisticated being Step 1, and the most sophisticated as Step 6. In this review, since we are only concerned with "best practice", we will only concern ourselves with examples of Steps 4, 5 and 6 evaluations.

Two keys to successful evaluations are:

(i) To ensure that the firms which respond in the evaluation are representative of all "treatment" clients, given that inevitably only a sample of clients will be included. This problem is overcome partly by absolute sample size and partly by statistical testing for sampling bias.
(ii) To accurately estimate what would have happened to the "treatment" firms if they had not been treated.

It is the latter that distinguishes the Evaluations referred to as Steps 4, 5, and 6 from those in Steps 1, 2 and 3. The former group explicitly tries to attribute performance change in the SME to the provision of the assistance. The latter merely seek to ensure the policy-maker can track the public funds were spent in an appropriate manner and, at best, obtain feedback on whether the recipient felt the contribution was helpful.

Table 6
The Six Steps: Monitoring and Evaluation

Monitoring	
Step I	Take up of Scheme
Step II	Recipients' Opinions
Step III	Recipients' views of the differences made by the Assistance
Evaluation	
Step IV	Comparison of the Performance of "Assisted" with "Typical" Firms
Step V	Comparison with "Match" Firms
Step VI	Taking account of selection bias

(i) Step 4 Evaluations

Two examples of Step 4 evaluations are presented in this section. The first is the evaluation of the economic impact of Small Business Development Centres (SBDCs) in the United States. The second is the appraisal of the Canadian Small Firms Loan Act (SFLA).

Chrisman and colleagues have undertaken assessments of the impact of SBDCs (Chrisman and Katrishen, 1994; Chrisman and McMullan, 1996) using a methodology first developed in Chrisman et al. (1985). SBDCs provide free, comprehensive, counselling, training and technical assistance services to small businesses. Training is viewed as a "group" activity, in the sense of being provided to classes of either potential or new business owners. Counselling, on the other hand, is the provision of "one-to-one" advice by specialists. SBDCs are generally a partnership between the Small Business Administration (SBA), local and state government, the private sector and educational institutions. Public money for SBDCs, coming from the Small Business Administration, is currently about 150 million USDs annually.

The Chrisman studies only examine counselling services, and so are not concerned with the training role of SBDCs. They take a (representative) sample of SBDC counselling[12] clients—the "treatment" firms. For established firms Chrisman et al. examine changes in sales and employment in "treatment" firms in 1990—before they received the coun-selling—with their sales and employment in 1991 after "treatment". For those firms who reported that they felt they had benefited from the Counselling [80%], a comparison is made with the "weighted average growth rates for US businesses on each measure". The assumption is that the difference between the performance of the "treatment" group and the weighted average is a good measure of the impact of the counselling.

However, this assumption is open to question for two reasons. First, because the "treatment" firms may differ from the "weighted average" firms in observable respects which influence performance. For example, the two groups of firms may differ in terms of age, size, sector or geography. Failure to account for these "observables" risks rendering invalid the assumption that, in the absence of treatment, these "treatment" firms would have performed in a manner similar to the "weighted average".

It is therefore necessary to take observable firm characteristic differences into account, where there is evidence that these may influence performance.[13] This is undertaken in the Step 5 analyses in which "treatment" firms are compared with another group of firms from which they do not differ in terms of key observables. The latter are often referred to as "match" firms on the grounds that they are selected to match with the "treatment" firms in terms of observables such as size, sector, geography and age.

---

[12]Note that Training clients are not included. In 1977 there were 15 times as many training as counselling clients in SBDCs. By the mid-1980s this ratio had fallen to $3:1$ and by the late 1990s it had fallen further to $1.5:1$.

[13]As an illustration, assume the counselling clients were primarily high-tech firms that, as a group, exhibit faster growth than were firms in more conventional sectors. Hence comparing SBDC clients with a weighted average of firms would be expected to yield differences in performance, but not necessarily because of the advice received, but because of the markets served by the clients. Similar arguments apply to factors such as size and age, where (surviving) younger and smaller firms would be expected to grow faster than larger and older small firms.

The second doubt is that, even if there were no significant differences between the "match" and the "treatment" firms in terms of observable characteristics, the two groups could differ in terms of "unobservables". The Step 6 evaluations seek to control for these.

Even bigger challenges are posed by attempts to estimate the contribution of Loan Guarantee Schemes such as the Canadian Small Business Loan Act (SBLA). The challenges are bigger because, as Riding and Haines point out, a key function of the Act is to facilitate the establishment of enterprises that would not otherwise have started in business. This type of calculation is probably best undertaken using time-series data in the format analysed by Barlow and Robson (1999) rather than by seeking responses from loan recipients because of the difficulties of interpreting replies.[14]

But, setting aside the question of new firms, Riding and Haines (1999) use two indicators of the additionality provided by the SBLA to established firms. First, they compare the age profile of SBLA firms with the lending profile of the Commercial banks. They find 14% of the portfolio of the SFLS is to firms that are less than one year old, compared with 5% for the banks. They infer that, without the SFLA, 9% of firms would have been un-funded.

A second group of established businesses benefiting from the SFLA are those who believe they would not have been funded without the Act. Riding and

Haines then compare the jobs created in the SBLA firms in 1995 with the national population. They then attribute the difference between the two to the SBLA.

This raises the same issues as the Chrisman et al. evaluations, by comparing the "treatment" group with the national population. It is that the "treatment" firms may differ from the national population in terms of both "observables" and "unobservables". Step 5 evaluations, to be discussed in the next sub-section, are examples of where explicit account is taken of "observables".

(ii) Step 5 Evaluation

An example of a Step 5 evaluation is that by Lerner (1999) of the Small Business Innovation Research Program (SBIR) in the United States. This programme allocated 1.1 billion USDs (in 1997) to small businesses seeking to undertake Research and Development. Phase I awards are now up to 100,000 USDs. At a later stage firms may re-apply for Phase II awards of up to 750,000 USDs.

In his evaluation Lerner hypothesises that "subsidy recipients should perform at least slightly better than their peers". He then takes a sample of firms in receipt of SBIR Phase I awards and identifies two matching samples. The first set of matches do not differ from the awardees ("treatment" firms) in terms of industry and firm size at the time of the award. The second matching sample is matched on geographic location and firm size.

---

[14]The difficulty of using loan respondents is that only firms which are in business, and which received a loan, can be asked about whether they would have been in business without the loan. Even for those attempting to answer as truthfully as possible, this is a difficult question since there are so many factors involved. We also suspect that many respondents do not answer truthfully. Some will underestimate the impact of the loan on the grounds that it is their foresight and determination that lead to the establishment of the business, rather than government funding. Conversely, some respondents may overestimate the impact—some may simply wish to please the interviewer. Others may think it is in their future interests to have such facilities available, even if they were not influential in starting their business. Clearly the researcher has little idea about the impact of these conflicting motivations.

This careful process ensures that, taking account of the "observables" of firm size, sector and geography the two groups of firms do not differ. Lerner then compares the changes in sales and employment over time of the two groups and finds the SBIR ("treatment") firms significantly out-perform the matches. He also finds that mean differences between the groups are not a reflection of the presence of extreme values (outliers).

A second example of a Step 5 evaluation is that by Maggioni et al. of the Italian Law 44. This Law provides government funding of up to 90% for capital investment in businesses started by young people under the age of 35 in the South of Italy, 30% of the government funding is in the form of low interest loans and the remainder is grant. In addition, young entrepreneurs are mandated to use the services of "mentors" for advice; no charge is made to the business for this. Finally, 30%–40% of the operating costs of the business during its first two years is also subsidised.

Maggioni et al. (1999) examines the effectiveness of the Law. The two year survival rate of these new firms is almost 80%, which is impressive for any economy, but particularly for businesses established by young people.[15] To test this, Maggioni et al. take a sample of 45 Law 44 firms in the Naples area and match these with 45 new firms from the local Chamber of Commerce. Matching takes place on the grounds that the two samples do not differ in terms of geography (all in Naples area), age (all new starts) and sector.

Maggioni et al. find the "treatment" firms are more "resistant to exit"[16] despite their debt levels being higher. However, they find no evidence of significantly faster sales or employment growth in the "treatment" group.

Whilst Step 5 evaluations, such as those by Lerner, and by Maggioni et al.,[17] take explicit account of "observables", we noted above that they do not seek to take account of "unobservables". In the case of small firms' policy initiatives, the key unobservable is that of selection.

There are two types of selection: Self-selection and Committee selection. Self-selection takes place when firms can choose whether or not to participate in a programme. If the programme is aimed at, for example, enterprises seeking to grow, then it is likely that the firms who apply to participate will be, on balance, more growth-orientated than those that do not apply. This is particularly the case where not all applicants are likely to be successful. The more growth-oriented applicants are therefore "self selecting" into the programme. This has potentially serious implications when comparing "treatments" with matches. It is that, even if the "treatments" actually received no funding/assistance, they would have been expected to perform better (grow faster) than the matches because they were more growth-oriented. Hence, when the performance of the two groups is compared over time, it is not clear

---

[15]As illustrations. Cressy and Storey (1996) find that about 60% of new firms survived for a two-year period. For UK firms registered for VAT the survival rate after 2 years is 70%. In Germany, Bruderl et al. (1992) find a two-year survival rate of 75%. Cressy and Storey find that businesses established by young people, under the age of 25, have a survival rate, over four years, of 30%, whereas those started by individuals between the ages of 55–65 have a 70% survival rate.

[16]This is the term used by Maggioni et al. to capture barriers to exit as assessed by the business owners.

[17]Other examples of Step 5 evaluations include those conducted in Atlantic Canada such as those of Thomas and Landry (2001).

whether any observed differences are attributable to initial differences in growth orientation (self-selection) or to the impact of the programme.

What independent evidence is there for self-selection into public programmes? KPMG (1999) in their examination of the UK Loan Guarantee Scheme (SFLGS) say:

"86% of firms in our Survey reported that they were growth orientated. This suggests that the SFLGS appealed to firms who were more growth orientated than the general SME population" (p. 4).

What is more difficult to demonstrate is whether they were more growth-oriented than a group of SMEs matched with SFLGS applicants on "observables" such as sector, size and geography. In the case of either SBIR or Law 44, is there any intuitive reason for suspecting the presence of self-selection, after taking account of matching?

It might be argued that all government programmes, especially those focusing on encouraging growth, are likely to attract better-networked (informed) and more motivated firms. Bennett and Robson (1999) provide some partial evidence for this. They show that for UK Business Links, which focused their advisory services on small businesses seeking to grow, that receiving a site visit and having a written brief/contract was correlated with historic employment growth. After taking account of "matching", however, it is more difficult to make a strong intuitive case for self-selection. It therefore becomes an empirical question as to whether self-selection is actually present within programmes.

A more powerful intuitive case can be made for the presence of Committee selection. This applies when not all applicants to a Programme/Scheme are successful. This is clearly the case in the SBIR Program, where typically about 10 Phase I applications are made for every award made, and only half of those progress to a Phase II award. Although it is not discussed by Maggioni et al., there is also Committee Selection present in Law 44, since under one quarter of all applicants are successful.[18]

As Lerner discusses, Committee Selection could also be subject to political influence but, in principle, the merits of the proposal in terms of the policy objectives should be the prime consideration. Hence, for SBIR, selection should be based on the technical merits of the proposal, whereas for Law 44 selection should be on the basis of the commercial strength of the business plan.

If the Committee is a good selector—that is, it can identify the good from the less good project—then comparing the performance of awardees with the matches will mean the awardees will always perform better—irrespective of whether they received the award or not. Observed differences in the performance of the awardees and the matches may therefore reflect the skill of the Committee in its selection. It does not necessarily reflect the impact of the programme.

To summarise, when the awardees are compared with the matches, in the presence of Committee Selection, it is not clear to what extent differences in performance reflect the benefits of the programme or the extent to which it reflects the ability of the Committee to select.

In principle, it is expected that there will be a positive impact of Committee selection—otherwise allocation could be

---

[18]OECD (1997) p. 101 reports that 4500 business plans were evaluated and 1000 were approved. In practice this may deflate the approval rate since decisions on the some of the applicants were still pending.

random and the Committee would serve no useful function. It is plausible, however, to argue that Committees could exercise a "negative" or political influence in the manner implied by Lerner. He suggests that, whilst there is no concept of "geographical equity" in the SBIR provisions, it is noteworthy that all states have received at least one award in recent years. He implies this may reflect early SBIR awards, which were heavily concentrated amongst states with many high tech firms. In this sense the Committee impact could be negative because the "best" firms do not necessarily obtain the awards, which are given to less good firms in more favoured geographical areas.

Overall, Step 5 evaluations risk suffering from both self-selection and Committee-selection bias. The expected overall effect of this is to over-estimate the impact of programmes by underestimating how the "treatment" group would have performed in the absence of the treatment. This occurs because the controls/matches are an imperfect proxy for the treatment group because of both sample selection and committee-selection.

(iii) Step 6 Evaluations

Step 6 evaluations seek to overcome these limitations. Several address the issue of self-selection, but none, to this author's knowledge, fully address Committee selection.

Analytically we can consider that our task as evaluators is to assess the impact of policy (I). However, observed impact may be considered to comprise both Selection (S) and Actual impact (A). Selection (S) comprises both Self-Selection (SS) and Committee-Selection (CS). Stage 5 evaluations measure 1 rather than A whereas Stage 6 evaluations seek to quantify S in both its forms (SS and CS).

This section provides four examples of Step 6 evaluations. The first are more

advanced analyses of both the SBIR and Law 44 programmes discussed in the above section. The third is an assessment of the UK Enterprise Initiative (EI) (Wren and Storey, 2002). Finally, we examine grants to small businesses in Northern Ireland and the Republic of Ireland (GI) (Roper and Hewitt-Dundas, 2001; Wallsten, 2000) in his evaluation of SBIR is concerned with somewhat different issues from Lerner. Wallsten examines whether SBIR leads to additional private sector R&D expenditure, but is concerned that prior work may have encountered the problem of endogeneity. In this case, although there is clearly a correlation between firms receiving awards and R&D, this may be because firms doing more R&D win more awards. This, in principle, is therefore a selection issue. Wallsten's findings are that firms with more employees and more patents win more awards, but the grants themselves do not appear to affect employment. Taking more robust account of selection therefore questions the real impact of this $1 billion programme.

Del Monte and Scalera (2001) have also recently reviewed the impact of Law 44. They argue that it is not appropriate to examine the success of a "start up" programme by comparing the survival rates of "assisted" and "natural" firms and expecting the former to exceed the latter. This is because the objective of the programme is to encourage individuals, who otherwise would not have done so, to start a firm. This emphasises the importance of clarity in specifying the objectives of policy (Storey, 1999). The key, and surprising, empirical finding from Del Monte and Scalera (2001) is that it is the larger Law 44 firms that are the least likely to survive. This suggests policy-makers need to encourage firms, in their own interest, to reduce the scale of their grant application.

We now turn to examine two examples of Step 6 evaluations. Section 2 of this chapter described the UK Enterprise Initiative (EI) in which small firms were able to obtain subsidised access to advice from vetted external consultants. The subsidy was available for up to 15 days assistance at a rate of 50%. Wren and Storey (2002) examine the element of the Enterprise Initiative devoted to Marketing.[19] The programme operated between 1988 and 1994 incurring a total public subsidy of 275 million GBP.

The GI programmes reviewed by Roper and Hewitt-Dundas are currently in operation in both Northern Ireland and the Republic of Ireland. These grants are for both fixed capital and for "soft" services such as marketing or export assistance or workforce training.

Wren and Storey (2002) specifically address (self-) selection by estimating impact through a two-stage procedure originally outlined by Heckman (1979). It is able to achieve this since records are available both of all enquirers—in the geographical area studied—and all those who decided to proceed and obtain the subsidised advice. The key policy result is that participation in EI does enhance the probability of survival and growth of a sub-group of middle-sized small firms. However, the key methodological result is that a failure to take explicit account of (self-) selection bias leads to this impact being over-estimated by a factor of more than three in the longer run.[20]

Roper and Hewitt-Dundas (2001) review the impact of grants in Northern Ireland and the Republic of Ireland. They recognise the potential impact on the evaluation of Committee-Selection, if the objective of policy-makers is to target assistance towards small firms most likely to grow—the so-called "picking winners" policy. They find the selection and impact indicators to be non-significant for Republic of Ireland firms. Three conclusions are compatible with this finding: First, that a "picking winners" policy does not exist; second that, whilst it is the objective of policy, it is not being implemented. Finally, whilst such a policy might have existed, it did not influence performance. For Northern Ireland, the significant selection term implies assistance is directed towards slower growing firms, by inducing faster employment (but not sales) growth after "treatment".

To conclude therefore, there is a very strong case for Step 6 evaluations that take account of both self- and committee selection. The empirical case is that, where they have been undertaken, self-selection is generally present and failure to account for it leads to over-estimation of programme impact. Perhaps even more disconcerting is that there are no studies which explicitly take account of committee selection, yet it is this type of selection which, for certain programmes, is most likely to influence perceived outcomes. Expressed baldly, failure to take account of committee selection is likely to significantly overestimate the impact of some programmes.

Learning the Lessons

We have seen above that Lerner is certainly correct that substantial sums of public money are devoted, throughout the world, to policies designed to assist small firms. It may be the case that, within the US, sophisticated policy eval-

---

[19]Other elements were product and service quality, manufacturing and service systems, design, business planning financial and management information systems. Marketing, however, was the most popular of the Initiatives, accounting for almost one quarter of the 114,000 projects.

[20]Taking no account of self-selection EI appeared to raise the survival rate of firms by up to 16% over an eight-year period. However, this fell to 5% when self-selection was incorporated.

uation has been rare, but this is at least partly because of that country's avowed philosophy of having "no policy" in this area. This is much less true for other parts of the world. In countries such as Canada, Sweden and the UK more evaluations are taking place, and the evaluations themselves are better, in the sense of being more sophisticated. In short, the science exists.

Given the ease and applicability of the science, two troubling issues remain. The first is why, even within the same country, some items of policy are more likely to be evaluated. The second is why best practice methods are not always implemented.

The greater frequency of evaluations of some small enterprise policy instruments/areas than others is apparent in the UK and a plausible case may be made that evaluations are only undertaken, and made public of "successful" programmes. For example, its Loan Guarantee Scheme has been externally evaluated on four occasions since its inception in 1981 (Robson Rhodes, 1984; NERA, 1990; PEIDA, 1992; KPMG, 1999). Broadly, on all occasions it has been given "a clean bill of health". Perhaps not surprisingly, Kuusisto et al. (1999) in their Delphi study of "experts" report "the most commonly cited successful intervention" in the UK policy arena to be the Loan Guarantee Scheme.

The converse is the case for the Business Expansion Scheme (BES) and its successor the Enterprise Investment Scheme (EIS). Both of these Schemes provided tax breaks for individuals or groups of individuals purchasing equity in small enterprises. In their Delphi review, Kuusisto et al. report the view of "experts" that the least successful intervention in the SME policy area was BES. This was introduced in 1983, abolished in 1993, reintroduced as the Enterprise Investment Scheme in 1994 and continues today. Despite this "chequered history", it has only been evaluated once—by KPMG—shortly before its abolition in 1993. No external evaluation of EIS has been undertaken.

This variation in frequency of evaluation is shown in Table 7. It shows that some items of policy have never been evaluated,[21,22] whereas others, such as the LGS are periodically assessed. The items that appear never to be assessed in some cases appear to be ones where the small business community appears most exercised.[23,24]

---

[21]This is not to imply there have been no studies of the impact of bureaucratic burdens on SMEs. Rather, to the author's knowledge, there have been no studies of the effectiveness of these policies on SMEs. For example, an Enterprise and Deregulation Task Force existed for many years yet no external evaluation was conducted of its impact upon SMEs.

[22]It is also not to imply that there have been no "external" evaluations/assessments. For example, the Enterprise Investment Scheme has recently been "evaluated" by BDO Stoy Hayward (1999) but only to make recommendations as to improving take-up, not to evaluate whether the Scheme should exist, or what its benefits are.

[23]This appears similar to the point made by Hoy (1997). He, however, compared the topics within small business and entrepreneurship upon which academics published articles in leading journals with the stated agenda of small business owners at the White House Conference. He found that overlap of "interest" to be modes, but markedly more than a decade earlier.

[24]Surveys of small business owners in the UK, such as those by SBRT and FSB, generally indicate that "the state of demand" is their key concern. After that, depending on the state of the macro-economy, the issues of access to labour, access to finance and recently the growth of bureaucratic burdens are high on the list.

Table 7
SME Policy Items in the UK

1. Reduction of Bureaucratic Burdens	No external evaluation
2. Tax Incentives	No external evaluation
3. Legislative Exemptions	No external evaluation
4. Late Payment Legislation	No external evaluation
5. Loan Guarantee Scheme	4 external evaluations
6. Enterprise Investment Business Expansion Scheme	1 external evaluation

Five key public policy issues therefore arise and each will be dealt with in turn:

(i) Which items of policy are evaluated?
(ii) What factors influence whether evaluations are conducted internally or externally?
(iii) Who should conduct external evaluation?
(iv) How can evaluation be undertaken to the highest possible standards?
(v) What should happen as a result of the evaluation?

(i) Which Items of Policy Are Evaluated?

UK experience suggests SME policy evaluation is more likely to take place where the policy will obtain a "clean bill of health" than where the outcome is less certain. This is particularly true for policies where the objectives are "fuzzy", examples of which are policies to minimise bureaucratic burdens or late payment legislation.

The simple answer to the question is that ALL items of policy, once they have been in place for a short period of time—say, three years—should automatically be subject to some form of evaluation.

(ii) What Factors Influence Whether Evaluations Are Conducted Internally or Externally?

Those evaluations undertaken by external organisations are—on balance—more likely to enter the public domain than those conducted "in-house". Almost by definition, it is difficult to know whether those items of polity above have been the subject of "internal" evaluation. Nevertheless, we do know that governments have a much greater opportunity to ensure the evaluation is favourable (if that is what is required) when it is undertaken "in-house". It was precisely this which the House of Commons Trade and Industry Select Committee (1999) accused the UK government of in its "massaging" of the findings from the internal evaluation of the SMART[25] programme.

The above experience suggests that *all* items of policy should be evaluated externally, so there is no opportunity for selecting internal evaluation where there is a greater likelihood that the results will

---

[25]Small Firms Merit Award Scheme for Research and Technology. This is modelled on the United States SBIR Program and was introduced in 1986. No official external evaluation has been funded. The Select Committee said: "We have no grounds for serious criticism of the SMART programme; far from it. . . . We do however have grounds for complaint at the apparently scant regard the department pays to its evaluation of its own schemes and the use of evidently selective and unattributed evidence to inform Parliament through the Annual Department Report of the proven outcome of schemes."

not enter the public domain if they are unpalatable.

(iii) Who Should Conduct External Evaluations?

The central conceptual issue here is that of "regulatory capture", initially articulated by Stigler (1971). The key values of the external assessment are that the results are more likely to enter the public domain where the analysis is prepared by an independent organisation, likely to take a dispassionate and objective view. It is appropriate here to repeat the point made by Kuusisto et al. (1999) that, on balance, official external evaluations have been more favourable than those evaluations that were undertaken independently.

The problem of regulatory capture is that even an "independent" or external organization that undertakes considerable work for government risks being "captured." Such organisations may be influenced to be "reasonable" by the risk of losing the goodwill of an important client, with the clear implication of not obtaining future work. This is most likely to influence the behaviour of private commercial organisations—and particularly small ones that are seeking to develop a reputation in the market. It is less likely for academic organisations to be less driven by the need for "repeat" business. Nevertheless, even this distinction between private consultancies and academic organisations is becoming increasingly blurred, so some risk of "capture" is present, irrespective of the type of organisation undertaking the evaluation.

"Capture" takes two forms. The first is that the bureaucrat whose programme is being evaluated, and whose Department is financing the evaluation, exercises a strong influence upon those organisations invited to tender, and ultimately upon the chosen evaluator. In this situation there is a powerful incentive to employ a "tame" evaluator. The second form of "capture" is to seek to influence the outcome of the evaluation during its progress.

There is, however, a key dilemma in this area. It is that evaluators build up expertise by working in a particular subject area, so that working on several evaluations, for example of SME policy, is likely to enhance the skills of the evaluator. This advantage has to be set against the increasing risk of "capture".

There is no simple solution to this problem. The introduction of "quotas" for consultants would clearly be both unwieldy and lose the benefit of learning on the part of the evaluator. However if evaluation were to be "built in" to policy, as will be recommended in the next two sections, then responsibility for the letting of external contracts should move to a specialist part of government, unrelated to the Department responsible for that programme. Ideally, that should be in the Finance or Audit departments that would obtain the funding from central earmarked sources.

(iv) How Can Evaluation Be Undertaken to the Highest Possible Standards?

Given the findings of the paper the following constitute characteristics of good practice:

- Objectives have to be clearly specified in the legislation and "converted" into targets that make it clear when the legislation is deemed to be a success and when it is deemed to have failed.
- A budget for evaluation is set aside in the legislation to conduct the evaluation, together with a statement on the methodology to be used to conduct the evaluation. This has to be prepared by the Ministry of Finance (see below) who would be consulted on the extent to which the "targets" in the legislation were amenable to evaluation. It may be necessary to begin the monitoring for estimating the

impact of the legislation prior to the legislation being implemented.

- All items of policy, once they have been in place for about three years, should automatically be subject to evaluation.
- All policy items should be evaluated externally approximately every six years.
- All external evaluations are to be managed by an independent Audit Office, reporting to the Ministry of Finance, but conducted by non-governmental organisations.[26]
- The (anonymised) data collected in the evaluations to be made available to bona fide researchers.
- The methodology for the evaluations will vary but it is to be expected that it will be conducted over a significant period of time— say, five years and begin, ideally, before the legislation is implemented. It would be expected to combine both leading edge quantitative (statistical) as well as qualitative approaches.
- Copies of all evaluations would automatically be published and be distributed to politicians of all parties and the media.

(v) What Should Happen as the Result of Evaluation?

The key theme of the above recommendations is that evaluation is *not* "the end of the line". Instead it has to become better integrated into the process of policy making, rather than being grudgingly conducted to find out, many years after the policy was implemented, whether or not it worked. Using evaluation as an "end of the line" tool risks it being seen as a threat to all those engaged in the policy process—those designing legislation and those implementing programmes.

The task of those promoting evaluation is to move from evaluation being seen as a threat, to engaging the support of all personnel implementing programmes. Their support is crucial since successful evaluation requires good data being collected by staff implementing programmes. The problem is that such staff—perhaps understandably—regard their prime responsibility as delivering a service to their clients rather than "filling in forms". Given they are not predisposed to help, if they view the data collected as being used to undermine the programme, it makes them much more reluctant to collaborate.

The key point therefore is that evaluation should not be "the end of the line", but part of the process by which programmes and policies are modified and improved in the light of experience. Achieving this requires changes in the behaviour of several groups. The first are the legislators. They need to be made aware that new legislation on programmes will be assessed, and that the specification of clear objectives and targets is central to that assessment. Programmes need clear criteria for assessing whether they are judged successful or unsuccessful and it is the responsibility of the legislators to ensure that clarity is present. The legislators also have a responsibility for ensuring there is an appropriate budget and an agreed approach to conducting the evaluation.

Once enshrined in legislation, this sends a powerful signal to those managing and implementing programmes that evaluation is taken seriously. It emphasizes that collecting information on customers/clients it not "clerical box-ticking", but rather a vital ingredient to ensure programme improvement.

However, it is after the evaluation is completed that the real change is needed. Too frequently the evaluation is

---

[26]In the United States the General Accounting Office (GAO) is probably the nearest example.

either "parked" or is the subject of acrimonious debate between the evaluators and the sponsoring/managing organisation. Neither outcome is desirable, yet frequently occur when the sponsoring/managing organisation feels it has had the evaluation imposed upon it. This emphasises the need, yet again, for the evaluation to be part of the programme when is begins and not viewed as an add-on.

Where evaluations are successful, in the sense of changing policy, is where the objectives of programmes become revised in the light of the evaluation evidence. For example, programmes may have several objectives/targets and the evaluation may show that some targets are clearly met, whereas others are not. The evaluation provides the unique opportunity for a dialogue about objectives and targets between the sponsoring and the managing departments. Failure to meet some targets may, in the light of experience, be viewed as of little importance, whereas the achievement of others may imply that it has been set too low.

In short, the evaluation provides the basis for a dialogue between the sponsoring and management organisation, which is intended to lead to the setting of more appropriate targets for the future. Far from being the "end of the line", the evaluation provides the basis for setting future objectives and targets for policy. In other cases, of course, because of changed circumstances or because programmes are poorly managed, their closure could be recommended, but this happens relatively infrequently.

Conclusions

This paper has reviewed that rationale for public policy in support of SMEs in developed countries. It begins with the assumption that public policy is justified by evidence of market failure and that the test of success is whether the intervention is beneficial to the economy.

The two most frequently cited reflections of market failure are information imperfections and the presence of externalities or spillovers. Programmes for subsidised training, education, information provision and finance are justified on the grounds that small, and particularly new or nascent firms, are poorly informed consumers of advisory services. This leads to such services being under-used, leading to the subsequent under-performance of the ventures. The case for public subsidy is further strengthened by the existence of positive externalities—such as enhanced job creation and competitiveness—associated with enhanced performance. This chapter, however, has pointed out that justifying public programmes on the grounds of information imperfections infers subsidies should only be "once-off", so as to encourage learning. In contrast, justifying public programmes on the grounds of spillovers implies a more continuing public commitment.

Within developed countries there is a wide range of philosophical approaches in public policy towards small business and Entrepreneurship. At one end of the spectrum is the United States, which views small business policy as almost synonymous with competition and the interests of the consumer—although, in practice, having major programmes such as SBIR in place. There is a clear contrast with EU countries, historically motivated by a desire for job creation, which seem to have an almost bewildering range of small firm support programmes.

This chapter has reviewed these programmes and concludes that there is a striking absence of clear objectives and targets in the legislation. This makes the conduct of evaluation extremely difficult. Despite these problems, the chapter reviews SME programmes in four countries—USA, UK/Ireland, Canada and Italy—and the techniques used by academic researchers to estimate impact. All the evaluations are examples of good practice, but the level of sophistication does vary sharply. The central task for the researcher is to adequately compare the performance of the firms that participate in public programmes with a relevant group of firms that do not participate, so being legitimately able to attribute the difference in the performance of the two groups to programme participation. Whilst identification of the participants [the treatment group] is not always easy, in most instances this is handled satisfactorily by researchers. Unfortunately, the non-treatment group, in most studies, is frequently inadequately derived. Too few studies take account of the selection bias endemic in such groups, so placing a major question mark over such research. In terms of the classification provided in this chapter, only evaluations that reach Step VI should be viewed as reliable. This is the challenge for researchers and journal editors!

The audience for this study is not only the research community, but also those formulating and implementing public programmes for SMEs. The chapter concludes by making eight recommendations for this audience. These range from the clear specification of Targets and Objectives to the procedures to be used for evaluating policy. It emphasises that evaluation is not "the end of the line" in the policy-making process. Instead evaluation needs to be built-in to policy making when legislation is being formulated and it needs to engage all those involved in delivering public policies to small enterprises. Once conducted, evaluations are the ideal vehicle for re-assessing the objectives and targets of small firm policies in the light of evidence, making them more strongly focused on the market failure they are designed to overcome. There is the suggestion that public programmes to assist SMEs are subject to "regulatory capture" in the sense that they focus more heavily upon the interests of politicians and

bureaucrats, than upon the small firms they are intended to assist. The task of those responsible for such programmes is to be transparent in formulating objectives and in facilitating studies that accurately assess whether such objectives have been met.

Overall the key message is that, throughout developed economies, there are a wide range of publicly funded programmes to assist small firms. Whilst the espoused philosophy underpinning these programmes varies, the presence of presumed market failure is a common theme. This review concludes that a combination of a reluctance of bureaucrats to submit their programmes to careful scrutiny, and the application of much weak science where this has taken place, means this continues to be a very fruitful area for research. It is this author's hope that this opportunity will be exploited in the coming years.

References

Acs, Z. and D. Andretsch (1988). Innovation in large and small firms. *American Economic Review*, **78**, 678–690.

Acs, Z., B. Carlsson and C. Karlsson (1999). *Entrepreneurship, Small and Medium Enterprises and the Macroeconomy*. Cambridge University Press, London.

Audrestch, D.B. (2002). The dynamic role of small firms: Evidence from the US. *Small Business Economics*, **18**, 13–40.

Barlow, D. and M.T. Robson (1999). Have unincorporated businesses in the UK been constrained in their ability to obtain bank lending? Paper presented at "Funding Gaps Controversies" Conference. University of Warwick, UK, 12–13 April.

BDO Stoy Hayward (1999). *The Enterprise Investment Scheme: Why Investors and Companies do not use the Scheme*. Confederation of British Industry, London.

Belfield, C.R. (1999). The behaviour of graduates in the SME labour market:

Evidence and perception. *Small Business Economics*, **12**(3), 249–259.

Bennett, R. and P. Robson (1999). Intensity of interaction in supply of business advice and client impact: A comparison of consultancy, business associations and government support initiatives for SMEs, ESRC Centre for Business Research. WP.142, University of Cambridge.

Bester, H. (1985). Screening versus rationing in credit markets with imperfect information. *American Economic Review*, **75**, 850–855.

Birch, D.L. (1979). *The Job Generation Process*. MIT Program on Neighborhood and Regional Change.

Bolton, J.E. (1971). *Small Firms: Report of the Committee of Inquiry on Small Firms*. Cmnd 4811. London: HMSO.

Boter, H., D. Hjalmarsson and A. Lundstrom (1999). *Outline of a Contemporary Small Business Policy*. Swedish Foundation for Small Business Research, FSF, Stockholm.

Bruderl, J., P. Preisendorfer and R. Ziegler (1992). Survival chances of newly founded business organizations. *American Sociological Review*, **57**, April, 227–242.

Burrows, R. (ed.) (1991). *Deciphering the Enterprise Culture*. London: Routledge.

Chrisman, J.J. (1995). The small business development center program in the USA: A statistical analysis of its impact on economic development. *Entrepreneurship and Regional Development*, 7, 143–155.

Chrisman, J.J. and E. Katrishen (1994). The economic impact of small business development center counseling activities in the United States: 1990–91. *Journal of Business Venturing*, **9**, 271—280.

Chrisman, J.J. and W.E. McMullan (1996). Static economic theory, empirical evidence and the evaluation of small business assistance programme: A reply to Wood. *Journal of Small Business Management*, **34**(2), 56–66.

Chrisman, J.J., R.R. Nelson, F. Hoy and R.B. Robinson Jr. (1985). The impact of SBDC consulting activities. *Journal of Small Business Management*, **23**(3), 1–11.

Cowling, M. and D.J. Storey (1998). *Job Quality in SMEs*. European Foundation for the Improvement of Living and Working Conditions. Dublin.

Cressy, R. and D.J. Storey (1996). *New Firms and their Banks*. National Westminster Bank, London.

Curran, J., R. Berney and J. Kuusisto (1999). *A Critical Evaluation of Industry SME Support Policies in the United Kingdom and the Republic of Ireland—Introduction to SME Support Policies and their Evaluation*. Ministry of Trade and Industry, Finland, Studies and Reports 5/1999.

Dc Meza, D. (1999). SME Policy in Europe. In D.L. Sexton and H. Landstrom (eds.), *Handbook of Emrepreneurship*. Oxford, UK: Blackwells, pp. 87–106.

Dc Meza, D. (2002). Overlending?. *Economic Journal*, **112**(477), F17–F31.

Dc Meza, D. and C. Southey (1996). The borrowers curse: Optimism, finance and entrepreneurship. *Economic Journal*, **106**, 375–386.

Dc Meza, D. and D.C. Webb (1987). Too much investment: A problem of asymmetric information. *Quarterly Journal of Economics*, **102**, 281–292.

Del Monte, A. and D. Scalera (2001). The life-duration of small firms born within a start-up programme: Evidence from Italy. *Regional Studies*, **35**(1), 11–21.

Dennis, W. (1999). Research mimicking policy: Entrepreneurship small business policy in the United States. In D.L. Sexton and H. Landstrom (eds.), *Handbook of Entrepreneurship*. Oxford, UK: Blakcwells, pp. 64–82.

Department of Trade and Industry (1994). *Science Parks and the Growth* of High Technology Firms. London: HMSO.

Department of Trade and Industry (1998). *Our Competitive Future: Building the Knowledge Driven Economy.* London: HMSO.

ENSR (1997). *The European Observatory for SMEs.* Fifth Annual Report. EJM, Zoctermeer, Netherlands.

Heckman, J.J. (1979). Sample selection bias as a specification error. *Econometrica,* **47**, 153–161.

House of Commons Trade and Industry Committee (1998). *Small and Medium Sized Enterprises.* 6th Report. London: HMSO.

House of Commons Trade and Industry Committee (1999). *Small Business and Enterprises.* 13th Report, London: HMSO.

Hoy, F. (1997). Relevance in entrepreneurship research. In D.L. Sexton and R.W. Smilor (eds.), *Entrepreneurship 2000.* Chicago: Upstart Publishing Company, pp. 361–376.

Klette, T.J., J. Moen and Z. Grilliches (2000). Do subsidies to commercial R&D reduce market failure? Microeconometric evaluation studies. *Research Policy,* **29**(4–5), 471–495.

KPMG (1999). *An Evaluation of the Small Firms Loan Guarantee Scheme.* London: Department of Trade and Industry.

Kuusisto, J., R. Berney and R. Blackburn (1999). *A Critical Evaluation of SME Support Policies in the United Kingdom and the Republic of Ireland—an In Depth Delphi Study of Selected SME Support Policies and their Evaluation.* Ministry of Trade and Industry. Finland, Studies and Reports 6/1999.

Lerner, J. (1999). The government as venture capitalist: The long-run impact of the SBIR program. *Journal of Business,* **72**(3), 285–318.

Llisteri, J.J. (1997). Credit guarantee schemes: Preliminary conclusions. *Financier,* **4**, 95–112.

Lundstrom, A. and L. Stevenson (2001). *Entrepreneurship Policy for the Future.* Stockholm: Elanders Gotab.

Maggioni, V., M. Sorrentino and M. Williams (1999). Mixed consequences of government aid in the new venture process: Evidence from Italy. *Journal of Management and Governance.*

Mason, C.M. and R.T. Harrison (2000). Venture capital: Rationale, aims and scope. *Venture Capital,* **1**(1), 1–47.

Ministry of Economic Affaires (2000). *The Entrepreneurial Society: More Opportunities and Fewer Obstacles for Entrepreneurship.* The Hague, Holland.

National Economic Research Associates (1990). *An Evaluation of the Loan Guarantee Scheme.* Department of Employment, Research Paper No. 74.

National Federation of Independent Businesses (2001). *Small Business Policy Guide.* Washington DC.

NUTEK (1998). *Europartinariat Northern Scandinaria 1996: Effects and Experience.* Swedish National Board for Industrial and Technical Development, Stockholm.

OECD (1996). *Best Practice Policies for Small and Medium Sized Enterprises.* Paris.

OECD (1997). *Best Practice Policies for Small and Medium Sized Enterprises.* Paris.

OECD (1998). *Best Practice Policies for Small and Medium Sized Enterprises.* Paris.

OECD (2000). *OECD Small and Medium Emerprise Outlook.* Paris.

PEÍDA (1992). *Evaluation of the Loan Guarantee Scheme.* London: Department of Employment.

Riding, A.L. and G. Haines Jr. (2001). Loan guarantees: Costs of default and benefits to small firms. *Journal of Business Venturing,* **16**(6), November, 595–612.

Robson, R. (1984). *A Study of Small Businesses Financed under the Loan*

Guarantee Scheme. London: Department of Trade and Industry.

Roper, S. and N. Hewitt-Dundas (2001). Grant assistance and small firm development in Northern Ireland and the Republic of Ireland. *Scottish Journal of Political Economy*, **48**(1), February, 99–117.

Rowley, C. and A. Peacock (1974). *Welfare Economics: A Liberal Restatement*. Oxford, UK: Martin Robertson.

Stigler, G.J. (1971). The economic theory of regulation. *Bell Journal of Economics*, **2**, 3–21.

Stiglitz, J.E. and A. Weiss (1981). Credit rationing in markets with imperfect information. *American Economic Review*, **73**, 393–409.

Storey, D.J. (1994). *Understanding the Small Business Sector*. London: Routledge, ITP.

Storey, D.J. (1999). Six steps to heaven: Evaluating the impact of public policies to support small businesses in developed economies. In D.L. Sexton and H. Landstrom (eds.). *Handbook of Entrepreneurship*. Oxford, UK: Blackwells, pp. 176–194.

Thomas, T. and B. Landry (2001). Evaluating Policy Outcomes in Federal Economic Development Programs in Atlantic Canada, ACOA, New Brunswick.

United Nations (2000). *Best Practice in Business Incubation*. Geneva: UN/ECE.

Wallsten, S.J. (2000). The effects of government-industry R&D programs on private R&D: The case of the Small Business Innovation Program. *RAND Journal of Economics*, **31**(1), Spring, 82–100.

Westhead, P. (1997). *Students in Small Business: An Assessment of the 1994 STEP Student Placement Scheme*. Small Business Research Trust, Milton Keynes, UK.

Wren, C. and D.J. Storey (2002). Evaluating the effect of "soft" business support upon small firm performance. *Oxford Economic Papers*, **54**, 334–365.

Entrepreneurship Policy for the Future: Best Practice Components
by Lois Stevenson* and Anders Lundström*

Background and Introduction

Policy think-tanks, economic development organizations and governments all over the world are emphasizing the importance of becoming more "entrepreneurial economies". We see this in documents and discussions of the OECD (OECD, 1995; 1998), the European Union (European Commission, 1998), APEC, UNIDO, the InterAmerican Development Bank, and others, and we hear it in (government) Ministers' speeches. This interest is being driven by the obvious shift in the industrial structure of economies—from large firm to small firm dominance, from a capital base to a knowledge base, and from relatively stable, controlled industrial environments to highly dynamic and constantly changing ones. Globalization, liberalization, democratization, technological developments and the Internet are all contributors to this shift. Acs and Audretsch (2001), as one example, address the factors which give rise to the emergence of the entrepreneurial society. However, these changes do mean an increased role for entrepreneurship. There is more opportunity to pursue innovations, the cost of starting a business has dropped considerably, small firms have more capacity to compete in niches of the marketplace, and more

people are choosing to follow their "own dream" rather than to stay in paid employment.

There is a growing body of research, which, number one, links higher levels of entrepreneurial activity, measured in terms of turbulence rates, to economic growth, and number two, which demonstrate the contribution of NEW firm entry, not only to job creation, but to innovation, total factor productivity growth, and economic renewal. Audretsch and Thurik (2001) have found that, in OECD countries, a shift towards "smallness" and higher levels of self-employment, over the long term, results in growth acceleration and reduced unemployment in an economy. The work of the GEM research suggests that as much as 30 percent of the differences in GDP growth rates may be attributed to differences in levels of entrepreneurial activity (Reynolds et al., 2001).

The practical reality is that, on an annual basis, we are seeing a considerable level of turbulence in the stock of firms—existing firms fading away and new firms entering the market, and of employment churning—jobs being created and lost by the entry, exit, expansion and downsizing of firms. This has important implications for governments. To replace the lost businesses and jobs every year *and* to maintain growth rates

Originally appeared as the Keynote Presentation at the 46th World Conference of the International Council for Small Business, Taipei, Republic of China, June 18, 2001.
*Swedish Foundation for Small Business Research (FSF).

in the economy, they need a constant supply of new entrepreneurs. The question is what policies and measures are needed to create and support the emergence of these new entrepreneurs? This dilemma shifts the emphasis away from firms and firm performance to individuals and their entrepreneurial propensities and skills, in other words, to issues of motivation, capacity and choice.

So, we see that Entrepreneurship policy is emerging as an important area of economic policy development, although, at this point, it is a not a very well-defined policy area. Many countries are now exploring what they need to do to create a more dynamic and competitive "entrepreneurial economy", but their work is often impeded by the lack of definition of entrepreneurship as a concept, the lack of clarity between SME *and* Entrepreneurship policy, and the lack of knowledge about precisely how to respond to the emergence of an "entrepreneurial society". Presently, what we see is "fuzziness", ambiguity, a lot of experimentation with policy measures and institutional structures, an eagerness to learn from the experiences of other countries and governments . . . and a *lot of "talk"* (which is why the title of our forthcoming book in the Entrepreneurship Policy for the Future Series starts with *Beyond the Rhetoric*). In other words, there is a basic lack of "know-what" and "know-how" and of course, a small amount of inertia.

This sets the stage for the remainder of this paper in which we share some of the results from our year-long study of what governments in ten economies are doing to shift from SME policy to Entrepreneurship policy and some of the lessons learned from their collective experience. We provide a comprehensive and systematic description of how this new policy base can be created. This includes our definition of entrepreneurship policy, its key components and a presentation of the policy typologies and good practices which emerged.

Of the ten economies selected for the study, one can see a lot of diversity, a deliberate criteria in our selections. Six were EU countries and four were APEC economies. They ranged in size from 4 million to 275 million in population. GDP per capita ranged from US$13,000 to US$33,000. They exhibited different levels of GDP growth, population growth and immigration growth over the past four years. Some have high levels of entrepreneurial activity and some have low levels. They have varying shares of SME employment in the economy, ranging from 53 percent in the United States to 80 percent in Taiwan. They represent a diversity of political and ideological orientations. Some have longer histories with SME policy than others.

We wanted to explore what this diverse set of economies was doing to actively promote entrepreneurship as a key policy element, and how they were doing it. Analysis of what we found would enable us to arrive at a fuller articulation of the framework that we used as the basis for the study.

The ten economies were Australia, Canada, Finland, Ireland, the Netherlands, Spain, Sweden, Taiwan, the United Kingdom and the United States. We made visits to each country, conducted interviews with government officials, academics and business associations, reviewed government policy documents, searched Websites, and prepared comprehensive reports on the national situation of each economy (Stevenson and Lundström, 2001). We then applied analysis to the collective approaches evident in the ten cases and more fully developed our Entrepreneurship Policy framework, including objectives, policy areas and measures, and performance indicators (Lundström and Stevenson, 2001; Stevenson and Lundström, forthcoming 2002). Finally, we pulled together, what we considered the "best practice" experiences in each of the Entrepreneurship Policy areas. This con-

Table 1
A Comparison of Features of SME versus Entrepreneurship Policy

Feature	SME Policy	Entrepreneurship Policy
Objective	Firm growth, productivity growth	Growth in entrepreneurial activity (number of business owners and firms)
Target	Existing firms Businesses as "entity"	Nascent entrepreneurs/new business starters Individuals (people) as "entity"
Targeting	"Pick winners" (i.e., growth sectors, firms)	General population/subsets (i.e., women, youth)
Client group	Easy to identify	Difficult to identify "nascents"
Levers	Direct financial incentives (e.g., tax credits, loans, guarantees)	Non-financial, business support (e.g., networks, education, mentoring)
Focus	Favourable business environment (i.e., tax regime, marketplace frameworks, reduced red tape and paper burden)	Entrepreneurial climate and culture (i.e., few barriers to entry, recognition of entrepreneurship in society)
Delivery system	Well-established	Lots of new players (need orientation)
Results orientation	More immediate (results in four year cycle)	More long-term (results can take longer)
Consultation and advocacy	SME associations	Forums do not generally exist

tributes to a more common vision of Entrepreneurship Policy and a clearer articulation of what it is, what it includes and how it is implemented, in practice.

Formulating the Problem

One of our basic premises, entering the research, was that there are several problems in the SME policy area, particularly in the areas of definition and evaluation, both of which suffer from a lack of precision. In part of our work, we examine the differences between SME and Entrepreneurship Policy orientations. A full discussion of these distinctions goes beyond the scope of this paper, but a basic comparison of differentiating features is presented in Table 1.

In general, we suggest that governments need to reorient their policies:

1) more towards individuals and individual behaviour and less towards SMEs as firm entities;

2) more towards measures to develop the supply of competent entrepre-

neurs and less towards "picking winners" among existing firms or sectors;

3) more in favour of measures to support the early phases of the entrepreneurial development process, including the nascent as well as the start-up phase; and

4) more in favour of developing an entrepreneurship culture, while still maintaining a focus on creating a more favorable business environment.

We also suggest that more thought should be given to how to create the right environment and circumstances to *motivate* and stimulate individuals to become entrepreneurs. This includes "enabling" policies both to help them acquire the appropriate *skills* and learning, and to surround them with *"opportunity"* (i.e., access to start-up resources and supports). These three elements, Motivation, Skills and Opportunity, are the basis of our Entrepreneurship Policy Foundations framework and are key to the creation of a more "entrepreneurial economy". We illustrate this framework in Figure 1.

There is a high degree of interdependence between these three elements. Stressing one area and ignoring the others will inevitably lead to sub-optimal results. At present, it appears that governments focus primarily on certain parts of the "Opportunities" area. Only a few

Figure 1
Entrepreneurship Policy Foundations

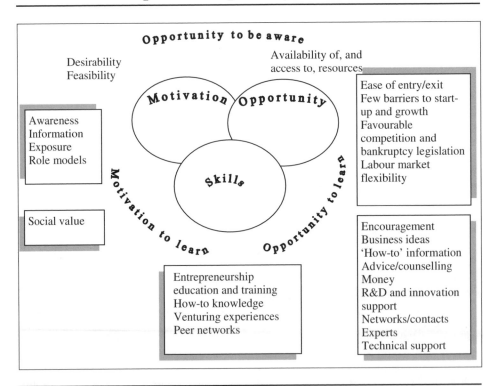

Source: Adapted from Stevenson, L. (1996)

in our study have progressed towards an integrated, comprehensive approach.

Our proposed definition of Entrepreneurship Policy is:

"policy measures taken to stimulate entrepreneurship,

- aimed at the pre-start, start-up and early post start-up phases of the entrepreneurial process,
- designed and delivered to address the areas of Motivation, Opportunity and Skills,
- with the primary objective of encouraging more people to consider entrepreneurship, to move into the nascent stage and proceed into start-up and early phases of a business."

"Entrepreneurship Policy in Practice"

"Entrepreneurship Policy in practice" . . . so, what did we find? We found evidence in all ten cases of an increasing focus on the "entrepreneurial economy". All of them are undertaking some entrepreneurship development activities, but some are further down the road than others in terms of embracing Entrepreneurship Policy. The most advanced policy efforts are in the Netherlands, where the government adopted an Entrepreneurship Policy in 1999 (Ministry of Economic Affairs, 2000). In 2000, the Finnish Government approved a government-wide, multi-departmental, two-year Entrepreneurship Project (Ministry of Trade and Industry, 2000) and the UK government adopted the mission of making the UK "the best place in the world to start a business" (Small Business Service, 2000). Other governments make reference to entrepreneurship as a part of their overall economic development agendas. For example, Sweden identifies "good entrepreneurship" as one of its pillars (NUTEK, 1999; Ministry of Industry, Employment and Communications,

2001), Ireland is focusing on "technology entrepreneurship" (Enterprise Ireland, 2001), and Australia has launched a national "Promoting Young Entrepreneurs" initiative as part of its new innovation agenda, *Backing Australia's Ability* (Industry, Science and Resources, 2001).

We noted that not all governments see things in the same way. To some extent their emphasis on entrepreneurship as a policy issue depends on to what extent it is already embedded in the values of its society. For example, in the US it is embedded in the American constitution as a key aspect of a free enterprise system. In Taiwan, it is embedded in families and a small business culture where 80 percent of the labour force is employed by small and medium sized firms. In such societies, people aspire to being their own boss, of having their own business. In contrast, Gallop polls reveal that people in many European countries much prefer to be a paid employee than to be self-employed (Gallop Europe, 2000).

Some governments look to entrepreneurship for employment growth, like Spain and Finland, which have higher levels of unemployment relative to other countries in this study; others look to it more as a source of wealth creation and economic prosperity, for example Ireland and Australia; and some see it more as a solution for domestic social issues, for example, labour market integration of ethnic groups and economically disadvantaged regions. We discuss these different policy typologies later in this paper. For now, we make the point, that regardless of context, all ten governments are incorporating entrepreneurship elements somewhere in their policy formulations and measures.

A collective categorization of these Entrepreneurship Policy measures revealed six major areas of emphasis:

1) promotion of an entrepreneurship culture and more favourable attitudes;

2) integration of entrepreneurship education in the schools and all levels of post-secondary education;
3) reduction of barriers to entry, elimination of obstacles to entrepreneurship and proactive measures to make it easier for enterprises to enter the market;
4) provision of seed financing and loans/equity for new businesses;
5) start-up business supports, such as mentoring programs, incubators, one-stop shops, peer networks, and online start-up portals aimed at increasing the number of new local businesses; and
6) tailored efforts to increase the business ownership participation rates and to meet the specific needs of under-represented target groups, such as youth, women, ethnic minorities, technology entrepreneurs, Aboriginals, etc.

The framework of these entrepreneurship policy measures is illustrated in Figure 2.

From this, we can see a fit between these policy measures and our Entrepreneurship Policy Foundations. Start-up financing, business support and reduction of entry barriers fall within the definition of the "Opportunity" aspect, promotion falls within the area of "Motivation", and entrepreneurship education falls within the domain of "Skills" and "Motivation". All of these are applied to a diverse range of potential entrepreneurial populations (i.e., target groups) to generate an increased rate of new firm formation.

The objectives of these policies are aimed at creating an entrepreneurship culture and increasing the supply of new entrepreneurs and new businesses as well as their survival and growth. At the time we did our interviews, only four governments made definitive policy statements, setting quantifiable targets for increasing new business start-ups—

Ireland, the Netherlands, Spain, and the UK. Others framed their entrepreneurship policy objectives in more general, non-quantifiable terms, like improving the entrepreneurial culture or climate.

While none of these policy areas is really new to anyone who has been working in the SME policy area for awhile, what IS new is their specific application to the objectives of encouraging a growth in the number of start-ups and increasing the supply of new entrepreneurs. What is also refreshing is the growing acceptance that one has to start focusing on the supply side of entrepreneurship, and that to influence a steady stream of new businesses one has to start by influencing potential entrepreneurs.

This has implications for the development of new business support approaches and services, new business support institutions, orientation of new actors (such as teachers), new orientations to more established processes (like examining barriers to entry as part of the process of reducing administrative burden) and new thinking about economic development, with entrepreneurship at the base; entrepreneurship as a distinct policy area!

For each of the policy measures, we categorized the collective approaches of our 10 cases, into "maps" which better articulated the multiplicity of approaches and innovations. By examining these in detail in our book on "best practices" (Stevenson and Lundström, forthcoming 2002), including lessons learned, critical success factors and innovations and trends, readers will obtain an enhanced view of how to think about these areas. The maps, in particular, may provide a valuable tool for other policymakers interested in adopting a more systematic and cohesive approach to entrepreneurship policy. We illustrate an example of one of these "maps" in Figure 3. In this case, it is the Framework of Entrepreneurship Promotion Options, selected

Figure 2
Framework of Entrepreneurship Policy Measures

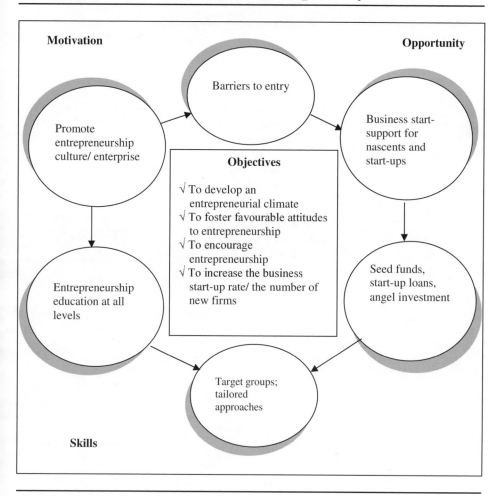

because entrepreneurship promotion is presently such an underdeveloped area of policy focus in most countries.

Entrepreneurship Policy Typologies

Although still in the final stages of model construction, we next present our Typology of Entrepreneurship Policies. So far in this paper, we have provided a collective picture of entrepreneurship policy and its components.

However, individual governments display considerable diversity in how, and to what extent, they combine and implement combinations of these policies. Often, the lines between SME policy and E-Policy are blurred, as we have already mentioned. Some governments are "adding-on" entrepreneurship "bits" within existing SME programs and services, only starting to think about start-up policy issues. Others have adopted a "niche" entrepreneurship policy. And

Figure 3
Framework of Entrepreneurship Promotion Options

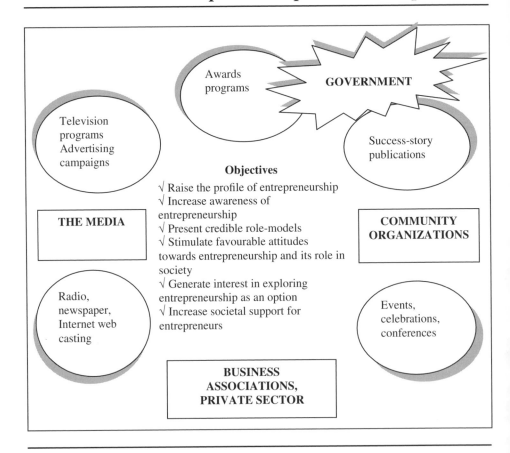

others have an overarching entrepreneurship policy which embraces all of the elements outlined above. These, we have organized into a set of Entrepreneurship Policy Typologies which are described in Figure 4. Briefly the typologies are:

1. *SME Policy "Add-on"*—in which case a focus on starting and new firms or the broader stimulation of entrepreneurship is "added-on" to existing SME programs and services, where they tend to be somewhat marginalized and weakly resourced.

2. *"Niche" Entrepreneurship Policy*—in which case the government formulates targeted entrepreneurship around specified groups of the population. There are two types of niche policies. In Type one, these target groups represent segments of the population which are under-represented as business owners. They might include women, youth, ethnic minorities, the unemployed, or Aboriginals, as examples. The objective is to address specific barriers these groups have to business start-up, as a way of solving unemployment or

Figure 4
Entrepreneurship Policy Typologies

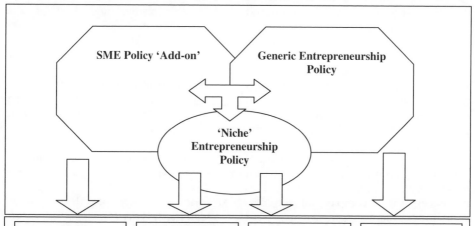

Characteristics	Characteristics	Characteristics	Characteristics
Job creation through new firms: Micro-and local enterprise; Start-up info, micro-loans, advisory services, etc. Tends to be marginally resourced, 'add-on' focus.	*Social inclusion: labour market integration; employment creation: Targets under-represented groups; role models, enterprise centres, loan programs, etc.*	*Wealth creation and innovation: Targets technology entrepreneurs - new grads, technologists; R&D, seed-cap, Vencap, incubators, networks.*	*Economic growth: Entrepreneurship culture; ease of entry and exit; entrepreneurship education; one-stop shops; some targeting; inter-ministerial.*

labour market integration problems or advancing social inclusion objectives. We saw this approach most vividly in the US, but it is evident in several other countries as well. In Type two, "technology entrepreneurship policy", the objective is to generate high-growth potential businesses based on R&D, technology or knowledge inputs by targeting people with the highest potential for starting these kinds of firms—scientific researchers, inventors, university graduates, and people with technology experience. Ireland is cur-

rently the most aggressive with this policy orientation, followed by Australia. The focus is R&D support, venture capital support, university based incubators and incentives for graduates and researchers to build technology-based firms.

3. *Generic Entrepreneurship Policy*—a cohesive entrepreneurship policy approach encompassing all of the policy objectives and measures outlined in the first part of our presentation. We saw this most vividly in the Netherlands and, to a great extent, in the UK and Finland.

Of course, countries do not fall neatly within these categories, as you may expect. For example, governments which "add-on" an entrepreneurship focus to their existing SME support programs and services will often offer special programs and services to identified target groups, that is a "niche" entrepreneurship policy element. In cases, like Taiwan and the US, where the SME policy label is used to cover a wide range of activity, we also see evidence of lots of entrepreneurship promotion and some elements of "technology entrepreneurship policy" (e.g., incubators, venture capital, and R&D support). In addition, we observe that a technology entrepreneurship policy does not necessarily encompass all entrepreneurship policy components. For example, they do not, at this point, make provision for incorporating entrepreneurship education in university programs, although mentoring and consultancy is often provided to the founding entrepreneurs. And so on.

The distinctions of each of these policy approaches are being explored further in Stevenson and Lundström (forthcoming 2002).

Structure

Structures for developing and implementing entrepreneurship policies and measures vary across countries. There appears to be a considerable amount of experimentation taking place in search of the optimal structure. We noted three prevailing approaches, each one with its own set of problems and challenges.

1) Taiwan and the US, for example, have legislated SME policy mandates and designated SME authorities, the Small and Medium Enterprise Administration and the Small Business Administration. These are *umbrella organizations with special authorities* to develop, coordinate and deliver SME policy objectives. The UK's new Small Business Service

is fashioned in a similar way. This is one approach.

2) The second approach is the *horizontal, multi-ministry* one adopted in the Netherlands, Finland and Spain. In this case, multi-ministries and levels of government partner in the delivery of a common vision for increasing the level of entrepreneurship and business creation activity in the country. The Ministry responsible for economic affairs may *coordinate* the policy implementation, but there is a great deal of consensus and cooperation in its delivery across departments and governments.

3) And the third approach is what we call the *"vertical" or "silo" approach*. In this structure, several departments and levels of government may be delivering small business programs and services, each responsible for its own sector, region or objective, with minimal incentive to collaborate in an integrated fashion. Australia, Canada, and to some extent, Sweden would fall into this category. In this latter case, any entrepreneurship development activity tends to take place at the local, regional level.

Because a cohesive Entrepreneurship Policy is impacted by a number of government policy areas—regulatory, labour market, taxation, regional development, technology, social inclusion, financing, education, trade and investment, sector, economic and even immigration policy, a horizontal approach makes sense, but in reality, this is difficult without strong central and mandated leadership. The search for the optimal structure continues!

Performance Indicators—Trends, Measures and Outcomes

The final area we want to cover relates to the development of performance indicators for entrepreneurship policy. The move to any new policy area demands new thinking about how progress will be measured. What performance indicators are needed? What types of evaluation should be undertaken? What are the appropriate benchmarks against which to monitor developments over time, or in relationship to other regions or nations? In this section, we focus on some of the emerging developments in this area of entrepreneurship policy, based on the insights gained from our ten cases.

A number of trends are worth highlighting. First of all, with the increasing emphasis on the "entrepreneurial economy" we notice two things. There is less interest in measures motivated from a neo-classical point of view, i.e., less concern with external effects or imperfections in the market, and there is less interest in individual firms, i.e., measuring the impacts of "picking the winner" strategies. Instead, a whole new category of performance indicators is emerging. These are referred to as measurements of "general entrepreneurship trends" and measurements of the "entrepreneurship climate/ culture". From our case studies, it is evident that Finland and the Netherlands are particularly focused on articulating these measures. Indicators to measure increases in the entrepreneurial climate/ culture include things like increases in the entrepreneurial potential of the population, increases in the preconditions for becoming an entrepreneur, decreases in start-up obstacles, and improvements in social attitudes towards entrepreneurship. Finland proposes to track, at the regional level, changes in entrepreneurial attitude, role identity, motivation level and intent to start a business, changes in the self-employment level, and changes in the level of entrepreneurial activity among women, youth, immigrants and academics. These could be classified as measures of the environment for entrepreneurship.

In the Netherlands, the government has established a set of performance indicators which include the level of business start-ups, exits and growth firms (measures of "dynamism"); increases in the number of sole-traders (measure of social value attached to entrepreneurship); reduced time needed and cost to start a business and reduced barriers to hiring the first employee (measures of reduced administrative burden); the number of professors who teach entrepreneurship and the attitudes of students towards entrepreneurship (measures of the impact of entrepreneurship education inputs); and business entry, exit, and turbulence rates in each of 25 cities (a measure of local/regional policies).

In the UK, increases in social attitudes towards entrepreneurship and the number of nascent entrepreneurs are being used to measure increases in the entrepreneurs climate/ culture, and reduced burden to comply with government regulation, to measure reduction in obstacles to business entry (Small Business Service, 2001).

We observe a trend to develop performance indicators for specific entrepreneurship policy/ program areas like entrepreneurship education, entrepreneurship promotion, start-up financing, administrative obstacles to business entry, etc. We also see the use of new indices to measure entrepreneurial vitality in a region or country, such as:

— "business formations per capita", which is a measure of the business start-up propensity in the population;
— "enterprises per capita", a measurement of the density of entrepreneurs in the population;
— the Total Entrepreneurial Activity Index, which measures the prevalence rate of entrepreneurial activity in a region/ country; and

— business "turbulence", a measurement of the business dynamics of entries and exits.

Static and dynamic measures like these allow international comparisons on a country-by-country basis, which in turn, leads to international benchmarking of entrepreneurship levels. This capability mirrors the existing capability and practice of countries to benchmark their SME sector against that of others (a pattern we also see in many of the cases in this study).

At this point, the development and adoption of these sorts of performance indictors and measures is in very early stages and certainty not wide spread. Only a few economies have made progress in this area and then only recently. But the importance of entrepreneurship in a government's policy mix is being raised as a result of the ability to identify and quantify such inputs, outputs and outcomes.

Driving forces making these developments possible are current research linking entrepreneurial activity to economic growth, attempts to define the intervening variables, and development of methodologies and instruments to collect data and track trends over time. The work of Paul Reynolds and his 21-country GEM research team to track nascent entrepreneurs (Reynolds et al., 2000) and the work of Finnish researchers at the University of Vaasa (Vesalainen and Pihkala, 1999; 2000) to track the movement of the population through all phases of attitude to pre-intent to start-up action, to give only two examples, are leading to the identification and development of the key measures of entrepreneurial activity. Another aid to this process is the work of the European Union which has developed a list of general indicators based on EU-member practices under the BEST Action Plan to Promote Entrepreneurship and Competitiveness (Commis-sion of the European Communities, 2000; 2001).

Best Practices

Finally, we draw attention to some of the "best practice" approaches to each of the Entrepreneurship Policy that we found in our study. The matrix in Table 2 sorts these measures by policy area.

Concluding Comments

Gradually, governments are finding their way along the path from small business to Entrepreneurship policy. The economies in this study have diverse structures, diverse philosophical underpinnings, diverse ideologies and social goals. But regardless of this, entrepreneurship is playing an important role in their societies, not just because entrepreneurs create jobs but because at the end of the day, it is not just about business; it is about people having the freedom to express their creativity, to imprint their style on the work they do, to turn their knowledge, skills and abilities into their own businesses, to create flexibility around their life conditions and personal interests and to make choices over which they have more control.

As governments realize the significant implications of business entry and exit "churn rates" and dynamism of the small business sector for innovation and growth, it will be hard for them to ignore the need for enhanced entrepreneurship support in all the areas outlined in this paper. The average life of a business is getting shorter, innovation is being driven at a faster rate and businesses are in the constant process of starting, expanding, contracting and disappearing. With this activity, jobs are also being created and lost. We need new businesses to replace the ones exiting for reasons of bankruptcy, retirement, marginality and lack of competitiveness, and to help create new jobs to replace the old ones. To influence a steady stream of new businesses, one has to start by influencing potential entrepreneurs. There is evidence in this study that governments are seeking to be more strategic in this task.

A few additional insights and lessons learned about this process are:

- According to Wennekers and Thurik (2001), *"small firms and new firm start-ups may not be necessary for regional growth in the short run, but perhaps they are the seeds of future growth and are of central importance for long run economic development."* Understanding more clearly where entrepreneurship policies are situated in relationship to the more established policy areas will be helpful to governments that want to move to a more integrated economic development approach.
- An E-Policy approach is an integrated one. It requires actions in each of the foundation areas of Motivation, Skills and Opportunity and at each stage of the entrepreneurial process.
- An emphasis on removing obstacles will not be sufficient in stimulating higher levels of entrepreneurial activity IF entrepreneurship is not already sufficiently embedded in the culture (lesson learned from Finland and the Netherlands).
- *"Skill in opportunity recognition, capacity to act on opportunities and respect for entrepreneurship as a career option are necessary conditions to stimulate entrepreneurial activity, but are not sufficient to drive it to high levels in a society"* (Hindle and Rushworth, 2000).
- Entrepreneurship education and promotion activity go hand-in-

hand. "Societal-readiness" is a critical factor in success of attempts to integrate entrepreneurship in the classroom (lesson learned from Finland).
- Government policy must embrace the notion that the "opportunity to be aware" of entrepreneurship as an option and the "opportunity to learn" about the entrepreneurial process are as legitimate and important as the opportunity to access economic resources and markets, which is where government action is primarily focused at present.
- In the development and implementation of Entrepreneurship Policy, "structure" matters.
- The implementation of Entrepreneurship Policy may require, not only a shift in thinking, but new forms of institutional structures and relationships, more partnerships and cooperative actions between federal and regional governments, between multiple ministries and with educational institutions, community-based organizations, business associations, the media, the financial community and the private sector. Everyone has a role to play.
- The presence of "entrepreneurship champions" cannot be overstated! These might be located in universities, schools, local economic development offices, business associations or government offices, but they are essential to advancing and fostering the entrepreneurship agenda.
- We stress the need for more research on the relationship between entrepreneurial activity and economic growth and the relationships between; 1) motivation and business entry; 2) business entry and opportunity; and 3) business entry and skills.

Table 2

Approaches and Innovations in Entrepreneurship Policy Areas—From Ten Cases

Promotion	Education	Barriers to Entry	Seed Capital and Start-Up Loans	Start-Up Supports	Performance Indicators
Television series (US, CA, TW)	Commission on Entrepreneurship and Education (NL)	Review procedural, regulatory, legislative and cost barriers to new business entry (NL, SP, UK, FL, SW)	Micro-loans (US, CA, SW, SP, TW)	One-stop shops (several cases)	Measures for general entrepreneurship climate, e.g., social attitudes towards entrepreneurship, increases in "entrepreneurial potential" (FL, NL, UK)
Advertising campaigns (SW, NL)	Entrepreneurship as part of National Curriculum Guidelines (AS, NL, UK, FL)	Review Competition Policy; deregulation and privatisation (AS, NL, SW, FL)	Small business loan guarantee programs (CA, US, NL, SP, UK, TW)	Use of Web portals to provide information, training and advice to new and potential starters (US, CA, AS, IR, UK, NL)	General entrepreneurship trends (e.g., business entry, survival, growth and exit rates; self-employment rates) (NL, UK, US)
Radio programs (NPR in the US)	Teaching resources for each grade level and subject area (CA, NL, FL, AS)	Bankruptcy Reform to reduce "cost" of failure (NL, UK, FL)	Tax incentives to encourage angel investments (several cases)	Mentoring programs including special mentors for starters (IR, UK)	Monitoring of SME sector performance (most cases)

Table 2
Continued

Promotion	Education	Barriers to Entry	Seed Capital and Start-Up Loans	Start-Up Supports	Performance Indicators
Positive newspaper and magazine coverage (US, CA)	Professional development for teachers	Review of social security and labour market rules (to reduce "quiet disincentives") and barriers to hiring the first employee (NL, FL, SP)	Angel networks and databases (CA, US, UK)	Small business incubators as start-up policy (IR, AS, TW, US, NL)	Measuring impact of entrepreneurship policy measures, such as reductions in cost of starting a business (NL, FL, UK)
Nurturing the media (US)	Student venture programs (most cases)	Simplify tax reporting and reduce tax burden (IR, UK)	Education initiatives to improve financial competency of new entrepreneurs (CA, TW)	Advice and counselling services for new starters and fledging entrepreneurs (all cases)	Small business access to financing (NL, UK)
Awards (all cases)	Entrepreneurship Education Resource Centres (NL, CA, US, FL, AS)		R&D and seed funds to support innovation (CA, US, IR, AS, NL)	Professional development for business advisers (UK, IR, CA, US, AS)	
Events and conferences (TW, US, CA, SW, UK)	Entrepreneurship education for all post-secondary programs of study (NL)		Streamlining loan processes to reduce cost of making small loans (US, CA)	Tailored services for target groups (most cases)	
Promotion of youth entrepreneurship (most cases)			Income support for unemployed people who want to start small businesses (CA, SW, UK, NL)		

Practical Implications of the Study

This study has resulted in the development of a number of tools which policymakers, in particular, may find useful—the definition of entrepreneurship policy; the Entrepreneurship Policy Foundations Framework; the Parameters of Entrepreneurship Policy; the Framework of Entrepreneurship Policy Measures; "maps" of options in each of the policy measure areas; a checklist to assess to what extent entrepreneurship is taken seriously by governments in any particular geographic area; and a road map to our "Entrepreneurship Policy Square" (graphically illustrated in Lundström and Stevenson, 2001).

How can these be used? We have emphasized the importance of context, i.e., that a good practice in one context may not obviously be a good practice in a different context. Therefore, countries should examine their economic, cultural and social dimensions to assess the conditions into which an integrated entrepreneurship policy would be introduced. This might include:

> ➤ Conducting a self-assessment by going through the checklist to see what the country is already doing.
> ➤ Analyzing which entrepreneurship policy measures are currently underway in the areas of Promotion; Entrepreneurship Education; Networks; Administrative, Regulatory, Legislative and Tax Burden; Target Groups; Business Support Services; Start-up and Seed Financing; and Research.
> ➤ Summarizing lessons learned about activity (or lack of it) in each of the different areas, for example, which are given the highest versus lowest priority.

> ➤ Analyzing the existing resource allocation between measures in the SME policy area and the Entrepreneurship policy area.
> ➤ Reviewing the preliminary list of performance indicators in use in other countries to determine which ones could be used to measure future performance.
> ➤ Considering the short run and long run implications of adopting a comprehensive and integrated entrepreneurship policy approach.

Although in most cases, the shift into entrepreneurship policy formulation is in its infancy stages, we are beginning to see how it is playing out in practice. This paper sheds some light on this process and provides useful insights for others as they embark on a similar journey.

References

Acs, Zoltan J. and David B. Audretsch (2001). "The Emergence of an Entrepreneurial Society." Presentation for acceptance of the 2001 NUTEK-FSF International Award for Entrepreneurship and Small Business Research, Stockholm.

Acs, Zoltan J. and David B. Audretsch (1990). *Innovation and Small Firms.* Cambridge: MIT Press.

Audretsch, David and Roy Thurik (2001). "Linking Entrepreneurship and Growth." STI Working papers 2001, Directorate for Science, Technology and Industry: OECD, Paris, May.

Boter, Hakan, Dan Hjalmarsson and Anders Lundström (1999). *Outline of a Contemporary Small Business Policy.* Swedish Foundation for Small Business Research, Stockholm.

Commission of the European Communities (2001). "2001 BEST Procedure Report." Commission Staff Working Paper, Brussels, 29.10.2001, SEC(2001) 1704.

Commission of the European Communities (2000). *Report on the Implementation of the Action Plan to Promote Entrepreneurship and Competitiveness*. Commission Staff Working Paper. Brussels, 27.10.2000, SEC(2000). 1825-Vol.1.

EIM (1999). "Benchmark entrepreneurship." In *Dutch Benchmark Ondernemerschap*. Zoetermeer, the Netherlands.

Enterprise Ireland (2001). *Driving Growth through Regional Enterprise*. Dublin. February.

European Commission (1998). *Fostering Entrepreneurship in Europe: Priorities for the Future*. Communication from the Commission to the Council. Brussels, 07.04.1998, COM(98) 222 final.

Gallop Europe (2000). "Flash Barometer 83 Entrepreneurship." Prepared for the Directorate General—Enterprises, European Commission, Brussels. September.

Hindle, Kevin and Susan Rushworth (2000). *Yellow Pages Global Entrepreneurship Monitor, Australia 2000*. Swinburne University of Technology, Melbourne, Australia.

Industry, Science Resources (2001). *Developing Australia's Innovation Action Plan*. Canberra, Australia.

Lundström, Anders and Lois Stevenson (2001). *Entrepreneurship Policy for the Future*, Special Edition, SME Forum 19–20 March, Växjö. Swedish Foundation for Small Business Research, Stockholm.

Ministry of Economic Affairs (2000). *The Entrepreneurial Society: More opportunities and fewer obstacles for entrepreneurship*. The Hague (Dutch version 1999; English version 2000).

Ministry of Industry, Employment and Communications (2001). *Sweden's Action Plan for Employment*. Stockholm. May.

Ministry of Trade and Industry (2000). *Enterprise and SME Policy in Finland*. Helsinki. September.

Ministry of the Economy (2000). *La Pequena y Mediana Empresa en Espana: Politicas y Realizaciones*. Government of Spain, Madrid.

NUTEK (1999). *Growth 2000—an industrial policy for the new millennium*. Stockholm, September.

OECD (1998). *Fostering Entrepreneurship*. OECD. Paris.

OECD (1995). *Thematic Overview of Entrepreneurship and Job Creation Policies*. Paris.

Reynolds, Paul D., S. Michael Camp, William D. Bygrave, Errko Autio and Michael Hay (2001). *Global Entrepreneurship Monitor, 2001 Executive Report*. Babson College, Kauffman Foundation and London Business School.

Small Business Service (2000). *Think Small First: A National Strategy for Supporting Small and Medium Sized Enterprises in the UK*. Department of Trade and Industry, London.

Small Business Service (2001). "Think Small First—Performance Monitoring." January.

Stevenson, Lois and Anders Lundström (2001). *Patterns and Trends in Entrepreneurship/SME Policy in Ten Economies*. Swedish Foundation for Small Business Research: Stockholm.

Stevenson, Lois and Anders Lundström (forthcoming 2002). *Beyond the Rhetoric: Defining Entrepreneurship Policy and its Best Practice Components*. Swedish Foundation for Small Business Research, Stockholm.

Stevenson, Lois (1996). *The Implementation of an Entrepreneurship Development Strategy in Canada: The Case of the Atlantic Region*. The Atlantic Canada Opportunities Agency (ACOA)/OECD. Paris.

Vesalainen, Jukka and Timo Pihkala (1999). "Entrepreneurial Identity, Intentions and the Effect of the Push-Factor." Academy of Entrepreneurship Journal 5: 2, 1–24.

Vesalainen, Jukka and Timo Pihkala (2000). "Barriers to Entrepreneurship—Educational Opportunities." Proceedings of the IntEnt-conference. Tampere. July.

Wennekers, Sander and Roy Thurik (2001). "Institutions, entrepreneurship and economic performance." In Anders Lundström and Lois Stevenson, *Entrepreneurship Policy for the Future*, Special Edition, SME Forum 19–20 March 2001, Växjö, Sweden. Swedish Foundation for Small Business Research, Stockholm.

Wennekers, Sander and Roy Thurik (1999). "Linking entrepreneurship and economic growth." *Small Business Economics* 13(1) 27–55.

Rationales for Public Policy
by Alistair Nolan

Do Markets Fail Entrepreneurs? And Are Markets Enough for Poor Localities?

This chapter examines the economic bases for public policies that aim to encourage self-employment and entrepreneurship in local economies. Frequently, the rationale for policy is assumed and implicit, rather than being clearly stated. Two related questions need to be considered: *i*) what grounds exist for entrepreneurship policy *per se*?, and *ii*) are there reasons why policy should be designed, implemented or targeted at the local level?

In seeking to foster entrepreneurship government has an undisputed role in ensuring the presence of high-quality framework conditions. These conditions include: well-functioning institutions; competitive markets for goods, services and labour; a transparent, fair, non-punitive and predictable system of corporate taxation; a propitious macroeconomic environment; and bankruptcy legislation that facilitates resource reallocation while properly protecting creditors. Aside from providing good framework conditions, the standard premise for policy intervention refers to failures in the markets that support entrepreneurial activity.

Market failure arises from systematic divergences between the private and social costs and benefits associated with transactions in the market concerned. Such divergences can occur for a number of reasons. These include the public good characteristics of certain services, information problems of various sorts, and non-competitive market structures, perhaps being dominated by one or a small number of firms. Gaps in the provision of goods and services can also exist owing to economies of scale in their supply—a consideration discussed below in relation to the market for venture capital. Concerns that market failure restricts the level of entrepreneurship usually focus on alleged shortcomings in the supply of debt and equity to new and small firms. But difficulties are also reported in other important markets, such as for industrial real estate, business development services and training. The relevant empirical and theoretical debates are reviewed later in this chapter.

Public support is sometimes advocated for small and medium-sized enterprises as a group on the basis that these provide large numbers of jobs. Calls have also been made for the public sector to support the minority of small businesses that grow rapidly and account for a disproportionately large share of new private sector jobs. Similarly, arguments have been made for public intervention to help the growing numbers of entrepreneurs from particular groups in society (the young, women, etc). Arguments of this sort—which depend solely on the weight that

Originally appeared in *Entrepreneurship and Local Economic Development: Programme and Policy Recommendations*, by Alistair Nolan, published by the Organisation for Economic Co-Operation and Development, 2003.

some category of firm has in employment, incomes or growth—are extremely weak. To be valid they would need to provide reasons why markets systematically fail to properly allocate resources to such firms and entrepreneurs.

Various Arguments for Policy Rest on External Benefits from Entrepreneurship

Another set of arguments exists for supporting entrepreneurship that does not depend on failures in the markets on which entrepreneurs depend. These arguments assume that the creation of new firms gives rise to *positive externalities*. An externality is an outcome of a market transaction that affects others who have not participated in the transaction. An externality can create benefits—a positive externality—or costs—a negative externality. In broad terms, society gains from increasing activities that produce positive externalities (possibly through subsidisation) and decreasing activities that have negative externalities (possibly through taxation). Within such a framework, attention has been drawn to the fact that when an entrepreneur creates a business, valuable information is provided to other actual and potential entrepreneurs. That is, the establishment of a firm generates a positive externality. Information is supplied, for instance, on what products sell and what business strategies work. Even

business failure sends useful signals to others. However, entrepreneurs are not rewarded for producing this information. Therefore, it is claimed, the amount of entrepreneurial activity is below a level that economists would describe as socially optimal.[1] If imitation plays a significant role in diffusing entrepreneurship—as discussed in Chapter 2—the plausibility of such an account is strengthened. However, this policy rationale is theoretical only, with as yet no substantiating empirical basis.

A related line of argument draws again on the idea that entrepreneurship spreads in part through the influence of imitation. If potential entrepreneurs are prone to imitate actual entrepreneurs, then places that have few entrepreneurs today—perhaps a locality with a history of dependence on large-scale industry—will be more likely to experience low rates of entrepreneurship tomorrow, other things unchanged. An implication of this form of path dependency is that public policy would be needed to impart a shift to a higher level of entrepreneurial activity. However, the possibility that rates of entrepreneurial activity might be partially determined by demonstration effects has not been analysed empirically. The path-dependency case may have a basis in fact—and feels true-to-life for many practitioners—but whether it is important relative to other influences is not known.

---

[1]Theory indicates that if an economic activity such as entrepreneurship produces positive externalities then it should be subsidised up to the point where the amount of the subsidy equals the value of the external benefit associated with the next unit of activity. In practice, however, policymakers will not know when this condition has been achieved. This is mainly because it is extremely difficult to assess the value of benefits (and costs) that occur outside a market. Precisely because these benefits are external to the market no monetary value is expressed for them. In the case in point, if a market existed in which actual and potential entrepreneurs could buy the information produced by enterprise creation then policymakers would have an indication of how much this information was worth. But such a market is absent. In some fields of economics a great deal of attention has been given to estimating the size of externalities using a range of innovative techniques. However, this report found no studies that attempt to assess information externalities associated with entrepreneurship.

Other positive externalities might be traced to a set of area regeneration effects from entrepreneurship. For example, start-ups might attract other firms to a locality by increasing the availability of services or by enlarging the local pool of trained workers. New firms might also make a location more attractive to live in. In so doing, they could help to counter the downward economic spiral that results when the best-qualified and most employable individuals emigrate from localities in decline. Increased start-up activity might also lower the unit costs of providing public utilities. And the value of housing could rise as new firms are created—a phenomenon witnessed in the vicinity of some business incubation schemes. New companies in a poor locality could also help to retain incomes that would otherwise have been spent elsewhere. Indeed, the variety of interactions between firms and the places that host them is considerable. Anecdotal accounts suggest that such processes can also be important quantitatively. However, policy arguments based on regeneration externalities are undermined by a lack of empirical studies of enterprise demographics and local economic development.[2]

The Costs and Distribution of Unemployment Have Also Played a Part in Policy Thinking

Another strand of policy thinking rests on consideration of the social costs of unemployment. Unemployment and underemployment have obvious direct and indirect economic and social costs for communities as well as individuals. For any population group—local, regional or national—there are benefits in having the unemployed move into employment. If measures are available to reduce joblessness that cost less than the full cost of unemployment their adoption merits consideration. Encouraging entrepreneurship is potentially one such measure. Indeed, Cowling and Hayward (2000) found significant overall public savings from a full cost-benefit assessment of a local self-employment scheme in the United Kingdom. However, the available evidence indicates that the cost-effectiveness of entrepreneurship support is limited to a small fraction of the unemployed, and that pro-entrepreneurship strategies deliver relatively small numbers of jobs over the short-run. Nevertheless, promoting entrepreneurship in order to reduce unemployment could entail an automatic area-based targeting of programmes if, as is frequently the case, unemployment is geographically concentrated (for example, a 1998 study in the United Kingdom found that half of the unemployed live in the sixty-five most deprived local authorities[3]).

A related argument for policy focuses on spreading the burden of unemployment. The difficulty of re-entering the labour force increases as the duration of unemployment lengthens. Therefore, reducing the prevalence of long-term unemployment could enhance welfare even if total unemployment is unchanged. However, as a rationale for policy this argument again turns on the cost-effectiveness of entrepreneurship promotion—relative to alternative policy measures—as a vehicle for

---

[2]By contrast, a large number of comprehensive quantitative studies have been undertaken of local and regional income and employment effects stemming from discrete and generally large commercial investments, investment subsidies and infrastructure projects. Examples are described in Foley (1992).

[3]Department of the Environment, Transport and Regions, index of local deprivation, 1998.

employment creation and improved social cohesion. As previously described, cost-effectiveness generally exists for only a minority of the unemployed. Furthermore, this minority tends not to include persons with the weakest attachments to the labour market.

A policy of targeting business support to specific areas might be justified if it were shown that the social benefits of enterprise are particularly high in some types of locality. For instance, it is reasonable to expect that the social benefits of entrepreneurship in poor communities could be greater than in wealthier localities. But this will not be the case for all poor communities. For instance, the cost-effectiveness of pro-entrepreneurship programmes is likely to be low in circumstances of severe economic and social distress. Enterprise survival times, for example, will generally be shorter than in localities with more conducive trading environments. In fact, promoting entrepreneurship in low-unemployment localities might yield greater economic benefits on account of lower displacement effects (Metcalf *et al.*, 2000).

A further basis for intervention is where this can yield other forms of benefit—not related directly to employment or local regeneration—that would not have arisen in the absence of policy. For instance, efficiency gains can result from stimulating various forms of collaboration among firms. In this connection, a catalytic public sector role in developing business networks can be

relatively inexpensive (see Chapter 10). In addition, many firms fail for reasons not directly related to the underlying viability of the business. For example, the inability to manage cash flow is responsible for a high share of new and small-firm mortality. Measures to help attenuate such "unnecessary" business failure—such as mentoring and training—could generate economic and social benefits. Economic benefits could arise because it is unlikely that the process of reallocating resources following company closures is cost-less.[4] Economic and social benefits could arise because of savings from lower unemployment (even if this is temporary) and a reduction in the distress that afflicts individuals and households when a business fails. In principle, all of the benefits described in this paragraph can be realised without distorting the essential process whereby markets allocate resources to highest-value uses.

Intervention at the Local Level Has Potential Advantages

Once it is decided that there are economic grounds for public action, intervention by subnational governments may have particular advantages. The combination of major spatial variations in entrepreneurial activity and the scope for superior resource mobilisation and allocation through local programmes highlight the importance of local flexibility in the design and implementation of policy.[5] Local authorities have a role

---

[4]This is especially so when the value of assets is specific to a particular use (see Williamson, 1985). However, asset specificity is most common in manufacturing. It is less relevant to the micro-enterprises, often in the service sector, that are frequent in poorer localities.

[5]However, centralised co-ordination and/or implementation of programmes will also be necessary. In the most general terms, if local policies have important effects on the welfare of other localities then inefficient resource allocation (from a national standpoint) could occur in the absence of central control. If policies entail economies of scale then they might best be implemented centrally. Central co-ordination can also provide a degree of economic insurance because interregional recessions and growth are often not perfectly correlated. And centralised policy is required on equity grounds. This is because policies that have redistributive

to play in matching programmes to varied local circumstances. Managerial training programmes, for example, are often best delivered through local bodies, or decentralised offices of national programmes. These local institutions can adapt schemes to an area's specific needs. They can also operate near to trainees, allowing these to undertake training without spending excessive time away from the workplace. Even the manner in which enterprise agencies present themselves may need to be tailored to the locality, as support agencies can be perceived as part of a social structure that is alien to some residents of deprived communities.

There are also occasions when enterprise creation might require strategic guidance from a local authority. This is particularly so when problems of co-ordination among numerous economic agents are serious. For instance, when localities are subject to acute economic shock—such as a major factory closure—local rates of self-employment usually rise sharply. However, many of the unemployed making a transition to self-employment choose easy-entry markets, especially if those who have lost jobs possess low or medium skills. This problem of "flocking" to sectors with low entry barriers will lead to further distress as firms in oversupplied markets earn small margins or cease to trade. Such distress can be prevented, or mitigated, if local enterprise support agencies promote diversification and discourage overcrowding in the relevant markets.

Governments, local and central, must also be concerned with policy failures. That is, they need to correct policies that impede the efficient functioning of markets or worsen existing market failures. For example, inappro-priate spatial planning can exacerbate the difficulties of finding a place to work that many nascent businesses confront. Policy options are available that have few if any distortionary effects on the markets concerned. For instance, measures such as increasing the flow of information and advice for starting, financing and managing entrepreneurial ventures, encouraging public awareness of entrepreneurship, and promoting beneficial collaborative behaviour among entrepreneurs (such as in mutual credit guarantee schemes and inter-firm networks) are unlikely to involve policy failure.

Discrimination on grounds of race, gender, age or disability clearly calls for a public response, although this response need not be specific to any particular level of government. Discrimination has been claimed most often in connection with the treatment of loan applications by banks.

The following sections of this chapter discuss alleged market failures in connection with the supply to new and small firms of finance, business advisory services, physical workspace and training.

Finance

Various characteristics of small firms can create negative perceptions among banks considering loan applications (see Box 5.1). An extensive literature has examined purported market failure in the supply of debt and equity to small firms, as well as financial impediments to self-employment. The empirical evidence is somewhat inconclusive but increasingly errs to the view that market failure is less important than previously supposed. Many policy analyses insist on survey findings that a significant share of entrepreneurs report difficulties in gaining access to finance. However, such

---

effects at the local level may become financially unsustainable owing to the movement of wealthier individuals out of redistributing areas and the movement of poorer individuals towards such localities.

reports do not necessarily constitute evidence of market failure. For instance, in responding to surveys entrepreneurs may have a bias towards explaining poor enterprise performance in terms of developments external to the firm and its management. Access to finance is just such an external consideration.[6] Indeed, it has been shown that the views of entrepreneurs do not always accord with those of more "objective" observers such as credit rating agencies (Cressy and Olofsson, 1997).[7]

Credit Markets Do Not Function as a Textbook Market Should

The market for credit for small firms does not function as a neo-classical market should. In a textbook market good projects should be funded regardless of the resources of the proprietor. In practice, collateral-based lending predominates, with the interest rate relatively unimportant as a means of discriminating between projects having different levels of perceived risk. For example, Astebro and Bernhardt (1999)

show that while Canadian banks are increasingly interested in funding start-ups and small enterprises, loan applications are almost exclusively evaluated against the entrepreneur's personal creditworthiness rather than an assessment of project merits.[8] In the United States during the early 1990s some seventy per cent of all commercial loans were secured (Cowling, 1998). Such findings suggest particular problems for individuals with few financial assets or low personal creditworthiness and who wish to start a business.

In recent years banks in many countries have moved heavily into small-firm transactions. Indeed, banks have a growing commercial interest in cultivating a portfolio of small-firm clients.[9] Competition and rising costs in other markets—such as personal deposit taking—have reduced business for some banks. Banks can also benefit from lending to small firms as a way of marketing a range of banking services. Indeed, fee income from small-firm clients, for services other than lending,

---

[6]More telling perhaps are responses from employees maintaining that a lack of capital is a key reason for not becoming self-employed (see Blanchflower and Oswald, 1998).

[7]However, Egeln et al. (1997) compare firms' subjective assessments of financial restrictions with credit-rating data. The authors find a relatively high correlation between self-classification and the "objective" data.

[8]At the same time, the creditworthiness of owners was not seen to correlate strongly with business success. The banks considered by Astebro and Bernhardt were thus found to be doing a relatively poor job in allocating loanable funds. While the receipt of a bank loan was seen to be a significant positive predictor of a firm's survival, other sources of debt were more than twice as effective in increasing business survival. Indeed, higher-quality projects tended to select nonbank sources of debt, where terms were better (it was also found that the number of sources of finance appeared to be a good predictor of project quality). The authors show how the use of additional variables to predict business survival could significantly reduce bank loan losses. The variables used include the number of owners of the firm, the human capital of the entrepreneur(s), the availability of equity, whether the company was new or bought from a previous owner, and whether the firm was a franchise. The authors note that the failure to properly evaluate start-ups affects bank profitability. It may also limit potentially able firms by sending incorrect signals to other actors. It is not clear, however, that these important findings lead to a public policy conclusion. Successful banks will presumably be alert to such research—which was in fact sponsored by a bank—and modify lending practice accordingly. Other banks will be forced to follow suit or risk losing market share.

[9]See for example "Small business offers bankers rich pickings", *Financial Times*, 11/08/2000.

Box 5.1. Bank Lending and the Financial Structure of Small and Nascent Firms

The financing of new and small businesses typically differs from that of medium-sized and large firms. Small businesses usually depend for finance on the entrepreneur's own capital, retained profits, trade creditors, other creditors (such as fiscal authorities in the case of an allowance for deferred payments of corporation tax), and short-term credit in the form of hire-purchase, leasing and bank overdraft. The lack of equity and long-term debt capital, combined with a reliance on short-term credit, is reflected in a high debt to equity gearing ratio and low liquidity.

Characteristics of new and small firms that are likely to create negative perceptions among banks considering loan applications include the following:

- A high level of perceived risk owing to a high rate of enterprise failure and a general vulnerability to adverse market conditions. Amongst other causes this vulnerability can stem from reliance on a small number of products and/or a restricted market. Dependence on only a small number of products might also deter longer-term bank lending if product life cycles are short (bootstrap financing—financing out of cash flow—is irrelevant to many new-technology-based firms owing to very short product lifecycles).
- The lack of a track record, in the case of start-ups.
- The inability of some small-scale firms to provide collateral. Lenders may request personal guarantees as security for a loan. Such guarantees can be socially counterproductive if they deter Directors from taking the risks necessary to continue the expansion of their businesses. In addition, the intangible and highly specific nature of the assets of many new-technology-based firms can present obstacles in posting collateral.
- High bank transaction costs (for example in assessing and obtaining collateral) as a proportion of the amounts lent.
- Frequently, a relative lack of accounting expertise and of the skills required for proper presentation of business plans and loan applications. More generally, banks (and venture capital funds) may wish to see evidence of multidisciplinary business skills in a firm's management (including financial awareness, marketing skills, technical knowledge of the business, etc.) that may be unusual in small owner-managed companies.
- Risk associated with cash flow deficiencies. Cash flow problems can arise from a lack of financial management expertise, rapid growth, and the fact of having a small number of products (with a larger number of products cash flow surpluses and deficits may cancel out). Innovative firms that supply new markets also face inherent difficulties in forecasting the scale and timing of capital requirements and may need substantial funds at short notice.

usually exceeds income from loans. There is evidence from the United States that competition in financial services has helped to supply the needs of lower-income groups. The demand for micro-loans for example is being met in part through credit cards which, despite carrying high rates of interest on debt, can involve low introductory rates, low transaction costs and low total costs (by comparison with specialised providers of micro-finance) (Glackin, 2002). Increased attention by banks to the small firms sector may have served to narrow previously reported funding gaps. Public policy may also have had an impact. In the United Kingdom, for instance, a secondary effect of the Small Firm Loan Guarantee Scheme has been to raise awareness among some bankers of business opportunities in the small firms sector (although the primary impact of this policy in reducing funding gaps appears to have been small). Similarly, in the United States, the Community Reinvestment Act has made many banks more alert to the commercial opportunities available in low-income areas.

Evidence Exists Both For and Against Market Failure

Attempts to demonstrate failures in the supply of debt have used a number of criteria. Some studies have sought to assess the effects of individual wealth on the likelihood of entry into self-employment. However, a positive association between wealth and entrepreneurship might simply reflect a greater propensity, or opportunity, for entrepreneurial activity among the affluent. It could also be a result of the tendency of children of wealthy parents to inherit family-owned businesses. To eliminate these possibilities research has examined whether windfall gains such as lottery wins, which bear no relation to the existing wealth of the recipients, increase the likelihood of entry to self-employment. This line of enquiry has revealed ample evidence that asset windfalls increase the probability that agents enter entrepreneurship, which is consistent with borrowing constraints (Blanchflower and Oswald, 1998; Taylor, 1998). Other research shows a positive relationship between the real value of housing equity and the rate of creation of unincorporated businesses, again indicating a collateral constraint on bank lending (Barlow and Robson, 1999). Similarly, house prices have been shown to be the single most important determinant of loan size under the United Kingdom's Small Firm Loan Guarantee Scheme (Cowling, 1998). And using data on one thousand six hundred companies, Carpenter and Petersen (1999) showed that the growth of small firms is constrained by the availability of internal finance, which supports an external constraints hypothesis.[10] As described earlier, there is also robust evidence, particularly from the United States, of discrimination in credit markets against certain ethnic minorities (Blanchflower et al., 1998).

---

[10]Other studies use a related but different approach, examining the existence of a relationship between cash flow and investment. In an efficient capital market there should be no systematic relationship between the two. Firms would be indifferent whether funds came from internal or external sources. Using such an approach, Audretsch and Elston (1994) find evidence for liquidity constraints on a sample of German small firms from 1977 to 1985. However, Kaplan and Zingales (1997; 2000) have called into question the theoretical and empirical suitability of investment-cash flow sensitivities as an indicator of financial constraints. The authors note, *inter alia*, that such sensitivities can also be seen in large firms—such as Hewlett-Packard—that are hard to classify as financially constrained. Why these sensitivities exist is still unclear.

When firms increase in size they require a wider range of sources of finance. At the same time, greater size can bring efficiencies in obtaining financial resources. Various authors have found that liquidity constraints are more severe for smaller companies. For instance, Audretsch and Elston (1999) showed that small German firms are relatively disadvantaged in terms of access to finance.

However, there is also a considerable weight of evidence suggesting that market failure is not significant. Cressy and Toivanen (1999) found a regime of symmetric information between borrowers and banks in the United Kingdom, with "good" entrepreneurs receiving larger loans on better terms than "bad" entrepreneurs. Calcagnini *et al.* (1999) find empirical support for the proposition that small-firms in Italy are no more likely to be credit constrained than larger firms. A succession of recent Annual reports on small firm finance by the Bank of England tends to the view that credit constraints on small companies are not critical. And Hughes (1997) found little evidence for generic market failure in either the supply of debt or equity to small firms in the United Kingdom.

Ongoing contributions to the theory of credit markets also suggest that constraints are unlikely to be binding (see Box 5.2). Indeed, economists are increasingly coming to the view that while some investment projects with a positive net present value do go unfunded, market failure in the provision of debt is not widespread (Berger and Udell, 1992). If market failure does occur it appears to be more isolated than systemic and perhaps does not merit a major public policy response. As described by Cressy and Olofsson (1997), summarising a variety of empirical studies in Europe:

"There are both supply and demand constraints in some European countries. However, the evidence also suggests that in others the gaps are confined to specific financing modes (debt or equity), to specific sectors/types of firm (e.g. high-tech), and that they may also be a function of the state of the economy (recession or boom). The association of perceived funding gaps with other 'real' factors like management skills [. . .] also weakens the argument for governments simply 'throwing money' at the problem."

One of the financing modes in which constraints may be serious is the supply of the smallest-sized loans. Collateral is not taken by banks for such loans because the costs of assessing the collateral's worth, and collecting it in the case of default, are too high relative to the size of the loan. In this connection, where banks rely on personal credit history, and there are persons who combine potentially viable projects with poor credit histories, public intervention can be valuable in principle. Schemes to facilitate access to loans in the smallest size class are detailed in Chapter 9.

The Supply of Equity May Be More Problematic than the Supply of Debt

The supply of small volumes of equity may be more problematic than the provision of debt, especially for start-ups and new-technology-based firms.[11] This is largely because venture capitalists face costs in assessing, monitoring and managing investments that vary little with the size of the investments they make. This makes smaller investments

---

[11]Nevertheless, debt and equity gaps should not be treated as unrelated because banks may be more willing to lend to a company they had previously refused a loan to if the firm can obtain additional equity (Cressy and Olofsson, 1997).

Box 5.2. Theory Increasingly Suggests that Credit Gaps Are Not Decisive

Stiglitz and Weiss (1981) provided the theoretical basis of much concern regarding constraints in lending to small firms. The analytical starting point is that banks do not possess the same information on investment proposals as entrepreneurs in new and small firms. The authors show that if banks and borrowers do not have the same information on a project's risk (expressed in terms of variation around a mean return) then the interest rate cannot be used to efficiently allocate loanable funds. This is because raising the interest rate will only attract more risky projects. Entrepreneurs who know their projects are less risky will hold them back when the interest rate rises. This happens because borrowers who know that their projects have a high risk also know that they will have a high return if the venture goes well. However, if the venture goes badly the downside is the same for two projects with identical expected mean returns. This is because protection against extreme downside losses is afforded by legislation on limited liability. So borrowers with risky projects can bear a higher interest rate than borrowers with less risky investment proposals.

However, the Stiglitz/Weis analysis depended on projects differing only with respect to their risk. Other models have been proposed. In particular, DeMeza and Webb (1987) considered what would happen if the key distinction that entrepreneurs make between investment projects is based on each proposal's expected mean return. In this case a higher interest rate would attract borrowers who believe their projects have a lower risk of failure. In practice, uncertainty exists with respect to both the risk of projects and their expected mean return. Consequently, there is also uncertainty as to the role of the interest rate in project selection (Cosh and Hughes, 1994).

In more recent work DeMeza (1999) has argued against Stiglitz and Weiss using a model in which *laissez faire* will result in *excessive* lending. Furthermore, overlending is in this paper compatible with the presence of lending gaps. DeMeza also presents evidence suggesting that overoptimism among entrepreneurs merits caution in bank lending. He concludes that policies that make entry harder, such as strict bankruptcy laws or higher taxes on success, may lead to increased lending and higher quality entrepreneurship. In support of this contention evidence is cited from the United States where in States with generous bankruptcy laws it appears more difficult for low-income households to obtain loans (see Gropp *et al.*, 1997).

Parker (2000) takes the debate in a different direction by examining the decisions that entrepreneurs make over time—in the presence of credit constraints—regarding whether to enter and remain in entrepreneurship. He considers the fact that entrepreneurs can alter their decisions to save in order to overcome credit gaps and finance a business. Empirical evidence is presented from the United States showing that entrepreneurs do indeed have a greater incentive to save than employees. That is, the return from saving is higher for entrepreneurs. While welfare losses still occur in Parker's model as a consequence of constrained borrowing, this research casts further doubt on claims that credit gaps are a binding constraint.

relatively unattractive. In addition, mobilising investment resources is a time-consuming process. This fact, combined with regulations that restrict the share of a venture fund that can be held by any individual partner, creates incentives to raise large-volume funds (Lerner, 1999). Consequently, selecting large average investments makes sense for fund managers who need to invest large-volume resources.

Analysts have drawn a distinction between so-called primary and secondary equity gaps. The primary gap represents the smallest size of investment required by most formal venture capital firms. The secondary gap is the minimum equity investment considered by privately operated business angel networks (the term "business angel" refers to an informal private equity investor). Mason and Harrison (1997) observed primary and secondary equity gaps in the United Kingdom of around 638 000 ECU and 128 000 ECU respectively (they also observed a trend towards growth in the average size of venture capital investments). In the United States, in the early 1990s, publicly supported early-stage venture capital companies reported minimum investment thresholds of around US$1 million. In 2000 the average size of early-stage equity investments in the United Kingdom was around £1.4 million (Mason and Harrison, 2002). Across Europe the average venture capital investment in 2001 exceeded 2.2 million Euro (data provided by the European Venture Capital Association). The size of equity gaps will vary somewhat from country to country, and possibly across regions within countries, in response to a variety of institutional, regulatory and market characteristics.

Scale issues are also important for other reasons. Smaller venture capital funds account for the bulk of formal equity investment in start-ups. For the reasons described above, large funds seek large investments in management buy-outs, mergers and acquisitions and business development. But because of their size the smaller funds are limited in the degree to which they can hold diversified investment portfolios. They thus incur relatively greater risk than larger funds (in addition to the greater risk inherent to early-stage investments). Small funds can also register higher operating costs on account of a greater need for assistance in early-stage firms. And small funds may find it difficult to finance additional rounds of investment in their investees, which is most likely to be needed by the companies that succeed and grow. This inability to provide later-stage financing can undermine a small fund's ability to fully profit from its investments (Murray, 1994). Equity guarantee and enhancement schemes can help to address these problems. Such schemes are considered in Chapter 9.

Inadequate Demand Could Also Constrain Equity Investment

Demand factors can also constrain firms in adopting optimal financial structures. Among many entrepreneurs knowledge of external equity investment processes appears to be limited. At an extreme, one Canadian survey showed that a high proportion of small-firm owners did not know that equity markets exist (Feeney et al., 1999). Furthermore, venture capitalists often demand a significant equity stake in the firm as well as Board participation. But entrepreneurs frequently decline access to external equity, being averse to surrendering even a minimal degree of control over the enterprise. This is especially so in family-owned firms. Consequently, many businesses are undercapitalised. This adds to their risk, which in turn deters providers of debt. A policy implication is that programmes to expand the supply of debt might be counterproductive in some cases. A greater willingness to accept external equity would facilitate growth and survival in many small firms. Demand for external equity might be increased through tax policies and possibly education, training and information.

Furthermore, it is a frequent assertion that a lack of good projects is a prime constraint on the expansion of venture capital activity. For example, in Canada, some ninety per cent of investment applications are rejected by business angels because of quality concerns (Feeney et al., 1999). A scarcity of high-quality investment proposals has also been reported in the United Kingdom (Mason and Harrison, 2002). Policies that help to improve the quality and presentation of investment projects might expand access to equity finance (see Chapter 9).

Business Development Services

Many persons starting a company have only a vague conception as to how they will undertake the formation of the enterprise and its management. Fielden et al. (2000) found that thirty-five per cent of potential new business owners believe they would benefit from ongoing practical advice from a mentor in a related line of business.

Whether the market works well in providing advisory and information services to new and small firms is a contested subject, but market failure may be less frequent than is claimed. The Internet is augmenting information supply to small firms, and many providers of technical and managerial information have a strong interest in demonstrating products, equipment and services to potential small-firm clients. Hundreds of "how-to" books and journals are available to new entrepreneurs. In addition, manufacturers associations, chambers of commerce, universities and other bodies often provide a broad range of technical and managerial services tailored to small-firm requirements. Nevertheless, survey

work conducted by the North American Business Incubators Association has found a scarcity of private advisory services for the earliest stages of enterprise creation.

Feller (2001) notes that market failure arguments in this field take a variety of forms, but that the market failure rationale is attracting increasing reservations, at least as concerns services for manufacturing. The problem rests on alleged imperfections in the market for information, on the sides of both demand and supply, as outlined in the following paragraphs.

On the demand side, small firms are said to incur higher costs in information search and screening processes. However, a more widespread use of new information and communications technologies is likely to lower relative disadvantages for smaller companies in information search. Even so, screening costs may be high for small firms relative to their turnover. A further demand-side argument is that small and micro-enterprises do not know their real assistance needs, especially in a context of rapidly changing technologies, production methods and managerial practices. Exacerbating such a situation, small-scale entrepreneurs may limit external contacts on account of a self-help psychology (Curran and Blackburn, 1992). However, some observers would hold that over the long-term it is incumbent on entrepreneurs to be aware of the importance of continuous and autonomous skills and information acquisition. Some commentators take the above-mentioned arguments further and posit that for certain business services, and at certain times, small firms will fail to constitute a source of effective demand large enough for private supply to emerge.

On the supply side, the elevated costs of marketing services to large numbers of small enterprises—relative to expected revenues—is held to be a barrier to private sector outreach. For instance, it has been seen that some management consultancy companies have first designed and marketed major service packages—such as in technology management—for and to the large-firm market. Similar products tailored to the needs of smaller companies have been developed and marketed only later.

An argument that combines elements of demand- and supply-side constraints runs as follows: possessing a limited internal division of labour, small enterprises must contract in the skills that are scarce within the firm. However, if the volume of services demanded is small, and there is some indivisibility in their supply,[12] then markets can fail to provide the missing skills. Whether such purported market failures are constraints in practice, or whether these arguments are essentially theoretical, is underresearched. Nevertheless, there are some types of services that are unlikely to be established by private agents without public support and which can be important in promoting entrepreneurship and generating economic and social benefits. In particular, pre-start advisory and screening services for low-income or unemployed individuals need some public stimulus as, in addition to involving high transaction costs, these clients are easily discouraged by a requirement to pay. Temporary public support to expand the availability of some types of advisory service might also be justified where this aims to increase awareness (and absorptive capacity) among small firms regarding the commercial benefits of adopting particular business practices (such as ICT and its emerging applications).

As Storey (forthcoming, 2003) points out, the nature of the alleged market failure is directly relevant to the form that public intervention should take. If the assumption is that firms are unaware of the possible benefits from using external advice then the appropriate policy response should involve a onetime demonstration of these benefits. If the assumption (or evidence) is that markets systematically fail to supply the necessary services in the right amounts then a policy to rectify this situation should entail continuous measures. However, Feller (2001) observes that claims of market failure are highly generic. Their real-world significance depends on the particular—and in practice varied—structure of inter-firm relationships in given industries and regions. Inter-firm (and social) relationships often represent key sources of information and advice. So whether alleged market failures for business services necessitate a public response depends in particular cases on the extent of information supply from private and not-for-profit sources.

Finally, it needs to be borne in mind that even if market failure is confirmed, the policy response need not, and probably should not, involve direct public provision of business services. Appropriate regulation of private providers—and in some circumstances the subsidisation of their use—can have advantages. Regulation can, for instance, encourage competition among service providers. As previously noted, one argument that has been made for public intervention holds that this is justified in order to raise awareness among small firms of the benefits from using certain business services. If successful, this could increase effective demand and stimulate the private supply of services. In the framework of such an argument, the logical option would be to support the use of private service providers in the first place in order to bring about such demonstration effects.

---

[12]For example, entrepreneurs sometimes attest that engineering firms are unwilling to service frequent small job requirements.

Business Accommodation

The supply of industrial real estate is often problematic. Westall *et al.* (2000) concluded that "One of the key barriers to enterprise in disadvantaged areas is appropriate premises; that is premises that offer affordable and flexible rents". The authors note little investment in workspace for disadvantaged communities in the United Kingdom. A lack of available premises was also observed to be a key reason why micro-enterprises choose to relocate. Survey data for western Germany from the early 1990s revealed that almost ninety per cent of firms in business incubators considered that the rented space that these programmes offer had played a significant role in the development of the company (OECD, 1999c).

Supplying industrial accommodation often holds little attraction for private investors without public support. In economically distressed areas there may be difficulties in securing tenants—especially if auxiliary infrastructure is poor—and long time periods in recovering investment outlays. Moreover, opportunities for higher returns often exist in other forms of real estate. There can also be serious problems in the supply of accommodation for new and small firms in dynamic property markets. These difficulties principally relate to the superior returns available from using real estate for office space and/or housing. Such uses do not involve the high transaction costs of invoicing and collecting payments from numerous small firms, tracking rent arrears, maintaining an optimum level of occupancy, and overseeing the movement of firms in and out of the property (OECD/LEED-SOFIREM, 2000).

Furthermore, corporate property investors are often averse to the risk entailed by unknown business propositions such as enterprise start-ups. They sometimes demand a quality of covenant from prospective tenants that many new ventures cannot meet, even if these have business plans accepted by external financiers. For the private property developer an adequate covenant might require the submission of audited accounts for a number of previous years showing profits in excess of the annual rental, or one year of rent paid in advance on a rolling basis.

Training

For a variety of reasons small firms may express insufficient demand for training. The opportunity cost of time spent away from the firm can be especially high in a small venture—even though the potential benefits from training are considerable in firms with a minimal internal division of labour. Training can be expensive, while small firms face high levels of uncertainty in their investment decisions, including investments in training (Kitching and Blackburn, 2002). Firms may be particularly concerned about their inability to appropriate the benefits of investments in training. This apprehension is likely to be acute in the smallest firms, which are generally unable to match the compensation packages offered by larger companies and which experience relatively high rates of turnover among managerial staff. Indeed, the share of managers that undertakes formal external training is a positive function of firm size (OECD, 2000a). Entrepreneurs in some small firms may also be unaware of what types of training have greatest potential impact on business performance.

On the supply side of the training market, the training provided may be inappropriate to the specific needs of the smallest category of firms. In part this is because providers of training face high costs in tailoring programmes to the diverse needs of many small firms. Supplying generic forms of training entails lower costs for trainers.

Concluding Remarks on Rationales for Policy

The strongest grounds for policy intervention appear to be the correction of failures in a number of markets on which entrepreneurs depend. Policy justifications premised on employment effects appear weak. This is because there is only a limited population over which enterprise support is a cost-effective alternative to unemployment insurance, while employment creation from the birth of new firms tends to be small over the short-run. At present, there is insufficient empirical evidence to base policy solely on regeneration and other externalities from enterprise births. Nevertheless, the local economic impact of enterprise creation is likely to be multi-faceted and possibly significant (and certainly merits further investigation, as described in Chapter 11). Where discrimination exists against minorities, women, the disabled or other groups, corrective and preventive policies are essential (indeed, preventive policies might be justified at all times).

Market failure justifies public action if failure is confirmed, and if policy is likely to produce a situation superior to the "do nothing" option. However, the identification of market imperfections does not imply that the public response should be a direct one. For example, commentators have noted that techniques used by banks to assess creditworthiness can operate to the disadvantage of poorer individuals—regardless of inherent creditworthiness. So, for some banks, making regular mortgage repayments is more likely to be taken as an indicator of good credit standing than is a history of regular rental payments. And making regular loan repayments appears to be considered as better evidence of creditworthiness than consistent payments into a savings account (Metcalf *et al.*, 2000). An appropriate response for public authorities wishing to change banking practice might be indirect, working with the banking industry, exercising moral suasion and encouraging the examination of alternative criteria in credit assessment. Part II of this book addresses possible policy responses to key issues of market failure discussed in this chapter.

Bibliography

Astebro, T. and I. Bernhardt (1999), *Bank loans as predictors of small-business start-up survival*, paper presented at the Conference "Funding Gap Controversies", 12–13 April 1999, Warwick University.

Audretsch, D.B. and J. Elston (1999), *Do funding gaps exist in Germany?*, paper presented at the Conference "Funding Gap Controversies", 12–13 April 1999, Warwick University.

Barlow, D. and M. Robson (1999), *Have unincorporated businesses in the UK been constrained in their ability to obtain bank lending?*, paper presented at the Conference "Funding Gap Controversies", 12–13 April 1999, Warwick University.

Berger, A.N. and G.F. Udell (1992), *Some Evidence on the Empirical Significance of Credit Rationing*, Journal of Political Economy, Vol. 100, No. 5, pp. 1047–1077.

Blanchflower, D.G., P.B. Levine, and D. Zimmerman (1998), *Discrimination in the Small Business Credit Market* paper presented at the OECD/CERF/CILN Conference on Self-Employment, September 1998.

Blanchflower, D.G. and A.J. Oswald (1998), *What Makes an Entrepreneur?*, Journal of Labour Economics, Vol. 16, No. 1.

Calcagnini, G., D. Iacobucci, and D. Ticchi (1999), *Are small firms more likely to be credit-rationed than larger firms?*, paper presented at the Conference "Funding Gap Controversies", 12–13 April 1999, Warwick University.

Carpenter, R.E. and B.C. Petersen (1999), *Is the growth of small firms constrained by internal finance?*, paper presented at the Conference "Funding Gap Controversies", 12–13 April 1999, Warwick University.

Cosh, A. and A. Hughes (1994), *Size, financial structure and profitability: UK companies in the 1980s*, in Finance and the Small Firm, edited by Hughes, A., and D.J. Storey, Routledge, 1994.

Cowling, M. and R. Hayward (2000), *Out of Unemployment*, Research Centre for Industrial Strategy, United Kingdom.

Cowling, M. (1998), *Regional Determinants of Small Firm Loans Under the UK Loan Guarantee Scheme*, Small Business Economics, 11: pp. 155–167, 1998.

Cressy, R. and C. Olofsson (1997), *European SME Financing: An Overview*, Small Business Economics, Vol. 9, No. 2, April 1997, pp. 87–96.

Cressy, R. and O. Toivanen (1999), *Is there adverse selection in the credit market?*, paper presented at the Conference "Funding Gap Controversies", 12–13 April 1999, Warwick University.

Curran, J. and R. Blackburn (1992), *Local Economies and small firms: a view from the ground*, paper presented at the 15th National Small Firms Policy and Research Conference, Southampton, cited in Westall et al. (2000).

DeMeza, D. (1999), *Overlending*, paper presented at the Conference "Funding Gap Controversies", 12–13 April 1999, Warwick University.

DeMeza, D. and D. Webb (1987), *Too much investment: a problem of asymmetric information*, Quarterly Journal of Economics, 102, 281–292.

Egeln, J., G. Licht, and F. Steil (1997), *Firm Foundations and the Role of Financial Constraints*, Small Business Economics, Vol. 9, No. 2, April 1997, pp. 137–150.

Feeney, L.S., G. Haines Jr., and A.L. Riding (1999), *SME owners' awareness and acceptance of equity capital: implications for lenders*, paper presented at the Conference "Funding Gap Controversies", 12–13 April 1999, Warwick University.

Feller, I. (2001), *Program Theory, Evaluation Design, and Operational Modalities for Industrial Extension*, paper prepared for the DATAR/OECD World Congress on Local Productive Systems, January 2001, Paris.

Fielden, L.S., M.J. Davidson, and P.J. Makin (2000), *Barriers encountered during micro and small business start-up in North-West England*, Journal of Small Business and Enterprise Development, Vol. 7, No. 4.

Foley, P. (1992), *Local Economic Policy and Job Creation: A Review of Evaluation Studies*, Urban Studies, Vol. 29, Nos 3 and 4, pp. 557–598.

Glackin, C.E. (2002), *What Does it Take to Borrow?*, Journal of Microfinance, Vol. 4, No. 1, Spring: pp. 115–135.

Gropp, R., J. Scholz, and M. White (1997), *Personal bankruptcy and credit supply and demand*, Quarterly Journal of Economics, CX11(1), pp. 217–51.

Hughes, A. (1997), *Finance for SMEs: A UK Perspective*, Small Business Economics, Vol. 9, No. 2, April 1997, pp. 151–166.

Kaplan, S.N. and L. Zingales (1997), *Do Investment-Cash Flow Sensitivities Provide Useful Measures of Financing Constraints?*, Quarterly Journal of Economics, Vol. CXII, Issue 1 (February), pp. 169–216.

Kaplan, S.N. and L. Zingales (2000), *Investment-Cash Flow Sensitivities Are Not Valid Measures of Financing Constraints?*, Quarterly Journal of Economics, May, pp. 707–712.

Kitching J., and R. Blackburn (2002), *The Nature of Training and Motivation to Train in Small Firms*, Department for

Education and Skills, Research Brief No. RB330, March 2002.

Lerner, J. (1999), *"Public Venture Capital": Rationales and Evaluation*, paper presented at the Conference "Funding Gap Controversies", 12–13 April 1999, Warwick University.

Mason, C.M. and R.T. Harrison (2002), *Closing the Regional Equity Gap? A critique of the Department of Trade and Industry's Regional Venture Capital Funds Initiative*, Hunter Centre for Entrepreneurship, University of Strathclyde, Glasgow (*E-mail: colin.mason@strath.ac.uk*).

Mason, C.M. and R.T. Harrison (1997), *Business Angel Networks and the Development of the Informal Venture Capital Market in the UK: Is There Still a Role for the Public Sector?*, Small Business Economics, Vol. 9, No. 2, April 1997, pp. 111–123.

Metcalf, H., T.V. Crowley, T. Anderson, and C. Bainton (2000), *From Unemployment to Self-Employment: The Role of Micro-Finance*, International Labour Office, London.

Murray, G. (1994), *The second "equity gap": exit problems for seed and early stage venture capitalists and their investee companies*, Internationl Small Business Journal, 12 (4), 59–76.

OECD/LEED-SOFIREM (2000), *Good Practice in Business Incubation*, Local Economic and Employment Development (LEED) Programme, Notebook No. 28.

OECD (2000a), *Management Training in SMEs: Draft Synthesis Report*, DSTI/IND/PME (2000) 5.

OECD (1999c), *Business Incubation: International Case Studies*, OECD, Paris.

Parker, S. (2000), *Saving to Overcome Borrowing Constraints: Implications for Small Business Entry and Exit*, Small Business Economics 15: pp. 223–232.

Stiglitz, J.E. and A. Weiss (1981), *Credit Rationing in Markets with Imperfect Information*, American Economic Review, Vol. 71, No. 3, June.

Storey, D.J. (forthcoming, 2003), *Entrepreneurship, Small and Medium-Sized Enterprises and Public Policies*, in Acs, Z.J. and D.B. Audretsch, "Handbook of Entrepreneurship Research: An Interdisciplinary Survey and Introduction".

Taylor, M. (1998), *Self-Employment and Windfall Gains in Britain: Evidence from Panel Data*, paper presented at the OECD/CERF/CILN International Conference on Self-Employment, Burlington, Ontario, Canada, September 1998.

Westall, A., P. Ramsden, and J. Foley (2000), *Micro-Entrepreneurs: Creating Enterprising Communities*, Institute of Public Policy Research and New Economics Foundation.

Williamson, O. (1985), *The Economic Institutions of Capitalism*, (New York: The Free Press).

Research Mimicking Policy: Entrepreneurship/Small Business Policy Research in the United States

by William Dennis, Jr.

An assessment of entrepreneurship/ small business (E/SB) policy research in the United States must begin with an extraordinary irony: the current elevated status of and interest in E/SB can be traced to a single piece of research, the *Job Generation Process* (Birch 1979). This report's most influential finding—that new and small businesses generate a vastly disproportionate share of the net new jobs—now laces policy debate and repeatedly emerges in the popular media. Yet, policy research that directly considers a growth (entrepreneurship) or a size (small business) variable appears infrequently in the policy, economics, public finance and management literatures and, outside of Birch's job generation thesis, rarely surfaces in policy debate.

The most obvious consequence of this information shortage is that policy-making is less informed about entrepreneurial and small businesses than it would otherwise be. But a strong case can be made that small business and entrepreneurship have neither suffered from it (on a relative, rather than an optimal, basis) nor is fundamental policy toward them unsound. The supporting evidence lies in the result. American E/SBs seem to be doing as well as E/SBs almost anywhere in the world and have

for the past several years. Moreover, if share of employment and GDP are appropriate measures, entrepreneurial and small business are, at worst, competing evenly with their larger counterparts. Direct research may not exist to explain the success, but the United States is doing something right (OECD 1997).

The thesis of this chapter is that E/SB policy research in the United States mimics American policy. Research reacts rather than leads. The limited amount of E/SB policy research contributes little to the direct formulation of policy impacting them. Further, to date it contributes little to our understanding of the externalities associated with entrepreneurship and small business. Policy-makers are left to make decisions affecting these businesses from theory and research on competition and specific issues, experientially based frames-of-reference and raw political calculation.

The term "policy research" as used in this chapter refers to the analysis of primary material without prejudice to the methodology(ies) employed. The purpose of the definition is to clearly separate research from the plethora of papers, backgrounders, analyses, testimonies and argument that in legislative centers frequently carries the term

Originally appeared in *A Handbook of Entrepreneurship*, edited by D. Sexton and H. Landstrom, published by Blackwell Publishing, 2000.

"research." Many of the latter are thoughtful pieces, carefully constructed from secondary materials. Others are little more than hastily drafted propaganda lacking any semblance of intellectual detachment or merit. Thus, to make a meaningful and objective division, I have drawn a definitional line between primary and secondary research.

The remainder of this chapter is organized as follows: the second section provides a brief overview of E/SB policy in the United States and its association with E/SB policy research. The third outlines the state of E/SB policy research in the United States and discusses its six principal characteristics. The fourth section provides an extended example of the interface between policy and policy research to illustrate the six characteristics. The final section offers observations from the American experience that may help Americans and non-Americans alike to understand the direction E/SB policy research needs to take.

No Policy as Policy

The United States has no small business or entrepreneurship policy. Instead, it has a competition policy in which small business and entrepreneurship play an important role (Aoyama and Tietz 1996; Dennis 1998). The essential characteristic of that policy is to maintain government neutrality among competitors, regardless of size. Activities and programs do exist to reduce size advantages. However, they are not intended to offset economies of scale derived from markets so much as to offset economies of scale resulting from government demands (interventions). Small business policy is also increasingly mixed with a social policy designed to attain greater equity among social groups (Aoyama and Tietz 1996). Despite such departures from the "neutrality among competitors" model, the focus of E/SB policy in the United States is clear if not always consistent.

Revealing is the declaration of policy found in the first sentences of the Small Business Act of 1953, the law establishing the US Small Business Administration and the closest thing the United States has to a framework for policy governing American entrepreneurial and small business. The exposition of "small business policy" in the United States, begins:

> The essence of the American economic system of private enterprise is free competition. Only through full and free competition can free markets, free entry into business, and opportunities for the expression and growth of personal initiative and individual judgment be assured. The preservation and expansion of such competition is basic not only to the economic well-being but to the security of this Nation. Such security and well-being cannot be realized unless the actual and potential capacity of small business is encouraged and developed (15 USC §631(a)).

Small business is not mentioned in its own policy outline until the eightieth word. Three references to competition precede it. Even security is a forerunner. Competition, and implicitly the consumer, is the overriding concern of the law, not entrepreneurial or small business per se.

The logical extension of the competition policy is that no special treatment should be extended to any competitor or any group of competitors. From this framework, programs favoring (subsidizing) one competitor over another regardless of size, financial condition or other factors are irrational. Public intervention to assist competitors can only be justified when markets are distorted and not functioning efficiently. Manifestation of the competition policy has increasingly centered on entry and de-emphasized control of questionable competitive practices.[1] Visible results included deregulation of the trucking, airlines, telecommunications and financial services industries as well as frequent removal of local impediments to home-based businesses—all to reduce or eliminate entry barriers. At the same time, enforcement of competition regulating measures such as Robinson-Patman has all but disappeared.

Subtle Changes in Policy Direction

A subtle change in the dominant policy began to occur in the late 1970s and early 1980s. Birch's (1979) *The Job Generation Process* empirically demonstrated that entrepreneurial and small business do more than simply enhance competition. They are also uniquely involved in the employment process and local economic development. The perspective on entrepreneurial and small firms shifted as a result. The altered view offered intellectual justification for exploring a wider range of policy impacts on E/SBs and gave policymakers a rationale to intervene in their support.

Meanwhile, research associated with the SBA Office of Advocacy demonstrated that government is an important source of market distortion for E/SBs. Government-imposed burdens disproportionately impact (adversely) smaller firms, thereby artificially upsetting the competitive balance among large and small (Cole and Tegeler 1980; Berney 1981; Faucett et al. 1984; Gaston and

Carroll 1984; Arthur Andersen 1979). Government-created advantages and disadvantages are not legitimate, while market created advantages and disadvantages are. The result is an equity argument for small business exemptions, exclusions, phase-ins, alternative sets of rules and so forth for various government burdens. (Another American characteristic is that the grievance should typically be redressed through elimination or minimization of the burden, rather than the offer of a compensating initiative.) These arguments become critical because as economic regulation has declined dramatically since the late 1970s, the increase in social regulation has more than offset it.

The small business lobby began its ascent a few years earlier. It brought demands to the political system, and new influence to the ballot box. Increasingly, the lobby forced policymakers to ask, How does this affect small business?[2] Policymakers posed the question not so much for analytic, as for political purposes. Yet, once this simple question became a common inquiry, a new demand was created for E/SB policy research.

In 1976, the small business lobby pushed through creation of the Office of Advocacy at SBA, not to run programs, but to provide E/SB policy research and to serve as an in-house advocate. On the philosophic premise that government regulations are an artifice that disadvantages small business's competitive position, the small business lobby also led the successful effort to pass the Regulatory Flexibility Act (Reg Flex) in 1980. The law requires federal agencies to produce small business impact state-

---

[1] I am grateful to Jim Morrison for drawing my attention to this point.

[2] *Fortune* magazine recently used a poll of White House staff, Congressmen, Congressional staff, and Washington insiders to produce a ranking of the most powerful lobbies in the nation's capital (Birnbaum 1997). The small business lobby, i.e., the National Federation of Independent Business, ranked fourth. It trailed only the AARP (seniors), American-Israel Public Affairs Committee and the AFL-CIO (organized labor confederation).

ments on any significant rule-making and to provide a different, presumably less burdensome, set of regulations for smaller firms when appropriate. The implication of this legal requirement is that agencies must conduct research to determine small business impacts. Though the agencies have treated this mandate as a pariah, requiring the stronger Small Business Regulatory Enforcement Fairness Act (SBREFA) of 1997, Reg Flex laid the ground for creation of an extensive body of small business policy-oriented research. Finally, the Small Business Economic Policy Act of 1980 required the President to provide the Congress an annual report on the state of small business and *competition*. The Act's declaration of policy incorporates the shift to more direct support of E/SBs, but its most visible result is the annual State of Small Business report.

Policy Today

Competition policy still reigns. However, political strength, the externality of job generation and the concept of disproportionate impacts, altered the policy landscape. Small business can now expect to receive a reasonable share of any tax reduction and "carve-outs" from major legislation are increasingly a fact of life.[3] Barbieri (1998) identified over twenty examples of carve-outs at the federal and state levels including paperwork in the Occupational Health and Safety Act (OSHA), exemption from the Family and Medical Leave Act and allowance of the smallest businesses to opt out of the Federal Electronic Payments System. These carve-outs can play a pivotal role in the larger debate, as the process of amending "Superfund" illustrates. Environmentalists want to remove small business from parts of the legisla-

tion in fear that without relief for these firms, the toxic clean-up program will be lost in its current form. Big businesses want to keep them in because that is the only way the program will be radically changed.

The Clinton Administration would alter the policy focus further. It is intent on moving from the competition model. It would de-emphasize the existing competition policy and focus on social programs, e.g., micro loans, and providing growing business with affirmative assistance (an industrial policy), e.g., the extension service for manufacturers in the National Institute of Standards and Technology. The Congress has resisted, particularly with regard to the latter. Thus, the 1990s has brought little practical change in policy direction.

Interest in small business impacts continues to grow. The demand for E/SB research increases as a result. Quantitative estimates of impacts are particularly desired. But not even the Department of the Treasury appears capable of or willing to produce relevant E/SB estimates. NFIB in the late-1970s and SBA in the mid-1980s attempted to construct E/SB models. The attempts were not successful, but they identified a need. A prominent tax economist restated the issue arguing for

> a robust model of the formation of small businesses and their contribution to the economy. Only through the development and empirical testing of such a model will it be possible to identify any beneficial externalities arising from the formation and growth of small business, and to isolate the parameters that are both crucial to these processes and amenable

---

[3]Opposition to the concept, sometimes referred to as regulatory subsides, is also rising. See, Pierce (1998) as an example.

to policy influence. (Holtz-Eakin 1995: 393)[4]

The State of E/SB Policy Research

E/SB policy research is a rational extension of the competition policy. If policy does not consider the size or growth variable, why bother to research it? If there is no research on these firms, why is there a need for data containing a size or growth variable? And, why is there a need for financial support to pay for the research? If E/SBs thrive in a competitive atmosphere, what more is needed? It is not coincidental that E/SB policy research to date centers on entry, the centerpiece of a competition policy.

The state of E/SB policy research in the United States can be summarized in the following six propositions:

(1) The volume of E/SB policy research is small and inadequate to address the most basic questions.

(2) Policy research in the United States has an issue-specific, not group-based, focus, except for women and minorities.

(3) The people who produce policy research on issues affecting small business and their publication outlets are not often associated with academic business schools.

(4) Funding for E/SB policy research is minimal and on a project-by-project basis.

(5) A prime reason for the lack of policy-oriented research is a lack of data.

(6 If a policy cycle begins with issue development, proceeds to the legislative process and ends with policy evaluation, most E/SB policy research currently addresses issues in the middle or latter stages.

Now let's examine each proposition in greater detail.

The Volume of E/SB Policy Research Is Small and Inadequate to Address the Most Basic Questions

Policy decisions affecting these firms are usually made without the benefit of research findings. While there is reason to believe this condition is changing for the better, the lack of research, enabling the development, analysis and evaluation of policy initiatives, "dumbs down" the public policymaking process.

Many, including the author, have lamented the general lack of policy research with an E/SB focus or at least incorporating E/SB impacts. Brockhaus (1987) attempted to add rigor to the consensus opinion when he compared the topics that delegates to the 1986 White House Conference on Small Business voted of greatest concern to the topics addressed in three academic journals and three E/SB proceedings. He found the two groups of topics were almost totally divorced. Owners found policy issues highly relevant; the academic community did not. Hoy (1997) effectively updated the Brockhaus investigation using policy priorities from 1995 White House Conference as a baseline and found virtually the same thing.

Banks and Taylor (1991) addressed the issue differently. They surveyed samples of E/SB owners and academics to determine perceptions of the most pressing business issues. Four of the top ten issues cited by E/SB owners in the Banks and Taylor survey were policy matters including "regulations and paperwork," which topped the list. Regulations and paperwork did not even make the academic top ten nor did any other policy issue.

These authors selected a narrow range of issues and publication outlets. Expand

---

[4]I am grateful to the NFIB Education Foundation for permission to include this quotation.

the ranges and the outlook is not as bleak. Make program evaluation the topic. Chrisman and McMullen (1996), Wood (1994),[5] Moini (1998) and Masten et al. (1995) published traditional program evaluations. Brewer and Genay (1995) explored a potential program modification in recent issues of the *Journal of Small Business Management (JSBM)* as examples. While one can argue with their use of small samples and the sophistication of the analyses, these are truly instances of E/SB policy research published in a small business journal.

Moreover, the contributions found in the *JSBM* represent a small portion of the program evaluation literature. Researchers at ABT Associates authored a three-volume series analyzing experiments in Massachusetts and Washington designed to use the unemployment compensation system to help unemployed people become self-employed (ABT 1992, 1994, 1995). Cadwell (1997) recently provided an evaluation of state export promotion programs for the US Small Business Administration (SBA). Lerner (1996) examined the value of the Small Business Innovation Research (SBIR) program for the National Bureau of Economic Research. The General Accounting Office evaluated problems in SBA's 8(a) program for the United States Congress (GAO 1995). In fact GAO produces eight to ten such reports and testimonies every year on topics ranging from estimates of credit subsidies (GAO 1997) to administration of employment taxes (GAO 1996). The foregoing constitute a few selected examples of program (or possible program) evaluations produced outside E/SB-specific journals.

Beyond evaluation, the Office of Advocacy in the SBA has supported about 750 separate pieces of policy-oriented research over the past two plus decades (Phillips 1998). Since 1982, it has also produced the annual State of Small Business report, which though not directly policy research, provides notable statistical background and descriptive material. No other source can claim an equivalent output. Omitting program evaluation, it is likely that all sources combined do not match Advocacy's production. The largest general E/SB research program run in the private sector belongs to the NFIB Education Foundation and it produces or sponsors an average of six or seven pieces in a typical year as well as a monthly economic report. The smaller, RISE business, a private, unaffiliated small business research foundation has begun to produce a limited number of published monographs.

Research volume is only half of the equation. The breadth and variety of issues, issue areas, programs and initiatives that impact E/SBs makes the existing volume of policy research inadequate for the need. This inadequacy means that participants in the legislative process often cannot respond to reasonable inquiries from policymakers seeking information on relevant questions. For example: the Chairwoman of a House Ways and Means subcommittee asked witnesses representing small business owners to respond in writing to several technical questions that arose from testimony presented in support of a proposal allowing the self-employed to deduct health insurance premiums from their federal income tax (Johnson 1998). The witnesses argued their case primarily on the grounds of equity, i.e., since corporate businesses are allowed the deduction, noncorporate businesses should be allowed the deduction as well. But the Chairwoman was interested in impact,

---

[5]Technically, the exchange does not fit the working definition of research. However serious debate on the proper methodology to evaluate a program appears to be a qualifying exception.

particularly the deduction's impact on the number of people with insurance coverage. Witnesses could answer perhaps one-quarter of her questions without new research, much of it complicated and requiring data collection. In this instance, the legislative process moved forward without the information.

If unsatisfied demand from policymakers is the measure of need, there truly is a shortage of E/SB policy research. But what of research on externalities, i.e., the impacts of E/SBs? Externalities, too, is an area ripe with interesting and influential research questions. This field is particularly appropriate for academics who are squeamish about conducting research directly on policy issues. After all, *The Job Generation Process* (Birch 1979) was a study of E/SB externalities, and the work's influence has been immeasurable.

Business formation is the single area where substantial externality research can be found. The Babson Entrepreneurship Research Conference, despite its changing focus, still constitutes a significant effort to understand the creation and growth of business enterprise. The same is true of the Entrepreneurial Research Consortium and work such as the Wells Fargo/NFIB Starts and Stops series (Dennis 1997).

A number of critical areas badly need exploration. Small business advocates boast of the people employed. But how do small business owners select their employees and how do they train them? And what is the value of that training? Schiller (1981) demonstrated that small employers provide more training to employees on their first jobs than do larger firms. Subsequent studies on the training issue can be cited, but not a number commensurate with the topic's importance. Critics like Bellman and Groshen (1998) prefer to discuss the wages and benefits in small and emerging businesses. Though E/SBs do not come off as well on this count as on

others, the subject can't be ignored. And then there are topics like innovation. The strong research base begun in early 1980s has eroded. The same appears true of regulation—and community. Why have so few examined the E/SB contribution to community? In fact, E/SB externalities beg for investigation.

Policy Research in the United States Has an Issue-Specific, Not a Group-Based, Focus Except for Women and Minorities

The impacts of policy on entrepreneurial and small business, and vice versa, are customarily subordinate to the larger issue. The problem created by this approach for E/SB policy research is that resources (money and talent) and interest are consumed investigating the broader questions. Little is left to examine impacts on E/SBs.

The primary question posed in most policy debates is the overall impact of a proposal on overreaching issue areas, e.g., the budget, employment and inflation. The interests or wishes of specific groups, including entrepreneurial and small business, are measured against larger needs. This approach demonstrates the American preoccupation with business environment and the rules of the game: Get the fundamentals right and "good things" will happen to individuals and groups. The most powerful opponent of various small business efforts to obtain tax incentives, equity, simplification or just plain reductions, therefore, becomes "revenue neutrality," i.e., maintaining a balance between revenues and expenditures. The first research consideration in a tax bill is its budgetary impact. Analysis of the primary macro impacts— economic growth, employment and inflation—follow. Small business impacts (other than political, which are increasingly common) are calculated only as a residual from the analyses of provisions that exclusively or largely affect small or growing businesses.

A Request for Proposal (RFP) from the National Institute of Disability Rehabilitation Research (NIDRR 1998) illustrates the theme. NIDRR's RFP lists one of its five research priorities as identifying and evaluating effective workplace supports to improve the employment outcomes of disabled persons. The tasks include evaluating the effectiveness of tax credits and Medicare "buydowns," examining employer perspectives, along with other research pieces. There are two points to note: the issue focuses on disabled people and implicitly views small business as one of many potential means to assist them. Second, the agency sponsoring the research is the agency of the disabled, not the agency of small business.

The body of policy research on issues affecting small business can be substantial, while the body of E/SB policy research on the same issue is negligible. The minimum wage presents an excellent example. The literature on the issue is extensive. Most appears in economics publications. It includes assessments of employment impacts (e.g., Welch et al. 1995), impacts on the poor and poverty (e.g., Neumark and Wascher 1997) and impacts on training received by employees (e.g., Hashimoto 1982). Yet, the literature and policy debate revolve around larger issues, i.e., employment, prices, poverty and the impact on employee groups, such as minority teenagers. The impacts on small businesses are largely ignored, though it is clear that retailers and owners of business in rural areas feel vastly more impacted than others (Dennis 1996). The concerns of these owners apparently are inadequate to stimulate research interest.

The focus on issue-specific E/SB policy research puts an implicit premium on issue-based knowledge, such as, taxes, in contrast to group-based knowledge, e.g., small business. (The discussion of research funding later in this chapter steers the reader in the same direction.) This priority means that the

bibliographic search must focus on the topic including associated publication outlets rather than on E/SBs and its research publication outlets. The priority also means that at least on one level, academics in the business school operate at a disadvantage compared with those in the traditional disciplines and participants in the policy process. That observation leads to the third point.

The People Who Produce Policy Research on Issues Affecting Small Business and Their Publication Outlets Are Not Often Associated with Academic Business Schools

As many or more can be found in the traditional disciplines, notably economics, and the publication outlets in those fields. E/SB policy researchers are also as likely to be nonacademic, i.e., from government or the private sector, as academic. Research conducted by the former usually does not appear in the journals, but in government, association or private business reports.

Brockhaus (1987), Hoy (1997) and Banks and Taylor (1991) are all relevant in this context. The first two investigated the E/SB policy research published in E/SB-oriented journals and proceedings. The latter two examined attitudes of researchers in business schools. The researchers' results were largely negative. But even by expanding the scope of issues and publications examined, E/SB policy research from those it is assumed would be most productive and interested in these questions, i.e., the business schools, is minimal.

Later in this chapter the author provides a detailed example of a contentious policy issue and the E/SB research involved. Not one pertinent study in this example was produced by an individual associated with a business school. The useful studies were produced by people in schools of health policy, public health, economics and public finance (or outside academe). In fact, there have been more

National Bureau of Economic Research (NBER) working papers published on entrepreneurship, small business and self-employment policy since 1996 than appeared during that same time period in articles in *Journal of Small Business Management (JSBM)*, *Entrepreneurship Theory and Practice (ETP)* and *Journal of Business Venturing (JBV)* combined.

The pertinent product from government, including SBA, is vastly greater in quantity than from business schools.[6] Most of the federal reports are lodged in the National Technical Information Service's archives. Unfortunately, studies and reports from the states, economic development organizations, and private groups have no similar central depository, restricting their accessibility for research and policy purposes.

The implications of the business school's divorce from E/SB policy research are a smaller research volume, one less informed about micro questions and a surrender of the policy agenda. Most critically, the business perspective is suborned to other interests. We will examine later the lack of policy research in the developmental stage, a place where the business school might play a key role.

Funding for E/SB Policy Research Is Minimal and on a Project-by-Project Basis

The resources available for E/SB policy research are scattered. Disbursement is usually ad hoc and tied to a specific issue rather than an ongoing program. Government resources for this type of work are often found in project or program evaluation.

The primary exception has been SBA's Office of Advocacy, which has main-tained a continuing research program since its inception in the late 1970s. Funding has ranged from a high of $4.5 million in the early 1980s to a low of $500,000. Resources of the office became so limited that it was forced to terminate its competitive research grant program (recently reinstated). However, this program has been the one consistent source of support for E/SB policy research. Other federal agencies, such as the Economic Development Administration (EDA) and the Minority Business Development Administration (MBDA), both in the Department of Commerce, have records of supporting E/SB research with policy implications. (Birch produced *The Job Generation Process* under a grant from EDA.) Still other agencies conduct research in-house and publish it in agency journals, e.g., *Statistics of Income Bulletin* (IRS) and the *Monthly Labor Review* (Bureau of Labor Statistics). But Advocacy has been the public sector's principal supporter of E/SB research, despite hard times.

Private foundations in the United States also finance considerable amounts of policy research. A review of contributors to Washington's think-tank community, e.g., American Enterprise Institute, Brookings Institution, CATO, Heritage Foundation, Urban Institute, makes that clear. However, the foundations that fund policy research generally do not include small business specific projects (or at least generally have not), and the largest grant-making foundations focusing on ESBs are not in the policy research business. The Coleman, Kauffman, Lowe and Price foundations do not include E/SB policy research among their funding priorities.[7]

---

[6]Some double counting occurs because of the way Advocacy issues research contracts. Advocacy prefers to award its contracts to private businesses. As a result, grantees may appear under the name of their consulting firm rather than their academic institution.

[7]The Kauffman Foundation appears increasingly interested in policy matters but has yet to show interest in an ongoing policy research program.

An exception is the Robert Wood Johnson Foundation's (RWJF) ongoing interest in small business and health.[8] RWJF, one of the nation's largest, may have spent more money on small business policy research than any organization in the country excluding the SBA. Its sponsorships include demonstration projects (with accompanying research) among small employers not providing employee health insurance (e.g., Helms et al. 1992; McLaughlin and Zellers 1992) as well as policy evaluations in its State Initiatives in Health Care Reform program (e.g., Cantor et al. 1995; Acs et al. 1996; Long and Marquis 1996). But RWJF's concern is health, not small business. The motive supporting such research is locating means by which small business can provide more employee health insurance. Other foundations provide smaller amounts on occasion to support E/SB policy-oriented research. The Institute for Justice (1996, 1997), for example, employed a consortium of foundations to sponsor the research and publication of its series on government barriers to entry-level entrepreneurial opportunity in seven cities.

Private businesses and business organizations also support E/SB policy research, often as an adjunct to their marketing activities. The Employee Benefit Research Institute (EBRI), a nonprofit research organization in Washington, for example, marshaled a consortium of thirty-three private businesses and nonprofit groups, many in the financial services industry, to sponsor the 1998 Retirement Confidence Survey. One of the project's three modules focused on small business.

A researcher who intends to pursue an E/SB policy-oriented project has no logical or obvious funding source. This is more true today than previously because of the decline in SBA support.

Success can be achieved in the public or private sector, in a nonprofit or for-profit organization, but the sponsor will likely dictate the topic, with small business only an ancillary consideration. Different projects probably will require different sponsors. Most support has been relatively modest, though projects such as RWJF's demonstrations (and evaluations) and the Department of Labor's on transforming unemployed people to self-employed people, can involve significant dollars.

A Prime Reason for the Dearth of Policy-Oriented Research Is a Lack of Data

While this difficulty is not unique to E/SB policy research, the lack of timely, detailed, enterprise-specific numbers remains a significant research liability. This does not suggest that the available data have been exhausted. IRS's public use (research) file, for example, has not been explored to any notable extent for E/SB policy questions. The new Longitudinal Enterprise and Establishment Microdata (LEEM) file allows examination of growth questions that other countries have been able to do for years. However, data limitations cause the research questions posed to be more restricted than they would otherwise be.

The United States has a relatively poor statistical system if one is interested in the business size variable (Phillips and Dennis 1997). It has virtually no system for the growth variable. Enough reasonable assumptions and manipulations can be made so that available data will allow the modeling of economic impacts of significant issues (e.g., CONSAD 1994, 1998). However, that type of policy research requires considerable up-front investment and is not applicable for all relevant questions. Moreover, as the budgets of statistical agencies tighten and resistance to questionnaires from

---

[8]The Henry J. Kaiser Family Foundation has a similar interest.

business owners stiffen, the capacity of government statistical agencies to provide more and better data diminishes.

Private-sector databases, e.g., Dun & Bradstreet's New Incorporations and Business Failures series, Wells Fargo/NFIB's Business Stops and Starts and NFIB's Small Business Economic Trends, supplement public data sources to a modest degree. They will probably do so more in the future (Phillips and Dennis 1997). However, private institutions cannot and arguably should not replace the Federal government's role in data collection and dissemination.

E/SB researchers as a group rely on ad hoc surveys to collect much of their data. Aldrich and Baker (1997) calculated that surveys were used to conduct entrepreneurship research published in selected outlets during the 1990s about five times as often as were public databases. There is no reason to believe a similar ratio does not hold for E/SB policy research (except tax-related questions). This massive use of surveys carries its own liabilities. Among the more notable are:

- inconsistency of sample, definition, and inquiry across surveys,
- poor survey construction in too many instances; inadequate response rates,
- public inaccessibility (often), and
- lack of context on all but the immediate question.

E/SB policy research will never reach complete legitimacy without the development of better and more plentiful data sets.[9] These sets unfortunately can take years to create and are costly. Despite a proposal for significant revision of the American statistical system from then-Council of Economic Advisors Chairman, Michael Boskin, no major change in the nation's data collection system appears imminent. Still, those conducting E/SB policy research would do well to invest more time and energy in locating better data sets before resorting to their own surveys.

If a policy cycle begins with issue development, proceeds to the legislative process and ends with policy evaluation, most E/SB policy research currently addresses issues in the middle or latter stages.[10] The dominant reason is that those interested in entrepreneurial and small firms are more likely to defend the status quo, i.e., the competition policy, than they are to initiate change (even through repeal). There are related considerations—cost and the ability to raise funds for a future shared benefit rather than a "present danger," the lack of planning and lead time, comfort with the traditional arguments based on equity, appeals for sympathy as an underdog and, implicitly, political strength. By default, the demand for E/SB policy research at the early stages of the policy cycle is limited. When advocates and other sponsors do press the initiative, they usually draw on available material. An example is Stuart Butler's (1981) *Enterprise Zones: Greenlining the Inner City*, which argues for enterprise zones, an innovative proposal in which entrepreneurs and their businesses are envisioned as central actors in inner-city revitalization. The book was well-

---

[9]This includes restructuring current sets, e.g., the inclusion of small, closely held C corporations in the Bureau of the Census's *Characteristics of Business Owners* set.

[10]A considerable amount of research produced by SBA involves externalities and is, therefore, insensitive to a policy cycle. Hopkins (1995), for example, attempted to quantify the cost of federal regulation to small business. These data can be used in a variety of legislative and nonlegislative contexts, not exclusively for a particular proposal(s).

documented, well-written and well-argued. It also drew exclusively on secondary materials.

There are limited instances when research plays a role in the earlier stages. Many appear related to tax policy where revenue estimates have been calculated for years. One example involves estate and gift taxes where proponents of their elimination provided notable developmental research. Wagner (1993) and Beach (1996), among others, conducted econometric studies to quantify economic benefits from the repeal. Wagner's work appeared before the issue was taken up, and Beach appeared during consideration. It should also be noted that these projects centered on the overall issue, with E/SBs just a part of it.

Advocates are most likely to produce research when they are combating an initiative. The health example in the next section illustrates the point—so does *The Economic Impact of Mandated Family Leave on Small Businesses and Their Employees* (Barnett and Musgrave 1991). Both health and family leave studies emerged well after the issues were framed and debate begun. Research on the former appeared early enough to influence the course of events; the latter probably did not.

On the other hand, advocates are unlikely to devote resources to evaluating enacted legislation. The premium for them is passing or defeating the initiative, not maximizing or minimizing its impact once the decision has been made. They usually exhibit minimal interest in evaluation, meaning that their later stages research product is practically nil.

Government focuses on the end of the cycle. Since the agencies administer the policy or program, they have a corollary responsibility to evaluate their actions. These evaluations, almost by definition, involve the analysis of primary data, i.e., research. Several examples of government or government-sponsored evalua-

tions were cited earlier. But government also participates in the E/SB policy formulation stages, e.g., ABT Associates (1992, 1994, 1995). It is the entity most likely to do so. However, government-sponsored early-stage research appears much less important as it relates to E/SB than it does for many other interests because:

- E/SBs demand less from government than do most interests, which diminishes the pressure for E/SB-oriented government initiatives.
- Basic E/SB policy is not sympathetic to intervention on their behalf.
- Government, as others, think in terms of overarching issues and questions rather than group impacts, at least business group impacts.

An Example: Mandated Employee Health Insurance

A particularly contentious issue appeared in Washington during the first half of the 1990s that illustrates well the six propositions just discussed. The exception, to a degree, is the volume of research produced. The amount of research published on this issue is atypically large, reflecting both the stakes and the ideological splits involved. However, given the immense implications and multiplicity of important topics within the primary issue, the volume is probably less than might have been expected. With respect to the other five points, the issue is a prototype. The legislative example is The Health Security Act of 1993, President Clinton's unsuccessful attempt in 1993 and 1994 to effectively nationalize health care in the United States.

Health care in the United States is financed through a combination of private and public insurance. Those age 65 years and over are covered by a public system (Medicare) while the poorest are covered by a different public system (Medicaid). The remainder of the public obtains private insurance either through employer-sponsored plans or through individual policies. Most employed people and their families are covered by employer-sponsored and subsidized health insurance.[11] However, employee health insurance is a "benefit," and not all employers provide it, nor do all employees choose to be covered if they must contribute a portion of the premium.

Universal health insurance coverage was high on President Clinton's agenda when he entered office. The new President proposed the Health Security Act of 1993 to achieve that objective as well as to retard the rapidly escalating costs of health care. Central to the President's proposal was mandatory employer-provided employee health insurance. All employers would be required either to provide health insurance or to pay a significant penalty. The President subsequently revised his proposal to provide subsidies for small businesses to help them finance the cost, but the health insurance mandate was fundamental to the program from the onset.

Small business was integral to the President's proposal for two reasons: First, almost half of the 23 million employed uninsured were tied to small workplaces (fewer than twenty-five employees). Fewer than 30 percent of firms with less than five employees provided health insurance coverage, though the percentage increased as firm size rose. Second, the remainder of the President's plan could not be financed without the revenues from mandatory coverage.

The literature on the issue of mandatory provision of employer-paid employee health insurance, particularly the tie between small employers and insurance provision, should have been massive. Not only is the health insurance mandate issue not new in health policy circles, but one assumes that a Presidential initiative the magnitude of Health Security Act would have its central features developed from prior inquiry. Unfortunately, that was not the case. The literature on the mandate was practically nonexistent before the debate and then during and after it.

I reviewed the most prominent journals in health policy to ascertain the extent and nature of E/SB policy research published during the relevant period.[12] The primary debate on the Health Security Act occurred between 1993 and 1994. The review arbitrarily covered the ten-year period, 1989–98. Three themes emerged from the analysis:

(1) While all three journals bulged with articles on health care reform, assessments of the Health Security Act or parts thereof, and various health policy ideas, comparatively little focused on small business, entrepreneurship, self-employment or small groups.[13] Only about twenty

---

[11]The federal government also subsidizes employer-sponsored health insurance by the tax exclusion of premium costs. It does not do the same for health insurance purchases made directly by individuals.

[12]A list of journals was developed with the help and advice of Robert B. Helms, Director of Health Policy Studies at the American Enterprise Institute in Washington; Michael A. Morrisey, Professor, Department of Health Care Organization and Policy, Department of Public Health, University of Alabama–Birmingham; and, Wilbur A. Steger, President, CONSAD Research Corporation in Pittsburgh. It includes *Health Affairs, Inquiry* and the *Journal of Health Politics, Policy and Law*.

[13]"Small group" is an insurance term. While small firms are not always equivalent to small groups, they approximate one another for all practical purposes.

from hundreds of articles proved applicable.

(2) Before the introduction of the Health Security Act (January 1, 1993, for purposes of article classification), just five topical articles appeared that fit the author's working definition of E/SB policy research. Four of the five were published in *Health Affairs* (Helms et al. 1992; McLaughlin and Zellers 1992; Zellers et al. 1992; Edwards et al. 1992) and one in *Inquiry* (Kronick 1991); the *Journal of Health Politics, Policy and Law* published none. An equivalent number of thoughtful pieces, not qualifying under my definition of research, ran in all three. The preponderance of this research discussion appeared after the fact and played no role in the policy debate.

(3) The emphasis throughout the literature of this period was not on the health insurance mandate, the principal debate topic involving entrepreneurial and small business. Rather, the main topic proved to be the issue of small group reform, irrelevant if the Health Security Act were enacted. The reasons for this focus are not totally clear; however, it is fair to speculate that research dollars, data, complexity of the issues and timeliness all played a role.

Major actors in the debate, Washington-based think tanks and government, provided most of the policy research surrounding the Health Security Act. Lewin, Data Resources Inc. (DRI), O'Neill and O'Neill (sponsored by American Enterprise Institute [AEI]) and the Congressional Budget Office estimated job impacts, for example. The Heritage Foundation, among others, offered a proposal of its own, and Lewin modeled its impacts. The Employee Benefit Research Institute (EBRI) and SBA offered data from the Current Population Survey (Bureau of the Census) on the incidence of health insurance coverage in smaller firms. However, the National Federation of Independent Business (NFIB), a small business advocacy organization, was the only group to provide policy research specifically on small firms. Its most sophisticated inquiries, conducted by CONSAD Research Corporation, modeled job losses, jobs affected, change in wages, and government subsidies by firm size (measured in employees), industry and state (CONSAD 1994). A second iteration modeled business closures by firm size and employment losses (CONSAD 1995). Variants of the CONSAD model simulated the small business impacts of Senator Kennedy's short-lived proposal, those of Congressmen Gephardt and Gibbons and health insurance mandates in Washington state. Though small business was central to the argument on both sides of the Health Security Act and its variations, only the NFIB-sponsored CONSAD studies and one considerably more modest NFIB research piece became part of the debate.

The data on smaller businesses was not satisfactory to address many of the primary research questions posed. For example, though controlling costs was a principal objective of the Health Security Act, data on premiums paid by small employers for a particular benefit package was either weak or nonexistent. The critical insurance price/employer purchase elasticity used to model the Health Security Act was not size specific. And perhaps, most egregiously, the number and location of impacted firms had to be drawn from establishment rather than enterprise data. An exception was provision of employee health insurance coverage by firm size.

Since the death of the Health Security Act, the nonacademic research community, excluding the Robert Wood Johnson Foundation. has conducted or sponsored relatively little E/SB policy research on health related matters. An econometric analysis projecting impacts of the Expanded Portability and Health Insurance Coverage Act (CONSAD 1998) is an exception. In contrast, the bulk of the academic literature on small business and health appeared during this time, well after the Health Security Act debate was over.

Conclusions

The United States lags parts of Europe in E/SB policy research. Americans have nothing like the more than twenty years of policy research conferences the United Kingdom has enjoyed. There are no organizations equivalent to the Swedish Foundation for Small Business Research or the Entrepreneurship and the Small Business Research Institute (also in Sweden). The State of Small Business report was an American invention, but the European Observatory for SMEs is now in the same league as are similar reports from Australia to Poland, from Japan to Canada. Government support for E/SB policy research often found elsewhere does not exist in the United States, particularly in recent years. Yet the United States maintains advantages. Perhaps the most important are private-sector involvement and a large cadre of academics interested in E/SBs, if not particularly interested in the policy aspects.

Does the American experience with E/SB policy-oriented research to date hold any lessons for ourselves or for others? The following are a few observations:

The quality and quantity of E/SB policy-oriented research is not necessarily related to the quality of policy impacting E/SBs. De facto E/SB policy in the United States has proven reasonably successful without it. Perhaps, its absence has allowed (required) policymakers to fall back on fundamental principles, i.e., the value and importance of competition, rather than research results on marginal questions. Researchers working in small

business policy would do well to devote resources to investigating the relationship and influence of the growth and size variables on competition and vice versa. However, the competition policy is ebbing, and government demands on E/SBs are rising. A successful policy model is changing, and policymakers have no idea of its consequences. E/SB research is necessary to establish the impacts of these alternate policy models. Are they improvements or do they undermine a relatively successful policy direction?

The Job Generation Process (Birch 1979) has been enormously influential. Some complain, tacitly if not explicitly, that it is too influential, even distorting general policy debate (Brown et al. 1990; Davis et al. 1993; Pierce 1998). Though filled with policy implications, Birch's report is not a policy document per se. It is research exploring E/SB externalities. Externalities research is particularly conducive to the academic setting due to unlimited time lines and its essential neutrality on specific issues. Academe can leave interested parties and government to organize, finance and conduct (or have conducted) research on more immediate and direct policy proposals. Though self-interest is usually the motivation behind such research (government must usually be considered an "interested party"), useful material often emerges.

E/SB policy-oriented research in the United States involves widely varying segments of American interest, both public and private: government, academe, trade groups, business associations, private foundations and for-profit businesses. Those planning to use E/SBs to advance their agendas and E/SB owners promoting their own interests are in the mix, but there is no leadership or organizing entity and no centralized research agenda. Such dispersed activity has all the inherent advantages and disadvantages of a highly decentralized system, though it is probably the only arrangement that will work in the United States. Others may prefer a more centralized system, but private-sector involvement should never be marginalized.

American business schools should encourage greater interest in E/SB policy research. Policy is clearly an essential part of today's environmental equation. It is, therefore, highly relevant and offers significant opportunities in a largely unexplored area.

If there are few small business support programs (or if they consume minimal resources), there is no need to spend limited research resources evaluating them. A negligible body of such research also minimizes the opportunity to confuse what is central with what is peripheral.

Mathematical models measuring impacts must be developed sooner rather than later. Quantification of impacts is central to policymaking in Washington (less so at the state and local levels). Federal agencies and others frequently use models to appraise general impacts. Small business must operate models to appraise small business impacts if it wishes to compete.

International research cooperation and participation is increasingly valuable. E/SB researchers often encounter similar questions even when the specific issues and their contexts are quite different. And, even when the specific issues and their contexts are quite different, they are increasingly traded across national boundaries. Mutual efforts allow researchers to leverage resources (intellectual and financial) and reduce repetitive effort. The best example is the Entrepreneurial Research Consortium, which involves over a hundred researchers from nine countries. Moreover, the ongoing sharing of ideas and experiences among policy organizations regarding such policies as compulsory privatized retirement systems can rapidly move relevant policy from one national context into another.

References

ABT Associates, Inc. 1992. *Self-Employment Programs for Unemployed Workers*. Unemployment Insurance Occasional Paper 92-2, Employment and Training Administration, US Department of Labor: Washington, DC.

ABT Associates, Inc. 1994. *Self-Employment as a Reemployment Option: Demonstration Results and National Legislation*. Unemployment Insurance Occasional Paper 94-3, Employment and Training Administration, US Department of Labor: Washington, DC.

ABT Associates, Inc. 1995. *Self-Employment Programs: A New Reemployment Strategy, Final Report on the UI Self-Employment Demonstration*. Unemployment Insurance Occasional Paper 95-4, Employment and Training Administration, US Department of Labor: Washington, DC.

Acs, G., Stephen, H., Long, M., Marquis, S. and Farley Short, P. 1996. Self-insured Employer Health Plans: Prevalence, Profile, Provisions, and Premiums. *Health Affairs* 15(2): 266–73.

Aldrich, H. E. and Baker, T. 1997. Blinded by the Cites? Has There Been Progress in Entrepreneurship Research? In D.L. Sexton and R.W. Smilor (eds.), *Entrepreneurship 2000*. Chicago: Upstart, pp. 377–400.

Aoyama, Y. and Tietz, M.B. 1996. *Small Business Policy in Japan and the United States: A Comparative Analysis of Objectives and Outcomes*. Institute for International Studies. Berkeley: University of California.

Arthur Andersen & Co. 1979. *Analysis of Regulatory Cost on Establishment Size for the Small Business Administration*. Office of Advocacy, Small Business Administration, Contract No. SBA-263-OA-79, October.

Banks, M.C. and Taylor, S. 1991. Developing an Entrepreneur and Small

Business Owner-defined Research Agenda. *Journal of Small Business Management* 29(2): 10–18.

Barbieri, D. 1998. *Legislative Definitions of Small Business.* Washington, DC: NFIB Education Foundation.

Barnett, W.S. and Musgrave, G.L. 1991. *The Economic Impact of Mandated Family Leave on Small Businesses and Their Employees.* Washington, DC: NFIB Education Foundation.

Beach, W.W. 1996. The Case for Repealing the Estate Tax. In A.M. Antonelli and C.L. Shortridge (eds.), *Why America Needs a Tax Cut.* Washington, DC: Heritage Foundation.

Belman, D. and Goshen, E.L. 1998. Is Small Business Beautiful for Workers? *Small Consolation: The Dubious Benefits of Small Business for Job Growth.* Washington, DC: Economic Policy Institute.

Berney, R.E. 1981. *Small Business Policy: Subsidation, Neutrality, or Discrimination.* Working Paper No. 1180–1, Economics Department. Pullman, WA: Washington State University.

Birch, D.L. 1979. *The Job Generation Process.* Cambridge: MIT Program on Neighborhood and Regional Change.

Birnbaum, J. 1997. Washington's Power 25. *Fortune*, December 8, pp. 144–52.

Brewer, E. and Genay, H. 1995. Small Business Investment Companies: Financial Characteristics and Investments. *Journal of Small Business Management* 33(3): 38–56.

Brockhaus, R.H. 1987. Entrepreneurial Research: Are We Playing the Correct Game? *American Journal of Small Business* 11(3): 43–50.

Brown, C., Hamilton, J. and Medoff, J. 1990. *Employers Large and Small,* Cambridge: Harvard University Press.

Butler, S.A. 1981. *Enterprise Zones: Greenlining the Inner City.* New York: Universe Books.

Cadwell, C. 1997. *State Export Promotion and Small Business*, Office of Advocacy, Small Business Administration, Contract No. SBA-5659-ADV-90, August.

Cantor, J.C., Long, S.H. and Marquis, M.S. 1995. Private Employment-based Health Insurance in Ten States. *Health Affairs* 14(2): 199–206.

Chrisman, J.J. and McMullen, W.E. 1996. Static Economic Theory, Empirical Evidence, and the Evaluation of Small Business Assistance Programs: A Reply to Wood. *Journal of Small Business Management* 34(2): 56–66.

Cole, R.J. and Tegeler, P.D. 1980. *Government Requirements of Small Business.* Lexington, MA: Lexington Books.

CONSAD Research Corporation. 1994. *Employment and Related Economic Effects of Health Care Reform.* Prepared for the National Federation of Independent Business, Washington, DC, April.

CONSAD Research Corporation. 1995. *The Impact of Health Care Reform on Business Closures, and Associated Job Losses.* Prepared for the National Federation of Independent Business, Washington, DC, January.

CONSAD Research Corporation. 1998. *The Projected Impacts of the Expanded Portability and Health Insurance Coverage Act on Health Insurance Coverage.* Prepared for the National Federation of Independent Business, Washington, DC, June.

Davis, S.J., Haltiwanger, J. and Schuh, S. 1993. *Small Business and Job Creation: Dissecting the Myth and Reassessing the Facts.* National Bureau of Economic Research, Working Paper No. 4492, Cambridge, MA, October.

Dennis, W.J., Jr. 1996. *Small Business Problems and Priorities.* Washingron, DC: NFIB Education Foundation.

Dennis, W.J., Jr. 1997. *Wells Fargo/NFIB Series on Business Starts and Stops.* Washington, DC: NFIB Education Foundation.

Dennis, W.J., Jr. 1998. Small Business Policy in the United States. In

A. Lundström, H. Boter, A. Kjellberg and C. Öhman (eds.), *Svensk småföretagspolitik: Struktur, resultat och internationella jämförelser (Small Business Policies in Sweden: Structure, Results and Internaltional Comparisons)*. Örebro, Sweden: Swedish Foundation for Small Business Research.

Edwards, J.N., Blendon, R.J., Leitman, R., Morrison, E., Morrison, I. and Taylor, H. 1992. Small Business and the National Health Care Reform Debate. *Health Affairs* 11(1): 164–73.

Employee Benefit Research Institute. 1998. *1998 Retirement Confidence Survey*. Washington, DC: Employee Benefit Research Institute.

Faucett, J. and Associates. 1984. *Economies of Scale in Regulatory Compliance: Evidence of the Differential Impacts of Regulation by Firm Size*. Office of Advocacy, Small Business Administration, Contract No. SBA-7188-OA-83, December.

Gaston, R.J. and Carroll, S.L. 1984. *State and Local Regulatory Restrictions as Fixed Cost Barriers to Small Business Enterprise*. Office of Advocacy, Small Business Administration, Contract No. SBA-7167-AER-83, April.

General Accounting Office (GAO). 1995. *Small Business Administration: Case Studies Illustrate 8(a) Program and Contractor Abuse*, December 13, T-OSI-96-1.

General Accounting Office (GAO). 1996. *Tax Administration: Employment Taxes and Small Business*, November 8, T-GGD-97-21.

General Accounting Office (GAO). 1997. *Small Business Administration: Credit Subsidy Estimates for Sections 7(a) and 504 Business Loan Programs*, July 16, T-RCED-97-197.

Hashimoto, M. 1982. Minimum Wage Effects on Training on the Job. *American Economic Review* 72(5): 1070–84.

Helms, W.D., Gauthier, A.K. and Campion, D.M. 1992. Mending the Flaws in the Small-group Market. *Health Affairs* 11(2): 7–27.

Holtz-Eakin, D. 1995. Should Small Businesses Be Tax-favored? *National Tax Journal* 11(2): 387–95.

Hopkins, T.D. 1995. *A Survey of Regulatory Burdens*. Office of Advocacy, US Small Business Administration, Contract No. 8029-OA-93.

Hoy, F. 1997. Relevance in Entrepreneurship Research. In D.L. Sexton and R.W. Smilor (eds.), *Entrepreneurship 2000*. Chicago: Upstart, pp. 361–75.

Institute for Justice (1996 and 1997), Washington, D.C., seven monograph series. Berliner, Dana. *How Detroit Drives Out Motor City Entrepreneurs;* ———, *Running Boston's Bureaucratic Marathon;* Bolick, Clint, *Brightening the Beacon: Removing Barriers to Entrepreneurship in San Diego;* ———, *Entrepreneurship in Charlotte: Strong Spirit, Serious Barriers;* Bullock, Scott G., *Baltimore: No Harbor for Entrepreneurs;* Mathias, Donna G., *Entrepreneurship in San Antonio: Much to Celebrate, Much to Fight For,* and, Mellor, William H., *Is New York City Killing Entrepreneurship?*

Johnson, N. 1998. Letter to April 23rd House of Representatives Ways and Means Committee hearing witnesses, regarding follow-up questions on health insurance data, May 1.

Kronick, R. 1991. Health Insurance 1979–1989: The Frayed Connection between Employment and Insurance. *Inquiry* 28(4): 318–32.

Long, S.H. and Marquis, S.M. 1996. Some Pitfalls in Making Cost Estimates of State Health Insurance Coverage Expansions. *Inquiry* 33(1): 85–91.

Lerner, J. 1996. *The Government as Venture Capitalist: The Long-Run Impact of SBIR*. NBER Working Paper No. 5753. Cambridge, MA: National Bureau of Economic Research, September.

Masten, J.G., Hartmann, B. and Safari, A. 1995. Small Business Strategic Planning and Technology Transfer: The Use of Publicty Supported Technology Transfer Agencies. *Journal of Small Business Management* 33(3): 26–37.

McLaughlin, C.G. and Zellers, W.K. 1992. The Shortcomings of Voluntarism in the Small-group Insurance Market. *Health Affairs* 11(2): 28–40.

Moini, A.H. 1998. Small Firms Exporting: How Effective are Government Export Assistance Programs? *Journal of Small business Management* 36(1): 1–15.

National Institute of Disability Rehabilitation Research. 1998. *Federal Register.* Washington, DC: Geovernment Printing Office, April 14, pp. 18300–6.

Neumark, D. and Wascher, W. 1997. *Do Minimum Wages Fight Poverty?* Cambridge, MA: National Bureau of Economic Research, Working Paper No. 6127.

Organization for Economic Cooperation and Development. 1997. *OECD Economic Surveys: United States, 1996–1997.* Paris: OECD, pp. 151–72.

Phillips, B.D. 1998. Director of the Office of Economic Research, Small Business Administration, conversation with author June 10.

Phillips, B.D. and Dennis, W.J., Jr. 1997. Databases for Small Business Analysis. In D.L. Sexton and R.W. Smilor (eds.), *Entrepreneurship 2000.* Chicago: Upstart, pp. 341–60.

Pierce, R.J., Jr. 1998. Small Is Not Beautiful: The Case Against Special Regulatory Treatment of Small Firms. *Administrative Law Review* 50(3): 537–78.

Schiller, B.R. 1981. *Human Capital Transfers From Small to Large Businesses.* Office of Advocacy, US Small Business Administration, Contract No. SB-1A-00067-1.

State of Small Business: A Report of the President (annual). Washington, DC: Office of Advocacy, US Small Business Administration.

United States Code Annotated. 1998. St. Paul, MN: West Publishing.

Wagner, R.F. 1993. *Federal Transfer Taxation: A Study in Social Cost.* Costa Mesa, CA: Center for the Study of Taxation.

Welch, F., Murphy, K. and Deere, D. 1995. Employment and the 1990–91 Minimum Wage Hike. *American Economic Review* 85(2): 232–43.

Wood, W.C. 1994. Primary Benefits, Secondary Benefits and the Evaluation of Small Business Assistance Programs. *Journal of Small Business Management* 32(3): 65–75.

Zellers, W.K., McLaughlin, C.G. and Frick, K.D. 1992. Small-Business Health Insurance: Only the Healthy Need Apply. *Health Affairs* 11(1): 174–80.

Evaluating the Effect of Soft Business Support upon Small Firm Performance
by Colin Wren and David J. Storey

1. Introduction

Virtually all industrialised countries now utilise taxpayers' money to offer "soft" business support to small and medium-sized enterprises (OECD, 2000). This support is in the form of advisory assistance, the dissemination of best practice, encouragment of partnerships, gateway services and so on, which make recognition of the particular kinds of market failure facing these firms. It is provided directly by public agencies, such as by ALMI in Sweden, or indirectly, through subsidised private-sector consultancies, such as Law 44 in Italy or the regional Funds in France. Expenditure on "soft" business support is substantial and probably growing. A recent Swedish report estimates that advisory services to small firms absorbed 7–8% of net industrial costs (Lundström *et al.* 1988), while in Italy spending on small firm tutoring under Law 44 has exceeded 300 million ECU since its inception. In the UK, public support to the small firm sector, which is directed primarily through the Business Link framework, is currently estimated to be around £650 million per annum (Gavron *et al.* 1998). It is in addition to the more traditional forms of "hard" support, such as the loan guarantee schemes which exist in the US, Canada, France, and the Netherlands, the subsidised small firm loans such as Law 488 in Italy, and the small firm capital grants which are available under UK regional policy.

Despite the considerable sums of money involved, the evaluation of small firm policies is remarkably undeveloped (see Roper and Hewitt-Dundas, 2001). Storey (1999) identifies several kinds of evaluation which are undertaken by public agencies and others. These range from the straightforward monitoring of take-up; to questionnaire surveys of firms in which the recipients are in effect asked to attribute the policy effect; to comparisons of treated firms with control groups, which are matched according to characteristics such as firm size and activity. However, inference is problematic in these studies, since even in the matched samples the policy effect is measured simply as the difference in performance for firms of a given characteristic. Further, no account is taken of selection, whether through agency selection or self-selection by firms, even though this problem in evaluation is often remarked upon (e.g. Venetoklis, 1999), and it has long-been recognised in the labour-market literature (e.g. O'Higgins, 1994). This problem seems especially acute for the soft business support, even though these measures form a key part of the UK Government's programme to raise industrial competitiveness (Cm 4176, 1998).

This paper evaluates the impact of soft business support upon the performance of small and medium-sized enterprises (SMEs). It considers the subsidised advice to SMEs for marketing, provided

Originally appeared in *Oxford Economic Papers*, 2002, Volume 54, Number 2.

by private-sector consultants through the Consultancy Initiatives scheme of the UK Enterprise Initiative.[1] It examines the direct effect of this support on the sales turnover of firms, and its impact on two other indicators of small firm performance: employment, which is an important policy concern, and survival, which is perhaps the critical issue in small firm policy.[2] The paper makes two important contributions. The first are the empirical findings, which are widely applicable and relevant to Governments with soft small business assistance policies. The second contribution is to identify the issues which need to be considered in such evaluations, and to provide an example of how these can be addressed by applying econometric techniques and taking explicit account of selection bias. This approach is of general interest, although it is recognised that it may not be applicable to all kinds of business support measure, and may not extract all of the information which is of interest to policymakers.

The consultancy advice is found to have a marked effect on SME performance, but only for firms which are neither too small nor too large in size. This provides support for more recent changes to UK small firm policy, which have concentrated resources more heavily on the mid-range SMEs through the Business Links framework. In relation to the smaller SMEs, survival is not affected by participation in the scheme, while there is evidence that the scheme's effect varies over the economic cycle. The selection results suggest that, compared with all firms expressing an interest in the scheme, the supported firms have low-growth but high-survival characteristics. The failure to take account of this selection effect substantially alters the measured effect, which is approximately halved. Scaling-up the effects we find the scheme had a substantial impact on output, but the magnitude of this makes us believe that the wider effects, such as displacement, are also important, which has implications for the Government's competitiveness programme.

Overall, the study shows that the soft support for marketing had a substantial direct impact on the performance of some small firms. Equally important, it demonstrates the need to control for selection effects and to evaluate these programmes in terms of clearly identified performance measures, such as survival or the growth in sales or employment. It suggests important areas for improving the effectiveness of these measures and saving taxpayers money, both in relation to the kinds of SME which are targeted and the potential sensitivity of the impact to macroeconomic conditions.

The next section describes the Consultancy Initiatives, and the nature of selection. Section 3 sets out the approach for correcting for potential selection bias, Section 4 outlines the sample and data, and Section 5 presents the selection results. The modelling framework and

---

[1]The Enterprise Initiative operated between 1988 and 1994, and was something of a ground breaker. Robson and Bennett (2000) report that prior to the Enterprise Initiative less than 10% of eligible small businesses used public-sector support, whereas Keeble *et al.* (1992) find that the useage of the Enterprise Initiative was over 30% among small firms, and the CBI (1994) that 56% of its SME membership had used it. The Enterprise Initiative is an early and excellent example of the business support which is now offered to industry, exhibiting all the main characteristics of this support (see Wren, 2001).

[2]It is only relatively recently that firm failure has been considered in relation to industrial assistance, but the studies consider "hard" assistance. These include Kennedy and Healy (1985), O'Farrell and Crouchley (1987) and Lavy (1994).

results for survival are presented in Sections 6 and 7. The framework and results for turnover and employment are reported in Section 8. Section 9 considers the overall effectiveness of the scheme, and conclusions are drawn in Section 10.

2. The Scheme

The Consultancy Initiatives scheme formed a key part of the 1988 Enterprise Initiative (Cm 278, 1988), designed to raise UK economic performance. Its purpose was to "improve the competitiveness of small and medium-sized enterprises by improving the quality of management through subsidised consultancy in key strategic functions" (DTI, 1989a). The rationale for the scheme was market failure based on asymmetric information, with SMEs either unaware or unwilling to use outside consultancy advice, which was seen as expensive and of limited relevance (DTI, 1989b). An important role for the scheme therefore was to demonstrate the value of this advice to firms. From January 1988 it offered support in the areas of marketing, product and service quality, manufacturing and service systems, and design; and from April 1988 in business planning and financial and management information systems. When the scheme terminated in September 1994, 114,400 projects had been approved for support from 145,800 applications, involving a total £275 million in public subsidy.

Each of the six business areas was known as an Initiative. In this paper we focus on the Marketing Initiative, which was the most popular of the Initiatives, accounting for around a quarter of cases. The aim of the Marketing Initiative was to provide firms with a marketing strategy, either in new or existing markets at home or abroad. It offered subsidised advice in the areas of promotion, pricing, distribution and after-sales service, and market research on product demand, competitors and emerging markets. The Government-sponsored evaluation of the Consultancy Initiatives found that most projects were undertaken for reasons of expansion, such as the development of new products, exporting or as a response to rapidly changing markets (DTI, 1994). The administration of the Marketing Initiative was delegated to four (later five) regional Scheme Contractors. An account of the scheme is provided by Wren and Storey (1998), so that here we give only a brief outline.

The procedure for selection under the Marketing Initiative (and the Consultancy Initiatives more broadly) was multiple and sequential, arising from both self-selection and the Government selection criteria. Three main stages of selection are identified in Fig. 1, along with several sub-stages. In the First Stage (the Approval Stage) firms applied to their local Department of Trade and Industry (DTI) Office to assess eligibility (Stage 1a). Eligible firms consisted of British-based SMEs in manufacturing or services, which were independent or part of a group, but which in either case had less than 500 employees.[3] Subject to this they received a Business Review of up to two days by a DTI-appointed Enterprise Counsellor to assess their suitability for an Initiative, after which time successful applicants were approved for the scheme (Stage 1b). The Business Review was carried out for free and typically lasted half a day.

If the Enterprise Counsellor recommended assistance and the firm decided to proceed, then in the Second Stage (the Completion Stage), a private Consultant

---

[3]Most activities were eligible for the scheme, but excluding agriculture, fishing, forestry, energy, extraction and mining.

Figure 1
Stages of Selection*

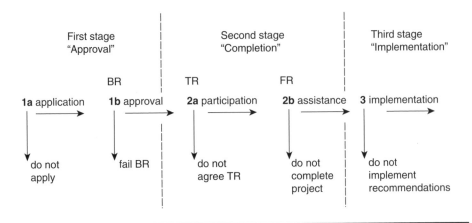

*Notes: BR = Business Review, TR = Terms of Reference and FR = Final Report. Firms self-select at Stages 1a, 2a, 2b and 3 and the Government selects at Stage 1b. For our sample 4326 firms enter the Second Stage, but 944 firms select out at Stage 2a and a further 542 select out at Stage 2b, so that 2840 firms enter the Third Stage.

appropriate to the firm's needs was appointed by the relevant Scheme Contractor. Terms of Reference for the project were agreed between the firm and Consultant (Stage 2a). A firm could nominate a consultant, possibly at the consultant's prompting, which was known as a "seeded case", or an approach could be made directly by a consultant known as a "direct case", but there was no guarantee that this consultant would be appointed to the project. The daily rates which the Consultants could charge were approved by the Scheme Contractor based on DTI guidelines, and were fixed for the duration of the project. On completion of the project and submission of a Final Report to the DTI (Stage 2b) firms received assistance towards the consultancy. If the firm dropped out, the Consultant was reimbursed for the cost of the Terms of Reference only. Finally, in the Third Stage (the "Implementation" Stage) the firm decided whether to implement

the Consultant's recommendations or not (Stage 3).

Government assistance was in the form of a grant for between five and 15 days of the Consultant's time. This was at a rate of 50%, but at a higher rate of two-thirds in urban and regional policy areas designated as experiencing high unemployment and other social problems. A short time after completion the Enterprise Counsellor returned to the firm to review the project and to discuss the implementation of the Consultant's recommendations. From June 1989 financial assistance was available to very small firms (normally less than 25 employees) for an extra five days consultancy to alleviate financial constraints associated with implementing the recommendations. This post-completion assistance was scrapped in July 1993, when the grant rate was reduced to 50% in the policy areas and to one-third elsewhere. Firms could receive assistance for a maximum of two projects under different Initiatives, but this was reduced to one project from April 1991.

3. *Methodological Approach*

Broadly, from a choice-theoretic base and under reasonable assumptions, we can derive a linear relationship for a representative firm i between the project outcome y_i and the assistance amount AID_i as follows:[4]

Treatment group (t):
$$y_{it} = \beta_{1t}x_{it} + \beta_{2t}AID_i + u_{it} \quad (1)$$

where x_i is a vector of explanatory variables which determine the project outcome in the absence of assistance, β_1 and β_2 embody various parameters in the underlying model, such as factor prices, the production technology and the cost of private funds, and u_i is an error term, which is assumed to be independent of x_i.

Equation (1) defines the relationship for firms receiving assistance, i.e. the treatment group. In a similar way, we can define a relationship for the non-treatment firms

Non-treatment group (n):
$$y_{in} = \beta_{1n}x_{in} + u_{in} \quad (2)$$

Selection bias occurs when the mean project outcome for the treatment group differs from that of the comparison group of non-treatment firms even in the absence of assistance. In this case, the non-treatment firms fail to give the counter-factual position for the treatment firms, so that $E(y_{it}|AID_i) \neq E(y_{in})$. The bias arises when the treatment firms are non-randomly assigned from the population of firms comprising both treatment and non-treatment groups. For example, it might be that only the firms with "good" characteristics take up the business support, so that the project outcome y_{it} is wrongly attributed to the policy effect AID_i, when in fact it is due to the x_{it}, making policy seem more effective than it really is.

In the presence of selection bias, the OLS regression of (1) yields inconsistent estimates of β_{2t} (and β_{1t}). Further, a dummy variable for treatment/non-treatment status is inappropriate, since the selection cannot be treated as exogenous. We now consider a procedure for eliminating the effect of selection bias in both the treatment and non-treatment equations. For simplicity, we suppose there is a single stage of selection. This means the model is given by (1), (2) and[5]

Selector equation: $I_i^* = \gamma z_i + u_i$, (3)

where I_i^* is a continuous latent variable indicating the propensity for treatment, z_i is a set of characteristics determining treatment with coefficients γ and u_i is an error term. The observed project outcome y_i is defined by the selector equation $y_i = y_{it} \Leftrightarrow I_i^* > 0$ and $y_i = y_{in} \Leftrightarrow I_i^* \leq 0$.

3.1 Correcting for Selection Bias

Formally, selection bias arises when the stochastic element of the selector

---

[4]The linear relationship is derived in Wren (1994). The project outcome is employment, but for generality we allow it to include other measures of firm performance, such as turnover or survival. A more elaborate model based on financial constraints is inappropriate, since the rationale for the scheme is a market failure based on asymmetric information, i.e. a lack of firm information rather than a lack of cash. The model is sufficient for our purpose since it exhausts the available data. It is considered further in Wren (1999).

[5]Lavy (1994) uses an alternative single-equation method, due to Goldberger (1972), in which the Government assigns the firms to the treatment and non-treatment groups.

equation is correlated with the stochastic elements of the treatment and non-treatment equations.[6] Assuming the error terms in (1) to (3) are jointly normal, and letting σ_t and σ_n denote the covariances between u_{ti}, u_{ni}, and u_i respectively, the conditional expectations of the error terms in (1) and (2) are $E(u_{it}|I_i^* > 0) = \sigma_t \phi(\gamma z_i)/\Phi(\gamma z_i)$ and $E(u_{in}|I_i^* \leq 0) = -\sigma_n \phi(\gamma z_i)/[1 - \Phi(\gamma z_i)]$, when ϕ and Φ are the standard normal density and distribution functions (see Maddala, 1983). This suggests a two-stage estimation procedure, due to Lee (1976). First, we obtain estimates of γ in (3) using the probit ML method with observations on the indicator variable I_i ($I_i = 1 \Leftrightarrow I_i^* > 0$ and $I_i = 0 \Leftrightarrow I_i^* \leq 0$), giving $\hat{\gamma}$. Second, we use this to estimate (1) and (2) with an additional regressor in each case, respectively as follows

$$\lambda_{it} = \phi(\hat{\gamma}z_i)/\Phi(\hat{\gamma}z_i) \quad \text{and}$$
$$\lambda_{in} = \phi(\hat{\gamma}z_i)/[1 - \Phi(\hat{\gamma}z_i)] \qquad (4)$$

With the inclusion of λ_{it} and λ_{in} as additional regressors, the residuals in (1) and (2) have zero conditional means and the estimates of β_{1t}, β_{2t}, and β_{1n} are consistent.

This procedure corrects for selection bias on observables, as given by the z_i in (3). However, selection bias may also arise from unobservables, as represented by the error term u_i in (3). For example, it might be that even after using the z_i to control for factors which are measurable, the treatment firms are still qualitatively

different from the non-treatment firms, perhaps because of their superior motivational drive or entrepreneurial ability.

The procedures when selection is on unobservables are considered by Heckman and Hotz (1989). These involve differencing the treatment group equation before and after the assistance, but given the nature of our analyses described below, we are unable to implement these procedures.[7] Instead, we carry out the correction for selection on observables outlined above, and then check that this aligns the project outcomes for the treatment and non-treatment groups, save for the effect of assistance. Specifically, after including the λ_{it} and λ_{in}, we examine if the estimated coefficients on the non-policy terms x_i are the same between (1) and (2), i.e. $\beta_{1t} = \beta_{1n}$. If they are not significantly different, then it gives us some confidence that we have correctly determined the counter-factual position, and hence the scheme effect.

3.2 The Non-treatment Group

For our sample we take all those applicants satisfying the Business Review at the end of the First Stage of selection in Fig. 1. The analysis therefore applies to all those firms entering the Second Stage of selection, whether they are subsequently assisted or not. This means the treatment group are those firms receiving assistance and entering the Third Stage of selection, while the non-

---

[6]When the stochastic elements of (1) and (3) are correlated, then $E(y_{it}|I_i^* > 0) = \beta_{1t}x_{it} + \beta_{2t}AID_i + E(u_{it}|I_i^* > 0)$, so that OLS gives inconsistent estimates of β_t when $E(u_{it}|I_i^* > 0)$ is non-zero. The selectivity bias has aspects of the classic omitted variable problem, with $E(u_{it}|I_i^* > 0)$ representing the omitted variables. The same follows for the non-treatment group when the stochastic elements of (2) and (3) are correlated.

[7]Our analysis of firm survival is not of the linear form suggested by (1) and (2), since we use duration data to maximise a log-likelihood with a Weibull survivor function. In the case of firm growth, the dependent variable y_i is the annualised growth rate calculated from the time of the Business Review, and this exhausts the available data.

treatment group are those firms entering the Second Stage but which do not go on to receive assistance and hence enter the Third Stage. In the case of the non-treatment group it might be argued that we should draw these from the population of all eligible SMEs. However, we do not think that this is problematic, and indeed we believe it offers certain advantages, providing a strong test of the scheme's effect.

To see this, suppose that the selection at the First Stage means that the firms entering the Second Stage are intrinsically different from the other eligible SMEs, e.g. they are fast-growing whereas other SMEs are slow growing. Then the kind of question we address is whether the fast-growers grow even faster when they are assisted. Attempting to correct for selection bias at the First Stage seems disadvantageous. This is because not only must we explain why the other SMEs are slow growing, but it poses considerable and possibly insurmountable difficulties in obtaining data on a comparable basis for other firms over the life of the scheme. It means that we are not concerned with the substantial number of firms which were unaware or, for whatever reason, chose not to apply for the scheme, or were turned down at the Business Review.[8] While the reasons for the non-take up of Government schemes are of policy interest, these lie outside our scope.

The advantage of restricting the analysis to just those firms entering the Second Stage of selection is that all of these firms revealed an interest in the scheme by undertaking the Business Review and they were successfully screened by the Enterprise Counsellor. This is likely to reduce any unobserved heterogeneity between the treatment and non-treatment firms. It gives us a sufficient number of observations with which to form a non-treatment group, since around a third of the firms satisfying the Business Review did not go on to receive assistance.

Finally, it can be seen from Fig. 1 that at the Second Stage there are in fact two sub-stages of selection, so that in place of (3) there are two selector equations (for Stages 2a and 2b), and in place of (2) there are two non-treatment equations (one for firms not agreeing the Terms of Reference, and one for firms agreeing the Terms of Reference but not submitting a Final Report). Catsiapis and Robinson (1982) extend the Heckman-Lee correction procedure to multiple selection rules. This does not greatly affect our analysis, except that there are now two selection terms to be included in the treatment equation, and two such terms to be included in each of the non-treatment equations. Further, since selection at Stage 2b depends on selection made at Stage 2a then it is a sequential-decision model, and in estimating γ we should allow for any correlation between the error terms of the selector equations (Maddala, 1983). In the case of the Third Stage we do not observe selection, and this is subsumed in our estimate of β_{2t} in (1), but in any case it seems that virtually all of the assisted firms implement the Consultant's recommendations (DTI, 1994).

---

[8]A major factor for non-take up seems to have been a lack of awareness. Of 733 SMEs surveyed by the DTI (1994) which were not assisted under the Consultancy Initiatives, 87% had heard of the Enterprise Initiative but only 13% realised that it covered consultancy advice. Of the consultancy-based projects implemented by these firms, 23% would have been eligible for the scheme, but the vast majority of these firms chose to meet the costs in full themselves.

4. The Data

The sample is drawn from one of the regional Scheme Contractors for the Marketing Initiative, covering the geographical areas of the West and East Midlands of England, the South West of England and South Wales. The sample includes all eligible firms which satisfied the Business Review, giving details of 4326 firms over the scheme's life, but for the years 1988–91 only in the case of the South West. Of the firms in our sample, 2840 (65.7%) submitted a Final Report to the local DTI Office and received assistance, so that these are the treatment firms. Of the 1486 non-treatment firms, 944 failed to agree the Terms of Reference with the Consultant and the remaining 542 firms agreed the Terms of Reference but failed to submit a Final Report (see Fig. 1).

The firm-level data used in our study derive from three sources: the record cards on the sample firms held at the local DTI Offices; a questionnaire survey carried out by the Centre for Small and Medium-Sized Enterprises at the University of Warwick; and a follow-up telephone survey of non-respondents. The available data are set out in Table 1, along with the variable labels and descriptive statistics. The Table indicates whether each variable is based on the information collected from the record cards or surveys, and whether the data are available for all firms or for some sub-group.

In the case of the record cards these give the date of the Business Review, and the dates when either the firm selected into the scheme at Stages 2a and 2b or it withdrew. Characteristics of the establishment plant visited by the Enterprise Counsellor are known, including its activity, location, sales turnover, and employment at the time of the Business Review, and whether the firm is located in a policy area and the project is seeded. Direct projects are coded the same as projects in which there was a change of Consultant, but only 88 projects (2.0%) are "direct", whereas 967 (22.4%) are seeded. For the firms agreeing the Terms of Reference the Consultant's daily rate and the number of whole days of consultancy received are known, as are the grant amount and post-completion assistance for the firms submitting a Final Report.

The survey was carried out in 1996, and its purpose was two-fold. First, it sought to determine whether the firm had survived until this date. Second, for the survivors it sought information on the firm at that time, including its activity, location, turnover, employment, legal status, exports, the take-up of other Government SME schemes (including the other five Consultancy Initiatives) and if it had worked with a marketing consultant since the project. A postal questionnaire was sent to all 4326 sample firms, and followed-up, from which 2799 firms (64.7%) were classified as surviving.[9] For the surviving firms 1136 useable responses were generated, i.e. 40.6%, which is a reasonable response rate given that the survey was carried out up to eight years after the project commenced.

For a working definition of firm survival we are guided by Storey and Wynarczyk (1996), who define a firm death where a change occurs in at least three attributes as follows: name, location, ownership and sector. The definition of a firm closure is always problematic, particularly in the case of small firms, but Storey and Wynarczyk

---

[9]The questionnaire was sent out under a covering letter from the DTI. It was followed-up by a second postal questionnaire a few months later, and by a telephone survey of firms using the number in the record card, which was checked using the BT directory.

Table 1
Firm-Level Variables

Variable Description and Label	Min.	Max.	Mean	CV
(a) Record Cards				
All firms:				
DATE: no. of years that the Business Review occurred after the beginning of 1988, measured in years	0.10	6.95	2.52	0.66
IND1 to IND9: dummy variables for firm's activity under divisions of the 1980 Standard Industrial Classification	0	1	—	—
AREA1 to AREA23: dummy variables for location in counties in study area	0	1	—	—
TURN: turnover at time of Business Review (£m, 1994 prices)	0	99.3	0.97	2.81
TURND: dummy variable for missing TURN data	0	1	0.18	—
EMP: number of employees at time of Business Review	1	451	17.8	0.48
EMPD: dummy variable for missing EMP data	0	1	0.16	—
GT: grant rate available to firm	0.33	0.67	0.59	0.15
POL: dummy variable for higher grant rate policy areas	0	1	0.62	—
POLCH: dummy variable on POL for lower grant rates from July 1993	0	1	0.06	—
SEED: dummy variable for whether project "seeded"	0	1	0.22	—
DIRECT: dummy variable for whether project "direct"	0	1	0.02	—
Firms agreeing terms of reference:				
DURTR: period between the Business Review and the Terms of Reference, measured in years	0	2.69	0.17	0.99
CONDR: Consultant's daily rate (£'s, 1994 prices)	149	585	417	0.19
CONPD: number of days of consultancy	0	15	11.6	0.47
Firms submitting final report:				
AID (= GT * CONDR * CONPD): assistance (£'000s, 1994 prices)	0.37	5.38	3.43	0.31
POSTAID: post-completion assistance (£'000s, 1994 prices)	0.78	1.67	1.28	0.15
(b) Surveys				
All firms:				
SURVIVE: dummy variable for survival to 1996	0	1	0.65	—
Survivors:				
SURVEY: dummy variable for firms responding to survey	0	1	0.41	—
Useable responses:				
TURN96: turnover in 1996 (£m, 1994 prices)	1	79.29	2.50	2.53
EMP96: employment in 1996	1	1700	37.5	2.08
INDEP: dummy variable for independent firms	0	1	0.92	—
EXPORT: proportion of output which is exported	0	1	0.10	2.05
ASS1 to ASS15: dummy variables for assistance received under each of 15 other schemes	0	1	—	—
MARK: dummy variable for employment of a marketing consultant since termination of the scheme	0	1	0.31	—

Notes: Some variables have missing values, which are not included in the descriptive statistics. Monetary variables are at first quarter 1994 prices using a quarterly GDP deflator. CONDR, AID and POSTAID are exclusive of Value Added Tax. CV = coefficient of variation.

conclude that this definition is operationally the closest to an economic death in a situation of highly-imperfect information. In practice, it proved a sharp discriminator since few firms experience a change in only two of these attributes. We are unable to determine the reasons for failure, e.g. takeover or liquidation, but small firms experience a lower death rate from takeover (Dunne and Hughes, 1994), and in fact very few of these firms are acquired.[10] Further, for a firm to be considered as non-surviving a change in legal ownership must be accompanied by a change in economic function, i.e. either in its activity or its location.

4.1 Characteristics of the Sample Firms

A breakdown of the sample firms by the year of the Business Review, sales turnover, employment size, and sector is given in the Appendix. It shows that the proportion of firms receiving treatment increases with time and firm size (except for the very largest firms), and it is higher for service sector firms. The survival rate decreases the longer is the observation period and is higher for larger firms, which provides some comfort for the validity of our definition of survival. Not unexpectedly, the survey response rate increases the later in time is the project, but we allow for this and other response-rate biases in our subsequent analysis.

The number of firms satisfying the Business Review peaked in 1989 but then declined, reflecting a number of factors. This includes the initial very heavy promotion of the scheme, the recession of the early 1990s, which reduced interest in the scheme, the smaller size of our study area from 1992,

and amendments to the scheme which no doubt lessened its attractiveness, such as the reduction in grant rates and restriction on take-up. Table 1 shows the mean sales turnover of the sample firms is £970,000 (1994 prices), and the mean employment size is 18 (the median is 12). Turnover and employment could each not be ascertained for about one-sixth of firms, but the turnover cases mainly comprise prospective start-ups in the early years of the scheme which the Scheme Contractor coded as missing.[11] The firms are divided more or less equally between the manufacturing and service sectors.

Table 1 shows 62% of the sample firms are located in the higher grant rate policy areas. The average grant payment is £3,430, but only 257 of these firms received post-completion assistance to help implement the Consultant's recommendations, averaging just £1,280. The average Consultant daily rate of the firms agreeing the Terms of Reference is £417, but this is lower for the firms that did not go on to submit a Final Report at £367. Eighty-nine per cent of the treatment firms received 10 or more days consultancy and 79% received the maximum of 15 days consultancy (the average was 13.6 days), while 87% of the firms that did not go on to submit a Final Report had no more than one day's consultancy and 26% had no consultancy at all (the average was 0.9 days).

5. The Selection Results

To estimate the selector equations for the Second Stage of selection (i.e. equations such as (3) for Stages 2a and 2b) we use a bivariate probit model with sequential selection. As regressors z_i we take the firm and project characteristics

---

[10]Where a firm did not respond to our survey then it was classified as surviving where its name and address in the BT directory corresponded to the DTI record card. For these firms we do not know if the ownership changed.

[11]For only 137 firms are both employment and turnover not known. Employment is known for all firms from January 1990.

shown in Table 1. These include variables which are not in x_i in (i) and (2), which helps identify the selection rule. They are the Consultant's daily rate (CONDR), the time taken to agree the Terms of Reference (DURTR) and the date of the Business Review (DATE).[12] We believe the first two terms impact on the motivation of the Consultant and firm to submit a Final Report, but not the scheme effect, while the latter term is included as the understanding of the scheme seems to have improved with time. The terms are described more fully below. Other variables, which are included in both z_i and x_i are quadratic terms in turnover and employment (TURN2 and EMP2), which are suggested by the Appendix (see above discussion), and the position of the national economy at the time of the Business Review (GDP), which is important given the sharp cycle in economic conditions which characterised the study period.[13] The results are given in Table 2.

The first equation in Table 2 shows the factors affecting the probability of a firm agreeing the Terms of Reference, and the second equation the probability of a firm then going on to complete the consultancy and submitting a Final Report (see Fig. 1). We consider the equations together. They suggest that the probability of treatment increases at a decreasing rate with employment size (EMP) and that a negative relationship exists for firms with around 150 employees or more, perhaps because the assistance amount is effectively capped under the scheme (at the grant rate times the Consultant's daily rate times 15 days consultancy), making the scheme less attractive and then unattractive to larger SMEs. The coefficient on the variable for the missing turnover date (TURND) indicates that the prospective start-ups have a strong probability of completion once they have agreed the Terms of Reference.

The higher grant rate in the policy areas (POL) and seeding (SEED) increases the probability of treatment, but the change in grant rate (POLCH) and direct projects (DIRCET) are insignificant (the former includes only a small number of cases, while the latter includes a mixture of effects). The probability of completion increases with the Consultant's daily rate (CONDR), which is highly significant. We believe that it reflects the Consultant's commitment rather than any index of quality. However, it decreases with the length of period taken to agree the Terms of Reference (DURTR), which suggests that there projects experienced difficulty.

The sign on the coefficients for the date of the Business Review (DATE) indicate that later projects were less likely to

---

[12]In terms of eqs (1) to (3) identification requires that there are variables in z_i which are not in x_i and that these variables are exogenous to (1) to (2). It is not possible to test for exogeneity, but when CONDR, DURTR and DATE are included in our regression equations (such as Equation III in Table 3) we find they are insignificant. Otherwise the variables in x_i and z_i are identical, except that the x_i include assistance terms AID and POSTAID (Table 1), and in the growth analysis the x_i also include some variables collected for surviving firms as part of our survey. The AID term is defined as GT*CONDR*CONPD, but our later analysis suggests its effect arises from the consultancy period CONPD and not the consultant's daily rate CONDR, which gives further support to CONDR as an identifying variable. For reasons of endogeneity in the estimation of the selection equations we exclude CONDR and DURTR from Stage 2a of selection, and the period of consultancy CONPD from both Stages.

[13]There was strong growth up to the end of 1989, a two-year period of declining output and then a recovery from early 1992. Our variable is based on the quarterly index of GDP, of which the percentage change in output over the three months following the quarter in which the Business Review took place proved to be the best measure.

Table 2
Selection Results for the Second Stage

Variable	Terms of Reference (Stage 2a)		Final Report (Stage 2b)	
Constant	0.573	(9.82)	−0.930	(5.82)
GDP	0.012	(1.13)	0.003	(0.15)
Firm characteristics:				
TURN	0.035	(1.34)	0.060	(1.25)
TURN2	−0.00019	(0.14)	−0.00096	(1.23)
TURND	−0.042	(0.78)	0.261	(2.59)
EMP	0.0041	(2.72)	0.0024	(0.71)
EMP2	-0.13×10^{-4}	(2.49)	-0.99×10^{-5}	(0.72)
EMPD	−0.032	(0.52)	0.060	(0.60)
Project characteristics:				
POL	0.133	(3.19)	0.338	(5.00)
POLCH	0.051	(0.34)	−0.158	(0.43)
SEED	0.701	(13.47)	0.488	(3.28)
DIRECT	−0.128	(0.72)	0.132	(0.38)
CONDR	—	—	0.0040	(13.72)
DURTR	—	—	−0.801	(6.24)
DATE	−0.078	(4.39)	0.126	(3.22)
Rho		0.625 (21.00)		
Log-likelihood		−3546.24		
n		4326		

Note: Bivariate probit estimates with sequential selection. Figures in parentheses are t-ratios. Rho is the estimate of the correlation coefficient between the error terms of the selection equations. CONDR, DURTR and DATE are identifying variables. Industry (IND) and area (AREA) dummies are included but not shown.

agree the Terms of Reference, but that once agreed they were more likely to complete. We think that this reflects an increased understanding of the scheme, indicating that the quality of the projects coming forward improved with time. When it is newly introduced it is reasonable that firms are ill-informed about how the scheme operates, so that they agree the Terms of Reference but later drop out. However, as firms pass their experience on to other firms through the usual business channels they are able to exercise greater judgement in agreeing the Terms of Reference and are more likely to complete.[14]

[14]Since the coefficients on the GDP term are insignificant, and remain insignificant what the DATE term is omitted, we believe that this pattern is unrelated to economic events.

We examined the sensitivity of our parameter estimates in Table 2 by dropping the variables in turn, but the selection results were robust to this. In our subsequent analyses we use the parsimonious version of these results to form our selection terms, i.e. the λ_t and λ_n from (4) for each stage of selection. Identification of these terms is through the exclusion restrictions described above, but also through their non-linear functional form.

6. Modelling Firm Survival

We consider firm survival from the time of project implementation, and so define the time origin as the date of the Business Review, analysing the firm's lifetime until its closure. Duration data have been much used in recent studies, such as Mata and Portugal (1994) and McCloughan and Stone (1998), and like these studies our data are right-censored, in that for the survivors we observe only that these firms survived until 1996. For non-surviving firms there is further censoring in that we also do not observe the lifetimes of these firms, but only that they did not survive until the time of the survey.[15] In this way our data are similar to that used in some other studies, such as Cressy (1996).

Conventional statistical methods such as OLS are inappropriate for analyzing survival data. Briefly our approach is as follows. For firm i let τ_i denote the period of observation from the time origin, and let δ_i be an indicator variable such that $\delta_i = 1$ if $T_i > \tau_i$ (survivor) and $\delta_i = 0$ if T_i

$\leqslant \tau_i$ (non-survivor), where T_i is a continuous non-negative random variable representing the lifetimes of firms in the absence of censoring. Assuming the pairs (τ_i, δ_i) are independent and identically distributed then the log-likelihood function $\log L$ is

$$\log L = \sum_i \{\delta_i \ln S(\tau_i) + (1 - \delta_i) \ln[1 - S(\tau_i)]\} \qquad (5)$$

where $S(\tau_i)$ is the survivor function, representing the probability that a firm survives for a length of time τ_i ($\geqslant 0$). Estimation of (5) requires knowledge of the survivor function $S(\tau_i)$, and we model this using the Weibull distribution. This is a popular and well-known functional form and is both a proportional hazards and accelerated failure model (see Kiefer, 1988). In conditional form this survivor function is

$$S(\tau_i | x_i) = \exp\left[-(\tau_i / \beta x_i)^\alpha\right] \qquad (6)$$

where α is the shape parameter and the other notation is as before. This is a flexible form of distribution, but which assumes monotonic behaviour in the underlying hazard rate. When $\alpha > 1$, the hazard rate increases with the length of time from the time origin and there is positive duration dependence (and conversely), while $\alpha = 1$ is the exponential distribution.

As explanatory variables x_i for inclusion in (6) there is an extensive literature. One virtually consistent finding is that survival is positively related to firm size

---

[15]The duration data is unlike that used in some other studies, where the lifetimes of the non-survivors are known. However, it can be accommodated straightforwardly in the estimation procedure through the specification of the log-likelihood function in (5) below. For each firm we observe whether it survived or not, or equivalently for each firm we have observations on the survivor function S or on $1 - S$. The data for both survivors and non-survivors can then be used together to maximise the log-likelihood, giving the estimates of the parameters of S, from which the hazard rates and firms' lifetimes can be constructed.

(Storey, 1994). Mata and Portugal (1994) find that the nature of entry is important, with larger entrants and those firms with multiple plants more likely to survive, while Phillips and Kirchhoff (1989) show that start-ups which experience some employment growth are more likely to survive. Audretsch and Mahmood (1994) find that survival is higher for firms in industries which are either fast growing or where innovation is less important, and Dunne *et al.* (1989) show that age affects survival positively even when size and ownership are held constant.

We are able to pick up these kinds of influence by including our variables for the firm and project characteristics in Table 1, but the main omissions are firm age and ownership. Dunne *et al.* (1989) find that age affects failure strongest in very young firms, and to some extent our variable for the missing turnover data will capture this. In any event, it is not clear that age will vary systematically between the treatment and non-treatment firms, since while younger firms may be more in need of marketing advice they have less resources with which to commit to this. Ownership is known for the survey firms only, but the vast majority of these are independent (see INDEP in Table 1), and in our growth analysis we find that the other estimates are robust to the exclusion of this term. In either case, the semi-parametric analysis presented below indicates that survival increases more or less monotonically with the length of the observation period, which suggests that these data omissions are not serious.

We specify the assistance as the grant amount AID = GT * CONDR * CONPD, and then subsequently examine the role of each of the composite terms. We include POSTAID for the post-completion assistance to allow for an increased effect of assistance in those firms receiving additional support to help implement the Consultant's recommendations. We also include the GDP and selection terms for each stage. Finally, we write $\delta \equiv$ SURVIVE in (5), and measure the survival duration in years from the implementation date to the middle of 1996, i.e. $\tau \equiv 8.5 -$ DATE in (6), where DATE = 0 at the beginning of the scheme in 1988 (see Table 1).

7. *The Results for Firm Survival*

To examine the monotonicity of the hazard function, and hence the appropriateness of the Weibull survivor function, we first undertook a semiparametric analysis of the survival data using the method of Han and Hausman (1988).[16] This is a proportional hazards model which leaves the underlying baseline hazard function unrestricted in order to condition on the firm and project characteristics. It involves organising the firms into groups according the length of the observed duration, and then applying an ordered logit model to these data. The results from this analysis are illustrated in Fig. 2. This shows the empirical survivor function calculated from the raw data, and the smoothing introduced by conditioning on our variables. It also plots the conditional hazard rate.

Apart from a few exceptions, the conditional survivor function in Fig. 2 declines monotonically. This is encouraging since the survival rate is calculated for each group from a different cohort of firms, i.e., those firms taking the Business Review in each quarter. It suggests that we have successfully controlled for the trade cycle and that our data omissions are not serious. In the case of the conditional hazard rate there is evidence

---

[16]The model is described in Greene (1998). We cannot use the Cox proportional hazards model as our duration data are censored for both survivors and non-survivors.

Figure 2
Semiparametric Survival and Hazard Rates*

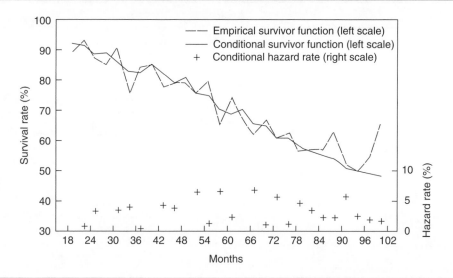

*Notes: The survival data are organised by the length of the observed duration into 28 three-month groups from the time of the Business Review until mid-1996. The conditional survivor function is obtained according to the method of Hans and Hausman (1988), conditioning on EMP, EMPD, TURN, TURND, POL, SEED, AID, POSTAID and GDP. The conditional hazard rates cannot be calculated for all observations owing to some upward-sloping segments in the conditional survivor function.

of an increasing and then decreasing failure rate, i.e. non-monotonic, but fitting a quadratic time trend to the hazard rate gives only weak support for this, while a constant hazard rate is not rejected. Together with our other evidence, it suggests the Weibull survivor function is not overly restrictive.[17]

7.1 Parametric Analysis

The results from maximising the log-likelihood function in (5) with the Weibull survivor function in (6) are given in Table 3. Equations I and II report the results for the treatment firms, with and without selection terms, while Equations III and IV repeat these

---

[17]The empirical survivor function for the firms taking the Business Review in each year is reported in the Appendix. When calculated separately for the treatment and non-treatment firms the survival rate diminishes monotonically with the observation period in each case. The treatment firms have a higher probability of survival in each year, and an exponential ordered score test shows that this is highly significant ($\chi^2 = 25.37$; $\chi^2_{0.01} = 6.63$), but this makes no allowance for selection or other effects. In Wren and Storey (1998) "double-log" plots of the empirical survival data for treatment and non-treatment firms are shown to be roughly parallel and linear. The former supports the proportional hazards assumption, while the latter is implied by the Weibull function.

Table 3
Regression Results for Firm Survival

Equation	I	II	III	IV
Shape parameter (α):	1.354 (6.05)	1.080 (6.63)	1.119 (8.58)	1.053 (8.75)
Coefficients (β):				
constant	11.022 (3.13)	13.355 (5.90)	10.836 (6.22)	10.211 (11.53)
EMP	0.085 (2.03)	0.153 (2.20)	0.176 (3.20)	0.193 (3.14)
EMP2	−0.00020 (1.79)	−0.00036 (1.95)	−0.00038 (2.56)	−0.00041 (2.43)
POL	0.130 (0.16)	0.106 (0.10)	−1.519 (2.30)	−2.064 (2.88)
SEED	−2.015 (1.33)	−2.036 (2.08)	−1.289 (1.59)	−1.400 (1.87)
GDP	0.472 (2.01)	0.816 (2.48)	0.433 (2.50)	0.494 (2.62)
assistance terms:				
AID	0.141 (0.41)	−0.149 (0.30)	0.417 (1.31)	1.003 (4.17)
POSTAID	1.832 (1.54)	2.837 (1.52)	2.497 (1.66)	2.782 (1.56)
selection terms:				
λ_t^a	−4.541 (0.90)	—	−2.727 (0.89)	—
λ_n^a	—	—	−0.946 (0.83)	—
λ_t^b	5.167 (1.65)	—	5.737 (2.15)	—
λ_n^b	—	—	−0.497 (0.53)	—
Log-likelihood	−1687.42	−1688.95	−2647.04	−2651.37
n	2840	2840	4326	4326

Notes: ML estimation of (5) with (6). Figures in parentheses are t-ratios. Equations I and II are for the treatment firms, with and without selection terms, and Equations III and IV are for all firms. The variables are described in Table 1 and text. They include all of the variables in the selection equation shown in Table 2, except the identifying variables CONDR, DURTR and DATE, but EMPD, TURN, TURN2, TURND, POLCH and DIRECT are not shown as they are nowhere significant. The λ are the selection terms in (4) for Stages 2a and 2b; where the superscript indicates the stage (a or b) and the subscript denotes whether the firm proceeded to the next stage (t) or not (n). These are reported in full. Industry (IND) and area dummies (AREA) are included but not shown.

estimations for all firms by stacking the data for the treatment and non-treatment firms. In Equation III we include the relevant selection terms on both the treatment and non-treatment equations.[18]

The non-treatment firms should give the counter-factual position, so that in the absence of the assistance we expect the treatment firms to have the same survival pattern as these. We examined this in Equation III by placing dummy variables on the shape parameter, constant term, explanatory variables (except AID and POSTAID) and the selection term λ_t^a for the non-treatment firms, but as a group these were insignificant ($\chi^2(8) = 11.89$; $\chi^2(8)_{0.05} = 15.51$).[19] Individually, the only

---

[18]In Equation III λ_n^a and λ_n^b are zero for the treatment firms, λ_n^a and λ_t^b are zero for those firms agreeing the Terms of Reference but not submitting a Final Report, and λ_t^a and λ_t^b are zero for those firms not agreeing the Terms of Reference.

[19]Using estimates of the selection terms in place of their true values affects the standard errors of the parameter estimates, but the method of correcting for this is inappropriate. This applies throughout the analysis. With the exception of the POL and AID terms, visual inspection of Equations I and III reveals that the parameter estimates are similar between these equations, and the same applies to II and IV.

significant difference occurred for the POL term, but since the treatment firms in the higher grant rate policy areas tend to receive more assistance, this is correlated with the AID term in Equation I ($r = 0.49$) and hence poorly determined. For this reason, we prefer Equation III to I, in which the correlation between the AID and POL terms is much lower ($r = 0.28$), and hence in which we believe the estimates are better determined.

The estimate of the shape parameter α in Equation III suggests that the hazard rate increases at a decreasing rate with the length of time over which the firms are observed, but a constant hazard rate cannot be rejected ($\chi^2 = 1.85$; $\chi^2_{0.10} = 2.71$). The same conclusion is reached when Equation III is regressed using the data for each year. Survival increases at a decreasing rate with employment size, and is negative for firms with around 200 employees or more. This is consistent with larger firms being more at risk from takeover, but our subsequent analysis makes us think that these are distressed firms which are more prone to failure. There is evidence of a mild negative effect in seeded projects, while firms in the higher grant rate policy areas have higher failure rates, which perhaps reflects the less favourable industrial structure of these areas.[20] Survival is pro-cyclical with economic conditions, but when the GDP term is excluded the constant hazard rate is rejected ($\chi^2 = 5.78$; $\chi^2_{0.05} = 3.84$), which gives us some confidence that the GDP term is picking up the effect of recession.

If the selection terms are omitted from III, Equation IV shows that the AID term is highly significant. This contrasts with Equations I and II in which the assistance term remains strongly insignificant. The reason is that the assistance and selection term λ_t^b are both zero for the non-treatment firms, and hence correlated for the sample as a whole ($r = 0.50$), so that the AID term picks up the effect of λ_t^b when it is omitted in IV. However, in Equation I, which includes treatment firms only, the correlation between AID and λ_t^b is much lower, and actually negative ($r = -0.29$), so that the AID term remains insignificant when λ_t^b is omitted in II. This latter point is important, as it implies that the insignificance of the AID term in Equation III does not arise from correlation with the included selection term, but that the assistance genuinely has no effect.

We examined the sensitivity of the estimates to the model assumptions, but the results concerning the AID term were unchanged. This included omitting the POL and other terms. The technique for correcting for selection bias is based on a jointly normal error distribution, so in place of (6) we maximised (5) with an accelerated failure survivor model in which the error term is normally distributed (see Dolton et al. 1994). We also maximised (5) with a log-logistic survivor function to allow for an increasing and then decreasing hazard rate, but the results were unsatisfactory, indicating that survival is negatively related to employment size. Finally, if assistance improves a firm, but makes it more vulnerable to takeover, then this may account for a poor measured effect. However, we do not think this is the case, since under our definition of a firm closure the takeover would have to be accompanied by a change in economic function.

The significant selection term in Equation III of Table 3 suggests that firms with high survival characteristics are more likely to select themselves for assistance, but potentially there is still a problem of endogeneity. One possibility

---

[20]Firms in these areas have maturer products, an older age structure and higher costs, and this seems to dominate their greater access to financial assistance.

is that these firms are more likely to receive assistance because they have a greater chance of seeing the project through to the Final Report. However, defining the time origin as the date of agreement of the Terms of Reference, rather than the date of Business Review, we found that the results were little changed.[21] Another possibility is that firms with high survival characteristics are less in need of assistance and may be prepared to accept smaller grant amounts, so that assistance would appear more effective than it really is. Given the insignificance of the AID term, the direction of the bias suggests it is not a problem, but we examined it by including interaction terms between AID and those measured variables which are associated with firm survival to see if they enhanced its effect. However, the coefficients on these terms were insignificant and negative.

7.2 The Role of Firm Size

While the scheme has no effect on survival overall, firm size plays an important role in selection and survival, and it is possible that this lack of effectiveness may be due to a poor effect in certain size classes of firm. There are two reasons for this. First, smaller SMEs do not have a substantive track-record, so that the Consultant may have difficulty in gauging the appropriateness of the advice to firms, while a lack of managerial capacity or financial resources could

mean that these firms have difficulty in implementing the Consultant's recommendations. Second, assistance is effectively capped under the scheme at relatively small amounts for larger SMEs, so that the benefit of the scheme to these firms may be small or even negligible. The correlation between turnover and employment is not especially strong ($r = 0.40$), so that we consider both these measures of firm size.

With the AID term in spline form we searched on firm size to maximise the value of the log-likelihood. For each of turnover and employment this gave us three size groups, which we refer to as small, medium and large SMEs. The size groups are defined in Table 4, which also reports the estimated coefficient on the AID term for each group. These coefficients differ significantly between the groups shown (turnover: $\chi^2(3) = 12.44$; employment: $\chi^2(3) = 19.57$; $x^2(3)_{0.05} = 7.81$), which is also the case when Not Classified firms are excluded. We now consider the results in Table 4 for the different size groups. Given that the lifespan of the scheme is characterised by a sharp cycle in economic conditions, we investigate for variations in the effect of assistance both prior to and after the onset of recession towards the end of 1989.[22]

7.2.1 Small SMEs. The effect of assistance in small SMEs is negative and insignificant, whether they are consid-

---

[21]We estimated Equation III with the smaller sample of 3382 firms selecting into the scheme at Stage 2a. Using an exponential ordered score test there was no significant difference in the empirical survivor function for the non-treatment firms between those selecting out at Stage 2a and those selecting out at Stage 2b.

[22]Wren and Storey (1998) report the results when a quadratic time trend in τ is included on the AID term in Equation III. This shows that the effect of AID decreases and then increases with time, reaching a minimum in early December 1989. This pattern remains the same when the quadratic term is interacted with TURN or EMP to allow for firm size. The alternative of an exponential function was insignificant, while a test for a structural break on the shape parameter at this time was also insignificant. Since the quadratic function smooths the actual response pattern, and may be dominated by the skewed distribution of firm sizes, in testing for the effect of firm size we split the sample into two sub-periods.

Table 4
Coefficients on AID for Firm Survival

Category of Firm	Definition	Number of Treated Firms	Estimated Coefficient
(a) Sales turnover:			
Small SME	£0–£300,000	790	−0.123 (0.40)
Medium SME	£300,000–£2m	1347	0.616 (2.02)
Large SME	£2m+	194	−0.721 (1.19)
Not Classified	—	509	0.300 (0.82)
(b) Employment:			
Small SME	1–5	558	−0.209 (0.66)
Medium SME	6–80	1757	0.532 (1.72)
Large SME	81+	130	−2.046 (2.03)
Not Classified	—	395	0.452 (1.30)

Note: ML estimates of Equation III of Table 3 with the AID term in spline form. The size groups are defined at the time of the Business Review. Figures in parentheses are t-ratios. Not Classified are cases where turnover or employment is not known. Log-likelihoods are −2640.62 and −2637.60 respectively and $n = 4326$.

ered by turnover or employment. This may be related to the difficulty of these firms in implementing the Consultant's recommendations, which is consistent with the introduction in 1989 of the post-completion assistance for smaller firms. While individually insignificant the effect varies over time, with firms more likely to fail if assisted just prior to the recession (not shown). A similar poor effect was found for the sectoral schemes in the late 1970s, which led firms to mistakenly take-on extra capacity shortly before the recession of the early 1980s (Lambert, 1985; Potter, 1985). Insignificant coefficients were also obtained for the missing data, although a significant positive effect was found for the earlier period in the case of turnover. These mainly comprise start-up projects, so that the assistance seems to have

had qualitatively different effects in these firms.

7.2.2 Medium SMEs. The main result from Table 4 is that the scheme has a significant positive effect on the survival of medium-sized SMEs. The estimates are the same before and after the recession. The effect of the assistance on the survival of medium-sized firms is evaluated at the variable means in Table 5, and are virtually identical between the turnover and employment size groups. For firms taking the Business Review in 1988, the scheme raises their probability of survival to 1996 from around 0.56 to 0.60, and for firms assisted in 1994 from 0.89 to 0.90.[23] When the selection terms are omitted the measured effect roughly doubles from 1 to 20% after two years and from 4 to 7% after eight years. Com-

---

[23]For firms assisted in 1988 the scheme lowers the hazard rate from around 0.086 to 0.075 and for firms assisted in 1994 from around 0.070 to 0.062.

Table 5
Predicted Survival Probabilities

Cohort	Sales Turnover		Employment	
	Treatment	Non-treatment	Treatment	Non-treatment
1994	0.899	0.887	0.898	0.887
1993	0.847	0.826	0.841	0.825
1992	0.792	0.768	0.787	0.769
1991	0.741	0.710	0.739	0.714
1990	0.693	0.658	0.686	0.659
1989	0.647	0.608	0.642	0.609
1988	0.603	0.564	0.595	0.565

Note: Based on the estimates in Equation III of Table 3 for medium-sized firms. Calculated at the mid-year.

pared with all firms satisfying the Business Review, this tells us that the medium-sized SMEs selecting themselves for assistance have higher survival characteristics.

7.2.3 Large SMEs. The effect of assistance on the survival of large SMEs is negative, and significantly so in the case of employment, but there is not significant difference over time. The benefit of the scheme for these firms is likely to be very small, but since they are willing to commit resources to obtain assistance it suggests that the opportunity cost of their time and effort is also small, i.e. that alternative productive used are not good. It implies that they are poor performing or distressed firms, and that they are perhaps using the assistance to fund similar work, so that the AID terms is picking up an unobserved selection effect.

Overall, these results are encouraging since medium-sized firms account for

58% of the sample treatment firms by turnover and 72% by employment size. To examine the different elements of the composite assistance term AID (see Table 1), we entered the grant rate (GT), the Consultant's daily rate (CONDR) and the period of consultancy (CONPD) separately in place of the AID term for the medium-sized firms.[24] We found that the grant rate and daily rate were insignificant, so that the role of these is to cause selection into the scheme (see POL and CONDR in Table 2). The period of consultancy is significant, which means that the effect of the scheme increases with the intensity of the consultancy. It might be thought that CONPD is picking up the mere presence of assistance (although the coefficient of variation is much greater for this than either GT or CONDR), but if instead we include a dummy variable for firms receiving assistance we find that it is insignificant. The implication is that project success is associated with receiv-

---

[24]We also considered these in quadratic form and a decomposition of the AID term around the means, but the basic result was unchanged.

ing at or near the maximum of 15 days consultancy.[25]

Finally, a potential criticism of this kind of analysis is that it is contingent on the exact size groupings chosen. To examine the sensitivity of our results to the choice of the size group we further sub-divided our three groupings into a total of ten size groups for each of turnover and employment, and then estimated the AID term in spline form for these. Except for one case only, the obtained coefficients were negative for firms in the small and large size groups but positive otherwise, providing strong support the pattern shown in Table 4. We also omitted the quadratic employment term in Equation III and other regressors, but the broad pattern was not affected by this. This suggests that the scheme did have significant positive effects, but only in SMEs which were neither too small nor too large in size.

8. The Effect on Firm Growth

The effect on firm growth is examined for the surviving firms, making use of the data collected through the survey. These data are available for 1136 of the 2799 surviving firms, although from the time of the Business Review to the survey, sales turnover growth is known for only 909 firms and employment growth is known for only 1008 firms. Seventy-five per cent of the survey firms are treated compared with 70% for all survivors.

As a first step, we ran a ML probit equation for selection of the surviving firms into the survey, giving a further selection term such as (4), denoted λs. These selection results are reported in Wren and Storey (1998), and they confirm the impression given by the Appendix. The survey firms are those most recently taking the Business Review and they tend to be drawn from around the middle of the employment distribution. Further, the Consultants have higher daily rates and are more likely to be seeded.

The analysis is based on (1) to (3), but in which there are three selector equations (for Stages 2a, 2b and the survey), and the dependent variable is defined as the annualised growth rate, i.e. $y = \ln(\upsilon_{96}/\upsilon_{88+DATE})/\tau$, where $\upsilon = $ TURN, EMP and $\tau \equiv 8.5 - $ DATE (see Table 1). The annualised growth rate is discussed by Hall (1987) and used by Evans (1987). The growth rates for firms taking the Business Review in each year are reported in Wren and Storey (1998). This shows that the sample firms grew at an average annual rates of 5.2% by turnover and 2.6% by employment, but that while the turnover growth decreases with the length of the observation period τ, the employment growth rate increases. This indicates that job growth was strongest in the late 1980s, while sales growth occurred in the 1990s as the economy recovered from recession, but was largely jobless.[26]

For each of turnover and employment, we jointly estimated equations for the treatment and non-treatment firms i as follows ($\upsilon \equiv $ TURN, EMP)

$$\ln(\upsilon_{96}/\upsilon_{88+DATE})_i/\tau_i = \\ \beta_{1\upsilon}x_i + \beta_{2\upsilon}AID_i + u_i \qquad (7)$$

---

[25]One interpretation of this is that CONDR is signalling those projects where the consultancy (rather than the implemented project) was unsuccessful or broke down (i.e. where it was not at or near the maximum of 15 days), but rather tan select out of the scheme, these firms submitted a Final Report in order to claim the grant. Certainly, few firms withdrew from the scheme once the consultancy had commenced, with the DTI (1994) reporting that only 4% of the firms which selected out at Stage 2 did so after the Consultant had started work.

[26]This does not contradict our earlier finding of a positive correlation between turnover and employment which relates to the variables in levels.

where

$$u_i \sim N(0, \sigma_i^2) \quad \text{and}$$
$$\sigma_i = f_\upsilon(\text{DATE}_i, \upsilon_i, \text{GDP}_i, \text{AID}_i) \qquad (8)$$

The right-hand side of (7) is the growth function, which varies between turnover and employment. As before, the regressors x_i are the firm and project characteristics in Table 1, but in this case they include the information collected through the survey. These capture the main influences on growth (see McCloughan, 1995), but again firm age is an omission for which the same points apply as before. We include terms for assistance AID, post-completion assistance POSTAID and the output term GDP. Selection terms, including λ_s, are also included, and the identification of these terms is the same as before. The standard deviation σ_i of the error term u_i is made to depend on DATE in (8), as the variation in growth rates increases the shorter is the observation period. Numerous studies suggest that σ_i is also affected by firm size υ, and we include GDP and AID in f_υ, on which we say more below. It is assumed that f_υ is linear.

We regress (7) and (8) using maximum likelihood techniques. The results for turnover and employment are given in Table 6, which we consider together. As a test of the counter-factual position, we examined the constancy of the non-assistance terms between the treatment and non-treatment firms. These restrictions could be accepted in either case, but only with the inclusion of AID in f_υ. This implies that the support reduces the variability of growth rates of assisted firms. The estimates in Table 6 of the other terms in f_υ indicate that the variation in growth increases the shorter is the period of observation, the better is the state of the economy and the smaller is firm size, which all seem plausible.

The coefficients on the x_i in Table 6 show that firm growth decreases with initial firm size, which is consistent with that found elsewhere, although initial employment [turnover] size has a positive effect on turnover [employment] growth. Growth is lower for firms which are independent, server mainly UK markets, are located in the policy areas and for projects which are classified as "direct". Post-completion assistance has no additional effect on turnover, while the assistance has no effect at all on employment in these projects. Projects receiving post-completion assistance therefore seem relatively poor in nature, although Table 3 suggests that they have higher survival rates. Some other assistance schemes have positive growth effects.

8.1 The Effect of Assistance

The coefficients on AID in Table 6 indicate that marketing assistance has significant positive effects on turnover and employment. Using the same firm size groups as before, (7) was re-estimated with spline terms on AID, and the results are given in Table 7. This shows that assistance has significant growth effects in medium-sized firms, even stronger effects in small SMEs, but an insignificant effect on the sales of large firms.

The estimates were robust to changes in the specification, and were unchanged when the equations were regressed for the treatment firms only or separately for each size group. We tested for differences before and after the recession, and significant differences were obtained, but only in the case of small firm employment growth, again indicating that assistance was less effective when given to these firms just prior to the economic downturn. As a further test, year dummies were placed on the AID terms. These suggested slightly stronger short-run effects in small SMEs, but they were not significantly different from one another.

Evaluating the estimated coefficients in Table 7 at the variable means indicates

Table 6
Regression Results for Firm Growth

Variable	Sales Turnover	Employment
Firm characteristics:		
TURN	−0.092 (7.89)	0.029 (3.11)
TURN2	0.0025 (3.52)	−0.00011 (2.47)
TURND	—	0.113 (5.88)
EMP	0.0016 (5.78)	−0.0022 (4.48)
EMP2	—	0.50×10^{-5} (2.46)
INDEP	−0.135 (3.90)	−0.079 (4.07)
EXPORT	—	0.555 (1.79)
Project characteristics:		
POL	−0.061 (2.64)	—
DIRECT	−0.118 (1.49)	—
AID	0.035 (2.75)	0.030 (3.89)
POSTAID	—	−0.030 (1.71)
ASS1	0.098 (1.62)	0.090 (2.53)
ASS2	—	0.083 (4.35)
Selection terms:		
λ_t^a	0.006 (0.05)	−0.057 (0.68)
λ_n^a	0.084 (1.49)	0.036 (1.10)
λ_t^b	−0.037 (0.49)	0.033 (0.81)
λ_n^b	0.004 (0.09)	0.042 (1.31)
λ_s	0.025 (0.18)	0.021 (0.26)
Standard deviation (f_υ):		
Constant	0.114 (9.86)	0.134 (11.61)
DATE	0.067 (22.36)	0.028 (13.04)
GDP	0.014 (5.13)	0.003 (1.51)
υ (TURN, EMP)	−0.0025 (1.02)	−0.0003 (4.42)
AID	−0.0054 (1.82)	−0.0055 (2.00)
Log L	−186.84	186.71
n	909	1008

Note: ML estimation of (7). Figures in parentheses are t-ratios. Dependent variable: $\ln(\upsilon_{96}/\upsilon_{88+\text{DATE}})/\tau$, where $\upsilon \equiv$ TURN, EMP and $\tau \equiv 8.5 -$ DATE. The variables are described in Table 1 and text. They include all of the variables in the selection equation shown in Table 2, except the identifying variables CONDR, DURTR and DATE, but EMPD, SEED, GDP, POLCH, MARK and a constant term are not shown as they are insignificant in both equations. There are no non-zero observations on EMPD in the employment equation and likewise for TURND in the turnover equation. The λ are selection terms, of which λ_s is the survey selection term, and the others are described in Table 3. These are reported in full. ASS1 = Business Expansion Scheme and ASS2 = Investors in People. Industry (IND) and area (AREA) dummies are included but not shown.

Table 7
Coefficients on AID for Firm Growth

Category of Firm	Definition	Number of Assisted Firms	Estimated Coefficient
(a) Sales turnover:			
Small SME	£0–£300,000	207	0.0669 (5.78)
Medium SME	£300,000–£2m	407	0.0263 (2.33)
Large SME	£2m+	70	0.0012 (0.13)
(b) Employment:			
Small SME	1–5	152	0.0507 (6.45)
Medium SME	6–80	568	0.0249 (3.52)
Large SME	81+	43	0.0294 (2.03)

Note: ML estimates of eq. (7) with the AID term in spline form. The size groups are defined at the time of the Business Review. Figures in parentheses are t-ratios. Log-likelihoods are −171.23 and 196.85, and the number of observations are 909 and 1008 respectively.

strong impacts. The assistance caused the sales and employment of small SMEs to increase at annual rates of around 20% (from £127,000 to £151,000 in sales and from 3.2 to 3.9 employees when calculated at the means).[27] In the case of medium-sized SMEs the annualised growth rates are about 10% (from £846,000 to £921,000 and from 19.8 employees to 21.8), and for large firms employment also grew at 10% per annum (from 146 to 162 employees). These effects were robust to all our tests. However, once allowance is made for non-survival the expected sales growth of a typical assisted medium-sized SME (survivor or non-survivor) is a much more modest 3.2% per annum.[28] Likewise, the expected annual employment growth rate of a typical assisted medium-sized firm is 2.3%.

The selection terms in Table 6 are jointly significant, and when omitted the estimated coefficients on the AID terms remain significant but the annual growth rate falls by 6–8% in each case: to around 12% for small firms and to around 4% for medium and large-sized SMEs.[29] This underscores the importance of correcting for selection bias. It implies that the firms which selected themselves for the scheme had lower growth-rate charac-

---

[27]For employment these are based on the post-December 1989 estimates. The estimated coefficients before and after the recession with *t*-ratios are 0.0272 (2.59) and 0.0696 (7.27).

[28]By typical we mean a firm assisted at the mean implementation date (i.e. $\tau = 6.076$). At an annualised growth rate of 10% the average turnover of this firm grows from £0.846m to £1.510m by 1996, but since only 68% of these firms survive to 1996 the expected turnover is £1.026m at 1996. This gives an annualised growth rate of 3.2%. This is less than the average annual growth rate of all our survey firms (at 5.2%), but as we see the assisted firms have characteristics associated with lower growth.

[29]These reductions are slightly larger when the survey selection term ls is left undeleted.

teristics, and since they also had higher survival probabilities it suggests that they were the less dynamic firms. Finally, the factors underlying the success of assistance were examined, but again the significance of the composite term AID = GT*CONDR*CONPD derived from the period of consultancy.

9. The Effectiveness of the Marketing Initiative

In order to gauge the success of the Marketing Initiative we calculate its direct impact on output and employment, and compare this to its cost. It does not constitute a full economic appraisal, since the Marketing Initiative in effect provides a feasibility study, so that we do not know the cost of implementing the projects, and hence the firm surpluses. It also makes no allowance for the possible indirect effects. We utilise our estimates on the effect of assistance on survival and growth over the life of the scheme to calculate its average impact at 1996. This is disaggregated, so that we allow for different effects in the firm size groups shown in Tables 4 and 7 and for the different survival probabilities of firms assisted in each year in Table 5. These effects are then weighted according to the number of firms in each group.

Overall, we find that the scheme led to an average increase in sales turnover at 1996 of £138,700 and an average increase in employment at 1996 of 4.8 jobs. This may be compared with average assistance over the life of the scheme at 1996 values (using a 5% discount rate) of £4,600. When translated to the scheme as a whole it suggests that the Marketing Initiative was responsible for increased

sales of around £2,100m and an extra 72,500 jobs (all at 1994 prices). Even allowing for administration costs, these are remarkably strong impacts, which indicate that the scheme was highly cost-effective.

The magnitude of these policy effects leads us to question our approach as a basis for determining the impact of policy, but in fact the estimates are consistent with the Government-funded survey-based evaluation of the Marketing Initiative.[30] This found that on average actual or planned fixed capital expenditure was £41,200, and that firms put the increase in turnover at £58,700 and employment at 2.2 jobs, anticipating that these would rise to £252,300 and 3.7 jobs in two-years time (DTI, 1991a). These two-year effects were even stronger for a later sample of firms, which put them at £463,400 and 8.0 respectively (DTI, 1991b). Of course, this does not mean that these effects necessarily arose from the marketing assistance, and there remains the possibility of a spurious attribution. This concern is heightened when we learn that "most firms already had a clear idea of the project they wished to carry out prior to the assisted consultancy" (DTI, 1991a, p. 11). Nevertheless, there are special features of our study which make us believe that we have correctly identified the scheme effect.

First, the non-treatment firms undertook the Business Review, i.e. they were considering investment, and there is evidence from the DTI surveys that many of these projects went ahead in some form, especially since the assistance was small in relation to total project costs. Hence, we are not simply picking up

---

[30]The Government-funded evaluation drew up a panel of 420 assisted firms spread more or less equally across the six Consultancy Initiatives. The firms were first interviewed in late 1988/early 1989 (DTI, 1989b) and followed up with a second interview about a year later (DTI, 1991a). To counter any biases a second panel of 316 firms was later drawn up (DTI, 1991b, 1994).

the effect of investment in treatment firms compared with non-investment by the non-treatment firms. Indeed, it is the non-treatment firms which have the characteristics associated with relatively higher growth. Second, the correction for selection bias is based on observables only, but since both the treatment and non-treatment firms were successfully screened for the scheme then this is likely to reduce any unobserved heterogeneity. Finally, when questioned every firm reported that the assistance had affected its project in some way, i.e. existence, scale, timing, or quality, and the DTI surveys reckoned that between 40% and 50% of the benefit was in fact due to the consultancy (DTI, 1991b).

While the impact on sales from the Government-funded evaluation of the Marketing Initiative look to be within a few orders of magnitude of our own, we caution against making direct comparisons because of the different durations over which the benefits are measured. The average effect of the scheme on turnover of £138,700 is large in relation to the assistance of just £4,600, but a full economic appraisal would also compare this with the average capital and labour costs, of which the DTI surveys puts the former at £41,200. Perhaps of greater concern is the large aggregate impact on output of £2,100m. This does not include the indirect effects of the scheme, and it seems that there must have been substantial displacement effects. The issue has not been explored here, and it is largely ignored in small firm policy evaluation literature, but it seems worthy of future investigation. It is clearly an important issue in the design of these schemes, which form a key part of the Government's competitiveness programme.

10. Conclusions

This paper applies robust techniques to assess the direct impact of the publicly-supported "soft" advisory assistance on the performance of small and medium-sized enterprises. It focuses on the marketing advice provided by private consultants under the UK Enterprise Initiative, looking at its effect on sales turnover, employment and survival. It also takes account of selection into the scheme. Overall, it finds that the scheme encouraged the use of outside consultants, which altered the nature of projects, and impacted upon important aspects of small firm performance. In this way it seems to have demonstrated the value of this kind of outside advice to firms and overcome a substantial market failure.

Using survival as a measure performance a key result is that for smaller firms as a group there is no impact. Policy is however effective in the mid-range SME firms, raising survival rates by about 4% over the longer run and increasing growth rates in surviving firms by up to 10% per annum. This provides strong support for recent changes in UK small firm assistance, which has been concentrated more heavily on the mid-range SME firms through the Business Links framework. The treated firms have lower growth characteristics but higher survival probabilities compared with all firms which apply for the business support. When no account is taken of this selection effect then the measured effects are approximately halved.

The direct effects of the marketing assistance are extremely strong, so that on average £1,000 in assistance generates around £30,000 in increased sales turnover and creates one extra job. The magnitude of these effects draws attention to the possibility of displacement. Further, while the scheme seems to have been successful at raising the awareness of firms to the value of outside advice, having been applied once, there must be doubts about whether such an initiative could be repeated in the UK on such a cost-effective basis.

Acknowledgements

The authors are grateful to Don McPhie, Bob Brown, and Ron Cantrell for help with the collection and interpretation of the DTI data, to Philip Hamilton, Miles Storey, and Trent Surveys for help with the survey work and to funding from the Marketing Council. The paper has benefited from comments and discussions with Tim Barmby, Peter Dolton, Stuart Fraser, Patrick McCloughan, and Don McPhie. The paper has also benefited from presentations at the Universities of Lancaster, Leicester, Newcastle and Warwick, and from participants at seminars held at HM Treasury in December 1999 and at the DTI in November 2000. The authors gratefully acknowledge the comments of anonymous referees.

References

Audretsch, D. and Mahmood, T. (1994). "The rate of hazard confronting new firms and plants in US manufacturing", *Review of Industrial Organisation*, 9, 41–56.

Catsiapis, G. and Robinson, C. (1982). "Sample selection bias with multiple selection rules", *Journal of Econometrics*, 18, 351–68.

CBI (1994). *Management Development: A Survey of Small and Medium-Sized Businesses*, Confederation of British Industry with Touche Ross, London.

Cm 278 (1988). *DTI—The Department for Enterprise*, Department of Trade and Industry, HMSO, London.

Cm 4176 (1998). *Our Competitive Future: Building the Knowledge-Driven Economy*, Department of Trade and Industry, HMSO, London.

Cressy, R. (1996). "Are business startups debt-rationed?", *Economic Journal*, 106, 153–70.

Dolton, P.J., Makepeace, G.H., and Treble, J.G. (1994). "The youth training scheme and the school-to-work transition", *Oxford Economic Papers*, 46, 629–57.

DTI (1989a). *The Enterprise Initiative*, Department of Trade and Industry, London.

DTI (1989b). *Evaluation of the Consultancy Initiatives, A Report by Segal Quince Wicksteed*, Department of Trade and Industry, London.

DTI (1991a). *Evaluation of the Consultancy Initiatives—Second Stage, A Report by Segal Quince Wicksteed*, Department of Trade and Industry, London.

DTI (1991b). *Evaluation of the Consultancy Initiatives—Third Stage, A Report by Segal Quince Wicksteed*, Department of Trade and Industry, London.

DTI (1994). *Evaluation of the Consultancy Initiatives—Fourth Stage, A Report by Segal Quince Wicksteed*, Department of Trade and Industry, London.

Dunne, P. and Hughes, A. (1994). "Age, size, growth and survival: UK companies in the 1980s", *Journal of Industrial Economics*, 42, 115–40.

Dunne, T., Roberts, M., and Samuelson, L. (1989). "The growth and failure of US manufacturing plants", *Quarterly Journal of Economics*, 104, 671–88.

Evans, D.S. (1987). "The relationship between firm growth, size and age: estimates for 100 manufacturing industries" *Journal of Industrial Economics*, 35, 567–81.

Gavron, R., Cowling, M., and Westall, A. (1998). *The Entrepreneurial Society*, Institute of Public Policy Research, London.

Goldberger, A.S. (1972). "Structural equation methods in the social science", *Econometrica*, 40, 979–1001.

Greene, W.H. (1998). LIMDEP, version 7.0, Econometric Software, New York.

Hall, B.H. (1987). "The relationship between firm size and firm growth in the US manufacturing sector",

Journal of Industrial Economics, 35, 583–606.

Han, A. and Hausman, J. (1988). "Semi-parametric estimation of duration and competing risk models", Department of Economics, MIT, Cambridge, MA.

Heckman, J.J. and Hotz, V.J. (1989). "Choosing among alternative nonexperimental methods for estimating the impact of social programs: the case of manpower training", *Journal of the American Statistical Association*, 84, 862–74.

Keeble, D., Bryson, R., and Wood, P. (1992). "Small firms, business services growth and regional development in the United Kingdom", *Regional Studies*, 25, 439–57.

Kennedy, K.A. and Healy, T. (1985). *Small-scale Manufacturing Industry in Ireland*, The Economic and Social Research Institute, Dublin.

Kiefer, N.M. (1988). "Economic duration data and hazard functions", *Journal of Economic Literature*, 26, 646–79.

Lambert, J.T. (1985). "Ferrous foundry industry scheme", Government Economic Service Working Paper no. 77, Department of Trade and Industry, London.

Lavy, V. (1994). "The effect of investment subsidies on the survival of firms in Israel", Discussion Paper 94.04, The Maurice Falk Institute, Jerusalem.

Lee, L.F. (1976). "Estimation of limited dependent variable models by two-stage methods", PhD dissertation, Department of Economics, University of Rochester.

Lundstrom, A., Boter, H., Kjellberg, A., and Ohman, C. (1998). "Svensk Smaforetags-politik: Struktur, Resultat och Internationella Jamforelser", FSF, Orebro, Sweden.

Maddala, G.S. (1983). *Limited Dependent and Qualitative Variables in Econometrics*, Econometric Society Monographs No 3, Cambridge University Press.

Mata, J. and Portugal, P. (1994). "Life duration of new firms", *Journal of Industrial Economics*, 42, 227–45.

McCloughan, P. (1995). "Simulation of concentration development from modified gibrat growth-entry-exit processes", *Journal of Industrial Economics*, 43, 405–33.

McCloughan, P. and Stone, I. (1998). "Life duration of foreign multinational subsidiaries: evidence from UK northern manufacturing industry, 1970–93", *International Journal of Industrial Organisation*, 16, 719–47.

OECD (2000). *OECD Small and Medium-Sized Enterprise Outlook*, Organisation for Economic Cooperation and Development, Paris.

O'Farrell, P.N. and Crouchley, R. (1987). "Manufacturing-plant closures: a dynamic survival model", *Environment and Planning A*, 313–29.

O'Higgins, N. (1994). "YTS, employment and sample selection bias", *Oxford Economic Papers*, 46, 605–28.

Phillips, B. and Kirchhoff, B. (1989). "Formation, growth and survival: small firm dynamics in the US economy", *Small Business Economics*, 1, 65–74.

Potter, D. (1985). "The non-ferrous foundry industry scheme", Government Economic Service Working Paper no. 78, Department of Trade and Industry, London.

Robson, P.J.A. and Bennett, R.J. (2000). "The use and impact of business advice by SMEs in Britain: an empirical assessment using logit and ordered logit models", *Applied Economics*, 32, 1675–88.

Roper, S. and Hewitt-Dundas, N. (2001). "Grant assistance and small firm development in Northern Ireland and the Republic of Ireland", *Scottish Journal of Political Economy*, 48, 99–117.

Storey, D.J. (1994). *Understanding the Small Business Sector*, Routledge, London.

Storey, D.J. (1999). "Six steps to heaven: evaluating the impact of public policies to support small businesses in developed economies", in D. Sexton and H. Landstrom (eds), *Handbook of Entrepreneurship*, Blackwell, Oxford.

Storey, D.J. and Wynarczyk, P. (1996). "The survival and non survival of small firms in the UK", *Review of Industrial Organisation*, 11, 211–29.

Venetoklis, T. (1999). *Process Evaluation of Business Subsidies in Finland: A Quantitative Approach*, Government Institute for Economic Research, Helsinki.

Wren, C. (1994). "The build-up and duration of subsidy-induced employment: evidence from UK regional policy", *Journal of Regional Science*, 34.3, 387–410.

Wren, C. (1999). "Methodologies for evaluating the new business support", DTI Seminar on Assessing the Supply-Side Benefits of Business Support, HM Treasury, London.

Wren, C. (2001). "The industrial policy of competitiveness: a review of recent developments in the UK", *Regional Studies*, 35.9, 847–60.

Wren, C. and Storey, D.J. (1998). "Estimating the impact of publicly subsidised advisory services upon small firm performance: the case of the DTI marketing initiative", Working Paper no. 58, SME Centre, University of Warwick, Warwick.

Appendix
Characteristics of Sample

	No. of Firms	Proportion Treated (%)	Proportion Surviving (%)	Response Rate (%)
All firms	4326	66	65	41
(a) Year				
1988	913	59	53	33
1989	1014	62	58	31
1990	857	66	63	39
1991	702	72	71	42
1992	358	74	77	60
1993	308	71	84	49
1994	174	72	88	54
(b) Turnover (£'000s, 1994 prices)				
1–100	622	59	53	36
101–250	624	61	65	43
251–500	875	66	67	44
501–1000	660	67	69	42
1000+	784	71	71	42
Not classified	761	67	60	34
(c) Employment size				
1–5	879	64	60	41
6–10	508	64	69	43
11–25	1686	68	67	39
26–50	320	71	76	48
51–100	127	74	84	59
101–200	96	77	78	40
201+	34	67	77	35
Not classified	676	59	51	33
(d) Sector				
Primary and utilities	34	59	62	38
Metals, chemicals, and extracting	214	57	66	39
Metal goods and engineering	1045	66	67	44
Other manufacturing	770	61	60	34
Construction	209	65	59	33
Distribution and hotels	755	66	66	41
Transport and communications	117	62	58	32
Banking and financial services	883	70	64	43
Other services	299	71	70	48

Note: The proportions which are treated or survive are calculated for all sample firms, while the survey response rate is calculated for surviving firms only. In (a) the year is the date of the Business Review; in (b) a quarterly GDP index is used as deflator; and in (d) the sectors are Divisions 1 to 9 under the 1980 SIC (five firms in horticulture are included with Division 1).

Best Papers in the Field of Education

Introduction
by Kevin Hindle and George Solomon

Entrepreneurship education as a discipline and field of academic investigation was virtually ignored in the literature and as well as in the contemporary press until the early 1970s. Beginning in 1953, with the creation of the U.S. Small Business Administration and the developing interest in teaching entrepreneurship at schools such as Harvard, researchers, scholars, and teachers began serious inquiry into examining a set of propositions. Central among these propositions were could entrepreneurship be taught at all? If so, what pedagogy would you use to teach and which metrics could you use to measure what you taught?

In the early days, the dominant problem for development of an entrepreneurship pedagogy was a widely held belief among the general population and many academics that entrepreneurs were "born, not made." In other words, there was widespread suspicion that entrepreneurship was an inherent trait not easily developed and nurtured. A second important problem was a failure to distinguish entrepreneurship education from small-business education and the attendant belief that all one had to do was teach general principles of management and condense them for small business. Against this somewhat hostile backdrop, researchers, scholars, and teachers who genuinely believed that many aspects of entrepreneurship could be taught and that the core subject matter was a distinct area began serious inquiry into the development of an

accepted scholarly field of study into entrepreneurship education.

The first article, "The Chronology and Intellectual Trajectory of American Entrepreneurship Education 1876–1999" by Katz, provides a solid foundation to the chapter on entrepreneurship education. He begins by exploring the roots of entrepreneurship education, exploring the first course offerings in the United States and the evolution of entrepreneurship education through an extensive review of the literature including creating a comprehensive chronological table of significant events, studies, and milestones in entrepreneurship education. The article then presents some interesting data and trend analysis on the growth of courses, followed by a discussion of infrastructure elements and the issues surrounding the growth of publication outlets and credibility of scholarly research. This excellent article sets the stage for the chapter.

The second article, "The State of Entrepreneurship Education in the United States: A Nationwide Survey and Analysis" by Solomon, Duffy, and Tarabishy examines the current state of entrepreneurship education by reporting on a survey examining entrepreneurship education both in the United States and some selected international colleges and universities. Their results report the evidence that institutions are receiving major endowments for entrepreneurship education in the form of chairs, professorships, and centers. A surprising trend emerged from the data regarding entrepreneurship education and the use of technology. Growth in entrepreneurship education has accelerated over the last two decades. The dilemma is for the field to stay on the "cutting edge." This article provides data on the pedagogies being used in entrepreneurship programs and some trends for future development of courses in small business and entrepreneurship.

The third article, "Measuring Progress in Entrepreneurship Education" by Vesper and Gartner is another empirically based review of curriculum offerings at business schools, primarily in the United States. Vesper and Gartner's survey attempts to rank entrepreneurship programs and offer some insight into the dilemma of the ranking process. The authors conclude that there is no universally accepted set of criteria for ranking such programs and that a number of problems exist when academics attempt to rank an entrepreneurship program other than their own. They offer as a solution to the lack of a universally accepted set of criteria the "Malcolm Baldridge National Quality Awards." To the authors' credit, they raise the issues of methodological deficiencies in program ranking and criteria development and attempt to offer a plausible solution to both issues.

The fourth article, "Emerging Structures in Entrepreneurship Education: Curricula Designs and Strategies" by Plaschka and Welsch is a provocative piece, raising a number of compelling questions regarding the field of entrepreneurship education. Published in 1990, this article was one of a wave of scholarly pieces focused on challenging the field of entrepreneurship education's academic credibility and integrity. As entrepreneurship education grew in importance and relevance to the emerging field of entrepreneurship, it became critical to examine the pedagogical and intellectual issues surrounding the teaching of entrepreneurship principles.

Against the background of the professional climate at the dawn of the 1990s, Plaschka and Welsch examine whether entrepreneurship is a recognizable field whose theories support the foundation of learning. They also offer commentary on the state of management education in the United States and raise some important issues, especially in light of the Porter and McKibben study, critical of the lack of active participation in economic development process and the minimal emphasis on entrepreneurship. The authors present two *emerging structures of entrepreneurship education* and explain how these structures, applied to enhance established curricula, may provide a vehicle for change.

The fifth and final article, "Pedagogical Methods of Teaching Entrepreneurship: An Historical Perspective" by Solomon, Weaver, and Fernald provides a historical overview of the U.S. Small Business Administration's examination of small-business management and entrepreneurial education curricula and pedagogies. The authors examine the existing literature on both entrepreneurship and small-business management education. They then offer some suggestions for curriculum design in small-business management and entrepreneurial education, closely followed by an examination of course structures. The essence of the paper is a chronological review of four major surveys on entrepreneurial education with discussion and descriptive analysis of the various teaching formats (for example, courses, seminars) and pedagogies (for example, business plans, field-case consulting) used by professors in teaching the essential elements of small-business management and entrepreneurship.

These five articles collectively provide the reader with a strong initial overview of the issues surrounding the teaching and offering of entrepreneurship education. Of course, in a field now growing exponentially, the choice of just five articles is a judgment call that can only be indicative, not prescriptive. There is a plethora of outstanding articles, any of which could have been included in the chapter. Our hope is that our choices may act as a stimulus for readers to engage with a literature whose importance is now matched by its abundance.

The Chronology and Intellectual Trajectory of American Entrepreneurship Education, 1876–1999

by Jerome A. Katz

Since the first entrepreneurship class—held in 1947—the academic discipline of entrepreneurship's growth is described using a chronology of three domains—courses, supplemental infrastructures and publications. A 100+-item chronology of entrepreneurship education in the USA from 1876 through 1999 is offered and analyzed. The major findings are (1) in the USA, the field has reached maturity and (2) growth is likely outside business schools and outside the USA. The major problems include a glut of journals, a narrowing focus on top-tier publications, potential American stagnation and a shortage of faculty overall exacerbated by a shortage of PhD programs.

Keywords: History; Infrastructure; Entrepreneurship education; Entrepreneurship programs; Entrepreneurship chairs; Entrepreneurship centers; Entrepreneurship textbooks; Entrepreneurship research; Entrepreneurship endowments; Legitimization; Publications glut; Stagnation; Entrepreneurship journals

---

1. Introduction

It has been more than 50 years since Myles Mace taught the first entrepreneurship course in the United States. Held at Harvard's Business School in February 1947, it drew 188 of 600 second-year MBA students (Jeff Cruikshank, 1998, personal communication). In 1994, more than 120,000 American students were taking entrepreneurship or small business courses (Katz, 1994), and at the start of the new millennium that number is thought to have increased by 50%, although no new studies have been conducted. From that first class in 1947, an American infrastructure has emerged consisting of more than 2200 courses at over 1600 schools, 277 endowed positions, 44 English-language refereed academic journals and over 100 centers. The growth is impressive, even exceptional, but it raises a key question: What are the prospects for and the impacts of such growth for the 21st century?

Assessing the prospects for an academic discipline is better approached

Originally appeared in *Journal of Business Venturing*, 2003, Volume 18, Number 2.

less as a science and more as a speculative enterprise, guided by the lessons of history. In that vein, this paper offers the first detailed chronology of entrepreneurship education in the United States, both as a basis for providing preliminary answers to the above questions and as a common historical basis for others' speculations on the future of the field.

2. Methodology

The chronology itself reflects a publication trajectory of papers from the past 10 years on the infrastructure of the academic discipline of entrepreneurship (Katz, 1991a,b,c, 1994). These papers reflect a preference for errors of inclusion, rather than errors of exclusion. When respondents or archival sources indicated more than one event may have had an impact, each of the events was included. The paper also is eclectic and inclusive about what is meant by "entrepreneurship." It uses the "prairie populist" model (Katz, 1991c) in which "entrepreneurship" refers to a collection of academic disciplines and specialties including entrepreneurship, new venture creation, entrepreneurial finance, small business, family business, free enterprise, private enterprise, high-technology business, new product development, microenterprise development, applied economic development, professional practice studies, women's entrepreneurship, minority entrepreneurship and ethnic entrepreneurship. The advantage of the term as used here is that it is very similar to the way the general public views entrepreneurship and its myriad subspecialties—i.e., as one field. The intent is to establish a definition and chronology that is inclusive, in the hopes of crafting as comprehensive a list as possible, leaving subsetting-by-definition to others with particular theoretical models to promote.

Katz (1991c, 1994) focused on three major venues—publications, courses and supplemental infrastructure elements—

and those continue to be the focus in this Executive Forum. The methodology underlying the construction of the chronology was multifaceted, but straightforward, including the following:

- Review of key primary and secondary historical source documents were used including Block and Stumpf (1992), CEEB (1997), Christy and Jones (1982), Cooper (1998), Dainow (1986), Dennis (1997), Katz (1991a,b,c, 1994), Gorman et al. (1997), Herbert and Link (1982), McMullan and Long (1987), Meyer (2001), Peterson's Guide (1998a,b), Robinson and Haynes (1991), Sandberg and Gatewood (1991), Solomon and Fernald (1991), Solomon et al. (1994), Vesper (1993), Vesper and Gartner (1997) and Zeithaml and Rice (1987).

- Review of the websites of some of the major programs in the field, including the National Entrepreneurship Survey, eWeb, the Babson College entrepreneurship program and the Entrepreneurship Division of the Academy of Management.

- Review of responses to a series of queries about the history of the field posted to the ENTREP-L (entrepreneurship), FAMLYBIZ (family business) and SMALL-BUSINESS-ISSUES Internet discussion lists.

- Direct discussion with many of the faculty and other professionals in the field who had direct involvement or direct knowledge of the key actions and actors involved, including Karl Vesper, who developed one of the first listings of courses; Charles Hofer, who was involved in the creation of the dissertation awards; Jeff Cruikshank, who is writing a history of entrepreneurship education at the Harvard Business School;

Charles Matthews, about the Small Business Institute program; Bert Twaalfhoven, about European activities; Nancy Rothwell of the Institute for Scientific Information; and Ellen Thrasher and J. Hardy Patten of the US Small Business Administration.

3. Results

The chronology developed is given in Table 1. As noted above, the key ques-

Table 1
Chronology of Entrepreneurship Education in America

1876	Francis Walker's *The Wages Question* published. (First major work by an American university academic considering the entrepreneur. His 1884 book *Political Economy* will further extend his model for the entrepreneur. Walker was an influential theorist, having served at one point as President of the American Economic Association.)
1887	Hatch Act passed. (Created agricultural experimental stations, the forerunners of modern incubators and research parks.)
1893	49 agricultural experimental stations.
1911	Joseph Schumpeter published *The Theory of Economic Development* (in German).
1913	Schumpeter arrived in America and taught in Columbia.
1914	Smith-Lever (Agricultural Extension) Act passed. (Created agricultural extension to widely disseminate improved farming methods developed at experimental stations to farmers. The prototype of government sponsored business development services.)
1915	F.W. Taussig published *Principles of Economics*. (A textbook that makes the argument that the role of the entrepreneur is not merely innovation, but also wealth creation, which serves as the basis even today for a uniquely American definition of entrepreneurship.)
1921	Frank Knight published *Risk, Uncertainty and Profit* providing the first complete definitively American model of the entrepreneurial process.
1923	Cooperative Extension Service formally organized to deliver advice to farmers on agricultural and business practices.
1932	Schumpeter began teaching at Harvard.
1934	Schumpeter's *The Theory of Economic Development* translated into English.
1941	US Senate convened its special committee to study the problems of American small business. Report issued in 1942 with several recommendations for protecting and developing small business during and after the war, including using university resources for training small businesses and helping them innovate.
1945	Rudolph Weissman's *Small Business and Venture Capital* published by Harper. (One of the first books to argue for the importance of small business in the economy and the pioneering effort in venture capital.)
1946	The Research Center for Entrepreneurial History started by Schumpeter and Arthur Cole at Harvard. (First research center with entrepreneurship as its major focus.)
1947	(Feb.) Management of New Enterprises, first MBA entrepreneurship course started at Harvard. Myles Mace was the faculty member. 188 students took the course.

Table 1
Continued

1949	*Explorations in Entrepreneurial History* began publication at Harvard. (First research journal focused on entrepreneurs. Ceased publication in 1969.)
1950	William Hoad's *Small Business Casebook* (also known as *Cases in Small Business*) published as a monograph. (First collection of business cases focussing on small businesses.)
1951	Coleman Foundation created. (The first foundation with entrepreneurship education as a major focus. Makes program grants and has endowed chairs.)
1951	*Outline and Source Material for Small Business Education* (1950) by William Hoad published by the US Department of Commerce. (One of the pilot projects leading to the creation of the SBA, this delivered small business training through universities.)
1952	Pearce Kelley and Kenneth Lawyer's *Case Problems in Small Business Management* published by Prentice-Hall. (First commercially published small business text/trade book, contained short cases about small businesses.)
1953	US Small Business Administration started.
1953	Grant Moon reported that the University of Illinois offers a course in "small business or entrepreneurship development."
1953	C. Roland Christensen's *Management Succession in Small and Growing Enterprises* first published. (First major work on growth-oriented business, also a classic contribution to the eventual field of family business.)
1953	Entrepreneurship and Innovation offered at New York University by Peter Drucker.
1954	Small Business Management, first MBA small business course offered at Stanford.
1954	*Cases in the Management of Small, Family-Controlled Manufacturing Businesses* published at Indiana University. (First family business-specific case book.)
1954	Grant Moon began teaching a small business course at the University of South Dakota.
1955	New York (State) Bureau of Business and Distributive Education implemented a nondegree course, *Small Business Management; Adult Course Outline* in state colleges (Library of Congress Call No. 59021189).
1956	International Council for Small Business formed (called the National Council for Small Business Management Development until 1977).
1958	MIT's entrepreneurship course offered by Dwight Baumann.
1959	SBA Research Initiative launched. (First major government effort to use academics for substantive research on entrepreneurship. Included projects by Pickle, 1964; Hoad and Rosko, 1964; Mayer and Goldstein, 1961.)
1961	David McClelland's *The Achieving Society* published.

Table 1

Continued

1961	Halsey Broom's *Small Business Management* published by Southwestern. (This is the first book on small business focused expressly on the college text market. It remains in publication, with Justin Longenecker as Broom's successor.)
1963	*Journal of Small Business Management* (*JSBM*) began. (First refereed scholarly journal devoted to mainstream entrepreneurship/small business research.)
1963	First endowed position, the Bernard B. and Eugenia A. Ramsey Chair of Private Enterprise, created at Georgia State University.
1964	Service Corps of Retired Executives (SCORE) started.
1964	Collins, Moore and Umwalla's *The Enterprising Man* first published as a research monograph.
1965	H. Schrage's "The R&D entrepreneur: profile of success" comes out in *Harvard Business Review*. (First major work on high-technology entrepreneurship.)
1967	Norman Smith's *The Entrepreneur and His Firm* published. (First research contrasting high-growth entrepreneurs to slower-growth small business owners. One of first secondary analyses in entrepreneurship.)
1967	First contemporary MBA entrepreneurship courses introduced at Stanford and New York Universities. (In these courses, focus is on wealth-creation vs. firm creation, the hallmark of small business courses.)
1967	Approximately two schools offering courses in entrepreneurship (Vesper, 1999, personal communication).
1968	First undergraduate entrepreneurship concentration, Babson College.
1969	McClelland and Winter's *Motivating Economic Achievement* published. (First major study of entrepreneurship training with detailed outcome assessment.)
1970	Leon Danco held first interdisciplinary seminar on family business.
1970	First modern entrepreneurship center, the Caruth Institute of Owner-Managed Business, was established at Southern Methodist University.
1970	First major academic research conference, *Symposium on Technical Entrepreneurship*, chaired by John Komives and Arnold Cooper at Purdue. (Library of Congress Call No. 72177979/r883.)
1970	Sixteen schools offering courses in entrepreneurship (Vesper, 1999, personal communication).
1971	Peter Kilby's *Entrepreneurship and Economic Development* published. (Seminal early compilation of entrepreneurial theory and research.)
1971	"Black is beautiful, is it bountiful?" by Jeffry Timmons came out in *Harvard Business Review*. (First major published work on minority entrepreneurship.)
1971	First MBA entrepreneurship concentration, University of Southern California.
1972	Small Business Institute program launched by US Small Business Administration at Texas Tech University. By the end of the year, 20 schools were participating. (SBI sponsored student-performed field consulting projects to small businesses.)

Table 1
Continued

1972   Patrick Liles' *New Business Ventures and the Entrepreneur* text with cases first published. (First contemporary model entrepreneurship case text. Howard Stevenson was lead author for the current edition.)

1972   First undergraduate entrepreneurship concentration, University of Southern California.

1973   Association of Private Enterprise Education formed.

1973   Lawrence Klatt's *Small Business Management: Essentials of Entrepreneurship* published. (One of the first texts to cross over from small business to entrepreneurship.)

1974   Gordon Baty's *Entrepreneurship: Playing to Win* (Reston Publishing) was first published. (The first trade volume to get significant use in entrepreneurship courses—also one of the first texts devoted exclusively to the contemporary approach to entrepreneurship.)

1974   Entrepreneurship Interest Group of the Academy of Management formed under the direction of Karl Vesper.

1975   Students in Free Enterprise (SIFE), supporting collegiate entrepreneurship and free enterprise, started by Robert Davis of the National Leadership Institute.

1975   Karl Vesper reported 104 colleges/universities with entrepreneurship courses (Vesper, 1993).

1975   Al Shapero published "The displaced, uncomfortable entrepreneur" in *Psychology Today*. (One of the first major articles about entrepreneurs in the popular press.)

1975   Small Business Institute Directors Association founded.

1974   Five endowed positions (Katz, 1991a).

1976   Heizer Award for Dissertations in New Venture Creation first awarded.

1975   *American Journal of Small Business* (after 1988, *Entrepreneurship: Theory and Practice*) first published.

1976   *Entrepreneur Magazine* began publication.

1977   First nine pilot Small Business Development Centers (SBDCs) were started in California (2), District of Columbia, Florida, Georgia, New Jersey, Maine, Missouri and Nebraska.

1979   *Inc. Magazine* began publication.

1979   First SIFE student business competition (four schools represented).

1979   Harold Livesay's *American Made* published (launching point for the "entrepreneurial decade" of the 1980s).

1979   David Birch published "The Job Generation Process" working paper for MIT's Program on Neighborhood and Regional Change. (Provided impetus for government interest in entrepreneurship as the engine of economic growth.)

1979   263 postsecondary schools with courses in entrepreneurship or small business (Solomon et al., 1994).

1980   First of Don Sexton's "State of the Art" conferences held at Baylor University.

1980   Eleven endowed positions (Katz, 1991a).

1980   Public Law 96-302 passed, formalizing Small Business Development Centers (SBDCs).

Table 1

Continued

1981 First Babson Entrepreneurship Research Conference and first publication of *Frontiers of Entrepreneurship Research* (Vesper, 1981).

1981 SIFE's annual competition drew 100 schools.

1982 First undergraduate entrepreneurship course in a Marketing Department (University of Illinois-Chicago).

1982 *Encyclopedia of Entrepreneurship*, edited by Kent, Sexton and Vesper.

1982 315 postsecondary schools with courses in entrepreneurship or small business (Solomon et al., 1994).

1983 First entrepreneurship course in an engineering school, University of New Mexico.

1983 Association of Collegiate Entrepreneurs (ACE) formed.

1983 Neil Churchill and Virginia Lewis published "The five stages of small business growth" in *Harvard Business Review*.

1983 *The Business of Art* first published. (First text/trade volume focused on contemporary entrepreneurship training for a specific profession.)

1984 First Price-Babson College Fellows Program offered. (Pioneering training program for tenure-track and adjunct faculty in entrepreneurship.)

1984 Robert Hisrich and Candida Brush published "The woman entrepreneur: management skills and business problems" in *JSBM*. (First major work on women entrepreneurs.)

1984 First single campus business plan competitions at Babson College and University of Texas-Austin (known as MOOT).

1984 Collegiate Entrepreneurs of Illinois Conference. Group became Collegiate Entrepreneurs of the Midwest (CEM) in 1985 and the Collegiate Entrepreneurs Organization (CEO) in 1997.

1985 *Journal of Business Venturing* began publication.

1985 Peter Drucker's *Innovation and Entrepreneurship* first published. (This volume legitimized entrepreneurship among traditional Business School faculties and greatly increased the visibility of entrepreneurship among Business school alumni.)

1986 First national business plan competition held, under the direction of Tim Mescon, University of Miami.

1986 Vesper reported 253 colleges/universities with entrepreneurship courses (Vesper, 1993).

1986 590 postsecondary schools with courses in small business or entrepreneurship (Solomon et al., 1994).

1986 Gary Liebcap's *Advances in the study of entrepreneurship, innovation and economic growth* began publication. (First major annual research series specifically with a focus on entrepreneurship.)

1987 *Journal of Business Venturing* added to Social Science Citation Index.

1987 Entrepreneurship Interest Group of the Academy of Management became the Entrepreneurship Division.

1987 First National Business Plan Competition, San Diego State University. (First of the enduring national "open" business plan competitions.)

1987 *Family Business Review* began publication.

1988 *Small Business Economics* began publication.

Table 1
Continued

1991   *Special Issue of Entrepreneurship: Theory and Practice* on the infrastructure of the academic discipline of entrepreneurship.

1991   102 endowed positions (Katz, 1991a).

1991   57 undergraduate and 22 MBA programs with entrepreneurship concentrations (Robinson and Haynes, 1991).

1991   1060 postsecondary schools with courses in entrepreneurship or small business (Solomon et al., 1994).

1992   *Small Business Economics* added to Social Science Citation Index.

1992   Center for Entrepreneurial Leadership created at the Ewing Marion Kauffman Foundation. (The largest foundation with a direct interest in entrepreneurship education.)

1993   Vesper reports 370 colleges/universities with entrepreneurship courses (Vesper, 1993).

1993   EGOPHER begins operation. (First Internet site devoted exclusively to entrepreneurship education. Succeeded by eWeb—www.slu.edu/eweb—in 1995.)

1993   SBA Online FTP and Gopher sites began operation.

1993   Jerome Katz and Robert Brockhaus' *Advances in Entrepreneurship, Firm Emergence and Growth* began publication. (First major annual research series specifically focused on mainstream entrepreneurship.)

1994   First of three special September issues of *Simulation and Gaming* appeared on entrepreneurship education. Others appeared in September of 1995 and 1996.

1994   First ETP/NFIB Award for dissertations in Small Business given.

1995   Over 450 schools participating in the Small Business Institute program.

1995   *Journal of Small Business Management* added to Social Science Citation Index.

1996   SBA withdrew its share of funding for the Small Business Institute program.

1996   Lisa Gundry and Aaron Buchko's *Field casework* published by Sage. (First entrepreneurship text supplement series from a commercial publisher.)

1996   First Family Business major offered, Texas Tech University.

1997   SIFE has 264 schools competing at their annual gathering.

1997   Service Corps of Retired Executives (SCORE) began delivering consulting assistance over the Internet.

1998   SBA preliminary results showed 1400 postsecondary schools with courses in entrepreneurship or small business http://www.gwu.edu/~nes).

1998   SBI programs at 220 schools (Matthews, 1999).

1998   208 endowed positions (Katz, 1999).

1998   VuSME, the Virtual University for Small and Medium Enterprises, went on the World Wide Web. (First entrepreneurship distance education program deployed by a university, in this case a consortium of four schools.)

1999   (Summer) "Special Research Forum on International Entrepreneurship" to be published in *Academy of Management Journal*. (First special issue of a mainstream management journal dedicated to a theme in mainstream entrepreneurship.)

tion is what are the prospects for and the impacts of such growth for the next millenium? The answer is given using the three domains forming the chronology—courses, other infrastructure elements and publications.

3.1. Growth of Courses

The number of courses continues to grow at a fast rate as illustrated in Fig. 1, but controversy exists regarding what "counts" as growth. Vesper (1993) looks only at 4-year and graduate programs and only those teaching "entrepreneurship," defined as business start-up, especially among high-growth firms. Solomon et al. (1994), in a study conducted for the United States Small Business Administration (SBA), include entrepreneurship and small business courses, as well as 2-year postsecondary schools. So, Vesper (1993) shows courses growing from 4 schools in 1968, 16 schools in 1970, 370 in 1993, all the way to 504 in 2001 (Vesper and Gartner, 2001)—a rate of approximately 15 schools a year, while the Solomon et

Figure 1
Growth in Number of Endowed Positions and Schools with Entrepreneurship Courses

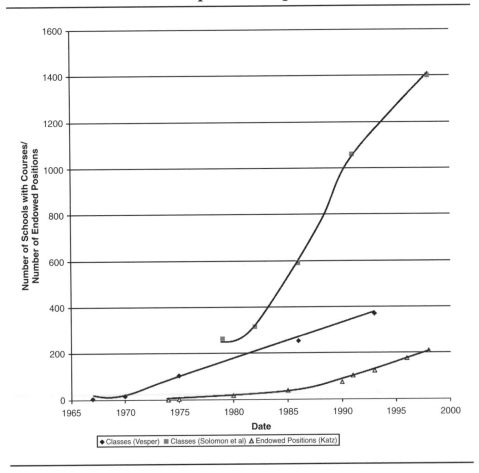

KEYSTONES OF ENTREPRENEURSHIP KNOWLEDGE

al.'s survey reports growth from 263 schools in 1979 to 1400 in 1998 (approximately 57 schools a year).

The Vesper/Gartner/University of Southern California and Solomon/Weaver/Fernald/SBA results are beginning to show greater divergence. The SBA studies show greater growth in small business courses than entrepreneurship, while the opposite is true for the USC compendium. The SBA sample is more representative, but the USC survey is more precise. In many ways, the results are not comparable and not resolvable. Both show growth and both show that growth is greater for some courses than others.

Neither group is adequately sampling outside of business schools in the USA or surveying schools and programs outside of North America. Vesper initially included engineering schools, but has discontinued the practice. Entrepreneurship courses in other university venues are growing, but no research to date covers this change. Examples of such courses include microfinance and indigenous business organization courses in sociology and economic development (Malecki, 1994), high-tech entrepreneurship in engineering schools (Vesper, 1993; Roberts, 1991), home economics (Heck et al., 1995), vocational education (e.g., International Consortium for Entrepreneurship Education), professions newly awakened to the need for training in the management of small profession-based businesses (Caplin, 1983; Katz, 1991b) and the traditional home of agricultural extension.

Similarly, growth of entrepreneurship courses and majors in Europe and Asia has been profound, but largely untracked, except for efforts by the European Foundation for Entrepreneurship Research, which focuses largely on top-tier European business schools. Vesper and Gartner (2001) found a similar pattern with 80% North American and 20% elsewhere, primarily Europe, in their sample of 128 respondents. Since most overseas programs are fewer than 10 years old, it shows the phenomenal growth of entrepreneurship education *outside* the USA.

In contrast, the early-adopter half of the roughly 3000 North American colleges with business programs have courses in place now. The remaining late-adopter schools will continue to draw out their adoption processes. Virtually, all schools with American Assembly of Collegiate Schools of Business (AACSB) accredited MBA or 4-year degrees, as well as nearly all nationally ranked schools, are already teaching entrepreneurship. These schools are generally offering multiple courses, including MBA concentrations or undergraduate majors in entrepreneurship. One web-based listing (Katz, 2001) identified 233 such schools worldwide, with 195 in the USA. Moving from courses to majors is the likely pattern of future growth for American business schools' entrepreneurship efforts.

3.2. Growth of Infrastructure Elements

In Fig. 1, it is also possible to see the remarkable growth in endowed positions, taking off after a slow start in the 1960s and 1970s and now doubling on average every 4 years (Katz, 1991a, 1994, 1999). Katz (1999) reports some slowing in the USA due to saturation, but indicates that growth overseas continues to climb. The American saturation point is indicated by endowed positions in most schools with entrepreneurship concentrations or centers. Even as schools add multiple chairs, the overall pace, while still fast, is no longer meteoric.

The bulking up of endowments was funded largely through the stock market boom of the late 1990s. For example, since 1995, several top-tier business schools have aggressively grown their center or program endowments past US$10 million each. For comparison, centers in the early 1990s had endowments between US$500,000 and US$1 million, with the largest reported endowment of US$4.5 million as a significant exception (Katz, 1994). These "bulked-up" centers and programs could lead to a broader range of program possibilities, in terms of support for faculty without endowed positions, student groups, incubators, consulting services, libraries and other settings.

Beginning in 1963, following the establishment of the first endowed position, the discipline of entrepreneurship's wealth has grown to exceed US$440 million with more than 75% of the funds accrued since 1987. The breakdown includes, at an average of US$1.05 million each, 277 chair and professorship endowments; at an average of US$1 million each, 100 center endowments; and 9 program endowments with a combined value of US$50 million. For comparison, *Business Week* reports that the endowments to major business schools as institutions since 1984 have totaled US$975,000,000 (http://www.business week. com/bschools/faqsnfigs/aacsb/aacsbgift.htm). It is possible that no other area in American business education draws on a larger or more widely dispersed financial foundation. Even with the dot-com bust of 2000 and the stock market declines of 2000 and 2001, the majority of American millionaires still come from the ranks of entrepreneurs, and a return to endowment bequests similar to the early 1990s is the most likely prospect.

3.3. Growth of Publications

Publications had several high-water marks in terms of books, throughout the field's history. However, it is not possible to discern a trend in the identification of books likely to have a major impact on the academic discipline. In lieu of that, it is possible, however, to find some indication of the growth of popular literature in the areas of entrepreneurship and small business.

The number of trade and textbooks in entrepreneurship and related disciplines continues to grow dramatically. A comprehensive survey conducted in 1995 showed 625 titles in print (Katz and Green, 1996). A 1998 replication using Amazon.com produced initial lists of 3555 titles in small businesses and 1132 in entrepreneurship, which when combined and cleaned produced a list of 2723 active titles. This approach suggests a dramatic rise in the number of trade and text volumes, conservatively shown to be doubling every year.

Impressive in the recent numbers, but somewhat slower in growth, are academic journals. Largely a phenomenon of the period since 1987, the number of journals have doubled every 3 years on average (http://eweb.slu.edu/booklist. htm). As shown in Table 2, 44 refereed entrepreneurship journals are accepting papers as of May 2001, with a new one starting approximately every 4 months (i.e., three new journals a year) since 1987. By comparison, in 1996, the rate was one journal starting every 6 months (i.e., two new journals a year).

With such growth, it is probable that journal supply is growing faster than researcher supply. For example, the Entrepreneurship Division of the Academy of Management grew from 600 to 800 members in a 10-year period (1987–1996), while the number of journals grew from 3 to 26 during the same time. Adjusting for increases in journal size and frequencies of publications, there were approximately 1200% more journal pages available per entrepreneurship professor per year in 1997 than in 1987. This makes a simple but elegant argument in favor of our soon hitting a limit to growth.

3.4. A Research Caveat

Before speculating on the future, it is important to note the major limitation of this particular Forum so far, namely its focus on the North American market. At several points in the Forum, the

Table 2
English-Language Refereed Journals in Entrepreneurship and Small Business Operating or Announced as of December 1999

1. *Academy of Entrepreneurship Journal*
2. *Asian Journal of Business and Entrepreneurship*
3. *Creativity and Innovation Management*
4. *Economic Analysis: A Journal of Enterprise and Participation*
5. *Enterprise and Innovation Management Studies*
6. *Entrepreneurial Executive*
7. *Entrepreneurship Development Review*
8. *Entrepreneurship, Innovation and Change*
9. *Entrepreneurship and Regional Development*
10. *Entrepreneurship: Theory and Practice*
11. *Enterprise and Innovation Management Studies*
12. *Family Business Review*
13. *International Journal of Entrepreneurial Behaviour and Research*
14. *International Journal of Entrepreneurship*
15. *International Journal of Entrepreneurship and Innovation*
16. *International Journal of Entrepreneurship and Innovation Management*
17. *International Journal of Technological Innovation and Entrepreneurship*
18. *International Small Business Journal*
19. *Journal of Applied Management and Entrepreneurship*
20. *Journal of Business and Entrepreneurship*
21. *Journal of Business Strategies*
22. *Journal of Business Venturing*
23. *Journal of Creative Behavior*
24. *Journal of Developmental Entrepreneurship*
25. *Journal of Enterprising Culture*
26. *Journal of Entrepreneurship*
27. *Journal of Entrepreneurship Education*
28. *Journal of Extension*
29. *Journal of International Business and Entrepreneurship*
30. *Journal of Microfinance*
31. *Journal of Private Enterprise*
32. *Journal of Private Equity*
33. *Journal of Small Business and Enterprise Development*
34. *Journal of Small Business and Entrepreneurship*
35. *Journal of Small Business Management*
36. *Journal of Small Business Strategy*
37. *Journal of Technology Transfer*
38. *New England Journal of Entrepreneurship*
39. *Small Business Economics*
40. *Small Business and Enterprise Development*
41. *Small Enterprise Development: An International Journal*
42. *Southern Africa Journal for Entrepreneurship and Small Business*
43. *Small Enterprise Research: The Journal of SEAANZ*
44. *Venture Capital*

An up-to-date list, including nonrefereed journals, is maintained at http://eweb.slu.edu/booklist.htm

alert reader will have noticed mention of program elements outside of North America. These are the tip of an unexplored iceberg. Today, entrepreneurship education outside North America is growing dramatically. While the number of schools is in the hundreds and programs in the one- to two-dozen range, the effort is starting at the top business schools and working down through the rest of schools. Already there are more PhD students in entrepreneurship outside North America than inside, and the number of highly capable researchers is growing very dramatically. While endowments significantly lag those of North America, there is more government commitment to funding. For instance, Germany funded nearly two-dozen entrepreneurship chairs in the late 1990s. In short, the worldwide market for entrepreneurship education is becoming more competitive in terms of programs for the brightest MBA students, PhD programs and endowed positions. With most of the new entrepreneurship journals being started outside the USA and substantial growth of European entrepreneurship, especially in the newly emerging economies of eastern Europe, American entrepreneurship programs will face unprecedented global competition for students in the classroom and mindshare in the media.

4. Implications

The American business schools' distinctive approach to entrepreneurship education has enjoyed more than 50 years of growth, with accelerated growth in the 1990s when courses, endowed positions, centers and publications began doubling every 3–5 years. What are the implications of these trajectories of growth for the field of entrepreneurship education in America?

4.1. The Major Findings

4.1.1. Maturity in Business Schools. In a field more than 50 years old, it is safe to say that the life cycle of entrepreneurship education in United States business schools is at the threshold of the maturity stage. This arguably is characterized by:

- Two widely recognized and consistent approaches: entrepreneurship (wealth-creation focussed courses) and small business (form-creation focussed courses);
- For each approach, there is considerable standardization across the industry (notably the reliance on the number, type and teaching approach to courses) (Plaschka and Welsch, 1990; Solomon et al., 1994);
- The presence of the service in the major venues, notably nearly all AACSB accredited business schools, as well as more than 1000 nonaccredited ones (Solomon et al., 1994);
- A complete educational infrastructure, consisting of more than 300 endowed positions, more than 100 centers, more than 40 refereed academic journals and more than a dozen professional organizations in the United States alone (Katz, 1994);
- An emerging segmentation of the discipline marked by the growth of specialized professional groups and publishing venues in economics, economic development, finance and high-technology; and
- Legitimization by various external sources, including
  ○ National rankings of entrepreneurship programs in the mainstream media (*US News and World Report, Business Week*) and
  ○ Inclusion of four top-tier entrepreneurship journals in the Social Science Citation Index (*Entrepreneurship and Regional Development, Journal of Business Venturing, Journal of Small*

Business Management, Small Business Economics).

4.1.2. Growth Outside of Business Schools. While entrepreneurship education in American business schools may be reaching maturity, demand in other markets is growing. Since the late 1990s, demand for entrepreneurship trade books has nearly doubled each year. Entrepreneurship offerings continue to grow in schools of agriculture, engineering, the learned professions, and arts and science, usually with minimal or no involvement by business school entrepreneurship faculty (cf. examples such as Carnegie-Mellon, Colorado, Cornell, Iowa, Laval, Minnesota, Missouri at Kansas City). If new approaches are developed there, business schools are not likely to know, much less benefit. The real risk to business schools would be if a new paradigm of entrepreneurship education emerged from these new sources, supplanting the model developed in American business schools and refined over the last 50 years. The 21st century entrepreneurship education would be certain to look nothing like its 20th century predecessor.

4.2. The Major Problems
4.2.1. The Publications Glut. Simply put, there are too many journals for faculty in entrepreneurship today. Few schools can buy more than a fraction of the journals, and most are not indexed or available on the major services like EBSCO, ProQuest, Lexis-Nexis or Info-Trac. With too many journals chasing too few good papers, the newer journals will face difficulties demonstrating the quality to get into indexes, into libraries and onto lists of journals approved for tenure decisions. In short, a shakeout could be coming unless the field grows much faster or the journals restructure themselves.

Ironically, the field arguably *still* needs journals—with niche journals being a likely area for sustainable growth. In looking at the number of papers presented at research conferences, areas like international entrepreneurship, women's entrepreneurship and entrepreneurship education have sufficient paper flow to warrant dedicated outlets. Using electronic publishing models, it would be possible to create journals able to survive financially on very small subscriber bases. For schools seeking legitimacy or visibility, such electronically published niche journals could be attractive. For commercial publishers, such journals have been risky. The *Journal of Small Business and Entrepreneurial Finance* and the *Franchising Research* were folded due to poor financial performance. Meanwhile, more than a dozen new general market entrepreneurship journals were started by commercial publishers.

4.2.2. Legitimization and Publication. While there is a glut of new and unproven journals in entrepreneurship, the leading-edge researchers in entrepreneurship, especially those at AACSB-accredited institutions, are increasingly focused on publishing in an even more select venue, the top-tier management journal. This is another indicator of reaching the maturity stage. Not only are articles on entrepreneurship appearing in top-rated management journals, but there are more journals devoting special issues to entrepreneurship topics, including: "International Entrepreneurship" in the *Academy of Management Journal* (October 2000), "Privatization and Entrepreneurial Transformation" in the *Academy of Management Review* (July 2000) and "New and Evolving Organizational Forms" in the *Academy of Management Journal* (December 2001).

Legitimization like maturity poses challenges. The greatest one is socialization of junior professors new to the field. For example, where should they publish? If they aim for mainstream management journals and away from mainstream entrepreneurship journals, we are likely to see research more generic (to appeal across management disciplines) and less relevant. The field of strategic management has achieved this type of "success" over the past 20 years, but seems to have done so largely at the cost of estranged relationships with the strategic planners in the business world. The orthodoxy and mainstream opportunities that have come as entrepreneurship education's payoff for success also pose the very real threat of less variance in thinking, in depth or quality of relation to the entrepreneurial community, and in the distinctiveness of the domain of entrepreneurship research.

4.2.3. Avoiding Stagnation. Can American entrepreneurship education cope with maturity? The big problem is avoiding stagnation. This is particularly possible where the internal business school "market" is rich—with abundant financial resources, publication outlets, students and programs to absorb faculty time. Entrepreneurs are warned about the danger success brings—getting "complacent with success" and forgetting about the energy, innovation and market orientation that originally made them successful.

The maturity of the field noted above, when contrasted with the explosive demand for entrepreneurship training and education outside of business schools and outside America, suggest America has reached a "complacent with success" phase. Historically, eager entrepreneurship faculty, on the prowl for mindshare that could turn into endowments, have emphasized innovation. Entrepreneurship was one of the first disciplines to have students consult (Gundry and Buchko, 1996) or to formally organize the use of adjunct faculty (e.g., the Price-Babson Fellows Program or Katz, 1995). Today, however, collegiate entrepreneurship education has institutional-

ized its original model for growth, creating a new orthodoxy. If the American business schools are going to generate a new generation of frame-breaking paradigms, they must once again consider embracing the "lean and hungry" mindset of their earlier stages.

4.2.4. Challenges in the Faculty Pipeline. Today, lack of faculty at every rank is the number one limiting factor of the growth of the field. At higher ranks, this shortage is reflected in the more than 20 open endowed positions, a number that grows almost monthly as new positions are created. At the introductory course levels, it is reflected in the high percentages of adjunct (i.e., nontenure track, part-time) faculty being used to teach entrepreneurship, even in some of the most famous business schools in America. It also is reflected by the growth of entrepreneurship and small business education across the university because demand has outstripped the supply of business courses and business faculty. Currently, the greatest growth of entrepreneurship faculty can be witnessed in programs outside the United States. American business-school-based entrepreneurship faculty represents a decreasing proportion of the community of entrepreneurship educators, both across the university and around the world. This means the previously taken-for-granted ability of American business-school-based entrepreneurship professors to set the agenda or *desiderata* for the field of entrepreneurship as a whole is on the decline. In the 21st century, entrepreneurship education will become a worldwide product with multiple national and niche competitors competing for intellectual mindshare, students and trainees.

4.2.5. PhD Programs in Entrepreneurship. A second fundamental weakness for entrepreneurship education worldwide is a lack of PhD programs providing faculty in entrepreneurship. Based on lists from eWeb and the Vesper and Gartner (2001) *Compendium*, only 12 schools offer PhD's specific to entrepreneurship [Calgary (Canada), Case Western, Colorado, European Doctoral Consortium, Georgia, Harvard, Imperial (UK), Swinburne (Austrailia), Jyvaskyla (Finland), Vaxjo (Sweden) Indiana, Jonkoping (Sweden)], although more than two dozens offer PhD's in management or marketing or even education where students can specialize (and receive support) in entrepreneurship (http://eweb.slu.edu/phdlist.htm). As a result, most of the holders of endowed positions come from other disciplines and, of the 1600+ schools teaching entrepreneurship or small business, the majority still make do with adjunct faculty rather than standing professors (Katz, 1991c, 1995).

Entrepreneurship education worldwide needs to aggressively grow the faculty from the ground-up. The Academy of Management Entrepreneurship Division has developed a white paper on doctoral education in entrepreneurship to lead the way in this effort. Doctoral faculty, trained in the history and specifics of entrepreneurship education, educated to perform leading-edge as well as mainstream research, and imbued with the challenge to look at the broader societal context in which entrepreneurship education is enmeshed, would do much to strengthen and adapt the field of entrepreneurship education. Trained in this way, the graduates would be in a position to make contributions in the 21st century to rival those of the pioneers from the last half of the 20th century.

5. Conclusion

Depending on how broadly one wishes to define entrepreneurship, it is more than 50 or perhaps even more than 100 years old. In America, it has grown to become an infrastructure of tremendous size, scope and wealth. It also has just gone through one of its periods of greatest growth, perhaps growth that was so fast that it might have outstripped the available intellectual resources. For American business school entrepreneurship professors, this means that they will face increasing competition for the brightest students and the best ideas and the premiere venues for publication from not only entrepreneurship faculty around the world, but from entrepreneurship faculty members in the office next door. In a way, this reflects the broader acceptance of entrepreneurship as a discipline of value in academia, and that is a tremendous success for a field that 20 years ago was uncertain of itself or its value.

For the American entrepreneurship academics in business schools, there are major questions to be asked in the near future about where work should be directed in terms of subject and market, how the competing demands of research, teaching and service should be balanced and, most fundamentally, how to maintain an entrepreneurial attitude in an academic industry that has tasted success in a big way.

The good news is that entrepreneurship education is certain to continue as a major and growing academic discipline worldwide. There are too many academics, too much established infrastructure and too much demand from students, firms and governments to let entrepreneurship fall into disuse or disarray. And from the standpoint of establishing the discipline worldwide, entrepreneurship education is succeeding beyond anyone's past predictions. One future uncertainty is the form or forms of entrepreneurship education that dominate in the new century. The next new paradigm could come from anywhere on the globe, emerging from the new infusions of culture, business settings and institutional influences. For the 20th century's history of entrepreneurship education, the world turned to America for inspiration. For the 21st century version, the world could turn anywhere.

Acknowledgements

Part of the research and the chronology for this paper was developed under contract from the OECD to the author for a working paper entitled "A Brief History of Tertiary Entrepreneurship Education in the United States" and is used here with permission. Sweden's Entrepreneurship and Small Business Research Institute (ESBRI) also provided assistance. The author wishes to thank Kimberly Green, Cheryl Nietfeldt, Magnus Aronsson, Claudette Jenkins and Maria Byström for their assistance and advice. Extensions and updates of this chronology will be available online at http://eweb.slu.edu/chronology.htm.

References

Block, Z., Stumpf, S.A., 1992. Entrepreneurship education research: experience and challenge. In: Sexton, D.L., Kasarda, J.D. (Eds.), The State of the Art of Entrepreneurship. PWS-Kent, Boston, pp. 17–42.

Caplin, L., 1983. The Business of Art. Prentice-Hall, Englewood Cliffs, NJ.

College Entrance Examination Board, 1997. Index of Majors and Graduate Degrees—1998. College Entrance Examination Board, New York.

Christy, R., Jones, B.M., 1982. The Complete Information Bank for Entrepreneurs and Small Business Managers. The Center for Entrepreneurship and Small Business Management, Wichita, KS.

Cooper, A., 1998. Entrepreneurship: the past, the present, the future. Keynote address to the 1998 Annual Meeting of the US Association for Small Business and Entrepreneurship, Clearwater, FL.

Dainow, R., 1986. Training and education of entrepreneurs: the current state of the literature. J. Small Bus. Entrepreneurship 3 (4), 1–23.

Dennis, W.J., 1997. The Public Reviews Small Business. NFIB Education Foundation, Washington, DC.

Gorman, G., Hanlon, D., King, W., 1997. Some research perspectives on entrepreneurship education, enterprise education and education for small business management: a ten-year literature review. Int. Small Bus. J. 15 (3), 56–77.

Gundry, L., Buchko, A., 1996. Field Casework: Methods for Consulting to Small and Startup Businesses. Sage, Thousand Oaks, CA.

Heck, R.K.Z., Owen, A.J., Rowe, B.R. (Eds.), 1995. Home-Based Employment and Family Life. Auburn House, Westport, CN.

Herbert, R.F., Link, A.N., 1982. The Entrepreneur Praeger, New York.

Katz, J.A., 1991a. Endowed positions: entrepreneurship and related fields. Entrepreneurship: Theory Practice 15 (3), 53–67.

Katz, J.A., 1991b. Educating entrepreneurial professionals: identification of the critical market. J. Private Enterp. 7 (1), 105–120.

Katz, J.A., 1991c. The institution and infrastructure of entrepreneurship. Entrepreneurship: Theory Practice 15 (3), 85–102.

Katz, J.A., 1994. Growth of endowments, chairs, and programs in entrepreneurship on the college campus. In: Hoy, F., Monroy, T.G., Reichert, J. (Eds.), The Art and Science of Entrepreneurship Education, vol. 1. Baldwin-Wallace College, Cleveland.

Katz, J.A., 1995. Managing practitioners in the entrepreneurship class. Simul. Gaming 26 (3), 361–375 (September).

Katz, J.A., 1999. eWeb's 1999 Survey of Endowed Positions in Entrepreneurship and Related Fields. St. Louis University. (http://www.eweb.slu.edu/chair.htm).

Katz, J.A., 2001. eWeb's Listing of Majors in Entrepreneurship and Related Fields.

St. Louis University. (http:// www. eweb.slu.edu/ent_college_list.htm).

Katz, J.A., Green, R.P., 1996. Academic resources for entrepreneurship education. Simul. Gaming 27 (3), 365–374.

Malecki, E., 1994. Entrepreneurship in regional and local development. Int. Rev. Reg. Sci. 16 (1–2), 119–153.

McMullan, W.E., Long, W.A., 1987. Entrepreneurship education in the nineties. J. Bus. Venturing 2, 261–275.

Meyer, G.D., 2001. The Evolution of Entrepreneurship Education: Current State of the Art. Plenary address to the ICSB World Conference. (http://www-bus.colorado.edu/faculty/meyer/evol utn/index.htm).

Peterson's Graduate Programs in Business, Education, Health, Information Studies, Law and Social Work Peterson's, Princeton, NJ.

Peterson's Graduate Programs in the Humanities, Arts and Social Sciences, 1998b. Peterson's, Princeton, NJ.

Plaschka, G.R., Welsch, H.P., 1990. Emerging structures in entrepreneurship education: curricular designs and strategies. Entrepreneurship: Theory Practice 14 (3), 55–71.

Roberts, E.B., 1991. Entrepreneurs in High Technology. Oxford, New York.

Robinson, P., Haynes, M., 1991. Entrepreneurship education in America's major universities. Entrepreneurship: Theory Practice 15 (3), 41–52.

Sandberg, W.R., Gatewood, E.J., 1991. A profile of entrepreneurship research centers: orientations, interests, activities, and resources. Entrepreneurship: Theory Practice 15 (3), 11–24.

Solomon, G.T., Fernald, L.W., 1991. Trends in small business and entrepreneurship education in the United States. Entrepreneurship: Theory Practice 15 (3), 25–40.

Solomon, G.T., Weaver, K.M., Fernald, L.W., 1994. A historical examination of small business management and entrepreneurship pedagogy. Simul. Gaming 25 (3), 338–352.

Vesper, K.H., 1981. Frontiers of Entrepreneurship Research—1981. Babson College, Babson Park.

Vesper, K.H., 1993. Entrepreneurship Education. Entrepreneurial Studies Center, UCLA, Los Angeles, CA.

Vesper, K.H., Gartner, W.B., 1997. Measuring progress in entrepreneurship education. J. Bus. Venturing 12 (5), 403–421.

Vesper, K.H., Gartner, W.B., 2001. Compendium of Entrepreneur Programs. University of Southern California, Lloyd Greif Center for Entrepreneurial Studies, Los Angeles (http:// www.marshall.usc.edu/entrepreneur/ postoffice/Compendium/index.html).

Zeithaml, C.P., Rice, G.H., 1987. Entrepreneurship/small business education in American universities. J. Small Bus. Manage. 25 (1), 44–50.

The State of Entrepreneurship Education in the United States: A Nationwide Survey and Analysis*

by George T. Solomon, Susan Duffy, and Ayman Tarabishy

This paper presents the current state of entrepreneurship education in the United States and internationally as reported by participants in the 1999–2000 National Survey of Entrepreneurship Education. Survey results indicate a small but growing trend in the number of courses, concentrations and degrees in the academic fields of small business management and entrepreneurship. There is also evidence that institutions are receiving major endowments for entrepreneurship education in the form of chairs, professorships and centers. A surprising trend emerged from the data regarding entrepreneurship education and the use of technology. Of those that responded to the survey only 49% indicated that they offer information on the web regarding entrepreneurship and new venture creation to students and entrepreneurs. Also, 30% of those who responded indicated that they offer on-line management and technical assistance for students and entrepreneurs. Finally, 21 percent of the respondents indicated they use distance-learning technologies in their entrepreneurship education courses or concentrations. Growth in Entrepreneurship Education has accelerated over the last two decades. The dilemma is for the field to stay on the "cutting edge." To continue to be a vibrant member of the academic community, pedagogies must reflect the changing times.

Keywords: entrepreneurship education, United States, survey

---

1. Introduction

The past decade (1990–1999) witnessed enormous growth in the number of small business management and entrepreneurship courses at both the 2 and 4-year college and university level. This expansion of educational offerings has been fueled in part by dissatisfaction with the traditional Fortune 500 focus of business education voiced by students and accreditation bodies (Solomon &

Originally appeared in *International Journal of Entrepreneurship Education*, 2002, Volume 1, Number 1.

*The authors wish to thank the Kauffman Center for Entrepreneurial Leadership for their support. The authors also wish to thank Dr. Erik Winslow for his support and editorial advice.

Fernald, 1991). The dilemma is not that demand is high but that the andragogy selected meets the new innovative and creative mindset of students. Plaschka & Welsch (1990), recommend an increased focus on entrepreneurial education and more reality and experientially-based pedagogies such as those recommended by Porter & McKibbin (1988). If entrepreneurship education is to produce entrepreneurial founders capable of generating real growth and wealth, the challenge to educators will be to craft courses, programs and major fields of study, that meet the rigors of academia while keeping a reality-based focus and entrepreneurial climate in the learning experience environment.

This paper reports on the results of the 1999–2000 George Washington University/Kauffman Center for Entrepreneurial Leadership nationwide survey on entrepreneurship education.

2. *Literature Review*

The following examination of the literature presents the historical context of entrepreneurial education; a comparison between entrepreneurial education and traditional business education; a review of the conceptual distinction between small business courses and entrepreneurship courses; and an examination of entrepreneurship education methodologies and evaluation strategies.

2.1. Historical Context

Entrepreneurship education has experienced remarkable growth in the last half century. Within fifty years the field evolved from a single course offering to a diverse range of educational opportunities available at more than 1500 colleges and universities around the world (Charney & Libecap, 2000). The field's earliest roots are traced to Japan where in 1938, Shigeru Fujuii, Professor Emeritus at Kobe University, initiated the first efforts in applied education in entrepreneurship (McMullen and Long, 1987).

Courses in small business management began to emerge in the 1940's (Sexton and Upton, 1984) and in 1958, Dwight Baumann, an engineering professor at MIT, introduced what may have been the first course in entrepreneurship in the United States (McMullen and Long, 1987).

The early prediction that "... the number of course offerings should increase at an expanding rate over the next few years" (Vesper, 1985, p. 380) held true. In 1985, 253 colleges or universities offered courses in small business management or entrepreneurship and in 1993, 441 entrepreneurship courses were available to interested students (Vesper, 1994). By 1999, Foote reported student enrollment in entrepreneurship classes at five top U.S. business schools increased 92 percent from 1996 to 1999 (from a total of 3,078 to 5,913) and the number of entrepreneurship classes offered increased 74 percent. A recent estimate suggests that entrepreneurship and small business education may now be offered in as many as 1200 post secondary institutions in the United States alone (Solomon, 2001) with educational experiences ranging from traditional course work to integrative curricula that include marketing, finance, new product development and technology (Charney & Libecap, 2000).

2.2. Differentiating Traditional Business Education from Entrepreneurship Education

Although small business management and entrepreneurship courses have experienced remarkable growth in the last several decades, there is consensus that the field is far from maturity (Robinson and Hayes, 1991). As the field evolves, discussion continues regarding the field's relevance, course content, pedagogy, and effectiveness measures (Solomon, Weaver, and Fernald, Jr., 1994). Early discussions focused on the need for entrepreneurship education and questioned whether entrepreneurship courses were not simply traditional management courses with a new label (King, 2001). While there is general agreement that the core management courses offered in traditional business programs are essential for success in any business career, (Vesper and McMullan, 1987; Block and Stumpf, 1992), there are fundamental differences between business principles applied to new ventures and those applied to large corporations (Davis, Hills, and LaForge, 1985).

Unlike the functional "specialist" focus of traditional business programs such as accounting, marketing or finance, entrepreneurial education requires a "generalists" approach that integrates and combines a variety of functional skills and knowledge (Hills, 1988; Block and Stumpf, 1992). Entrepreneurship education is also differentiated by stage of development, the central problem of new venture. Traditional management education presents the functional format as if it were equally applicable to ventures at all levels of development, from an idea onward as though no differentiation by stage of development is required" (McMullan and Long, 1987, p. 267). Courses and programs in entrepreneurship education must focus on early lifecycle development challenges; particularly those related to startup (Vesper and McMullan, 1987) such as opportunity recognition, market entry, protecting intellectual property, the legal requirements of new businesses and severe resource constraints. Educational content must also address the lack of specialized functional expertise, the ways in which some organizational objectives differ from mature firms, and the finite time span available to generate profits (Loucks, 1982; Hills, 1988).

A core objective of entrepreneurship education that differentiates it from typical business education is "to generate more quickly a greater variety of different ideas for how to exploit a business opportunity, and the ability to project a more extensive sequence of actions for entering business . . ." (Vesper and McMullen, 1988. p. 9). Business entry is fundamentally a different activity than managing a business (Gartner and Vesper, 1994); entrepreneurial education must address the equivocal nature of business entry (Gartner, Bird, and Starr, 1992). To this end, entrepreneurial education must include skill-building courses in negotiation, leadership, new product development, creative thinking and exposure to technological innovation (McMullen and Long, 1987; Vesper and McMullen, 1988). Other areas identified as important for entrepreneurial education include awareness of entrepreneurial career options (Hills, 1988; Donckels, 1991); sources of venture capital (Vesper and McMullan, 1988; Zeithaml and Rice, 1987); idea protection (Vesper and McMullan, 1988); ambiguity tolerance (Ronstadt, 1987); the characteristics that define the entrepreneurial personality (Hills, 1988; Scott and Twomey, 1988; Hood and Young, 1993) and the challenges associated with each stage of venture development (McMullen and Long, 1987; Plaschka and Welsch, 1990).

The integrated nature, specific skills, and business lifecycle issues inherent in new ventures differentiate entrepreneurial education from a traditional business education. An additional comparison, within the context of entrepreneurial education, can be made between small business management courses and entrepreneurship courses—a distinction not always addressed in the literature (Zeithaml and Rice, 1987).

2.3. Small Business Management and Entrepreneurship Courses

Unlike many specialized business courses, courses in both small business management and entrepreneurship focus on the total firm. These courses provide a breadth of creative managerial skills and knowledge that is the "closest approach to the original concept of professional management education offered at colleges and universities" (Zeithaml and Rice, 1987, p. 50). Both types of courses frequently provide students with opportunities to gain the knowledge and skills needed to generate a business concept, determine its feasibility, launch and operate a business, and develop exit strategies (Solomon, Weaver, and Fernald, Jr., 1994). Although small business management and entrepreneurship courses are closely related, there are also important conceptual differences between the two education types (Zeithaml and Rice, 1987; Solomon and Fernald, Jr., 1993). Small business management courses focus on achieving normal sales, profits and growth within an existing business. The traditional objective of small business management programs is to provide students with management know-how related to managing and operating small, post-startup companies including "setting goals and objectives, leading, planning, organizing and controlling from a small business perspective" (Solomon and Fernald, 1993, p. 5). In contrast, entrepreneurship education focuses on originating and developing new growth ventures (Guglielmino and Klatt, 1993; Marchigiano-Monroy, 1993) with an emphasis on high profitability, rapid growth, and expedient exit strategies (Solomon, et al., 1994).

2.4. Moving beyond the Nature versus Nurture Debate

Continued rapid growth in both small business management courses and entrepreneurship courses offers some credibility for the assumption that skills relevant to successful entrepreneurship can be taught (Solomon and Fernald, 1991). In a study of entrepreneurial program graduates, Clark, et al. (1984) found evidence to suggest that the teaching of entrepreneurial and small business management skills aided new venture creation and

success. A survey of 100 chief executives in entrepreneurial firms found that respondents believed that "while personality traits are difficult to influence, the vast majority of knowledge required by entrepreneurs can be taught" (Hood and Young, 1993). Additional support for this view comes from a ten-year (1985–1994) literature review of enterprise, entrepreneurship and small business management education that reported ". . . most of the empirical studies surveyed indicated that entrepreneurship can be taught, or at least encouraged, by entrepreneurship education" (Gorman, Hanlon & King, 1997, p. 63).

Given the relationship between entrepreneurial activity and economic development and the widely accepted notion that entrepreneurial ventures are the key to innovation, productivity and effective competition (Plaschka and Welsch, 1990), the question of whether entrepreneurship can be taught is obsolete. Ronstadt (1987) posed the more relevant question regarding entrepreneurial education: what should be taught and how should it be taught?

2.5. Education Methodologies

2.5.1. Course Content. Despite general agreement that entrepreneurship can be taught, there is little uniformity in program offerings (Gorman, Hanlon and King, 1997). This may be a function of an emerging field with a limited, but growing, body of knowledge. As researchers and scholars develop frameworks and sets of hypotheses for the study of emerging business successes and failures, the content of courses will evolve based on what is needed and what can be taught for the successful development of a new venture (Block and Stumpf, 1992). According to Ronstadt, the program focus of "the old school" was on action; the business plan; and exposure to experienced visitors who inspired students through stories and practical advice. This era of entrepreneurship education was "one venture" centered and was essentially based on the premise that entrepreneurial success was a function of the "right human traits and characteristics" (1990, p. 76). "The new school", while still action oriented, builds and relies on some level of personal, technical or industry experience. It requires critical thinking, ethical assessment and is based on the premise that successful entrepreneurial activities are a function of human, venture and environmental conditions. This newer form of entrepreneurship education also focuses on entrepreneurship as a career process composed of multiple new ventures and the essential skill of networking or "entrepreneurial know-who" (Ronstadt, 1990, p. 80).

Another view from McMullan and Long calls for entrepreneurial education programs to have some of the core functional elements of a business administration program, but to present those functions from the "vantage point of a start up" (1987, p. 11). In addition to entrepreneurship-specific content, such as the social, psychological, historical and economic aspects of entrepreneurship, the program should include skill practice in one-on-one negotiations, oral presentations and persuasive writing. Courses should be structured around a series of strategic development challenges including opportunity identification and feasibility analysis; new venture planning, financing and operating; new market development and expansion strategies; and institutionalizing innovation (McMullan, Long and Vesper, 1988).

Real-time entrepreneurial activities include "projecting new technological developments, strategically planning, assisting in attracting necessary resources, and arranging for joint ventures" (vesper and McMullen, 1988, p. 11). Ideally students should create multiple venture plans, practice identification of opportunities, and have extensive exposure to entrepreneur role models.

Student interaction with these role models may occur in several important ways including having entrepreneurs serve as coaches and mentors (Hills, 1988; Mitchell and Chesteen, 1995), classroom speakers (Hills, 1988), and interview subjects (Hills, 1988; Solomon et al., 1994; Truell, et al., 1998). Effective entrepreneurial education requires students to have substantial hands-on experience working with community ventures so that they can learn to add value to real ventures and thus be prepared to add value to their own ventures (McMullan and Long, 1987).

2.5.2. Pedagogy. In addition to course content, educators are challenged with designing effective learning opportunities for entrepreneurship students. Sexton and Upton suggested that programs for entrepreneurship students should emphasize individual activities over group activities, be relatively unstructured, and present problems that require a "novel solution under conditions of ambiguity and risk" (1984, p. 24). Students must be prepared to thrive in the "unstructured and uncertain nature of entrepreneurial environments" (Ronstadt, 1990). This kind of experience is offered to students in innovative entrepreneurship programs recognized by the United States Association for Small Business and Entrepreneurship (USASBE). Highlights of these programs include the following activities:

- A rigorous business plan evaluation by an outside panel of business leaders held just prior to graduation. Students who do not pass this "final" evaluation do not graduate and must wait another year for a second chance to complete degree requirements (Ball State University);
- An internal business plan competition where qualifying MBA teams present business plans to a panel

of six judges comprised of investment advisers and venture capitalists. The winning team receives $10,000 and an additional $20,000 in 2-for-1 matching dollars for committing to invest their winnings in the business startup (University of Louisville);

- In addition to coursework, internship activities and networking events, students apply for university-based venture funds and incubator facilities. This startup "hatchery" offers students the opportunity to learn about the risks, problems, and rewards that make up the entrepreneurial experience (Miami University of Ohio).

Offering students opportunities to "experience" entrepreneurship and small business management is a theme among many entrepreneurial education programs. The most common elements in entrepreneurship courses continue to be venture plan writing, case studies, readings, and lectures by guest speakers and faculty (Vesper, 1985; Klatt, 1988; Kent, 1990; Gartner and Vesper, 1994). The typical elements of small business management courses include class work, tests, and a major project, which is usually a consulting project (Carroll, 1993). Project based, experiential learning is widespread in entrepreneurial education and may take myriad forms such as the development of business plans (Hills, 1988; Vesper and McMullan, 1988; Preshing, 1991; Gartner, and Vesper, 1994; Gorman et al., 1997); student business start-ups (Hills, 1988; Truell et al., 1998); consultation with practicing entrepreneurs (Klatt, 1988; Solomon et al., 1994); computer simulations (Brawer, 1997); and behavioral simulations (Stumpf, et al., 1991). Other popular activities include interviews with entrepreneurs, environmental scans (Solomon, et al., 1994), "live" cases (Gartner and Vesper, 1994), field trips, and the use of

video and films (Klatt, 1988). Student entrepreneurship clubs are also widespread (Vesper and Gartner, 1994).

Anticipated changes in course pedagogy include a greater use of various types of cases, increased international considerations, a more intense focus on stategy formation and implementation, and an increase in the use of computers for various purposes (Ahiarah, 1989). Computer simulations provide entrepreneurial students "with multiple experiences of simulated new venture decision making" (Clouse, 1990, p. 51). The use of computer simulations described by Brewer, et al. (1993) affords students realistic entrepreneurship experiences that develop skills in complex decision-making and offer instant feedback.

Pedagogy is also changing based on a broadening market interest in entrepreneurial education. New interdisciplinary programs use faculty teams to develop programs for the non-business student and there is a growing trend in courses specifically designed for art, engineering and science students. In addition to courses focused on preparing the future entrepreneur and small business manager, instructional methodologies should also be developed for those who manage entrepreneurs in organizations; potential resource people (accountants, lawyers, consultants) used by entrepreneurs; and top managers who must provide vision and leadership for corporations which must innovate in order to survive (Block and Stumpf, 1992).

2.6. Entrepreneurship Education Evaluation Strategies

Evaluation of entrepreneurship education encompasses assessment of both the individual student and the program as a whole. Current student assessment methodologies combine traditional and entrepreneurial techniques. Conventional business education evaluation strategies of tests and written case studies are supplemented by innovative assessment methods that include having students evaluate each other's venture plan; having venture capitalists evaluate students' venture plans; using a live case for the final examination; and "adopting a grading policy under which any student who manages to raise $10,000 or more on the basis of a plan developed in the course receives an automatic 'A'" (Vesper, 1986, p. 383). To adequately measure the impact entrepreneurial education has on students' knowledge and attitudes, "a uniform method of evaluation which permits comparisons between students, faculty, pedagogical method, course content, and other variables is needed" (Block and Stumpf, 1992).

Measuring program success is also vital to the evolution of the field. While student acceptance (Block and Stumpf, 1992) and number of students graduated (McMullan and Long, 1987) are requisite measures of effectiveness, these indicators are not adequate. The fundamental measure of effectiveness of entrepreneurial education should be measured by socioeconomic impact produced (McMullan and Long, 1987; Block and Stumpf, 1992). Evaluation should consider the number, types and growth rate of companies produced (McMullan and Long, 1987), the contribution to the economy in terms of employment, and the degree of career satisfaction of students (Block and Stumpf, 1992). A challenge to the academic entrepreneurship education community is to develop solid theoretical bases upon which to build pedagogical models (Robinson and Hayes, 1991) and systematic evaluation strategies. "Like any new venture, these programs must be given room to breathe, flexibility of movement in order to develop their educational products, and protection to grow and flower into healthy maturity" (Ronstadt, 1990).

3. Methodology

The George Washington University developed a mail survey to examine the current state of entrepreneurial education in the United States and internationally and to evaluate the extent and breadth of entrepreneurial education methods and course offerings during the 1999–2000 academic year. The study also sought to examine pedagogical developments and trends, as well as any relations between and among students, course offerings and teaching pedagogy. Finally, the study sought to examine what innovative and creative teaching pedagogies were being introduced into the classroom such as use of the Internet and educational technologies.

The content of the survey is organized as follows:

1. Identify institutional academic entities—two-year community and junior colleges, four-year colleges and universities and international colleges and universities—which were offering small business and entrepreneurial educational programs.
2. Examine trends in entrepreneurial education in both the United States and internationally and closely examine the multiple course offerings, concentrations and majors at both the undergraduate and graduate level.
3. Explore teaching pedagogies and assessments employed both in and outside of the class setting.
4. Identify the traditional and non-traditional pedagogies and assessment techniques employed given the non-traditional foci of the filed.

Over 4000 questionnaires were initially mailed to 2 and 4-year colleges and universities both in the United States and internationally. After a month, a follow-up postcard was sent including an incentive offer to stimulate response rate. Finally, 240 qualified responses were received both through the mail and through online submissions.

In order to conduct meaningful data analysis, the data were analyzed using the Statistical Package for the Social Sciences Personal Computer Plus software (SPSS PC+). Data regarding type of institution were recoded and broken into three discrete groupings [two-year community and junior colleges, four-year colleges and universities, and international universities and colleges]. The questions regarding trends in entrepreneurial education, which offered respondents the opportunity to select as many of the responses as they perceived applicable to their institution, were coded using the multiple response technique of SPSS PC+. An analysis of the survey data is the focus of the next section.

3.1. Results

The results of the survey are presented as responses to specific questions on the survey.

1. **Please indicate what type of academic institution your school represents.** The responses to this question indicated that 80 percent of the respondents to the survey were four-year colleges and universities, that 13 percent of the respondents to the survey were two-year community and junior colleges and that 6 percent of the respondents to the survey were international universities and colleges.

2. **What year did your educational institution first start offering courses on Entrepreneurship?** A frequency analysis of the data indicates that the range of years in which schools started offering courses on Entrepreneurship was from 1978 to 1999. The modal year that the educational institution started offering courses on Entrepreneurship and or Small Business was 1982.

3. **What types of courses are offered in the area of Entrepreneurship and or Small Business in your educational institution?** As shown in Figure 1, the data indicate for all respondents, 2-year colleges, 4-year colleges and universities and international colleges, Small Busi-

Figure 1
Course Offerings in Entrepreneurship

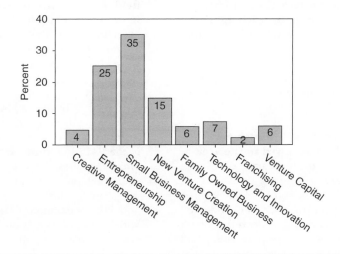

Table 1
Courses Offered by Institution

2-Year Colleges	4-Year Colleges and Universities	International Colleges and Universities
1. Small Business Management	1. Small Business Management	1. Entrepreneurship
2. Entrepreneurship	2. Entrepreneurship	2. Small Business Management
3. New Venture Creation	3. New Venture Creation	3. New Venture Creation

ness Management was the most frequently offered course offering [35 percent of all respondents], second was Entrepreneurship [25 percent of all respondents] and third was New Venture Creation [15 percent of all respondents].

When the data were further analyzed by specific type of educational institution, the results in Table 1 were obtained. The data indicate that 2-year colleges are predominantly teaching Small Business Management courses. The 4-year colleges and universities are also predominantly teaching Small Business Management, and International colleges and universities are predominantly teaching Entrepreneurship. The researchers believe that for future studies, terms such as *"entrepreneurship, new venture and small business management"* should be operationally defined to reduce any response bias.

4. **What types of endowments has your school received in the area of Entrepreneurship and or Small Business?** As shown in Figure 2, respondents were given three choices: Endowed Center, Endowed Professor and Endowed Chair. Because some respondents had multiple forms of endowments, the researchers regrouped the data to better display the range of endowments currently existing in 2 and 4-year colleges and universities. As shown, the data indicate that Endowed Center was the most popular type of endowment to educational institutions. Endowed Center was closely followed by schools with endowed professorships; a combination of Endowed Center and Endowed Chair; and all three forms of endowments: Endowed Center, Endowed Professor and Endowed Chair.

5. **Does your school offer a course, field of concentration or degree in Entrepreneurship?** As shown in Figure 3, the data indicate among 2-year colleges, "Courses" were the primary academic vehicle offering Small Business Management and Entrepreneurship education with "Concentrations" in most cases, a distant second. Some institutions did offer "Degree Programs" in Entrepreneurship and Small Business. These data indicate that among those responding, Small Business Management and Entrepreneurship courses were widely offered but "Concentrations" and "Degree Programs" lagged far behind.

Figure 2
Type of Endowments

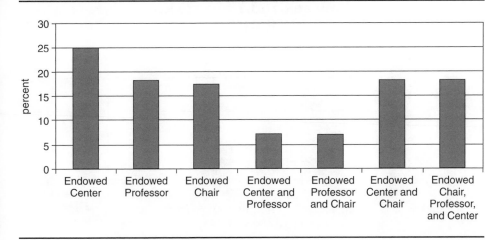

Figure 3
Course Offerings, Concentrations and Degree Programs in Various Entrepreneurial Education Areas at 2-Year Colleges

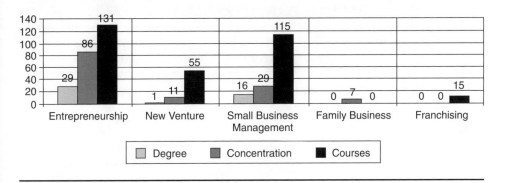

As shown in Figure 4, the data indicate that among 4-year colleges and universities "Courses" were the primary academic vehicle offering; Small Business Management and Entrepreneurship "Concentrations" again were a distant second. The majority of degree programs (20) were in Entrepreneurship.

6. **What are the most popular in-class pedagogical methods used in teaching Entrepreneurship and or Small Business in your educational institution?** The data reveal that all three populations—2-year colleges, 4-year colleges and universities, and international colleges and

Figure 4
Course Offerings, Concentrations and Degree Programs in Various Entrepreneurial Education Areas at 4-Year Colleges and Universities

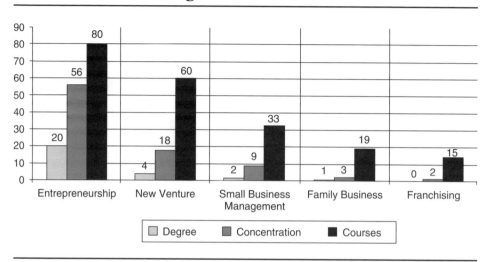

Table 2
In-Class Pedagogical Methods

2-Year Colleges	4-Year Colleges and Universities	International Colleges and Universities
1. Case Studies	1. Creation of Business Plans	1. Creation of Business Plans
2. Creation of Business Plans	2. Case Studies	2. Case Studies
3. Discussions	3. Guest Speakers	3. Lectures by business people and guest speakers

universities—tend to employ the same basic in-class teaching methods (see Table 2).

7. **What are the most popular pedagogical methods outside the classroom in teaching Entrepreneurship and or Small Business in your educational institution?**

The top three most popular methods used outside the classroom are shown in Table 3. The data reveal that all three populations—2-year colleges, 4-year colleges and universities, and international colleges and universities—tend to employ the same basic external

Table 3
External Classroom Pedagogical Methods

2-Year Colleges	4-Year Colleges and Universities	International Colleges and Universities
1. Internships	1. Small Business Consulting	1. Small Business Consulting
2. On-Site Visits with Small Business Owners	2. Internships	2. On-Site Visits with Small Business Owners
3. Community Development and Small Business Consulting	3. On-Site Visits with Small Business Owners	3. Internships

Figure 5
School/Center Offer Information on the Internet Regarding Entrepreneurship and New Venture Creation

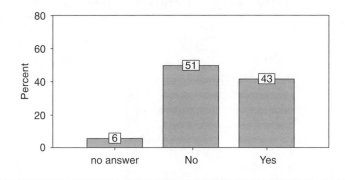

teaching methods, with 2-year colleges more focused on Internship programs than the other two populations.

8. **Does your school/center offer information on the web regarding Entrepreneurship and New Venture Creation to both students and entrepreneurs?** The data indicate that 51 percent of the educational institutions do not offer information on the web regarding Entrepreneurship while 43 percent do offer information on the web (see Figure 5).

9. **Do you offer management and technical assistance on-line for students and entrepreneurs?** The data indicate that 23 percent of the educational institutions responding to our survey offer some technical assistance on-line (see Figure 6).

10. **Do you offer Distance Learning in entrepreneurship via the Internet?**

Figure 6
Offer Management and Technical Assistance On-Line for Students and Entrepreneurs

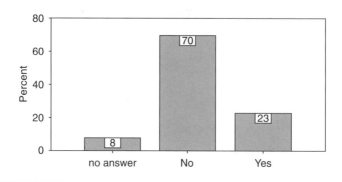

Figure 7
Offer Long-Distance Learning

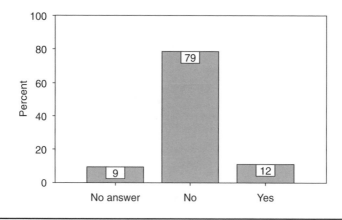

The data indicate that 21 percent of the educational institutions responding to the survey offer Distance Learning (see Figure 7).

11. **Do you require web-based assignments as part of your entrepreneurship curriculum?** The data

indicate that 52 percent of the educational institutions responding to the survey do require web-based assignments as part of the entrepreneurship curriculum (see Figure 8).

12. **What are the most popular periodicals used in the class?** The data

Figure 8
Web-Based Assignments for the Entrepreneurship Curriculum

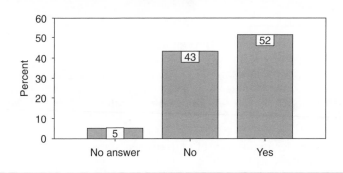

Figure 9
Periodicals Used in Class

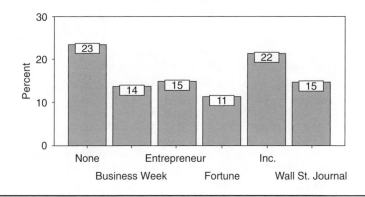

indicate that the most popular periodicals used in class are: Inc. Magazine (22 percent), Entrepreneur (15 percent), Wall St. Journal (15 percent) and Business Week (14 percent) (see Figure 9).

Table 4 provides the summary for multiple questions asked in regard to the educational institution outreach efforts in the area of entrepreneurship. The questions are in the left column of the table with the results in the right column broken down into a Yes, No or No Response categories.

3.2. Discussion of Findings

Based on previous national surveys on entrepreneurial education (Solomon, 1988; Solomon and Fernald 1991;

Table 4
Outreach Efforts

Questions	Yes	No	No Response
Does your school offer Executive Development courses in Entrepreneurship?	29%	65%	6%
Does your school offer Continuing Education programs in Entrepreneurship?	45%	48%	7%
Does your school offer Internship opportunities with small local companies?	73%	18%	9%
Does your school work with local, state and federal government agencies in support of entrepreneurship?	72%	23%	5%
Is your school involved with any outreach programs that teach entrepreneurship to secondary and elementary schools?	39%	55%	6%
Does your school keep track of Alumni who started their own business?	42%	48%	11%
Does your school participate in Business Plan competitions?	42%	52%	6%

Solomon and Fernald, 1993; and Solomon, Weaver and Fernald, 1994) results of the 1999–2000 data indicate that there is a growth trend in terms of courses, concentrations and degrees in the academic fields of small business management and entrepreneurship. The data also show that entrepreneurial educators are increasingly using diverse experiential teaching and evaluation pedagogies. The growth of small business management and entrepreneurship courses is an occurrence that is not likely to dissipate soon. More importantly the data show a rise in course offerings, majors in the field and funding through endowed chairs. In fact, studies now point to the fact that endowments in entrepreneurship education are growing at an exponential rate (Katz, 1994).

Based on the data presented in this paper, there is a need to move to away from the use of traditional non- technology based forms of teaching and evaluation methods to the use of more educational technologies such as the Internet-based assignments and the use of knowledge portals. This opens the door for new methods of both teaching and learning. Not all technologies and educational methods using the Internet might be the correct or best suited tool and approach. Early experiences with distance learning have not proven successful for some colleges and universities. Yet, the point is to start integrating the use of the internet in the entrepreneurial education process. According to noted management expert Peter Drucker, "Technology will force the educators to restructure what they are teaching (BizEd, 2001). For example the use of video conferencing and streaming of video case studies shows promise as a viable use of educational technology. The ability to bring new 'live' perspectives from different geographic locations and schools adds to the richness of the content and educational experience.

As educators move away from tests in favor of self-directed 'project' centered educational techniques, such as personalized business plans, it makes sense to create a class structure that facilitates this form of learning. Also, given the nature of learning and knowledge acquisition, educators need to explore ways that they can virtually provide knowledge to students 24/7. Recent developments in the educational and training sector, including "Small Business Classroom", show much promise as indicated by cofounder Hattie Bryant.

One of the most surprising results of the survey was the relationship between various entrepreneurship education pedagogies and the limited use of educational technologies. Given the tremendous growth in personal, business and academic technology, one might assume that a higher percentage of entrepreneurship educators would have adopted and used various educational technology tools such as the Internet, online chat rooms and distance learning. These results show that entrepreneurial educators are beginning to employ educational technologies into their teaching. However, educators need to lobby for more resources from their administrations in order to introduce more educational technologies into the classroom and consider requiring students to purchase laptops for lectures and labs. Since 1994, the National Center for Education Statistics (NCES) has surveyed schools to measure what proportion of them is connected to the Internet. As of the fall of 2000, almost all schools in the United States have access to the Internet. Our results indicate that only 49 percent of the educational institutions surveyed offered information on the web regarding Entrepreneurship and that 30 percent of the educational institutions in our survey offered technical assistance on-line.

3.3. Conclusion

The George Washington University (GWU) School of Business and Public Management (SBPM) Department of Management Science conducted the 1991–2000 National Survey of Entrepreneurship Education. The primary aim of the project was to conduct research into entrepreneurial education. The first step in the research was a review of the literature on entrepreneurship and in particular entrepreneurial education. The second step was to send a mail survey to identify academic institutions that were offering small business and entrepreneurial educational programs. The third step examined trends in entrepreneurial education in both the United States and internationally regarding the development of multiple course offerings, concentrations and majors at both the undergraduate and graduate level. The results showed various new trends and one of them was in entrepreneurship education and technology.

If entrepreneurial educators are to broaden their teaching approaches, they need to move away from traditional methods and look to the full range of educational technologies as tools that will expand their reach to other schools and more students. Also, with the quantity and quality of information available on the Internet, students and faculty can use this resource to more easily acquire the needed knowledge to develop feasibility studies and business plans, gain access to market data and research industry and economic trends. As colleges and universities are beginning to realize that long distance learning is a part of regular learning, entrepreneurship and small business courses need to capitalize on this opportunity. The Internet is playing a major role in allowing this new type of education to take place.

Clearly, for entrepreneurship to embrace the 21st century, educators must become more competent in the use of academic technology and also expand their pedagogies to include new and innovative approaches to the teaching of entrepreneurship. Cyberspace has virtually erased time and distance and the Internet is transforming the theory of education into the practice of implementation. Professors are beginning to use this medium for communicating with other educators to learn how to improve and expand their courses. Entrepreneurship educators are also experiencing this phenomenon. For example, The George Washington University, under a grant from the Coleman Foundation, created an entrepreneurship education website for the Distributive Education Clubs of America (DECA). In addition to downloadable teaching modules, the site provides a message board where teachers from different schools can share knowledge by exchanging ideas and resources. Users are also encouraged to use the "comment" option to give feedback to the GWU curriculum development team regarding course materials. The entrepreneurship education modules are continually updated and improved to best meet the real-time needs of the user community.

Recently, Newsweek published a special article entitled "The Classroom of the Future" (Newsweek 10-29-01), in which leading teachers, inventors and entrepreneurs shared their vision for what schools will be in 2025. Among the viewpoints expressed by Steve Jobs was "One of the issues as a society going forward is to teach in the medium of the generation. The medium of our times is video and photography. We see things changing. We are doing more and more with movies and DVDs. The drive over the next twenty years is to integrate multimedia tools into the medium of the day." Some entrepreneurship educators are already beginning to teach using the "medium of the day" with the help of courseware products such as Prometheus, developed by Bo Davis at The George Washington University. In addition to offering students and teachers the opportunity to interact via email, bulletin boards and live discussion formats, Prometheus and other course management programs also integrate multimedia options into the course. Students can access a course site, download a posted journal article, watch an instructional video or DVD and return a completed assignment from any Internet connection. Educators can follow up with individualized online coaching and feedback to the student. "A good deal of teaching will still be done in the classroom, but much of it will take place off campus and in groups. Much will occur online, and much will be accomplished through self-study. Perhaps the single most important medium will be special tools that are adapted for use at home, with built-in visual and audio feedback mechanisms" (Drucker, BizEd, Nov/Dec 2001).

Linda Darling-Hammond, a professor of education at Stanford University, expressed her view that "Technology will support individuals becoming citizens of the world. Teachers will become coaches, directing students to the resources they need to solve problems—a guide on the side helping students find answers online, rather than a sage on stage. Teachers will understand how students are learning and access lots of different ways to help a particular student learn" (Newsweek, 10/29/01). For example, rather than offering students a few traditional options to research new venture feasibility, educators can invite the institution's resource librarian to hold a tutorial on written, electronic and multimedia resources now easily accessible in most libraries. With some basic instruction, students in a matter of hours can mine data that was once the time-intensive domain of only the most advanced researchers. A final viewpoint shared by Senator Maria Cantwell expresses the notion that "The real issue is not the technology—the hardware is going to change—but the interactive nature of the education. People who interact with information retain more of that information. But most important, perhaps, education will become part of a larger more robust community" (Newsweek, 10/29/01).

We at The George Washington University Council for Family and Entrepreneurial Enterprises believe in and are working on, the creation of Entrepreneurship Knowledge Portals as the next educational technological frontier. These portals represent one alternative to improving entrepreneurship education pedagogical approaches, as they create centralized locations where educators can come, share and learn. The mission of an **Entrepreneurship Knowledge Portal** is to provide a one-stop shop for educators to come and review what other schools are offering in entrepreneurship education and share their own ideas on innovations in entrepreneurial education.

The field of entrepreneurial education has experienced tremendous growth in the United States. The results of this study represent a stream of research that began in 1978 with the examination of the current *state of entrepreneurship education*. In the last twenty years, a great many changes have occurred including gains in the academic acceptance and credibility for the field of entrepreneurship education. The American dream is to start your own business, not work for someone else. American colleges and universities as well as their international counterparts are responding to this growing interest and realizing what major public policy makers now believe: that small and medium enterprises will continue to be the economic generators capable of propelling their economies into the next millennium.

References

Ahiarah, S. (1989). "Strategic management and entrepreneurship courses at the undergraduate level: Can one inform the other?" *Proceedings of the 1989 Small Business Institute Director's Association National Conference*, Arlington, VA, pp. 60–66.

Baumol, W. J. (1968). "Entrepreneurship in economic theory," *American Economic Review*, 58, 64–71.

——— (2001). "What Peter Drucker has to say about business schools and management education as original, provocative as all his observations have been for the past 50 years." BizEd (pp. 13–17).

Block, Z. and Stumpf, S. A. (1992). "Entrepreneurship education research: Experience and challenge." In D. L. Sexton and J. D. Kasarda, (Eds.) *The state of the art of entrepreneurship*, pp. 17–45. Boston, MA: PWS-Kent Publishing.

Brawer, F. B. (1997). "Simulation as a vehicle in entrepreneurship education." *ERIC Digest*, Number 97-1, ED 433–468.

Brewer, B., Anyansi-Archibong, C. and Ugboro, I. O. (1993). "Using computer simulation technology in entrepreneurship and small business education." *Proceedings of the International Council for Small Business*, Las Vegas, NV, 217–229.

Charney, A. and Libecap, G. (2000). "Impact of Entrepreneurship Education." Insights: A Kauffman Research Series. Kauffman Center for Entrepreneurial Leadership.

Carroll, J. J. (1993). "Course and curriculum design in developing and changing nations: Problems following the U.S. model." *Proceedings of the International Council for Small Business*, Las Vegas, NV, 254–263.

Clark, B. W., Davis, C. H. and Harnish, V. C. (1984) "Do courses in entrepreneurship aid in new venture creation?" *Journal of Small Business Management*, 2, 26–31.

Davis, C., Hills, G. E. and LaForge, R. W. (1985). "The marketing/small enterprise paradox: A research agenda." *International Small Business Journal*, 3, 31–42.

Donckels, R. (1991). "Education and entrepreneurship experiences from secondary and university education in Belgium." *Journal of Small Business and Entrepreneurship*, 9(1), 35–42.

Foote, D. (1999, April 19). "Show us the money!" *Newsweek*, pp. 43–44.

Gartner, W. B. and Vesper, K. H. (1994). "Executive Forum: Experiments in entrepreneurship education: Successes and failures." *Journal of Business Venturing*, 9, 179–187.

Gartner, W. B., Bird, B. J. and Starr, J. A. (1992). "Acting as if: Differentiating entrepreneurial from organizational behavior." *Entrepreneurship Theory and Practice*, 16(3), 13–32.

Gorman, G., Hanlon, D. and King, W. (1997). "Some research perspectives on entrepreneurship education, enterprise eduction, and education for small business management: A ten-year literature review." *International Small Business Journal*, April/June, 56–77.

Guglielmino, P. J. and Klatt, L. A. (1993). "Entrepreneurs as self-directed learners." *Proceedings of the International Council for Small Business*, Las Vegas, NV, 206–216.

Hills, G. E. (1988). Variations in university entrepreneurship education: An empirical study of an evolving field. *Journal of Business Venturing*, 3, 109–122.

Hills, G. E. and Welsch, H. P. (1986). Entrepreneurship behavioral intentions and student independence characteristics and experiences. In R. Ronstadt, J. A. Hornaday, R. Peterson & K. H. Vesper (Eds.), *Frontiers of entrepreneurship research*, 73–186. Wellesley MA: Babson College.

Hood, J. N. and Young J. E. (1993). Entrepreneurship's requisite areas of development: A survey of top executives in successful entrepreneurial firms.

Journal of Business Venturing, 8, 115–135.

Kate, J. A. (1994). Growth of endowments, chairs and programs in entrepreneurship on the college campus. In Frank Hoy, Thoms G. Monroy & Jay Reichert (Eds.) The Art and Science of Entrepreneurship Education, Volume 1 Cleveland: Baldwin-Wallace College, pp. 127–149.

Kent, C. A. (1990). Entrepreneurship education at the collegiate level: A synopsis and evaluation. In C. A. Kent (Ed.) *Entrepreneurship Education*, pp. 111–122. New York: Quorum Books.

King, S. W. (2001). Entrepreneurship Education: What the Customer values. *Proceedings of the 46th International Council for Small Business*. Taipei. Tiawan.

Klatt, L. A. (1988). A study of small business/entrepreneurial education in colleges and universities. *The Journal of Private Enterprise*, 4 (Fall): 103–108.

Loucks, E. L. (1982). Elaboration on education in entrepreneurship. In C. A. Kent, D. L. Sexton & K. H. Vesper (Eds.), *Encyclopedia of entrepreneurship*, pp. 344–346. Englewood Cliffs NJ: Prentice Hall.

Marchigiano-Monroy, T. (1993). Realities and emerging realities of adapting to changing global economic conditions: Rethinking the role of SBI/SBIDA in entrepreneurial education. *Proceedings of the 17th National Small Business Consulting Conference-Small Business Institute Director's Association*, 120–130.

McMullan, W. E. and Long, W. A. (1987). Entrepreneurship education in the nineties. *Journal of Business Venturing*, 2, 261–275.

McMullan, W. E., Long W. A. and Wilson, A. (1985). MBA concentration on entrepreneurship. *Journal of Small Bussiness and Entrepreneurship*, 3(1), 18–22.

Mitchell, R. K. and Chesteen, S. A. (1995). Enhancing entrepreneurial expertise: Experiential pedagogy and the new venture expert script. *Simulation and Gaming*, 26(3), 288–306.

Plaschka, G. R. and Welsch, H. P. (1990). Emerging structures in entrepreneurship education: Curricula designs and strategies. *Entrepreneurship Theory and Practice*, 14(3), 55–71.

Porter, L. W. and McKibbin, L. E. (1988). *Management Education: Drift or Thrust into the 21st Century?* New York: McGraw-Hill.

Preshing, W. A. (1991). Education by projects. *Journal of Small Business and Entrepreneurship*, 9(1), 55–59.

Robinson, P. and Hayes, M. (1991). Entrepreneurship education in America's major universities. *Entrepreneurship Theory and Practice*, 15(3), 41–52.

Ronstadt, R. (1987). The educated entrepreneurs: A new era of entrepreneurial education is beginning. *American Journal of Small Business*, 11(4), 37–53.

Ronstadt, R. (1990). The educated entrepreneurs: A new era of entrepreneurial education evolves. In C. A. Kent (Ed.) *Entrepreneurship Education*, pp. 69–88, New York: Quorum Books.

Schumpeter, J. A. (1934). *The theory of economic development*. Cambridge, MA: Harvard University Press.

Sexton, D. L. and Upton, N. E. (1984). Entrepreneurship education: Suggestions for increasing effectiveness. *Journal of Small Business Management*, 22(4), 18–25.

Sexton, D. L. and Upton-Upton, N. (1987). Evaluation of an innovative approach to teaching entrepreneurship. *Journal of Small Business Management*, 25(1), 35–43.

Scott, M. G. and Twomey, D. F. (1998). The long term supply of entrepreneurs: Student's career aspirations in relation to entrepreneurship. *Journal of Small Business Management*, 26(4), 5–13.

Solomon, G. T. (1988). "Small Business Management and Entrepreneurial Education in America: A National Survey Overview." *Journal of Private Enterprise*, November, 1988.

Solomon, G. T. (2001). Interview at The George Washington University School of Business and Public Management.

Solomon, G. T. and Fernald, L. W., Jr. (1991). Trends in small business management and entrepreneurship education in the United States. *Entrepreneurship Theory and Practice*, 15, 25–39.

Solomon, G. T. and Fernald, L. W., Jr. (1993). Assessing the need for small business management/entrepreneurship courses at the university level. *Proceedings of the 17th National Small Business Consulting Conference-Small Business Institute Director's Association*, 102–107.

Solomon, G. T., Weaver, K. M. and Fernald, L. W., Jr. (1994). "Pedagogical Methods of Teaching Entrepreneurship: An Historical Perspective." *Gaming and Simulation*, Volume 25 Number 3, 1993.

Stumpf, S. S., Dunbar, L. and Mullen, T. P. (1991). Simulations in entrepreneurship education: Oxymoron or untapped opportunity? *Frontiers of Entrepreneurship Research*, 681–694.

The Classroom of the Future, Newsweek, pp. 60–68, October 22, 2001.

Truell, A. D., Webster, L. and Davidson, C. (1998). Fostering entrepreneurial spirit: Integrating the business community into the classroom. *Business Education Forum*, 53(2), 28–29, 40.

Van Clouse, G. H. (1990). A controlled experiment relating entrepreneurial education to student's start-up decisions. *Journal of Small Business Management*, 28(2), 45–53.

Vesper, K. H. (1985). *Entrepreneurship education 1985*. Wellesley, MA: Babson College.

Vesper, K. H. (1986). New developments in entrepreneurship education. In D. L. Sexton & R. W. Smilor (Eds.), *The art and science of entrepreneurship*, pp. 379–387. Cambridge, MA: Ballinger.

Vesper, K. H. and McMullan, W. E. (1987). Entrepreneurship education in the nineties. *Journal of Business Venturing*, 2, 261–275.

Vesper, K. H. and McMullan, W. E. (1998). Entrepreneurship: Today courses, tomorrow degrees? *Entrepreneurship Theory and Practice*, 13(1), 7–13.

Zeithaml, C. P. and Rice G. H. (1987). Entrepreneurship/small business education in American universities. *Journal of Small Business Management*, 25(1), 44–50.

Measuring Progress in Entrepreneurship Education

by Karl H. Vesper and William B. Gartner

This article presents the results of a survey that ranked university entrepreneurship programs. The survey also explored how universities determined what courses constituted a program in entrepreneurship and how they determined the criteria that impact an entrepreneurship program's quality. We conclude the article with a discussion of the education pilot criteria for the Malcolm Baldrige National Quality Award that may be useful for measuring progress in entrepreneurship education.

A mail survey was undertaken in late 1994. This survey was sent to deans at 941 business schools in the United States, 42 in Canada, and 270 overseas. Of the 311 replies, 233 came from U.S. business schools, 16 from Canadian schools, and 62 from schools in other countries.

The top seven criteria suggested for ranking entrepreneurship programs were courses offered, faculty publications, impact on community, alumni exploits, innovations, alumni start-ups, and outreach to scholars. The most frequently offered entrepreneurship courses at both the undergraduate and graduate levels in the entrepreneurship programs surveyed were entrepreneurship or starting new firms, small business management, field projects/venture consulting, starting and running a firm, venture plan writing, and venture finance.

The survey uncovered a number of problems with how academics ranked other entrepreneurship programs. Evaluators did not specify the criteria they used to rank entrepreneurship programs. Evaluators did not offer their specific weights for each criterion used to judge a program. Finally, evaluators were not asked to provide a judgment of their depth of knowledge of other programs.

Since the criteria for determining what constitutes a high-quality entrepreneurship program is, at present, rather fluid and indeterminate, we thought it appropriate to borrow insights from a highly successful and visible evaluation effort in higher education, the education pilot criteria for the Malcolm Baldrige National Quality Award (MBNQA). For an MBNQA evaluation, organizations are assessed across 28 requirements that are embodied in seven categories.

Leadership. *This category examines senior administrators' commitment and involvement in creating and sustaining performance excellence that has a student focus, clear goals, and high expectations. In the context of entrepreneurship education, the leadership category entails describing the involvement and commitment of*

Originally appeared in *Journal of Business Venturing*, 1997, Volume 12, Number 5.

entrepreneurship program directors, business school deans, university administrators, advisory board members, and student representatives.

Information and Analysis. *This category examines how data and information are used to support the overall mission of the program. The focus of this category is towards identifying and specifying information and data that would be appropriate for evaluating the quality of an entrepreneurship program, as well as for making comparisons with other programs. We suggest that entrepreneurship programs begin to systematically collect information about issues such as demographic and performance measures of incoming students enrolling in entrepreneurship courses; comparative information on entrepreneurship, business school and university students; descriptions of the outcomes that specific entrepreneurship courses intend to generate and the measures of the efficacy of each course; and measures of the intended outcomes of the entrepreneurship program in terms of student performance, student satisfaction, and impact on the community (i.e., number of start-ups, students employed in new firms, students working in positions assisting new firms).*

Strategic and Operational Planning. *This category focuses on how a program sets strategic directions and key planning requirements. For an entrepreneurship program, such a requirement would entail generating a strategic plan that specifies the purpose and mission of the program, key student and overall program performance requirements, external factors impacting the implementation of the plan, internal resources and university barriers to change, and key critical success factors.*

Human Resource Development and Management. *This category examines how faculty and staff are supported and developed so as to satisfy the strategic goals of the program. While an entrepreneurship program might typically measure "faculty productivity" as an indicator of this category, the intention is actually towards specifying the resources and systems that impact the ability of staff and faculty to be productive.*

Educational and Business Process Management. *This category specifies key aspects of the design and delivery of the educational research and service components of a program, as well as an examination of the processes involved in improving these components. Rather than programs being compared to each other by the quantity of courses offered, this category requires that programs be measured on the logic, coherency, and efficacy of the educational experience that entrepreneurship students undertake.*

School Performance Results. *This category examines the outcomes of a program, such as student performance and improvement, improvement in services provided by the program, and faculty productivity. This category accounts for 23% of the total evaluation score. The primary focus of this category is determining the improvements in student performance. Such key measures might include student performance in specific courses, student demonstrations of key skills and knowledge through portfolios of original work that they create, measures of student satisfaction, and impact on the community (i.e., number of start-ups, students employed in new firms, students working in positions assisting new firms).*

Student Focus, and Student and Stakeholder Satisfaction. *This category describes the process for determining student and stakeholder needs and expectations, as well as making comparisons of student and stakeholder satisfaction among other programs. This category accounts for 23% of the total evaluation score.*

The MBNQA evaluation scheme forces us to become aware of the implicit goals, objectives, and pedagogical perspectives of our programs. We must not lose sight of the fact that entrepreneurship programs are and will be evaluated, and that we must, there-fore, be ready to offer criteria that we want our programs to be evaluated on. If uni-versity entrepreneurship educators do not step forward to assume leadership of our own field, others will surely come to the forefront to determine the rules of the game.

Introduction

This article discusses some of the logic involved in the development of criteria that might be useful for evaluating university entrepreneurship programs. Our intention is to surface some of the dilemmas and issues inherent in attempting to make comparisons across widely varying pedagogies and curricula. In addition, we hope to redirect the evaluation of entrepreneurship programs away from a dependence on what we perceive to be public relations efforts by many schools, and towards the use of discernible and measurable criteria that can evaluate the important aspects of an entrepreneurship program. We conclude the article with a discussion of criteria that may be useful for measuring progress in entrepreneurship education.

Are there criteria that one might utilize to make comparisons among various universities and colleges offering programs in entrepreneurship? While "Best College" lists are typically based on self-reported information that have been shown to be of questionable validity, and on information that is quantifiable but not necessarily germane to determining the quality of a university education (Gilley 1992), the public has a nearly insatiable demand for any information that might help them make better choices among all of the universities and colleges offering degrees. An interest in college rankings is reasonable and rational. A college degree is an expensive investment for most individuals and families. Prospective students want to have some inkling of the kinds of features

(e.g., small class sizes, world-renowned faculty, state-of-the-art facilities, etc.) that might differentiate among a "good, better, or best" education. A ranking might, therefore, be an appropriate measure of some of the criteria that could be used to make a distinction among different university programs. We are now seeing college-level entrepreneurship programs being evaluated with the same kinds of schemes used by magazines to evaluate other university programs.

For example, in the past two years, *Success Magazine* (Callan and Warshaw 1994, 1995) has ranked college-level entrepreneurship programs on evaluation of criteria that seem, on face value, to be reasonable. Colleges and universities are measured on four areas: (1) qualifications of faculty, (2) the variety and depth of the entrepreneurship curriculum, (3) academic standards and student scores, and (4) the quality and depth of resources. Yet, upon a closer look at the specific criteria measured in this survey, such measures as the GMAT (Graduate Management Aptitude Test) scores and GPA (Grade Point Average) scores of incoming students may not be a reasonable measure of these students' entrepreneurial capabilities. A measure that is used to predict success in school (i.e., GMAT) may be an inappropriate measure to use to predict success at starting and growing a business. In addition, measuring the quality and depth of resources at a university by measuring, for example, the number of computers per capita, may be easily quantifiable, but not necessarily correlated to improving the teaching and acquisition of entrepreneurial knowledge and skills. There are many specific measures that are used in these *Success Magazine* rankings that have a tenuous link to factors that might enhance the acquisition of entrepreneurship knowledge, skills, and abilities. A ranking of entrepreneurship programs might therefore be based on information that, while well-meaning, might be a very poor reflection of the relative quality of each specific entrepreneurship program. In the belief that entrepreneurship educators have important insights and a vested interest in the criteria used to evaluate entrepreneurship programs, we think it useful to begin a public discussion of some of the issues involved in generating these rankings.

Concurrent with an advisory role in the *Success Magazine* evaluation of university-level entrepreneurship programs, the first author had undertaken a survey that focused on the development of programs in entrepreneurship at business schools around the world. Over the last 20 years of surveys of entrepreneurship courses (Vesper 1974, 1975, 1976, 1978, 1979, 1980, 1985, 1990, 1993), a growing number of business schools have developed a series of courses in entrepreneurship, variously labeled as either a program, concentration, or major in entrepreneurship. This survey sought to discover what courses might comprise a program in entrepreneurship, as well as other elements that might impact the quality of an entrepreneurship program, such as faculty activities, community outreach, resources applied to entrepreneurship, and perspectives on measures of program efficacy and outcomes.

A Brief History of University-Level Entrepreneurship Education

Until 1970, very few universities offered entrepreneurship courses. The Harvard Business School introduced an entrepreneurship course in 1945, apparently in response to students who were returning from World War II military service to an economy that was in transition due to the collapse of the weapons industries. The course took hold and grew in popularity, although the tenure-track faculty member who began it apparently saw insufficient academic future in it and shifted his attention to the study of boards of directors in major corporations.

The subject of entrepreneurship was not generally fashionable in the decades that followed. This, in part, is reflected in the measures of the entrepreneurial activity in the United States economy during this time. During the 1950s and 1960s, the number of Schedule C's (Income from Business or Profession) filed with the U.S. Internal Revenue Service and the number of corporations per capita experienced a period of steady decline (Gartner and Shane 1995). The big corporations grew bigger.

But by 1970 the number of business schools offering courses in entrepreneurship had begun to change dramatically. Suddenly, there were 16 universities with such courses, of which 12 had started in the preceding two years. What caused this change is difficult to pinpoint. Measures of entrepreneurial activity, such as the number of Schedule C's and the number of corporations per capita stopped falling around 1969 and began to rise. New magazines celebrating entrepreneurship began to emerge: *Inc.*, *Venture*, *In-Business*, and *Entrepreneur*. Connotations of the term "entrepreneur" began to shift from notions of greed, exploitation, selfishness, and disloyalty to creativity, job creation, profitability, innovativeness, and generosity. The venture-capital community, while getting its start just after World War II, became established in the late 1960s as a professional occupational area of high visibility beckoning potential entrepreneurs to try entrepreneurship. Certain industry sectors, such as electronics, had cultivated a population of individuals who could create new products, both commercial and consumer, to put invested capital to work profitably. The advent of the microcomputer accelerated this trend, helping entrepreneurs by making possible the operation of businesses with greatly reduced economies of scale, while at the same time creating opportunities for new software firms that were low in capital intensity and high in margin, therefore, easy to start on a wave of high demand.

From this base of 16 universities and colleges offering entrepreneurship courses in 1970, the number of schools offering entrepreneurship courses had grown to over 400 by 1995. As the number of schools offering entrepreneurship courses grew, so did the number of schools offering more than one course in entrepreneurship. There began to be programs in this subject.

What Is an Entrepreneurship Program?

There appear to be at least 50 universities that offer four or more courses clustered in the area of entrepreneurship that allow students to take concentrations, majors, or degrees (Gartner and Vesper 1994). We recognize that there is a diversity of views among academics about what constitutes "entrepreneurship" as a field of study (Gartner 1990), as well as in what constitutes an entrepreneurship program. For example, entrepreneurship scholars have differing views on whether entrepreneurship must focus on organization creation, growing firms, innovation, value creation, and ownership. While previous surveys by Vesper (1974–1993) have defined entrepreneurship as business entry, whether by start-up or acquisition and whether

independently or within an established organization, the growth of university-level entrepreneurship programs has tended to broaden this viewpoint to include other topics such as family business, managing smaller enterprises, and managing high-growth businesses. As a way to categorize the variation in types of university-level efforts in entrepreneurship education, Plaschka and Welsch (1990) have suggested four different dimensions: number of courses offered (single to multiple), degree of integration (low to high), stages of business transition (e.g., inception, survival, growth, expansion, maturity), and number of disciplines. Their article suggested that entrepreneurship education is moving towards integrative, comprehensive, and holistic programs, that is, towards the vision of business education offered in Porter and McKibbin (1988).

It is not difficult to see how an initial focus on entrepreneurship as "a person who organizes and manages a business undertaking, assuming the risk for the sake of profit" (Webster), could expand into other topic areas. The process of starting a business introduces the possibility of starting a business with zero profit (non-profit entrepreneurship) or that of starting a new business within an existing business (corporate entrepreneurship). Linked to the process of start-up is the aftermath of start-up: small and growing businesses. The association of entrepreneurship with business entry also suggested to some schools a link between entrepreneurship and family business. Starting a business has family and estate implications. Running a family business might also have small-business implications. Inheriting a business could be connected to the issues of business entry.

The popularity of the term "entrepreneurship" has also propelled its application as an adjective. The term "entrepreneurial" has found a widening application, connoting innovativeness, initiative, job creation, creativity, ambition, perseverance, achievement, and success (Lumpkin and Dess 1996).

Finally, many wealthy individuals have given money to universities to promote entrepreneurship, and therefore many universities have sought to seek more funding using the "entrepreneurship" label. Sometimes entrepreneurship programs are created with this money, sometimes not, and in between are many combinations.

Given the variety of meanings of "entrepreneurship," the variety of different courses in entrepreneurship, and the variety of ways that the entrepreneurship label is used by universities to promote differing agendas, finding a reasonable way to rate and rank entrepreneurship programs is a challenge.

Rating Entrepreneurship Programs

Scholars debate about whether entrepreneurship programs should be rated and ranked: Every program is unique, and to some degree, incomparable. No two people would rate programs in exactly the same way. Aggregate results of ratings apply to no single program in particular. Programs are constantly changing, so ratings are constantly out of date. Criteria for ratings also change and are also out of date. Some schools are more visible than others, and nobody knows them all. Ratings are bound to be distorted by ignorance. Even so, rankings of entrepreneurship programs have occurred and seem to occur with greater frequency.

A number of magazines such as *Success* and *Business Week* have started rating and ranking entrepreneurship programs. (See Table 1.) These magazines will continue to do so because their readership wants this information and will buy these magazines to get it. Publication of ratings and rankings have powerful effects on universities. High-ranked programs receive more inquires, applications, and enrollments. Schools that depend on tuition income pay close attention to applications and enrollments, and therefore pay attention to how they fare in these ratings. Hence, ratings influence what schools offer.

Ratings and rankings can be constructive. Programs that make contributions to entrepreneurship education deserve to be recognized for it. If some programs have better features, then recognizing these programs through widely distributed publications can let other schools learn these better ways of operating. Competitive scrutiny can help ward off complacency and stimulate universities to strive for better ways of operating. Finally, public scrutiny and exposure can help weed out misleading advertising among the claims of different programs. Since ratings and ranking are bound to influence the direction of entrepreneurship programs, it makes sense to consider, with care, how the ratings should best be done to enhance the benefit of their influence.

A mail survey was undertaken in late 1994 to learn about entrepreneurship programs around the world. This survey sought to discover how universities ranked other university entrepreneurship programs, how universities determined what courses constituted a program in entrepreneurship, and how universities formed opinions about other criteria that might impact the quality of an entrepreneurship program, such as faculty activities, community outreach, resources applied to entrepreneurship, and perspectives on measures of program efficacy and outcomes. The survey was sent to 941 business schools in the United States, 42 in Canada, and 270 overseas. We recognize that this survey is not a complete and comprehensive survey of all four-year colleges and universities that might have an entrepreneurship program. But it is our opinion that the survey represents a broad and thorough

Table 1
Top-Rated U.S. Entrepreneurship Programs

Rank	School	Academic Points	Entrepreneur Magazine 1993	Business Week 1993	Success 1994 Top 25	Success 1995 Top 25	Success 1995 2nd 25
1	Babson College	1063	X	X	X	X	
2	Harvard Business School	904	X	X	X	X	
3	Wharton School	810	X	X	X	X	
4	Univ. of Southern California	499	X	X	X	X	
5	Univ. of Texas, Austin	421		X	X	X	
6	UCLA	408		X	X	X	
7	Wichita State	362	X		X		X
8	Univ. of Georgia	298		X	X	X	
9	Carnegie-Mellon	290		X	X	X	
10	Northwestern	283	X	X	X		X
11	New York Univ.	281		X	X	X	
12	Rensselaer	262	X	X	X	X	
13	Univ. of St. Thomas	245			X	X	
14	Baylor Univ.	224	X			X	
15	DePaul Univ.	215		X	X	X	
16	Stanford	176		X			X
17	Kennesaw State Univ.	162		X			X
18	Ball State Univ.	159	X	X		X	
19	Univ. of Arizona	147	X	X	X		X
20	Case-Western Univ.	136			X		X
21	Cornell Univ.	133			X	X	
22	Univ. of Minnesota	116			X	X	
23	Univ. of Colorado, Boulder	101			X	X	
24	San Diego State Univ.	97		X			
25	Boston Univ.	79			X	X	
26	U.C., Berkeley	72			X	X	
27	Univ. of So. Carolina	66			X	X	
28	Univ. of Washington	62					X
29	Fairleigh Dickinson Univ.	61			X		X
30	St. Louis Univ.	59					X
31	Southern Methodist Univ.	58		X			
32	Univ. of Maryland	38	X		X	X	
33	Purdue Univ.	38					
34	Illinois, Chicago	35					X
35	Georgia Tech	26					
36	Univ. of Illinois, Urbana	20		X			
37	Thunderbird	20					X
38	Fresno State	18					
39	Seattle Pacific Univ.	18					
40	Baldwin-Wallace	17					
41	Duke Univ.	16					
42	Univ. of Oregon	13					X
43	Miami, Ohio	13					
44	Ohio State	13					
45	Columbia Univ.	9					X
46	Univ. of Montana	9					
47	Univ. of So. Dakota	8					
48	M.I.T.	7					X

Table 1
Continued

Rank	School	Academic Points	*Entrepreneur Magazine 1993*	*Business Week 1993*	Success 1994 Top 25	Success 1995 Top 25	Success 1995 2nd 25
49	Rice Univ.	3					
50	Univ. of Nebraska	2					X
51	Central Arkansas	1					
	Brigham Young	0				X	
	Birmingham Southern	0					X
	Cal Poly Pomona	0					X
	Cal State Hayward	0					X
	Canisius College	0					X
	George Washington Univ.	0			X	X	
	Georgetown Univ.	0				X	
	Indiana, Bloomington	0					X
	Iowa	0					X
	James Madison	0					X
	Samford Univ.	0					X
	San Francisco State	0					X
	Wisconsin, Whitewater	0				X	
	Xavier	0					X

exploration of entrepreneurship courses and programs in existence.

Although the questionnaires were addressed to deans, they were answered by a variety of people, sometimes deans, and sometimes others to whom a dean had passed the questionnaire. Of the 311 replies, 233 came from U.S. business schools, 16 from Canadian schools, and 62 from schools in other countries.

Ranking Entrepreneurship Programs

Respondents were given a table that listed in three columns the schools whose entrepreneurship offerings have been noted as most prominent by three magazines: *Success* (1994), *Business Week* (1993), and *Entrepreneur* (1993). The schools were listed alphabetically. A fourth column of the table was provided so that respondents could rank the schools they regarded as the top ten

besides their own. Space was also provided for "write-ins." Some respondents ranked 10 schools. Some simply checked 10 schools without listing a rank. Other respondents included more than 10 schools. Of the 311 returned questionnaires, 62 provided ranking information. In all, respondents either ranked, checked, and/or nominated a total of 51 U.S., plus 4 Canadian, and 9 overseas schools.

To combine the different types of responses consistently, a weighting scheme was used under which a school ranked #1 by a respondent was assigned 30 points, #2 was assigned 29 points, #3 received 28 points, etc. If a school was only checked by a respondent, it was given the same number of points as if it has been the middle-ranked school on the array of schools that the respondent gave checks to. Self-rankings did not count. How schools ranked in total points allocated by this scheme can be seen in Tables 1, 2, and 3.

Table 2
Top-Rated Canadian Entrepreneurship Programs

Rank	School	Academic Points	Entrepreneur Magazine 1993	Business Week 1993	Success 1994 Top 25	Success 1995 Top 25	Success 1995 2nd 25
1	Univ. of Calgary	55	X				
2	HEC, Montreal	16					
3	York Univ., Toronto	9	X				
4	Univ. of Western Ontario	8					

Table 3
Top-Rated Entrepreneurship Programs Abroad

Rank	School	Academic Points	Entrepreneur Magazine 1993	Business Week 1993	Success 1994 Top 25	Success 1995 Top 25	Success 1995 2nd 25
1	Durham Univ., UK	29					
2	Swinburne, Australia	28					
3	Univ. of Stirling, UK	27					
4	Vaxjo, Sweden	17					
5	INSEAD, France	17					
6	Vincennes Univ., France	16					
7	Cranfield Institute, UK	16					
8	London Business School, UK	14					
9	Bocconi, Italy	1					

Table 1 presents the rankings of U.S. schools, Table 2 presents the rankings of Canadian schools, and Table 3 the rankings of schools of other countries. The reason for this separation is that the majority of respondents were from U.S. schools, and the comments that some of the respondents made, such as "I haven't a clue," indicated that their familiarity with U.S. schools was limited and their knowledge of schools in other countries was still less. The magazines whose published ratings were included in the questionnaire were all published in the United States, and all but one of them listed only U.S. schools. So there was clearly both a national bias and also imperfect knowledge of what was going on at other schools in this field.

The schools appearing last on the list in Table 1 all failed to receive any nominations to the "top ten" by respondents, yet they appear in the listing produced subsequently by *Success Magazine* in 1995. This is perhaps due, in part, to the fact that the two pollings took place at different times and both the offerings of schools and the knowledge that academics at other schools have about other programs are changing fairly fast. This flux in rankings seems likely to continue.

A number of issues should be noted in regard to these academic rankings. First, since the ranking form included rankings from three previous magazine evaluations, it is likely that these previous benchmarks may have influenced the academic responses. Second, as noted earlier, we received many written comments from academics indicating the paucity of information they had available for use in ranking various entrepreneurship programs. Except for the compendia of entrepreneurship course descriptions published by Vesper (1974–1993) and the Solomon (1986) national survey, little systematic evidence that compares and describes entrepreneurship courses and programs has been published and disseminated. It would seem likely that many of the academics in this survey are not familiar with this information, and would only have knowledge of other programs through anecdotal evidence or through newsletters, brochures, and flyers distributed by some of these programs. To the extent that the knowledge level of many of the academics who ranked the various programs is incomplete, we think it appropriate to view these rankings with some reservation. Finally, this survey did not provide direct links between the rankings and facts relevant to subsequent criteria thought to be important for ranking programs. For example, while academics indicated that "courses offered" was the most important criterion for ranking an entrepreneurship program, limitations of time and resources have not yet allowed investigation of the correlation between ranks given and actual numbers or the makeup of courses offered by each program.

Ranking Criteria

In order to determine how academics made judgments about the relative quality of various entrepreneurship programs, respondents were asked to indicate, with a rank ordering, what criteria should be used for rating entrepreneurship programs. The results can be seen in Table 4. The leading criteria are courses offered, faculty publications, impact on community, and innovations and accomplishments of alumni. The figures in Table 4 were computed by weighting responses in order of rank, with rank one receiving the highest weighting, and then adding the weights. The top rank was given 25 points, the next 24, and so forth, for as many criteria as the respondent ranked. It can be seen that courses offered was strongly the number-one criterion, with the next few substantially below it but fairly closely ranked to each other.

Courses Offered

The number-one criterion at the time of this survey, "courses offered," may seem enigmatic if described in those two words alone. Does it mean number of different courses, size of classes, number of credits or class sessions, something about the way the courses are taught, who is doing the teaching, or some other feature of the courses? Respondents were asked which of 22 types of courses (plus a blank for other write-ins) the respondent's school either had (as indicated by an established catalog number) or was planning to add. This list appears in Table 5. A challenge in interpreting the results for tabulation arose from the fact that while some respondents listed the catalog number, others simply put check marks. Our decision in the latter event was to regard the data as indicating that there was one course that treated all the topics checked. This may have resulted in under-counting the actual number of courses that were offered.

If the same catalog number was used for more than one of the courses on the list, then it was considered a single course for tabulating purposes and credit for that course was divided evenly among however many courses that number was used for. Sometimes a

Table 4
Ranking of Program Criteria by Other Academics

Criterion	Overall Rank n = 130	U.S. Rank n = 112	Non-U.S. Rank n = 28
1. Courses offered	1	1	1
2. Faculty publications	2	2	2
3. Impact on community	3	3	3
4. Exploits of alumni	4	4	4
5. Innovations	5	5	5
6. Alumni start-ups	6	6	6
7. Outreach to scholars	7	7	7
8. Competitions and awards won	8	8	13
9. Years of activity	9	9	12
10. Size of MBA program	10	10	11
11. Halo of school or university	11	14	8
12. Magnitude of resources	12	11	15
13. Alumni comments years later	13	13	14
14. Size of undergrad program	14	16	12
15. Incoming student qualities	15	15	9
16. Size of doctoral program	16	16	10
17. Faculty start-ups	17	16	17
18. Location	18	18	18

catalog number was the same for both undergraduate and graduate courses except for the first digit. This might mean there were two courses or it might mean that one course was offered to both categories of students, with undergraduates signing up under one number and graduate students under a different one for the same series of classes. Not being able to tell whether this is the case, we counted such courses as separate. This may have resulted in over-counting the actual number of different graduate and undergraduate courses offered.

Aside from the above difficulties of determining how many different courses were offered, there is another problem associated with using the number of different courses offered as a criterion for rating programs. It implies that entre-preneurship as a subject should be taught in separate courses, rather than as part of "regular" courses or infused throughout the curriculum. Not all schools see it that way. Some claim that the subject is covered as part of other courses. Should there be a second rating scheme for schools that take such an approach? But then, how should schools be evaluated that sometimes treat the subject with separate courses and other times infuse it in regular courses? should that make a third category, or possibly a whole array?

Faculty Publications

The importance of the second criterion, faculty publications, was significantly lower that that of courses offered. Unfortunately, there was no question that

Table 5
Number of Schools with Different Courses in Catalog or Planned

Courses Offered or Planned	Undergraduate		Graduate	
	In Catalog	Planned	In Catalog	Planned
Entrepreneurship or starting new firms	128	14	98	5
Small business management	109	5	31	2
Field projects/venture consulting	44	4	31	3
Starting and running a firm	34	2	18	1
Venture plan writing	31	3	23	1
Venture finance	30	4	30	6
Entrepreneurship for non-business majors	18	5	7	1
Family business	16	6	12	3
Venture opportunity finding/ screening	15	1	9	0
Venture marketing	13	0	12	5
Management of fast-growing firms	11	4	10	4
Venturing in (arts, nursing, Eastern Europe, technology, or other fields)	11	3	6	1
Creative thinking	10	1	7	2
Franchise development	9	3	9	2
International venturing	9	2	6	0
Law for entrepreneurs	9	5	5	3
Innovation evaluation	7	0	21	1
Technology transfer	6	2	22	4
Entrepreneurship for (bankers, software writers, biologists, or other fields)	5	1	4	2
Corporate venturing	4	1	15	6
Business entry via acquisition	3	2	8	1
Street smarts in business	2	0	2	0
Other (please attach catalog description)	20	0	18	1

asked which kinds of publications (such as books and journal proceedings, and magazine articles) or what about the publications (such as how often cited, whether data-based, how applied, nature of target audience, length) should be considered of most importance.

Impact on Community

The impact that the entrepreneurship program might have on the community ranked closely behind faculty publications in importance. Public symposia, student consulting projects, and company spin-offs from the university would be examples of this criterion. To determine which of these was most effective or valuable in evaluating an entrepreneurship program will require further investigation. Judging from the indicated importance of this criterion, however, such a study might be worthwhile. Foundations interested in the practical accomplishments of entrepreneurship programs might consider underwriting such a study.

Alumni Exploits

Alumni exploits include not only start-ups by alumni, but also alumni participation in the ventures of others as investors, partners, employees, or other helpers. Determining the number of graduates who have started companies has, to date, been beyond the resources of most schools. The few informal studies done by schools show a strong correlation between students who study entrepreneurship and, at some later time, start companies. It will never be possible to separate selection from training as the cause of these start-ups, but it should be possible, through detailed case studies, to uncover which elements of the educational process influence selected decisions and actions in alumni start-ups.

Innovations

This criterion could be interpreted either to mean innovations of the alumni of these programs or innovations in the programs, themselves. This criterion was ranked virtually on a par with alumni exploits. The conclusion for schools might be simply to regard introduction of innovations as important, whether in their own activities or those of their students. Part of the self-critique of a school desiring to be high-rated would be to ask, "What innovations have we been responsible for?" Innovative programs would seem more likely to be noticed.

Alumni Start-Ups

Although not the same thing as "alumni exploits," start-up accomplish-

ments could, logically, be included within it.

Outreach to Scholars

This criterion seems to refer to such program activities as hosting conferences, sponsoring journals, creating and distributing new teaching materials, publishing newsletters, and helping other schools. Faculty publications could be part of this.

Other Criteria

The following were all emphasized about equally as still important, but noticeably less so than the first seven criteria; awards and national competitions won, years in the business, number of MBA students, halo of the school, magnitude of resources, comments of alumni years later, number of undergraduate students, and qualities of incoming students. It is clear that performance on some of the "other criteria" is likely to influence performance on the first seven criteria. For instance, the magnitude of resources can affect a program's ability to score on any of the other dimensions. More years "in the business" (the length of time the program has existed) will have allowed time for more accomplishments to have occurred. A larger number of students, whether MBA or undergraduate, will provide a bigger population for luck, if nothing else, to work in producing alumni exploits.

Least Important Criteria (for Now?)

Finally, the criteria judged least important by respondents in rating programs were the following: number of doctoral students, faculty start-ups, and location. Low importance ratings on any of these criteria could be regarded with some surprise. The late provost emeritus of Stanford University, Frederick Terman, regarded Ph.D. production as the prime criterion for elevating the status of his engineering school, having noted from his earlier association with Harvard and

MIT, that Ph.D. production had been a winning strategy for those schools. The rating of faculty start-ups as a relatively unimportant criterion for judging entrepreneurship programs was also a surprise to us. It would seem that the creation of a new business would be a very relevant demonstration that an entrepreneurship faculty member had some practical knowledge to teach from. Finally, it would seem that location should be important for judging a program. It has long been observed that exceptionally high-performance entrepreneurship tends to cluster geographically. That is how "Route 128" and "Silicon Valley" became familiar terms. Presence of role models to serve as speakers and mentors to entrepreneurship students are elements that faculty commonly regard as very helpful in entrepreneurship courses, and such resources are certainly more available in metropolitan areas where, coincidentally, entrepreneurship programs are generally situated.

This study is a first cut at exploring criteria for evaluating entrepreneurship programs. In the future it seems likely that better information and further thought will change both the criteria and their weightings. At the same time, some schools will introduce new programs. Existing programs will expand, refine, and publicize their offerings. As all this happens, and people learn about these changes and innovations, the rankings of entrepreneurship programs should change as well, and become more meaningful. In the meantime, in the spirit of generating some discussion on this issue, we offer a framework for evaluating entrepreneurship programs and some opinions on specific criteria for measuring progress in entrepreneurship education.

Discussion

As we have suggested earlier in this article, the rankings of university entrepreneurship programs should be viewed with much skepticism. There are a number of problems with these rankings. Evaluators did not specify the criteria they actually used to rank entrepreneurship programs, just ones they considered important. Evaluators did not offer their specific weights for each criterion used to judge a program, they just ranked them. Finally, evaluators were not asked to provide a judgment about their depth of knowledge of other programs. Since the criteria for determining what constitutes a high-quality entrepreneurship program is, at present, rather fluid and indeterminate, we suggest that a discussion of measures of quality in entrepreneurship education should be placed in the context of the larger movement in higher education toward achieving quality and continuous improvement (Boyer 1990; Malcolm Baldrige National Quality Award 1995; Seymour 1992) and, particularly, the quality movement in business schools (Meisel and Seltzer 1995; Vance 1993). Rather than inventing evaluation criteria and processes for evaluating entrepreneurship programs, we thought it more appropriate to borrow insights from highly successful and visible evaluation efforts in higher education.

In our review of these evaluation schemes, we believe the Malcolm Baldrige National Quality Award (MBNQA) *Education Pilot Criteria: 1995* offers a very comprehensive and detailed format that may serve as a guide for identifying criteria for measuring quality in entrepreneurship education. The MBNQA was established in 1987 to promote quality improvement, recognize organizations that have made substantial improvements in quality, and foster the sharing of best-practices information. The MBNQA is one of the largest quality-improvement programs. Over one million copies of the MBNQA Criteria have been disseminated, though there have been only 546 applicants for the

Baldrige Award and less than 30 award recipients. The MBNQA Education Pilot Criteria are structured in a format similar to all MBNQA programs. Organizations are assessed across 28 requirements that are embodied in seven categories. For the education pilot criteria framework, these seven categories and their weights in the overall evaluation schema are (1) Leadership, 9%; (2) Information and Analysis, 7.5%; (3) Strategic and Operational Planning, 7.5%; (4) Human Resource Development and Management, 15%; (5) Educational and Business Process Management, 15%; (6) School Performance Results, 23%; and (7) Student Focus and Student and Stakeholder Satisfaction, 23%. The MBNQA is oriented towards helping organizations undertake substantial efforts at self-evaluation and study leading to significant improvements in organizational processes, structure, and outcomes. The MBNQA is primarily a diagnostic system that focuses on achieving results. While the MBNQA evaluation process is very elaborate and detailed, and cannot be easily summarized in a few sentences or pages, it is in the context of the MBNQA format that we offer some suggestions for how entrepreneurship programs might be rated. Further information about the MBNQA Education Pilot Program is provided at the end of this article.

Leadership

This category examines senior administrators' commitment and involvement in creating and sustaining performance excellence that has a student focus, clear goals, and high expectations. In the context of entrepreneurship education, the leadership category entails describing the involvement and commitment of entrepreneurship program directors, business school deans, university administrators, advisory board members, and student representatives. One way that senior-administrator commitment and involvement could be determined is by evaluating the centrality of entrepreneurship education to the university's mission. For instance, a high-quality entrepreneurship program might have "entrepreneurship" as a significant part of the mission statement of its business school. Entrepreneurship should, indeed, be part of the mission of the university as a whole. Ways that a leadership commitment to entrepreneurship might be measured might include how often entrepreneurship is described in university publications, such as its bulletin, catalogue, recruiting brochures, and other materials, as well as how often entrepreneurship is publicly championed in speeches, presentations, and articles by the key decision-makers in the university. Finally, there should be some emphasis on where an entrepreneurship program is placed in the administrative structure of the university. In many universities, the primary way a topic area gains prominence is through department status. Universities form departments as a way to focus faculty efforts, coordinate resources through a specified budget, and recruit students. Our primary concern in the leadership category is that the quality criteria demonstrate that entrepreneurship is an important focus of the university, and not merely an afterthought or tangential response to placate growing student interest in this topic, or a gesture to garner financial support from successful entrepreneurial alumni to use for other projects of non-entrepreneurship faculty. As evidence from the corporate-venturing literature suggests (Block and MacMillan 1993), a program within a large university is unlikely to flourish and innovate without the active support of top administrators, as well as the championing efforts of business school deans, and the cooperation of the school's voting faculty. The day of the 'one-man band" is probably over for significant programs.

Information and Analysis

This category examines how data and information are used to support the overall mission of the program. The focus of this category is towards identifying and specifying information and data that would be appropriate for evaluating the quality of an entrepreneurship program, as well as for making comparisons with other programs. This includes collection of information for comparisons and benchmarking to improve program performance. As we have indicated throughout this article, one of the major problems in conducting surveys of entrepreneurship programs has been the paucity of information that each program collects. We suggest that entrepreneurship programs begin to systematically collect information about such issues as demographic and performance measures of incoming students enrolling in entrepreneurship courses; comparative information on entrepreneurship, business school, and university students; descriptions of the outcomes that specific entrepreneurship courses intend to generate and measures of the efficacy of each course; and measures of the intended outcomes of the entrepreneurship program in terms of student performance, student satisfaction, and impact on the community (i.e., number of start-ups, students employed in new firms, students working in positions assisting new firms). While much of this information might seem onerous to collect, we posit that the growing trend towards quality management in higher education will require that this information, or information similar to it, be collected from all university units in the foreseeable future. Without such information on inputs, processes, and outcomes, it is difficult to adequately evaluate the performance of any program. The collection of relevant information will be critical for making sound comparisons among various entrepreneurship programs. There should also be a way to share it efficiently to minimize redundant inquiries.

Strategic and Operational Planning

This category focuses on how a program sets its strategic direction and develops its key planning requirements. The primary emphasis of this category is on aligning the strategic planning process with student needs and expectations, external factors, requirements and opportunities, internal capabilities, and resources, so that improvements can be made in student performance and in the service and research components of the program if they, too, are present. For an entrepreneurship program, such a requirement would entail generating a strategic plan that specifies the purpose and mission of the program, key student and overall program performance requirements, external factors impacting the implementation of the plan, internal resources and university barriers to change, and key critical success factors. The goal of this category is to generate a road map to guide the success of the program. A measure of this category would be whether a program has a strategic plan, or not.

Human Resource Development and Management

This category examines how faculty and staff are supported and developed so as to satisfy the strategic goals of the program. While an entrepreneurship program might typically measure "faculty productivity" as an indicator of this category, the intention is actually towards specifying the resources and systems that impact the ability of staff and faculty to be productive. What might be measured in this category could be the amount of resources devoted to enabling faculty to do research, helping faculty become better entrepreneurship teachers (through such activities as case writing and attending workshops, conferences, and training programs), and enabling staff to better serve students or work with entrepreneurial clients. The ability of faculty to generate academic publications or high teacher ratings, for example, are only two possible measures of the support provided to conduct such activities. In the MBNQA framework, faculty productivity is the result of efforts to enhance the well-being of faculty. Increasing productivity is difficult without the necessary resources to achieve such gains.

Educational and Business Process Management

This category specifies key aspects of the design and delivery of the educational research and service components of a program, as well as an examination of the processes involved in improving these components. This is the category in the evaluation scheme where such measures as "courses offered" have some bearing. This category recognizes a more comprehensive and detailed description of a program's pedagogy and curriculum. A high-quality program would articulate the logic of the course offerings (e.g., What is their purpose? What do they hope to achieve? Who are these courses designed for? How do these courses fit with the rest of the business school's curriculum?) and how new courses are designed and introduced. A high-quality program would need to describe how these courses are delivered and how the program measures the success of the delivery of these courses (e.g., student evaluations of courses and instructors, enrollment demand, complaints, attendance rates). A high-quality program would specify the kinds of support services available to help entrepreneurship students succeed (e.g., counseling, advising, internships, mentors). Finally, a high-quality program would show how research, scholarship, and the service activities of faculty are linked to achieving the educational mission of the program. Such a comprehensive descrip-

tion of the pedagogy and curriculum of an entrepreneurship program is a quantum change in the level of detail and thought necessary compared to a measure such as "courses offered." Rather than programs being compared to each other by the quantity of courses offered, this category requires that programs be measured on the logic, coherency, and efficacy of the educational experience that entrepreneurship students undertake.

School Performance Results

This category examines the outcomes of a program, such as student performance and improvement, improvement in services provided by the program, and faculty productivity. As may have been noticed earlier, this category accounts for 23% of the total evaluation score. The primary focus of this category is determining the improvements in student performance. In order to specify such improvements, a program must identify key measures and indicators of performance. As mentioned earlier, such key measures might include student performance in specific courses, student demonstrations of key skills and knowledge through portfolios of original work that they create, measures of student satisfaction, and impact on the community (i.e., number of start-ups, students employed in new firms, students working in positions assisting new firms). For research universities, programs should also be evaluated on faculty contributions to knowledge creation and transfer. Measuring the number of faculty publications is one, rather limited, approach to describing faculty productivity. Text books, professional and trade books, cases, teaching exercises, and activities such as consulting, counseling, and advising students and entrepreneurs might also be appropriate measures for certain university programs. Finally, the impact of a program's contribution to knowledge should not just be measured by counting the number of times a journal article is cited in a citation index, but also through evidence of impact on practitioner thought and action. Since entrepreneurship is an occupation, impact should ultimately be measured as an effect on practitioner activities.

Student Focus and Student and Stakeholder Satisfaction

This category describes the process for determining student and stakeholder needs and expectations, as well as making comparisons of student and stakeholder satisfaction among other programs. This category accounts for 23% of the total evaluation score. A high-quality entrepreneurship program would seek to determine the needs and expectations of current students, as well as future student needs and expectations, and the needs and expectations of other key stakeholders (e.g., parents, communities, alumni, employers, legislatures, and practicing entrepreneurs). In the MBNQA evaluation process, the concept of quality is determined by a thorough understanding of student and stakeholder needs. In many respects, the MBNQA process begins with this category. The quality of a program, is therefore, externally driven, rather than driven by what we, as educators and administrators, might want to posit as a key and important contribution. An entrepreneurship program should be "close to the customer," and information should be collected that demonstrates what students and stakeholders need and expect, as well as how a program best attempts to serve them.

Conclusions

The MBNQA is one approach to a comprehensive and detailed evaluation of an entrepreneurship program. What the MBNQA evaluation scheme does is force us to become aware of the implicit goals, objectives, and pedagogical perspectives of our programs. Our measures of the quality of entrepreneurship programs have to become more comprehensive and robust to reflect these issues. We do not know of any entrepreneurship program that has undertaken the kind of evaluation specified in the MBNQA process. But we think such efforts should help the refinement process. This may be the "higher road" towards improving entrepreneurship programs, rather than seeking to play the "ratings game" of satisfying superficial criteria. The evolution of entrepreneurship programs in colleges and universities is still in its infancy. More debate and dialogue among academics, administrators, students, and other stakeholders must be encouraged. The criteria for determining high-quality entrepreneurship education programs should not be become fixed at this time. Yet, we must not lose sight of the fact that entrepreneurship programs are and will be evaluated, and that we must, therefore, be ready to offer criteria that we want our programs evaluated on. If university entrepreneurship educators do not step forward to assume leadership of our own field, others will surely come to the forefront to determine the rules of the game.

References

Block, Z., and MacMillan, I.C. 1993. *Corporate Venturing.* Cambridge, MA: Harvard Business School Press.

Boyer, E.L. 1990. *Scholarship Reconsidered: Priorities of the Professoriate.* Princeton, NJ: Princeton University Press.

Callan, K., and Warshaw, M. 1994. The 25 best business schools for entrepreneurs. *SUCCESS* 41(7):37–50.

Callan, K., and Warshaw, M. 1995. The 25 best business schools for entrepreneurs. *SUCCESS* 42(7):37–49.

Gartner, W.B. 1990. What are we talking about when we talk about entrepreneurship? *Journal of Business Venturing* 5:15–28.

Gartner, W.B., and Shane, S.A. 1995. Measuring entrepreneurship over time. *Journal of Business Venturing* 10:283–301.

Gartner, W.B., and Vesper, K.H. 1994. Experiments in entrepreneurship education: Successes and failures. *Journal of Business Venturing* 9:179–187.

Gilley, J.W. 1992. Faust goes to college. *Academe* 78(3):9–11.

Lumpkin, G.T., and Dess, G.G. 1996. Clarifying the entrepreneurship orientation construct and linking it to performance. *Academy of Management Review* 21:135–172.

Lundquist Center for Entrepreneurship. 1994. Benchmarks in entrepreneurship education. Working paper, Charles H. Lundquist College of Business, University of Oregon.

Malcolm Baldrige National Quality Award. 1995. *Education Pilot Criteria: 1995*. Gaithersburg, MD: National Institute of Standards and Technology.

Meisel, S., and Seltzer, L. 1995. Rethinking management education: A TQM perspective. *Journal of Management Education* 19(1):75–95.

Plaschka, G.R., and Welsch, H.P. 1990. Emerging structures in entrepreneurship education: Curricular designs and strategies. *Entrepreneurship: Theory and Practice* 14(3):56–71.

Porter, L.W., and McKibbin, L.E. 1988. *Management, Education and Development: Drift or Thrust into the 21st Century?* New York: McGraw-Hill.

Seymour, D.T. 1992. *On Q: Causing Quality in Higher Education*. New York: MacMillan Publishing Company.

Solomon, G.T. 1986. *National Survey of Entrepreneurial Education*. (3rd Ed.) Washington, DC: Government Printing Office.

Vance, C.M. 1993. *Mastering Management Education*. Newbury Park, CA: Sage.

Vesper, K.H. 1974. *Entrepreneurship Education—1974*. Milwaukee, WI: Society for Entrepreneurship Research and Application.

Vesper, K.H. 1975. *Entrepreneurship Education—1975*. Milwaukee, WI: Society for Entrepreneurship Research and Application.

Vesper, K.H. 1976. *Entrepreneurship Education—A Bicentennial Compendium*. Milwaukee, WI: Society for Entrepreneurship Research and Application.

Vesper, K.H. 1978. *Entrepreneurship Education—A 1978 Update*. Milwaukee, WI: Society for Entrepreneurship Research and Application.

Vesper, K.H. 1979. *Entrepreneurship Education—1979*. Milwaukee, WI: Center for Venture Management.

Vesper, K.H. 1980. *Entrepreneurship Education—1980*. Wellesley, MA: Babson College Center for Entrepreneurial Studies.

Vesper, K.H. 1985. *Entrepreneurship Education—1985*. Wellesley, MA: Babson College Center for Entrepreneurial Studies.

Vesper, K.H. 1990. *Entrepreneurship Education—1990*. Wellesley, MA: Babson College Center for Entrepreneurial Studies.

Vesper, K.H. 1993. *Entrepreneurship Education—1993*. Los Angeles: University of California, Los Angeles, Center for Entrepreneurial Studies.

Emerging Structures in Entrepreneurship Education: Curricular Designs and Strategies

by Gerhard R. Plaschka and Harold P. Welsch

In 1987, the Internal Revenue Service reported 18.1 million businesses in the U.S. Only 7,000 of them would not qualify as small businesses. The implication is that 99.5% of all businesses are small if the cutoff of 500 employees is used (State of Small Business, 1988). The increase in business start-ups between 1981 and 1987 was 153% (from 92, 161 to 232, 948). More than one-half of the total job growth between 1980 and 1986 came from companies with 100 or fewer employees; companies with 500 or fewer employees represented 76.6% of the new job growth (State of Small Business, 1988, p. 36). That outcome has been labeled "The Great American Job Machine."

During the 1980–84 period of small business growth, a similar continuous growth pattern can be identified in entrepreneurship education. In 1985(a) Vesper reported an increase of over 50% (from 163 to 253) in universities that had entrepreneurship courses, and in his latest survey (1990), he reported a comparable rate of growth continued between 1985 and 1990. Solomon (1986) reported 418 educational organizations with formal entrepreneurship activities. American and European entrepreneurship programs have grown tenfold since 1958 (Kerr, 1988). Administrators expect that a future shift in program emphasis from a small business to an entrepreneurship perspective, with the potential for entrepreneurship to be integrated into MBA programs, will take place

within the next five years (Kerr, 1988). Hills and Welsch (1986), in a survey of almost 2,000 students, found that 80% expressed an interest in taking one or more courses in entrepreneurship/new ventures. Boberg and Kiecker (1988) also show that demand for entrepreneurship education will outstrip resources.

In the early 1980s, several institutions (Babson College, Baylor University, University of Southern California) held major conferences on this topic. Harvard hosted a colloquium in 1983 on "Entrepreneurship: What It Is and How to Teach It", and Ohio State University published *A National Entrepreneurship Education Agenda for Action* in 1984. Also in 1984, the Price Institute for Entrepreneurial Studies launched the Price-Babson College Fellows Program to create a mechanism to enable universities to attract and support entrepreneurship educators.

Growth is also evident by the proliferation of entrepreneurship centers, chairs, conferences, journals, and programs. The field is evolving rapidly in both academic and professional arenas. For example, Katz (1989) reported 93 endowed positions and chairs of entrepreneurship; Sandberg et al. (1989) identified 39 research centers; and the authors found more than 20 professional national and international entrepreneurship conferences.

Simultaneously, a related set of complementary activities has arisen. Those activities, such as entrepreneur of the

---

Originally appeared in *Entrepreneurship Theory and Practice*, 1990, Volume 14, Number 3.

year programs, entrepreneurship awareness programs, round table luncheons, seminars, vocational education, student entrepreneurship clubs and businesses, sponsors, endowments, university-based incubators, entrepreneur alumni groups, enterprise forums, volunteer assistance programs and workshops, have a symbiotic relationship. Another sign of maturation of the field is the proliferation of differentiated concepts in addition to the established one of entrepreneurship: intrapreneurship (Pinchot, 1985), interpreneurship (Hoy et al., 1989), and Infopreneur (Weitzen, 1988) are examples.

Is Entrepreneurship Recognized as an Established Discipline?

Entrepreneurship has struggled long and hard for an identity in an effort to be recognized and accepted. In its early years it had to deal with several problems. First, it had to get past the negative connotations that the "small business" label carried, i.e., "buying a job," lack of growth, lack of innovation, and the "ma and pa" image. Second, it had to establish itself as its *own* field, not one under the mantle of "small business." This involved achieving recognition for the field as an independent discipline even though there were few distinct criteria that made it unique.

Entrepreneurship fell into a "general management" category and later into a "small business management" category, neither of which allowed the field to become distinctive, i.e., it utilized "borrowed" or "stolen" principles that were not its own (Vesper, 1987). In fact, Vesper (1985a) concluded that in the late 1970s,

entrepreneurship was a "tangential activity, academically 'flaky,' and lacking in a scholarly body of knowledge. . . . Little research in entrepreneurship goes on and consequently the literature on it remains thin" (p. 64).

Even though Say (1816), Mill (1848), Schumpeter (1911), and Knight (1921) outlined and shed some original light on the concept of entrepreneurship, it was not until McClelland (1961) introduced the need for achievement and its possible impact on entrepreneurship that the initial formative stages of identity began. Utilizing the individual as the unit of analysis and applying psychological principles to help understand the motivations of entrepreneurs, other scholars began to contribute to the field. Hartman (1959), Hoad and Rosko (1964), Collins, Moore, and Unwalla (1964), Schrage (1965), Smith (1967), Leibenstein (1968), Collins and Moore (1970), Hornaday and Bunker (1970), and Palmer (1971) were among the early contributors who helped form the field.

To answer the question of when a field becomes recognized as an established discipline, it is necessary to examine the elements by which a field is judged. According to Greenwood (1957), Hall (1968), and Wilensky (1964), it is possible to identify several elements that a field needs to be distinguishable: (1) systematic theory and an established body of literature; (2) authority, professional associations, and communication sanction; (3) ethical codes and culture; and (4) career.

Systematic Theories

There has been a dramatic increase in the entrepreneurship literature in recent years. At least 12 academic journals[1] con-

---

[1]For example: *Entrepreneurship and Regional Development* (Ireland), *Entrepreneurship Development Review* (Canada), *Entrepreneurship Theory and Practice* (US), *Family Business Review* (US), *International Small Business Journal* (originally *European Small Business Journal*, UK), *Internationales Gewerbearchiv* (Switzerland), *Journal of Business Venturing* (US). *Journal of Small Business Management* (US), *Small Business Economics* (Netherlands).

centrate on entrepreneurship; about 20 annual conferences, at which approximately 700 papers are presented, have been identified; several series of entrepreneurship research collections (e.g. Frontiers of Entrepreneurship. Encyclopedia of Entrepreneurship, and collections of proceedings of professional societies) have appeared in the last decade. In addition, several bibliographies have emerged (Welsch, 1990; London Business School, 1988; Ronstadt, 1985a). It view of the number of references in the most recent years, it is evident that rapid growth is taking place.

Wortman (1989, p. 3) summarized the last ten years in entrepreneurship as "(a) a positive movement toward a commonly accepted definition of entrepreneurship and toward the definition of the boundaries of the field of entrepreneurship; (b) a division of entrepreneurship into individual (or independent) entrepreneurship and corporate entrepreneurship (intrapreneurship); (c) a movement toward more sophisticated research designs, research methods, and statistical techniques; (d) a shift toward larger data samples and the use of large data bases; and (e) a slight movement away from exploratory research toward causal research."

Unfortunately, there is yet no agreement on common terms, such as the definition of an entrepreneur (Gartner, 1988; Carland et al., 1988; Hebert & Link, 1989), or on parameters, such as industry types or types of entrepreneurs (Smith & Miner, 1983; Davidsson, 1988). Nor has there been agreement on an entrepreneurship conceptual framework that could advance and develop the field.

While several attempts at developing a comprehensive unifying framework have been made (Wortman, 1987, 1989; d'Amboise & Muldonney, 1988; Sexton, 1988; Brockhaus, 1988; Chell & Haworth, 1987; Low & MacMillan, 1988; Carsrud et al., 1986; Gartner, 1985; Kao & Stevenson, 1983), none of the authors has generated an integrated unified theory that has proved useful in a systematic advancement of the field.

Authority and Professional Associations

More formal disciplines are characterized by professional associations that operate through a network of formal and informal groups. The associations possess the power to criticize or to censure, since membership is viewed as a "sine qua non" of professional success. The associations perform their professional functions through a network of relationships that creates its own subculture, with adjustment to it a prerequisite for career progress. Professional associations in entrepreneurship are characterized by diverse groups representing a wide range of functions, including research, education and practice. The first modern international organization in entrepreneurship was the Recontres de St. Gall, founded in 1948.[2]

It is at the conferences of the associations that theoreticians-researchers mingle with practitioners, junior members meet with senior authors and professors, and colleagues join together to share recent information, developments, and innovations in the field. The interactions represent the professional culture fostered and encouraged by members in

---

[2]The authors identified over 20 organizations which are concerned with entrepreneurship including Academy of Management/Entrepreneurship Division, European Foundation for Entrepreneurship Research, European Foundation of Management Development, Family Firm Institute, International Council for Small Business with 5 affiliates, International Small Business, Small Business Institute Directors Association.

the field, and the conferences have helped establish the legitimacy of the discipline. Discussions held in the conferences pointed to the lack of a systematic knowledge base, which led to the realization that in-depth research studies in entrepreneurship were needed. Several Ph.D. programs in the country took on the challenge and allowed, and later encouraged, Ph.D. students to conduct dissertation research in entrepreneurship. This followed the tradition of several European universities (e.g. St. Gall, Vienna, Cologne) that had established doctoral programs two decades earlier.

Authority-based institutions like the Small Business Administration (SBA) and the White House Conferences on Small Business set standards across industries for which businesses qualify as "small," and have adopted regulations and norms on how businesses should operate. In addition, the SBA's various divisions provide financing, assistance, and information to small businesses, all of which are recognized as valuable contributions by the public. Also recognized as authorities in entrepreneurship are the National Federation of Independent Businesses (NFIB), and certain academic institutions specializing in entrepreneurship with endowed chairs, such as Babson, Baylor, Harvard, and Wharton.

Professional Culture

The image of robber baron villains of the 19th century has given way to the image of a successful entrepreneurial hero of the 1990s. The values and norms of the entrepreneur as a professional are based on the concepts of creativity, innovation, and opportunity development within a dynamic environment. Today, it is widely accepted that entrepreneurial activity is the key to innovation, improved productivity, and more effective competition in the marketplace. In the US, the image of the successful

entrepreneur was projected by the popular media as early as the 1920s. Henry Ford embodied the entrepreneurial "Zeitgeist" of the country, permeating the culture with his revolutionary concept of providing people with what they demanded.

Entrepreneurs like Thomas Watson, William Hewlett and David Packard, Ray Kroc, Walt Disney, and Steven Jobs embodied a new set of standards that incorporated creation of value where none had existed before, freedom to succeed or fail, and a legitimate possibility of acquiring wealth. In addition, risk taking, leadership, achievement, and an action orientation in pursuit of opportunities were recognized as important cultural components of entrepreneurship.

Occupational Career

Another measure of the professionalism of the field is whether it leads to an occupational position and career. Although several efforts are currently under way to establish entrepreneurship awareness programs, i.e., to communicate entrepreneurship as a career possibility, many individuals and students deciding on a career are still seeking a position that provides a "security blanket" for life. In the past, "secure" job opportunities were sought in such "stable" organizations as banks, government, and the automobile, insurance, steel, and aviation industries. However, recent changes in government deficits, and, in basic industries, mergers, acquisitions, and globalization have served to overturn many of the expectations of stability, continuity, and career progress. It appears that lifetime positions are vanishing faster than the myth on which they were based.

Facing uncertainty has become an underlying phenomenon in all career choices. Therefore, a career choice approach should be one based on creativity, vision, innovation, and identification of new opportunities. Unfortunately, most individuals do not perceive entrepreneurship, which exploits such uncertainties to its advantage, as a possible career alternative. Starting a new venture, however, is only one possibility among the entrepreneurial career choices (Clouse, 1989; Scott, 1988; Ronstadt, 1985b). Several career options exist within entrepreneurship. One can explicitly seek employment in a newly established firm, where the individual can experience the vision and see the zeal of the entrepreneur, and where the structure and activities are evolving and fluid (Gundry, 1989; Drucker, 1985). The individual is able to design concepts, in concert with the vision, zeal and personal expression of the entrepreneur, to help reduce the uncertainty and ambiguity.

Another option exists within established firms where institutional slack, flexibility, and freedom to fail are not in place. Such a fossilized situation may need an infusion of entrepreneurial activity to mobilize forces for renewal and change. As a change agent in a middle management role (Kanter, 1986; Pinchott, 1985), one may choose to assume a career risk when pursuing a new idea within an established setting, sharing in the reward if the project succeeds, or perhaps losing one's job if it does not.

A third option is to serve as an entrepreneurial executive (Kanter, 1989; Kao, 1989) in an established firm, creating a new product or service in terms of one's own vision and implementing ideas in one's own style. The entrepreneurial executive thus must be in a position to work within existing structures as well as to form new frameworks to help implement the innovation. Often board members and other stakeholders provide general approval and support while the entrepreneurial executive retains operational and financial responsibility.

The career options described are only some of the career alternatives open.

Current Status of Management Education

We have come to the point where individuals have recognized entrepreneurship as a discipline and a career, but business curricula and management education have recently been criticized for a variety of deficiencies. A number of studies have been undertaken recently to determine the status of business schools and to help guide future directions and objectives.

One criticism is that business schools follow a "product" approach rather than a "customer" approach to education. All too often, schools like to pump out whatever they have rather than what is needed. Neck (1981) suggests that the top-down approach to education and training does not seem to cater adequately to the needs of small businesses and entrepreneurs. He charges that the small business sector has been effectively removed from the planning, development, implementation, and evaluation of programs.

Criticisms also come from within the educational system. Two business school deans, Behrman and Levin (1984), charge that there is: (1) too much emphasis on theory and quantitative analysis; (2) too little emphasis on qualitative factors; (3) too much emphasis on tools, concepts, and models; (4) too much emphasis on bureaucratic management; and (5) too little emphasis on entrepreneurial activity. Their sixth criticism is that professors work on unreal rather than important problems.

Leavitt (1989, p. 39) summarized that "we have built a weird, almost unimaginable design for MBA-level education. We then lay it upon well-proportioned young men and women, distorting them . . . into critters with lopsided brains, icy hearts and shrunken souls. We perform less of that witchcraft in our programs for older executives, because they won't stand for it." He points out further that we do not teach our chauvinistic American students to think globally or to view themselves as world citizens or train them in habits of life-long learning or the most vital characteristic of "action." Nor do we teach them on the "critical visionary, entrepreneurial path finding process part of the managing process, and [even] less on the problem-solving and implementing parts" (p. 40).

Some of the criticisms are similar to those of Porter and McKibben (1988) on the future of management education: (1) lack of an international focus; (2) too narrow concentration in specializations; (3) lack of integration of disciplines; (4) lack of active participation in the economic development process; and (5) too little emphasis on entrepreneurship in the curricula.

Others charge that academics only talk to themselves and are too busy writing what interests other academics. Wojahn (1986) writes of complaints of students remembering classes that only taught them "tools." They did not receive much "practical advice" or "street smarts" as opposed to "analytic smarts." Byrne et al. (1988) report a Duke graduate who stated: "I can crunch numbers to death, but I didn't learn anything about managing, motivating and leading people" (p. 84). Cheit (1985) also reviewed thirteen complaints about business schools; one of the complaints concerned the inadequate attention given to entrepreneurship, technology, productivity, and international concerns. Leavitt (1989) joins the critics by charging that "we presently devote perhaps 80% of our pedagogical energy [to] generating a mountain of 'analysis' courses: financial analysis, economic analysis, decision analysis, marketing analysis, and lots more" (p. 40).

Fortunately, the overemphasis on analysis, tools, and theory has not been successful in "killing off the deepest roots of American individualism" (Leavitt,

1989, p. 41). The family has encouraged the children to act independently, autonomously and self-reliantly. However, to the hard-line analysts, teaching about vision and creativity looked wrong headed, second class, anti-intellectual— precisely what a proper education was intended to replace. Those analysts generally could not abide the intuitive, often non-rational and unyielding mental processes characteristic of pathfinding styles and shared a disdain for pathfinders and their alien cognitive styles (Leavitt, 1989).

Curriculum Experimentation with Entrepreneurship

As the criticisms of business education show, current analytical-functional, quantitative, tools-oriented, theoretical, left-side of the brain, overspecialized, compartmentalized approaches are not adequate to begin solving ill-defined, unstructured, ambiguous, complex, multidisciplinary, holistic, real world problems. A reformulated approach to business/management education must be generated to prepare the new generation to attack those problems. Recent developments in globalization, internationalization, communication systems, opening of closed economic systems, emergence of a pluralistic set of values, environmental demands, and changing lifestyles force us to consider alternative configurations of educational business programs.

Hence, educational programs and systems should be geared toward creativity, multidisciplinary and process-oriented approaches, and theory-based practical applications. What is needed is a more proactive, problem-solving, and flexible approach rather than the rigid, passive-reactive concept, and theory-emphasized functional approach. One possibility is experimentation in entrepreneurship education topics and approaches. Since "off-the-shelf" solutions are not available to solve such chaotic and fuzzy problems, different skills and knowledge must be discovered. They include pattern recognition, mapping, front-end experimentation, experiential projection, and prestructuring of chaos.

Several authors have contributed brilliant ideas about what should be taught in entrepreneurship (Grad & Shapiro, 1981; Brown, 1982; Loucks, 1982; Vesper, 1982, 1986; Zeithaml & Rice, 1987). For example, Ulrich and Cole (1987) analyzed learning styles of entrepreneurs and the implications of teaching methods. Trinkaus (1987) has called for incorporating "impinging issues" in a "loosely structured, but highly responsive manner" (p. 171). Sexton and Bowman (1987) found that students responded positively to learning by doing, assignments without any guidance, readings with no specific assignments, and research projects for products that had not yet been introduced to the marketplace. A comprehensive literature analysis of current methods in entrepreneurship education has been provided by Borycki (1989) and Curran and Stanworth (1989).

Unfortunately, these techniques are not widely used in current business educational systems. Instead, a more departmentalized, compartmentalized, limited range of inputs is entered into discrete areas for further detailed analysis. If entrepreneurship is an integrative activity based upon the capacity to understand very complex dilemmas regarding purpose, possibilities, and tools, as Stevenson (1986) suggests, then we must follow non-traditional processes in designing entrepreneurship programs. Such non-traditional processes include dealing with overwhelming complexity, multi-functional roles, multi-dimensional problem solving, unpredictability, uncertainty, and ambiguity. A holistic and multidisciplinary perspective is needed.

Models of Evolving Entrepreneurship Structures

The field of entrepreneurship has grown and matured to a decision point in terms of its future structure and design. An examination of a number of entrepreneurship programs shows that they are evolving along two dimensions: (1) the absolute number of entrepreneurship courses, and (2) the degree of integration of the entrepreneurship course(s).

Number of Entrepreneurship Courses

The first dimension of the emerging entrepreneurship structure is the number and types of courses that are offered and their standing in the curriculum. This dimension can vary from a single course to a comprehensive program, which may consist of a "complete" list of courses combined with a major. In between the two extremes, a smaller set of courses could be offered which compose a minor.

The initial course, labeled variously "Entrepreneurship" or "New Venture Creation," has "standard" contents such as "(1) venture design projects, (2) case studies, (3) readings and (4) lectures by guest speakers and the instructor" (Vesper, 1985b). Many of the new venture courses were influenced by the Small Business Institute (SBI) program, which was a field project program designed to assist existing businesses. The SBI program, however, did not address the question of how new ventures were created. Because of the publicity given to successful entrepreneurs in the popular media, students represented a market demand for knowledge about how to go into business and to create new businesses.

Spurred on by such strong demand, additional courses began to be added to the initial offering. It was soon found that there were commonalities between entrepreneurship and strategic management (Ahiarah, 1989). Both courses required the skills to deal with the business as a whole, but from slightly different perspectives. Both required a strategic vision, a broad mission statement, goal setting and formulation of objectives, identification of opportunities and threats, and evaluation of risks. These commonalities eventually led to a course sometimes labeled "Entrepreneurship Policy," which sometimes served as the capstone integration course required by American Assembly of Collegiate Schools of Business (AACSB). Additional courses were derived from the original entrepreneurship course in two different ways. One direction was a course in field studies only, to investigate the feasibility of initiating a new venture. The other direction was a combination of entrepreneurship and different functional areas, e.g., "New Venture Financing" and "Entrepreneurship Marketing" (Hills, 1988). The small combination of courses thus served as the basis for a minor in the curriculum. A decade after single entrepreneurship courses were introduced, the first graduate and undergraduate majors in entrepreneurship appeared. The objectives of the full programs or major were: (1) to identify and evaluate the characteristics of prospective entrepreneurs; (2) to evaluate the opportunities and risks of a political venture; (3) to assemble financial, technical and human resources to initiate a new venture; and (4) to create, develop, acquire or merge a business.[3]

Degree of Integration

"Degree of integration" represents the level of acceptance and support from a variety of different groups. They include the basic working groups of the dean, chairperson, immediate colleagues and students. Additional acceptance and support is sought from intra-university groups, such as other business faculty members and non-business colleagues, as well as inter-university groups, such as alumni, professional associations, small businesses, entrepreneurs, and the community.

Another measure of integration is the degree of cooperation/coordination provided by close working associates who teach other courses in which entrepreneurship could be introduced or expanded. An informal relationship that begins with a voluntary suggestion can progress to formal requirements in the curriculum specified in the school catalog.

A third measure of integration is the set of complementary entrepreneurship activities that show that the entrepreneurship course or program is established and entrenched at the university and is embodied in the curriculum. Such activities include active participation of entrepreneurs, entrepreneurship clubs or organizations, placement of entrepreneurship graduates, internships, field and laboratory projects (e.g., incubators), and establishment of an entrepreneurship center and an entrepreneurship advisory board.

Two Frameworks of Entrepreneurship Programs
Framework A

The first framework, A, can be envisioned if we combine the two dimensions of *Number of Entrepreneurship Courses* and *Degree of Integration* (Figure 1). We can present two continua

---

[3]Several lists of courses constituting "minors," "majors," or "programs" from five universities are included in Appendix 1. It should be noted that the programs are different from one another and that there is no standard or ideal design.

Figure 1
Emerging Structure "A" of Entrepreneurship Education

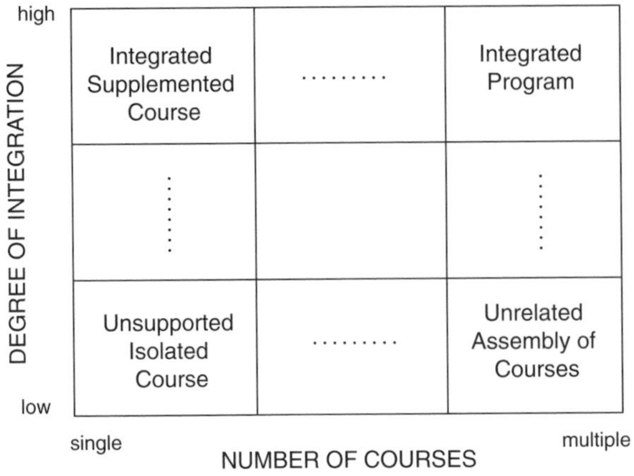

in a taxonomy where four "ideal" combinations can be described. The combination of a single course with low integration can be labeled *Unsupported Isolated Course*. The lone course is not fully accepted, is uncoordinated, and is not combined with other established curricula. This is a typical entrepreneurship course, "Entrepreneurship" or "New Venture Management," which has been placed on top of a traditional business program.

The combination of a single course with high integration can be labeled *Integrated Supplemented Course*. The lone course is well accepted and supported, is coordinated with other courses in the business curriculum as an elective or required course, and has a full range of complementary activities attached to it. A typical unitary supplement course may be combined with Small Business Institute activity and could be labeled "Entrepreneurship Policy."

A third combination involves a string of multiple courses with low integration. The *Unrelated Assembly of Courses* is a series of unrelated courses that are not

melded well into the curriculum. The courses, for example, could have arisen as an extension of established functional courses or out of a series of seminar courses thought up by individual faculty members without concern for how a course fits into the total curriculum. Examples would be "Effective Writing for the Entrepreneur," "Recordkeeping for the Small Business Owner," "Small Business Planning for Women," and "Estate Planning for the Small Business Owner." Schools that have such a collection of uncoordinated courses may appear to be making progress but, in reality, are doing a disservice to their students through the bead-stringing approach. Neither the design nor the structure of the curriculum is well thought out or planned.

The fourth combination of multiple courses that are well integrated both internally (with one another) and externally (with the curriculum), can be labeled the *Integrated Program*. It represents an "ideal state" of a mature structure that has evolved from earlier stages on the basis of experimentation, corrections, and refinements. This structure offers a full complement of coordinated courses based on a well-conceptualized growth-oriented framework.

A rational pathfinding process would assume a strategy that follows a diagonal direction in the matrix; i.e., as more courses are added, they become more integrated. The courses tend to support one another in a synergistic relationship as they move to the mature structure of an integrated program. However, not all programs develop along the diagonal path. Some schools find themselves market-driven to add entrepreneurship courses without an overall conceptual foundation, and never consider designing an integrated program. Other schools deliberately follow a strategy of introducing an entrepreneurship course and are satisfied with waiting for it to be integrated before considering additional courses. The schools use this course as an anchor, with a proven record of success, in an attempt to attain similar levels of integration of new courses they add.

Framework B

A second framework, B, is based on a model that incorporates two paths: (1) stages of transition in a firm; and (2) a functional approach, which adds entrepreneurship courses according to the disciplines that may be required in an entrepreneurial undertaking (Figure 2).

The dimension *Transition Stages* of this framework can be visualized around challenges, deficiencies, and crises that arise at different transitional stages in the firm's evolutionary process. Course contents can be designed to meet those difficulties, which seem to appear in stages similar to those of McMullan and Long's model (1987) along a sequential progression:

- Entrepreneurship Awareness
- Career Assessment
- Innovation and Creativity
- Opportunity Identification and Analysis
- Feasibility Analysis
- Business Planning

Figure 2
Emerging Structure "B" of Entrepreneurship Education

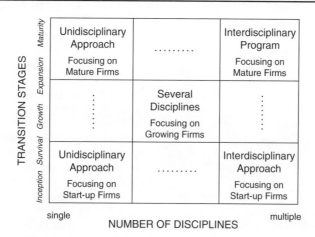

- Resource Assembling
- Assessment and Management of Risk
- New Venture Initiation
- Standardizing Operations
- Expansion Strategies
- Professionalizing Management Roles
- Evaluation of Results and Reformulation of Plans

The second dimension is the *Number of Disciplines* (or "Functional Fields") that may be represented in the entrepreneurship curriculum. These are the study areas (topics) that may be required in solving problems within the business. Typically, the "entrepreneurship course" is introduced in a management or marketing department or, in some cases, in departments of engineering. Often, more emphasis is placed within the course on the functional field in which the course is introduced (*Unidisciplinary Approach*). Many focus on the start-up stage of venture initiation. One or several courses may be added within that particular discipline, as instructors and administrators recognize that supplementary refinements and detailed expansion of topics are necessary.

Soon, it is recognized that several disciplines are required to prepare the entrepreneur for the myriad kinds of problems he/she will encounter. Later yet, the benefits of a multidisciplinary set of courses are recognized, and the synergy of an interdisciplinary program that has been blended around the entrepreneur is exploited (*Interdisciplinary Approach*). Various schools may stress different combinations of functional fields depending on their orientation. Management, marketing, and finance perhaps represent the most frequently added disciplines to a basic entrepreneurship course. Appendix 1 cites several examples of established programs, and the types and numbers of dis-

ciplines that are represented. Some stress more financial courses beyond the core entrepreneurship courses, while others stress more management courses in rounding their curriculum.

The uniqueness of the entrepreneurship programs can further be established when the two dimensions (*Transition Stages* and *Number of Disciplines*) are combined. The interesting question is how many different disciplines are represented in one of the courses. Are disciplines added in fits and starts according to the background and training of the instructors who are brought in? Or are disciplines systematically combined into the program according to some well-conceived plan?

Several programs have evolved into the middle ground area in terms of *Number of Courses* and *Degree of Integration*, as well as in combining *Transition Stages* of the business with *Number of Disciplines*, which may have direct implications for the entrepreneur.

Conclusion

Many programs are evolving on a trial and error or as needed basis, depending on the types of entrepreneurial projects currently undertaken in the program and on the feedback of students experiencing deficiencies, gaps, and difficulties in their courses. These are not necessarily poor approaches to program development as long as some mechanism or medium is systematically employed to document the feedback. One traditional method for collecting information for program design is attendance at professional conferences at which curriculum structures are compared and discussed. Written historical reviews can cover the origin, evolution, and maturation of a discipline as it becomes "professional" and accepted in the academic community.

On the other hand, if practitioners are an integral part of entrepreneurship education they can and should provide input to entrepreneurship curricula design. It may be possible for them to identify differences in relative importance of entrepreneurship content issues. These issues could be a function of various roles played by new venture entrepreneurs, intrapreneurs, or entrepreneurial executives. In addition, the stages of the business life cycle can also call for a diversified entrepreneurship education and training. For example, an entrepreneur who is restructuring the organization after a period of growth may demand different training from an entrepreneur who is starting a new venture; or an intrapreneur who is seeking financing for new product development in a mature company may need different training from an entrepreneurial executive.

The two examples show that educational needs may differ according to the stages of development and entrepreneurial career roles. Therefore, program designers should provide multiple alternative structures and learning mechanisms to meet the evolving needs of advancing firms. At the same time, program designers must be sensitive to career paths of people in or entering the entrepreneurship arena and take some responsibility for outlining the entrepreneurial career paths of business students.

However, at this point entrepreneurship is still growing or has just been introduced at most universities. Perhaps, after a more systematic theory and established body of knowledge has been accepted, it will be time to start differentiating entrepreneurship programs according to stages of development, career paths, and regional or cultural demands.

The proposed models in this paper can be used to study and design entrepreneurship programs. In further development of entrepreneurship curricula, *Degree of Integration* as well as *Transition Stages* should be considered major criteria in the design. Little is known about a systematic manner of studying the efficiency of these two approaches. Future research efforts should focus on the effectiveness of diverse entrepreneurship education program designs in order to optimize resources that must be allocated to their growth and development.

References

Ahiarah, S. (1989). Strategic management and entrepreneurship courses. At the undergraduate level: Can one inform the other? *Proceedings of the 1989 Small Business Institute Directors' Association National Conference*, Arlington, VA, 60–66.

d'Amboise, G., & Muldonney, M. (1988). Management theory for small business: Attempts and requirements. *Academy of Management Review*, *13*(2), 226–240.

Behrman, J. N., & Levin, R. I. (1984). Are business schools doing their job? *Harvard Business Review*, January–February, 140–147.

Boberg, A. L., & Kiecker, P. (1988). Changing patterns of demand: Entrepreneurship education for entrepreneurs. In B. A. Kirchhoff, W. A. Long, W. Ed McMullan, K. H. Vesper, & W. E. Wetzel (Eds.), *Frontiers of entrepreneurship research*, pp. 600–661. Wellesley, MA: Babson College.

Borycki, C. (1989). Entrepreneurship education research: Current trends and methods. Paper presented at the Fourth Annual National Conference, United States Association for Small Business and Entrepreneurship, October, 1989, Cleveland, Ohio.

Brockhaus, R. H. (1988). Entrepreneurial research: Are we playing the correct game? *American Journal of Small Business*, *12*(2), 55–61.

Brown, W. S. (1982). Commentary on entrepreneurship education. In C. A. Kent, D. L. Sexton, & K. H. Vesper

(Eds.), *Encyclopedia of entrepreneurship*, pp. 346–351. Englewood Cliffs, NJ: Prentice Hall.

Carland, J. W., Hoy, F., & Carland, J. C. (1988). Who is an entrepreneur? Is a question worth asking. *American Journal of Small Business, 12*(3), 33–39.

Carsrud, A. L., Olm, K. W., & Eddy, G. G. (1986). Entrepreneurship research in quest of a paradigm. In D. L. Sexton & R. W. Smilor (Eds.), *The art and science of entrepreneurship*, pp. 367–378. Cambridge, MA: Ballinger.

Cheit, E. F. (1985). Business schools and their critics. *California Management Review, 27*(3), 43–62.

Chell, E., & Haworth, J. M. (1987). Entrepreneurship and entrepreneurial personality—A review. In *London Business School Small business bibliography 1985–1986*, pp. 5–33. London: Business School Library.

van Clouse, G. H. (1989). The impact of entrepreneurship education on the new venture decision process: An empirical assessment. *Proceedings of 34th World Conference of the International Council for Small Business*, Quebec, pp. 394–406.

Collins, O. F., Moore D., & Unwalla, D. B. (1964). *The enterprising man* (3rd ed.). East Lansing: Michigan State Univ. Business Studies.

Collins, O. F., & Moore, D. (1970). *The organization markers. A behavioral study of independent entrepreneurs.* New York: Meredith.

Curran, J., & Stanworth, J. (1989). Education and training for enterprise: Some problems of classification, evaluation, policy and research. *International Small Business Journal, 7*(2), 11–22.

Davidsson, P. (1988). Type of man and type of company revisited: A confirmatory cluster analysis. In B. A. Kirchhoff, W. A. Long, W. Ed McMullan, K. H. Vesper, & W. E. Wetzel (Eds.), *Fron-tiers of entrepreneurship research*, pp. 88–105. Wellesley, MA: Babson College.

Drucker, P. F. (1985). *Innovation and entrepreneurship.* New York: Harper & Row.

Gartner, W. B. (1985). A conceptual framework for describing the phenomenon of new venture creation. *Academy of Management Review, 10*(4), 696–706.

Gartner, W. B. (1988). Who is an entrepreneur? Is the wrong question. *American Journal of Small Business, 12*(3), 11–32.

Grad, M., & Shapero, A. (1981). *Federal and state policies for entrepreneurship education, Small Business Administration.* Washington, D.C.

Greenwood, E. (1957). Attributes of a profession. *Social Work, 2*(3), 45–55.

Gundry, L. K. (1989). Creating catalysts, entrepreneurs, and visionaries: Enhancing our focus on small organizational settings in management education. *Proceedings of the Midwest Academy of Management*, Columbus, Ohio, 1989, pp. 217–221.

Hall, R. H. (1968). Professionalization and bureaucratization. *American Sociological Review, 33*(1), 92–104.

Hartman, H. (1959). Managers and entrepreneurs: A useful distinction? *Administrative Science Quarterly, 3,* 429–457.

Hebert, R., & Link, A. (1989). In search of the meaning of entrepreneurship. *Small Business Economics, 1*(1), 39–50.

Hills, G. E. (1988). Variations in university entrepreneurship education: An empirical study of an evolving field. *Journal of Business Venturing, 3,* 109–122.

Hills, G. E., & Welsch, H. P. (1986). Entrepreneurship behavioral intentions and student independence characteristics and experiences. In R. Ronstadt, J. A. Hornaday, R. Peterson, & K. H. Vesper (Eds.), *Frontiers of entrepreneurship* research, pp. 173–186. Wellesley, MA: Babson College.

Hoad, W. M., & Rosko, P. (1964). *Management factors contributing to the success and failure of new small manufactures.* Ann Arbor: University of Michigan.

Hornaday, J., & Bunker, C. (1970). The nature of the entrepreneur. *Personnel Psychology, 23*(1), 47–54.

Hoy, F., Reeves, C., McDougall, P., & Smith, P. (1989). Transitions and second generation entrepreneurship. Paper presented at the Babson College Entrepreneurship Research Conference 1989, St. Louis, MO.

Kanter, R. M. (1986). *The change masters: Innovation for productivity in the American corporation.* New York: Simon and Schuster.

Kanter, R. M. (1989). *When giants learn to dance: The post-entrepreneurial revolution in management, and careers.* New York: Simon and Schuster.

Kao, J. J. (1989). *Entrepreneurship, creativity and organization.* Engelwood Cliffs, NJ: Prentice Hall.

Kao, J. J., & Stevenson, H. H. (1983). Report of the colloquium on entrepreneurship. In J. J. Kao, & H. H. Stevenson, *Entrepreneurship. What it is and how to teach it*, pp. 1–24. Cambridge, MA: Harvard Business School.

Katz, J. A. (1989). Endowed positions in entrepreneurship and related fields. *Proceedings of the Fourth Annual National Conference*, United States Association for Small Business and Entrepreneurship, October, 1989, Cleveland, Ohio.

Kerr, J. R. (1988). Entrepreneurship and the Small Business Institute curriculum: Rationale, development and results. *Proceedings of National Conference of the Small Business Institute Directors' Association*, San Francisco, CA, pp. 27–30.

Knight, F. (1921). *Risk, uncertainty and profit.* Boston: Houghton Mifflin.

Leavitt, H. J. (1989). Educating our MBAs: On teaching what we haven't taught. *California Management Review, 31*(3), 38–50.

Leibenstein, H. (1968). Entrepreneurship and development. *American Economic Review, 58,* 72–83.

London Business School (1988). *London Business School Small business bibliography 1987.* London: Business School Library.

Loucks, E. L. (1982). Elaboration on education in entrepreneurship. In C. A. Kent, D. L. Sexton, & K. H. Vesper (Eds.), *Encyclopedia of entrepreneurship*, pp. 344–346. Englewood Cliffs, NJ: Prentice Hall.

Low, M. B., & MacMillan, I. A. (1988). Entrepreneurship: Past research and future challenges. *Journal of Management, 14*(2), 139–161.

McClelland, D. C. (1961). *The achieving society.* Princeton, NJ: Van Nostrand.

McMullan, W. Ed., & Long, W. A. (1987). Entrepreneurship education in the nineties. *Journal of Business Venturing, 2,* 261–275.

Mill, J. S. (1848). *Principles of political economy with some of their applications to social philosophy.* London: J. Parker.

Neck, P. H. (1981). Education and training for small business. *Proceedings of the International Symposium on Small Business*, Berlin, October.

Palmer, M. (1971). The application of psychological testing to entrepreneurial potential. *California Management Review, 13*(3), 32–39.

Pinchot, G. (1985). *Intrapreneuring.* New York: Harper & Row.

Porter, L. W., & McKibbin, L. E. (1988). *Management, education and development: Drift or thrust into the 21st century?* New York: McGraw-Hill.

Ronstadt, R. (1985a). *Entrepreneurship bibliography.* Dover, MA: Lord Publishing.

Ronstadt, R. (1985b). The educated entrepreneurs: A new era of entrepreneurial education is beginning. *American Journal of Small Business, 10*(2), 7–23.

Sandberg, W. R., Gatewood E., & Olm, K. (1989). Entrepreneurship research centers: Their interests, activities, and support of research. Paper presented at the Babson College Entrepreneurship Research Conference 1989, St. Louis, MO.

Say, J. A. (1816). *A treatise on political economy*, London: Sherwood, Neeley and Jones.

Schrage, H. (1965). The R&D entrepreneur: Profile of success. *Harvard Business Review, 43*, 56–69.

Schumpeter, J. (1911). *Theorie der wirtschaftlichen Entwicklung. Eine Untersuchung ueber Unternehmergewinn, Kapital, Kredit, Zins und Konjunkturzyklus* (1st ed.). Leipzig: Mohr.

Scott, M. G. (1988). Aspects of the long term supply of entrepreneurs: The U.K. experience of encouraging graduate enterprise. In B. A. Kirchhoff, W. A. Long, W. Ed McMullan, K. H. Vesper, & W. E. Wetzel (Eds.), *Frontiers of entrepreneurship research*, pp. 662–664. Wellesley, MA: Babson College.

Sexton, D. L. (1988). The field of entrepreneurship: Is it growing or just getting bigger? *Journal of Small Business Management, 26*(1), 5–8.

Sexton, D. L., & Bowman, U. N. (1987). Evaluation of an innovative approach to teaching entrepreneurship. *Journal of Small Business Management, 25*(1), 35–43.

Smith, N. (1967). *The entrepreneur and his firm: The relationship between type of man and type of company.* East Lansing: Michigan State University Press.

Smith, N. R., & Miner, J. B. (1987). Type of entrepreneur, type of firm, and managerial motivation: Implications for organizational life cycle theory. *Strategic Management Journal, 4*, 325–340.

Solomon, G. T. (Ed.). (1986). *National survey of entrepreneurial education* (3rd ed.). Washington, D.C.: U.S. Small Business Administration.

State of Small Business (1988). *The state of small business: A report of the president.* Washington, D.C.: Government Printing Office.

Stevenson, H. H. (1986). Harvard's experience with a new entrepreneurship program. In D. L. Sexton, & R. W. Smilor (Eds.), *The art and science of entrepreneurship*, pp. 389–402. Cambridge, MA: Ballinger.

Trinkaus, J. (1987). A contemporary topics course in small business. *Proceedings of National Conference of the Small Business Institute Director's Association*, San Antonio, TX, pp. 171–175.

Ulrich, T. A., & Cole, G. S. (1987). Toward more effective training of future entrepreneurs. *Journal of Small Business Management, 25*(4), 32–39.

Vesper, K. H. (1982). Research on education for entrepreneurship. In C. A. Kent, D. L. Sexton, & K. H. Vesper (Eds.), *Encyclopedia of entrepreneurship*, pp. 321–343. Englewood Cliffs, NJ: Prentice Hall.

Vesper, K. H. (1985a). *Entrepreneurship education 1985.* Wellesley, MA: Babson College.

Vesper, K. H. (1985b). New developments in entrepreneurship education. *Frontiers of entrepreneurship research 1985*, 489–520.

Vesper, K. H. (1986). New developments in entrepreneurship education. In D. L. Sexton, & R. W. Smilor (Eds.), *The art and science of entrepreneurship*, pp. 379–387. Cambridge, MA: Ballinger.

Vesper, K. H. (1987). Entrepreneurial academics. How can we tell when the field is getting somewhere? *Journal of Small Business Management, 25*(2), 1–7.

Vesper, K. H. (1990). Personal correspondence, June, 1990.

Welsch, H. P. (1990). *International entrepreneurship and small business bibliography.* International Council for Small Businesses, in press.

Weitzen, H. S. (1988). *Infopreneurs, Turning data into dollars.* New York: Wiley.

Wilensky, H. L. (1964). The professionalization of everyone? *American Journal of Sociology, 70,* 137–158.

Wojahn, E. (1986). Class acts. *Inc., 8*(4), 126–132.

Wortman, M. S., Jr. (1987). Entrepreneurship: An integrating typology and evaluation of the empirical research in the field. *Journal of Management, 13*(2), 259–279.

Wortman, M. S., Jr. (1989). Entrepreneurship research and its integration into the curriculum. *Paper presented at the 1989 Annual Meeting of the Academy of Management,* Washington, D.C.

Zeithaml, C. P., & Rice, G. H. (1987). Entrepreneurship/small business education in American universities. *Journal of Small Business Management, 25*(1), 44–50.

Pedagogical Methods of Teaching Entrepreneurship: An Historical Perspective
by George T. Solomon, K. Mark Weaver, and Lloyd W. Fernald

The past ten years have witnessed an enormous growth in the number of small business management and entrepreneurship courses at both the junior and senior college levels. This expansion of educational offerings has been fueled in part by dissatisfaction among students and by accrediting programs with the traditional big-business focus of business education (Solomon & Fernald, 1991). Plaschka & Welsch (1990) parallel the rapid growth in small business management courses with the rapid growth in small businesses in the United States. Additionally, calls for an increased focus on entrepreneurial education and more reality-based pedagogies, such as those issued by Porter & McKibbin (1988) in their review of the state of management education in America, have certainly helped fuel this growth.

This paper analyzes data reported on the U.S. Small Business Administration's (SBA) historical examination of small business management and entrepreneurial education curricula and pedagogies.

Introduction

The past ten years have witnessed an enormous growth in the number of small business management and entrepreneurship courses at both the junior and senior college levels. This expansion of educational offerings has been fueled in part by dissatisfaction among students and by accrediting programs with the traditional big-business focus of business education (Solomon & Fernald, 1991). Plaschka & Welsch (1990) parallel the rapid growth in small business management courses with the rapid growth in small businesses in the United States.

Additionally, calls for an increased focus on entrepreneurial education and more reality-based pedagogies, such as those issued by Porter & McKibbin (1988) in their review of the state of management education in America, have certainly helped fuel this growth.

This paper analyzes data reported on the U.S. Small Business Administration's (SBA) historical examination of small business management and entrepreneurial education curricula and pedagogies. The paper will first provide the reader with background literature in the field of small business management and entrepreneurial education. Next, will be a dis-

Originally appeared in *Gaming and Simulation*, 1993, Volume 25, Number 3.

cussion of curriculum design in small business management and entrepreneurial education followed by an examination of course structures in small business management and entrepreneurial education. The next section will provide a brief overview of previous surveys in small business management and entrepreneurial education. After establishing a conceptual basis, the paper will discuss the methodologies employed by the SBA, discussion of the findings and a then the conclusion.

Background
Growth in Small Business Management and Entrepreneurship Courses

The past ten years have witnessed an enormous growth in the number of small business management and entrepreneurship courses at both the junior and senior college levels. This expansion of educational offerings has been fueled in part by dissatisfaction among students and by accrediting programs with the traditional big-business focus of business education (Solomon & Fernald, 1991). Additional motivating forces appear to include a growing sensitivity to the fundamental differences between the management of new ventures and ongoing small companies and the management of large corporations (Hills, 1988).

Sexton and Bowman (1984) reason that both government emphasis on small business development and prevailing economic conditions are playing a crucial role in the expansion of small business management and entrepreneurial course offerings. Plaschka & Welsch (1990) parallel the rapid growth in small business management courses with the rapid growth in small businesses in the United States. Additionally, calls for an increased focus on entrepreneurial education, such as those issued by Porter & McKibbin (1988) in their review of the state of management education in America, have certainly helped fuel this growth.

Most fundamentally, the growth in these type of courses may be motivated by the fact that teachers and students alike enjoy them (Vesper, 1987; Vesper & McMullan, 1988). In spite of the rapid growth of course offerings demand for these courses continues to grow (Vesper & McMullan, 1988) because student demand remains high (Fernald & Solomon, 1993) and most people believe the field is far from reaching maturity (Robinson & Haynes, 1991).

In order to understand both the growth of small business management and entrepreneurial courses and the evolving educational methodologies, it is important to establish a conceptual difference between these two educational types—a differentiation that too often the literature fails to make (Zeithaml & Rice, 1987).

Differences in Small Business Management and Entrepreneurship Courses

Small business courses at the postsecondary level were first established in the 1940's (Sexton & Bowman, 1984) and dealt primarily with the managing and operating of small, existing companies. Entrepreneurship courses, which first emerged as academic offerings in the 1960's had as their major focus the activities involved in originating and developing new growth ventures (Guglielmino, 1993; Marchigiano-Monroy, 1993). The conceptual difference is a fine one that is often blurred in both the academic and real worlds.

The focus of both small business management and entrepreneurial education programs are to provide a breadth of creative and managerial skills and knowledge that is the "closest approach to the original concept of professional management education offered at colleges and universities" (Zeithaml & Rice, 1987, p. 50). While both small business management courses and entrepreneurship courses have experienced rapid growth, courses focusing on entrepreneurship have experienced the greatest growth. Vesper (1987) reasons that this is due in part to the "rise of the service economy, the baby boom, and the growth of certain technologies (e.g., computers and electronics)" (p. 2).

In spite of the rapid growth in entrepreneurial courses, there exists a popular debate concerning the feasibility of teaching entrepreneurial skills. The remarkable growth in programs and course offerings at the post-secondary level appear to offer some credibility for the assumption that skills relevant to successful entrepreneurship can be taught (Solomon & Fernald, 1991). The prevailing issue was what pedagogies were most appropriate for the transfer of entrepreneurial skills and knowledge?

Clark et al (1984), in a study of graduates of an entrepreneurial program, found evidence to suggest that the teaching of entrepreneurial and small business management skills did in fact aid in new venture creation and success. More recently, Ronstadt (1990) has argued that "strong indications exist that an entrepreneurial education will produce more and better entrepreneurs than were produced in the past" (p. 69). Encouraged by these conclusions the debate concerning the feasibility of teaching entrepreneurial skills is quickly being replaced by a debate concerning how entrepreneurship and small business management skills should be taught (Ronstadt, 1990).

Curricular Design
Learning Objectives
The learning objectives of the two educational types, small business management and entrepreneurship, are in some ways different. The traditional objectives of small business management programs have been in to provide students with management know-how relating to "setting goals and objectives, leading, planning, organizing, and controlling from a small business perspective" (Fernald & Solomon, 1993, p. 103). Entre-

preneurial education has had as its focus an action orientation primarily embodied in teaching students how to develop a business plan (Ronstadt, 1990).

A more lucid understanding of the needs of individuals preparing to become private entrepreneurs has led to a growing consensus concerning the objectives of entrepreneurial education (Hills, 1988). Gerry Hills (1988) has summarized this consensus in terms of three education objectives: (1) "to increase students' awareness and understanding of the new venture initiating process" (2) to increase "student awareness of the new-venture/smaller-company career option," and (3) to help the student "develop a fuller understanding of interrelationships between the business' functional areas" (p. 114). Ronstadt (1987) argues that entrepreneurial educational objectives should include skills relating to creativity, ambiguity tolerance, opportunity identification, venture evaluation, venture strategy, career assessment, deal-making, and networking.

Educational Providers
The rapid growth in small business management/entrepreneurship courses has to some degree been shaped by educational objectives. Most two- year and four-year college programs acknowledge that small business management and entrepreneurship education is "interfunctional and does not fully fit within any one business department," (Hills, 1988, p. 114) nor does it seem to fit solely within four year colleges. Ronstadt (1987) acknowledges the interesting fact that:

> Entrepreneurship courses are offered not only at business schools, but increasingly at community colleges, junior colleges and engineering schools (p. 38).

Traditional two-year schools have experienced a rapid growth in demand for small business and entrepreneurship courses (Anselm, 1993). The traditional role of the community college as a "post-secondary institution, with a bias toward job-oriented skills," (Anselm, 1993, p. 186) has mandated an involvement in offering small business as well as entrepreneurship courses. Often times these courses are "continuing education" courses geared toward the non-traditional student (Carroll & College, 1993).

Courses geared toward non-traditional students are not the sole province of the two-year schools. Solomon & Fernald (1991) report a rapid growth in "for-credit" and "not-for-credit" courses at the university level. The "not-for-credit" courses, designed in most cases for working professionals, are often times handled through special centers or institutes (Zeithaml & Rice, 1987) or are linked to the U.S. Small Business Administration's (SBA's) Small Business Institute (SBI) program or Small Business Development Centers (SBDCs) (Hills, 1988).

Course Offerings

The traditional approach in course offerings both for small business management and for entrepreneurship has been to offer one general course "usually aimed at the development of a new business and covering basic planning, market analysis, and procurement of venture capital" (Zeithaml & Rice, 1987, p. 48). A secondary course aimed at getting the student involved in a consulting experience or in a special venture project (Vesper, 1986) is sometimes included.

Vesper (1987) has concluded that the traditional paradigm of small business management and entrepreneurship education needs to be changed. Plaschka & Welsch (1990) argue that a much greater degree of integration is needed between small business and entrepreneurial courses and courses providing the requisite skills necessary for entrepreneurs

to be successful. They offer two models for the development of programs. The first has as its ideal type a "structure that offers a full complement of coordinated courses based on a well-conceptualized growth-oriented framework" (p. 64). The second model has as its ideal type either an interdisciplinary program focusing on skills necessary in a mature company or an interdisciplinary program focusing on skills necessary in a start-up company.

Ronstadt (1987) acknowledges that nearly all small business and entrepreneurial programs "will be composed of selective courses" (p. 48). This leads him to conclude that these courses must by necessity fit into existing curriculums. Ronstadt (1987) proposes a two module design encompassing issues relating to "know how" and "know who" (p. 47). His "know how" structure encompasses skills traditionally associated with small business management, while the "know who" structure focuses more on the entrepreneurial skills.

Gerry Hills (1988) suggests that a review of the types of courses that are developing in the field represent three emerging models for entrepreneurship education. These three models are built upon conceptual bases which include "the business plan, the business life cycle, and business functions" (p. 116). The "business plan" and "business life cycle" models focus on entrepreneurial skills while the "business functions" model focuses on small business management skills.

Course Structure
Existing Pedagogical Approaches

Ronstadt (1990) characterizes an "old school" of small business and entrepreneurship education that:

took an extreme, action-oriented approach to the subject. The motto of the old school was decidedly "go out and do it now". The business plan served as the academic heart of these courses. The rest of the curriculum was provided by experienced visitors who provided interesting stories, practical advice, and inspirational motivation (p. 73).

The description of a program at the University of Tennessee-Knoxville consisting of "lectures, case studies and field projects," (Miller, 1987, p. 4) is typical of the structure of most courses. In a recent survey of university courses, Carroll & College (1993) describes a small business management course as typically consisting of class work, tests, and a major project which is usually a consulting assignment. The entrepreneurship course consists of class work, tests, and a major project that usually is the development of a business plan.

Other courses described tend to fit the above description. Hills, (1988) in assessing the importance that business educators placed on teaching methods, discovered that:

> Entrepreneurship course features considered most important were development of a business plan project and entrepreneurs as speakers as role models. Cases ranked next in importance followed by lectures and assigned readings (p. 110)

Other teaching methods described included literature reviews, interviewing of entrepreneurs, working with a start-up entrepreneur, or the start-up of a small-scale business by a class. A survey conducted by Ahiarah (1989) revealed that the most used pedagogical tool for teaching small business management and entrepreneurship was a combination of lectures and cases.

The second most used tool was special projects which include live cases or case formulations. Other assignments included oral and written presentations, guest lectures, business plan preparations, and the use of films and videos. It is interesting that both Hills (1988) and Ahiarah (1989) found that assigned readings were the least preferred method.

The above may be explained by the findings of Hess (1987) in a comparison of the perceptions of business graduates' concerning the most important skills necessary for success and topics covered by a number of the most popular small business texts. His findings indicated that in most instances there was very little correlation between the emphasis areas of the text and the graduates' perceptions of important skills. Borycki (1989) and Curran & Stanworth (1989) both offer additional reviews of current methods in small business and entrepreneurship pedagogy.

Emerging Pedagogical Approaches

The "old school" as described by Ronstadt (1990) is beginning to give way to new methods of teaching small business and entrepreneurial skills. These new methods are arising from an increased understanding of entrepreneurship (Ronstadt, 1987) and a better understanding of entrepreneurship students. Sexton and Upton (1987) have proposed structuring courses around the psychological needs of entrepreneurship students. They conclude from their research that:

> entrepreneurship students can be depicted as independent individuals who dislike restraint, restriction, and the routine. They are capable of original thought, especially under conditions of ambiguity and uncertainty. Many of them need to develop better communication skills and to become more aware of how others perceive their

behavior (Sexton & Upton, 1987, p. 38)

These conclusions lead Sexton and Upton (1984) to propose that courses should be relatively unstructured and "pose problems which require novel solutions under conditions of ambiguity and risk" (p. 25). Additionally, an increasing awareness of the special needs of adult students (Weinrauch, 1984) and minority students (Mann, 1990) is leading to an assessment of how small business management and entrepreneurship can best be taught.

Ahiarah's survey (1989) included questions concerning anticipated changes in course methodology. The greatest increase was seen in the use of computers for various purposes followed by greater use of various types of cases, increased international considerations, and a greater focus on strategy formation and implementation. In a review of business schools, Vesper (1986) discovered a number of new and innovative approaches being tried. These approaches included a greater use of the personal computer in venture planning projects, the applications of programs that developed product prototypes, the use of feasibility studies for class projects, the use of live cases as opposed to written cases, the evaluation of student's venture plans by other students as well as by venture capitalists, and the use of activities diaries.

Based on this review of pedagogy, Carroll & College (1993) propose the use of several complementary methods which include lectures, cases studies, and computer simulations, projects based around the development of a business plan, formal presentations of business plans, role-playing, and experts as lecturers. One of the themes that run throughout these new methodologies is the use of computer simulations for teaching small business and entrepreneurial skills. Clouse (1990) concludes

that simulations provide entrepreneurial students "with multiple experiences of simulated new venture decision making" (p. 51).

Sims and Hand (1976) argue that a "complex simulation game can be the key to integrating the behavioral aspects of a managerial decision system" (p. 110). The use of computer simulations is seen by Brewer, et al. (1993) as a realistic way of providing students with entrepreneurship experience. They conclude that simulations can help develop skills in complex decision making and offer instant feedback to the student.

Assessment

In addition to the emergence of new course methodologies, new methods of assessing students are beginning to develop. Beyond the traditional use of tests and written case studies in grading students, Vesper (1987) has called for the use of school-based business creation as a basis upon which to assess the performance of students. Vesper (1986) previously noted two innovative programs of assessment. One program utilized live cases studies as final examinations. The other contained a policy that gave any student who managed to raise $10,000 in venture capital an automatic "A".

Despite all of the recent innovations in the teaching of small business management and entrepreneurship, there is still room for improvement. Robinson and Hayes (1991) lament the fact that the challenge for business schools is not to increase the breadth of offerings, but to increase the quality of offerings. They conclude that the greatest obstacle to quality growth is:

the lack of good solid theoretical bases upon which to build pedagogical models and methods. There is a need to develop and test entrepreneurship theories, models, and methods that go beyond an academic interest by being applicable to both the practitioner and the educator (p. 51).

Previous Surveys in Small Business Management and Entrepreneurial Education

Vesper

Vesper (1985) reported a 50 percent increase in the number of respondents (from 163 in 1976 to 253 in 1987) in universities that had entrepreneurship courses. In his latest survey, Vesper (1990) reported that the same rate of growth (50%) in response rate had continued between 1984 and 1988 in entrepreneurship courses at colleges and universities. Five schools reported graduate specializations or majors in entrepreneurship and eleven schools had undergraduate specializations or majors in entrepreneurship available to students. This pattern of growth is described by Vesper and McMullan (1988) as follows: "the number of schools with several courses in the subject which allows students to select majors or concentrations in the subject has grown from one or two in 1977 to around ten in the US".

Solomon and Sollosy

In 1977, Solomon and Sollosy conducted a limited survey of course offerings in small business and management at accredited four year colleges and universities (Solomon and Sollosy, 1977). Ninety three colleges and universities were found to have course offerings in small business management out of two hundred college catalogs and a mini survey of eighty colleges and universities. This survey was descriptive in nature and primarily used secondary sources and a small number of primary sources to collect course descriptions

and course syllabi. No analyses were performed on these materials. Based on this survey the U.S. Small Business Administration (SBA) decided to launch a more comprehensive and historical survey to examine the state of the small business management curriculum in the United States.

U.S. Small Business Administration

The U.S. Small Business Administration (SBA) conducted nationwide surveys in 1979, 1982, 1986 and 1992 (Solomon, 1979; Solomon and Eliason, 1983; Solomon, 1986). These surveys were cross-sectional mail surveys. The sampling frames included both institutional and individual level units of analysis. This was done to increase the coverage of the surveys. Recognizing the possible problems this might cause in terms of institutional multiple responses, checks for multiple responses were implemented at the SBA by culling duplicate course listings (See Table 1).

In each of the surveys, all responses were recorded and selected non-respondents were interviewed to ascertain if they in fact offered small business and entrepreneurship courses and programs. Some indicated that they did offer small business and entrepreneurship courses and programs and simply decided not to respond. Others did not at the time, offer small business and entrepreneurship courses and/or programs.

Survey Methodology

The focus of the SBA surveys was:

1. Which institutional academic entities—secondary–high school and vocational educational schools; post secondary two-year community and junior colleges and 4-year colleges and universities were offering small business and entrepreneurial educational programs.
2. Whether the program of study was credit/non credit and whether it con-

sisted of traditional courses or tailored seminars and short courses for the adult learner.

3. What teaching pedagogies and assessments were employed? Were these pedagogies and assessments non-traditional or traditional given the non-traditional focus of the courses?

An analysis of the four surveys' data, relative to the teaching and evaluation pedagogies employed by two and four year colleges and universities in course and seminar offerings in small business management and entrepreneurial education, is the focus of this paper.

Findings

Table 1 summarizes the four national surveys SBA conducted in 1979, 1982, 1986 and 1992 on course offerings and pedagogies in entrepreneurship and small business management. It can be seen that the number of responses grew from 263 responses in 1979 to 470 responses in 1992. For the entire period, 1409 responses were received from 1060 different colleges and universities. The table provides a breakdown of two year community and junior college responses as compared with four-year college and university responses. It also includes a breakdown of the total number of different schools which responded, eliminating duplicative entries received from, for example, and the same university for two of the four surveys. Collectively, the four surveys represent the largest and most comprehensive study to date of the extent of entrepreneurial education in the U.S with over 1,000 different colleges and universities reporting.

Tables 2 and 3 summarize the trend in small business management (SBM) and entrepreneurship (EP) course at two-year and four-year colleges and universities from 1979–1992. Both two and four-year colleges and universities use a variety of different teaching pedagogies including credit and non-credit courses, seminars

and workshops. While most of the course offerings are for credit, there has been an greater increase proportionately, in the number of seminars and workshops at two-year and four year institutions compared to traditional credit courses.

As shown in Table 2, in 1979, two-year colleges offering small business management courses used as the major teaching pedagogy, credit course, 159. Seminars 7, workshops 5, and non-credit courses 10, were a distant second. A similar trend existed for two year colleges offering courses in entrepreneurship. By 1992, the major teaching pedagogy for small business management courses was still credit courses 179. However, the number of seminars reportedly being offered has risen to 65, and the number of workshops had grown to 88. In total numbers for both small business management and entrepreneurship, credit courses were still the dominant teaching pedagogy 823, followed by workshops at 325, and seminars at 223.

Table 3 shows similar results for four-year colleges and universities. In 1979, the data indicated that four-year colleges and universities used as the major teaching pedagogy for small business management: credit courses, 114; seminars, 6; workshops, 16; and, non-credit courses, 0, were a distant second as teaching pedagogies. A similar trend existed for four year colleges and universities offering courses in entrepreneurship. By 1992, the major teaching pedagogy for small business management was still credit courses, 420. However, the number of seminars has risen to 107, and the number of workshops had grown to 57.

Tables 4 and 5 show the dramatic rise in the variety of teaching and evaluation pedagogies employed by two and four year colleges and universities in the small business management and entrepreneurship area. The major evaluation pedagogies used by two-year and four-year institutions include: (1) written tests; (2) development of business plans;

Table 1
Summary of 1979, 1982, 1986 and 1992
National Survey of Entrepreneurial Education

	Number of Responses	Total Population
1979 Resource Book		
Community & Junior College responses	146	
Colleges & Universities responses	117	
Total		**263**
1982 Resource Guide		
Community & Junior College responses	131	
Colleges & Universities responses	131	
Total		**262**
1986 Survey of Entrepreneurial Education		
Community & Junior College responses	202	
Colleges & Universities responses	212	
Total		**414**
1992 Survey of Entrepreneurial Education		
Community & Junior College responses	160	
Colleges & Universities responses	310	
Total		**470**
GRAND TOTAL:		**1409**
Unique Filtered Through		
First Level ('92)		all =
Second Level ('86)		**470**
Com. & JC's:	202 − 45 = 167	
Col. & Univ:	212 − 104 = 108	
Total		**275**
Third Level ('82)		
Com. & JC's:	131 − 35 = 96	
Col. & Univ:	131 − 39 = 92	
Total		**188**
Fourth Level ('79)		
Com. & JC's:	146 − 73 = 73	
Col. & Univ:	117 − 63 = 54	
Total		**127**
Total Unique (or the total number of different schools which responded to the surveys)		**1060**

Table 2

Small Business Management and Entrepreneurial Education Programs and Major Project Assignments

	1979 2 Year Colleges		1982 2 Year Colleges		1986 2 Year Colleges		1992 2 Year Colleges		Frequency
	Small Business	Entrepreneurship	Small Business	Entrepreneurship	Small Business	Entrepreneurship	Small Business	Entrepreneurship	
Courses, Workshops, and Seminars									
Credit Courses	159	8	170	15	238	36	174	23	823
Seminars	7	1	71	4	53	15	65	7	223
Workshops	5	0	91	3	117	15	88	6	325
Non-credit courses	10	1	20	7	39	4	20	10	111
Major Projects, Tests, and Experiential Learning Activities									
Tests	85	1	64	12	131	14	80	3	390
Business Plans	26	6	24	3	46	27	28	5	165
Cases	34	2	40	10	23	4	50	14	177
Consult Small Businesses (SBI)	0	0	1	0	2	0	2	0	5
Interview Entrepreneurs	5	1	3	0	2	0	6	2	19
Simulations	3	0	4	1	10	0	14	2	34
Individual Projects	8	0	10	1	12	0	10	1	42
Group Projects	4	0	8	1	8	0	3	1	25
Other	24	0	20	4	23	3	21	60	98

Table 3
Small Business Management and Entrepreneurial Education Programs and Major Project Assignments

	1979 4 Year Schools		1982 4 Year Schools		1986 4 Year Schools		1992 4 Year Schools		
	Small Business	Entrepreneurship	Small Business	Entrepreneurship	Small Business	Entrepreneurship	Small Business	Entrepreneurship	Frequency
Courses, Workshops, and Seminars									
Credit Courses	114	25	133	42	251	134	420	214	2183
Seminars	6	0	50	1	72	22	107	36	517
Workshops	16	0	43	0	63	3	57	5	512
Non-credit courses	0	0	88	6	4	0	10	1	220
Major Projects, Tests, and Experiential Learning Activities									
Tests	43	13	52	15	96	42	142	64	847
Business Plans	33	14	34	20	55	58	81	92	734
Cases	39	13	24	17	41	32	72	48	463
Consult Small Businesses (SBI)	32	10	37	3	56	11	151	44	279
Interview Entrepreneurs	3	0	1	1	4	4	7	7	46
Simulations	4	4	5	4	8	10	10	7	52
Individual Projects	9	2	12	6	20	15	23	10	97
Group Projects	3	3	6	5	14	8	17	12	68
Other	12	2	16	27	27	10	56	14	89

Table 4
2-Year Universities Individual Ratios (Individual/Total)

	1979 SBM	1982 SBM	1986 SBM	1992 SBM	1979 EP	1982 EP	1986 EP	1992 EP	Total Percent
Courses, Workshops, and Seminars									
Credit Courses	0.88	0.48	0.53	0.50	0.80	0.52	0.51	0.50	0.56
Seminars	0.04	0.20	0.12	0.19	0.10	0.14	0.21	0.15	0.15
Workshops	0.03	0.26	0.26	0.25	0.00	0.10	0.21	0.13	0.22
Non-Credit Courses	0.06	0.06	0.09	0.06	0.10	0.24	0.06	0.22	0.07
Total	1.00	1.00	1.00	1.00	1.00	1.00	1.00	1.00	1.00
Major Projects, Tests, and Experiential Learning Activities									
Tests	0.45	0.37	0.51	0.37	0.10	0.38	0.29	0.30	0.41
Business Plan	0.14	0.14	0.18	0.13	0.60	0.09	0.56	0.22	0.17
Cases	0.18	0.23	0.09	0.23	0.20	0.31	0.08	0.16	0.19
Consult Small Business Institute	0.00	0.01	0.01	0.01	0.00	0.00	0.00	0.00	0.01
Interview Entrepreneur	0.03	0.02	0.01	0.03	0.10	0.00	0.00	0.02	0.02
Simulations	0.02	0.02	0.04	0.07	0.00	0.03	0.00	0.02	0.04
Individual Projects	0.04	0.06	0.05	0.05	0.00	0.03	0.00	0.03	0.04
Group Projects	0.02	0.05	0.03	0.01	0.00	0.03	0.00	0.03	0.03
Other	0.13	0.11	0.09	0.10	0.00	0.13	0.06	0.22	0.10
TOTAL	1.00	1.00	1.00	1.00	1.00	1.00	1.00	1.00	1.00

Table 5
4-Year Universities Individual Ratios (Individual/Total)

	1979 SBM	1982 SBM	1986 SBM	1992 SBM	1979 EP	1982 EP	1986 EP	1992 EP	Total Percent
Courses, Workshops, and Seminars									
Credit Courses	0.84	0.42	0.64	0.71	1.00	0.86	0.84	0.84	0.69
Seminars	0.04	0.16	0.18	0.18	0.00	0.02	0.14	0.14	0.15
Workshops	0.12	0.14	0.16	0.10	0.00	0.00	0.02	0.02	0.10
Non-Credit Courses	0.00	0.28	0.01	0.02	0.00	0.12	0.00	0.00	0.06
TOTAL	1.00	1.00	1.00	1.00	1.00	1.00	1.00	1.00	1.00
Major Projects, Tests, and Experiential Learning Activities									
Tests	0.24	0.28	0.30	0.25	0.21	0.15	0.22	0.21	0.26
Business Plan	0.19	0.18	0.17	0.14	0.23	0.20	0.31	0.31	0.20
Cases	0.22	0.13	0.13	0.13	0.21	0.17	0.17	0.16	0.16
Consult Small Business Institute	0.18	0.20	0.17	0.27	0.16	0.03	0.06	0.15	0.19
Interview Entrepreneurs	0.02	0.01	0.01	0.01	0.00	0.01	0.02	0.02	0.02
Simulations	0.02	0.03	0.02	0.02	0.07	0.04	0.05	0.02	0.03
Individual Projects	0.05	0.06	0.06	0.04	0.03	0.06	0.08	0.03	0.05
Group Projects	0.02	0.03	0.04	0.03	0.05	0.05	0.04	0.04	0.04
Other	0.07	0.09	0.08	0.10	0.03	0.28	0.05	0.05	0.05
TOTAL	1.00	1.00	1.00	1.00	1.00	1.00	1.00	1.00	1.00

(3) the use of business cases; (4) consulting via the Small Business Institute program; (5) interviewing entrepreneurs; (6) simulations; (7) individual projects; and (8) group projects.

For Table 4, the data indicates that for two year colleges, the major evaluation pedagogy for the entire length of the study, 1979–1992, was tests. Tests were the most frequently cited method of evaluating learning in both small business management and entrepreneurship courses (41%). However, business plans (17%) and cases (19%) were becoming more widely used as evaluation pedagogy in both small business management and entrepreneurship.

For Table 5, the data indicate that for four year colleges and universities, the number one choice an as evaluation pedagogy for the entire length of the study, 1979–1992, was tests. Tests were the most frequently cited method of evaluating learning in both small business management and entrepreneurship courses (26%). However, business plans (20%) and Small Business Institute Consulting (19%) and Cases (16%) closely followed as preferred evaluation pedagogies.

Conclusion

This paper examined the data from four historical surveys on small business management and entrepreneurial education collected by the U.S. Small Business Administration (SBA). The results of the data indicated a definite growth pattern in small business management and entrepreneurship course offerings at both two and four-year colleges and universities. The data also indicated that experiential teaching and evaluation pedagogies were being employed.

The growth of small business management and entrepreneurship is an occurrence which is not likely to dissipate soon. More importantly, given the rise in course offerings, endowed chairs, majors and research it is important not to lose sight of the uniqueness of the phenomenon under discussion and investigation—the entrepreneur.

As stated earlier in this paper, the prevailing issue is what teaching and evaluation pedagogies are most appropriate for transferring of entrepreneurial skills and knowledge? Based on the data presented in this paper, the need is for less traditional forms of teaching and evaluation and more unique, unconventional methods.

Given the trends to date, it is hoped that educators and trainers will continue to move toward more unconventional, experiential-based teaching and evaluation methods. Traditional paradigms will not work when the focus of the learning is to broaden horizons and perceptions and in fact, move individuals to a different plane of thinking and action where the focus is for them to become "Paradigm Pioneers" and blaze new trails for others to follow.

The field of entrepreneurship must not suffer the fate of traditional teaching and become institutionalize to the point that we merely learn the "mechanics" of entrepreneurship, and lose sight of the "romance" of becoming that rare breed of capitalist known as the "Entrepreneur."

References

Adams C. R. & Song J. H. (1989). Integrating decision technologies: implications for management curriculum. *MIS Quarterly*, 13 (2), 199–209.

Ahiarah S. (1989). Strategic management and entrepreneurship courses at the undergraduate level: can one inform the other? *Proceedings of the 1989 Small Business Institute Directors' Association*, 60–66.

Anselm, M. (1993). Entrepreneurship education in the community college. *Proceedings of the International Council for Small Business*, 177–192.

Aronoff, C. E. & Cawley M. B. (1990). Family business: a new wave for business schools. In C. A. Kent (Ed.), *Entrepreneurship Education*, pp. 123–133, New York: Quorum Books.

Brewer, B., Anyansi-Archibong, C. & Ugboro, I. O. (1993). Using computer simulation technology in entrepreneurship and small business education. *Proceedings of the International Council for Small Business*, 217–229.

Brockhaus, R. H. (1991). Entrepreneurship education and research outside North America. *Entrepreneurship Theory and Practice*, *15*(3), 77–84.

Carland, J. C. & Carland J. W. (1993). Entrepreneurship curriculum design in developing and changing nations: problems in following the U.S. model. *Proceedings of the International Council for Small Business*, 243–253.

Carroll, J. J. & College G. C. (1993). Course and curriculum designs for transnational small business. *Proceedings of the International Council for Small Business*, 254–263.

Clark, B. W., Davis, C. H. & Harnish, V. C. (1984). Do courses in entrepreneurship aid in new venture creation? *Journal of Small Business Management*, *22*(2), 26–31.

Clouse, V. G. H. (1990). A controlled experiment relating entrepreneurial education to students' start-up decisions. *Journal of Small Business Management*, *28*(2), 45–53.

Eldredge, D. L. & Galloway, R. F. (1983). Study of the undergraduate business policy course at AACSB-accredited universities. *Strategic Management Journal*, *4*, 85–90.

Fernald, L. W. & Solomon, G. T. (1993). Assessing the need for small business management/entrepreneurship courses at the university level. *Proceedings of the 17th National Small Business Consulting Conference-SBIDA*, 102–107.

Guglielmino, P. J. & Klatt, L. A. (1993). Entrepreneurs as self-directed learn-ers. *Proceedings of the International Council for Small Business*, 206–216.

Hess, D. W. (1987). Relevance of small business courses to management needs. *Journal of Small Business Management*, *25*(1), 27–34.

Hills, G. E. (1988). Variations in university entrepreneurship education: an empirical study of an evolving field. *Journal of Business Venturing*, *3*, 109–122.

Kent, C. A. (1990). Entrepreneurship education at the collegiate level: a synopsis and evaluation. *Entrepreneurship Education*, pp. 111–122, New York: Quorum Books.

Kiesner, W. F. (1990). Post-secondary entrepreneurship education for the practicing venture initiator. In C. A. Kent (Ed.), *Entrepreneurship Education*, pp. 89–110, New York: Quorum Books.

Kirby, D. A. (1990). Management education and small business development: an exploratory study of small firms in the U.K. *Journal of Small Business Management*, *28*(4), 78–87.

Mann, P. H. (1990). Nontraditional business education for black entrepreneurs: observations from a successful program. *Journal of Small Business Management*, *28*(2), 30–36.

Miller, A. (1987). New ventures: a fresh emphasis on entrepreneurial education. *Survey of Business*, Summer 1987, 4–9.

Marchigiano-Monroy, T. (1993). Realities and emerging realities of adapting to changing global economic conditions: rethinking the role of SBI/SBIDA in entrepreneurial Education. *Proceedings of the 17th National Small Business Consulting Conference-SBIDA*, 120–130.

Porter, L. W. & McKibbin, L. E. (1988). *Management Education: Drift or Thrust into the 21st Century?* New York: McGraw-Hill.

Rabbior, G. (1990). Elements of a successful entrepreneurship/economics/education program. In C. A. Kent (Ed.), *Entrepreneurship Education,* New York: Quorum Books pp. 53–65.

Ray, D. (1990). Liberal arts for entrepreneurs. *Entrepreneurship Theory and Practice, 15*(2), 79–93.

Reid, S. (1987). Designing management education and training programs for service firm entrepreneurs. *Journal of Small Business Management, 25*(1), 51–60.

Robinson, P. & Haynes, M. (1991). Entrepreneurship education in America's major university. *Entrepreneurship Theory and Practice, 15*(3), 41–52.

Ronstadt, R. (1987). The educated entrepreneurs: a new era of entrepreneurial education evolves. In C. A. Kent (Ed.), *Entrepreneurship Education,* New York: Quorum Books, pp. 69–88.

Ronstadt, R. (1990). The educated entrepreneurs: a new era of entrepreneurial education is beginning. *American Journal of Small Business, 11*(4), 37–53.

Rushing, F. W. (1990). Entrepreneurship and education. In C. A. Kent (Ed.), *Entrepreneurship Education,* pp. 29–39, New York: Quorum Books.

Sexton, D. L. & Bowman, N. B. (1984). Entrepreneurship education: suggestions for increasing effectiveness. *Journal of Small Business Management, 22*(2), 18–25.

Sexton, D. L. & Upton, N. B. (1987). Evaluation of an innovative approach to teaching entrepreneurship. *Journal of Small Business Management, 25*(1), 35–43.

Sims, H. P. & Hand, H. H. (1976). Simulation gaming: the confluence of quantitative and behavioral theory. *Academy of Management Review, 1*(3), 109–113.

Smilor, R. W., Gibson, D. V. & Dietrich, G. B. (1990). *Journal of Business Venturing, 5,* 63–76.

Solomon, George T., and Sollosy, Marc (1977) *Nationwide Survey in Course Offerings in Small Business Management/Entrepreneurship,* International Council for Small Business.

Solomon, George T. (1979). *Small Business Management Resource Guides Vol. 1–6,* U.S. Small Business Administration.

Solomon, George T. and Eliason, Carol (1983). *Small Business Management Resource Guides Vol. 1–4,* U.S. Small Business Administration, American Association of Community and Junior Colleges and International Council for Small Business.

Solomon, George T. (1986). *National Survey of Entrepreneurial Education Vol. 1–6,* U.S. Small Business Administration, National Center for Research in Vocational Education and Training.

Solomon, G. T. & Fernald, L. W. (1991). Trends in small business management and entrepreneurship education in the United States. *Entrepreneurship Theory and Practice, 15*(3), 25–39.

Stevenson, H. H. (1986). Harvard's experience with a new entrepreneurship program. In D. L. Sexton & R. W. Smilor(Eds.), *The Art and Science of Entrepreneurship,* pp. 389–401, Cambridge, MA: Ballinger.

Vesper, K. H. (1986). New developments in entrepreneurship education. In D. L. Sexton & R. W. Smilor (Eds.), *The Art and Science of Entrepreneurship,* pp. 379–387, Cambridge, MA: Ballinger.

Vesper, K. H. & McMullan, W. E. (1988). Entrepreneurship: Today courses, tomorrow degrees? *Entrepreneurship Theory and Practice, 13*(1), 7–13.

Weinrauch, J. D. (1984). Educating the entrepreneur: understanding adult learning behavior. *Journal of Small Business Management, 22*(2), 32–37.

Williams, N. A. (1991). Curriculum recommendations for an insurance major. *CPCU Journal, 44*(3), 174–180.

Wolfe, J. (1975). A comparative evaluation of the experiential approach as business policy learning environment. *Academy of Management Journal, 18*(3), 442–452.

Zeithaml, C. P. & Rice, G. H. (1987). Entrepreneurship/small business education in american universities. *Journal of Small Business Management, 25*(1), 44–50.

Best Papers in the Field of Service Provision

Introduction
by Colin Dunn and Michael Schaper

Many entrepreneurs are good at going it alone, but the growth and development of small and medium-sized enterprises (SMEs) often rely on the guidance and support of external practitioners or advisers with specific expertise, knowledge, and skills that entrepreneurs may not have. These practitioners range from general business facilitators, accountants, and lawyers to people in business enterprise associations, business incubators, and people who work for governments and other agencies whose task it is to provide support for the SME operator. These people make a difference, and research has shown they improve the longer-term viability of new ventures, helping them get past those critical first five years. Enterprise facilitators and other specialists can help business builders avoid some of the roadblocks that can lead to failure and help identify the signposts to success by providing support and advice that can help businesses survive and grow.

We have selected a range of papers dating from 1999 that explore the relationship between the entrepreneur and the practitioner.

Trust

The overwhelming impression one receives from reading these papers is of the importance of trust in a relationship between an SME operator and the practitioner. This kind of trust usually comes about through a personal approach to assisting small and medium businesses.

Brochures, advertising, and mail-outs "were of little effect" (Breen 2002). From their work in the United Kingdom, Bennet and Robson (1999) concluded "that levels of use [of support agencies] and [their] impact depend on the extent to which trust-producing mechanisms exist." In their work with accountants, Gooderham et al. (2004) concluded that trust was built on the quality of the relationship between the firm and the accountant and that their accountant could be trusted to satisfactorily deal with the regulatory requirements of their business. The research by Chrisman and McMullan (2004) was of long-term clients of a small-business counseling service where *long term* was defined as more than five hours of counseling. They concluded that an SME operator can "gain valuable insights into the requirements necessary to start a successful business," indicating that such trust can be built up through publicly funded SME support agencies as long as the support methodology is right.

It appears from these research papers that where a learning partnership develops between an SME operator and external practitioner or support agency, then the level of trust grows and the relationship is seen as more productive.

Government or Private Sector—Which Is the More Effective Counseling Source?

Bennet and Robson (1999) found that in the United Kingdom the private sector dominates the provision of advice to

SMEs. They found that public-sector sources had low levels of trust (and were less effective) because they tended to have fewer "trust-producing mechanisms." Specialist professionals, customers, suppliers, and business friends were preferred sources of advice and support. Fischer and Reuber (2003) in their work on rapid-growth firms agreed, pointing out that these businesses preferred to obtain advice from their peers through networks rather than from government agencies and external providers. Their work indicated that government support might be best directed to assist these networks to grow and develop. On the other hand, Chrisman and McMullan (2004) indicated that government agencies can be very effective if the counseling methodology is right. This argument is based on their research where they examined the long-term clients of a U.S. Small Business Development Centre that had spent many hours working with each client.

What Can We Conclude from Our Five Papers?

Trust is critical in the effective provision of practitioner counseling. Trust can best be achieved (and thus be the basis for a successful counseling program) by the provision of more personal counseling services that have an emphasis on building a long-term professional relationship and one that helps build business support networks.

The Use of External Business Advice by SMEs in Britain
by Robert J. Bennett and Paul J. A. Robson

This paper reports new survey results on the extent, sourcing and impact of external business advice to SMEs in Britain. The survey, covering 2547 respondents, is the largest and most definitive assessment to date. Its results demonstrate the very wide extent of external advice: used by 95% of respondent SMEs, an increase from 85.8% in a similar survey in 1991. The analysis of the survey assesses sources of advice in terms of the level of trust that exists between the supplier and the SME client. The market appears to be strongly segmented and dominated by high trust specialist sources (accountants, lawyers), customers, suppliers and business friends. Business associations and government-backed sources play an important but lesser role. The recent government initiative of Business Link has, however, established an important market, used by 27% of respondents. Impact assessments confirm the significance of high trust private sector suppliers for the most crucial supplies of advice. Variations in use occur by SME type chiefly by size but also by sector and growth record. Generally levels of use vary by SME type to a greater extent than levels of impact.

Keywords: consultants; business services; Business Link; trust; business advice.

---

1. Introduction

The primary objective of this paper is to assess the extent and impact of external advice to small and medium-sized enterprises (SMEs) and to test whether different relationships of trust with the supplier influence levels of use and impact.

External advice and consultancy has increased rapidly since the mid-1980s. This has been a result of a variety of changes: the increased demand for specialist services that may be difficult to supply in-house, the innovation of new products that has created new markets for external suppliers, and increased outsourcing of activities formerly undertaken in-house (Howells and Green 1986, Kutscher 1988, Perry 1992, O'Farrell *et al.* 1993).

The growth in business services has been spectacular in most countries (Moulaert and Tödling 1995). In Britain,

Originally appeared in *Entrepreneurship and Regional Development*, 1999, Volume 11, Number 2.

employment has more than doubled in business service firms between 1981 and 1990 (Keeble *et al.* 1991), and has increased again in the late 1990s. Moreover, the use of external advice has been strongly linked to successful business growth (Harrington *et al.* 1991, Berry-Lound and Parsons 1994, Ilersis 1994, Bryson *et al.* 1997), particularly for the use of management training (Hendry *et al.* 1991, CBI 1993, 1995, Tordoir 1994). Previous surveys in Britain have shown that between 80 and 95% of businesses use external advice from one source or more.

However, despite interest in the growth of external business services, there have been few large-scale surveys over a complete range of external advice sources, which include public and quasi-public intermediaries as well as private sector market suppliers, nor has there been an assessment of why differences in suppliers arise. This paper seeks to fill these gaps using new information from a 1997 survey focusing on use of advice by SMEs of up to 500 employees. The empirical results relate specifically to Britain, however it should be possible to apply the conclusions to other countries where similar environments of regulation, self-regulation and trust operate to government client-supplier relations in the delivery of external business advice.

The authors first review the existing research on the extent of demand for different sources of external business advice. Particular attention is given to the literature assessing why different sources are used, focusing on the level of trust, regulation and quality control that operates between the client and the advisor. The authors then present the results of the new survey of sources of advice and their impact. Startup businesses are, in general, *excluded* from the discussion since they clearly have a special category of demand for advice supply. The authors chiefly seek to assess the role of external advice for established SMEs.

2. Sources of External Advice

A wide range of sources of advice is available to businesses in most countries, ranging in the private sector from professional and technical specialists to more generalized consultants, the social networks of the firm's owner(s), and its supply chain and customer links. In addition there is a wide range of sector-based trade and professional associations to which most businesses belong to at least one, and local associations such as chambers of commerce. In most countries there is also a range of public sector bodies that seeks to offer advice services to businesses.

2.1 Previous Evidence

There have been a number of previous studies of sources of advice to SMEs. General international reviews are given by Harrington *et al.* (1991), Illeris (1994) and Moulaert and Tödtling (1995). In Britain, as a basis for comparison with the authors' own survey presented later, the most recent studies are summarized in tables 1 and 2. Taking first the private sector suppliers, shown in table 1, all studies demonstrate these to be the chief source of advice for most companies. Among the private sector suppliers the chief sources of advice in rank order are accountants, next either banks or solicitors, and then business associations, or consultants. The market appears, therefore, to be dominated by professional specialists, followed by the rather special bodies of sector and local associations, and then a broad range of consultants. These results are comparable with those quoted by Harrington *et al.* (1991) or Illeris (1994). However, the comparative rankings in these surveys are not consistent, except for the primary role of accountants, nor are their sampling frames fully comparable. A further problem is interpreting the form and intensity of the advice offered.

Table 1
Previous Recent Surveys of Use of Private Sector and Business Association Advice Services by Source (% of Respondents Reporting Use). A Gap Indicates that a Survey Did Not Ask or Identify that Source Explicitly

Source	Keeble et al. (1992)	Curran & Blackburn (1994)	Barclays (1994)	CBI 1994	Doggett & Hepple (1995)	MORI (1994)*	Bank of England (1996)	Lloyds/SBRT (1998)
Date of survey	1991	1990/1	1993	1994	1994	1994	1996	1997
Accountant	62	74.4	93.7	35	77.3	29	19	—
Solicitor	—	67.6	—	—	19.5	7	—	—
Banks	42	36.3	38	35	63.9	7	7	—
Business friend/relative	—	—	17	—	—	2	—	—
Customers	—	—	—	—	—	6	—	—
Suppliers	—	—	—	—	—	6	—	—
Consultants	37	16.0	7	55.0	15.8	37	8	—
Non-executive director	—	—	—	32.1†	1.2	—	—	—
Chambers of commerce	—	23.7	2.3	—	—	5	14	31
Trade/professional associations	—	29.1	9.8	—	—	17	—	26
Respondents	1128	410	600	215	410	775	59	350
Sample frame	D & B in 3 types of areas, mostly under 100 employees	11 small service sectors in 7 areas	SMEs, 3–10 years old	CBI SME members	D & B mainly manufacturing. Turnover £0–200 m	D & B 10–200 employees	Technology-based firms. Turnover £0–100 m	SMEs 0–50 employees

*Refers to final source of advice (MORI 1994: 12).

†Refers to those having a non-executive director.

D & B is Dunn and Bradstreet.

Table 2
Previous Recent Surveys of Use of Public Sector-Backed Advice Services by Source (% of Respondents Reporting Use). A Gap Indicates that a Survey Did Not Ask or Identify that Source Explicitly

Source	Curran & Blackburn (1994)	Keeble et al. (1992)	SBRC (1992)	Barclays (1994)	CBI (1994)	MORI† (1994)	Doggett & Hepple (1995)	3i/MORI (1996)	3i/MORI (1997)	IoM/NCM (1996)	IoM/NCM (1997)	Bank of England (1996)	Lloyds/ SBRT (1998)
Date of survey	1990/1	1991	1991	1993	1994	1994	1994	1995	1996	1996	1997	1996	1997
TEC/LEC (includes SFS)	11.8	15	—	19	45	7	7	27	25	28	27	19	21
Business Link	—	—	—	—	5	1	—	11	14	42	48	22	26
Other Government*	19.5	31	33.4	—	55	16	10.5	20	16	—	—	—	—
Enterprise agencies	18.8	15	7	14	12	2	—	—	—	—	—	7	5
Regional/local development agencies	—	10	—	—	—	—	—	—	—	—	—	5	—
College/University	12.7	—	—	—	—	4	—	—	—	—	—	—	—
Local authority	—	13	—	—	—	7	—	—	—	—	—	—	3
Respondents	410	1128	2028	600	215	775	410	1067	62	196		59	
Sample frame	Service industries	D & B in 3 types of area, mostly <100 employees	D & B manufacturing & business services <500 employees	SMEs, 3–10 years old	CBI SME members		D & B manufacturing. Turnover £0–200 m	Owner managers Turnover £1–100 m D & B plus 31 portfolio		Exporters. Turnover £1–10 m		Technology-based firms. Turnover £0–100 m	

*Includes DTI Enterprise Initiative consultants.

†Refers to first Contact source of advice (MORI 1994: 12).

TEC = Training and Enterprise Council; LEC = Local Enterprise Company; SFS = Small Firms Service; BL = Business Link; SE = Scotish Enterprise; D & B = Dunn and Bradstreet.

Turning next to public sector sources, table 2 reviews the findings of recent studies of use of advice services in Britain. This table can be compared with the summary given by Storey (1994, table 8.6) covering the period up to 1992, i.e. before recent changes in the organization of government support services. Storey found that the use of any support agency varied from 1 to 55% of businesses, with most studies finding that less than 10% of businesses use public sector sources. Exceptions to this are, first, the study by Smallbone *et al.* (1993), but this probably includes many start-ups and does not control for area eligibility, and second, the SBRC (1992) survey results for 1991 (Keeble and Bryson 1996), and the Keeble *et al.* (1992) survey of 1991, where the Enterprise Initiative is shown to be used by over 30% of SMEs, with significant differences between areas. The CBI (1994) in a more self-selective survey of their members also found use of the Enterprise Initiative to be high, 55% of businesses surveyed. The Enterprise Initiative may, therefore, have stimulated a degree of external demand far greater than previously was the case. However, the messages from these surveys are confused by different sampling frames and different controls for the influence of other factors. Firm size is often an important factor influencing the extent to which external advice is sought, with major differences occurring between the smallest classes. Also, where start-ups are involved a much higher level of use of public external agents is generally made (Turok and Richardson 1991, Birley and Westhead 1992). Thus small differences in sampling frame or sample responses could make significant differences to the assessed use of different sources. Similarly, the type of advice field in which advice is sought, and the age, ownership, employment growth, production structure and level of exporting of the business are each also important factors likely to lead to differences in levels of external advice sought, which should be controlled for. It is clear, therefore, that to gain a proper insight into the extent and form of external advice, much better controls of sampling and analysis are required.

2.2 The Influence of Supplier Trust

The primary objective of the authors is to test the hypothesis that the choice of advisor, level of use and impact depends on the relationship of trust existing between the supplier and the SME.

Advice is a very specific kind of business service that delivers a largely intangible product.

The process of production of advice is usually an exchange process involving learning and exchange on both sides (Mills and Margulies 1980, O'Farrell and Moffat 1995, Tordoir 1994). Clark (1993) emphasizes four differentiating characteristics of business services: *intangibility*, *inseparability* (production and competition usually require no intermediary between client and supplier), *heterogeneity* (low level of standardization with tailoring to each client's needs), and *perishability* (excludability: each new client has to have the service re-tailored leading to low levels of repeat businesses for similar fields of service advice). Theses characteristics mean that advice services depend a great deal on personal relationships and exchanges, which in turn are governed by the very different institutional environments of each type of supplier.

Suppliers of advice fall into very different categories of regulatory regimes. These can be interpreted as generating different environments of trust that will be likely to lead to different extents and intensity of use of advisors. Zucker (1986) contrasts environments of (i) low trust, (ii) high personal trust, based on personal acquaintance and social relations between the client and suppliers, and (iii) high institutional trust where the client relies on whatever regulatory structures exist governing the behaviour of the supplier. External advisors fall into each of these categories and we expect these different regimes to have important implications for their level of use and impact. In an unregulated market, as for example that largely governing consultants, there is a low level of both personal and institutional trust. In contrast, friends and business associates fit within a regime of high personal trust and low institutional trust. Professional specialists, such as lawyers and accountants work within a regime of institutional trust derived from self-regulation, whilst government agencies are regulated by government. These concepts can be used to compare different sources of advice. The different levels of trust, and the balance between personal and institutional trust, lead to very different expectations about the extent and form of use of advice services for different sources. Levels of trust depend on institutional structures, hence the following discussion is presented for the context of Britain, which is relevant to interpretation of the subsequent survey.

2.3 Private Sector Suppliers

In the case of the two chief professional specialists, accountants and solicitors, advice is given within a very specific institutional framework of self-regulation, which should award them a high level of institutional trust. Accountants implement the statutory audit requirements, which apply to all SMEs except the very smallest (although exemptions from statutory audit for larger SMEs have been implemented since 1997). Solicitors implement a number of technical legal requirements, particularly related to loan and finance agreements for property and facilities/plant purchase or leasing. Both accountants and solicitors operate within a government-backed self-regulating framework of training, qualification, code of conduct, trading standards, discipline, enforcement, and group insurance. These are regulated by

the six accountancy associations and the Law Society. There have been criticisms of the depth of accountant and solicitor involvement with SMEs, which suggest that their impact on performance can be limited (Kirby and King 1997). There have also been considerable recent tensions within their associations between the few large and many small practitioners in each case and between accounting bodies and government (see the *Financial Times* 1996, 1998, *The Times* 1996). Despite these caveats, accountants and solicitors work within a strong self-regulatory framework that offers a professional status, level of trust and quality control of advice that is not likely to be achievable in most other areas of advice because of lower levels of regulatory and self-regulatory controls.

Bank financial advice is also bound by regulatory framework. However, although the core business of banks is finance, most commonly associated with account, overdraft and other loan facilities, banks also play a role in giving wide advice, but this area is *not* subject to strict regulatory control. Ennew and Binks (1996) argue that banks can draw on the basis of the trust and confidence clients have in them, their approachability, and the information that flows to them as a result of their financial dealings with clients.

However, despite these positive aspects of banking advice, their services have been much criticized for gaps in provision, particularly a narrow focus on overdraft facilities and/or absence of wider advisory capacity, and problems of service quality (Smith 1989, Bannock and Doran 1991, Cowling *et al.* 1991, Deakins and Hussain 1991). Indeed the loyalty of customers has been interpreted as a consequence largely of inertia, high costs of switching banks, and a belief that there is little difference between banks. Hence, whilst Doggett and Hepple (1995) find that clients are in contact with their bank frequently for advice, it has a relatively low rating for the quality of its services. Particularly negative views have focused on service charges for SMEs, inflexibility of financial products and inability to take a long-germ view (Cowling *et al.* 1991), which is contrasted with the attitude of German banks (Bannock and Albach 1991). Hence, although banks may gain advantage from a high level of institutional trust, and certainly are recognized as having a high level of professional integrity among their staff, the level of institutional trust on which they can draw will be relatively low for their advice compared to their mainstream finance services.

The role of business friends or relatives as advisors draws on the wider social networks of the owners and managers of SMEs. Their use will draw on personal trust, but will be limited by the extent to which the relevant experience exists within an owner or manager's personal networks. In some cases friends and relatives act as the preferred and most valuable route for many of the smallest owner-managers (Department of Employment 1991a), who are often resistant to giving out information and believe that "no one could know their business better than themselves" (Department of Employment 1991b: 23). Hence, for micro-businesses and owner-managers, friends and relatives may be the best way of getting value at a low price and with a high level of trust, with also a high level of confidentiality and retention of personal control by the owner.

Customers and suppliers are an important part of the information system of any business. At the most crucial level customers are a market signal of the success of the business's products and trading. Similarly, suppliers are a source of information on new technologies, opportunities to innovate, and reduction of costs. However, this essential flow of information may also develop into quite important exchanges of advice. These exchanges can range from the informal to formal contractual arrangements or alliances between businesses.

A specific aspect of the role of customers and suppliers as sources of advice can be through networks and local embeddedness. In part this is an extension of the social networks of friends and relations discussed above. Various assessments of international case studies have suggested that networks of individual and institutional trust may stimulate inter-firm linkages, exchanges of information and innovation in a highly context-dependent structure, i.e. is deeply locally embedded (Brusco 1982, Granovetter 1985, Sabel 1989). This means that coercive market power may be supplemented or replaced by supportive exchanges and continuing relationships. Some evidence of this structure is claimed for business service firms in Britain (O'Farrell and Wood 1998) and among financial service firms (Amin and Thrift 1992). However, in detailed surveys Curran *et al.* (1993) and Curran and Blackburn (1994) find little evidence in Britain of extensive or supportive local supplier networks for SMEs. Indeed they find a general decline in the social context of inter-firm relations, and weaker development in newer and more rapidly growing firms.

Consultants are a key aspect of the advice sources available to SMEs, and their role has been stimulated by government initiatives (particularly the Enterprise Initiative) and more recently through Business Link. Consultants range over a wide variety of different intensities of relationships with their clients, from short-term and very specific advice to broader advice on management strategy, product development, marketing, technology, etc. Kirby and Jones-Evans (1997) show, moreover, that the consultant's objectives and approach can vary considerably Wood *et al.* (1993) show that the demand for management consultancy and market research advice is strongly differentiated by firm size (higher for larger firms), by sector and to some extent by region, with consultancy covering a wide range of specialist and technical areas, from human resources and information technology to business strategy, marketing and logistics. Hence it is important to differentiate the type of firms in any assessment. Wood *et al.* (1993) also show that the demand for consultancy is for specialist rather than generalist skills in over 50% of cases, and for a mix of specialist and generalist skills in a further 25% of cases. The generalist consultant therefore satisfies no more than about 25% of the market demand. This suggests that the choice of source of advice will tend to give preference to professional specialists where they exist (as in accountancy, law, finance), so that consultants as a generic category will tend to seek to differentiate themselves by specialism and branding. Generally the source of trust drawn on when recruiting a consultant is reputation, branding and personal recommendation (Bryson 1997). These are essentially market mechanisms for signalling quality (Shapiro 1983). Hence consultants probably draw little on either personal or institutional trust and rely chiefly on market signals.

Sector and local business associations are used chiefly by a self-selecting group of businesses that choose to be members. Associations appear to fill a niche market for advice services where they "brand name capital", interrelated with a relatively high level of institutional trust based on their duty to members (usually written into their constitution; Bennett 1996) gives them a privileged route for access and exchange of advice with their members. Detailed studies of business associations demonstrate that they are chiefly supporting advice requirements of low cost, moderate frequency and duration, but high human asset specificity (knowledge skills) and high interconnectedness with similar and other transactions (Schneiberg and Hollingsworth

1991, van Waarden 1991, Taylor and Singleton 1993, Bennett 1996). The volume of association advice to members can, however, be quite considerable: enquiries per member per year range from zero to 106 in sector bodies (Bennett 1998), and average five per member per year in chambers of commerce.

2.4 Public Sector Suppliers

Previous surveys of public sector advice services reviewed in table 2 show that the Enterprise Initiative was the main government source used up to about 1993/94, then Training and Enterprise Councils become more important in the period 1993–1996, but since about 1996 the Business Link initiative becomes significant. Overall the level of use of government services reaches a maximum of 25–34% in most surveys. The concept of trust involved in these services is likely to be chiefly institutional, tending to rely on quality assurances, recommendations and awareness campaigns.

The Enterprise Initiative was launched in January 1988 and expanded in various stages (HM Government 1988, DTI 1990). Its key aspect was to subsidize the use of business planning, design, financial and information systems, manufacturing systems, marketing, and quality. It thus sought to stimulate most of the core areas of external advice that are the focus of this paper. Evaluations (SQW 1989, 1994) show the marketing aspect to be the most popular (about 30% of use), followed by quality (20%). Business planning, design and financial and information systems each had 10–15% take up, with manufacturing system consultancy the lowest at 6–8%. Most important in terms of the government's desired impact, about one-half of all users had never used external consultants before, and this was particularly high for use of marketing, business planning and design consultants. The Enterprise Initiative therefore had an important effect on expanding the experience of use of external advice. Satisfaction levels were generally high, scoring mean levels of 3.9–4.3 (on a satisfaction scale of 1–5). This is much higher than ratings of Government Department of Trade and Industry (DTI) services as a whole, where 59% of respondents found its assistance to be poor or very poor, and a further 24% found it to be only adequate (BCC 1994). Impact ratings and additionality of the Enterprise Initiative were also evaluated as extremely positive in the SQW (1994) study. Although the evaluation methodology has been criticized for selection bias and being too highly reliant on respondent ratings of actions in the absence of support (over 80% said that they would not have used a consultancy, would have delayed, or would have had a less detailed study) (Storey 1996, Wren and Storey 1998), Storey's estimates taking into account selection bias still show positive impact on short-term and especially long-term survival rates (4–5% better), and up to 9% increases in turnover and employment.

The Enterprise Initiative sought to stimulate the market for private consultancy. Hence it combined the benefits of a level of institutional trust for government-backed schemes with reliance on market signalling using brand and recommendation on which consultancy more typically rests. The Enterprise Initiative terminated in 1994, although some central DTI services continued for information and referral purposes (chiefly the Consultancy Brokerage Service—see DTI 1995a).

Business Link is an initiative, launched in 1992, to offer a national network of *local* business advice centres. In Scotland a system of "Business Shops" and in Wales "Business Connect" are similar bodies. However, the Scottish and Welsh approach has put less emphasis on a "one stop shop" and more on a "first stop shop" with referral to other agents. Business Link has focused on a core service of Personal Business Advisors, information provision and diagnostic assessment, supplemented by internal referral to specialist counsellors. Further referral is then possible to private sector, public sector or local partner bodies. Targeting has eventually focused on growth companies of 10–200 employees, but recently with increased flexibility to deal with business of all sizes including start-ups.

The trust characteristics of Business Link draws on the government-backing of institutional trust, but unlike the Enterprise Initiative it draws on internal consultancy expertise to a greater extent. Brand and recommendation may still play a role, but it is likely that the key element will rely on strengthening institutional trust through positive experiences, positive marketing, and internal quality controls. Evaluation of Business Links shows that they have conformed to a fairly narrow pattern with limited local innovation in services (Priest 1999), suggesting a narrow focus that should encourage market recognition. Take-up by late 1997 has been very large with market penetration covering 81,000 businesses, strongly related to firm size: 4% of the firms with 1–9 employees, 19% of firms with 10–49 employees, 36% of firms with 50–199 employees, and 41% of firms with >200 employees, or 7% overall (DTI 1997). However, there have been concerns about quality, particularly variation in quality between different local offices and different advisors, with government efforts to improve quality standards to a basic minimum (Roche 1997).

The Training and Enterprise Councils (TECs) and Local Enterprise Companies (LECs) also provide advice services. They were set up in England and Wales from April 1990 onwards, with all operational by October 1991, and all Scottish LECs operational in April 1991. The TECs play an important role as the local agents of many government advice programmes, chiefly vocational qualifications and apprenticeships. They provide grants or subsidies in these fields. Of the small firm's budget spent by TECs before Business Link was fully established, 13% went to information and advice, 32% to business counselling and consultancy, 27% to business skills training, and 28% to diagnostics and other services (DTI 1995b). Since the establishment of Business Link, the TECs have tended to become even more identified with these rather narrow fields of training advice. In Scotland TECs more closely integrate business advice with wider physical economic development projects. Like the other government programmes, TECs and LECs draw on institutional trust as well as relying on brand and recommendation.

Enterprise agencies provide a range of counselling, advice and business training that in the 1980s chiefly focused on pre-start and start-ups (about 80% of businesses counselled), as well as young established businesses (about 18% of business counselled), over half of the clients of which were previously unemployed (Bennett 1995, tables 4 and 5). The enterprise agencies are thus an important part of the advice system for very small and early-stage businesses, but the development of TECs/LECs (to which most enterprise agencies are now contracted) and Business Link (with which most enterprise agencies are partners), is likely to have reduced their level of direct use. Some reduction is already evident in the later dated surveys quoted in table 2.

The remaining public sector agents used for business advice (table 2) vary considerably between areas depending on the existence or not of given bodies, or their attitude to supplying business advice. Development agencies are very important in some areas, notably Scotland, Wales, rural areas (particularly through the Rural Development Commission) as well as in many older industrial cities. Universities, Colleges and local government vary considerably in their level of supply of advice and the intensity with which they become involved, although there is evidence of generally increasing levels of involvement by each of these bodies.

The findings of this earlier literature are summarized as follows. First, major differences in the level used of external advice, its source and field occur between different surveys. Generally most surveys have been relatively small samples and have inadequately controlled for differences between firms in their use of externalization. Size, age and sector appear to be significant factors influencing the level and source of external advice, which have not been fully controlled for in many previous studies.

Second, there have been significant changes over time in the mode of delivery and form of government support so that it is important to be clear about the period analysed and hence the institutional structures relevant at the time. The period 1988–94 saw a strong emphasis on the Enterprise Initiative as a central service. From about 1993 the TECs emerge as a local delivery system for business advice, and from about 1996 Business Link becomes more significant. It would be expected that some important contrasts would occur between these localized delivery structures and the more centralized system formerly followed.

A third aspect is the relationship of the advisor and the supplier. It is fairly clear from the discussion of previous findings that the likely extent of use of particular sources largely depends on the level of trust that the client has of the supplier. In the case of accountants and solicitors the high level of use appears to derive from a "professional trust" supported by government-backed self-regulation. This is a form of "institutional trust". This form of trust also applies to bank financial services, but applies less to bank general advisory services, and is not usually available to consultants. Consultants work in a low-trust relationship largely drawing on market signals of quality such as reputation, recommendation or previous experience. For business associations "constitutional trust" or institutional trust may characterize relationships where advice is backed by a confidentiality and high human asset skill specificity that puts these bodies in a special position with their clients. The use of friends and relatives relies on a "social trust", while the use of suppliers and customers will depend less on trust than on the high level of technical and tacit knowledge that each possesses, as well as the exercise of coercive market power.

Government agencies and initiative offering advice are clearly in a different position that cannot usually draw on any of these sources of trust or tacit knowledge. The use of such advice is therefore likely to depend on different factors. Whilst a level of institutional trust will exist for government-backed services, their use is likely to be mainly stimulated by financial subsidies and grants, their perceived quality, and will be considerably boosted by effective marketing (as occurred with the Enterprise Initiative). To the extent that these are the most important factors, the level of use will depend on the scale of grants and other supports available and the effectiveness with which awareness can be raised among clients.

3. Evaluating the Use of External Advice by SMEs

In the following empirical evaluation the authors use the 1997 Cambridge Centre for Business Research survey of SMEs (summarized in CBR 1998). This survey is the most recent in a wave of large-scale studies undertaken in previous years in 1991, 1993 and 1995. It is an important resource base for the present analysis because of its size and care in sampling design. In addition, its structure allows measurement of all the significant differences between firms, which can then be used as controls in the assessment.

3.1 Methodology

The survey is drawn by random sampling from the sampling frame of Dun and Bradstreet (D & B). D & B derives from credit ratings of firms and is recognized to under-represent sole proprietors, the self-employed, partnerships and micro-businesses. However for the main area of concern with established SMEs, it is a high quality data base, kept up-to-date continuously, with the firm's address, sector (based on main activity), and other important information. The surveyed firms were contacted by mail and 2474 responded (25%). Tests of non-response bias show this to be a valid data base (CBR 1998). The possible significance of non-response to each question is assessed in the text below. The sample drawn is stratified to include SMEs of under 500 employees, approximately equally from two broad industrial sectors: all manufacturing codes and business services. The survey strata are weighted towards medium/larger sized SMEs in order to obtain usable numbers for comparisons of each size group. The final sampling proportions are 74%, 1–49 employees; 22%, 50–199 employees; and 4%, 200–499 employees. Results cannot be aggregated to the whole population of SMEs without re-weighting because of the unequal sampling proportions, but can be treated as representative within each size group stratum.

In the 1997 survey (CBR 1998) the use of external advice is a significant addition to the methodology. External advice is defined as being linked with meeting the business's objectives, which are defined in the immediately preceding questions. It excludes basic information provision. Respondents were asked to identify each area and source of advice they had used to meet their business objectives in the previous 3 years, and to rate its impact. The types of external advice investigated are wide: including the services of other firms, public agencies and external consultants. The range of sources specified is broad enough to allow assessment of the full range of external sources. In addition to advice all other indicators of SME structures are surveyed. Attention is focused below on sector, employee size and growth history.

3.2 Use of Sources of Advice

The survey assesses the extent of use and level of impact of 13 external service suppliers. These cover the full range of external sources, falling into six categories: (i) professional specialists (accountants, solicitors, banks); (ii) professional generalists (consultants, but themselves composed of a wide range of highly specialized as well as generalist skills); (iii) market contacts through the supply chain (customers and suppliers); (iv) social contacts (family and business friends); (v) business associations (trade and professional bodies, local chambers of commerce); and (vi) government-sponsored agents (Business Link/Business Shop/business Connect, TECs, Rural Development Commission, enterprise agencies, etc.).

Overall the level of use of external advice has increased since the similar (SBRC 1992) survey: from 85.8% in 1991 to 95.0% of all respondents in 1997. This indicates that the scale of the market for external advice to SMEs remains large, is probably still increasing, and involves all SMEs. The different categories of supplier fall into a strongly differentiated rank order according to their level of use (table 3). Non-response to this question was extremely low (1.8%) and hence the results are believed to be fully reliable. In these and all following tables responses are adjusted where relevant to

the different respondent locations relevant to the different agents of TECs, LECs, and Business Link.

The specialist professionals are by far the most frequent source of external advice. Accountants (83%), banks (62%) and solicitors (56%) are each used by over one-half of all respondents, and the combined use of these three agents accounts for 42% of all external sources used. The market for external advice is therefore dominated by professional specialists. This is in line with the findings of other recent surveys (table 1). These figures themselves may also be underestimates since these three specialists are probably more likely to be used on a number of occasions.

Next in importance in terms of use are customers (47%) and suppliers (36%), together accounting for 17% of all external advisors. In a similar position is the use of a business friend or relative (38%). Like the professional specialists, the use of the business supply chain and a business friend or family relative suggests that the key focus for external inputs of advice is from individuals who possess two key characteristics: first, they are specialists, which appears to place a high emphasis on both high-level technical skills and/or tacit knowledge of the business through personal or market relations; second, they are probably in a position of high trust with their customers, drawing on their already developed trading or social relationships with the client. Together this "high trust" and the "professional specialist" group accounts for 68% of all external sources.

In comparison the role of the professional generalist of consultants is seventh ranked overall, used by 32% of respondents, accounting for 7% of total responses. The role of consultants covers a wide range of specialist as well as generalist fields of advice. They appear to be an important part of the market for external advice, but well behind those suppliers that draw on a level of institutional

Table 3
Use of Private and Public Sector Advice Sources by Sector, Firm Size, and Growth
(% of Respondents Reporting Use, Multiple Responses Allowed)

Advice Source	All	Manufacturing	Services	Micro	Small	Medium/Larger	Stable/Declining	Medium Growth	Fast Growth
Accountant	82.8	83.1	82.4	81.7**	85.0**	79.7**	77.3***	84.0***	89.8***
Solicitor	55.9	55.6	65.5	40.7***	66.6***	75.1***	45.3***	61.6***	68.7***
Bank	61.6	62.9	59.7	56.1***	66.9***	62.6***	53.6***	63.8***	70.0***
Business friend/relative	37.8	35.3***	41.3***	43.6***	33.6***	32.0***	34.7***	31.9***	43.3***
Customers	47.2	46.9	47.6	43.9***	48.1***	57.7***	41.2***	51.9***	52.4***
Suppliers	36.4	40.7***	30.4***	33.5***	37.3***	44.5***	33.2***	39.8***	41.6***
Consultants	31.9	31.6	32.4	19.9***	40.6***	46.6***	26.7***	38.6***	39.3***
Chambers of commerce	23.0	25.3***	19.8***	16.7***	29.2***	24.6***	18.4***	29.7***	25.0***
Trade/Professional Associations	31.4	28.1***	36.1***	25.1***	35.0***	41.6***	28.8*	35.2*	31.3*
Local Enterprise Agency	14.4	14.9	13.8	13.0	15.4	16.3	13.0	14.1	16.8
Local TEC	22.0	25.0***	17.6***	13.5***	26.9***	36.0***	18.0***	26.9***	26.9***
Local LEC	33.3	37.3	29.7	23.6*	46.3*	35.7**	16.7***	42.3***	55.6***
Business Link	26.6	31.2***	19.9***	18.9***	33.7***	29.5***	22.1***	32.0***	30.3***
Business Shop/Connect	13.2	14.4	11.8	11.8	12.8	15.0	8.8*	8.3*	22.4*
Rural Development Commission or Regional Agency	4.7	5.6**	3.5*	3.4*	5.8**	5.7**	3.2***	6.3***	7.2***
Used any external advice	95.0	95.2	94.8	92.2***	97.5***	96.4***	92.5***	96.6***	98.1**
N	2474	1445	1029	1080	1082	281	772	495	517

(*$p > 0.1$; **$p > 0.05$; ***$p > 0.01$) using Mann-Whitney test for two group comparisons, or the Kruskal-Wallis test for multigroup comparisons, between column entries.

Types of business: micro, <10 employees; small business, 10–99 employees; medium/larger businesses, 100–499 employees. Employment growth of business during last 3 years: stable/declining businesses with zero or negative growth; medium-growth $0 \leq 40\%$; and fast-growth $\geq 40\%$.

or personal trust. When added to the six previous private sector suppliers they bring the total responses to 75% of the market from the private sector. It is clear, therefore, that the overwhelming market for external business advice to SMEs is supplied by private sector suppliers themselves.

The business associations are a further specialist form of private supplier relying on a different structure of institutional trust, as well as brand name capital and identification as a collective supplier of specific advice. The sectoral associations (trade and professional associations) come eighth ranked of the sources of supply, used by 31% of respondents and accounting for 7% of all responses. The local associations of chambers of commerce are ranked tenth, used by 23% of respondents and accounting for 5% of responses. These figures are in line with estimates of their UK membership within the respective firm size categories of their membership (Bennett 1996, 1998). However, the overall scale of development of advice from associations is fairly modest, confirming earlier findings that the associations fill rather specific niches in the market drawing on their special position as collective bodies. Together the sectoral and local associations account for 11.4% of all responses. When added to the previous private sector groups of professionals, suppliers, customers, friends and consultants, the total private sector coverage of the market accounts for 86% of all responses.

The role of the government-sponsored suppliers therefore fills about 14% of the total responses with a lower take-up than almost all private sector suppliers of advice. It is also divided between a variety of agents. Ninth ranked in terms of respondent use is Business Link, used by 27% of respondents accounting for 5% of all responses. Local TECs and LECs are used by 23% of respondents (5% of all responses); and the Rural Development Commission and other regional agencies are the least used category of all, used by 4.7% of respondents accounting for 1% of all responses (although no account is taken here of eligibility levels for different regional agencies).

The local enterprise agencies are a rather specialist body. Their chief source of finance in almost all cases comes from government sources in the form of contracts from a TEC/LEC, Business Link, grants from central government or local authorities, as well as modest sponsorship from larger companies usually in the form of seconded staff. They are thus a government-funded agent, although they pride themselves on their entrepreneurial focus seeking to act like a private sector supplier. They fill a small niche, acting as adviser to 14.4% of respondents and accounting for 3% of all responses.

3.3 Use of Advice by Firm Type

Assessment of the variation in sources of advice by firm type shows that differences are significant for almost all categories except sector (table 3). The only statistically significant differences for sectors are for manufacturing, which is more likely to use suppliers, TECs and Business Link; service industries are more likely to use friends and sector associations.

Most important are differences by size of firm. There is a tendency for there to be significantly increasing external sourcing with increasing size of firm for the use of solicitors, customers, suppliers, consultants, sector associations, enterprise agencies and TECs. Only the use of a business friend or relative is higher for smaller firms. The largest differences between firms by size is in the use of consultants and TECs, which are twice as likely to use these sources in larger compared to smaller firms. Customers, suppliers, sector associations and Business Links are about 50% more likely to be used as an external source by larger firms.

Growth firms (in terms of employment numbers) generally have the highest use of most external suppliers, and declining forms the lowest use, except for the cases of chambers, TECs and Business Links, which all have the highest level of use among the slower growth firms. These bodies are all locally-based and serve to some extent similar markets. Hence it may be that they are focused on, or are found to be most useful by, slower growth firms. However, in all cases the differences between firms by employment growth history are fairly small, although it is statistically significant for 1 out of 13 sources.

The significant effect of firm size on use of sources is an important finding of the research. To illustrate how this effect operates over a finer mesh of firm size categories, the responses are retabulated in figures 1 and 2. These figures extend the previous insights generated in the surveys by O'Farrell *et al.* (1992, 1993). Two sources show something approximating an inverted "U" shaped distribution; i.e. highest for medium-sized firms

Figure 1
Use of Private Sector Advice Services by Firm Size (% of Respondents Reporting Use) (Source: Cambridge CBR)

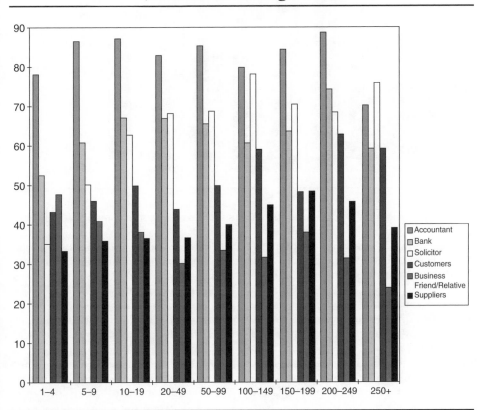

Figure 2
Use of Consultants, Business Associations and Public Sector Advice Services by Firm Size (% of Respondents Reporting Use)
(Source: Cambridge CBR)

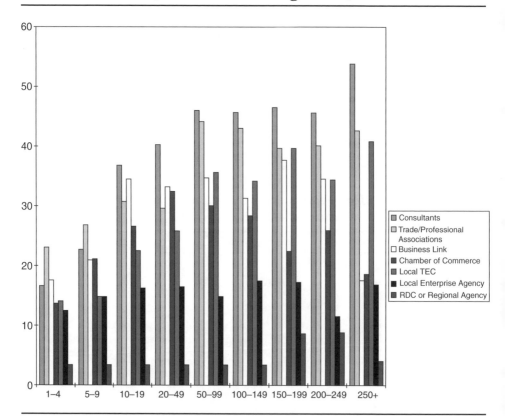

and lowest for small and large firms. These are accountants and banks. Two sources show little systematic influence of firm size: enterprise agencies and Rural Development Commission. Eight sources, that is the majority, show a rapidly increasing use by firms as we move from 1–4 employees to 50–99 employees, with a levelling off after that point. This applies to solicitors, consultants, sector associations, chambers, Business Link, TECs, and LECs. Whilst suppliers and customers tend to have generally a greater level of use with size, this is not a smooth change in figure 1.

There are some influences of sample size fluctuations, particularly for the largest firms of over 150 employees. Nevertheless an important conclusion can be drawn, that for most private sector sources the smallest use of external advice is for the smallest firms, with use increasing up to about 20–49, or 50–99 employees, and then either levelling off, or having an inverse "U" pattern. The overall pattern of use is shown in table 4 between the main categories of

Table 4
Summary of Use of Sources by Firm Size
(% of Respondents Using Each Source,
Multiple Responses Allowed)

Firm Size	All Private Sector (excluding business friends)	All Public Sector	Business Friends/ Relatives
1–4	90.4	29.0	47.5
5–9	94.3	32.8	40.8
10–19	96.1	45.2	37.9
20–49	96.8	45.6	30.2
50–99	97.7	50.3	33.6
100–149	96.7	45.8	31.7
150–199	98.3	55.2	37.9
200–249	100.0	51.4	31.4
>250	90.7	48.1	24.1

all private sources (except business friends/relatives), all public sources, and business friends/relatives.

Overall the analysis confirms the importance of the private sector as the dominant source of supply of external advice, with sectoral and local associations adding a further collective private source of supply, so that overall the private market supplies 86% of all external advice and accounts for 9 out of the top 10 ranked suppliers. It is clear, however, that government-backed suppliers have a specific niche where they are consulted in 14% of cases. Of these government sources the most widely used, by some margin, is Business Link, followed by TECs. Moreover, Business Link seems to have overtaken the chambers as a source of local advice in terms of numbers of users, despite their relative newness and known high level of quality variation across the country (Roche 1997). There is however considerable complexity in local delivery systems since many local Business Links are in fact part of the local chamber or TEC, or both. Also most enterprise agencies are part of the TEC, Business Link or chamber, so that this group of agents has to be looked at to a large extent as a single group with a variety of local brands and management. Taking this approach suggests that the local delivery system of supports of Business Link, TEC/LEC and chambers is an important addition to the market of external advice, but is very much secondary to that provided by the specialized private sector advisors.

3.4 Range of Sources of Advice Used

As is clear in table 3, most respondents in the surveys used several different sources of advice over the previous 3 years. Table 5 shows the range of sources used. The mean number of sources used was 4.5 and the mode was 4, within a strong clustering from two to seven sources. This is similar to other studies, e.g. O"Farrell and Moffat (1995) find an average of 3.9 to 4.2 sources and similar values are evident in Keeble *et al.* (1992),

Table 5
External Sources of Business Advice from Sole and Multiple Sources (Percentage of Respondents Using Each Source Who Use It as a Sole Service, or as One of Two, 3–5, or 6 or More Services)

Advice Source	Sole Source	2	3–5	6 or more
Accountant	52.7	70.6	89.1	95.8
Solicitor	9.1	24.3	53.1	83.9
Bank	4.8	32.2	62.2	87.5
Business friend/relative	4.2	10.2	32.8	62.8
Customers	6.7	15.3	39.8	78.0
Suppliers	3.0	5.9	24.9	68.6
Consultants	7.3	9.8	22.1	57.7
Chamber of Commerce	1.2	8.2	14.0	44.3
Trade/Professional Associations	5.5	11.0	22.0	56.4
Local Enterprise Agency	1.2	2.0	6.8	30.7
Local TEC or Scottish Enterprise	1.8	4.7	11.3	47.0
Business Link/Shop/Connect	2.4	5.1	15.0	50.1
Business Link	2.6	5.5	15.8	52.6
Business Shop & Connect	0.0	0.0	6.5	26.7
Rural Development Commission or Regional Agency	0.0	0.8	2.2	10.2
N (All)	165	255	1016	915

Curran and Blackburn (1994), Doggett and Hepple (1995). Vatne (1995) quotes a mean of 7 sources in his Norwegian case studies, which is unusually high.

Comparing the sources by their pattern of use, table 5 shows that accountants dominate the use of single sources. In cases where only two sources are used, accountants together with solicitors and/or banks are the dominant sources. Where three to five sources are used the spread of use among other private sector sources increases to 20–40%, but public sector sources reach 15% at the highest (that for Business Link). Only when six or more sources are consulted do public sector sources become used by a large proportion of respondents.

Table 5 therefore seems to indicate that there are rather different SME types in their use of services. A first group of SMEs uses a small number of sources and these focus highly on the private sector, especially technical professionals. Of the sample there are 6.7% users of a single source, 17% use one or two sources, and 30.9% are users of one, two or three sources. A second group of SMEs are heavy users of business advice, and it is these who use a significant number, but a diversified range, of public sector supports as well as private sector sources. A total of 37.1% of the sample fulfil this description and use six or more sources. For this group Business Link is used in 50% of cases, followed by TECs (47%) and enterprise agencies (31%). The third group of SMEs, which is 20–30% of the sample, is a mixture of the previous two groups, predominantly private sector users across a broad range of sources, but with some use of usually a single public sector source (among which Business Link is the most significant).

3.5 Impact

Turning to the assessed impact of the different suppliers there are some constraints on interpretation due to non-responses which range from 5.2 to 14.4% for different sources. For the Rural Development Commission, non-response is 32.5%, but most firms are not in eligible areas so this is of less concern. The non-responses are generally highest for all public sector and association bodies. They are also higher for the service sector, smallest firms and slow growth firms. There is probably, as a result, some over-estimation of impact since it is believed that many non-respondents did not respond because they gave a low impact rating to the services. If this is true, the over estimation of impact will be greatest for the public sector and association services.

Table 6 shows the impact perceived by respondents. Impact is measured on a 5-point scale from 1 (no impact) to 5 (crucial). Table 6 demonstrates that only customers and accountants achieve an impact rating of "important" or greater, on average (i.e. 3 or above). They are followed by friends, solicitors, suppliers, consultants and banks, which all have ratings between 2.7 and 3.0. There is then something of a gap in impact before we reach the intermediary collective and government-backed bodies, which all rate between 2.16 and 2.44. Within this rating the two collective associations differ considerably, with the sector bodies being the highest in impact of this intermediary group and the local chambers the lowest.

The survey thus indicates a rather marked differentiation in the significance of external suppliers in terms of their impact. This interrelates with the sort of advice that is being sought from or supplied to each firm. It is clear that there is an important differentiation of the specialist professionals, customers, suppliers and business friends, not only in terms of their much greater level of use as external suppliers, but also in terms of their much higher levels of general impacts. It is they that are the largest and most crucial market for external sources of business advice. In contrast, the role of intermediary collective associations and government-backed suppliers appears to be chiefly not only to fill gaps but also to provide advice of a less significant kind in terms of assessed impact.

The differentiation of impacts between sectors of firm (table 6), shows a relatively small level of differentiation of impacts. Differences between firms of different sizes generally show the impacts increasing with firm size, except for the use of friends. The largest differences between size groups are for solicitors and consultants, although the overall differences of impact with size are fairly small.

Employment growth differences in impact of advice between firms (table 7) are also generally small, with the fastest growth firms experiencing the highest impacts. The most significant differences between firms by growth record are for use of accountants, solicitors and customers. Similarly the most innovative firms generally have the higher levels of impact, but the difference between firms in level of impact are again fairly small, with the only significant differences being for use of accountants, customers and suppliers.

The results of this survey can be compared with other surveys assessing impacts. Unfortunately few other surveys have sought to assess impact across a wide range of sources of advice for a wide range of businesses. However, two other surveys do allow comparisons.

Table 6

Assessment of the Impact of the Sources of Advice; Mean Impact, and Impact by Sector and Firm Size (Mean Scores from 1 = No Impact, to 5 = Crucial Impact)

Impact	All		Manufac-turing		Services		Micro		Small		Medium	
	Mean	N	Mean	N	Mean	N	Mean	N	Mean	N	Mean	N
Accountant	3.10	1986	3.08	1165	3.13	821	3.0***	846	3.19***	900	3.16***	218
Solicitor	2.80	1349	2.72***	781	2.91***	568	2.64***	430	2.82***	702	3.09***	205
Bank	2.70	1480	2.71	884	2.70	596	2.61***	587	2.75***	706	2.88***	171
Business friend/relative	2.99	910	2.97	495	3.02	415	3.02	458	2.99	354	2.85	88
Customers	3.22	1136	3.17*	658	3.28	478	3.13***	459	3.24***	504	3.40***	161
Suppliers	2.78	882	2.79	578	2.78	304	2.74	352	2.77	395	2.92	125
Consultants	2.73	769	2.64**	445	2.86**	324	2.56***	210	2.77***	427	2.91***	127
Local Chamber of Commerce	2.16	551	2.24***	355	2.01***	196	2.01**	174	2.24**	304	2.16**	68
Trade/Professional association	2.44	753	2.49	393	2.39	360	2.38*	267	2.42*	362	2.59*	114
Local Enterprise Agency	2.28	345	2.28	207	2.29	138	2.24	136	2.28	161	2.36	44
Local TEC	2.40	500	2.42	336	2.35	164	2.36*	132	2.34*	270	2.61*	94
Scottish Enterprise	2.74	47	2.84	25	2.64	22	2.12	17	3.28	25	2.20	5
Business Link	2.36	580	2.38	401	2.31	178	2.21**	175	2.44**	326	2.32**	76
Business Shop & Connect	2.38	29	2.41	17	2.33	12	2.38	13	2.45	3	2.00	13
Rural Development Commission or Regional Agency	2.22	110	2.33	76	1.97	34	2.25	36	2.12	59	2.43	14
All	2.77	11427	2.75	6817	2.81	4610	2.72	4292	2.79	5478	2.89	1513

($^*p > 0.01$; $^{**}p > 0.05$; $^{***}p > 0.01$ tested as in Table 3).

Table 7

Assessment of the Impact of the Sources of Advice by Respondent's Growth History over Previous Three Years (Mean Scores from 1 = No Impact, to 5 = Crucial Impact)

Impact	Stable/ Declining		Medium Growth		Fast Growth	
	Mean	N	Mean	N	Mean	N
Accountant	2.97***	577	3.12***	408	3.23***	454
Solicitor	2.66***	341	2.73***	301	2.96***	350
Bank	2.65	403	2.63	309	2.72	358
Business friend/relative	2.92*	259	2.82*	153	3.03*	221
Customers	3.10***	307	3.12***	249	3.36***	267
Suppliers	2.75	250	2.79	194	2.72	213
Consultants	2.66	201	2.73	189	2.77	197
Local Chamber of Commerce	2.12	137	2.10	145	2.15	127
Trade/Professional association	2.50**	217	2.23**	171	2.48**	160
Local Enterprise Agency	2.21	97	2.19	68	2.41	86
Local TEC	2.22*	125	2.46	123	2.53*	131
Scottish Enterprise/LEC	3.00***	8	2.55***	11	2.07***	15
Business Link	2.28*	148	2.26*	144	2.52*	140
Business Shop & Connect	2.14	7	2.67	3	2.36	11
Rural Development Commission or Regional Agency	2.08*	25	1.93*	28	2.51*	37
All	2.70	3102	2.69	2496	2.85	2767

(*$p > 0.1$; **$p > 0.5$; ***$p > 0.01$; tested as in Table 3).

Doggett and Hepple's (1995) results, summarized in table 8, show that fairly positive ratings are received for all sources, with 70–90% rated good or very good. However, the professional specialists (accountants and solicitors), friends and consultants have the highest ratings of good, with the DTI and TECs having the lowest ratings. The Doggett and Hepple results in table 8 are also interesting because they compare external with internal advice. Only the other/ friend category exceeds the impact assessment of internal staff, but all sources have a higher frequency of use than internal staff. This survey appears to suggest stronger distinctions between sources than the present survey. This is less true in a satisfaction survey by 3i/MORI (1997). Although this shows the professionals having the higher levels of satisfaction, the DTI in this case gets a very high satisfaction rating.

The present survey thus shows similar but less marked differences between sources in their impact than that found in other surveys. However it is an important conclusion to be drawn from our assessment of impact that there are only relatively small systematic differences

Table 8
Percentage of Rankings of "Good" and "Fairly Good" of External and Internal Sources of Advice and Their Frequency of Use

	"Good"	"Fairly Good"	Frequency Advice Sought	
			≥6 per year	<6 per year
Accountant	53.7	42.1	49.6	50.4
Banks: principal	34.8	53.6	31.0	69.0
Banks: second/third	39.5	44.2	53.6	46.4
Solicitor	56.8	33.8	49.5	50.5
Consultants	53.3	36.7	46.3	53.7
Other/friends	64.0	36.0	—	—
TECs	21.7	52.2	23.1	76.9
Department of Trade and Industry	17.9	59.0	25.0	75.0
Internal staff	63.8	34.8	7.4	92.6

Source: adapted from Doggett and Hepple 1995: Table 15.

between types of SME firms in the levels of impact they experience, with firm size being the main and most significant differentiating characteristic between businesses. Generally, however (except for firm size), the differences in impact between firm types are not statistically significant. Moreover the average level of impact, at 2.93 across all sources, indicates that external suppliers are generally filling important rather than crucial needs of their clients. The important finding of the research is therefore that the most important contrasts exist in terms of the frequency of use of different sources of advice rather than type of client. This suggests a fairly marked segmentation of the market between different suppliers, which in turn directs attention to the type of services supplied and the business objectives that the services are seeking to support.

4. Conclusion

This paper has provided a large-scale assessment of the extent, sources and impact of external advice using new survey evidence of SMEs of up to 500 employees in Britain. It is the first large-scale coverage of all main sources of supply of SME advice, ranging from the private sector, through social networks, to business associations and government-backed agents. The results, although specific to Britain, also have a more general relevance.

A chief finding is confirmation of the large scale of external advice, 95% of all surveyed firms use at least one source, an increase from 85.8% in the similar SBRC (1992) survey of 1991. Second, a very marked differentiation of the scale of the market exists for different sources. Overall the private sector dominates, accounting for 86% of all responses.

Third, the conclusions are generally in line with previous studies, as summarized in tables 1 and 2. However, the larger sample size that the authors have been able to deploy, and the more recent date of the survey, does lead to a key difference in conclusion compared to the MORI (1994) survey, which was to a large extent a baseline survey for Business Link. The MORI survey is confirmed as significantly out of line with our analysis and the general pattern found in most other surveys. Since this survey was a key foundation and benchmark for Business Link evaluation it is suggested that its findings should be used by government only with great caution. It appears particularly inconsistent in its findings of high levels of use of consultants compared to professional specialists, and its low level of use of TECs and enterprise agencies.

The paper is primarily of significance, however, in confirming that the level of trust appears to explain the levels of use and impact of different sources of advice. Within the private sector in particular there appears to be confirmation of the hypothesis that levels of use and impact depend on the extent to which trust-producing mechanisms exist. Those suppliers that have a high level of specialization and draw great trust from professional self-regulation have the highest levels of use: accountants, solicitors and banks. These draw on institutional trust. The rather lower levels of use of business associations indicates both their weaker self-regulation, and hence the lower institutional trust of these suppliers, and also the smaller level of development of the advice services that they are concerned with. The existence of personal trust appears to be a strong force behind the use of business friends/relatives and suppliers and customers, although the latter will also exercise an important element of coercive market power. Consultants, whom we expect to be mainly dependent on market signalling, using reputation, branding and recommendation, have a relatively low level of use. This is suggestive of the difficulties of consultants breaking into a market for advice, which tends to be dominated by specialist suppliers who benefit from a higher level of trust derived from either institutional regimes or personal relationships.

The public sector sources all have a low level of trust, depending more on marketing and access to grants. They have a lower level of use than almost all private sector sources, except for Business Link, but this appears to have surpassed only chambers of commerce. However, the relationships between the public agents is complex, with TECs and LECs, local government, enterprise agencies and chambers of commerce all partners in delivery of Business Link, with many Business Link services delivered by these partners and many of the partner's services branded as Business Link. Looked at as a group these local suppliers are now contributing a considerable part of the supply of advice in Britain, and indeed are reaching a comparable level to that for the Enterprise Initiative which the similar SBRC (1992) survey found was used by 33.4% of respondents. It must be questioned, however, whether users are helped by fragmenting supply between these different agents at the local level. Certainly this appears to reduce their overall impact, as discussed below.

The impact levels of different sources also appear to be strongly interrelated with the level of specialization, and the levels of trust that we argue apply. Specialist professionals, customers, suppliers and business friends all have high levels of either personal or institutional trust. They are not only the main sources of supply but also those with the largest impact. They are thus the largest and most crucial part of the market for SME advice. In contrast, intermediary collective associations and government-backed suppliers appear chiefly to fill niche gaps with advice of a less significant kind in terms of perceived impact. Consultants fall between these two groups with a high impact chiefly for service industries and larger firms. In general, impact ratings vary much less by SME type than does the level of use, but differences are not generally statistically significant except for firm size. This suggests a fairly marked segmentation of the market between suppliers for different purposes, with impact varying more by choice of supply source than by firm type.

A further finding is the very significant differences in use of advice by firm size, but with different patterns for different sources. Most private sector sources experience rapidly increasing use from firms up to 20–49 or 50–99 employees in size, with a levelling off after that size. For banks and accountants, however, there is some evidence of an inverse "U" distribution. Public sources vary in the influence of size depending largely on their targeting and eligibility criteria. However, an interesting contrast exists between Business Link in England, which shows an inverse "U" distribution, and the similar Business Shop and Business Connect in Scotland and Wales, which shows a chief focus on firms of 10–49 employees and those of over 200 employees, almost the inverse of the Business Link targeting. The use of business friends and relatives is the only source that systematically declines as firm size increases, although this remains an important source, used by over 25% of firms, for all size classes.

The authors have also demonstrated an important difference between SMEs in their use of either a narrow or a wide range of (multiple) advice sources. Respondents appear to fall into three groups: first, those firms that use a narrow range of one, two or three sources, which are almost entirely drawn from the private sector; second, those firms that draw heavily on public sector sources do so chiefly among many other sources. A third group uses predominantly private sector sources with a single public source, most commonly Business Link. These differences between types of SME use of advice are the subject of further investigation.

The authors would expect many of these conclusions to hold true in other countries. Although the detailed environments of trust examined in this paper are specific to Britain, the general pattern of relationships between advisors and their clients should be similar in other countries. For example, Tordoir (1994) contrasts client-supplier "sparring" relations, where strong interpersonal relations are important, "jobbing relations" where technical specialists are primarily used, and "sales" relations where services are sold "off-the-shelf" in a pre-tailored form. The present results suggest that jobbing relations draw on high trust self-regulatory mechanisms and have, as a result, high levels of use and impact. Sparring relations appear to chiefly influence business consultants and to a lesser extent government initiatives such as Business Link. Here considerable effort has to go into re-tailoring advice and high reliance is placed on intense interactions. The effort involved tends to reduce the level of use compared with professional specialists, and the impact is also lower and more highly variable. As commented by Tordoir (1994: 228) "trust and good interpersonal 'chemistry' ", are important, but the present results suggest that they are extremely variable in extent.

As far as the full range of advisors has been compared in other international studies, the present results generally point in a similar direction (Harrington *et al.* 1991, Illeris 1994, Moulaert and Tödtling 1995). However, the interpretation of the range of use and impact in terms of institutional and trust-producing mechanisms clearly requires further international comparative research. In particular it is important to see how far differences in institutional environments affect the extent of use and impact of external business advice.

Acknowledgements

The Cambridge University Centre for Business Research and its SME survey are funded by the Economic and Social Research Council, whose support is gratefully acknowledged. The authors are also grateful for the additional support of the Cambridge University Newton Trust and Leverhulme Trust.

References

Amin, A. and Thrift, N. 1992 Neo-Marshallian nodes in global networks, *International Journal of Urban and Regional Research*, 16: 571–587.

Bank of England 1996 *The Financing of Technology-based Small Firms* (London: Bank of England).

Bannock, G. and Albach, H. 1991 *Small Business Policy in Europe: Britain, Germany and the European Commission* (London and Bonn: Anglo-German Foundation).

Bannock, G. and Doran, A. 1991 *Business Banking in the 1990s: A New Era of Competition* (Dublin: Lafferty Group).

Barclays Bank 1994 *Bridging the Skills Gap* (London: Barclays Bank).

Bennett, R. J. 1995 The re-focusing of small business services in enterprise agencies: the influence TECs and LECs, *International Small Business Journal*, 13(4): 35–55.

Bennett, R. J. 1996 Can transaction cost economics explain voluntary Chambers of Commerce? *Journal of Institutional and Theoretical Economics*, 152: 654–680.

Bennett, R. J. 1998 Business associations and their potential contribution to SMEs competetiveness, *Entrepreneurship and Regional Development*, 10: 243–260.

Berry-Lound, D. and Parsons, D. 1994 *Human Resource Information and Advisory Services to SMEs* (Horsham: Sussex HOST Consultancy).

Birley, S. and Westhead, P. 1992 A comparison of new firms in "assisted" and "non-assisted" areas in Great Britain, *Entrepreneurship and Regional Development*, 4: 299–338.

British Chambers of Commerce [BCC] 1994 *Government Services to Business: Small Firms Survey No. 8* (London British Chambers of Commerce and Alex Lawric).

Brusco, S. 1982 The Emilian model: productive decentralization and social integration, *Cambridge Journal of Economics*, 6: 167–184.

Bryson, J. R. 1997 *Business Service Firms, Service Space and the Management of Change* WP 62 (Cambridge: ESRC Centre for Business Research, University of Cambridge).

Bryson, J. R., Keeble, D. and Wood, P. 1997 The creation and growth of small business service firms in post-industrial Britain, *Small Business Economics*, 9: 345–360.

Centre for Business Research [CBR] 1998 *Enterprise Britain* (Cambridge: ESRC Centre for Business Research, University of Cambridge).

Clark, T. 1993 The market provision of management services, information, asymmetries and service quality—some market solutions: an empirical example, *British Journal of Management*, 4: 235–251.

Confederation of British Industry [CBI] 1993 *Finance for Growth: Meeting the Financial Needs of Small and Medium Enterprises* (London: Confederation of British Industry).

Confederation of British Industry [CBI] 1994 *Management Development: A Survey of Small and Medium Sized Businesses* (London: Confederation of British Industry with Touche Ross).

Confederation of British Industry [CBI] 1995 *Managing to Grow: Developing*

Management Competence in Small and Medium Sized Enterprises (London: Confederation of British Industry).

Cowling, M., Samuels, J. and Sugden, R. 1991 *Small Firms and Clearing Banks* (London: Association of British Chambers of Commerce).

Curran, J. and Blackburn, R. A. 1994 *Small Firms and Local Networks: The Death of the Local Economy?* (London: Paul Chapman).

Curran, J., Jarvis, R., Blackburn, R. A. and Black, S. 1993 Networks and small firms: constructs, methodological strategies and some finding, *International Small Business Journal*, 11(2): 13–25.

Deakins, D. and Hussain, G. 1991 Risk assessments with asymmetric information, *International Journal of Bank Marketing*, 11(1): 24–31.

Department of Employment [DE] 1991a *Keys to Growth for Owner-Managers Seeking in Expand* (London: Price Waterhouse and Department of Employment).

Department of Employment [DE] 1991b *A Survey of Owner-managed Business* (London: Department of Employment).

Department of Trade and Industry [DTI] 1990 *The Enterprise Initiative: An Introduction* (London: Department of Trade and Industry).

Department of Trade and Industry [DTI] 1995a *Consultancy Brokerage Service: Listing with CBS—Guidance Conditions* (London: Department of Trade and Industry).

Department of Trade and Industry [DTI] 1995b UK Management Training and Advisory Services for SMEs, in *Best Practice Policies Small and Medium Sized Enterprises* (Paris: Organisation for Economic Cooperation and Development), pp. 143–149.

Department of Trade and Industry [DTI] 1997 *Business Link Statistics, July–September 1987* (London: Business Link Directorate, Department of Trade and Industry).

Doggett, P. and Hepple, L. W. 1995 *Corporate Banking Survey 1995—England, Wales, Scotland and Northern Ireland* (London: Mees Pierson NY).

Ennew, C. T. and Binks, M. R. 1996 The impact of service quality and service characteristics on customer retention: small businesses and their banks in the UK, *British Journal of Management*, 7: 219–230.

Financial Times [FT] 1996 The voice trainer: the new President of the Chartered Accountants talks about his strategies for unity in diversity, *Financial Times*, 20 February 1998.

Financial Times [FT] 1998 Minister to ponder proposals for firms' regulation, *Financial Times*, 20 February 1998.

Granovetter, M. 1985 Economic action and social structure: the problem of embeddedness, *American Journal of Sociology*, 91: 481–510.

Harrington, J. W., MacPherson, A. D. and Lombard, J. R. 1991 Interregional trade in producer services: review and synthesis, *Growth and Change*, 22: 75–94.

Hendry, C., Jones, A., Arthur, W. and Pettigrew, A. 1991 *Human resources Development in the Small and Medium Sized Enterprise*. Research Paper No. 88 (London: Department of Employment).

HM Government 1988 *Enterprise Initiative*, Cmd 278 (London: HMSO).

Howells, J. and Green, A. 1986 Location, technology and industrial organisation in UK services, *Progress in Planning*, 6: 88–183.

Illersis, S. (1994) Proximity between service producers and service users, *Tijschrift voor Ecohomische en Sociale Geograpfie*, 85: 294–302.

Institute of Export/NGM Credit Insurance Ltd [IoM/NCM] 1997 *Fifth Surcey of International Services Pro-*

vided to Exporters (London: Institute of Export/NCM Credit Insurance Ltd).

Keeble, D. and Bryson, J. 1996 Small-firm creation and growth, regional development and the North-South divide in Britain, *Environment and Planning A*, 28: 909–934.

Keeble, D., Bryson, J. and Wood, P. 1991 Small firms, business service growth and regional development in the UK: some empirical findings, *Regional Studies*, 25: 439–457.

Keeble, D., Tyler, P., Broom, G. and Lewis, J. 1992 *Business Success in the Countryside: The Performance of Rural Enterprise* (London: HMSO).

Kirby, D. A. and Jones-Evans, D. 1997 Small technology-based professional contultancy services in the United Kingdom, *Service Industries Journal*, 17: 155–172.

Kirby, D. A. and King, S. H. 1997 Accountants and small firm development: filling the expectation, *Service Industries Journal*, 17: 294–304.

Kutscher, R. E. 1988 Growth of services employment in the US, in Guile, B. R. and Quinn, J. B. (eds), *Technology in Services: Policies for Growth, Trade and Employment* (Washington, DC: National Academy Press).

Lloyds Bank/SBRT 1998 Business support agencies, *Quarterly Small Business Management Report*, 5(4) (Milton Keynes: Small Business Research Trust, Open University).

Mills, P. K. and Margulies, N. 1980 Toward a pure typology of service organizations, *Academy of Management Review*, 5: 255–265.

MORI 1994 *"Business Links": The Business Advice Market among Small and Medium-sized Enterprises* (London: Department of Trade and Industry).

Moulaert, F. and Tödtling, F. (eds) 1995 The geography of advanced producers services in Europe, *Progress in Planning*, 43: 2–4, 274 pp.

O'Farrell, P. N. and Moffatt, W. A. R. 1995 Business services and their impact upon client performance: an exploratory interregional analysis, *Regional Studies*, 29: 111–124.

O'Farrell, P. N. and Wood, P. A. 1998 Internationalisation by business service firms: towards a new regionally-based conceptual framework, *Environment and Planning A*, 30: 109–128.

O'Farrell, P. N., Hitchens, D. M. W. N. and Moffat, I. A. R. 1992 The competitiveness of business service firms in Scotland and South East England: a matched pairs analysis, *Regional Studies*, 26: 519–533.

O'Farrell, P. N., Moffat, I. A. R. and Hitchens, D. M. W. N. 1993 Manufacturing demand for business services in a core and peripheral region: does flexible production imply vertical disintegration of busines services? *Regional Studies*, 27: 385–400.

Perry, M. 1992 Flexible production, externalisation and the interpretation of business service growth, *Service Industries Journals*, 12: 1–16.

Priest, S. P. 1999 Business Link SME services: targeting, innovation and charging, *Environment and Planning: Government and Policy*, 16.

Roche, B. 1997 *Enhanced Business Links: A Vision for the 21st Century* (London: Department of Trade and Industry).

Sabel, C. F. 1989 Flexible specialization and the re-emergence of regional economics, in Hirst, P. and Zeitlin, J. (eds), *Reversing Industrial Decline* (Leamington Spa: Berg).

Schneiberg, M. and Hollingsworth, J. R. 1991 Can transaction cost economics explain trade associations? in Czada, R. M. and Windoff-Héritier, A. (eds), *Political Choice: Institutions, Rule, and the Limits of Rationality* (Frankfurt am Main: Campus Verlag).

Segal Quince Wicksteed [SQW] 1989 *Evaluation of the Consultancy Initiative* (London: Segal Quince Wicksteed for Department of Trade and Industry).

Segal Quince Wicksteed [SQW] 1994 *Evaluation of the Consultancy Initiatives: Fourth Stage* (London: Segal Quince Wicksteed/HMSO).

Shapiro, C. 1983 Premiums for high quality products as returns to reputations, *Quarterly Journal of Economics*, 43: 659–679.

Small Business Research Centre [SBRC] 1992 *The State of British Enterprise: Growth, Innovation and Competitive Advantage in Small and Medium-sized Firms* (Cambridge: Small Business Research Centre, University of Cambridge).

Smallbone, D., North, D. and Leigh, R. 1993 The use of external assistance by mature SMEs in the UK: some policy implications, *Entrepreneurship and Regional Development*, 5: 279–285.

Smith, A. M. 1989 Service quality: relationships between banks and their small business clients, *International Journal of Bank Marketing*, 7(5): 28–35.

Storey, D. J. 1994 *Understanding the Small Business Sector* (London: Routlege).

Storey, D. J. 1996 *Assessing the Economic Impact of the DTI Marketing Initiative upon Small Firms, 1988–94* (Warwick: SME Centre, University of Warwick).

Taylor, M. and Singleton, S. 1993 The communal resource: transaction costs and the solution of collective action problems, *Politics and Society*, 21: 195–214.

The Times 1996 Those who adapt will flourish: Frances Gibb talks in his last week as secretary-general of the Law Society, 28 May 1996.

Tordoir, P. P. 1994 Transactions of professional business services and spatial systems, *Tijdschrift voor Economische en Sociale Geografie*, 85: 322–332.

Turok, I. and Richardson, P. 1991 New firms and local economic development: evidence from West Lothian, *Regional Studies*, 25: 71–86.

van Waarden, F. 1991 Two logics of collective action? Business associations as distinct from trade unions: the problems of associations of organisations, in Sadowski, D. and Jacobi, O. (eds), *Employers' Associations in Europe: Policy and Organisation* (Baden-Baden: Nomos), pp. 51–84.

Vatne, F. 1995 Local resource mobilisation and internationalisation strategies in small and medium sized enterprises, *Environment and Planning A*, 27: 63–80.

Wood, P. A., Bryson, J. and Keeble, D. 1993 Regional patterns of small firm development in the business services: evidence from the UK, *Environment and Planning A*, 25: 256–700.

Wren, C. and Storey, D. J. 1988 *Estimating the Impact of Publicly Subsidized Advisory Services upon Small Firm Performance: The Case of the DTI Marketing Initiation* (Warwick: SME Centre, University of Warwick).

Zucker, L. G. 1986 The production of trust: institutional sources of economic structure, 1840–1920, in Straw, B. M. and Cummings, L. L. (eds), *Research in Organizational Behaviour* (London: JAI Press).

Si/MORI 1997 *The 3i MORI Survey of Key Independent Businesses in Britain* (London: 3i).

The Small Business Assistance Dilemma: Is the Disparity between the Offerings of Support Agencies and the Needs of Businesses Irreconcilable?
by John Breen and Sue Bergin-Seers

There is a wide range of service providers who have varying motives for supplying assistance to small businesses in Australia. Despite the sizeable numbers of both suppliers and consumers of assistance it is believed that the marketplace for small business assistance operates inefficiently. This inefficiency is described as a disparity or misfit between the learning opportunities offered by service providers to small business and the learning needs of small business owner/operators.

This paper provides an analysis of the learning activity that currently exists in the small enterprise sector. The role of communication in bringing supply and demand closer together is discussed and a proposition is developed to alleviate the learning disparity via a more proactive approach to communication by service providers. Two small enterprise projects are used to test the proposition. The findings provide guidance for the more effective functioning of organisations that serve and support small businesses.

Introduction

The provision of assistance to small businesses is available from a range of service providers who have varying motives for supplying such assistance. At the same time there are almost one million small businesses in Australia that have a broad range of needs for assistance. Despite the large numbers of both suppliers and consumers of assistance there is strong evidence to suggest that the marketplace for small business assistance still operates inefficiently. On the supply side there are many provider offerings that are not taken up in large numbers while at the same time there are many operator needs that are not being satisfied. Such an inefficiency can best be described as a disparity or misfit between the learning opportunities offered by service providers to small business and the learning needs of small business owner operators.

Originally appeared in *Small Enterprise Research*, 2002, Volume 10, Number 1.

This paper begins with an analysis of the learning activity that currently exists in the small enterprise sector. The different perspectives of service provider and small business operator are considered and an introduction to the learning disparity follows. The role of communication in bringing supply and demand closer together is discussed and a proposition is developed to alleviate the learning disparity. The proposition suggests that the learning disparity can be decreased if there is a more proactive approach to communication taken by the service providers. Two small enterprise projects are used to test the proposition. The data suggests that the outcomes from the project support the proposition. The findings provide guidance for the more effective functioning of organisations charged with the provision of service to small businesses. Finally some suggestions for additional research are made.

The Small Business Assistance Landscape

Organisations that provide services to small business include government agencies and departments, educational institutions, quasi community organisations, industry associations and private operators such as accountants, lawyers and consultants. The assistance for small business provided by government has usually been motivated by economic considerations, notably to increase employment opportunities and economic development by having better functioning small businesses. Industry associations are generally trying to meet the needs of their membership, while the private operators are trying to earn an economic return.

Gibb (2000) categorises the different types of support offered to small business as assistance, intervention and training. He explains such support in two contexts. The first one focuses on

small business development policies and is usually within the context of subsidised programs of public intervention. The other view of support structures incorporates accountants, bankers, educational institutions, chambers of commerce and business networks, which are commercial services and part of the conduct of normal business activity. Howard and Hine (1997) describe three different forms of government assistance to small business in Australia. They include advisory services offered through quasi government agencies, which they argue, act as a multiplier agency; start-up support including training and financial assistance designed to offset unemployment; and finally business incubator development which aims to foster successful business operations.

On the demand side, the take up of small business assistance offerings by small businesses is inconsistent. Most businesses rely on their accountant for assistance with statutory taxation matters (Peacock 1997, Holmes and Nicholl 1990, Yellow Pages 1995), but are less likely to use accountants for business advice. Participation in government programs is low amongst small businesses, but it is particularly low in the smallest businesses. The government program that is attractive to the smallest businesses is the New Enterprise Incentive Scheme, which is designed for start-ups and attracts some funding subsidy (Industry Commission 1997). Gibb (1997) summarises the literature on small business training by indicating it does not appeal to small firms for a variety of reasons including time and resource concerns. Furthermore he argues that these concerns were first identified over 25 years ago and were still valid in the late 1990's. Holmes, Butler and Lennon (1995) reported on similar constraints to the take-up of training in the Australian small enterprise context.

In summary, the supply side of small business assistance consists of numerous players in both the government and private sector who offer a broad range of activities designed to help business operators carry out their business activities more effectively. On the demand side there is a large number of small businesses, with varying needs but with little inclination to participate in small business learning. There is clearly a disparity between the learning opportunities offered by service providers and those taken up by the small business operators. It is this mis-match that indicates the inefficiencies in the market and the need for greater compatibility among all involved.

Learning is important to small business survival, innovation and profitability (Chaston et al. 1999; Massey & Walker 1999). Small business has many of the characteristics of an effective business learning organisation (Gibb 1997), however, it has often been assumed that small business learning takes place in the same way as in large business. Service providers need to be aware of the influence of the small business founder in defining the business concept and mode of operation (Watson & Hogarth-Scott, 1998; Penn et al. 1998; Kerr & McDougall, 1999). The owner/operator has a key role in shaping the culture of the business, which is important as culture acts as a filter through which learning occurs (Guglielmi, 2000). Learning occurs as a result of critical reflection on one's own experiences and through active experimentation, not just through formal training (Drejer, 2000; Gibb, 1997). All businesses do not learn in the same way nor need support in the form that it is often interpreted by educators and support service providers (Kearney, 1998; Hawke, 1999).

In an ideal world the demand for small business support and the supply of such support should be matched, however that is rarely the case. Many service providers are inflexible in their offerings because of organisational constraints such as the time they have available for the delivery of services and the resources they have available for activities such as training. There is also a lack of understanding of small business learning needs.

On the demand side the learning needs of small business operators tend to be difficult to categorise because the needs are associated with the current status of the business and usually involve an immediate problem that needs to be solved. At a more strategic level, most small business operators don't realise they have a need for learning. They are generally too busy to go looking for support or are cynical about the impact of such support. Finally there is also a lack of awareness of what learning opportunities are available.

Therefore this disparity between the offerings of support agencies and the needs of small business operators is caused mainly by an awareness gap. That is, each side lacks an awareness of what the other has to offer or is seeking. It may be argued that if the communication between the two parties is improved, then the awareness of what learning opportunities are available will improve and lessen the disparity between offerings and needs.

Literature

The level of understanding about effective learning practices amongst service providers is often limited because of their narrow views about what constitutes learning. It is not generally understood that many small business owner/operators are often actively involved in informal learning. In the workplace, staff are regularly involved in activities that are not always viewed as learning, for example discussions with product representatives, attending seminars organised by suppliers, gleaning knowledge from new staff or borrowing approaches learned from their business competitors (Kerr & McDougall, 1999). Small business owner/operators learn in a variety of contexts. They learn from peers, learn by doing, learn by feedback from customers and suppliers, learn by coping, learn by experiment, learn by problem solving and opportunity taking and learn by mistakes (Gibb, 1997; Kearney, 1998).

Gibb (2000) identified a range of economic, product and knowledge factors, which inhibit small business service providers in the delivery of appropriate support. With respect to economic inhibitors the most appropriate delivery mechanism for small business support requires flexibility to suit the business operator, however such delivery is costly and often not economical for service providers (Kearney, 1998). Furthermore dealing with small business involves considerable investment in terms of establishing reputation, financing and customisation. Finally many support agencies are dependent on government funds for their existence and a shift in government policy can undermine their efforts and the returns available (Gibb, 1997).

The product related inhibitor refers to the fact that the support activity often lacks flexibility and relevance to the small business. The delivery is usually designed to suit the agency rather than the business. There are frequent complaints about the lack of understanding of the particular industry area and that the work tends to be content focused rather than process focused. Other criticisms include the use of generic programs rather than tailored activities, and the complicated bureaucratic procedures necessary to enable participation (Kerr & McDougall, 1999).

The knowledge obstacle refers to the lack of understanding of the culture of small business and their learning needs (Gibb, 1997; Kearney, 1998; Sparrow, 1999). Additionally, support services and agencies tend to assume that all small

businesses need assistance. They often do not fully understand that an informal, somewhat ad-hoc approach to change and development by businesses through on-the-job learning and use of business networks may adequately satisfy their needs and should not be underestimated (Kearney, 1998; Gibb, 1997; Gibb, 2000).

A number of factors influence the approach that small business operators take to support services. Small business operators are very cost conscious and will make a decision about utilising support by comparing the benefit of gaining the information against the cost of not accessing the information. Their attraction to support can also depend on the learning focus of the business operator, that is, do they operate their business as a learning organisation? Small businesses are usually attracted to learning when it aids in solving problems and enables the seizing of opportunities (Gibb, 2000). They tend to be very focused on their immediate problems.

"Small business operators are only interested in assistance which contributes to the solution of today's problems, as they simply do not have the time to engage in generic support, with a potential pay-off in the future"
(Kearney, 1998:15, quoting Annual Review of Small Business, 1997).

Gibb (2000) found that small business operators report on a series of obstacles that inhibit their involvement in support activities. These obstacles have been classified as economic, structural and attitudinal factors.

Economic factors, which are seen as obstacles to small business involvement in support activities include the general lack of resources among small business operators and also their priorities whereby the most pressing priority takes precedence. Small business operators also find that time and resources used in chasing support or in implementing change tend to disrupt their productivity. With respect to structural obstacles, small businesses lack sufficient personnel and in particular specialty staff to follow-up support opportunities or to sustain an informed effort.

The small business attitudinal factors that inhibit involvement in support activities include the fact that training and outside support is not valued in the same way as learning on the job. Business operators are busy and often have a limited understanding of the small business support sector and the support options available to them. Furthermore the autocratic, individualistic behavioural traits of owner/operators often lead to rejection of a critical assessment of their management abilities. Some operators are also deterred because of previous unsuccessful experiences, which causes apprehension about becoming involved again. Finally, some operators have a distrust and resentment of officialdom and prefer to avoid dealings with government agencies.

The communication effort of the support providers usually depends on their drive to offer successful services and their degree of business familiarity. For small business operators the level of their communication effort usually depends on the urgency of their information need. It is feasible that improved communication may provide a better level of understanding of each party's views and should therefore improve the efficiency of small business support provision. However, there is less likelihood of the average small business operator changing their behaviour as they usually only react to urgent needs. Therefore there is only likely to be less disparity between supplier offerings and operator needs in the longer term if service providers are able to change their behaviour and communicate more with small business operators. Such an observation suggests the following proposition.

The disparity between the offerings of support agencies and the needs of small business operators can be decreased if there is a more pro-active communication focus undertaken by the service providers.

The remainder of this paper outlines two projects that involved a pro-active communication strategy among small business service providers. These two projects are used to assess the above proposition within a real world context.

Methodology
Project 1

The first project as described by Bergin (2000) was designed to help prevent injuries in small business. The service provision involved a partnership between a local municipal council and the state work safety regulating body. A project officer was appointed to take specific responsibility for the delivery of the project. He was supported by a steering group of stakeholders from the two partnering organisations. The project objective was to work with small businesses to help them improve their safety practices.

A number of services were developed by the provider to help achieve this objective. Firstly information about injury risks and safety practices was available in print form through brochures and the project officer was available in person to discuss the material with small business operators. Secondly, display posters that promoted the safety message to employers and their employees were made available and a press campaign was undertaken to announce this fact.

A further stage of the project involved workplace visits. The project officer provided information on workplace safety to 308 businesses in industrial estates where it was determined that industries with poorer safety records were more likely to be located. An analysis of workplace injury data helped identify those industries with a poor safety record. The project officer was skilled in conducting workplace risk assessments and offering this service was an important part of the workplace visits. Thirteen percent of the businesses visited also undertook a workplace risk assessment. Furthermore, the project officer was available to arrange for the provision of training designed to deal with injury prevention. As a result of the workplace visits a group of 13 owner/operators attended work place safety seminars.

This project represented a good example of the scenario described in the introduction, a service provider with an array of services that could be supplied to small business and a community of small businesses that have been identified with a problem—injuries in the workplace. The impact of such injuries include expensive insurance claims, potential legal battles and costs to the community in terms of an additional drain on health resources, as well as injured workers unable to carry out their normal work duties. This project provided an excellent opportunity to assess the different strategies used by the service provider to attempt to engage the small business operators.

Project 2

The second project reported by Breen, Bergin, Sims & Ali (2001) was designed to assist businesses that indicated a disposition to growth. The project developed out of a partnership between a local municipal council and a university research unit and had the objective of increasing employment by providing specific support to those businesses identified with a propensity to grow. A survey of 409 businesses was used to identify pro-growth businesses and further inter-

views were used to ascertain their support needs and any impediments that restricted their growth ambitions.

An initial model for support was proposed. It involved housing an information officer at one of the local small business enterprise centres and having them available to help any business that sought support. After further discussions with a group of 25 pro-growth businesses this model was modified to provide a more pro-active focus with the information officer being required to make initial contact with identified growth oriented businesses, rather than wait for the business to contact the officer.

The project officer was therefore used as a representative of all the service agencies offering support to small business. In the role as a facilitator he was involved in providing face-to-face contact with 25 businesses selected from a list of 85 growth businesses. The facilitator helped identify business growth needs and was responsible for linking the businesses with the most appropriate support agency in accordance with the businesses' identified needs.

On this occasion there were multiple service providers with many services that were available for small businesses to access. This project involved using a specific matching strategy on the basis of lengthy consultation with small business operators. Furthermore the project was confined to selected businesses—those identified as having growth potential. This scenario provided an opportunity to assess a pro-active facilitation strategy used in an attempt to provide support to small business operators.

Results

The broad-brush approach of using brochures, advertising and mail outs as described in the first project was of limited effect. The evaluation of the project indicated that the small business operators showed little recognition of these strategies. In general small business operators were not pro-active, they did not see workplace injuries as an immediate problem, so they had no cause to seek help.

The more specific approach of identifying target groups of small businesses and making direct contact with them through a visit to the workplace was much more successful. The project officer was seen as knowledgeable and non-threatening and was generally welcomed by the business with comments such as:

"User friendly"

"Very good, (we) know some of the problems but the officer gave us more information"

"Good, realistic recommendations" (Bergin, 2000)

There was a need to change the focus of the visit from specific falls prevention to more general coverage of occupational health and safety issues.

"Various approaches were tried with interesting results that shaped the way in which the project was delivered. Generally, small business did not consider falls as a problem in their workplace as other OHS issues were perceived as a bigger problem. This resulted in the initial consultation with small businesses being changed from providing falls prevention advice to providing general OHS advice. This increased the likelihood of getting a foot in the door and involving small business in the project." (Quote from the Project Officer, Bergin 2000)

This change in focus was in response to the more pressing need of business operators for advice on safety matters. This need was driven by the increased likelihood of inspections from the work safety regulatory body resulting in possible fines and increased insurance premiums where poor practices were detected.

The evaluation of the project (Bergin 2000) found that a majority of the firms involved considered the project to be a supportive means of assisting small firms to improve workplace occupational health and safety. Businesses involved wanted to see the project continue as an ongoing service. Bergin (2000) reported that small businesses were accepting of a supportive approach that was one-to-one, industry focused and provided practical information.

The second project was initially going to use the more broad brush or "shotgun" approach of advertising and use of brochures. However, after consultation with business operators it was decided to use a more specific approach of targeted visits to business premises and holding face-to-face interviews with the operator. This communication process was considered essential in order to ensure that the support model truly met the needs of business.

"The support should provide a human face to assist business operators in their quest for information . . . Because it may take too long for businesses to find out about this service a person should visit the business." (Focus Group Feedback, Breen et al, 2001)

This approach was quite successful in engaging the business operator in discussion of their business needs and in ultimately being able to provide support to the business. A total of 55 referrals to different support agencies were made for the 25 businesses that were visited. Some of the outcomes resulting from these referrals included four new jobs being created, two businesses entered new export markets, and eight businesses developed new marketing plans. All of these outcomes were facilitated by the project and may not have occurred if not for the strategy developed. the positive feedback on the process included:

> "Will definitely seek support from the department again"

> "Yes, we will use the service again, . . . it was the best thing out of the visit"

> "I think it was worthwhile . . . I may have been able to find the contacts provided on my own . . . but probably not. The facilitator gave me direct names and contacts, which were needed and extremely useful." (Breen et al, 2001)

In fact, 95 percent of the business felt the visits from the facilitator had increased their awareness of support services available and of those who had increased their awareness, most felt it had significantly increased. A majority of the respondents (55%) rated their increased awareness at 4 or above on the scale of 1–5.

Both of the projects reported that the business owners improved their knowledge of the services or agencies available and were able to access the required assistance. An evaluation of project 1 found that business operators said that they had learned from the visit and that they were more aware of safety and also had implemented some improvements as a result of the visit. Similarly with the second project a majority of the firms indicated that they had improved their knowledge of what support was available. Additionally, the opportunity to reflect on their business and to have an objective view of their activities was seen as a valuable learning experience.

Discussion

Both projects spent a great deal of time meeting with the small business operators in order to identify their specific needs. These visits formed part of a communication strategy that was developed as a result of the feedback received from small businesses during the planning and pilot stages of each project. The earlier attempts to use more general approaches through advertising and brochures were found to be lacking in personal contact and were too easily ignored by busy business operators.

The outcomes of the two projects indicated that small business assistance providers involved had developed a better understanding of the needs of small business. They did their homework and by talking to small business operators they developed an understanding of the small business culture and their learning needs. The service provider personnel involved in the projects understood the importance of practical, tailor-made support. As a result of their involvement in the projects they were able to adjust their support offerings or refer businesses to other providers better able to meet the identified needs. The service providers also recognised that not all businesses were ready or able to utilise the support available. They therefore instituted a more targeted approach in order to identify those firms who could best learn from the experience and then concentrated the support on those firms.

The small business operators involved in the projects had an improved understanding of the support opportunities available to help them. They also reported a better understanding of their own needs as a result of discussions with the more pro-active agencies. The small business operators valued the approach used and found the flexibility of support offerings more to their liking and indicated that they would be interested to hear of other opportunities in future. The outcomes represent a learning partnership between the small business operator and the support agency as Gibb (1997) recommended. Overall it is a much more efficient use of resources.

These results indicate there is support for the proposition espoused earlier in this paper. That is the disparity between offerings of support agencies and the needs of small business operators can be decreased if there is a more pro-active communication stance taken by the service providers. The disparity is not irreconcilable. Where there was dialogue between the two players, then it was possible for the service provider to target their offerings more effectively and to address the needs of the operators more accurately. The implications of this finding is that where there are more targeted offerings by small business assistance providers to the small business operators, there will be greater take up of services and a more efficient use of resources.

Small Business owner/operators do not hold all the answers nor are they able to solve all the problems that their businesses face. There is a part to be played by service providers in facilitating organisational and individual learning within the client's business context (Massey & Walker, 1999). Support agencies with the right approach are able to reinforce this learning in order to help develop better and more effective firms.

It is only by valuing these natural activities that owner/operators can better appreciate the role that learning already plays in their business. Similarly, by reflecting on operational issues, support agencies can gain valuable insights into how small businesses learn (Kearney, 1998). Kerr & McDougall (1999) argue that one-off injections of knowledge are not efficient. They support an approach by service providers which promotes learning at all times, where learning is integrated with work, and where learning is managed by the individual. The

challenge for service providers and government agencies is to add value to the owner/operator's learning from experience, in a way that brings greater meaning to the experience (Hawke, 1999; Gibb, 1997). Failure by service providers to tap into this natural learning focus may help explain why small enterprises are not large users of structured support.

Conclusion

This paper has argued that a more targeted and pro-active communication strategy undertaken by small business service providers results in a better matching of the service availability with the needs of small business operators. The results of the two projects support the arguments of Hull (1987) that there is a role for intermediaries, and Gibb (1997) that publications and guides are of limited use without a process of personal discussion and dialogue. The paper provides a better understanding of what support strategies work and is therefore of assistance to government policy makers in this sector. If other agencies use these strategies and find them successful then it should allow for more efficient use of scarce resources. Finally this paper is of benefit to assistance agencies in that it will help to generate a greater understanding about the dynamics of interaction with small business.

Although this paper found that there is support for the stated proposition, there is a need for further research across more cases to clearly establish the proposition. Furthermore there is also an opportunity to investigate the situation from the supply side. That is by examining the impact of improved communication between the small business and the assistance provider on the supplier agencies. Finally, a follow-up study to determine the longer-term impact of such a proactive strategy on small businesses and the service provider agencies would also be most useful.

References

Bergin, S. (2000). "Small Business Falls Prevention Project Evaluation." Victoria University, Melbourne.

Breen, J., S. Bergin, R. Sims, and S. Ali (2001). "Business Growth Facilitation Project Report." Victoria University, Melbourne.

Chaston, I., B. Badger, and E. Sadler-Smith (1999). "Small Firm Organisation Learning: Comparing the Perceptions of Need and Style Among UK Support Service Advisors and Small Firm Managers." *Journal of European Industrial Training* **23**(1): 36–43.

Department of Workplace Relations and Small Business (1997). *Annual Review of Small Business.* Canberra, Australian Publishing Service.

Drejer, A. (2000). "Organisational Learning and Competence Development." *The Learning Organisation* **7**(4): 206–220.

Garratt, B. (1999). "The Learning Organisation 15 Years On: Some Personal Reflections." *The Learning Organisation* **6**(5): 202–206.

Gibb, A. (1997). "Small Firms' Training and Competitiveness. Building Upon the Small Business as a Learning Organisation." *International Small Business Journal* **15**(3): 13–29.

Gibb, A. (2000). "SME Policy, Academic Research and the Growth of Ignorance, Mythical Concepts, Myths, Assumptions, Rituals and Confusions." *International Small Business Journal* **18**(3): 13–55.

Guglielmi, K. (2000). "Crisis Induced Learning in a Small Business: A Case Study", (Thesis). University of Connecticut.

Hawke, G. (1999). "Factors Influencing Active Learning in Small Enterprises. Sydney", University of Technology Sydney, Research Centre for Vocational Education and Training: 8.

Hill, R., T. Bullard, P. Capper, K. Hawkes, and K. Wilson (1998). "Learning About Learning Organisations: Case Studies of Skill Formation in Five New Zealand Organisations." *The Learning Organisation* **5**(4): 184–192.

Holmes, S., G. Butler, and J. Lennon (1995). "Small Business: A Review of Training Needs", in Industry Taskforce on Leadership and Management Skills, *Enterprising Nation: Renewing Australia's Managers to Meet the Challenges of the Asia-Pacific Century—Research Report Vol 1*, AGPS, Canberra.

Holmes, S., and D. Nicholls (1990). *Small Business and Accounting*, Allen & Unwin, Sydney.

Howard, D., and D. Hine (1997). "The Population of Organisations Life Cycle (POLC): Implications for Small Business Assistance Programs", *International Small Business Journal*, Vol 15, No 3, pp 30–41.

Hull, C. J. (1987). "Helping Small Businesses Grow: An Implementation Approach", London: Croom-Helm.

Industry Commission & Department of Industry, Science and Tourism (1997). *A Portrait of Australian Business: Results of the 1995 Business Longitudinal Survey*, AGPS, Canberra.

Kearney, P. (1998). *Big Pictures From the Small End of Town: 1998 Small Business Professional Development Programme Evaluation Report.* Canberra, Office of Vocational Education and Training.

Kerr, A., and M. Mc Dougall (1999). "The Small Business of Developing People." *The International Small Business Journal* **17**(2): 1–10.

Massey, C., and R. Walker (1999). "Aiming for Organisation Learning: Consultants as Agents of Change." *The Learning Organisation*, **6**(1): 38–44.

Peacock, R. (1997). "Small Business in South Australia: A Snapshot", *Small Enterprise Series No. 32*, University of South Australia, Adelaide.

Penn, D., W. Ang'wa, R. Foster, G. Heydon, and S. Richardson (1998). "Learning in Smaller Organisations." *The Learning Organisation* 5(3): 128–137.

Sherman, H. (1999). "Assessing the Intervention Effectiveness of Business Incubation Programs on New Business Start-Ups." *Journal of Developmental Entrepreneurship* 4(2): 117–133.

Sparrow, J. (1999). "Using Qualitative Research to Establish SME Support Needs." *Qualitative Market Research: An International Journal* 2(2): 121–134.

Watson, K., and S. Hogarth-Scott (1998). "Small Business Start-ups: Success Factors and Support Implications." *International Journal of Entrepreneurial Behaviour & Research* 4(3): 217–238.

Yellow Pages (1995). *A Special Report on Finance and Banking Issues*, Pacific Access, Melbourne.

Outsider Assistance as a Knowledge Resource for New Venture Survival
by James J. Chrisman and W. Ed McMullan*

An emerging theory of outsider assistance as a knowledge resource suggests that new ventures obtain a unique blend of tacit and explicit knowledge through the judicious use of outside assistance. Using data from a longitudinal study of one outsider assistance program at a point in time four to eight years beyond the provision of startup counseling assistance, we present evidence supporting the theory. Results suggest that the ventures studied enjoyed survival rates in excess of those in the general population. More importantly, logistic regression analysis indicates a positive, curvilinear relationship between survival and the time spent in venture preparation under the direction of an outside counselor, a proxy measure of new knowledge acquired. We conclude with a discussion of the directions future research should take to test more fully the relationships implied by the theory.

Over the last 20 years, a considerable body of research has accumulated in the United States that suggests outsider assistance can have a substantial impact on new venture startup, survival, and performance (Chrisman and Katrishen 1994; Nahavandi and Chesteen 1988; Pelham 1985; Robinson 1982). For example, outsiders may assist entrepreneurs to develop an effective network (Hansen 1995), to build a management team (Rice 2002), to raise capital (Bygrave and Timmons 1992), and to prepare a business plan (Smeltzer, Van Hook, and Hutt 1991). Much of the research conducted has focused on the Small Business Development Center (SBDC) because of the ubiquitous nature of the program, its extensive clientele, and the large amount of resources expended on it.[1]

Recently, Chrisman and McMullan (2000) found that the impact of the

Originally appeared in *Journal of Small Business Management*, 2004, Volume 42, Number 3.
*The authors wish to acknowledge the Pennsylvania Small Business Development Center for supporting this research and an anonymous reviewer for comments made on an earlier draft of this manuscript.

[1]There have been numerous additional unpublished studies of the SBDC program. For example, the Oregon SBDC commissioned Dun & Bradstreet in 1996 and 1997 and the Oregon Employment Development in 1997 and 1998 to conduct independent impact studies. In all four cases the results validated the findings of the impact studies reported in the literature (Cutler 2001).

SBDC's counseling interventions appeared to persist over a period of three to five years with a disproportionately large number of firms not only surviving but also doing well in terms of growth in both sales and employment. In that study recipients also reported that their ventures contained a disproportionate number of innovations. However, some have suggested that these findings may be a result of positive self-selection or, in other words, unique attributes of the entrepreneurs or ventures studied that make them more likely to be successful but are not captured even in matched sample comparisons (Storey 2000).

In contrast to the U.S. experience, the results of studies of different program interventions created in Britain to assist entrepreneurs have been less positive (Storey 1994; Stanworth and Grey 1991). For example, Storey (1994) observes, ". . . The more justifiable inference from robust research in this area is that it is difficult to isolate an impact which training has upon small business performance. . . . considerable doubts over the effectiveness of small business training have to be registered and contrasted with 'received wisdom'. . . ." (pp. 292–293).

Some Swedish scholars have used business and strategic startup classes as control variables in studies of determinants of venture startup, survival, and profitability (Dahlqvist and Davidsson 2000). The findings of those studies again raise important questions about the elements that might be useful for effective program design. Drawing on the European experience Davidsson (2002a) concluded:

"As regards more mundane entrepreneurs there are several studies that show weak, zero or even negative correlation between taking startup courses or counseling on the one hand, and successfully launching and/or running a business on the other (Dahlqvist and Davidsson 2000; Dahlqvist, Davidsson, and Wiklund 2000; Honig and Davidsson 2000; Maung and Ehrens 1991; Tremlett 1993). This is double embarrassing, for it may be interpreted as showing that a) those who have entrepreneurial talent do not come and take the courses or counseling, and b) those who actually come are not turned into successful entrepreneurs" (P. 6).

Following this point, in an email addressed to the authors of this study Davidsson (2002b) referenced a conversation with a distinguished European colleague in which they both concluded that they had seen very little evidence of positive benefits accruing from entrepreneurial courses and counseling. He continued, "We both agreed, however, that one reason for this was negative self-selection: Less experienced entrepreneurs are more likely to take such courses. In addition, we found it likely that the results were in part due to the fact that the 'entrepreneurship assistance industry' boomed in the late 80s and early 90s, meaning that a lot of courses were probably delivered by people who were pretty clueless about the realities of entrepreneurship and small business practice." Given the contrasting experiences of researchers in the United States and Western Europe, it is clear that more work needs to be done to determine if there is a causal relationship between outsider assistance and new venture survival and performance after controlling for potential confounding effects such as client self-selection. Such work is necessary because of the importance of entrepreneurship to economic development (Birch 1987; Schumpeter 1934). It must be ensured that scarce resources allocated to foster entrepreneurship in both the public and private sectors are well spent and that future investments to promote and to enhance entrepreneurship are directed to the highest and best uses possible.

The purpose of this article is to develop further a theory of outsider assistance as a knowledge resource and to present additional evidence of the importance of outsider assistance to entrepreneurial survival. To do so, this article reports the results of a longitudinal study of the SBDC program in Pennsylvania. The remainder of the article presents the theoretical foundations, methodology, results, and conclusions of the study.

Theory of Outsider Assistance as a Knowledge Resource

An emerging theory of outsider assistance expounded by Chrisman (1999) and Chrisman and McMullan (2000) is predicated on the notion that outsider assistance can be a valuable source of knowledge to entrepreneurs. However, those authors make it clear that the value of outsider assistance does not come simply or mainly from the knowledge that an outsider imparts to an entrepreneur. Rather, the value of outsider assistance primarily comes from the opportunity for knowledge generation that it provides to an entrepreneur in the context of a specific venturing decision.[2] Thus, it is argued that a contextual learning process, directed and facilitated by an experienced outsider, may lead to the creation of a combination of tacit and explicit knowledge. *Tacit knowledge* is defined as knowledge that is experientially based and is difficult to codify, to replicate, and to transmit; *explicit knowledge* is defined as knowledge based on facts and theories that can be codified, replicated, and transmitted to others more easily (Berman, Down, and Hill 2002; Grant 1996).[3]

Because the combination of tacit and explicit knowledge gained through outsider assistance is contextual, is experiential, and is hard to codify, to replicate, and to transmit, it possesses the properties of value, rarity, imperfect inimitability, and nonsubstitutability that Barney (1991, 1997) suggests are necessary for sustainable competitive advantage. In summary, the emerging theory of outsider assistance as a knowledge resource suggests that outsider assistance can lead to the creation of knowledge that provides a basis for sustainable competitive advantage, which will, in turn, influence venture survival and performance.[4]

The remainder of this section discusses the components that appear

---

[2]The idea that outsider assistance is a knowledge resource is supported by Honig (2001), who found that contact with an assistance agency was a significant human capital indicator in distinguishing nascent entrepreneurs from intrapreneurs.

[3]Tacit knowledge can be of value to entrepreneurs in at least two ways: The first is its contextual value to a specific venturing opportunity, and the second is its more general value to future venturing, or more precisely, to the creation of subsequent ventures over an entrepreneur's career (Ronstadt 1988). Although this study controls for previous entrepreneurial experience in the empirical analysis, the theoretical discussion focuses on the value of the contextual knowledge for which the outsider assistance was sought.

[4]Although the theory emphasizes the tacit knowledge component, we should not lose sight of the fact that the generation of explicit knowledge also is integral to the success of the counseling process. It is the combination of the two that is expected to lead to competitive advantage. Without explicit knowledge, tacit knowledge may lack the foundation and focus needed for effective application. Without tacit knowledge, explicit knowledge will lead only to competitive parity because while valuable, it generally is not rare and always is imitable.

necessary for effective knowledge development through outsider-assistance programs and comments on characteristics of the SBDC program with respect to these components.

The Knowledge Gap

As a precondition, this study's theory assumes that in many cases there is a gap between the knowledge possessed by entrepreneurs and the knowledge required for successful venturing. For example, Drucker (1985) noted that the most likely reason for such a large failure rate among new business startups is because most people do not know what they are doing. Of course, for outsider assistance to do any good, an entrepreneur also must recognize that a knowledge gap exists; otherwise outsider assistance will not be sought.

A knowledge gap can exist in any one of four areas: know-why, know-what, know-how, and know-who (Malecki 1997). Know-why deals with scientific knowledge, whereas know-what deals with facts and techniques. These forms of explicit knowledge can be codified, replicated, and transmitted (Phillips 2002) and, therefore, are not likely by themselves to lead to sustainable competitive advantage. On the other hand, know-who and know-how are both forms of tacit knowledge. They are more difficult to codify or to copy. Know-who involves developing a network of relationships. Know-how involves a process of learning by doing that typically integrates both know-why and know-what with contextual experience. Both know-how and know-who possess the characteristics necessary for the development of sustainable competitive advantage (Phillips 2002). Furthermore, both may be developed through outsider interventions.

Based on previous research (Chrisman and McMullan 2000; Chrisman 1989), it appears that the SBDC's primary mission is to provide a mix of know-what

and know-how to its clients. However, the know-who necessary for building effective network relationships with suppliers, customers, lenders, and other stakeholders also may be imparted through the counseling process.

Stage of Venture's Development

Although the generation of know-how is assumed to be valuable in general, we suggest that the potential impact of such knowledge may vary depending on the stage of development of the venture. Specifically, McMullan and Long (1990) theorized that decisions made during the opportunity identification stage have a larger overall impact than decisions made at later stages of a venture's development. They also suggest that knowledge gained during the early stages of the development of a venture is applied more easily, because when a business is still just a concept it has fewer rigidities to constrain adaptation. In fact, the fluidity of a venture in its early stages and the importance of initial decisions to its future survival and growth have been expounded by a number of scholars (Barney 1986; Bouwen and Steyaert 1990; Bird 1988; Stinchcombe 1965). Therefore, it is expected that outsider interventions could have a large impact on the startup, survival, and performance of nascent ventures.

The SBDC program assists clients who are seeking to start a new business as well as clients who are seeking to improve the operations of existing businesses. This study focuses specifically on the long-term impact of SBDC counseling on the subsequent survival propensities of nascent entrepreneurs who started businesses.

Self-Selection

Unfortunately, not all ventures are conceived with equal potential for survival and growth. Consequently, the potential value of the knowledge imparted to entrepreneurs starting such ventures also will vary. For example, coaching someone on the intricacies of basketball will be less likely to lead to a career in the National Basketball Association if the person is five feet tall rather than seven feet tall. Ironically, whereas Storey (2000) suggests that the selection methods used to screen out ventures with low potential for success may be an obstacle to measuring the impact of outsiders accurately, Chrisman and McMullan (2000) suggest that such screening methods may be among the most important components of effective assistance programs. The recent work by McMullan, Chrisman, and Vesper (2002) illustrates the difference in outcomes that occur between programs that serve clients with unequal potential.

The SBDC offers its service to all comers and in that sense does not screen its clients directly. Rather, it uses a self-selection mechanism that involves a precounseling workshop intended to screen out would-be entrepreneurs who are less committed or who have an idea with low potential for success (Rech 1999).

Strengths of the Advisers

Regardless of knowledge gaps, client selection, and a venture's stage of development, outsider intervention will not be effective unless advisers are well trained, capable, and experienced. Advisers must be able to steer clients' efforts effectively toward the development of useful knowledge. Furthermore, advisers must be able to impart knowledge in a way that allows clients to blend that knowledge into their own understanding of their situations. In some ways an effective adviser to an entrepreneur must possess the same skills and must perform the same functions as an effective doctoral supervisor.

Although McMullan, Chrisman, and Vesper (2001) show that clients' subjec-tive assessments of quality have little relationship with venture outcomes, the continued evidence of client satisfaction combined with the positive economic performance of the ventures of coun-seled clients does suggest the strength of the advisers employed by the SBDC (Chrisman and Katrishen 1994; Naha-vandi and Chesteen 1988; Pelham 1985). More specific to this study, the SBDC has made a point of hiring counselors who both are educated and are experienced in the development of new and small enterprises. The majority of these coun-selors are full-time professionals with advanced degrees (Rech 1999). Further-more, counselors are expected to engage in a minimum of 40 hours of professional development per year (PASBDC 1977). Finally, each state SBDC is subjected to periodic review by an accreditation team from the Association of Small Business Development Centers.

Timing of Service Delivery

McMullan, Chrisman, and Vesper's (2002) review of several successful edu-cation and training programs suggests that just-in-time delivery might be more effective for developing entrepreneurs than an education program intended to have a delayed fuse. Because many of the important attributes of the knowl-edge gained through the outsider-assistance process are related to its contextual and experiential components, knowledge not in use for an extended period of time may become stale and even irrelevant. For example, Long, Taylor and McMullan (2000) found that after a 10-year lag graduates of a high school course in entrepreneurship were not involved in more startups propor-tionally than the general public. Just-in-time delivery is a component of the counseling provided by the SBDC. Clients seek assistance from the SBDC during the process of starting a business or making modifications to an existing business.

Type of Intervention

Chrisman and McMullan (2000) have suggested that the use of counseling rather than consulting may be a key to the success of outsider assistance. Consulting is distinguished from counseling in this study as follows. The primary function of consultants is to perform a task or set of tasks for their clients and to provide advice. By contrast, the primary function of counselors is to facilitate the performance of a task or set of tasks by their clients. While counselors also provide advice and may complete some of the work themselves, their key contributions are the direction and mentoring provided to clients and the feedback provided on the quality of the clients' work.

Outsiders, no matter how well trained, by definition cannot transfer valuable contextual, experiential knowledge to entrepreneurs. Such knowledge must come through the efforts of the entrepreneurs themselves. However, trained outsiders can provide guidance and direction to facilitate and to enhance the knowledge gained by entrepreneurs in the process of preparing to start a venture. Through this process clients gain both tacit and explicit knowledge pertinent to a specific venturing opportunity.

As noted in previous studies (Chrisman and McMullan 2000; Chrisman 1999), the SBDC program engages in the types of intervention defined in this study as counseling. Counselors meet with clients to gain an appreciation of the situation and provide initial advice and direction. A letter of understanding is prepared outlining the specific tasks to be performed by both parties, with a strategic business plan being the usual outcome of the process. From there, periodic meetings are scheduled to review progress. Rech (1999) suggests the rule of thumb is that clients spend three to four hours working on their business preparations for every hour spent with a business counselor.

The process continues for as long as the client believes that he or she has something further to gain. This is an important point because it suggests there may be practical limits to the amounts of knowledge that can be gained through outsider interventions or, at least, that there might be diminishing returns associated with continuing interventions over time.

Hypotheses

As suggested previously, the blend of tacit and explicit knowledge gained through outsider assistance accrues through a process of intervention that depends on the knowledge gap of clients, the stage of venture development, a selection or screening process, the skills of the advisers, just-in-time service delivery, and a counseling rather than a consulting approach to knowledge creation and transfer.

There are several ways in which the theory of outsider assistance as a knowledge resource might be tested. First, one could compare matched samples of assistance users and nonusers, as Robinson (1982) did in his study of the benefits of outsiders in strategic planning. Second, one could compare users of different assistance programs so as to isolate, for example, the value of just-in-time service delivery, or counseling versus some other form of intervention. Third, one could compare the performance of clients who received differential amounts of assistance from a single program. Both the second and third approaches have the additional advantage of avoiding or at least of minimizing the potential problem of selection bias noted by Storey (2000).[5]

---

[5]Here the term *selection bias* is used to refer to the potential for bias that might exist if clients of outsider-assistance programs differ in some meaningful way from nonclients that is not controlled through a matched sampling methodology.

In this study, a test is performed of the first method using a comparison rather than a control group to determine differences in survival propensities for SBDC clients versus nonclients. The relevant hypothesis is as follows:

H1: Entrepreneurial ventures started with the assistance of the SBDC are more likely to survive for at least four years than ventures in the general population.

A test also is performed of the third method described previously by testing the influence of the amount of time spent by clients in the counseling process on their survival propensities. Here the time an entrepreneur spends in preparing to venture under the guidance of a trained counselor is used as a proxy for the amount of knowledge gained, with the assumption that time and knowledge are related positively, to a point.[6] Thus, allowance is made for the possibility that the relationship between clients' level of involvement with outsiders and survival propensity may be curvilinear (inverted U-shaped) rather than linear. The idea that the value of knowledge may be subject to diminishing (and eventually even negative) returns has been supported recently by Berman, Down, and Hill's (2002) study of the value of shared experience among team members in the National Basketball Association. The two hypotheses that follow are

H2: There is a positive relationship between the time entrepreneurs spend preparing to start a venture under the guidance of the SBDC and survival.

H3: There are diminishing returns to scale in the relationship between the time entrepreneurs spend preparing to start a venture under the guidance of the SBDC and survival.

Methodology

Long-term clients, defined as those who received five or more hours (average of 20) of counseling, of the Pennsylvania Small Business Development Center (SBDC) program in the years 1992, 1994, and 1996 were surveyed first in 1994, 1996, and 1998, respectively, to obtain data on their performance one year after receiving assistance (that is, 1993, 1995, and 1997). In the first quarter of 2001 a follow-up study was conducted of those cohorts of preventure clients. This article pertains to the results of that study.

The sample for the current study was composed of all clients who had responded to the initial questionnaires concerning the performance of their businesses one year after receiving SBDC assistance and who had indicated that they successfully had started a firm during or following the counseling process. These clients were selected for the sample because they had started businesses and because data were available from an earlier period. This previously collected data enabled us to track performance over a longer period of time for the cohorts of responding clients served in 1992, 1994, and 1996. Having these data also allowed for more stringent tests to be conducted on the representativeness of the respondents to the current study than would have been pos-

---

[6]Since tacit knowledge by definition cannot be measured directly, it was necessary to use a surrogate. Using number of hours as a surrogate for the measurement of both tacit and explicit knowledge is consistent with the measure of collective experience employed by Berman, Down, and Hill (2002). Finally, this study's approach also is aligned with Rice's (2002) case studies, which showed that the outputs of business assistance are related to, among other things, the amount of time spent by all parties in the business assistance process.

sible had such data been unavailable.[7] These tests were important because the samples selected for this study were one step removed from the original client populations. However, previous analyses of these samples indicated that they were representative of the long-term client populations served in the three time frames with respect to first-year performance and perceptions of the SBDC programs.

Mail questionnaires to clients were sent and were followed by a second mailing to nonrespondents to increase the sample size and to be able to test for response bias. In total, a total of 159 usable responses were received from the 576 clients who had responded to the previous impact studies for an overall response rate of 27.6 percent.[8]

Tests for Response Bias

A series of tests were conducted to determine if the responses to the questionnaire were representative and unbiased. First, t-tests and chi-square tests were used to compare initial performance as reported in the original studies of respondents and nonrespondents. No differences were found with respect to initial size, industry, or perceptions of the benefits of SBDC counseling. Overall, then, these tests indicated that the respondents were representative of the initial samples of clients used in this study.

Furthermore, the responses were compared to the first and second mailings of the current questionnaire along each of the variables used in this study. No significant differences between respondents to the two mailings in terms of any of these variables were found. It should be noted that respondents to the second mailing were nonrespondents to the first mailing. Relative to early respondents, late respondents tend to be more similar to nonrespondents (Kanuk and Berenson 1975; Oppenheim 1966). Therefore, it was concluded for this study that there was no statistical reason to conclude bias with respect to any of the variables used here.

The Data

To achieve the purposes of this study, data from the original surveys in 1994, 1996, and 1998 were used, as well as data obtained from the survey conducted in 2001.

In the original studies clients were asked, among other things, to indicate the industry sector in which they competed from among the following categories: retail, service, wholesale, manufacturing, construction, and other. To preserve degrees of freedom in this study, industry was measured as a categorical variable. Ventures in retail or service industries were coded as "1," and ventures in other industries were coded as "0." Clients were asked to indicate the year their venture was started. This number was subtracted from 2000, the last full year prior to the study, to measure age (for example, 2000 − 1993 = 7 years old). Finally, clients were asked to provide initial employment levels for their first year of operation.

---

[7] It also allowed for the use of data collected from the earlier studies, which reduced the size of the questionnaire and helped increase response rates. As well, this served to reduce the possibility of common method variance somewhat since the data were collected at two points in time.

[8] Response rates broke down as follows: 31 of 132 clients from the 1992 study (23.5 percent); 65 of 267 clients from the 1994 study (24.3 percent); 63 of 177 clients from the 1996 study (35.6 percent). It also should be noted that not all clients responded to every question. Therefore, the effective sample size was reduced to 141 due to missing data for this study's test of H2 and H3.

In the follow-up study, several questions pertinent to this study were asked. First, clients were asked whether their businesses were still in operation in order to measure the dependent variable, survival. Second, they were asked whether they had prior ownership or management experience prior to startup. Both questions required categorical responses, which were coded as "1" for responses of yes and "0" for responses of no. Third, clients were asked to provide their highest level of education. The following scale was used: (1) less than high school; (2) high school; (3) some college; (4) technical school; (5) two-year associate's degree; (6) four-year bachelor's degree; (7) master's degree; and (8) Ph.D. degree.

Finally, to measure the independent variables data on the number of hours clients spent working on business preparations under the guidance of the SBDC were collected. Clients were instructed to estimate the time spent in direct contact with an SBDC counselor as well as any time spent on work prompted by the advice or direction provided by their SBDC counselor(s). Since this question depended on clients' ability to recall events that occurred in the past, nine response categories were provided: (1) 25 hours or less; (2) between 26–50 hours; (3) between 51–75 hours; (4) between 76–100 hours; (5) between 101–125 hours; (6) between 126–150 hours; (7) between 151–175 hours; (8) between 176–200 hours; and (9) more than 200 hours. It was believed that this approach provided a scale that would yield sufficient variance to test the study's hypotheses and sufficient breadth in the response categories to allow clients to respond with reasonable accuracy.

The square of clients' responses to this question was used to test the third hypothesis pertaining to diminishing returns.

Comparison Data

To test the first hypothesis, a comparison group was required. Data were obtained to make the comparison with the survival rates of this sample from a recent study conducted by Boden (2000) of survival rates in the general population between 1992 and 1996, a time frame that was reasonably consistent with the time frame of this study.

Control Variables

Testing the second and third hypotheses required an analysis of the relationship between the amount of time spent by clients on business preparations and survival using binominal logistic regression. To ensure that the results were not spurious, a number of control variables were included in the analysis, the operationalizations of which were described earlier.

Initial size suggests the resources available at the time of founding as well as the scale of entry. Since initial size is expected to be related to survival (Cooper, Woo, and Dunkelberg 1989), first-year employment was controlled for in this study's analysis. Up to the point where the venture moves beyond the liabilities of newness and adolescence, the probability of failure among startups tends to increase over time (Durand and Coeurderoy 2001; Bruderl and Schussler 1990; Stinchcombe 1965). Therefore, age was controlled for in this study's analysis. Survival rates may also vary by industry (Stearns et al. 1995; Bruderl, Preisendorfer, and Ziegler 1992) so a variable was included measuring industry in the regression equation. Scholars have suggested that the previous entrepreneurial experience and education of the entrepreneur may influence venture survival (Cooper, Gimeno-Gascon, and Woo 1994). Thus, both experience and education were controlled for in the analysis.

Table 1
Descriptive Statistics

Variables	Mean	Standard Deviation	Number
Survival	0.805	0.397	159
Industry	0.465	0.500	159
Age	5.201	1.785	159
Initial Employment	3.355	5.962	148
Previous Experience	0.401	0.492	157
Education	4.949	1.857	158
Hours of Preparation	2.586	2.320	152

Results

Before turning to a detailed analysis of survival rates, a brief discussion of the demographic characteristics of the sample are provided.

As shown in Table 1, 80.5 percent of the respondents indicated that their ventures had survived through the year 2000. Approximately 47 percent of the ventures were started in retail or service industries. The average venture had 3.35 full-time equivalent employees in their first year of operation and was slightly over five years old at the time of the study.[9]

In terms of education the largest group of respondents possessed a four-year bachelor's degree (28.5 percent). However, almost half of the responding clientele reported an education level below a bachelor's degree, broken down as follows: less than a high school education (0.6 percent); high school degree (13.9 percent); some college (13.3 percent); technical school (12.0 percent); or a two-year associates degree (9.5 percent). At the other end of the continuum, 22.2 percent of the respondents obtained a master's (17.1 percent) or Ph.D. (5.1 percent). With regard to whether clients previously had owned or had managed a business, 40.1 percent responded in the affirmative. Finally, translating the scaled measure of number of hours into actual hours suggests that clients spent an average of approximately 65 hours in preparation for start up under the guidance of an SBDC counselor (2.586 × 25).[10]

Testing Hypothesis One

To test the first hypothesis, an adjusted rate of survival was used for each cohort of preventure clients in order to account for undeliverable questionnaires, most of which probably represented discontinued businesses. Adjusted survival rates for the 1992, 1994, and 1996 cohorts were 65.2 percent, 60.7 percent, and 70.1 percent, respectively (64.6 percent overall).[11]

---

[9]Average full-time equivalent employment in 2000 was 5.29.

[10]Since clients received an average of 20 hours of counseling the average number of hours of preparation was consistent with the rule of thumb of three to four hours of work on business preparations for every hour spent with a business counselor noted by Rech (1999).

[11]The unadjusted survival rates of the three client cohorts were 83.9 percent for 1992 clients, 80.0 percent for 1994 clients, and 79.4 percent for clients served in 1996. However, there was

Then the adjusted survival rates for SBDC clients were compared to Boden's (2000) research on business dissolutions. Boden used a unique database available through the Small Business Administration that combined the Census Bureau's 1992 Survey of Minority-Owned Businesses and 1992 Women-Owned Business Survey with the Business Information Tracking Series for 1989–1996. He found that 47 percent of all businesses started across industry groupings, gender, and ethnic background in 1992 had survived through 1996.

Using chi-square tests of goodness of fit, it was found that the survival rates for the three SBDC cohorts studied were each significantly greater than the 47-percent survival Boden (2000) found in the general population, testing at the 1-percent level. Thus, H1 was supported. It would appear that obtaining professional outsider assistance at an early stage in the development of a venture is related to its long-term survival (four to eight years).

Testing Hypotheses Two and Three

To test the second and third hypotheses, a binary logistic regression model with survival as the dependent variable was used.

As shown in Table 2, both H2 and H3 were accepted. Thus, controlling for age, size, industry, experience, and education there was a significant, positive relationship between the number of hours clients spent in preparation under the guidance of SBDC counselors and the probability of survival, supporting H2. Furthermore, there was a significant, negative relationship between the square of the number of hours and the probability of survival, supporting the premise of H3 that there are diminishing returns associated with the value of guided preparations by entrepreneurs. With regard to the control variables, only employment at the time of startup was related significantly to the probability of survival, reinforcing the points made by Cooper, Woo, and Dunkelberg (1989) on the importance of initial size.

Conclusions

This article has elaborated further on an emerging theory of outsider assistance as a knowledge resource (Chrisman and McMullan 2000; Chrisman 1999) and has presented evidence that more directly supports the presence of a causal linkage between such assistance and venture survival. The hypothesized relationships between outsider assistance and survival were tested in two ways: first, through a test with a comparison sample from the general population of ventures that started in a similar period to our sample; and, second, through a test of the relationship between time spent in guided preparation and survival, with appropriate controls for a number of variables that were linked conceptually and empirically to venture survival and performance in other studies.

Unfortunately, it is not possible to measure knowledge acquisition directly.

---

a large number of undeliverable questionnaires to account for 30 of 132 from the 1992 sample (22.7 percent); 64 of 267 from the 1994 sample (24.0 percent); and 21 of 177 from the 1996 sample (11.9 percent), for a total of 115 of 576 (20.0 percent). This study assumed that all of these ventures were discontinued. Thus, the survival rate of the clients for each cohort was multiplied by the number of deliverable questionnaires to obtain an estimate of the number of survivors. Then this number was divided by the total number of firms surveyed from that cohort to get adjusted estimates of survivals by year. Thus, for 1992 it was estimated that there were 86 survivors [$0.839 \times (132 - 30)$], yielding an effective survival rate of 65.2 percent (86/132). Using a similar procedure the survival rate of the 1994 client cohort was estimated at 60.7 percent and the survival rate of the 1996 cohort at 70.1 percent.

Table 2
Logistic Regression Analysis for Probability of Survival[a]

Variables	Beta	Standard Error
H2: Time Spent in Guided Preparation	0.972*	0.455
H3: Square of Time in Preparation	−0.101*	0.046
Industry	−0.069	0.456
Age	−0.023	0.133
Initial Employment	0.315*	0.143
Previous Experience	0.456	0.519
Education	−0.153	0.122
Constant	0.175	1.122

[a] −2 log likelihood: 124.68; model chi-square: 18.63**; overall hit rate: 79.43 percent; goodness of fit: 156.28; Cox and Snell R^2: 0.124; degrees of freedom: 7; number: 141.
*$p < 0.05$.
**$p < 0.01$.

As others have done (Berman, Down, and Hill 2002), time spent in guided preparation for startup was used as a proxy measure. The authors of this study believe that measure both was reasonable and was appropriate for capturing the underlying concept in which there was interest. Furthermore, it was recognized that the relationship between time spent and knowledge acquired probably would not be linear, in that the value of later, additional units of time spent in preparation for startup would be less than the value of earlier increments of time spent in preparation. The authors' expectations were confirmed in every case, and all three of our hypotheses were supported by the results of this research.

Implications for Practice

Based on this study's analysis it appears that preventure clients can gain valuable insights into the requirements necessary to start a successful business from the counseling provided by the SBDC program. Given what has been learned through studies conducted in the past (for example, Chrisman and Danforth 1995; Chrisman 1989), it appears that the knowledge entrepreneurs gain involves a deeper appreciation of the strategic situation of their ventures and how to exploit the opportunities present in the environment. This strategic appreciation appears to be a function of directing clients' efforts toward strategic planning in order to determine potential sources of competitive advantage through innovation and market positioning (Chrisman and McMullan 2000; McMullan and Long 1990). In any case, this study provides further confirmation that offering free publicly funded, professional-quality counseling to members of the general public on demand generally makes sense from an economic perspective.

Directions for Research

Besides a need to replicate this study in other venues there also is a need to develop better measures of knowledge. Unfortunately, because tacit knowledge cannot be measured directly it is important to select proxies that tap into the domain of the construct. For example, in the context of outsider assistance as a knowledge resource Rice's (2002) multi-case study of coproduction of business assistance suggested that the reported amount, intensity, and breadth of counseling is related to subjective measures of business performance. Perhaps these three dimensions of counseling, combined with an approach to capture the relevant contributions of the client entrepreneurs, together might provide a better indication of the amount of knowledge accumulated during the counseling process.

There are also a number of important research questions that remain to be answered. For example, studies are needed that will help to determine the value of the various components of the assistance process. While this study provides some evidence in support of an overall theory that an outsider-assistance program with a number of prespecified features will be effective, it is necessary to delve deeper to gain a stronger appreciation of the results for programs that use different delivery and screening methods, to reach ventures with different potentials or in later stages of development, or to seek to impart knowledge using other methods. This study did not isolate these various characteristics and therefore can conclude only that the combination of characteristics described does appear to facilitate the generation of useful knowledge. However, without further comparisons, other combinations that work equally well may be overlooked.

More specifically, there may be certain features of outsider-assistance programs that have larger impacts than others, or certain configurations that work better for ventures starting under different sets of circumstances. For example, following on Charney and Libecap (2000), it is necessary to know how the payoffs compare over time among outsider-assistance programs, entrepreneurial education, and general business education when it comes to successful venturing. Knowledge is desired about how the content and delivery of entrepreneurial knowledge should be adjusted to take into account factors such as level of preparedness (for example, age, education, experience) and timing of need. Answers to these questions are necessary to give a better understanding of how to contribute to the success of new ventures for economic development and growth.

References

Barney, J. B. (1986). "Strategic Factor Markets: Expectations, Luck, and Business Strategy," *Management Science* 32(10), 1231–1241.

——— (1991). "Firm Resources and Sustained Competitive Advantage," *Journal of Management* 17(1), 99–120.

——— (1997). *Gaining and Sustaining Competitive Advantage*. Reading, MA: Addison-Wesley.

Berman, S. L., J. Down, and C. W. L. Hill (2002). "Tacit Knowledge as a Source of Competitive Advantage in the National Basketball Association," *Academy of Management Journal* 45(1), 13–31.

Birch, D. (1987). *Job Creation in America*. New York: Free Press.

Bird, B. (1988). "Implementing Entrepreneurial Ideas: The Case for Intention," *Academy of Management Review* 13(3), 442–453.

Boden, R. J. Jr. (2000). *Analysis of Business Dissolution by Demographic Category of Business Ownership*.

Washington, DC: Office of Advocacy, U.S. Small Business Administration.

Bouwen, R., and C. Steyaert (1990). "Construing Organizational Texture in Young Entrepreneurial Firms," *Journal of Management Studies* 27(6), 637–649.

Bruderl, J., P. Preisendorfer, and R. Ziegler (1992). "Survival Chances of Newly Founded Business Organizations," *American Sociological Review* 57(2), 227–242.

Bruderl, J., and R. Schussler (1990). "Organizational Mortality: The Liability of Newness and Adolescence," *Administrative Science Quarterly* 35(3), 530–547.

Bygrave, W. D., and J. A. Timmons (1992). *Venture Capital at the Crossroads.* Boston, MA: Harvard School Press.

Charney, A., and G. D. Libecap (2000). *The Impact of Entrepreneurship Education.* Kansas City, MO: Insights, A Kaufman Research Series.

Chrisman, J. J. (1989). "Strategic, Administrative, and Operating Assistance: The Value of Outside Consulting to Preventure Entrepreneurs," *Journal of Business Venturing* 4(6), 401–418.

——— (1999). "The Influence of Outsider-Generated Knowledge Resources on Venture Creation," *Journal of Small Business Management* 37(4), 42–58.

Chrisman, J. J., and G. W. Danforth (1995). "Strategy as a Determinant of the Perceived Value of Outsider Assistance in New Ventures: An Exploratory Study," *Journal of Small Business Strategy* 6(2), 47–68.

Chrisman, J. J., and F. Katrishen (1994). "The Economic Impact of Small Business Development Center Counseling Activities in the United States: 1990–1991," *Journal of Business Venturing* 9(4), 271–280.

Chrisman, J. J., and W. E. McMullan (2000). "A Preliminary Assessment of Outsider Assistance as a Knowledge Resource: The Longer-Term Impact of New Venture Counseling," *Entrepre-*

neurship Theory and Practice 24(3), 37–53.

Cooper, A. C., F. J. Gimeno-Gascon, and C. Y. Woo (1994). "Initial Human and Financial Capital as Predictors of New Venture Performance," *Journal of Business Venturing* 9(5), 371–395.

Cooper, A. C., C. Y. Woo, and W. C. Dunkelberg (1989). "Entrepreneurship and the Initial Size of Firms," *Journal of Business Venturing* 4(5), 317–332.

Cutler, M. E. (2001). Memorandum to State Senator Mae Yih. Oregon Small Business Development Center, Eugene, May 9.

Dahlqvist, J., and P. Davidsson (2000). "Business Startup Reasons and Firm Performance," in *Frontiers of Entrepreneurship Research.* Ed. P. Reynolds, E. Autio, C. Brush, W. Bygrave, S. Manigart, H. Sapienza, and K. G. Shaver. Wellsley, MA: Babson College, 46–54.

Dahlqvist, J., P. Davidsson, and J. Wiklund (2000). "Initial Conditions as Predictors of New Venture Performance: A Replication and Extension of the Cooper et.al. Study," *Enterprise and Innovation Management Studies* 1(1), 1–17.

Davidsson, P. (2002a). "What Entrepreneurship Research Can Do for Business and Policy Practice," *International Journal of Entrepreneurship Education* 1(1), 1–20.

——— (2002b). E-mail correspondence from Per Davidsson August.

Drucker. P. F. (1985). *Innovation and Entrepreneurship.* New York: Harper and Row.

Durand, R., and R. Coeurderoy (2001). "Age, Order of Entry, Strategic Orientation, and Organizational Performance," *Journal of Business Venturing* 16(5), 471–494.

Grant, R. M. (1996). "Toward a Knowledge-Based Theory of the Firm," *Strategic Management Journal* 17(Winter Special Issue), 109–122.

Hansen, E. L. (1995). "Entrepreneurial Networks and New Organizational Growth," *Entrepreneurship: Theory and Practice* 19(4), 7–19.

Honig, B. (2001). "Learning Strategies and Resources for Entrepreneurs and Intrapreneurs," *Entrepreneurship Theory and Practice* 26(1), 21–35.

Honig, B., and P. Davidsson (2000). "The Role of Social and Human Capital among Nascent Entrepreneurs," paper presented at the annual meeting of the Academy of Management, Toronto, Canada, August.

Kanuk, L., and C. Berenson (1975). "Mail Surveys and Response Rates: A Literature Review," *Journal of Marketing Research* 22(4), 440–453.

Long W. A., M. Taylor, and W. E. McMullan (2000). "Creating an Enterprise Culture: A Ten-Year Follow-Up Study," paper presented at the annual meeting of the Entrepreneurship Education Forum, Chicago, Ill., November.

Malecki, E. (1997). *Technology and Economic Development: The Dynamics of Local, Regional, and National Competitiveness.* Toronto, Canada: Longman.

Maung, N. A., and R. Ehrens (1991). *Enterprise Allowance Scheme: A Survey of Participants Two Years after Leaving.* London, UK: Social and Community Planning Research.

McMullan, W. E., J. J. Chrisman, and K. H. Vesper (2001). "Some Problems in Using Subjective Measures of Effectiveness to Evaluate Entrepreneurial Assistance Programs," *Entrepreneurship Theory and Practice* 26(1), 37–53.

——— (2002). "Lessons from Successful Innovations in Entrepreneurial Support Programming," in *Innovation and Entrepreneurship in Western Canada: From Family Businesses to Multinationals.* Ed. J. J. Chrisman, J. A. D. Holbrook, and J. H. Chua. Calgary, Canada: University of Calgary Press, 207–223.

McMullan, W. E., and W. Long (1990). *Developing Entrepreneurial Ventures.* San Diego, CA: Harcourt Brace Jovanovich Inc.

Nahavandi, A., and S. Chesteen (1988). "The Impact of Consulting on Small Business: A Further Examination," *Entrepreneurship Theory and Practice* 13(1), 29–40.

Oppenheim, A. N. (1966). *Questionnaire Design and Attitude Measurement.* New York: Basic Books.

Professional Development Program Implementation and Assessment Criteria (PASBDC) (1997). *Professional Development Program Implementation and Assessment Criteria.* Philadelphia: Pennsylvania Small Business Develoment Center.

Pelham, A. (1985). "Should the SBDC Program Be Dismantled?" *American Journal of Small Business* 10(2), 41–51.

Phillips, P. W. B. (2002). "Regional Systems of Innovation as Modern R&D Entrepots: The Case of the Saskatoon Biotechnology Cluster," in *Innovation and Entrepreneurship in Western Canada: From Family Businesses to Multinationals.* Ed. J. J. Chrisman, J. A. D. Holbrook, and J. H. Chua. Calgary, Canada: University of Calgary Press, 31–58.

Rech, C. (1999). Telephone interview with (former) Associate State Director of the Pennsylvania Small Business Development Center program. March.

Rice, M. (2002). "Coproduction of Business Assistance in Business Incubators: An Exploratory Study," *Journal of Business Venturing* 17(2), 163–187.

Robinson, R. B. Jr. (1982). "The Importance of 'Outsiders' in Small Firm Strategic Planning," *Academy of Management Journal* 25(1), 80–93.

Ronstadt, R. (1988). "The Corridor Principle," *Journal of Business Venturing* 3(1), 31–40.

Schumpeter, J. A. (1934). *The Theory of Economic Development.* Cambridge, MA: Harvard University Press.

Smeltzer, L. R., B. L. Van Hook, and R. W. Hutt (1991). "Analysis of the Use of Advisers as Information Sources in Venture Startups," *Journal of Small Business Management* 29(3), 10–20.

Stansworth, J., and C. Grey (1991). *Bolton 20 Years On: A Review and Analysis of Small Business Research in Britain, 1971–91*. London, UK: Small Business Research Trust.

Stearns, T. M., N. M. Carter, P. D. Reynolds, and M. L. Williams (1995). "New Firm Survival: Industry, Strategy, and Location," *Journal of Business Venturing* 10(1), 23–42.

Stinchcombe, A. L. (1965). "Social Structure and Organizations," in *Handbook of Organizations*. Ed. J. G. March. Chicago, IL: Rand McNally, 142–193.

Storey, D. (1994). *Understanding the Small Business Sector*. London, UK: Routledge.

Storey, D. (2000). "Six Steps to Heaven: Evaluating the Impact of Public Policies to Support Small Business in Developed Economies," in *Handbook of Entrepreneurship*. Ed. D. Sexton and H. Landstrom. Oxford, UK: Blackwell, 176–193.

Tremlett, N. (1993). *The Business Startup Scheme: 18-Month Follow-Up Survey*. London, UK: Social and Community Planning Research.

Support for Rapid-Growth Firms: A Comparison of the Views of Founders, Government Policymakers, and Private Sector Resource Providers*

by Eileen Fischer and A. Rebecca Reuber

The paper contrasts the perspectives of firm owners, government policy advisers, and external resource providers on how rapid-growth firms should be supported. Qualitative data were analyzed to identify similarities and differences in groups' perspectives. The research indicates that each group sees its roles as critical. Policymakers and external resources providers have incentives to interact with rapid-growth firms. Rapid-growth firms have incentives to obtain advice from government sources and external resource providers but prefer to obtain advice from their peers. These findings suggest a network-based approach to the support of rapid growth that is consistent with a new Ontario-based program, the Innovators Alliance.

Introduction

Firms that grow very rapidly, often defined as those having a sales growth rate of at least 20 percent per year for five consecutive years[1], are a phenomenon that is attracting considerable and

Originally appeared in *Journal of Small Business Management*, 2004, Volume 41, Number 4.
*The authors gratefully acknowledge the comments and suggestions of Nancy Carter at key stages of this research; the assistance of Fulcrum Partners in organizing a conference that was instrumental to this research; and the financial support of the conference by the Royal Bank of Canada, Industry Canada, and the Business Development Bank of Canada. Leytha Miles and Laurie Hutchison of the Innovators Alliance generously provided information about their program. The research was supported financially by the Entrepreneurship Research Alliance II, led by Jim Brander at the University of British Columbia, and by the Social Science and Humanities Research Council of Canada.
[1]How to measure organizational performance most effectively, especially of new and small firms, is a substantial research topic in itself (Brush and Vanderwerf 1992; Chandler and Hanks 1993; March and Sutton 1997), and there is not one agreed-upon definition of a rapid-growth firm. Indeed, different definitions are likely to identify different sets of rapid-growth firms within a population (Delmar and Davidsson 1998). Since the focus here is on public policy and rapid growth, we use the definition frequently used within that context, while recognizing that alternate definitions exist.

growing interest from the public sector. Mirroring interest in the business media, such as the publication of the annual *Inc.* 100 list of America's fastest growing firms and the corresponding *Profit* 100 list of Canadian firms, governments are allocating resources to studies of the characteristics of rapid-growth firms, for example, in the United Kingdom (Department of Trade and Industry 1994; Storey 1996), the European Community (Birley et al. 1995), and Canada (Baldwin 1994; Johnson, Baldwin, and Hinchley 1997). While rapid-growth firms can provide high returns for investors and can become lucrative clients of consultants and banks, governments tend to focus on their value as job creators. David Birch (1987, 1995), who coined the term "gazelles" to refer to firms in the highest growth percentiles and argued that they play a disproportionate contribution to job creation, was awarded the first Nutek Prize, a Swedish "baby Nobel Prize," recognizing research in the field of small business and entrepreneurship (Hopkins 1997).

Although their impact on job creation has put rapid-growth firms on the public policy agenda, a key question has yet to be answered. It concerns the most effective role of government in supporting rapid growth. Indeed, the more general question is whether governments should be involved in supporting private enterprise at all. One school of thought advocates a relatively passive role of government: to create an overall environment that is supportive of new business development but without providing specialized assistance to selected industries or firms (for example, Levie 1994; Lohmann 1998). Another school of thought advocates a more active role involving the development of specialized policies and programs that allow new and small firms to overcome systematic disadvantages in the market (for example, Levy 1994; Hallberg 1999; Collinson 2000).

Given the growth over the past two decades in many countries of a specialized industry, often involving public sector entities, to proffer advice to new and small firms [see, for example, studies by Bennett and Robson (1999) and Gibson (1997), as well as websites maintained by the United States Small Business Administration (http://www.sbaonline.sba.gov) and by Industry Canada (http://strategis.ic.gc.ca)], it can be assumed that this more active role is the one more often preferred by policymakers. The general propensity to establish policies and programs, together with the keen interest in supporting rapid growth in particular and the emerging recognition that effective policies and programs need to be customized to segments within the population of small and new firms (Delmar and Davidsson 1998; Reuber and Fischer 1999; Chell and Baines 2000), underscores the importance of answering the question: How, if at all, can governments support rapid-growth firms effectively?

In order to address this question, we used a grounded theory approach (Glaser and Strauss 1967; Strauss and Corbin 1998) that was informed by a sensitivity to the multiple yet interrelated ways that different groups might have constructed their understanding of the phenomenon socially constructed (cf. Berger and Luckmann 1967). While there has been much prior research on entrepreneurial performance, with firm growth normally a dependent variable, there have been too few studies on rapid-growth firms as a distinct category to provide the basis for a theory refinement and testing approach. A grounded theory approach allowed for systematic exploration of the research question, generating, as opposed to testing, a conceptual model and also enabled exploration of the multiple perspectives on the phenomenon.

The next section of the paper discusses the previous research that has been done on rapid-growth firms, highlighting the implications for public policy of their distinctive characteristics, followed by a discussion of the research methods used. Taking the perspective that realities are socially constructed within, and enacted by, communities of practice (Berger and Luckmann 1967; Fleck 1979; Orr 1990; Lave and Wenger 1991; Brown and Duguid 2000), we started with the premise that three principal groups of individuals are knowledgeable about and have a vested interest in the success of rapid-growth firms. The first includes founders of rapid-growth firms, whose beliefs about rapid growth have direct consequences for the ways in which they manage their firms. The second consists of government policymakers, whose beliefs influence the programs, policies, and allocation of public resources (if any) targeted toward rapid-growth firms. The third is comprised of external resource providers (such as venture capitalists, bankers, and consultants), whose beliefs can influence both rapid-growth firm owners and policymakers seeking advice. Qualitative data were collected and analyzed from each of these groups. After describing these collection and analysis processes, the research findings are presented, followed by a discussion of implications for the development of policy initiatives to support rapid-growth firms.

Literature Review

The question of how governments can support rapid-growth firms most effectively is a difficult one because of the elusiveness of clear prescriptions for rapid growth. Some factors found to be associated with high-growth firms, such as having a greater sensitivity to opportunity (Feeser and Willard 1990); adaptability, flexibility and creativity (Lohmann 1998); or a distinctive temporal orientation (Fischer et al. 1997), are too abstract to yield meaningful practical guidelines for policymakers. Other factors found to be associated with high-

growth firms, such as innovation and venture capital backing (for example, Timmons and Bygrave 1986; Christensen and Bower 1996; Johnson, Baldwin, and Hinchley 1997) are less abstract but are outcome oriented and so leave unresolved the issue of what enables these outcomes to be achieved. In addition, paths to growth can differ systematically by firm-level factors such as age, size, and strategy and environment-level factors such as industry and geographic location (Covin, Slevin, and Covin 1990; Siegel, Siegel, and MacMillan 1993; Delmar and Davidsson 1998; Henderson 1999).

Moreover, rapid growth is arguably more difficult to sustain than to obtain and is often a mixed blessing for the growing firm. The research literature identifies common managerial issues associated with rapid growth, issues that are related to people, processes, and resources. The issues related to people stem from the fact that rapid-growth firms will double or even triple in size very quickly. The constant influx of new employees means that stress levels are high, skill levels are often inadequate, disaffection from the organization is common, and turf battles abound (Kotter and Sathe 1978; Hambrick and Crozier 1985). Furthermore, the founders may have strong start-up skills but may not possess the skills required to manage subsequent growth (Willard, Krueger, and Feeser 1992).

The issues related to processes are interrelated with those of people. The communication and decision-making systems and processes that exist in firms prior to a surge in growth rarely are adequate when the number of key managers has grown three-, four- or five-fold in a matter of months. Firms sometimes compound the problem by trying to adopt formalized, bureaucratized procedures that fit poorly both with their existing culture and with their need to stay nimble and to be innovative (Hambrick and Crozier 1985; Fombrum and Wally 1989).

Finally, the issues related to resources also are related to those involving people. One scarce resource is cash flow: The funds needed for working capital drain away the profits that growth can bring. Because of constant change, rapid-growth firms cannot realize efficiencies that may be possible in more stable environments; moreover, these firms always have to plan for and operate in business environments that are larger than their current financial resources (Kotter and Sathe 1978). This means, among other things, that existing employees who are pushed very hard may feel inadequately compensated (Hambrick and Crozier 1985). In addition, rapidly growing firms often need to recruit large numbers of new people with specialized skills, who may be difficult to locate and/or to attract (Kotter and Sathe 1978). Recruiting and training new people takes the time of key staff members within the firm, putting pressure on yet another scare resource—their attentional resources (Hambrick and Crozier 1985).

Given the difficult management issues associated with rapid growth, it is not surprising that it can result in ultimately poor performance. The same characteristics associated with high growth rates also can be associated with high failure rates (cf. Henderson 1999). Examining the growth of *Inc.* 500 firms from 1992 to 1996, Gartner and Markman (1999) find that sales growth is unrelated to profitability and, indeed, that employment growth is related negatively to profitability, and they conclude that rapid growth is likely to place strains on a firm's ability to operate efficiently and effectively. Studying a subset of *Inc.* 100 firms to identify the factors associated with success and failure, Hambrick and Crozier (1985) argue that "on first thought, it is hard to be very concerned about a company that is growing at over 50 percent per year. It seems like a

phenomenal success, where the entrepreneurs' dream has come completely true. But an extraordinary number of rapid-growth firms stumble severely, with unfortunate fates ranging from sharp sales and earnings declines to being acquired at a price far below what the business should have been worth, and even to bankruptcy. Instead of being a time for contentment, a period of rapid growth is a time for wariness" (32).

Thus, on the one hand, a firm that manages rapid growth successfully is seen as a valuable community resource: an important engine of economic development and an appropriate target of attention from policymakers. On the other hand, the reasons for its success are likely to be idiosyncratic and difficult to codify and transfer to other firms. Its continued growth is likely to be uncertain, and it is difficult to predict what type of attention from policymakers would be effective in sustaining growth. These gaps in our understanding of how rapid growth might be supported motivated the present study.

Research Methods

As has been mentioned, the grounded theory approach adopted here involved a sensitivity to different ways that reality may be constructed by different groups. The steps involved in this approach included a review of the prior literature (outlined above); an attempt to identify groups that might, a priori, be expected to have somewhat differing (albeit interrelated) understandings of the same phenomenon; the collection of data from members of the distinctive groups; and an iterative approach to the interpretation of this data. Our methodological approach integrates the standard procedures for developing grounded theory (Glaser and Strauss 1967; Strauss and Corbin 1998) with the guidelines offered by methodologists who emphasize sensitivity to multiple interpretive perspectives (Coffey and Atkinson 1996; Denzin and Lincoln 1994; Smircich and Stubbart 1985). More detail on the identification of groups, the collection of data and the interpretation of that data is provided below.

Group Identification and Data Collection

As an initial step, in-depth interviews with two firm owners and two public policy advisers were undertaken, were audiotaped, and were transcribed. They ranged in length from one to two-and-a-half hours. These interviews focused on the challenges and success factors the respondents believed to be associated with initiating and sustaining rapid growth and dealt with the possible roles outsiders can play. The interviews with public policy advisers focused on the ways that the government was attempting to assist rapid-growth firms. Extensive notes were taken by the interviewers both during and after the interviews.

As a result of an initial analysis of these data, additional data collection, involving an additional group of individuals, was undertaken. The group added was external resource providers and included venture capitalists, lenders, and consultants. Our first stage of data collection and analysis indicated that these groups are consulted heavily when public policy advisers are considering what should or should not be done for rapid-growth firms. Moreover, they are sometimes influential stakeholders in rapid-growth firms, so their perspectives, too, may inform day-to-day behavior in the firms. In the next phase of data collection, therefore, a number of firm owners, public policy advisers, and resource providers (venture capitalists, bankers, and consultants) concerned with rapid-growth firms were contacted regarding their willingness to participate in a one-day conference on the topic. To ensure that they had thought about key issues beforehand, those who could attend the conference were sent an open-ended questionnaire with the following three questions: (1) What distinctive characteristics or start-up factors lead to rapid firm growth? (2) What are the needs of, and obstacles faced by, early stage rapid-growth firms? and (3) What is the role of "outsiders"—governments, investors, bankers, or consultants—in nurturing rapid-growth firms?

The written responses to these open-ended questions constituted a supplementary source of data that complemented the interviews already conducted. They were not disseminated to conference attendees.

In the final phase of data collection, the one-day conference was held. Participants were six owners (all founders) of rapid-growth firms, three public policy advisers, four venture capitalists, four bankers, six consultants, the authors of this paper, two other business school academics, and a business journalist. The day involved both plenary discussions and breakout sessions where smaller groups discussed those questions listed above. Verbatim transcripts of the plenary discussions and breakout groups were created by professional court reporters.

Data Analysis

For the analysis, all of the texts created from each stage of the data collection (the interview transcripts, the written responses to the questionnaires, and the transcripts of the group discussions) were reviewed by the authors. The material from members of each group was separated initially, so that commonalities in the perspectives of members of each could be identified. The analysis proceeded, as is common in interpretive studies, by first categorizing and coding passages in the texts that seemed to be related (Huberman and Miles 1994; Coffey and Atkinson 1996; Strauss and

Corbin 1998). The categories were informed partially, but not completely, by the structure of the questions asked in the second and third phases of data collection: The analysis remained open to the emergence of new themes and issues. Coded passages in each category were grouped together, and instances of both agreement and disagreement were noted. Higher-order groupings of the initial categories were created in an iterative manner that attempted to account for negative cases if possible, to regroup categories where necessary, and to create a simple but insightful account of the key similarities and differences among groups. To enhance the credibility of the account (cf. Coffey and Atkinson 1996), a third business school academic, who did not participate in the preliminary phases of analysis but who attended the conference, reviewed the penultimate interpretation to assess its coherence and consistency. The results of this process are discussed in the next section.

Description and Interpretation of Findings

From the outset, a working assumption for this research was that individuals within a specific group would tend to share similar perspectives on the phenomenon of rapid-growth firms as a result of their shared social constructions of reality. However, the analysis undertaken allowed this assumption to be challenged; that is, variations among individuals within groups and across groups were explored, just as were within-group and between-group similarities. While the analysis suggested that there were some commonalities in the perspectives shared by those within groups, not surprisingly it also suggested that individuals did not always completely buy into the perspective that seemed dominant among members of their group. This divergence was largely

manifested as differences in the strengths of the views held, rather than as outright disagreements. Moreover, as some groups had considerably more representatives than others, the possibility for recognizing the disparity within the larger groups was probably greater. This information is important to keep in mind when considering the findings below, since it would be an unwarranted overgeneralization to assume that all members of each group viewed matters in exactly the same way.

What can be said is that distinct differences in perspectives did emerge. These have been organized into three distinct categories: external resource providers (including consultants, bankers, and venture capitalists), public policymakers, and rapid-growth firm owners. Table 1 summarizes key points of difference and similarity across the three perspectives as related to the roles of each group in supporting rapid growth, as well as the virtue of rapid growth itself.

To ensure that the group membership of each informant is clear and that their anonymity is maintained, everyone who either provided an initial interview or participated in the conference was assigned an identifier. Firm owners are referred to as OWNER 1 through OWNER 8. The public policy advisers, representing both the federal and provincial levels of government, are referred to as PPA 1 through PPA 5. The venture capitalists are VC 1 through VC 4. The bankers are BANKER 1 through BANKER 4. The consultants are CON 1 through CON 6.

The External Resource Provider Perspective: Rapid-Growth Firms as Lucrative Opportunities

Investors, bankers, and consultants certainly can be seen as three distinct groups of external resource providers. While there are differences among these groups, our analysis suggests that there

Table 1
Three Perspectives on Rapid-Growth Firms

Issue	External Resource Providers	Public Policy Advisers	Firm Owners
What are the roles of management in rapid growth?	Management is key but can be bought. Management needs to be receptive to outside help.	Management is key, but outside advice can help.	Management's vision and experience are key.
What are the roles of external resource providers in supporting rapid growth?	External resource providers are a key ingredient in supporting rapid growth.	External resource providers can be beneficial, but peer mentors can substitute.	External resource providers are sometimes necessary, especially in technical areas, and are often expensive.
What are the roles of governments in supporting rapid growth?	Governments have no direct role to play.	Governments have multiple, critical roles to play, including the provision of introductions, information and training.	Governments can be helpful, but public support is not necessary and cannot be relied on.
Is rapid growth good?	Rapid-growth firms are good for (our) business.	Rapid-growth firms are good for the economy and are politically beneficial.	Controlled growth is preferable because of the management challenges of rapid growth.

were many more commonalities in terms of their perspectives on rapid-growth firms. We believe these are reflected below, in that members of each group made compatible statements on the topics discussed, but we have used the naming system described above so that statements from consultants, bankers, and venture capitalists can be identified separately.

External Resource Providers Are One Ingredient in the Recipe for Success. External resource providers readily acknowledged that management is a key ingredient for rapid growth. However, this group felt that lack of management skills was not necessarily an obstacle, since outside managers or advisers could be brought in readily to replace founders who lacked the requisite skills.

Indeed, not surprisingly, external resource providers viewed themselves as very useful for rapid-growth firms. In addition to money, resource providers felt they could provide management with insights the firms themselves could not generate. For instance, CON 3 noted, "One of the interesting aspects that we, as service providers, can offer, is a lot of very useful benchmarking information for gazelles to not only sort of identify where they stand now, but how they position themselves for the future."

The perspective of this group was not merely that they could be helpful, however. Often, they viewed themselves as essential to the success of rapid-growth firms. While it can, in many cases, be argued that rapid-growth firms are reliant on external resource providers for financing, this group tended to believe that it was not just money that had to be sourced partially from external sources. CON 1 believes that "[one characteristic of a firm that will grow rapidly] is that they know they cannot do it all themselves. They look for help. . . . The lead people [in a rapid-growth firm] need to know the industry well and be

able to run the company well in the early stages. Alternatively, they need to know their limitations and be anxious to bring in the right management to run the company."

The implication here is that willingness to seek outsiders' help is hallmark of a firm able to grow rapidly. Moreover, the rugged individualism sometimes stereotypically associated with entrepreneurs is considered an impediment to rapid growth.

Governments Have No Direct Role to Play. As a group, external resource providers tended to believe that governments should, as BANKER 1 said, "Get out of the way," and as VC 2 said, "Stay out of the way." For some, this meant that they should not attempt to offer any assistance, while for others, it meant that they should minimize the interferences of bureaucracy, thereby creating a more hospitable business climate. VC 1 put this idea as follows: "I am not sure government should have direct involvement in rapid-growth firms. I would prefer to have government set general policies to encourage venture investment, technical training, research and development, etc."

The notion, then, that governments had any constructive role to play, much less a critical one, did not seem evident among members of this group.

Rapid-Growth Firms Are Good for (Our) Business. Consultants, investors, and bankers all recognized that many rapid-growth firms fail, often in spectacular ways. Nonetheless, the external resource providers included in this study viewed rapid-growth firms as a desirable target market because of the potential upsides associated with them. Some evidence of this comes from the fact that BANKER 1, BANKER 3, and BANKER 4 all were willing to offer financial support for studying rapid-growth firms. BANKER 1 stated that "two years ago we had nine people dedicated to nothing but these kinds of high growth companies and helping with either quasi-equity or venture capital type investments. Today we have 61."

All of the venture capitalists in the study viewed themselves as specialists in identifying rapid-growth firms, and each of the consultants had or was developing special services targeted toward rapid-growth firms.

The Public Policy Perspective: Rapid-Growth Firms as a Breed for which to Be Cared and Cloned

Rapid-Growth Firms Are a Resource for the Economy. Public policy advisers from both levels of government could justify readily the necessity of ongoing government attention to and support of rapid-growth firms given their strong belief that such firms are engines of the economy. Materials supplied by PPA 4 and PPA 5 stated that their government "has recognized the importance of [rapid growth] firms over the past three years to the [regional] economy. These firms create high value added jobs, are innovators, achieve higher growth in sales and profits, are high R & D performers, and are more likely to make capital investments and are export oriented."

Not all public policy advisers were so unquestioning of the virtue of rapid growth. PPA 2 noted, for instance, that many do not have profit performance that is matched to their sales growth. Overall, however, there was a sense that rapid-growth firms were good for the economy and could provide leadership by example to other small and medium-sized businesses in the region.

This sense is reflected in the efforts that PPA 4 and PPA 5 undertook to inventory those firms that met certain criteria they felt were indicative of future growth potential. They had invested considerable resources in having field officers in various regions identify the firms in their areas that had been growing at more than 25 percent per annum, had at least 10 employees, and had been in business for at least three years so that they could be included in a database of rapid-growth firms in their jurisdiction.

External Resource Providers Can Be Beneficial. Public policy advisers were neither dismissive of external resource providers nor were convinced that they were an absolute necessity. The view that they can be helpful, but may not always be necessary, was nicely stated by PPA 3: "I have met a few entrepreneurs who know everything and who really don't need to have any outside information from anybody else. But I haven't met many like that. And regardless of whether or not they are open to a board of advisers, or they are open to a professional, they are seeking out information and knowledge in one way or another. They may be doing a lot of reading or going to the Chamber of Commerce gathering, you know, getting information from other business owners, friends. They are doing something to advance their learning. It's different for everybody. It's not one formula that's going to meet everybody's needs." As this quotation suggests, public policy advisers tended to view mentoring from business peers as a reasonable substitute for external resource providers in at least some cases.

Public policy advisers expressed the view that rapid-growth firms needed some input from outsiders, but that this didn't mean they should be dependent upon them. PPA 1 said, "[Firms in the early stages of rapid growth] need a group of outside advisers. . . . [But] frequently the ones who are running for help are the wrong ones. You don't want to get too close to the ones that are running for help."

Governments Have Multiple, Critical Roles to Play. As would be expected, the public policy advisers felt it was possible for them to provide assistance to rapid-growth firm owners. This is revealed by public initiatives at both levels of government. For instance, picking up the idea that outside advice could come from peers, PPA 3 reported on the results of a focus group that one government agency had done with rapid-growth firm owners as follows: "Mentoring and brokering [of mentors] was probably the most critical thing that government could do. So if I'm an entrepreneur—I will give you an example of a young entrepreneur who wants to manufacture guitars who has found a new material and manufacturing technology that would allow him to make really inexpensive guitars, who wanted to meet with [name] who makes drums and cymbals that are all over the world. He just wanted to have an introduction on the phone so he could arrange to go to wherever it is and to have dinner with the guy, that's all he wanted, to have a chance to pick his brain, ask him questions and maybe have the drum and cymbals guy make connections for him. And I think that role, mentoring role is extremely important."

Facilitating peer relationships among rapid-growth firm owners was not the only initiative public policy advisers were undertaking, however. PPA 2, for instance, had invested considerable resources in a report that would identify unique success factors associated with rapid-growth firms based on the premise that this would help them and other firms to prosper. PPA 3 was considering ways in which the government could influence business school curricula so that graduating students would be more prepared to develop and to manage rapid-growth firms.

More than merely feeling they could be helpful, however, both the federal and provincial public policy advisers felt they had to be involved. This was evident in the fight for survival of the unit devoted to rapid-growth firms which PPA 4 and PPA 5 described. They noted that, in a time of government cutbacks, they had managed thus far to convince the senior officials in their governments to continue funding for the units devoted to identifying and to assisting rapid-growth firms. The continued funding of units solely dedicated to rapid-growth firms suggests that this was regarded by key members of the government as something of a necessity. This was not solely because of the aid that could be given to these firms: One of the purposes of inventorying rapid-growth firms in particular geographic areas was to provide politicians with local economic development "success stories" to talk about in their regional meetings and speeches.

The Firm Owner Perspective: Rapid-Growth Firms as an Act of Disciplined Imagination

Rapid-Growth Firms Require Visionary Leaders. Perhaps not surprisingly, given that firm owners have "been there and done that," this group stressed management qualities over all others as that which distinguished rapid-growth firms. They did not dispute that unique products, growing markets, and access to capital were necessary but clearly viewed them as insufficient.

Like other groups, they believed management required such characteristics as those described by OWNER 4: "experience, industry knowledge, and leadership." Beyond these skills, however, owners stressed another quality which had to do with seeing a potential for growth and making it happen. This quality is captured in the following description by OWNER 1 of what characterized an early stage firm with rapid growth potential—"a competent senior management team that has a shared vision and proven expertise in marketing and delivering the products/services the gazelle has to offer." OWNER 6 described the quality that would allow an envisioned future to become a reality as follows: "Rapid-growth firm managers need to have ego. And a visionary 'never big enough' attitude." OWNER 8 described his partner's vision as being "like a light bulb": "[He] came up with the initial idea. He described the idea and he was able to get it across to people that there was real potential here."

In stressing the importance not only of skills and knowledge but of vision or disciplined imagination, rapid-growth firm owners seemed to reject the notion that a firm with rapid growth potential necessarily could be recognized a priori and could be targeted at an early stage for assistance or for support either by governments or by external resource providers. That is, founders believe that no one except founders can cause rapid growth to happen. OWNER 5 expressed this, saying, "Rapid-growth firms happen because of the people involved. I don't think they can be reliably identified until after the fact. Investors are good, but how can they decide what will be a winner? I don't think you could formalize a procedure for identifying [potential rapid-growth firms]. I think you're going to have a lot of trouble trying to reduce it to a key set of questions or personality profiles and things like that because although everyone will come up with their anecdotes of someone who could identify a gazelle, they're probably missing the 900 or so that goofed up and aren't going to tell you."

The Sometimes-Necessary Evil of External Resource Providers. The owner–managers viewed external resource providers as being a necessity for some purposes (such as the provision of financing) and in these instances as unavoidable irritants. OWNER 1 described how, for example, long-term strategic plans were unrealistic as guides to action but were necessary to placate funders: "There will be a lot of issues that are going to arise. If you pretend that you've planned for them, you're just kidding yourself. And, generally, you're doing that [creating a long term strategic plan] because the business community, the banking community, for instance, wants to see a detailed plan. So you do that in order to meet the needs of the reader recognizing that the plan will fall by the wayside pretty quickly.

Business owners gave the impression that they were skeptical about what resources other than capital outsiders could provide. Some simply believed that those with the vision required to manage a rapid-growth firm would be resistant to outside help. For example, OWNER 6 said, "I believe that a true entrepreneur . . . will never fully utilize the benefits of consultants and investors other than for capital. A 'gazelle-type' leader is not easily persuaded away from his visionary ideals."

Other owner–managers stressed that at times they needed the help of, for example, accountants or lawyers but found them to be at best mixed blessings. OWNER 5 gave the following account of his firm's original use of such external resource providers and of his subsequent attitude toward them:

> When we started the company, none of us were true financial accountants or legal or any of that kind of stuff. We knew how to make our stuff and hopefully how to market it, but we did need legal and accounting advice. Of course, we had to go and make our original business plan, put it all together, and the first thing we found out is how much all this legal and accounting advice costs. If I was providing consulting services I would never have the gall to charge these rates. Then what happened is we said to them that we had to write this business plan, and you guys actually turn out to be a good chunk of that. How

many hours do we need [to budget to pay for legal and accounting advice]? They were the only thing we were off in our business plan for the first five-year business plan in terms of the number of hours and the dollars we actually had to pay. They underestimated like mad.

It was valuable advice and we needed the advice and I'm not disputing that. It's just that the price was high. It made us gun shy for going for other things, like advertising help . . . It really is a price issue, and, in fact, are we really getting value for that money in the early stages of the company when you don't even know whether you're going to have a product out there half the time or whether people are going to buy it?

Now, most of my legal agreements we do. I use common sense, or I go to some other company in the same business. I have a lot of agents around the world, so I went and got some examples of agency agreements that I use internationally rather than going to a lawyer. If I go to a lawyer it would cost me $6,000. To go and get it from some related company but not a competitor, it cost me nothing except for a little bit of effort.

The end of this quotation highlights a persistent theme among firm owners. Because of the value they placed on the quality of management and in particular on experience, their peers—owners of other rapid-growth firms—were seen as invaluable sources of relevant and useful advice.

Even among business owners who sometimes relied on external resource providers, there was a sense that firms needed to be wary of these would-be predators. OWNER 4 stated that "[professional advisers] are just out to make money. They won't tell me when I'm full of shit, and they want to sign me up for five years." OWNER 1 phrased his beliefs in the form of a message to external resource providers: "For those of you who are supplying services to companies, whether they be gazelles or not, you're using the euphemism of 'How do I help them?' I think what you're really asking is 'How do I make money from them?' For those of you in venture capital companies, how many of you are saying, 'How can I give a fair value for their business?' You're not saying that. You're saying 'How do I buy in cheaply, perhaps even before they recognize their real value?' There's a high degree of mistrust because now [that my business has grown larger] I'm hearing from so many people that would like to give me help, or buy in at low rates, or give me advice that I may or may not need, but since I can now pay for it, I probably should not want it."

Government Is neither Necessary nor Negative. Compared with external resource providers, the firm owners tended to view government as "low-risk" service providers. OWNER 4 expressed this attitude in saying, "We take everything the government has in terms of trade shows. We take everything that the Business Development Bank offers in consulting and advice. We go and say this is a resource." While government resources might be low risk, they could also be low return. Typical of this view was OWNER 5, who felt governments could not design programs or policies that provided proper incentives or assistance to firm owners. He stated, for instance that "research and development tax credits should be irrelevant to good decisions on what to develop."

Others believed that some programs provided by government agencies could be of value. OWNER 6, for example, demonstrated enthusiasm for roles the government could play, saying, "Government can be fantastic support for export advice and monetary incentives. Government could also be searching the world for the best technology [rapid-growth firms] can use but may not have the resources to learn about.

An underlying theme among this group was that firms never could rely on governments for assistance. Firm owners might be willing to take what the government offered, but they needed to be able to function without looking to governments for help and without counting on them to create a more favorable business climate.

Rapid Growth Is Not Necessarily a Good Thing. While the firm owners in this group were chosen because they had been able to grow their businesses at high rates for at least five years, they did not value growth for its own sake. OWNER 1 gave voice to the rationale behind ambivalence toward growth that he and his partners felt: "We'll only continue [to grow] at this pace if we must, so as not to miss key windows of opportunity. Otherwise, our business strategy calls for a more sedate pace. We call it aggressive but manageable growth." Manageable growth levels could vary from time to time and from firm to firm. OWNER 4 noted that at times his firm has "literally slowed down our growth while we trying to get the organization more tuned . . . If we didn't do that, we wouldn't have been around today."

The viewpoints of firm owners reflect the previously cited research findings indicating that growth was not an unmixed good and that controlled growth needs to be a higher priority than rapid growth. While government policymakers and private sector resource providers appear to laud rapid growth per se, firm owners themselves often do not.

Interpretation and Implications: (How) Should Governments Support Rapid-Growth Firms?

An essential first point to make here is that this study is not attempting to determine which perspective is "right" or to dismiss the beliefs of any group as naive or wrong-headed. One key assumption of this study is that different groups socially construct different realities and that these differing realities have powerful implications for behaviors. In a study such as this one, it is an understanding of understandings that is sought, since differences in understanding can lead to confusion and to failed communications at best and to conflict, hostility, and wasted resources at worst. What this study makes clear is that there are sufficiently many differences in perspectives among private-sector resource providers, governments, and firm owners that the potential for unfortunate outcomes is considerable. That which resource providers or public policymakers think governments should do is not necessarily that which firm owners want or will use, for a variety of reasons.

External resource providers want access to rapid-growth firms and to potential rapid-growth firms both for altruistic reasons (in order to provide advice they perceive as essential to firms' growth) and for less altruistic reasons (they can provide a lucrative, ongoing revenue stream). Similarly, public policymakers want access to these firms for altruistic reasons (again, in order to provide support which they perceive as valuable for firms) and for less altruistic reasons (they provide politically valuable evidence of economic development). Rapid-growth firms as a group, however, have mixed feelings about being identified as such, much less as being targeted for support. Those firms that do become known tend to be seeking publicity for specific strategic reasons (for example, attracting outside investors). On the other hand, the firm owners in this sample suggested that they sometimes avoided publicity to keep competitors at bay and often were indifferent to it since it served little purpose in their markets.

While firm owners may be relatively neutral about the value of government-backed policies and programs to assist them, they tend to be less suspicious of government assistance than that of private sector resource providers. The obvious gap that exists between the perspectives of firm owners and external resource providers thus may correspond to a role that governments are well suited to play. Firm owners are skeptical of, and sometimes are hostile toward, external resource providers who might offer valued information at critical times. Yet rapid-growth business owners want (in addition to a positive overall business climate) timely and appropriate information.

If governments can help to address this gap in a way that private-sector resource providers do not, the problem for them is how to develop inventory and retrieval mechanisms to provide for the needs of firms in a wide variety of industries and stages of development and how to satisfy these needs in the just-in-time fashion required by rapid-growth firms operating with very narrow windows of opportunity. If rapid-growth firms cannot reliably access information and introductions from their governments in a timely fashion, credibility will be lost and resources will be wasted.

The answer may lie in the fact that owners of rapid-growth firms are most comfortable learning and obtaining advice from their peers (in particular owners of other rapid-growth firms) but may not have the time or access to develop effective peer networks. They

require access to a wide range of information, but at unpredictable times and with a short shelf life, and so they prefer to obtain it in a reactive rather than proactive manner, focusing on the specific information that is required in a specific situation (cf. Sexton et al. 1997). This importance of peer and just-in-time support suggests that a network-based approach to policy initiatives in the area might be appropriate.

Although it has been argued that the owners of small firms are not interested in networking (Curran and Blackburn 1994), subsequent researchers have found that while this may be true for owners of low-growth firms, owners of high-growth firms understand that they need to engage in networking activities in order for their firms to develop needed ties beyond their personal circle of contacts and their local communities (Aldrich 1999; Chell and Baines 2000; Huggins 2000; Hite and Hesterly 2001). Hite and Hesterly (2001) argue that the ties in a firm's network will become less personal and will become more calculative and intentionally managed as the firm grows. Thus, we should expect that owners of rapid-growth firms will be interested in a network-based approach to policy that is aimed at supporting rapid growth.

One possibility along these lines is to conceptualize a network of rapid-growth firms as a cluster based on the demographic characteristic of firm growth. Much has been written about the role of clusters in promoting economic growth in both developed and developing economies (for example, Saxenian 1994; Rabelotti 1995; Humphrey and Schmitz 1996; Pouder and St. John 1996; Swann, Prevezer, and Stout 1998). However, clusters normally are defined as being specific to a particular geographic region and industry—for example, information technology in Silicon Valley, machining in Tokyo's Ota Ward, and shoemaking in Brazil's Sinos Valley. The benefits from interfirm learning that such clusters can provide, though, is that which is sought in developing support for rapid-growth firms. What would it take to develop a growth-based cluster?

An experiment along these lines is the Innovators Alliance, established by the Ontario Ministry of Enterprise, Opportunity & Innovation in June 1999 (see the website http://www.innovators.org). Financial support is provided by the government at a decreasing level over four years and by external resource providers (such as consulting firms, law firms, and banks) that wish to become affiliates. There are currently 150 members, all of whom are chief executive officers (CEOs) of rapid-growth firms. To be eligible for membership, a CEO's firm must have a head office in Ontario; have a minimum growth rate of 50 percent over three years; employ at least 20 people or have annual sales greater than $2 million; and employ no more than 500 people (although members with firms larger than this may remain in the organization as mentors). There is a permanent staff of three people.

There are eight local chapters of the organization across Ontario, all of which have monthly peer-to-peer meetings, where firm owners can discuss issues with each other. The value of these meetings is indicated by the high show rate: Roughly 70 percent of the local members are in attendance at any given meeting. The discussion at these gatherings is considered explicitly confidential in order to encourage openness and collaboration. In addition, there is an annual conference focused on specific issues and informal networking opportunities, such as a province-wide golf tournament.

Recently, members of the Innovators Alliance have had access to a members-only website, which has a bulletin board facility so that members can post questions and can receive comments and suggestions from other members. Although it is too early to determine how used or useful this system will be, the type of material posted to-date reflects the finding in this study that firm owners value concrete, operational information from their peers. For example, one topic that generated interest was how to set up a customer service relations department. Members responded with comments about the benefits of such an entity, things to watch out for, and practical suggestions for compensation and how the relationship between the department and a direct sales team might be structured. Another topic that generated interest was employee-shared ownership plans. Here, not only did members provide operational advice but, in one case, also recommended a consultant who had helped them considerably in implementing such a plan. Such a referral is likely to be particularly valuable, given the high degree of skepticism of consultants among firm owners in this study.

Thus, the Innovators Alliance reflects a model of support provision that is consistent with the findings of this research. It provides a forum for a wide range of rapid-growth firm owners to consult with each other on an ongoing basis as they require advice and reflects the importance of management as a key determinant of rapid growth. It has a funding model that is reflective of external resource providers' financial incentives and public policymakers' political incentives to become known to rapid-growth firms and to assist their growth. Moreover, it provides for regular interaction among these firm owners, private-sector resource providers, and government policymakers.

Regular interaction and a concomitant increase in mutual trust are necessary steps in understanding the needs of rapid-growth firms. Entrepreneurship research in the area of exporting, for example, has recognized that available support services are not used by those who, theoretically, could benefit the most from them, and has prescribed better market segmentation and targeting practices (Seringhaus and Rosson 1990; Crick 1995; Gray 1997; OECD 1997; Orser et al. 1999). The same prescription appears to be valid for providers of resources and services to rapid-growth firms, but it is only through "getting close to the customer" and understanding that "one-size-fits-all" policies are unlikely to be effective that market segmentation and targeting practices can be improved.

It is too early to determine what the long-term success of the Innovators Alliance will be. Membership is growing, as are the number of affiliated external resource providers. Different communication mechanisms are being explored. Due to its exclusivity to rapid-growth firms, it is highly focused, embodies shared attitudes, and has a low level of direct market competition, all of which have been shown to be important to effective network initiatives (Huggins 2000). Cautious optimism therefore is warranted.

Conclusion

Rapid-growth firms are attracting the attention of policymakers worldwide because of their contribution to job creation and economic development. Although they frequently need assistance to sustain their growth, it is difficult to determine appropriate policy initiatives, given their idiosyncratic and unpredictable requirements. The objective of this research was to develop a theoretical basis on which to identify guidelines for such initiatives, based on the perceptions of firm owners, policymakers, and private-sector resource providers such as venture capitalists, bankers, and consultants.

The research findings indicate that policymakers and external resources providers have incentives to interact with rapid-growth firms, but, although rapid-growth firms also have an incentive to interact with these other two groups,

they prefer to obtain advice from their peers. These findings provide tentative support for a network-based approach to the support of rapid growth by governments.

The theoretical contribution of the paper lies in its recognition of rapid-growth firm owners as knowledgeable and purposive actors actively engaged in acquiring and assessing different sources of support and advice. Much of the literature on assistance to new and small firms is focused on the differential impact of receiving or not receiving assistance from particular programs and/or on the effectiveness of the support obtained (for example, Chrisman and McMullan 2000). A construct frequently missing in this body of work is the value and content of alternate sources of support. The research presented in this paper suggests that owners of rapid-growth firms draw on diverse sources of support and are continually assessing their relevance and cost-effectiveness. Measures of the effectiveness of any one focal program therefore are likely to be confounded with support and advice provided elsewhere.

Furthermore, given that rapid-growth firm owners view support and resources obtained externally in a nuanced and specific way, they are more apt to discern positive and negative features of particular offerings than they are to classify them as "useful" or "not useful." This has implications for the measures used to evaluate specific programs or sources of advice. Much of the research in this area is based on questionnaire data, where respondents are provided with a list of programs or sources of advice and are asked to rate their usefulness on a Likert-type scale. The findings presented here suggest that this measurement scheme is not likely to capture the specifics of what is valued and what is not valued.

The paper suggests two directions for future research. The first is to examine the segments that exist among owners of new and small firms in the market for support services. It may be that other populations of owners, such as nascent entrepreneurs (Carter, Gartner, and Reynolds 1996) or established, slower-growth firms view support provision in a different way than did the rapid-growth firm owners in this study. Further, it may be that there are relevant segments within the population of owners of rapid-growth firms differentiated, for example, by industry or geographic location. A second possible direction for future research is to study longitudinally network-based approaches to the support of rapid growth. A social capital perspective (Coleman 1988; Portes and Sensenbrenner 1993) would be particularly interesting here—to examine whether and how regular interaction among firm owners, public sector advisers, and private-sector resource providers impacts the trust, reciprocity, information flows, and shared norms among and within different groups of participants. This research suggests that improvements in these areas would be welcomed by all concerned.

References

Aldrich, Howard (1999). *Organizations Evolving*. Thousand Oaks, CA: Sage Publications.

Baldwin, John (1994). *Strategies for Success: A Profile of Growing Small and Medium-Sized Enterprises (GSMEs) in Canada*. Ottawa: Statistics Canada.

Bennett, Robert J., and Paul J.A. Robson (1999). "The Use of External Business Advice by SMEs in Britain," *Entrepreneurship & Regional Development* 11(2), 155–180.

Berger, Peter, and Thomas Luckmann (1967). *The Social Construction of Reality: A Treatise in the Sociology of Knowledge*. Garden City, NY: Doubleday.

Birch, David (1987). *Job Creation in America*. New York: Free Press.

—— (1995). *Who's Creating Jobs?* Cambridge, MA: Cognetics, Inc.

Birley, Sue, Dan Muzyka, Caroline Dove, and Gerda Rossell (1995). "Finding the High-Flying Entrepreneurs: A Cautionary Tale," *Entrepreneurship: Theory & Practice* 19(4), 105–111.

Brown, John Seely, and Paul Duguid (2000). *The Social Life of Information*, Boston, MA: Harvard Business School Press.

Brush, Candida G., and Pieter A. Vanderwerf (1992). "A Comparison of Methods and Sources for Obtaining Estimates of New Venture Performance," *Journal of Business Venturing* 7(2), 157–170.

Carter, Nancy M., William B. Gartner, and Paul D. Reynolds (1996). "Exploring Start-Up Event Sequences," *Journal of Business Venturing* 11(3), 151–166.

Chandler, Gaylen N., and Steven H. Hanks (1993). "Measuring the Performance of Emerging Businesses: A Validation Study," *Journal of Business Venturing* 8(5), 391–408.

Chell, Elizabeth, and Susan Baines (2000). "Networking, Entrepreneurship and Microbusiness Behavior," *Journal of Small Business Management* 12(3), 195–215.

Chrisman, James J., and W. Ed McMullan (2000). "A Preliminary Assessment of Outsider Assistance as a Knowledge Resource: The Longer-Term Impact of New Venture Counseling," *Entrepreneurship: Theory & Practice* 24(3), 37–53.

Christensen, Clayton M., and Joseph L. Bower (1996). "Customer Power, Strategic Investment, and the Failure of Leading Firms," *Strategic Management Journal* 17(3), 197–218.

Coffey, Amanda, and Paul Atkinson (1996). *Making Sense of Qualitative Data*. Thousand Oaks, CA: Sage Publications.

Coleman, James S. (1988). "Social Capital in the Creation of Human Capital," *American Journal of Sociology* 94(Supplement), S95–S120.

Collinson, Simon (2000). "Knowledge Networks for Innovation in Small Scottish Software Firms," *Entrepreneurship & Regional Development* 12(3), 217–244.

Covin, Jeffrey G., Dennis P. Slevin, and Teresa Joyce Covin (1990). "Content and Performance of Growth-Seeking Strategies: A Comparison of Small Firms in High- and Low-Technology Industries," *Journal of Business Venturing* 5(6), 391–412.

Crick, David (1995). "An Investigation into the Targeting of U.K. Exporting Assistance," *European Journal of Marketing* 29(8), 76–94.

Curran, J., and R.A. Blackburn (1994). *Small Firms and Local Economic Networks: The Death of the Local Economy*. London: Paul Chapman.

Delmar, Frédéric, and Per Davidsson (1998). "A Taxonomy of High-Growth Firms," in *Frontiers of Entrepreneurship Research*. Ed. Paul D. Reynolds, William D. Bygrave, Nancy M. Carter, Sophie Manigart, Colin M. Mason, G. Dale Meyer, and Kelly G. Shaver. Wellesley, MA: Arthur M. Blank Center for Entrepreneurship, Babson College, 399–413.

Denzin, Norman, and Yvonna Lincoln (1994). "Introduction: Entering the Field of Qualitative Research," in *Handbook of Qualitative Research*. Ed. Norman Denzin and Yvonna Lincoln. Thousand Oaks, CA: Sage, 1–17.

Department of Trade and Industry (1994). *Competitiveness—How the Best UK Companies Are Winning*. London: Government of Great Britain.

Fischer, Eileen, A. Rebecca Reuber, Moez Hababou, William Johnson, and Steven Lee (1997). "The Role of Socially Constructed Temporal Perspectives in the Emergence of Rapid-Growth Firms," *Entrepreneurship Theory & Practice* 22(2), 13–30.

Fleck, Ludwick (1979). *Genesis and the Development of Scientific Fact*. Chicago, IL: University of Chicago Press.

Feeser, Henry R., and Gary E. Willard (1990). "Founding Strategy and Performance: A Comparison of High- and Low-Growth High-Tech Firms," *Strategic Management Journal* 11(2), 87–98.

Fombrum, Charles J., and Stefan Wally (1989). "Structuring Small Firms for Rapid Growth," *Journal of Business Venturing* 4(2), 107–122.

Gartner, William B., and Markman, Gideon D. (1999). "Is Growth Profitable? A Study of *Inc.* 500 Fast Growth Companies," in *Frontiers of Entrepreneurship Research*. Ed. Paul D. Reynolds, William D. Bygrave, Sophie Manigart, Colin M. Mason, G. Dale Meyer, Harry J. Sapienza, and Kelly G. Shaver. Wellesley, MA: Arthur M. Blank Centre for Entrepreneurship, Babson College, 633.

Gibson, Alan (1997). "Business Development Services: Core Principles and Future Challenges," *Small Enterprise Development* 8(3), 4–14.

Glaser, Barney, and Anselm Strauss (1967). *The Discovery of Grounded Theory*. New York: Aldine.

Gray, Brendan (1997). "Profiling Managers to Improve Export Promotion Targeting," *Journal of International Business Studies* 29(2), 387–419.

Hallberg, Kristin (1999). *Small- and Medium-Scale Enterprises: A Framework for Intervention*. Washington, D.C.: Small Enterprise Unit, Private Sector Development Department, The World Bank.

Hambrick, Donald C., and Lynn M. Crozier (1985). "Stumblers and Stars in the Management of Rapid Growth," *Journal of Business Venturing* 1(1), 31–45.

Henderson, Andrew D. (1999). "Firm Strategy and Age Dependence: A Contingent View of the Liabilities of Newness, Adolescence, and Obsolescence," *Administrative Science Quarterly* 44(2), 281–314.

Hite, Julie M., and William S. Hesterly (2001). "The Evolution of Firm Networks: From Emergence to Early Growth of the Firm," *Strategic Management Journal* 22(3), 275–286.

Hopkins, Michael (1997). "Help Wanted." *Inc. Magazine*, May 20, 35–41.

Huberman, Michael, and Matthew Miles (1994). "Data Management and Analysis Methods, in *Handbook of Qualitative Research*. Ed. Norman Denzin and Yvonna Lincoln. Thousand Oaks, CA: Sage, 413–427.

Huggins, Robert (2000). "The Success and Failure of Policy-Implanted Inter-Firm network Initiatives: Motivations, Processes and Structure," *Entrepreneurship & Regional Development* 12(2), 111–135.

Humphrey, John, and Hubert Schmitz (1996). "The Triple C Approach to Local Industrial Policy," *World Development* 24(12), 1859–1877.

Johnson, Joanne, John Baldwin, and Christine Hinchley (1997). *Successful Entrants: Creating the Capacity for Survival and Growth*. Ottawa: Statistics Canada.

Kotter, J., and V. Sathe (1978). "Problems of Human Resource Management in Rapidly Growing Companies," *California Management Review* 21(2), 29–36.

Lave, Jean, and Etienne Wenger (1991). *Situated Learning: Legitimate Peripheral Participation*. Cambridge, UK: Cambridge University Press.

Levie, Jonathan (1994). "Can Governments Nurture Young Growing Firms? Qualitative Evidence from a Three-Nation Study," in *Frontiers of Entrepreneurship Research*. Ed. William D. Bygrave, Susan Birley, Neil C. Churchill, Elizabeth Gatewood, Frank Hoy, Robert H. Keeley, and William E. Wetzel Jr. Wellesley, MA: Arthur M. Blank Centre for Entrepreneurship, Babson College.

Levy, Brian (1994). "Technical and Marketing Support Systems for Successful Small and Medium-Size Enterprises in Four Countries," *Policy Research Working Paper No. 1400*. Washington, D.C.: Policy Research Department, Private Sector Development Department, The World Bank.

Lohmann, David (1998). "Strategies of High-Growth Firms in Adverse Public Policy and Economic Environments," in *Frontiers of Entrepreneurship Research*. Ed. Paul D. Reynolds, William D. Bygrave, Nancy M. Carter, Sophie Manigart, Colin M. Mason, G. Dale Meyer, and Kelly G. Shaver. Wellesley, MA: Arthur M. Blank Centre for Entrepreneurship, Babson College, 16–29.

March, James G., and Robert I. Sutton (1997). "Organizational Performance as a Dependent Variable," *Organization Science* 8(6), 698–706.

Organization for Economic Cooperation and Development (OECD) (1997). *Globalization and Small and Medium Enterprises (SMEs). Volume 1: Synthesis Report* and *Volume 2: Country Studies*. Paris: Organization for Economic Cooperation and Development.

Orr, Julian (1990). "Sharing Knowledge, Celebrating Identity: Community Knowledge in a Service Culture," in *Collective Remembering*. Ed. David Middleton and Derek Edwards. Newbury Park, CA: Sage.

Orser, Barbara, Eileen Fischer, Sue Hooper, Rebecca Reuber, and Allan Riding (1999). *Beyond Borders: Canadian Businesswoman in Trade*. Ottawa: Department of Foreign Affairs and International Trade Canada.

Portes, Alejandro, and Julia Sensenbrenner (1993). "Embeddedness and Immigration: Notes on the Social Determinants of Economic

Action," *American Journal of Sociology* 98(6), 1320–1350.

Pouder, Richard, and Caron H. St. John (1996). "Hot Spots and Blind Spots: Geographical Clusters of Firms and Innovation," *Academy of Management Review* 21(4), 1192–1225.

Rabellotti, Roberta (1995). "Is There an Industrial District Model? Footwear Districts in Italy and Mexico Compared," *World Development* 23(1), 29–41.

Reuber, A. Rebecca, and Eileen Fischer (1999). "Domestic Market Size, Competences, and the Internationalization of Small- and Medium-Sized Enterprises," in *Research in Global Strategic Management* 7. Ed. Alan M. Rugman and Richard W. Wright. Stamford, CT: JAI Press Inc., 85–100.

Saxenian, AnnaLee (1994). *Regional Advantage: Culture and Competition in Silicon Valley and Route 128.* Cambridge, MA: Harvard University Press.

Seringhaus, Rolf, and Phillip Rosson (1990). *Government Export Promotion: A Global Perspective.* New York: Routledge.

Sexton, Donald L., Nancy B. Upton, Larry E. Wacholtz, and Patricia P. McDougall (1997). "Learning Needs of Growth-Oriented Entrepreneurs," *Journal of Business Venturing* 12(1), 1–8.

Siegel, Robin, Eric Siegel, and Ian C. MacMillan (1993). "Characteristics Distinguishing High-Growth Ventures," *Journal of Business Venturing* 8(2), 169–180.

Storey, David J. (1996). *The Ten Percenters—Fast-Growing SMEs in Great Britain.* London: Deloitte & Touche.

Smircich, Linda, and Charles Stubbart (1985). "Strategic Management in an Enacted World," *Academy of Management Review* 10(4), 724–736.

Strauss, Anselm, and Juliet Corbin (1998). *Basics of Qualitative Research: Techniques and Procedures for Developing Grounded Theory,* 2nd ed. Thousand Oaks, CA: Sage.

Swann, G.M. Peter, Martha Prevezer, and David Stout (1998). *The Dynamics of Industrial Clustering: International Comparisons in Computing and Biotechnology.* Oxford: Oxford University Press.

Timmons, Jeffery A., and William D. Bygrave (1986). "Venture Capital's Role in Financing Innovation for Economic Growth," *Journal of Business Venturing* 1(2), 161–176.

Willard, Gary.E., David A. Krueger, and Henry R. Feeser (1992). "In Order to Grow, Must the Founder Go?: A Comparison of Performance between Founder- and Nonfounder-Managed High-Growth Manufacturing Firms," *Journal of Business Venturing* 7(3), 181–194.

Accountants as Sources of Business Advice for Small Firms

by Paul N. Gooderham, Anita Tobiassen, Erik Døving, and Odd Nordhaug

In many countries small business accountants play an important role as business advisers for small firms in addition to providing basic accounting services. However, while some small firms make extensive use of external accountants as business advisers, a substantial proportion uses them only to a minor degree. On the basis of small firms in Norway the aim of this article is to contribute to our understanding of the determinants of such variations. Our study reveals that the quality, rather than the longevity, of the relationship between firm and authorized accountant is an important antecedent of the degree to which small firms use accountants as business advisers. In addition, the study indicates that the competency orientation of firms also functions as an important determinant.

Key Words: accountants; business advisory services; small firms

Introduction

In a number of countries accountants who have small firms as their client base have been developing services over and above traditional accountancy services. As such they have increasingly "depicted themselves as multidisciplinary practices, one-stop shops for an extensive array of services, including financial advisory, management consulting, and legal services" (Greenwood et al., 2002: 58). In the case of Norway, which constitutes the setting for this study, NARF (Norges Autoriserte Regnskapsføreres Forening [The Norwegian Association of Autho-

rized Accountants]), the main professional association for accountants with a small firm focus, has for the past five years been actively encouraging its membership to regard itself as business advisers. The main task of this article is to extend our knowledge of the characteristics of those small firms who use business advisory services stemming from accountants.

To date little is known about which factors are important for small firms in making use of accountants as sources of business advice. On a general level what is known is that the smaller the firm the less likely it is that external

Originally appeared in *International Small Business Journal*, 2004, Volume 22, Number 1.

advice will be sought (Bennett and Robson, 1999) and that it would be naive to assume that most owner-managers of small firms are particularly driven by a need to improve their skills bases (Stanworth and Gray, 1992). Chell and Baines' (2000) study indicates that it is entrepreneurs in the sense of individuals who are driven by a need to create wealth and accumulate capital who are the most likely to use external sources of advice. But according to Chell and Baines these are a minority. For many small firm owners, autonomy and independence are more important than growth (Low and Macmillan, 1988). The implication of research into public authority sponsored consultancy services to small firms (see for example Kvitastein, 1997; Wilks, 2000) is that acting as a business adviser, in the sense of motivating small firms to adopt and integrate key competencies, is a complex process that requires a high degree of relational competence.

In the first part of this article we first briefly discuss the most salient features of the Norwegian context. We then delineate the difficulties small firms face in obtaining critical competencies for business development. Thereafter we outline the conditions that have contributed to making the authorized accountant in Norway a significant source of business advisory services for small firms. In the final phase we derive three propositions regarding the likelihood of the small firm using its accountant as a business adviser, which are then empirically tested.

Backdrop

The subject matter of this article is small firms in Norway. In Norway small firms are defined as having 1–19 employees (Spilling, 2000). About 95 percent of Norwegian firms occupy this category, and among these, about 80 percent are micro-firms in that they have fewer than 5 employees. Our study analyzes variations in the use these firms perceive they

make of authorized accountants as business advisers, that is to say services that exclude basic or statutory financial accounting services.

In order to meet statutory requirements regulated by Norwegian law, firms are obliged to produce annual financial accounts. Rather than doing this in-house two-thirds of all small firms in Norway employ the services of an external authorized accountant for this purpose (Dagens Næringsliv, 2003). It should be noted that in Norway all persons that offer accounting services to others have to be authorized in accordance with Norwegian law. A prerequisite for authorization is a minimum of two years of higher education within economics and business administration, as well as two years relevant practice. There are approximately 4000 authorized accountants in Norway serving in excess of 200,000, mostly small, firms. They typically work in practices of five or fewer associates.

Competence as a Strategic Resource

Business advisory services encapsulate a range of competencies that are critical not only for survival, but also for competitive advantage. Teece et al. (1997: 516) have argued that sustainable competitive advantage is dependent on "the firm's ability to integrate, build and reconfigure internal and external competencies to address rapidly changing environments." In general terms critical competencies necessary for competitive advantage, or at least competitive parity, must either be developed internally and/or they must be accessed through the agency of consultancies engaged in the transfer of best practices across firms.

For small firms both of these are problematic (Langley and Traux, 1994). The uncertainty under which they operate combined with their lack of resources makes research and development problematic (Chell and Baines, 2000; Marshall et al., 1995; Nordhaug and Gooderham, 1996; Wynarczyk et al., 1993). This means that small firms have a particular need to obtain business advice from external sources (Birley and Westhead, 1992; Storey, 1994). However, in regard to availing themselves of mainstream consultancies, small firms, because of their relative lack of purchasing power, are viewed as unattractive clients. In a Norwegian survey 75 percent of the country's established consultancies reported that they either had no or only sporadic contact with small or medium-sized firms (Jevnaker, 1996).

The significance of being able to access critical competencies was confirmed in a survey of a large sample of mostly small Norwegian firms (Nordhaug and Gooderham, 1996). About 8 out of 10 firms in the sample ranked the competencies of their management and employees as crucial to the firm. In contrast the resources that traditionally have been viewed as critical, such as financial resources, technology, machines and equipment, were generally regarded to be of relatively less importance for value creation. The study indicated that firms' emphasis on competence development stems from a need to improve and sustain intangible factors such as the quality focus of the firm and the quality of customer relations (Nordhaug and Gooderham, 1996).

Research in the UK indicates that a majority of small firm owner-managers have no professional, management or other formal qualifications (Stanworth and Gray, 1992). Given that the competence these qualifications represent is critical, this constitutes a problem for the growth and survival of the small firm. In addition, many of the owner-managers of small firms lack financial skills and knowledge of how financial control systems might be used to aid decision-making (Deakins et al., 2001). It is reasonable to suppose that the situation is similar for small firms in Norway. One

possible way for a small firm to acquire competencies is to employ qualified persons. However, smaller firms often have difficulties in obtaining competent persons because of their inability to offer competitive salaries and benefits (Jennings and Beaver, 1997). Consequently, they are particularly dependent on being able to access their environment for business advice.

Competencies and Learning in Small Firms

Jennings and Beaver (1997) maintain that small firm owner-managers require specific, transferable, managerial skills directly related to entrepreneurship and professional management within the operating environment of the business. According to Gibb (1997) a small firm's learning will be located in the context of the external relationships of the firm, and in the context of sharing and developing the collective and individual knowledge in the company. If we consider the external context, there are many possible business relationships small firms may learn from: for example, customers, suppliers, lawyers, associations, authorities, bankers and accountants (Bennett and Robson, 1999; Curran et al., 1993; Gibb, 1997).

Which supplier of business advisory services an owner-manager relies on when it comes to advice is to a large extent dependent on the relationship of *trust* between the supplier of advice and the owner-manager (Bennett and Robson, 1999). This is particularly due to the fact that advice is a specific kind of business service that involves a largely *intangible product*. The process of production of advice is often an exchange process involving learning on both sides (O'Farrell and Moffat, 1995). As a consequence, the quality of the *personal relationship* is critical in these exchanges (Bennett and Robson, 1999). As we will discuss later in this article, this quality of the personal relationship between Norwegian authorized accountants and the owner-manager of small firms is potentially greater than that which can be achieved by consultants.

Public Policy and Small Firms

Due to the recognition of the importance of small firms to developed economies (Gallagher et al., 1990; Mitchell and Reid, 2000), public authorities in Norway and other European countries have introduced a series of initiatives to improve their competence and business performance. Throughout the last decade a key aim of the Norwegian authorities has been to stimulate small firms to invest in competence resources. Core measures have involved ambitious business development programmes under the management of the Regional Development Agency (SND) and The Institute for Applied Technology (TI). It has been shown, however, that these programmes have had a negligible impact on the firms that have been involved (Kvitastein, 1997). In addition, it has been shown that public suppliers of business advice and training are among the least used by small firms in Norway for competence and technological development transfer (Nordhaug and Gooderham, 1996; NHO [Næringslivets Hovedorganisasjon (Confederation of Norwegian Business and Industry)], 1994). These outcomes are not unique to Norway. In the UK a majority of small firms are dissatisfied with government support services (Wilks, 2000). A survey carried out by the University of Strathclyde concludes that government services intended to help businesses fail to do so. Bennett and Robson's (1999) study indicates similar outcomes: government support agencies have significantly less impact on small firm clients than private-sector consultants and business associations.

There appears to be a number of reasons for these discouraging results.

In the Norwegian case there is clear evidence that a substantial part of the problem is getting the advice from SND and TI consultants integrated into the businesses they are trying to serve. This is primarily due to a lack of insight into the idiosyncratic cultures of their clients. Owner-managers of small businesses typically adhere to a self-employed or micro-firm culture of individualism (Gray, 1995 cited in Chell and Baines, 2000), which contrasts to the culture of state funded consultants. A second problem is that the consultants employed by SND and TI offer services that often assume order, standardization, accountability, control, systems and planning rather than the skills needed to "thrive in the chaos" in which small firms have to cope (Gibb, 1997). Accordingly, we will argue that other value creation agents must be identified for the small firm sector. Of the possible value creation business relationships external to small firms, we will focus on the role of the authorized accountant.

The Role of the Accountant

Small accountancy practices as exemplified by Norwegian authorized accountants are of significance as small firm business advisers for a number of reasons. First, as we have noted, unlike consultancies, their clients are primarily derived from the small business sector. Second, small firms are willing to pay more for business advisory services than standard accountancy services, so that authorized accountants have an incentive to develop such services (Gooderham and Nordhaug, 2000). Third, because of the longevity of their client relationships (Marriot and Marriot, 2000; Nordhaug, 2000) there is a potential to develop relational competence in respect to their clients characterized by intimacy and trust (Gooderham and Nordhaug, 2000). In many instances, the small firm client regards its authorized accountant as an integral part of the business. Fourth, another source of trust lies in the fact that accountants have, together with banks and solicitors, to work within a strong self-regulatory framework that generates high institutional trust among clients (Bennett and Robson, 1999). As we have indicated, in Norway accountants can only practice if they are in receipt of authorization from the State. The purpose behind this authorization is to ensure that the work of the accountant is executed in an adequate manner in accordance with prevailing laws and regulations.

In general research conducted in the UK supports the notion that accountants play a particularly important role for small firms, although the findings are somewhat diffuse in regard to the precise nature of the role they play as business advisers. Kirby and King (1997) found that for small firms accountants are among the most frequently used external sources of advice. The factors that appeared to be most important for the use of the accountant for non-statutory work (non-auditing and taxation) were the relationship established through statutory work followed by "perceived value for money" and previous advisory work undertaken by the accountant. However, it should be noted that neither factor was decisive for half of the firms in the sample.

Similarly Bennett and Robson (1999) found that although most small firms used several different sources of advice, specialist professionals are the most frequent source of external advice for small firms. Of these, accountants are the most used (compared to banks and solicitors). In addition, accountants are, together with customers, ranked as those external sources of advice that have greatest impact.

Marriot and Marriot (2000) conclude in their study that there appears to be significant potential for professional accountants to expand the management accounting services they provide to smaller companies. They conclude that accountants have a role to play in increasing the financial awareness of the owner-mangers and can provide a management accounting service to meet their needs and abilities. The current demand for the accountant's reporting services is driven by regulatory requirements, but it is possible to extend these services beyond these.

Deakins et al.'s (2001) study of small businesses also indicates that an important task for an accountant is to act as a consultant to the manager (invariably the owner). The tasks involved supplying advice on internal planning, decision-making and control, that is, in areas where an owner-manager of a small firm often lacks competence, as discussed previously. Accountants were shown to be of significant help to the manager-owner in running the firm particularly when it came to the introduction and implementation of changes. Such a role was also shown to be of critical importance in the early phase of the business. The contact between the accountant and the manager-owner was especially significant for the learning processes that occur in the business.

While the above findings are generally positive about the accountant as a small business adviser, they should be tempered by Greene et al.'s study (1998) from the North of England that indicates that small business owner-managers see little need for external support and advice. When they do seek advice this is because the advice is viewed as necessary in meeting requirements set by the law rather than because it adds value to the business. In these situations it is, however, generally the accountant who is the source of advice, once again suggesting that accountants are primary sources of business advice.

Propositions
Proposition 1
The research we have reviewed suggests that the relational competence

accountants are able to develop is an important factor in explaining their use as business advisers by small firms. In addressing variations in their use by small firms we propose therefore that:

> The stronger the relationship between the small firm and its accountant, the more likely it is that the accountant will be used as a business adviser.

As it is reasonable to suppose that relationships are developed over time we propose that: (1a) small firms with long-term relationships to their accountant are more likely to use their accountant as a business adviser.

We propose further that the use of accountants as business advisers will be affected by the perception of the accountant's competencies that has been developed by the firm. In other words: (1b) the more competent the accountant is perceived to be in respect to the delivery of statutory services the more likely it is that the small firm will use the accountant as a business adviser, and (1c) the more competent the accountant is perceived to be in respect to non-statutory services the more likely it is that the small firm will use the accountant as a business adviser.

Proposition 2

The small firm research we have reviewed points to a number of dimensions that make small firms more vulnerable than larger firms. In large part this vulnerability is resource-based in the sense that small firms lack the necessary routines and competencies for survival. However, resource-based theory would also lead us to suppose that the use small firms make of their accountants as sources of business advice will be a function of the resources at the disposal of the firm. That is we propose that:

> The more resources, tangible and intangible, a firm disposes the more likely it is that the accountant will be used as a business adviser.

One indication of a firm's resources is reflected in its size so that (2a) the larger the firm the more likely it is that the accountant will be used as a business adviser. Another resource lies in a firm's competency orientation or absorptive capacity, i.e. its willingness to absorb and to invest in new knowledge (Cohen and Levinthal, 1990). Thus (2b) the greater the receptiveness of the firm in regard to non-statutory advisory services, the more likely it is that the accountant will be used as a business adviser, and (2c) the more the firm is willing to pay for non-statutory advisory services, the more likely it is that the accountant will be used as a business adviser.

Proposition 3

The uncertainty faced by small firms does not only derive from endogenous factors, but also from exogenous factors in the sense of competitive pressures. The more competition faced by a small firm the less likely it will able to survive because its narrow resource base does not permit it to adapt its product or service spectrum. That is, small firms facing competitive pressures need to be able to source critical competencies for survival and development so that:

> The stronger the competitive pressures faced by the firm, the more likely it is that the accountant will be used as a business adviser.

In the next section of the article we will test these propositions while controlling for industry sector.

Empirical Analysis
Sample

Using a structured questionnaire in May 1998 we conducted a survey of small firms in Norway by telephone. A sample of 320 firms was generated randomly using client lists from a random selection of authorized accountants. Non-response was minimal with 305 firms cooperating. Of these, 65 percent had fewer than 5 employees, 24 percent had between 5 and 9 employees, and the remainder between 10 and 20 employees. Ninety percent of the interviews were conducted with the owner or manager of the firm. The remaining 10 percent were conducted with the deputy manager.

Although in the context of our sampling strategy non-response was minimal, the sampling strategy itself may be criticized in that the one-third of small firms that do not outsource the production of their annual financial accounts to authorized accountants were excluded from our sample. Given the cost involved in using an authorized accountant it is conceivable that the very smallest firms prefer to perform this task in-house. This might account for our sample being somewhat skewed in relation to micro-firms. As we noted earlier in the article, about 80 percent of small firms in Norway have fewer than 5 employees, whereas in our sample the proportion is 65 percent. By controlling for size in our empirical analysis this bias is taken into account.

Operationalization of Variables

In this section we present the operationalization of the variables.

Dependent Variable

The degree to which a small firm uses its authorized accountant as a business adviser: Scale from 1–6; 1 = not at all and 6 = to a very large degree.

Independent Variables

1a. Long-term Relationship with Accountant
Dichotomous variable: 1 = changed accountant in the last 5 years
2 = have not changed accountant in the last 5 years.

1b. Perceived Competence in Statutory Accountancy Services
The degree to which the firm perceives its authorized accountant as a competent source of statutory accountancy services. Scale from 1–6; 1 = very limited competence and 6 = very highly competent.

1c. Perceived Competence in Business Advisory Services
The degree to which the firm perceives its authorized accountant as a competent source of business advisory services. Scale from 1–6; 1 = very limited competence and 6 = very highly competent.

2a. Firm Size
Number of employees:
1 employee = 1
2–4 employees = 3
5–9 employees = 7
10–20 employees = 15.

2b. Receptiveness for Business Advisory Services
The degree of interest small firms have in their authorized accountants' attempting to sell them advisory services on a scale form 1–6; 1 = very little interest and 6 = very large interest.

2c. Maximum Rate for Business Advisory Services
The upper hourly billing rate the firm is willing to pay for business advisory services.
Do not know or under NKr 300 = 1
NKr 300–450 = 2
NKr 451–650 = 3
NKr 651 or more = 4

3. Degree of Competition
Scale from 1–6 with 1 = negligible and 6 = very hard.

Control Variable–Industry Sector
Retail sector, manufacturing industry and services sector.

Table 1
The Degree to which Small Firms Use Authorized Accountants as Business Advisers (*N* = 305)

Degree	Percentage
Very large	18.4
Large	26.2
Some	26.2
Small	13.8
Very small	9.2
Not at all	6.2
Total	100

Testing of Propositions

Prior to testing our propositions let us examine our dependent variable, that is the extent to which small firms use authorized accountants as business advisers for issues beyond statutory services. Table 1 indicates that nearly 45 percent of small firms claim that they use their accountant as a business consultant to a "large" or "very large" degree, while nearly 30 percent either do not use their accountant at all in this respect or do so only to a small degree. These findings indicate substantial variations.

However, given that these are subjective ratings there is a possibility that what is "very large" for one firm may be just "large" for another. Similarly "some" for one small firm may be "small" for another. To guard against this possibility we will conduct an additional analysis wherein we use a dichotomized version of the dependent variable with "very large" and "large" forming the one value and the other categories forming the other.

Table 2 features a correlation matrix containing the variables derived from our propositions. It indicates particular support for propositions 1b, 1c and 2b. In addition there is a significant correlation between degree of competition and the degree to which authorized accountants are used as business advisers. This lends some support to propositions 3 in that it suggests that competitive pressures do stimulate small firms to use their accountants as business advisers. The table indicates that small firms' receptiveness for business advisory services and their perception of their accountants' competence in statutory accountancy and business advisory services are interrelated.

In Table 3 column (a) we have employed linear regression analysis to test our propositions. Because the dependent variable is measured on a six-point ranked scale (see Table 1), the appropriateness of ordinary linear regression may be questioned. In order to accommodate possible deviations from the assumptions underlying "ordinary" regression analysis, we have also conducted an ordered logit regression analysis according to the methodology developed by McCullagh (1980). The ordered logit model used in Table 3 column (b) is similar to logistic regression for a binary dependent variable with the additional assumption that the impact of an independent variable is constant across levels of the dependent variable. Finally, we formed a binary dependent variable by collapsing "very large" and "large" into one category and all other responses into another (see Table 1). The results of binary logistic regression with regard to the new dichotomous variable are reported in Table 3 column (c).

Although the magnitude of coefficient estimates from ordinary regression, ordinal regression and binary logistic regression is not directly comparable, the sign and significance for each explanatory variable based on each of these alternative methods are identical with a single exception. The only notable

Table 2
Correlation Matrix for Variables Featured in the Propositions

	N	Mean	SD	Dependent Variable	1a	1b	1c	2a	2b	2c	3
Dependent Degree to which authorized accountant is used as business adviser	305	4.12	1.43	1.00							
1a. Long-term relationship with accountant	301	1.76	0.43	0.05	1.00						
1b. Perceived competence in statutory accountancy services	295	5.29	0.83	0.23***	0.06	1.00					
1c. Perceived competence in business advisory services	277	4.22	1.31	0.30***	0.05	0.30***	1.00				
2a. Firm size	304	4.87	4.16	0.05	-0.01	-0.05	-0.05	1.00			
2b. Receptiveness for business advisory services	293	3.95	1.39	0.25***	0.08	0.16**	0.21***	0.03	1.00		
2c. Maximum rate for business advisory services	305	2.07	1.13	-0.02	-0.02	-0.06	-0.12	0.01	-0.03	1.00	
3. Degree of competition	299	4.24	1.25	0.11*	0.02	0.01	0.05	0.13*	0.11	0.03	1.00

*$p < 0.05$.
**$p < 0.01$.
***$p < 0.001$.

Table 3
Determinants of the Degree to which Small Firms Currently Use their Authorized Accountants as Business Advisers

	(a) Linear regression	(b) Ordered logit[b]	(c) Binary logit[c]
1a. Long-term relationship with accountant	−0.080	−0.065	−0.218
1b. Perceived competence in statutory accoutancy services	0.255**	0.373**	0.441**
1c. Perceived competence in business advisory services	0.230***	0.351***	0.381***
2a. Firm size	0.019	0.014	0.003
2b. Receptiveness for business advisory services	0.155**	0.211**	0.196*
2c. Maximum rate for business advisory services	0.021	0.018	0.073
3. Degree of competition	0.085	0.108	0.081
Manufacturing[a]	0.085	0.285	0.703*
Services[a]	−0.088	−0.123	−0.171
R^2	0.147	0.163[d]	0.142[d]
F	4.80***		
−2 Log likelihood		816.5	319.5
Chi-square (d.f. = 9)		46.6***	39.9***

[a]Reference category: retailing.
[b]Cut points omitted for simplicity.
[c]Dependent variable recorded into two categories.
[d]Cox & Snell pseudo R^2.
$N = 261$.
Unstandardized coefficients.
*$p < 0.5$.
**$p < 0.001$ one-tailed.

difference is the coefficient for manufacturing in the binary logit estimation; this is due to a nonlinearity of the dependent variable within manufacturing. This strongly supports the assumption that the robustness of ordinary regression for a sample this large is strong enough to be confident in the sign and significance of the results. A comparison of Spearman and Pearson correlations does not reveal any substantial differences (not shown here), further strengthening our belief that although our measurement of the dependent variable possibly violates regression assumptions, these violations give rise to negligible errors only.

The analysis indicates that the relationship between the small firm and its accountant is important in that both propositions 1b and 1c are supported. However, the analysis indicates that the actual longevity of the relationship (proposition 1a) is not important.

In terms of the resources the firm disposes only one aspect of this, the receptiveness of the firm in regard to advisory services (proposition 2b), is significant.

With regard to the effect of competition (proposition 3) there is no significant effect. Tests were conducted for a possible "inverse-U" effect, but none was found. In regard to the control variable, apart from the binary logit estimation, the table indicates no sector differences.

Finally, it is important to note that with explained variance (R^2) at 0.147 there clearly remains a considerable research effort to acquire a more comprehensive understanding of the determinants of small firms' use of authorized accountants as business advisers. Logistic regression, whether binary or ordinal, does not provide a measure of explained variance directly comparable to R^2; the pseudo R^2 does however suggest the same conclusion.

Conclusions and Future Research Directions

It is often argued that long-term relationships often result in a high degree of trust between the parties involved (Ring and Van de Ven, 1992). It might, therefore, be deduced that because trust is an important factor in the purchase of advisory services (Bennett and Robson, 1999), the longevity of the relationship between the small firm and the accountant would be important in determining their use as business advisers. However, in terms of our study this is not the case. This means that a small firm's satisfaction with its accountant is actually independent of the duration of the relationship. Trust therefore seems to be more a result of the quality of the services delivered rather than the duration of the relationship. That finding is in line with previous research and our results indicate that

small firms are reluctant to change accountant even when they are dissatisfied (Marriot and Marriot, 2000). One possible explanation for this inertia may be the asymmetry of the information that may be assumed to exist between an accountant and a small firm. This asymmetry makes it difficult for an owner-manager to assess whether a new accountant will do a better job, so that the small firm chooses to stay with its existing accountant. Moreover, even though an owner-manger is not satisfied with her accountant, she may consider that the regulatory responsibilities are being sufficiently attended to.

Unsurprisingly our study indicates that the small firm must perceive its accountant as a credible deliverer of business advisory services if they are to be used in an advisory capacity. However, for a small firm to purchase business advice from its accountant the results of our study indicate that there are at least two conditions that must be fulfilled. First, the statutory service of the authorized accountancy must be perceived as being of high quality. Second, in line with Spilling's (2000) research, the small firm itself must have an ambition to grow or to develop in the sense that it is receptive to the advisory services being offered to it. If these two conditions are met, there is a significant increased tendency that owner-managers will use non-statutory services from authorized accountancy firms. Of these two conditions, it is the latter that we regard as representing an important challenge for future research.

It would appear that for a small firm to source business advisory services from its accountant it must have some critical degree of *strategic intent* concerning growth ambitions. Strategic intent is the willingness to set goals and aspirations that create a motivating gap between ambition and existing resources (Gooderham, 1995; Hamel, 1995; Hamel and Prahalad, 1989). The concept encompasses an active management process and provides consistency to short-term action while at the same time leaving room for reinterpretation as well as the emergence of new opportunities. A firm characterized by strategic intent will be more focused on developing its own competence (Rumelt, 1984), and therefore be particularly interested in business advice over and above statutory accountancy services because it may result in competence development within the firm.

However, we suggest that strategic intent alone will not lead to competence development and the use of business advisory services. The firm must also have a certain degree of absorptive capacity (Cohen and Levinthal, 1990: Gooderham, 1995). Absorptive capacity is a dynamic capability that is embedded in a firm's routines and processes making it possible "to recognize the value of new information, assimilate it, and apply it to commercial ends" (Cohen and Levinthal, 1990: 128). Our future research will seek to further explore the significance of these two factors—that is strategic intent and absorptive capacity—for the purchase of business advisory services and to explore their amenability to external influence.

Acknowledgements

We wish to thank the Norwegian Research Council (NFR) for its generous funding of our research and NARF for its unstinting cooperation with our project. We also wish to express our appreciation to two unknown referees for critical but very constructive comments at the various stages in the development of this article.

References

Bennett, T. J. and Robson, P. J. A. (1999) "The Use of External Business Advice by SMEs in Britain", *Entrepreneurship & Regional Development* 11(2): 155–80.

Birley, S. and Westhead, P. (1992) "A Comparison of New Firms in 'Assisted' and 'Non-assisted' Areas in Great Britain", *Entrepreneurship & Regional Development* 4(3): 229–338.

Chell, E. and Baines, S. (2000) "Networking, Entrepreneurship and Microbusiness Behavior", *Entrepreneurship & Regional Development* 12(3): 195–215.

Cohen, W. M. and Levinthal, D. A. (1990) "Absorptive Capacity: A New Perspective on Learning and Innovation", *Administrative Science Quarterly* 35(1): 128–52.

Curran, J., Jarvis, R., Blackburn, R. A. and Black, S. (1993) "Networks and Small Firms: Constructs, Methodological Strategies and Some Findings", *International Small Business Journal* 11(2): 13–24.

Dagens Næringsliv (2003) "To Av Tre Setter ut Regnskapet" [Two Out of Three Outsource their Annual Financial Reporting], URL (consulted March, 2003): http://www.dn.no/arkiv/article 43299.ece

Deakins, D., Logan, D. and Steele, L. (2001) "The Financial Management of the Small Enterprise", ACCA Research Report No. 64. London: The Association of Chartered Certified Accountants, Certified Accountants Educational Trust.

Gallagher, C., Daly, M. and Thomason, J. (1990) "The Growth of UK Companies 1985–87", *Employment Gazette* 98(2): 92–8.

Gibb, A. A. (1997) "Small Firms" Training and Competiveness: Building Upon the Small Business as a Learning Organization", *International Small Business Journal* 15(3): 13–29.

Gooderham, P. N. (1995) "Bedrifters Kompetansemålrettethet" [Firms' Focus on Competence], *BETA* 2(9): 44–55.

Gooderham, P. N. and Nordhaug, O. (2000) "Regnskapsføreren som Verdiskapingsagent i SMB-sektoren:

Status og Muligheter" [The Authorized Accountant as a Value Creation Agent in the SMB-Sector: Status and Possibilities], Working paper 1/2000. Bergen: SNF.

Gray, C. (1995) "Managing Entrepreneurial Growth: A Question of Control?", paper presented at the 18th Institute of Small Business Affairs national small firms conference, University of Paisley, Scotland, 15–17 November.

Greene, F., Kirby, D. and Najak, B. (1998) "Accounting for Growth: Ways Accountants Can Add Value to Small Businesses". A Report to the Research Board of the Institute of Chartered Accountants in England and Wales. London: Institute of Chartered Accountants in England and Wales.

Greenwood, R., Suddaby, R. and Hinings, C. R. (2002) "Theorizing Change: The Role of professional Associations in the Transformation of Institutionalized Fields", *Academy of Management Journal* 45(1): 58–80.

Hamel, G. (1995) "Corporate Challenge", *Executive Excellence* 12(3): 7–10.

Hamel, G. and Prahalad, C. K. (1989) "Strategic Intent", *Harvard Business Review* 67(3): 63–76.

Jennings, P. and Beaver, G. (1997) "The Performance and Competitive Advantage of Small Firms: A Management Perspective", *International Small Business Journal* 15(2): 63–75.

Jevnaker, B. (1996) "Privat sektor: konsulentfirmaer" [Private-sector: Consultancies], in O. Nordhaug and P. N. Gooderham (eds) *Kompetanseutvikling i Næringslivet* [Competence Development in Private-sector Firms]. Oslo: Cappelen Akademisk Forlag.

Kirby, D. A. and King, S. H. (1997). "Accountants and Small Firm Development: Filling the Expectation Gap", *The Services Industries Journal* 17(2): 294–304.

Kvitastein, O. (1997) *Evaluering av FRAM-programmet i SND* [Evaluation of the FRAM-Programme in SND], Research Report 84/97. Bergen: SNF.

Langley, A. and Traux, J. (1994) "Technology Creation and Technology Transfer", *Research in International Business and Finance* 11: 137–77.

Low, M. B. and Macmillan, I. C. (1988) "Entrepreneurship: Past Research and Future Challenges", *Journal of Management* 14(2): 139–61.

McCullagh, P. (1980) "Regression Models for Ordinal Data", *Journal of the Royal Statistical Society B* 42(2): 109–42.

Marriott, N. and Marriott, P. (2000) "Professional Accountants and the Development of a Management Accounting Service for the Small Firm: Barriers and Possibilities", *Management Accounting Research* 11(4): 475–92.

Marshall, J. N., Alderman, N., Wong, C. and Thwaites, A. (1995) "The Impact of Management Training and Development on Small and Medium-Sized Enterprises", *International Small Business Journal* 13(4): 73–5.

Mitchell, F. and Reid, G. C. (2000) "Problems, Challenges and Opportunities: Small Business as a Setting for Management Accounting Research", *Management Accounting Research* 11: 385–9.

NHO (1994) *Statusrapport for Samarbeidsprosjektet "Kom-opp"* [Status Report for the Joint-Project "Rise Up"]. Moelv: Næringslivets Hovedorganisasjon Hedmark/Opland.

Nordhaug, O. (2000) "Norske Regnskapsbyråer: Verdiskapere i SMB-sektoren" [Norwegian Authorized Accountants: Value Creation Agents in the SMB-sector], Report 2/2000. Bergen: SNF.

Nordhaug, O. and Gooderham, P. N. (eds) (1996) *Kompetanseutvikling i Næringslivet* [Competence Development in Private-sector Firms]. Oslo: Cappelen Adademisk Forlag.

O'Farrell, P. N. and Moffat, W. A. (1995) "Business Services and their Impact Upon Client Performance: an Exploratory Interregional Analysis", *Regional Studies* 29(2): 111–24.

Ring, P. S. and Van de Ven, A. H. (1992) "Structuring Cooperative Relationships between Organizations", *Strategic Management Journal* 13(7): 483–98.

Rumelt, R. P. (1984) "Towards a Strategic Theory of the Firms", in R. B. Lamb (ed.) *Competitive Strategic Management*, pp. 171–80. Englewood Cliffs, NJ: Prentice Hall.

Spilling, O. R. (2000) *SMB 2000: Fakta om Små og Mellomstore Bedrifter i Norge* [Facts about Small and Medium-Seized Enterprises in Norway]. Bergen, Norway: Fagbokfor-laget.

Stanworth, J. and Gray, C. (1992) "Entrepreneurship and Education: Action-based Research with Training Policy", *International Small Business Journal* 10(2): 11–20.

Storey, D. J. (1994) *Understanding the Small Business Sector*. London: Routledge.

Teece, D., Pisano, G. and Shuen, A. (1997) "Dynamic Capabilities and Strategic Management", *Strategic Management Journal* 18(7): 509–33.

Wilks, N. (2000) "Small Firms Unhappy with Support Services", *Professional Engineering* 13(20): 16.

Wynarczyk, P., Watson, R., Storey, D. J., Short, H. and Keasey, K. (1993) *The Managerial Labour Market in Small and Medium Sized Enterprises*. London: Routledge.

The ICSB International Office
by Susan Duffy

The International Council for Small Business (ICSB) International Office (IO) is located in the heart of Washington, D.C., at the George Washington University School of Business. This headquarter office is strategically positioned within minutes of important small and medium enterprise (SME) resource organizations, such as the World Bank Group, the U.S. State Department, and the Small Business Administration. Washington, D.C. is also home to more than 150 embassies, chancelleries, and diplomatic residences where colors, cultures, and languages weave a distinctly global fabric. In addition to hosting ICSB members and potential members who visit the region, the ICSB IO frequently welcomes formal delegations of public- and private-sector groups working to advance SME development around the world. Recent guests included groups from Mexico, China, Botswana, Nigeria, Russia, Australia, South Africa, Kosovo, and countries of North Africa and the Near Middle East.

The IO, led by Executive Director Susan Duffy, relies on support from a talented group of individuals that includes Executive Assistant Alex Reed and Special Projects Coordinator Laura Olson, as well as highly respected members of the School of Business Management Science Department: Erik Winslow, Sergio D'Onofrio, George Solomon, Ayman Tarabishy, and Janet Nixdorff. Together, this group offers extensive ICSB institutional knowledge and wide-ranging SME global networks to an energetic and innovative vision for the future.

The function of the IO headquarter office is threefold. First, the office is the hub of the day-to-day business of the organization. It serves as the central point of communication among and between the board of directors, ICSB affiliates and members, and other SME partners. The IO uses state-of-the-art technology to bridge the distance of time and space within its worldwide network. The IO also plays an integral role in specific projects that advance the organization as a whole, such as creating and maintaining the ICSB website, building the ICSB global brand, and developing strategic relationships with other SME-related organizations.

Second, the IO executive director works together with the ICSB president and each executive officer to carry out the annual work plan objectives of the sitting board. In this capacity, the IO serves as a source of continuity between successive boards by helping to ensure that annual objectives build on the prior year's outcomes to drive the organization forward.

Finally, the IO plays a significant ambassadorial role for ICSB both internally, by connecting members to each other, and externally, by seizing every opportunity to share global knowledge with the ever-expanding ICSB global network. The IO staff is dedicated to the mission of ICSB to connect researchers, policymakers, educators, and business service providers, so that together they can more effectively advance entrepreneurship worldwide.

The ICSB IO team invites you to visit when you are in Washington, D.C. Contact them at anytime at icsb@gwu.edu.

History of the International Council for Small Business

by Bob Brockhaus

The Early Years: 1956–1975

Before the International Council for Small Business (ICSB) adopted its present name, it was known as the National Council for Small Business Management Development (NCSBMD), and its beginnings started before that name was adopted. NCSBMD grew from a conference on small-business management development held in June 1956 at the University of Colorado. This conference was sponsored by the university and the U.S. Small Business Administration and was financed by a grant from the Ford Foundation. At that time, the U.S. Small Business Administration had completed two years of programs to cosponsor administrative management courses for small business. They were organized and conducted by educational institutions, with the assistance and cosponsorship of the U.S. Small Business Administration. The courses were held for two to three hours, one night a week, for a period of 8 to 10 weeks. The Ford Foundation financed the meeting for 40 of the course coordinators from all parts of the country. The subject of the conference was "The Problems of Training Small Business Executives." Its purpose was to pool the experience of small-business management course coordinators so that future training programs would be improved. Interest of the Ford Foundation was developed largely through the efforts of Wilford L. White, who was then the chief of the Managerial Assistance Division of the U.S. Small

Business Administration, and Delbert J. Duncan, then the dean of the University of Colorado School of Business. Planning and arrangements for the program and accommodations were delegated to Professor Robert S. Wasley, assistant to Dean Duncan, and to Wendell O. Metcalf of the U.S. Small Business Administration, who would later become president and one of the major lifelong supporters of ICSB.

The first conference was deemed so worthwhile by the participants that they voted to have another one the following year. It was held with the University of Colorado again acting as host. At the second meeting, in June 1957, the council was formally organized. Officers and an advisory board were elected, and a program of activities was developed. Bylaws were drafted during the following year and were presented, thrashed out, rewritten, and adopted at the third annual conference in June 1958 at the University of Pittsburgh. The officer positions included president, secretary, and treasurer. In addition to the officers, there were six members on the advisory board—two each from education, business, and government. In 1961, an organizational membership was added. The NCSBMD organizational structure remained basically the same, with the offices of secretary and treasurer being combined and then later separated once again. Later, the office of general vice president was established. To provide more opportunities to implement plans, in 1973 the term of office was changed from one year to two years. A major change occurred in July 1974, when the office of general secretary was added and Robert Bauer, a past president, took on these duties. This was the first paid position within the organization. For the next seven years, the arrangements for conferences and the overall management of the council were provided by Bauer, whose title was changed to executive secretary in 1980.

In retrospect, the strength and accomplishments of NCSBMD proved that the effort was worthwhile. Certainly, many members vouched for the fact that their personal lives had been enriched by the friends and acquaintances made through the council. However, there were problems, as Metcalf described:

There was the speaker who, just before the meeting, wrote a letter asking for his travel expenses. When informed that there was no money, he refused to come. In desperation the secretary wrote a skit to fill the spot on the program left open by the recalcitrant speaker. There was no time to memorize parts, and the scene was staged around a conference table with each conferee reading his prepared script. Certain members were "tapped" as they registered for the annual meeting, and after one hasty rehearsal, they put on the skit. To get around this indigent predicament the group began relying almost exclusively upon its own members for speakers. Of course, this multiplied the problems. It changed the situation from a paucity to an over-abundance of skilled speakers. Nearly all the members were professionals at presenting ideas before groups. How do you get a "pro" to listen to a "pro"—and like it? The idea to allow everyone to speak for five minutes was tried. This works fairly well, provided (1) the group is small, and (2) you have a first-class

heel to chair the meeting—one who will really cut off speakers at the end of their allotted times.

At each successive annual conference, the purpose and objectives of the council were continually studied, and worthwhile subjects were discussed. Surveys were conducted, and the results were reported to members on such topics as the subject matter in the small-business courses, the costs of organizing and conducting courses, promotional methods used, and the value of research for small-business management development. Very early, the importance of getting the opinions of businesspeople was recognized. They often appeared on the program to present their ideas on management development programs. Furthermore, the interests in small-business programs by big business and trade associations were recognized at annual conferences. At the fourth conference, held at the University of Illinois, the subject matter that should be covered in small business courses was discussed by a management specialist, a businessperson, an educator, and a government person. Also discussed was the utilization of the case method in some successful workshops for small-business owner–managers.

Research was discussed in significant detail for the first time at the fifth conference, held at the University of Wisconsin–Milwaukee. Nine of the 15 presentations dealt exclusively with research relating to small-business management. Full proceedings of each conference were published and issued to members each year. By general agreement, conferences were held in a different part of the United States each year, moving from the central geographic division to the eastern, back to the central division, then to the western division. Regional conferences in each of the three U.S. geographic divisions were also held.

The annual conferences were held in widely varying physical facilities: from a high-rise hotel in downtown Chicago to a conference center on the Pacific coast off Monterey Peninsula in California; from campus dormitories and student unions to a downtown motel three blocks from a civic center facility. This variety never hindered attendance or interest. The inquisitive, energetic nature of the members responded to the challenge of each new adventure. The pattern of a late-afternoon gathering and a meal on the day preceding the formal business followed by two and one-half days of programs became a tradition, as did the annual awards banquet. Committee meetings on the day preceding the formal program, at breakfasts during the days of the program, and on the afternoon following the formal program became a custom. The publication of annual proceedings was discontinued during much of the period. It is unknown whether it was apathy or some other factor that caused the demise of this publication. The change during the years to a more informal program may have been responsible. As a substitute, the council reprinted, for free distribution, those papers provided by speakers and not published elsewhere. The publication of proceedings of the annual conference was resumed in the third decade.

Early conferences often involved the attendees bringing family members along and making the conference part of their family vacation. Golf tournaments with small awards being made at the final banquet became a fixture for a number of years in the 1970s. The number of active participants at the annual conferences continued to increase in the mid-70s, with between 50 and 60 conferees involved in the program. In 1962, the first Outstanding Small Businessman Award was given. The U.S. Small Business Administration joined in the selection process by the late 1960s, and in 1965 the U.S. president presented the award.

It was at the eighth meeting that the first honorary lifetime memberships were awarded by the council. One was awarded to L. T. White and one to Wilford White. Plaques were presented to these men that were engraved, "For his lifetime service in Management Education, for his generous contribution in time and talent to this council and for his foresight in bringing NCSBMD into being, a grateful membership acknowledges its thanks." In 1971, the first Distinguished Service Award was presented to Wendell O. Metcalf, Washington, D.C. In 1973, another such award was given to Joseph C. Schabacker, Arizona State University, Tempe. Receiving the same award in the years that followed were Lillian B. Dreyer, Calvin and Company, Inc., San Francisco, California in 1974; James H. Thompson and Stanley Kloc Jr., both from West Virginia University, Morgantown, in 1975; and Robert O. Bauer, University of Wisconsin–Extension, Milwaukee, in 1976.

The ICSB Years: 1975 to the Present
Organizational Changes

In the mid-1970s, a proposal to legally incorporate was considered but was stopped because of the proposal to change NCSBMD's name to the International Council for Small Business. In June 1977, the name change was made. The following two years were spent on developing a general plan of reorganization that was adopted at the June 1979 meeting. However, the actual approval of the new constitution and bylaws took place at the June 1980 meeting. Under the new structure, there were offices of president, president-elect, immediate past president, and senior vice presidents (SVP) for programs, publications and research, development, external relations, finance and control, and for each of the affiliates, plus an executive secretary. Twenty-five years later, most of these positions still remain—a tribute to those who established the officer structure. The board of directors (BOD) had a chair, in addition to 10 other board members, but none of the officers were on the board. The officers could propose plans but needed to obtain board approval, and they needed to follow the directives of the board. Because none of the board members were officers, they could direct the officers to carry out what they wished to see accomplished without having to be involved in the actual performance of the tasks. While such a process works well in a corporation, a volunteer organization operates much differently. Within a few years, the board was revamped to include officers with fewer nonofficer board members.

The organizational structure has changed several times in the last 25 years. The biggest changes have been to the board structure. Today, there are eight executive officers (president, president-elect, past president, SVP finance, SVP marketing, SVP programs, SVP research and publications, and SVP membership and affiliates) who also serve on the BOD, along with the president of each affiliate, five general representatives, and a representative of the Wilford White Fellows and past presidents. The international president serves as chair of the BOD. Each is elected for a one-year term and can be reelected. Through all these changes and growth in the last 20 years, the structure of the council remained remarkably true to plan. The Report of the Strategic Planning Committee—authored by Donald Myers, a past president, Randy Vandermark, and committee chair Max Wortman Jr. in 1986 and implemented in 1987—laid a stable foundation for the growth that followed. It reconfirmed the council's commitment to its original mission and set the following objectives:

1. To become recognized as the primary source for educational resources in small and medium-size businesses and entrepreneurships in the world.

2. To develop at least one new chapter per year for the next five years as a precursor to affiliate development.
3. To develop at least two new affiliates during the next five years.
4. To hold at least one annual ICSB conference in one of the new chapters or affiliate host countries in the period 1988–1991.
5. To restructure the organization so that there is a more viable operations structure and to reflect more accurately the international posture of the organization.
6. To define the membership of the organization to be affiliates, chapters, and individuals where there is no overlapping geographic jurisdiction. This will more accurately reflect the international mandate.
7. To determine and obtain new sources of revenue for ICSB other than membership dues.
8. To establish an ongoing permanent chief operating officer and a permanent headquarters so that international members will always know who to contact and where the headquarters is located.

Affiliate Development

During the two years following the name change to ICSB, efforts were made to establish procedures for forming affiliates and holding conferences outside of the United States. In 1980, a new constitution and bylaws were adopted. At that time, the Canadian division became the first affiliate of ICSB, with Robert Bilodeau as its president. There was no official U.S. affiliate. In October 1981, the United States became the second affiliate of ICSB, and Gerry Hills became its first president, having just completed his two-year term as president of ICSB.

In 1982, Bob Brockhaus, from the United States, became the president and established the goal of ICSB becoming truly international—not just a North American organization with a few members from other parts of the world. Over the next 20 years, Brockhaus, as the executive director of ICSB, used his Saint Louis University funds to travel throughout the world, seeking to attract new members and affiliates. Each year the current officers, along with Brockhaus, worked to establish formal relationships with groups such as the International Small Business Congress, the World Association for Small and Medium Enterprises, and others interested in small business and entrepreneurship. In 1987, there were only two affiliates: the Canadian Council for Small Business and Entrepreneurship and the United States Association for Small Business and Entrepreneurship. In the following decade, seven more affiliates were added.

ICSB–Korea, 1987. Myers, Bob Butler, and Gene Bonk met Ki-Jong Ryu, the head of the Korean Federation of Small Business, and Yoon-Bae Ouh, of Soong Sil University, at a World Association for Small and Medium Enterprises meeting in 1984. Almost immediately, these key Korean leaders formed an ICSB chapter. Within a very short time, it reached the requisite level of 50 members, most of them industry, for affiliate status. Within five years, it had 100 members. Its first president, Ryu, was elected as Wilford White Fellow that same year, and Ouh became ICSB's first president from a Pacific Rim country. In 1993, acting for ICSB–Korea, its president, Sang Kyu Park, donated $5,000 toward the publication of the ICSB Membership Directory.

European Council for Small Business, 1988. Harold Welsch initiated European membership development during his 1985–1986 sabbatical year in Italy. During that year, he met with senior European small-business professors from various countries to structure a European affiliate. While Mark Weaver, SVP for Programs, participated in the European Small Business Seminar Program, Dieter Ibielski invited him to attend a meeting of current ICSB members interested in forming a chapter. Ibielski was the group vice president, and Josef Mugler of the Department of Small Business, University of Economics Vienna chaired the steering committee that began the application process. The European Council for Small Business (ECSB) joined ICSB in 1988 with 78 members "mostly academics", from 24 countries. Mugler was ECSB's first president. The members' aim was to influence all of Europe, exchange information on research projects and small-business projects, develop an international small-business literature database inquiry system, and organize conferences. ECSB's application for affiliate status included an application to host the ICSB World Conference in Vienna in 1991.

Southern African Entrepreneurship and Small Business Association, 1988. In the same year that the Southern African Entrepreneurship and Small Business Association (SAESBA) was formed, the U.S. Congress applied economic sanctions against South Africa, one of the member countries, because of its apartheid rule. The U.S. House of Representatives declared the "ineligibility of small business engaged in South Africa." The ICSB BOD contended that there was a clear need to encourage entrepreneurship in South Africa because the small-business sector could contribute considerably to that country's gross national product. The policy of ICSB was confirmed to be politically neutral. SAESBA held its well-attended 10th annual conference in Zimbabwe, the first conference site outside of South Africa. The venue is significant because it underscores the affiliate's original goal to make the organization regional. In 2004, SAESBA hosted the 49th ICSB World Conference in Johannesburg. It was well attended, with more than 2,000 participants from around the world. South African president Thabo Mbeki, along with several other ministers of state, were keynote speakers at the conference.

Small Enterprise Association of Australia and New Zealand, 1992. In 1987, the Council of Small Business Organizations of Australia (COSBOA) offered to join ICSB. This organization represented 150,000 individual businesses and more than 21 trade associations in Australia and New Zealand. COSBOA was obviously a major institution, and the ICSB BOD questioned its involvement with big business. Another affiliation initiative came from smaller firms and universities in Australia. Conflict ensued between the two organizations. COSBOA wanted to control the affiliate and name it for its own organization, not allowing educators to participate in the decision. The educators did not like the way COSBOA conducted business and were unwilling to cooperate with them. In the end, ICSB chose the educators and small-business owners over its rival because helping small business is the mission of ICSB. The new affiliate organized under the name Small Enterprise Association of Australia and New Zealand (SEAANZ) in 1992. They preferred the word *enterprise* to *business* in their name because of the connotations locally. According to Geoff Meredith, first president of SEAANZ, *enterprise* is used for small-scale operations that may be for profit or nonprofit, community or noncommunity, public or private sector.

The Entrepreneurship Forum (Singapore), 1994. A small core membership of Singapore businesspeople began meeting in the late 1980s and in 1992 formed a pro tem committee chaired by Teck-Meng Tan, dean of the School of Accountancy and Business at Nanyang Technological University, Singapore. The committee actively promoted ICSB among government and educational institutions as well as individuals and local firms in the private sector. By 1994, it had the requisite 59 members. The new affiliate elected Wee-Liang Tan as its president. Singapore hosted the ICSB World Conference in 1998.

ICSB–Puerto Rico and the Caribbean, 1996. This affiliate covers the Caribbean basin from its headquarters in Puerto Rico. Councilmember Jose M. Romaguera, a professor at the University of Puerto Rico, organized the affiliate, shepherded it through the application process, and was elected its first president in 1997. ICSB–Puerto Rico and the Caribbean cohosted four executive business roundtable meetings with ICSB from 1997 to 1999 and hosted the annual World Conference in 2002. Romaguera served as ICSB president in 2003–2004.

ICSB–Japan, 1998. Japan had been an ICSB chapter for a number of years but had never acquired enough members to form an affiliate. Masayoshi Fukuda, an international venture capitalist, consultant, and lecturer at Nihon University, visited the ICSB international office at Saint Louis University. Upon his return to Japan, he led the Japanese chapter to increase its membership from 22 to 55 to meet the requirements to be approved as an affiliate. Fukuda became the first president of the affiliate.

ICSB–Brazil, 1998. Latin America had long been a target of ICSB aspirations. Following considerable relationship-building among Gerald Hills, Bruce Kirchhoff, and Lois Stevenson, all past presidents and the Sao Paulo chapter officers, Brazil applied with 50 members and was admitted to the council.

ICSB–Republic of China, 1999. The Republic of China (ROC) had a chapter in Taiwan as early as 1986, but it took until 1999 to acquire affiliate status. Cheung Chang was the first president of the affiliate, and more than 90 people participated in its first annual meeting in February 2000. ICSB–ROC hosted the 46th ICSB World Conference in June 2001.

Conferences

The first conference outside of the United States or Canada was in 1991 in Vienna, Austria. The BOD was concerned that attendance might be small, given the cost of traveling from North America where most of the members resided. However, the opportunity to visit such a beautiful and historic city prevailed in the final decision. It also was an opportunity for the newly formed European affiliate to attract new members. Attendance by the Americans and the Europeans was outstanding. Moreover, the hospitality of the Europeans, the quality of the presentations, and social events ensured that future conferences outside of North America were no longer a concern. Just three years later, the conference was again held in Europe—this time in Strasbourg, France.

The third European conference was in 1996 in Stockholm, Switzerland. Attendance was the largest of any conference to that date, with more than 900 persons in attendance. A highlight of that conference was dinner in the City Hall, where the Noble Prize dinner is held. The menu for the ICSB award banquet was the same as that of a Noble Prize dinner.

The 1995 conference, held in Sidney, Australia, was the first in the Pacific Rim. This conference was the first where a head of state spoke to the attendees. The heads of state from Taiwan and South Africa participated in later conferences.

The last 15 years have offered important and educational opportunities for our members through our keynote presentations. Major ministers of government normally deliver plenary presentations as do the world's leading entrepreneurship researchers. The latter is primarily due to the Swedish Foundation for Small Business Research, which sponsors an annual recognition for the researchers who have made significant contributions to the entrepreneurial field. As part of the requirements for receiving this coveted prize, the hon-orees must present their research at the ICSB World Conference.

After deducting a stipend that is paid to ICSB, the host affiliate receives all of the profits from the conference. This procedure has allowed the affiliates to have complete control over the finances of the conferences and many of the program aspects of the conferences. Over the years, the social events have continued to grow in quality. The conference in 2004 in Johannesburg, South Africa, featured two dinners with outstanding entertainment that included ballet, operettas, native dances and music, and much more. In addition, the morning and afternoon teas and coffees had musical entertainment on three separate floors of the conference center. (See Table 1 for a complete list of all of our conferences.)

Finances

An analysis of ICSB financial statements from the early years shows that there was very little revenue, but expenses were minimal as well. By 1981, because of budgetary constraints, the majority of the functions were reallocated to the officers, and the official address of ICSB was moved to St. Louis, Missouri, where Brockhaus of Saint Louis University volunteered to provide the basic office functions without charging a fee. The World Conference during this period was organized by the officers of ICSB, and all losses or profits went to ICSB. Hills served as chair of the 1982 World Conference in Knoxville, Tennessee, the site of the 1982 World's Fair. The conference profit was marginal, but every year saw the financial reserves improve.

By 1987, the board decided to have a paid international office. After soliciting proposals, Saint Louis University was selected. Brockhaus, who had been the president of ICSB in 1983–1984, was named executive director, an unpaid position, and was an ex officio member of the BOD. Sharon Bower was appointed to a half-time paid position as

Table 1
ICSB Annual World Conferences

Year	Venue	Theme
1956	Boulder, CO	—
1957	Boulder, CO	—
1958	Pittsburgh, PA	—
1959	Urbana, IL	—
1960	Milwaukee, WI	—
1961	Newark, DE	—
1962	Kalamazoo, MI	—
1963	Tempe, AZ	—
1964	Stillwater, OK	—
1965	Ithaca, NY	—
1966	Carbondale, IL	—
1967	Boulder, CO	—
1968	Chicago, IL	
1969	Hartford, CT	—
1970	Lexington, KY	—
1971	Monterey, CA	—
1972	Milwaukee, WI	—
1973	Morgantown, WV	—
1974	Tuscaloosa, AL	—
1975	San Antonio, TX	—
1976	Tempe, AZ	—
1977	Wichita, KS	Small Business: Today's Innovator
1978	Cullowhee, NC	Small Business in the 1980s
1979	Quebec City, Canada	The World of Small Business: Problems and Issues
1980	Monterey Peninsula, CA	The Big World of Small Business
1981	Waco, TX	Small Business Management Development: The Next 25 Years
1982	Knoxville, TN	Energizing Small Business Management and Entrepreneurial Development
1983	Halifax, Nova Scotia, Canada	Management Consulting Resources for Small Business
1984	Chicago, IL	Developing Linkages for Small Business Professionals
1985	Montreal, Canada	Small Business in the Entrepreneurial Era
1986	Denver, CO	Venturing into Entrepreneurship and Small Business
1987	Vancouver, Canada	The Spirit of Entrepreneurship
1988	Boston, MA	Entrepreneurship: New Direction for a Global Economy
1989	Quebec City, Canada	The Entrepreneurs and the Challenges of the '90s
1990	Washington, DC	Entrepreneurship: A Capital Idea
1991	Vienna, Austria	Small Business and Partnership

Table 1
Continued

Year	Venue	Theme
1992	Toronto, Canada	Enterprising in Partnership with the Environment
1993	Las Vegas, NV	Free Trade: A Good Bet for Small Business
1994	Strasbourg, France	Small Business and Its Contribution to Regional and International Development
1995	Sydney, Australia	Skills for Success in SMEs
1996	Stockholm, Sweden	Creating New Frontiers: The Role of SMEs
1997	San Francisco, CA	Entrepreneurship: The Engine of Global Economic Development
1998	Singapore	Entrepreneurship at the Threshold of the 21st Century
1999	Naples, Italy	Innovation and Economic Development: The Role of SMEs
2000	Brisbane, Australia	Entrepreneurial SMEs: Engines of Growth in the New Millennium
2001	Taipei, Taiwan	SMEs in a Traditional-and-New Mixed Era
2002	San Juan, Puerto Rico	Entrepreneurial SMEs and Strategic Relationships: Making the Connection
2003	Belfast, Northern Ireland, United Kingdom	Advancing Entrepreneurship and Small Business
2004	Johannesburg, South Africa	Advancing the SME Agenda
2005	Washington, DC	Golden Opportunities for Entrepreneurship

executive administrator with responsibilities for day-to-day operations. She was also secretary of the BOD. The international office remained there until 2003, when Brockhaus, in anticipation of his retirement from Saint Louis University, requested that another location be selected. At that time, Brockhaus had been an officer of ICSB for over 25 years—longer than any other individual. For over 20 years, from 1981 until 2003, approximately half of the expenses of operating the international office were paid by Saint Louis University and the other half by ICSB. President Gene Gomolka, in his article in the 1993 *Bulletin* referring to the contributions of Saint Louis University, expressed his appreciation as follows: "Without their generosity and vision, the services that ICSB offers its members would be greatly curtailed."

In 2003, the international office was moved to George Washington University in Washington, D.C., with Susan Duffy serving as executive director. George Solomon, a past president who has been very active in various roles for more than 25 years, retired in 2004 from his senior position in the U.S. Small Business Administration and joined the George Washington University entrepreneurship faculty, where his understanding of the history of ICSB is valuable.

The officers in the last decade have restructured the revenue streams by adjusting the *Journal of Small Business Management* (*JSBM*) revenue format, revising the conference stipend received from host affiliates, assisting the affiliates to increase their memberships, and closely monitoring all expenses. A combination of subsidized expenses, development of new sources of funds, and the careful management of funds by the officers BODs over the last two decades have resulted in a financially stable organization today.

Publications

The ICSB has a long history of publications. *JSBM* was first published in February 1963, with the first editor being Clifford Baumback of the University of Iowa. Baumback was the author of one of the very first textbooks on small business and was well suited to assume this responsibility. In 1969, West Virginia University assumed the editorship of *JSBM* under the leadership of James Thompson and Stanley Kloc Jr. In 2000, the decision was made by ICSB and West Virginia University to seek an outside publisher. Sandra King-Kauanui was responsible for the negotiations with West Virginia University and the selection of a publisher. Blackwell Publishing was selected, and Chandra Mishra of Florida Atlantic University and Daniel McConaughy of California State University–Northridge assumed the positions of coeditors.

ICSB has two quarterly publications— *The Bulletin* and *JSBM*. The quarterly *JSBM* is not only the very first academic journals devoted exclusively to small business and entrepreneurship but is also considered one of the top three journals in this field of inquiry. The quarterly newsletter, *The Bulletin*, was first published on a regular basis in 1963. Currently, the BOD is considering an electronic version of *The Bulletin*. A third publication was the *President's Letter*, which was written in the 1960s through the 1980s. This letter updated the membership on organizational activities. It combined with the quarterly *Bulletin*, and *JSBM* in providing the membership with input from ICSB on a monthly basis. Later, it was incorporated as part of *The Bulletin*. There were other special publications over the years, with 1976 being an especially productive year under the presidency of Metcalf. An annotated bibliography, *Small Business Information Sources* compiled by Joe Schabacker was published. *Educational Programs in Small Business Management* was prepared from information provided by the members. Also, a collegiate student chapter manual was completed that year. In 1992, Welsch published *The International Entrepreneurship and Small Business Bibliography* for ICSB. Brockhaus prepared the first comprehensive *World Conference Manual* in 1987 that has been updated nine times.

Leadership

To have lasted for 50 years is testimony to the quality of the individuals who have provided leadership to ICSB. Over the past 50 years, tens of thousands have been members of ICSB, some only for a year, as one becomes a member simply by attending a World Conference, others for decades. Of these thousands, only 43 have served as president. All of these men and women spent years in service to ICSB prior to becoming president. Many have continued to provide guidance and support in many different ways following their term as president. Table 2 lists the people who have served as president and their term of office. Thirty-six were educators, four were primarily government officials, two were employed as entrepreneurship researchers by foundations, and one was a banker. These individuals not only contributed their leadership skills to ICSB, but 11 of them have also served as dean or held higher positions in a college or university. Another 11 have held endowed chairs or professorships in

Table 2
ICSB Past Presidents

A. M. Woodruff	1957–1958
Joseph C. Schabacker	1958–1959
R. Ralph Bedwell	1959–1960
Martin L. Schotzberger	1960–1961
Willis J. Wheat	1961–1962
Ralph C. Hook Jr.	1962–1963
Roy T. Shaw Jr.	1963–1964
Eugene Swearingen	1964–1965
Ray M. Ayres	1965–1966
William A. Toomey	1966–1967
William D. Boub	1967–1968
Shelden R. Wagner	1968–1969
Wilford L. White	1969–1970
Harold K. Charlesworth	1970–1971
Robert O. Bauer	1972–1974
Wendell O. Metcalf	1974–1976
Ole S. Johnson	1976–1978
Carl M. Franklin	1978–1980
Grant C. Moon	1980
Gerald E. Hills	1980–1982
Robert Bilodeau	1982–1983
Robert H. Brockhaus	1983–1984
Justin G. Longenecker	1984–1985
G. R. Butler	1985–1986
Donald D. Myers	1986–1987
Raymond W. Y. Kao	1987–1988
Harold P. Welsch	1988–1989
George T. Solomon	1989–1990
Bruce A. Kirchhoff	1990–1991
K. Mark Weaver	1991–1992
Eugene G. Gomolka	1992–1993
Lloyd W. Fernald Jr.	1993–1994
Ken O'Neill	1994–1995
Yoon-Bae Ouh	1995–1996
William J. Dennis Jr.	1996–1997
Lois Stevenson	1997–1998
Brian Gibson	1998–1999
J. Hanns Pichler	1990–2000
G. Dale Meyer	2000–2001
Klaas Havenga	2001–2002
Anders Lundström	2002–2003
José M. Romaguera	2003–2004
Sandra King–Kauanui	2004–2005

entrepreneurship or small business, and seven have served in senior government positions responsible for small businesses. Although there is no record maintained, it is expected that many of them also have served in leadership roles in their churches, communities, and in other civic organizations.

ICSB recognizes and honors their leaders and others who have contributed to the advancement of small business and entrepreneurship worldwide by bestowing the title of Wilford L. White Fellow on them. Table 3 lists those who have been so honored. White was one of the founders of NCSBMD when he was director of the Office of Management and Research Assistance of the U.S. Small Business Administration. From 1969 to 1970, he served as president of NCSBMD. The Wilford White Fellows program was established in 1977 when the honor was first bestowed. White was one of the first recipients. The June 1978 *Newsletter* had the following statement: "The death of Wilford L. White on April 18, 1978 will not bring to an end his outstanding contributions to our council. The Wilford L. White Fellow, a distinction conferred upon council members for significant service to small business will keep his name before us for years to come. We are thankful that Wilford himself was with us to receive one of the first of these awards last year."

As you read, there is still more unwritten history that has occurred since this summary was prepared. Each month and each year, ICSB continues to change as it seeks to provide its members and entrepreneurs and owners of small businesses around the world with increased knowledge about establishing and growing successful businesses that will enhance the life of all of the world's citizens.

Author's Note

As a past ICSB president who served as the volunteer executive director of ICSB for 23 years from 1981 to 2003, I have prepared the summary of the

Table 3
Wilford L. White Fellows

1. Ray W. Ayres (deceased)
2. Robert Bauer
3. Clifford Baumbach (deceased)
4. Ralph R. Bedwell
5. Robert Bilodeau
6. David L. Birch
7. Eugene Bonk
8. William D. Boub Jr.
9. Robert Brockhaus
10. John F. Bulloch
11. Robert G. Butler
12. Harold K. Charlesworth (deceased)
13. Thomas Dandridge
14. William J. Dennis Jr.
15. Lillian Dreyer
16. Lloyd W. Fernald Jr.
17. Carl Franklin
18. Eugene G. Gomolka (deceased)
19. Walter Good
20. Gerald E. Hills
21. Ralph Hook Jr.
22. Dieter Ibielski
23. Klaas Havenga
24. Frank Hoy
25. Ole S. Johnson (deceased)
26. Wilson Johnson (deceased)
27. Raymond W.Y. Kao
28. John L. Komives
29. Bruce Kirchhoff
30. Bong-Ja Kim (deceased)
31. Guy A. Laviguer
32. John K.C. Liu (deceased)
33. Justin Longenecker
34. Tan Teck Meng
35. Geoffrey Meredith
36. Wendell O. Metcalf (deceased)
37. Donald D. Myers
38. Grant C. Moon
39. Josef Mugler
40. John Chang I. Ni (deceased)
41. Philip A. Neck
42. Ken O'Neill
43. Yoon Bae Ouh (deceased)
44. Sang-Kyu Park
45. J. Hanns Pichler
46. Hans Jobst Pleitner
47. Ki-Jung Ryu
48. Joseph C. Schabacker
49. Martin Schotsberger
50. Roy T. Shaw (deceased)
51. John R. Sloan (deceased)
52. George Solomon
53. Lois Stevenson
54. Eugene Swearingen
55. Roy Thurik
56. William A. Toomey Jr.
57. Joop Vianen
58. Sheldon R. Wagner
59. K. Mark Weaver
60. Harold Welsch
61. John Welsh (deceased)
62. Willis J. Wheat
63. Wilford L. White (deceased)
64. Ken Wilson
65. Arch Woodruff

history of ICSB. Much of the material was adapted from a series of articles on the history of ICSB. The first was a July 1967 *JSBM* article written by Wendell O. Metcalf, one of the founders and a past president. In the July 1975 issue, Robert O. Bauer, another past president who also served as the executive secretary for seven years, wrote of the 10 years that followed. Metcalf started the third decade, but it was finished by Justin Longenecker, another past president who is the coauthor of one of the first textbooks on small-business management. The most recent 15 years are chronicled by Harold Welsch, a past president and longtime active leader.

It has been my privilege to be part of this effort for the last 25 years, and I am most excited about the years yet to come.

Appendix A
Curricula Vitae of the Book Editors

Rob van der Horst is a regional economist from the Erasmus University Rotterdam, The Netherlands. After ten years of applied regional economic research at the Netherlands Economic Institute (NEI), he joined EIM Business & Policy Research in 1986.

He has been responsible for a variety of (applied) economic research projects on entrepreneurship and SMEs. He was involved in projects in all EU countries, several Eastern European countries, the Russian Federation, Dubai, South Africa and Jamaica. He has been a consultant to the OECD and UNIDO.

He is the director of EIM's Brussels' office. He is also the executive director of the ENSR: the European Network for Social and Economic Research, bringing together research institutes in 32 European countries. From 1992 to 2004 he was the project director of 'The Observatory of European SMEs', a research project for the European Commission. In the framework of the Observatory project a large number of reports have been prepared about structure and developments of SMEs in Europe.

Rob van der Horst is currently serving as Senior-Vice President for Research and Publications of the ICSB.

Sandra King-Kauanui is currently an Associate Professor of Management & Entrepreneurship at California State Polytechnic University, Pomona. She teaches Entrepreneurship, Family Business and Organizational Behaviour. Since 1996, Dr. King-Kauanui has been an active member of the ICSB board serving as SVP of Finance and SVP of Research and

Publications. She is currently serving as President of the ICSB for 2004–2005.

Sandra has conducted research on various aspects of Entrepreneurship, including her recent work in spirituality and entrepreneurship, and in Family Business in various countries around the world, including Mainland China. As a result of her research, she has participated in over 60 research presentations in various international, national and regional conferences. In addition she has published her research in numerous academic journals.

Previous to her career as an academic, Sandra started and operated her own business for twenty years. Through her company, she, along with her employees, provided tax, financial and business planning for over five hundred entrepreneurs and family-owned businesses. For three years, she hosted a cable TV talk show featuring discussions on financial, business and tax planning ideas. The business was successfully transferred to the next generation when she began her career at the University.

Susan Duffy is the Executive Director of the International Council for Small Business (ICSB), a global organization of researchers, policy makers, practitioners and educators dedicated to advancing entrepreneurship and small business worldwide. Susan works with an international team of SME professionals to build global networks that disseminate research, share best practices, and support policy for small and medium enterprise development. Susan also runs the international headquarter office of

ICSB at the George Washington University (GWU) in Washington, DC, USA.

An educator for over ten years, Susan founded the GWU Women's Entrepreneurial Leadership Initiative. Built on primary research of current successful women entrepreneurs, this innovative curriculum combines core entrepreneurship courses with personal and professional development activities, including leadership training, network building and mentor support. Susan also lectures in Family Business Dynamics, Small Business Management and New Venture Environmental Scanning and received the GWU School of Business and Public Management's Undergraduate Teaching Award in 2002. Susan presents her work at national and international conferences and has published research articles on the *State of Entrepreneurship Education in the United States* and *Expanding the Field of Family Business Research*.

Before coming to the George Washington University in 1998, Susan was a family business owner in the commercial construction industry. She has held leadership positions in health care and worked as an organizational consultant in private and public work systems.

Susan has a Master's Degree in Applied Behavioral Science from the Johns Hopkins University in Baltimore, Maryland and a Bachelor's Degree in Nutrition Science from the Pennsylvania State University. Currently Susan is a doctoral candidate researching entrepreneurial learning at The George Washington University School of Business.

Appendix B
Curricula Vitae of the Associate Editors

Roy Thurik is professor of economics and entrepreneurship at Erasmus University Rotterdam and professor of entrepreneurship at the Free University in Amsterdam. He is scientific advisor at EIM Business & Policy Research in Zoetermeer, the Netherlands, the largest private small business research institute in the world. Roy's research focuses on the role of small firms in markets, on the role of business owners in firms and on the consequences and causes of entrepreneurship in economies.

He is research professor of entrepreneurship, growth and public policy at the Max-Planck-Institut zur Erforschung von Wirtschaftssystemen (Max Planck Institute for Research into Economic Systems) in Jena, Germany. He is a research fellow at two renowned Dutch schools: the Tinbergen Institute for Economic Sciences and the Erasmus Research Institute for Management.

He recently published "Innovation, Industry Evolution and Employment" with Cambridge University Press together with David Audretsch and "Entrepreneurship: Determinants and Policy in a European-US Comparison" with Kluwer Academic Publishers. He has published over ninety scholarly articles in leading international academic journals. He is associate editor of Small Business Economics: An International Journal.

J. Hanns Pichler is an ICSB Past-President and Professor emeritus (Economics), University of Economics and Business Administration, Vienna. He has an Honorary Doctorate in Economics, Catholic University Brussels. He is President of the Austrian Institute for SME Research. He is a Wilford White Fellow (ICSB) and received various other scientific, professional and public awards. He has published books, numerous articles, conference papers and other topical publications relating to SME structures, to SME policy formulation and entrepreneurship.

David Storey is Associate Dean (Research) at Warwick Business School. Professor Storey has a First Class Degree in Economics, a Diploma in Applied Statistics and a PhD in Economics. He also has two honorary Doctorates and holds the title of Visiting Professor at the Universities of Manchester, Reading and Durham and is an EIM Fellow. In 1998 he received the International Award for Entrepreneurship and Small Business Research from the Swedish Council.

He has just completed a four year appointment by the UK Secretary of State for Trade and Industry as a Member of the Small Business Council which advises the government on small business policy making.

David Storey's work has focussed on small firm growth and on the evaluation of the impact of public policies to assist SMEs. He is the author of several books on small firms, the best known of which is *"Understanding the Small Business Sector"*.

He has undertaken work for several overseas governments and organisations. For six years he was the Expert Advisor to the OECD SME Best Practice Working Party and, in 2005, is to produce for them a Handbook on SME policy evaluation. He reviewed SME policy and practice for the Inter American Development Bank (IADB). He was consultant for the first ever Survey of micro enterprises in Trinidad and Tobago, and advisor to IADB on small enterprise policy in Jamaica. In Europe he co-ordinated an EU-wide review of new technology based firms for DG XIII, is the UK partner in the SME Observatory for DG Enterprise and has acted as advisor to many member state governments on SME policy.

Lois Stevenson has been studying entrepreneurship and small business related issues for over 20 years from four perspectives: that of scholar, government policymaker, consultant, and entrepreneur. She spent ten years as a university professor (1979–89), seven years as Director, Entrepreneurship Development with a federal government regional agency in Atlantic Canada (1990–97), and seven years leading directorates for SME, innovation, and economic framework policies in Industry Canada (1997–2005). She has owned her own business and offered consultancy and advice to governments and international organizations on entrepreneurship policy and approaches.

She has published over 45 books, papers and articles on entrepreneurship/small business, served on the editorial board of journals, and initiated projects to integrate entrepreneurship in the education system and to support youth entrepreneurship, women's entrepreneurship, and highly innovative entrepreneurship. Her most recent research publications focus on analysis of national level entrepreneurship policies and practices in a range of countries.

Prof. Stevenson is a Past President of the ICSB; a Past President of the Canadian Council for Small Business and Entrepreneurship (CCSBE), a Wilford White Fellow, a Fellow of the IC^2 Insti-

tute of the University of Texas at Austin, a Price-Babson College Fellow and a member of the International Reference Council of the Swedish Foundation for Small Business Research.

George Solomon is Associate Professor of Entrepreneurship and Small Business at The George Washington University School of Business and serves as the Deputy Director for the Council for Entrepreneurial Enterprises. Dr. George T. Solomon is currently Director of Exhibitor Relations for the Academy of Management, Past President of the United States Association for Small Business and Entrepreneurship (USASBE) and the International Council for Small Business (ICSB).

George Solomon has published over 70 articles, edited two books of readings, contributed chapters to texts in small business and edited a number of reference materials in both the areas of Entrepreneurship/Small Business Management and Organizational Behaviour & Dynamics. He is a colleague of the Creative Education Foundation, a fellow of the United States Association for Small Business and Entrepreneurship and the Small Business Institute Director's Association and a Wilford White Fellow of the ICSB. In 1984, he was one of five federal employees worldwide to receive the Arthur S. Flemming award for excellence in government management. He currently serves as chair of the Wilford White Fellows for the International Council of Small Business.

George Solomon received his Doctorate of Business Administration (DBA) from The George Washington University School of Government and Business Administration, 1982, with a major in Entrepreneurship/Small Business Management and Organizational Behaviour & Development.

Kevin Hindle, Professor of Entrepreneurship at the Australian Graduate

School of Entrepreneurship, Swinburne University of Technology, Melbourne, Australia is the Australian Project Director of the *Global Entrepreneurship Monitor* (GEM). He is a researcher, educator, management consultant and private equity investor.

As a long-serving educator, Professor Hindle has developed and taught entrepreneurship for a range of award and executive development programs in Europe, Asia and America as well as Australasia. He is co-author of two textbooks on entrepreneurship. His several professional awards include winning the (American) Academy of Management Entrepreneurship Division and McGraw Hill Innovation in Entrepreneurship Pedagogy Award in 2004 and Australia's highest entrepreneurship education award, the Business/Higher Education Round Table (B-hert) Award for the Best Entrepreneurial Educator of the year.

As a researcher, Kevin Hindle has authored over eighty publications including more than fifty peer-reviewed papers in a range of respected international journals and conference proceedings. He is a ministerially appointed foundation member of Australia's National Innovation Awareness Council and on the advisory board of the International Danish Entrepreneurship Academy (IDEA). The unifying theme of all his work is to develop and execute constructive, internationally relevant research whose findings can be used to enhance the teaching and development of ethical entrepreneurs in Australia and the world.

Colin Dunn has been the President of the Small Enterprise Association of Australia and New Zealand (SEAANZ) since 2002 and is currently Senior Vice President – Finance and Control of the ICSB. He has been on the ICSB Board since 2000. His research interest is in entrepreneurship and reasons why entrepreneurs are like they are.

Colin Dunn is the Program Coordinator for RMIT University's (in Melbourne) Bachelor of Business (Entrepreneurship) degree program and has a long history of teaching enterprise and business at a school and tertiary level and has had a passion in supporting and developing at-risk youth enterprise programs in Australia. He is the author of a number of books on the subject.

Colin Dunn has an economics degree from Melbourne University, post-grad qualifications in computing, is a trained teacher, a CPA and is currently undertaking a Masters in Business (Research).

Michael Schaper, PhD, is the inaugural Small Business Commissioner of the Australian Capital Territory, Canberra and the president of ICSB's Oceania body, the Small Enterprise Association of Australia and New Zealand. Prior to this, he held the foundation professorial chair in small business & entrepreneurship at the University of Newcastle, Australia. Michael has worked in a variety of fields, including periods as the owner/manager of his own business and as the manager of a community-based SME advisory agency.